ENTRUSTED
WITH THE
GOSPEL

ENTRUSTED
WITH THE
GOSPEL

PAUL'S THEOLOGY IN THE PASTORAL EPISTLES

EDITED BY:

ANDREAS J. KÖSTENBERGER

AND TERRY L. WILDER

NASHVILLE, TENNESSEE

Entrusted with the Gospel:
Paul's Theology in the Pastoral Epistles

Copyright © 2010 by Andreas J. Köstenberger and Terry L. Wilder

ISBN: 978-0-8054-4841-2
Published by B&H Publishing Group
Nashville, Tennessee

Dewey Decimal Classification: 227.8
Subject Heading: PAUL, APOSTLE/THEOLOGY/BIBLE. N.T. PASTORAL EPISTLES

Contents

To all those who faithfully shepherd the flock entrusted
to their care by the Great Shepherd of the sheep

And to those who considered us faithful
to be able to teach others also

Hans Finzel and Walter Davis

PREFACE

After a lengthy period during which scholars paid relatively little attention to 1 and 2 Timothy and Titus, a spate of studies has come to appear in print (e.g., see the volumes by I. H. Marshall [1999], J. D. Quinn and W. C. Wacker [2000], W. D. Mounce [2000], L. T. Johnson [2001], R. F. Collins [2002], P. H. Towner [2006], and A. J. Köstenberger [2006]). However, except for a relatively small number of commentaries and studies written by evangelicals (primarily those works of Marshall, Mounce, and Towner), critical scholars have largely neglected evangelical scholarship on these letters. One need only look at M. Harding's book *What Are They Saying About the Pastoral Epistles?* (Paulist Press, 2001) to see that "they" have not been saying much about the many studies done by evangelical scholars on these epistles. To help fill this gap, this volume offers a collection of important essays written by evangelicals, many of whom have done specialized work on 1 and 2 Timothy and Titus. This book aims to examine Paul's theology in the Pastoral Epistles and inform readers on the current state of scholarship on these letters. We offer the articles in this volume to you in the spirit of 2 Tim 2:2—"And what you have heard from me in the presence of many witnesses, commit to faithful men who will be able to teach others also."

Andreas Köstenberger examines many of the hermeneutical and exegetical challenges that one faces when interpreting 1 and 2 Timothy and Titus. These issues range from authorship to church leadership to the role of women in the church—to name a few. Köstenberger is well qualified to write on such a topic given that over the years he has written many articles on various issues in the Pastorals. His most recent work is the commentary on these letters in the revised edition of the *Expositor's Bible Commentary* (2006).[1]

Terry Wilder contributes an article in which he looks at pseudonymity, the New Testament, and the Pastoral Epistles. The issue of authorship is the dominant issue in

---

[1] A. Köstenberger, "Pastoral Epistles," in *Ephesians–Philemon* (rev. ed.; vol. 12 of *The Expositor's Bible Commentary*; Grand Rapids: Zondervan, 2006), 487–625.

scholarship on these letters, and Wilder seeks to show that the early church clearly did not accept pseudonymity. He takes the criteria that scholars often use to show that the letters to Timothy and Titus were not written by Paul and applies them to a letter that virtually no one today would dispute. He shows that it is possible to go overboard with theories of pseudo-apostolic authorship and offers a brief defense of the authenticity of the Pastorals. Wilder did his Ph.D. dissertation on pseudonymity and the New Testament and, amongst other things, examined the disputed Pauline letters in that study.[2]

Alan Tomlinson looks at the purpose of 1 and 2 Timothy and Titus in view of their stated occasions as well as any broader purposes for writing suggested by the various structural markers within each of the Pastorals. He explores a controlling metaphor of estate stewardship and household language as a central element in understanding the Pastoral Epistles. The latter ideas (with 2 Tim 2:2) are those from which this book draws its title. This imagery and language tend to be neglected by New Testament scholars when considering the purpose of these letters and need to be considered afresh.

Ray Van Neste summarizes the position of those who argue that the Pastoral Epistles lack coherent structure and flow of thought. He does not respond to this critique comprehensively in this article,[3] but gives a few examples of different ways in which we see important levels of connection across these texts. He argues that 1 and 2 Timothy and Titus function well as first-century letters, and that we should read these three letters as coherent documents with a reasonable flow of thought. Each paragraph should be interpreted in light of its connection to the rest of the letter rather than abstracting a unit from the rest of the letter and speculating about its original setting.

Greg Couser notes that modern scholarship has largely taken a dismissive approach to issues other than ecclesiology in the Pastorals. Many have done so because they were convinced that the author of 1 and 2 Timothy and Titus was no real theologian in his own right. Couser's study focuses on the doctrine of God (*theo*logy) in these letters. His discussion lays out the main contours of the *theo*logy as well as to highlight some of the more incidental statements that contribute to a full understanding of the God of Timothy and Titus. Couser did his doctoral work on this issue and has written several articles on the Pastorals.[4]

Daniel Akin notes that various methods have been used in studying the Christology of the Pastorals and that each approach has merit in its own right. He attempts to allow the Pastorals to speak unhindered by external constraints as much as possible. He examines the Christology of 1 and 2 Timothy and Titus by treating each book

---

    2 Revised and published as *Pseudonymity, the New Testament, and Deception: An Inquiry into Intention and Reception* (Lanham, MD: University Press of America, 2004).

    3 A thorough response can be found in R. Van Neste, *Cohesion and Structure in the Pastoral Epistles* (JSNTSup 280; London/New York: T&T Clark International, 2004). Van Neste's thesis was written partly in reply to the work of J. D. Miller, *The Pastoral Letters as Composite Documents* (Cambridge: CUP, 1997).

    4 G. Couser, "God and Christian Existence in 1 and 2 Timothy and Titus" (Ph.D. diss., University of Aberdeen, 1992).

individually and inductively, noting common themes and emphases in the letters with summary and concluding observations based upon what he has discovered.

George Wieland notes that the study of salvation language in the Pastorals confirms the importance of salvation as a theme in each of these letters. Salvation language is not only prevalent, but in all three letters the concept of salvation plays a vital role in relation to each letter's purpose. Each of the three letters makes use of soteriological concepts to address particular concerns and advance specific interests. Wieland did his doctoral work on this subject.[5]

Ben Merkle maintains that not only is the church at the center of God's mission; it is also the center of Paul's words to Timothy and Titus (1 Tim 3:15). The letters to Timothy and Titus provide us with crucial information concerning the offices of elder or overseer and deacon—offices that are also depicted in Paul's earlier writings. There was no monarchical bishop when the Pastorals were written. Instead, as Merkle has also stated elsewhere, the terms *elder* and *overseer* (or *bishop*) were used interchangeably to represent the same office.[6] Deacons are not the primary leaders in the church, but they are vital because they allow the elders/overseers to focus on their main task of shepherding and teaching the congregation. The qualifications given for deacons are very much like those of the overseers. Both lists focus on the individual's character.

Paul Wolfe asks, "What picture regarding the use of Scripture emerges from the Pastoral Epistles?" Wolfe, who also did his doctoral work on this subject,[7] says it is the work of a mature biblical theologian, at home in the text of Scripture and using it subtly and powerfully to make proclamation, to correct doctrinal error and ethical deviation, and to provide guidance for the church in transition. In doing so, Paul sets a final example for his coworkers and the churches to pay close attention to the Word and handle it carefully.

Thor Madsen writes on the ethics of the Pastorals and maintains that although these letters manifest a unique style and tone, their core logic and content agree with the major epistles. Paul traces his exhortations back to supernatural changes wrought by God in Christ. He strengthens the church by locking in essential doctrines and raising up conservative leaders. The Pastorals also imply that ministry entails almost constant struggle against false doctrines, false disciples, and cavalier disobedience. Therefore, believers need to endure, keeping the faith while others swerve out of line, and overseers especially need to steel against discouragement. Madsen's doctoral dissertation explored the relationship between the fact of the new life in Christ and the obligation of Christians to rise to that reality.[8]

[5] Published as *The Significance of Salvation: A Study of Salvation Language in the Pastoral Epistles* (Carlisle: Paternoster, 2006).

[6] B. Merkle, *The Elder and Overseer: One Office in the Early Church* (Oxford/New York: Peter Lang, 2003); idem, *40 Questions about Elders and Deacons* (Grand Rapids: Kregel, 2008).

[7] B. P. Wolfe, "The Place and Use of Scripture in the Pastoral Epistles" (Ph.D. diss., University of Aberdeen, 1990).

[8] T. Madsen, "Indicative and Imperative in Paul and Ancient Judaism: A Comparative Study" (Ph.D. diss., University of Aberdeen, 1998).

Chiao Ek Ho says that the letters to Timothy and Titus articulate an underlying missionary outlook and a theology of mission à la Paul. Reading these documents as mission-oriented documents better approximates the historical reality of the growing church in Ephesus and Crete in the first century AD. Ho shows, as he did more fully in an earlier work,[9] that the Pastorals contain Paul's mission-thought structure and missionary heartbeat.

Howard Marshall provides a general overview of scholarship on the Pastoral Epistles since the turn of the century. The survey falls into two parts: (1) an annotated catalogue of commentaries on the letters; and (2) a look at special areas of interest that lists some of the questions that are currently on the table for further consideration. The overview concludes with a listing of recent contributions to the study of the letters. Marshall is well acquainted with the letters to Timothy and Titus; his commentary on the Pastorals is considered a standard work.[10]

A word of appreciation should be expressed to the fine folks at B&H Academic, especially Jim Baird, director of academic publishing, and Ray Clendenen, senior academic editor. Thank you for your friendship and willingness to publish this project. Thank you also to Jean Eckenrode, executive assistant at B&H, and Dean Richardson, production editor. What would we do without you!?

A special word of thanks should also go to Paul Wolfe, one of this book's contributors. In a conversation some time ago he mentioned to me (Terry) that he would like to publish a collection of essays like this but did not have the time to do so. After talking further, he graciously agreed to let us grab hold of the idea's reins to produce this volume—and voilà!

Above all, we thank the God and Father of our Lord Jesus Christ. Thank you for entrusting us with the gospel. May we be wise and effective stewards for you, our Master. "Now to the King eternal, immortal, invisible, the only God, be honor and glory forever and ever. Amen" (1 Tim 1:17).

Andreas J. Köstenberger
Wake Forest, North Carolina

Terry L. Wilder
Nashville, Tennessee

---

[9] C. Ho, "Do the Work of an Evangelist: The Missionary Outlook of the Pastoral Epistles" (Ph.D. diss., University of Aberdeen, 2000).

[10] I. H. Marshall (in collaboration with P. H. Towner), *A Critical and Exegetical Commentary on the Pastoral Epistles* (ICC; Edinburgh: T&T Clark, 1999).

CONTRIBUTORS

Daniel L. Akin (Ph.D, University of Texas at Arlington) is president and professor of Preaching and Theology at Southeastern Baptist Theological Seminary in Wake Forest, North Carolina.

Greg A. Couser (Ph.D., University of Aberdeen) is professor of Bible and Greek at Cedarville University in Cedarville, Ohio.

Chiao Ek Ho (Ph.D., University of Aberdeen) is principal of the East Asia School of Theology, Singapore.

Andreas J. Köstenberger (Ph.D., Trinity Evangelical Divinity School) is professor of New Testament and Biblical Theology, and director of Ph.D. Studies at Southeastern Baptist Theological Seminary in Wake Forest, North Carolina. He also serves as editor for the *Journal of the Evangelical Theological Society*.

Thorvald B. Madsen II (Ph.D., University of Aberdeen) is dean of Midwestern College, SBC, and associate professor of New Testament, Ethics, and Philosophy of Religion at Midwestern Baptist Theological Seminary in Kansas City, Missouri.

I. Howard Marshall (Ph.D., University of Aberdeen) is emeritus professor of New Testament Exegesis at the University of Aberdeen, Scotland.

Benjamin L. Merkle (Ph.D., Southern Baptist Theological Seminary) is associate professor of New Testament and Greek at Southeastern Baptist Theological Seminary in Wake Forest, North Carolina.

F. Alan Tomlinson (Ph.D., Southern Baptist Theological Seminary) is professor of New Testament and Greek at Midwestern Baptist Theological Seminary in Kansas City, Missouri.

Ray Van Neste (Ph.D., University of Aberdeen) is associate professor of Christian Studies and director of the R. C. Ryan Center for Biblical Studies at Union University in Jackson, Tennessee.

George M. Wieland (Ph.D., University of Aberdeen) is lecturer in New Testament at Carey Baptist College, New Zealand.

Terry L. Wilder (Ph.D., University of Aberdeen) is academic acquisitions editor for B&H Publishing Group in Nashville, Tennessee, and research professor of New Testament and Greek at Midwestern Baptist Theological Seminary in Kansas City, Missouri.

B. Paul Wolfe (Ph.D., University of Aberdeen) is headmaster of The Cambridge School of Dallas in Dallas, Texas. He was formerly associate professor of New Testament at Southwestern Baptist Theological Seminary in Fort Worth, Texas.

Chapter One

HERMENEUTICAL AND EXEGETICAL CHALLENGES IN INTERPRETING THE PASTORAL EPISTLES

ANDREAS J. KÖSTENBERGER

INTRODUCTION

Recent years have seen the publication of several major commentaries and monographs on the Pastoral Epistles.[1] This is a sign of the reinvigorated study of this body of writings that is of great practical significance for the church today. Interpreters of Paul's letters to Timothy and Titus are faced with several important hermeneutical and exegetical challenges. Hermeneutical challenges include the Pastorals' authorship, genre, and matters related to their historical background. Relevant exegetical issues pertain to the question of proper church leadership and other matters related to the two major ecclesiastical offices of elder or overseer and deacon, respectively. The following treatment is intended as a survey of recent scholarship on these significant issues.[2]

HERMENEUTICAL CHALLENGES

THE AUTHORSHIP OF THE PASTORALS

PATRISTIC EVIDENCE

The authorship of the Pastoral Epistles continues to be a major topic of scholarly debate. The authenticity of Paul's correspondence with Timothy and Titus went

---

[1] See esp. I. H. Marshall, *The Pastoral Epistles* (ICC; Edinburgh: T&T Clark, 1999); W. D. Mounce, *The Pastoral Epistles* (WBC 46; Nashville: Thomas Nelson, 2000); J. D. Quinn and W. C. Wacker, *The First and Second Letters to Timothy* (ECC; Grand Rapids: Eerdmans, 2000); P. H. Towner, *The Letters to Timothy and Titus* (NICNT; Grand Rapids: Eerdmans, 2006); and the reviews of these works in *JETS* 44 (2001): 550–53; 45 (2002): 365–66; 44 (2001): 549–50; and 51 (2008): 656–59.

[2] The following treatment draws on relevant portions of A. J. Köstenberger, "Pastoral Epistles," in *Ephesians–Philemon* (rev. ed.; vol. 12 of *The Expositor's Bible Commentary*; Grand Rapids: Zondervan, 2006), 487–625.

largely unchallenged until the nineteenth century.[3] In all probability, Paul's letters to Timothy were known to Polycarp (c. AD 117; 1 Tim 6:7,10 is cited in *Philippians* 4.1).[4] The first unmistakable attestation is found in the second-century writers Athenagoras (c. AD 180; *Supplication* 37.1) and Theophilus (later 2nd cent. AD; *To Autolycus* 3.14). Both of these writers cite 1 Tim 2:1–2 and allude to other passages in the Pastorals. Irenaeus (c. AD 130–c. 200), likewise, in several passages in his work *Against Heresies* (e.g., 1.pref.; 1.23.4; 2.14.7; 3.1.1), cited each of the letters and identified their author as the apostle Paul. Clement of Alexandria (c. AD 150–c. AD 215; *Stromateis* 2.11) noted that some Gnostics who perceived themselves to be the targets of the denunciation of 1 Tim 6:20–21 rejected Paul's letters to Timothy. The Muratorian Canon (later 2nd cent. AD) included all three letters in the Pauline corpus.

Marshall's overall assessment of the patristic evidence regarding the Pastorals is noteworthy especially since, as will be further discussed below, he himself does not hold to Pauline authorship: "It can be concluded that the PE [Pastoral Epistles] were known to Christian writers from early in the second century and that there is no evidence of rejection of them by any writers except for Marcion [a mid-second-century AD heretic who excised most of the Old Testament and the New Testament from his truncated version of the canon]."[5] Consequently, the Pastorals became part of the established New Testament canon of the church, and the Pauline authorship of the Pastorals was not seriously questioned for a millennium and a half.

RECENT CHALLENGES

It was only in the nineteenth century that an increasing number of scholars have claimed that the Pastorals are an instance of pseudonymous writing in which a later follower attributed a given piece of writing to his revered teacher in order to perpetuate that person's teachings and influence.[6] At first, this view may seem surprising, since all three Pastoral Epistles open with the unequivocal attribution, "Paul, an apostle of Christ Jesus," or a similar phrase (1 Tim 1:1; 2 Tim 1:1; Titus 1:1). It seems hard to fathom how someone other than the apostle Paul could have written those letters, attributed them to the apostle, and these letters could have been accepted

---

[3] For brief surveys, see R. F. Collins, *Letters That Paul Did Not Write* (Wilmington, DE: Michael Glazier, 1988), 89–90, who names as the earliest challengers of the Pastorals' authenticity Schmidt (1804), Schleiermacher (1807), Eichhorn (1812), Baur (1835), and later Holtzmann (1885); and E. E. Ellis, "Pastoral Letters," in *Dictionary of Paul and His Letters* (ed. G. F. Hawthorne and R. P. Martin; Downers Grove, IL: InterVarsity, 1993), 659.

[4] See the discussion in Marshall, *Pastoral Epistles*, 3–8 (including the tables on pp. 4–5).

[5] Ibid., 8. See also G. W. Knight III, *Commentary on the Pastoral Epistles* (NIGTC; Grand Rapids: Eerdmans, 1992), 14, citing Guthrie, *Pastoral Epistles*, 19–20, and W. G. Kümmel, *Introduction to the New Testament* (trans. H. C. Kee; 2nd ed.; Nashville: Abingdon, 1975), 370, to the effect that from the end of the second century, the Pastorals are regarded without question as Pauline and are attested as strongly as most of the other Pauline letters.

[6] See the thorough survey and adjudication in T. L. Wilder, "Pseudonymity and the New Testament," in *Interpreting the New Testament: Essays on Methods and Issues* (ed. D. A. Black and D. S. Dockery; Nashville: Broadman & Holman, 2001), 296–335. See also D. A. Carson, "Pseudonymity and Pseudepigraphy," in *Dictionary of New Testament Background* (ed. C. A. Evans and S. E. Porter; Downers Grove, IL: InterVarsity, 2004), 856–64.

into the New Testament canon as Pauline while in fact having been the product of someone else, with all of this having taken place without any intent to deceive or any error on the church's part.

Indeed, as will be seen, the Pauline authorship of the Pastoral Epistles is by far the best conclusion on the basis of all the available evidence, and several major problems attach to any alternative proposals. While important *doctrinal* issues are at stake, the first important matter requiring adjudication is a *historical* matter. The following set of questions needs to be addressed:

(1) Is pseudonymous letter-writing attested in the first century AD?
(2) If so, was such a practice ethically unobjectionable and devoid of deceptive intent?[7]
(3) Could letters known to be pseudonymous have been accepted by the early church?
(4) If so, is the Pastorals' pseudonymity more plausible than their authenticity?[8]

I. HOWARD MARSHALL'S "ALLONYMITY" PROPOSAL

I. Howard Marshall recently addressed these issues and came to the conclusion that "the way in which the thought [in the Pastorals] is expressed, both linguistically and theologically, poses great problems . . . which seems to make it unlikely that he [Paul] himself wrote in these terms to trusted colleagues."[9] For this reason he rejected the Pauline authorship of the Pastorals. At the same time, however, Marshall found the theory of pseudonymity wanting due to the deceptive intent inevitably involved in such a practice.[10]

In an effort to find a *via media* between the (for him) Scylla of Pauline authorship and the Charybdis of pseudonymity, Marshall posited a view he called "allonymity" or "allepigraphy," according to which "somebody close to a dead person continued to write as (they thought that) he would have done."[11] According to Marshall, Timothy and Titus were only the purported, but not the real, recipients of the Pastoral Epistles, which were instead addressed to leaders of congregations in Ephesus/Asia Minor and Crete, respectively.[12] Moreover, Marshall proposed that 2 Timothy was substantially

---

[7] For a forceful argument against this contention, see E. E. Ellis, "Pseudonymity and Canonicity of New Testament Documents," *Worship, Theology and Ministry in the Early Church* (ed. M. J. Wilkins and T. Page; JSNTSup 87; Sheffield: JSOT, 1992), 212–24.

[8] For a thorough discussion of these issues, see esp. D. Guthrie, *New Testament Introduction* (4th ed.; Downers Grove, IL: InterVarsity, 1990), 607–49, 1011–28.

[9] Marshall, *Pastoral Epistles*, 79. See Marshall's entire discussion on pp. 57–92.

[10] Ibid., 80–83.

[11] Ibid., 84.

[12] Ibid., 85.

the work of Paul and formed the basis for the "allonymous" writing of 1 Timothy and Titus.[13] This, of course, turns the traditional (and canonical) sequence on its head, since it would make 2 Timothy—not 1 Timothy or Titus—the first of the Pastoral Epistles to be written.

How plausible is this theory? Perhaps an example will help to illustrate the nature of Marshall's proposal. If Marshall's line of reasoning is applied to his own commentary (which Marshall acknowledges to have been written "in collaboration with" Philip Towner), perhaps several hundred years from now, some might claim that the commentary was actually not written by Marshall himself but compiled subsequent to his death by Towner based on Marshall's notes and perhaps also based on some of his previous publications—not to mention oral interchanges and conversations or informal notes, such as e-mail messages, and so on, during Marshall's lifetime. With the passing of time, doubtless a plausible case could be construed along those lines. While plausible, however, such a theory would obviously not square with the facts, since Howard Marshall is demonstrably still alive and did publish his commentary during his lifetime and is the person responsible for his work (the degree of collaboration by Towner is another issue). Marshall would therefore rightfully protest any such attribution of his work to a posthumous author. One wonders whether Marshall's attribution of the Pastorals' authorship to an "allonymous" writer similarly gives short shrift to the apostle and his role in writing these letters.

ARGUMENTS ADVANCED AGAINST PAULINE AUTHORSHIP

Differences in Style and Vocabulary   What, then, is the evidence set forth for the pseudonymity of the Pastorals, and how should one assess it? First, attention has frequently been drawn to the *differences in style and vocabulary* between the Pastorals and the undisputed Pauline Epistles.[14] The Pastorals feature words not used elsewhere in Paul, such as the terms "godliness" (εὐσέβεια), "self-controlled" (σώφρων), or the expression ἐπιφάνεια rather than παρουσία to refer to Christ's return (but see 2 Thess 2:8 where ἐπιφάνεια is used). At the same time, characteristic Pauline terminology is omitted: "freedom" (ἐλευθερία), "flesh" (versus Spirit; σάρξ), "cross" (σταυρός), and "righteousness of God" (δικαιοσύνη θεοῦ).

As scholars have increasingly recognized, however, conclusions regarding authorship based on stylistic differences are highly precarious, not the least because the sample size of the writings in question is too small for definitive conclusions on the basis of word statistics alone.[15] Moreover, the difference between public letters sent

---

[13] Ibid., 86.

[14] See Mounce, *Pastoral Epistles*, xcix–cxviii. Other common objections to the Pauline authorship of the Pastorals are the difficulty of harmonizing Paul's movements mentioned in the Pastorals with those recorded in Acts and the alleged late church structures reflected in the Pastorals (see discussion below).

[15] For an incisive treatment, see B. M. Metzger, "A Reconsideration of Certain Arguments against the Pauline Authorship of the Pastoral Epistles," *ExpTim* 70 (1958–59): 91–94 (see esp. the four questions listed on p. 93).

to congregations (the 10 letters traditionally attributed to Paul, with the possible exception of Philemon) and personal correspondence such as the Pastoral Epistles must be taken into account.[16] The fact that Paul, in the case of the Pastorals, sensed that he was nearing the end of his life and that there was an urgent need to ensure the preservation of sound doctrine for the postapostolic period would appear to account adequately for the Pastorals' emphasis on qualifications for leadership, church organization, and the faithful passing on of apostolic tradition.

Ancient Pseudonymous Epistles But what about the claim, second, that pseudonymous writing was a common and commonly accepted ancient literary device? A careful screening of the relevant evidence yields the conclusion that while pseudonymity was not uncommon for apocalyptic writings, Gospels, or even Acts, pseudonymous *letters* were exceedingly rare.[17] The following observations can be made.

(1) Of the two extant *Jewish* sources, the "Epistle" of Jeremiah and the *"Letter" of Aristeas* are really misnomers, for neither can properly be classified as epistle: the former is a homily; the latter represents an account of the circumstances of the translation of the Hebrew Scriptures into Greek.[18]

(2) In the apostolic era, far from an *acceptance* of pseudonymous epistles, there was actually considerable *concern* that letters be forged; thus Paul referred to the "distinguishing mark" in all his letters (1 Cor 16:21; Gal 6:11; Col 4:18; 2 Thess 3:17; Phlm 19) and makes perturbed reference to the circulation of "a letter as if from us" (2 Thess 2:2).

(3) In the second century, Tertullian reports that an Asian presbyter was removed from office for forging a letter in Paul's name (*On Baptism* 17); both *3 Corinthians* and the *Epistle to the Laodiceans* are transparent attempts, in customary apocryphal fashion, to fill in a perceived gap in canonical revelation (cf. 1 Cor 5:9; 2 Cor 2:4; 7:8; Col 4:16);[19] and the end-of-second-century bishop of Antioch, Serapion (died AD 211), sharply distinguished between apostolic writings and those that "falsely bear their names" (ψευδεπίγραφα; cited in Eusebius, *Eccl. Hist.* 6.12.3).

---

[16] See esp. M. P. Prior, *Paul the Letter-Writer and the Second Letter to Timothy* (JSNTSup 23; Sheffield: JSOT, 1989), and P. H. Towner, *1–2 Timothy & Titus* (IVPNTC; Downers Grove, IL: InterVarsity, 1994), 34–35.

[17] R. Bauckham, "Pseudo-Apostolic Letters," *JBL* 107 (1988): 487, observes the rarity of apocryphal or pseudepigraphal apostolic letters in relation to other genres and conjectures that the reason for this "may well have been the sheer difficulty of using a pseudepigraphal letter to perform the same functions as an authentic letter." He concludes that "among the letters surveyed there is no really good example of a pseudepigraphal letter that achieves didactic relevance by the generality of its contents."

[18] Bauckham considers it "misclassified" and a "dedicated treatise" (ibid., 478). Bauckham also discusses several didactic letters (*1 En.* 92–105; Epistle of Jeremiah; *1 Baruch*; *2 Bar.* 78–87).

[19] Bauckham calls *Laodiceans* "a remarkably incompetent attempt to fill the gap . . . nothing but a patchwork of Pauline sentences and phrases from other letters, mainly Philippians" (ibid., 485). *Third Corinthians* is part of the late second-century *Acts of Paul*.

On the basis of this evidence it seems doubtful that the early church would have been prepared knowingly to accept pseudonymous letters into the Christian canon.[20]

Church Structure and the Alleged "Early Catholicism" of the Pastorals A third common argument presented in favor of the pseudonymity of the Pastorals is that the *church structure* found in these letters reflects, not the first-, but the second-century church. This pattern can most clearly be seen in Ignatius of Antioch (c. AD 35–107), who advocated a monarchical episcopate and a three-tiered ecclesiastical hierarchy (e.g., *Eph.* 2.2; *Magn.* 3.1; *Trall.* 2.2; 3.1).[21] However, it can be shown that in the Pastorals the terms "overseer" (ἐπίσκοπος) and "elder" (πρεσβύτερος) refer to one and the same office (Titus 1:5,7; cf. Acts 20:17,28), so that they attest to a two- rather than three-tiered structure and thus reflect an earlier rather than later time of composition.[22]

What is more, it is manifestly not the case that it was only in the second century that the church developed an interest in proper church leadership. Paul and Barnabas appointed elders in the churches they established already prior to AD 50 (Acts 14:23; cf. 11:30; 15:2; 20:28–31; 21:18). There is therefore nothing novel about Paul's instruction to Titus to "appoint elders in every town" (Titus 1:5). Paul's letter to the Philippians, in all likelihood written prior to the Pastorals, is addressed to the "overseers and deacons" at Philippi (Phil 1:1), which perfectly coheres with the two-tiered structure presupposed in the Pastorals (see 1 Tim 3:1–13). The emphasis on proper qualifications for overseers and deacons in the Pastorals also supports a first-century date because a second-century writer would likely have expected his readers to be already familiar with this type of information.[23]

Alleged Fictive Historical References An important fourth issue that is often not given adequate weight in the discussion is the significant number of *historical particularities* featured in the Pastorals. While it is just possible that a later imitator of Paul fabricated these pieces of information to lend greater verisimilitude to his epistle, it seems much more credible to see these references as authentic instances in Paul's life

---

[20] This is true despite B. Metzger's conclusion that "since the use of the literary form of pseudepigraphy need not be regarded as necessarily involving fraudulent intent, it cannot be argued that the character of inspiration excludes the possibility of pseudepigraphy among the canonical writings" ("Literary Forgeries and Canonical Pseudepigrapha," *JBL* 91 [1972]: 22). See especially J. Duff, "A Reconsideration of Pseudepigraphy in Early Christianity" (unpublished Ph.D. thesis; Oxford Univ., 1998), who concludes that the value of a text was closely linked to its true authorship; that pseudonymity was generally viewed as a deceitful practice; and that texts thought to be pseudonymous were marginalized.

[21] See Mounce, *Pastoral Epistles*, lxxxvi–lxxxviii, 186–92, who cites Polycarp, Clement of Rome, Clement of Alexandria, and Irenaeus as referring to a two-tiered structure, using *episkopos* and *presbyteros* interchangeably.

[22] F. M. Young, "On *Episkopos* and *Presbyteros*," *JTS* 45 (1994): 142–48, ventures the "admittedly tentative" hypothesis that the origins of the ἐπίσκοπος and the πρεσβύτερος are distinct. However, Young's interpretation of the Pastorals in light of Ignatius (rather than vice versa) seems precarious (if not methodologically fallacious).

[23] D. A. Carson and D. J. Moo, *An Introduction to the New Testament* (rev. ed.; Grand Rapids: Zondervan, 2005), 564.

and ministry.[24] Why would a later pseudonymous writer go through the trouble of inventing numerous details such as the following for no other reason than to add verisimilitude to his writing?

> Make every effort to come to me soon, for Demas has deserted me, because he loved this present world, and has gone to Thessalonica. Crescens has gone to Galatia, Titus to Dalmatia. Only Luke is with me. Bring Mark with you, for he is useful to me in the ministry. I have sent Tychicus to Ephesus. When you come, bring the cloak I left in Troas with Carpus, as well as the scrolls, especially the parchments. Alexander the coppersmith did great harm to me. The Lord will repay him according to his works. Watch out for him yourself, because he strongly opposed our words.
>
> At my first defense, no one came to my assistance, but everyone deserted me. May it not be counted against them. But the Lord stood with me and strengthened me, so that the proclamation might be fully made through me, and all the Gentiles might hear. So I was rescued from the lion's mouth. . . . Greet Prisca and Aquila, and the household of Onesiphorus. Erastus has remained at Corinth; Trophimus I left sick at Miletus. Make every effort to come before winter. Eubulus greets you, and so do Pudens, Linus, Claudia, and all the brothers. (2 Tim 4:9–21)

Within the framework of a theory of pseudonymity, all of the above details would of necessity need to be viewed as fictional. However, there is little (if any) extant instance of this kind of "fictive epistolary" genre in the first or second century AD. Moreover, an entirely different kind of hermeneutic would be required to decode such a letter. All incidental details would need to be discarded, and only the didactic portions, once separated from the nondidactic ones, would be exegetically significant.

In light of the virtual impossibility of separating between the incidental and the didactic material and in view of the negative ethical implications of a procedure that involves the invention of large sections of an epistolary writing, the Pauline authorship of the Pastorals seems considerably more plausible than pseudonymous (or allonymous) alternatives.

CONCLUSION

The Pauline authorship of the Pastorals continues to enjoy the support of the preponderance of the evidence. As the discussion above has shown, none of the

---

[24] Contra Bauckham who believes that the author of the Pastorals "has thought himself into situations in Paul's ministry and . . . has filled out whatever historical information was available to him with historical fiction" (p. 492; echoing Holtzmann). Bauckham even ventures the conjecture that Timothy might have written the Pastorals himself (p. 494)! Also contra the "mediating position" of J. D. G. Dunn, *The Living Word* (London: SCM, 1987), 82, who believes that Paul is "the fountainhead of the Pastorals tradition" and that the Pastorals reexpress for a later situation "the voice of the Pauline tradition for a new day"; and N. Brox, "Zu den persönlichen Notizen der Pastoralbriefe," *BZ* 13 (1969): 76–94, who considers the personal references to represent "typical situations in the ecclesiastical office, which are historicized and attributed to Paul."

arguments advanced against the Pauline authorship of the Pastorals require their pseudonymity or allonymity. For this reason the conclusion by Carson and Moo is apt: "The Pastorals are much more akin to the accepted letters of Paul than they are to the known pseudonymous documents that circulated in the early church."[25]

The above-mentioned factors receive additional weight through the recent survey of the relevant ancient evidence conducted by Terry Wilder, who arrived at the following three conclusions:

(1) The early church used both the authorship and the content of a given writing as criteria for authenticity; hence it would not knowingly have allowed pseudo-apostolic works to be read publicly in the churches alongside apostolic ones.

(2) There is no evidence for pseudonymity as a convention among orthodox Christians.

(3) The early church did not regard with indifference the fictive use of an apostle's name.[26]

As Wilder notes, both the external and the internal evidence clearly favor the Pauline authorship of the Pastorals. Many of the Fathers—Ignatius, Polycarp, Clement of Alexandria, Tertullian, Irenaeus, Eusebius, and the Muratorian Canon—accepted Pauline authorship, and arguments against the Pauline authorship from the internal evidence consistently fail to convince.[27]

To sum up: the internal evidence strongly suggests the Pauline authorship of the Pastorals, and all views positing pseudonymity or allonymity face considerable difficulties.[28] Contrary to widespread assertions or insinuations, it is not true that it is more scholarly and "enlightened" to attribute the Pastorals to someone other than Paul, nor is such a position backed up by the best historical or literary evidence.

---

[25] Carson and Moo, *Introduction to the New Testament*, 563. Similarly, D. Guthrie, "The Development of the Idea of Canonical Pseudepigrapha in New Testament Criticism," *VE* 1 (1962): 43–59. This, of course, in no way precludes the possibility that Paul may have employed an amanuensis, as he frequently did in other instances. See R. N. Longenecker, "Ancient Amanuenses and the Pauline Epistles," in *New Dimensions in New Testament Study* (ed. R. N. Longenecker and M. C. Tenney; Grand Rapids: Zondervan, 1974), 281–97; E. R. Richards, *The Secretary in the Letters of Paul* (WUNT 2/42; Tübingen: Mohr-Siebeck, 1991); and Ellis, "Pastoral Letters," 663–64.

[26] Wilder, "Pseudonymity and the New Testament," 307. Wilder provides a very thorough review of biblical scholarship on the issue of pseudonymity, including the above-mentioned contribution of Marshall. Wilder's primary problem with Marshall's theory is the difficulty of determining which parts of the Pastorals rely on authentic Pauline material and which ones do not on the basis of the existing form of these epistles (319).

[27] See ibid., 324–27.

[28] The viability of the apostolic authorship of the Pastorals is underscored by W. Mounce's advocacy of this view in his Word Biblical Commentary contribution. Quinn and Wacker, *First and Second Letters to Timothy*, on the other hand, contend in the introduction to their work that the Pastorals were written in the post-Pauline period (AD 70–100) in order to counter the tendency of disparaging the apostle owing to his shameful end as a purported criminal (p. 20). Regarding the recipients, Quinn and Wacker conjecture that "not only Titus and Timothy but also the places to which the letters are addressed may have a typical or representative function" (p. 22). Quinn and Wacker believe that Titus was the first of the Pastorals to be written.

THE GENRE OF THE PASTORALS AND THE ROLE OF BACKGROUND

If Paul wrote the Pastorals, then, what kinds of letters did he write, and what is their relevance for today? The Pastorals' genre and the role of background in interpreting specific passages are two other critical broader issues. At the outset, it is worth noting that while the common label for these letters is "Pastoral Epistles," the role of Timothy and Titus was not actually that of permanent, resident pastor of a church. Rather, these two men served as Paul's apostolic delegates who were temporarily assigned to their present locations in order to deal with particular problems. For this reason the Pastorals are not so much advice to younger ministers or generic manuals of church order as they are Paul's instructions to his special delegates, issued toward the closing of the apostolic era at a time when the aging apostle would have felt a keen responsibility to ensure the orderly transition from the apostolic to the postapostolic period.

If the Pastorals are occasional documents, therefore, to what extent does this require an ad hoc hermeneutic that methodically limits their scope of reference to the original situation at hand? This approach was taken, among others, by Gordon Fee, who viewed all of 1 Timothy, for example, as narrowly constrained by the injunction in 1:3, claiming that "the whole of 1 Timothy . . . is dominated by this singular concern" and that "the whole of chs. 2–3 is best understood as instruction vis-à-vis the behavior and attitudes of the FT [false teachers]."[29] William Mounce, too, consistently interpreted virtually every detail in the Pastorals narrowly in light of Paul's original context. Thus 1 Timothy 3 was viewed in light of a "leadership crisis" in the Ephesian church, in the conviction that "almost every quality Paul specifies here has its negative counterpart in the Ephesian opponents."[30]

Overall, it appears that Fee's contention that the entire letter constitutes an ad hoc argument narrowly constrained by the situation at Ephesus arguably represents an unduly sharp reaction against the traditional "church manual" approach that views the letter as containing timeless instructions for church leadership. Two main lines of critique may be raised. First, Fee unduly diminished the structural markers in 1 Tim 2:1 and 3:15–16 that set off chaps. 2–3 from chaps. 4–6 respectively. As especially 1 Tim 3:15 makes clear (see also 1 Tim 2:8), Paul's injunctions in chaps. 2–3 are not confined to the Ephesian situation but stipulate "how people ought to conduct themselves in God's household" (NIV) in general.

What is more, the solemn descriptive terms for the church in 1 Tim 3:15, "the church of the living God, the pillar and the foundation of the truth," speak decisively against the contention that these instructions are of value merely for

---

[29] G. D. Fee, "Reflections on Church Order in the Pastoral Epistles, with Further Reflection on the Hermeneutics of *Ad Hoc* Documents," *JETS* 28 (1985): 142–43.

[30] Mounce, *Pastoral Epistles*, 153.

first-century AD Ephesus. In a previous interchange with Kevin Giles, a proponent of a culturally relative approach to the interpretation of the Pastoral Epistles, several specific passages in Paul's first letter to Timothy were discussed that Giles claimed were limited to their original context.[31] According to Giles, the following passages in Paul's first letter to Timothy ought to be interpreted in culturally relative terms:

(1) Paul's injunctions on the care of widows in 1 Tim 5:3–16: since in our culture widows are "not necessarily destitute, or in need of male protection," this passage does not apply today.

(2) Men today do not pray "with lifted hands" (1 Tim 2:8), and women do not "literally obey" Paul's instructions in 1 Tim 2:9–10; hence 1 Tim 2:12 should likewise not be considered normative.

(3) In chap. 3, Paul "insists" that overseers and deacons be married, while today unmarried men are ordained; hence, again, 1 Timothy 3 does not apply.

(4) While Paul in 1 Tim 5:17 urges that church leaders be treated with "double honor," "church teachers are not necessarily paid double to other ministers" today; this passage, too, no longer applies.

(5) Slavery, "endorsed" in 1 Tim 6:1–2, has clearly been found unacceptable by subsequent history; hence this passage is outdated as well.

As pointed out, however, apart from faulty or doubtful exegesis, the difficulty with such proposals is their failure to distinguish between general norms and specific applications. In the case of widows, for example, the general norm is that the church should care for widows who have no other means of support. This applied in Paul's day as well as in ours. In Paul's day, the specific application was for widows over 60 years of age to be put on a list. While the church's outworking of the general scriptural norm may be different today, the norm still applies. The other points listed above can likewise be answered by a consistent application of this general norm/specific application distinction.[32]

Another problem with an ad hoc approach to the interpretation of the Pastoral Epistles is the manifest implausibility of an extreme application of this mirror-reading hermeneutic to every single injunction contained in the Pastorals. To be consistent, the proponents of such an approach would seem to have to argue that the false teachers taught all of the following, and were in every instance corrected by Paul:

---

[31] See A. J. Köstenberger, "Women in the Church: A Response to Kevin Giles," *EvQ* 73 (2001): 205–24, esp. 207–12.

[32] See also T. D. Gordon, "A Certain Kind of Letter: The Genre of 1 Timothy," in *Women in the Church: A Fresh Analysis of 1 Timothy 2:9–15* (ed. A. J. Köstenberger, T. R. Schreiner, and H. S. Baldwin; Grand Rapids: Baker, 1995), 53–63.

(1) The church ought not to pray for those in authority.

(2) God wants only some people to be saved.

(3) Church leaders ought not to be above reproach, or at least the false teachers were not.

(4) They ought not to be faithful to their wives, or at least the false teachers were not.

(5) They ought not to be hospitable or able to teach, or at least the false teachers were not.

(6) They ought to be given to drunkenness, or at least the false teachers were.

(7) They ought to be violent and quarrelsome, or at least the false teachers were.

(8) They ought to be lovers of money, or at least the false teachers were, and so on.

Perhaps some of the above may be true, but *all* of the above? Were the false teachers truly not able to teach but overseers in Paul's churches should be? Was Paul's point truly the false teachers' lack of hospitality, which he sought to offset with his injunction that overseers in his churches must open their homes to others? Hermeneutical consistency on the part of those advocating an ad hoc hermeneutic would seem to require this (or else require an inevitably arbitrary adjudication of which of Paul's statements were constrained by the false teachers), but, as shown, this approach leads to rather extreme results.

In the end, it seems, this kind of hermeneutic denies Paul, the author, the ability to make any pronouncements in a Pastoral or any letter that transcend his immediate circumstances. However, not only does this seem to impose an unreasonable constraint on authorial intention; this approach is also not logically compelling. The presence of an injunction to hospitality does not require the absence of this trait in the current leadership or false teaching regarding the need for hospitality on the part of church leaders. Hence a warrant for this type of ad hoc hermeneutic is lacking. At the very least, one ought not to make one's conjectured reconstruction of the Ephesian context the paradigm or absolute premise on the basis of which abiding implications for the church today are precluded or rendered presumptively unlikely from the very outset.

Especially in conjunction with the structural markers of 1 Tim 2:1 and 3:15–16, it is at least equally plausible that the reference to the false teachers in 1 Tim 1:3 informs Paul's comments in the remainder of chap. 1 and then again in chaps. 4–6, while the comments in 1 Tim 2:1–3:16 are more positive in orientation. Perhaps Johnson is correct that Timothy needed support and counsel on how to deal with the false teachers in Ephesus, which led Paul to interweave personal instructions with those on community life. Johnson called this the *mandata principis* ("commandments of the ruler") letter and cited several ancient parallels.[33] One final hermeneutical issue regarding the interpretation of the Pastorals needs to be addressed: their literary integrity and likely structure.

LITERARY INTEGRITY AND STRUCTURE

"Until recently," Ray Van Neste summarizes the state of scholarship on the topic, "one of the widely accepted tenets of modern scholarship regarding the Pastoral Epistles was that they lacked any significant, careful order or structure."[34] This was not confined to liberal critics; even an otherwise conservative commentator such as Donald Guthrie wrote, "There is a lack of studied order, some subjects being treated more than once in the same letter without apparent premeditation. . . . These letters are, therefore, far removed from literary exercises."[35] And A. T. Hanson, an opponent of the Pauline authorship of the Pastorals, maintained, "The Pastorals are made up of a miscellaneous collection of material. They have no unifying theme; there is no development of thought."[36]

Yet, in the last decade, the pendulum has swung away from such assessments. Over against those who have argued against the literary unity and integrity of the Pastoral Epistles, Van Neste has demonstrated, in the most careful study of the topic to date, that there is "evidence of a high level of cohesion in each of the Pastoral Epistles" and that "all three letters show evidence of care in their design."[37] I. Howard Marshall, likewise, noted that "there is a growing body of evidence that the Pastoral Epistles are not a conglomerate of miscellaneous ideas roughly thrown together with no clear plan, purpose or structure. On the contrary, they demonstrate signs of a coherent structure and of theological competence."[38]

In light of assessments such as these, it appears that the literary integrity and coherence of the Pastoral Epistles has been amply rehabilitated against charges of incoherence by their critics. It remains to provide brief discussions of the literary plan of 1 and 2 Timothy and Titus.

1 TIMOTHY

William D. Mounce divides the structure of 1 Timothy as follows: I. Salutation (1:1–2); II. The Ephesian problem (1:3–20); III. Correction of improper conduct

---

[33] See L. T. Johnson, *Letters to Paul's Delegates: 1 Timothy, 2 Timothy, Titus* (The New Testament in Context; Valley Forge, PA: Trinity Press International, 1996), 106–7, 168.

[34] R. Van Neste, *Cohesion and Structure in the Pastoral Epistles* (JSNTSup 280; London/New York: T&T Clark, 2004), 1.

[35] D. Guthrie, *The Pastoral Epistles* (2nd ed.; TNTC; Grand Rapids: Eerdmans, 1990), 18.

[36] A. T. Hanson, *The Pastoral Epistles* (Grand Rapids: Eerdmans, 1982), 42.

[37] Van Neste, *Cohesion and Structure*, 285. Contra J. D. Miller, *The Pastoral Letters as Composite Documents* (SNTSMS 93; Cambridge: Cambridge Univ. Press, 1997).

[38] I. H. Marshall, "The Christology of Luke-Acts and the Pastoral Epistles," in *Crossing the Boundaries: Essays in Biblical Interpretation in Honour of Michael D. Goulder* (ed. S. E. Porter, P. Joyce, and D. E. Orton; Biblical Interpretation 8; Leiden: Brill, 1994), 171.

in the Ephesian church (2:1–4:5); IV. Personal notes to Timothy (4:6–16); V. How Timothy is to relate to different groups in the church (5:1–6:2a); and VI. Final instructions (6:2b–21).[39] On the whole, this outline is sound, especially in drawing a line of demarcation between 1:20 and 2:1[40] and in identifying 5:1–6:2a as a separate literary unit. However, it seems preferable to see 3:16 as concluding Paul's instructions that began in 2:1[41] and to see him as starting a new major unit in 4:1 with reference to the last days.[42] If so, the discussion of the literary plan of 1 Timothy may proceed as follows.[43]

Overview of Structural Proposals (1 Timothy)		
Mounce	*Towner*	*Köstenberger*
1:1–2 Salutation	1:1–2 Opening	1:1–2 Opening
1:3–20 Ephesian Problem	1:3–6:21a Body	1:3–20 Personal Charge
2:1–4:5 Correction	1:3–3:16 Part 1	2:1–3:16 Congregational Matters
4:6–16 Personal Notes	4:1–6:21a Part 2	4:1–6:2a Further Charges
5:1–6:2a Different Groups	6:21b Benediction	6:2b–19 Final Exhortation
6:2b–21 Final Instructions		6:20–21 Closing

Paul's first letter to Timothy immediately turns to the subject at hand: the need for Timothy to "command certain people not to teach other doctrine" in the church at Ephesus (1:3–4). Paul's customary thanksgiving follows after his initial comments regarding these false teachers and is, in fact, a thanksgiving to God for Paul's own conversion, since Paul himself at one point persecuted the church of God (1:12–17). At the end of the first chapter, Paul even mentions two of these false teachers by name: Hymenaeus and Alexander (1:20).

After this, Paul transitions ("First of all, then"; 2:1) to a section where he sets forth instructions for the church, in keeping with his purpose cited in 3:14–15: "I write these things to you, hoping to come to you soon. But if I should be delayed, I have written so that you will know how people ought to act in God's household,

---

[39] Mounce, *Pastoral Epistles*, cxxxv (note that the numbering is off in that Mounce has two II. and two IV.). Similarly, Guthrie, *Pastoral Epistles*, 63–64, whose major divisions are I. 1:1–20; II. 2:1–4:16; III. 5:1–6:2; and IV. 6:3–21. Even less structure is discerned by T. D. Lea and H. P. Griffin, *1, 2 Timothy, Titus* (NAC 34; Nashville: Broadman & Holman, 1992), 17, who divide the letter into I. 1:1–2; II. 1:3–20; and III. 2:1–6:21.

[40] Contra P. H. Towner, *The Letters to Timothy and Titus* (NICNT; Grand Rapids: Eerdmans, 2006), ix, who keeps 1:3–3:16 as a single unit and gives insufficient attention to the markers "first of all" and "then" at 2:1. However, Towner, unlike Mounce, rightly discerns a break between 3:16 and 4:1 (ibid., x).

[41] See the interaction with Fee, "Reflections on Church Order in the Pastoral Epistles," 145, in Köstenberger, "1–2 Timothy, Titus," 504, 509–10.

[42] This critique pertains to Mounce as well as Guthrie and Lea/Griffin.

[43] See Köstenberger, "1–2 Timothy, Titus," 497. See also the proposed structure by Marshall, *Pastoral Epistles*, 30, who divides the letter between 1:3–3:16 and 4:1–6:21a.

which is the church of the living God, the pillar and foundation of the truth." This makes clear that 2:1–3:16 constitutes a section apart from chap. 1 on the one hand and chaps. 4–6 on the other, both of which are dominated by Paul's concern with the false teachers. While such concerns are not completely absent from chaps. 2–3, these chapters are taken up with Paul's more positive instructions to Timothy on how to govern the church. This includes instructions on prayer (2:1–8), women's roles in the congregation (2:9–15), and qualifications for church leadership, both overseers (3:1–7) and deacons (3:8–13). The section concludes with a presentation of the "mystery of godliness," possibly drawing on a piece of liturgy (3:16).

Chapter 4, then, opens with the dramatic phrase "Now the Spirit explicitly says" (4:1), setting the work of the false teachers squarely in the context of the end times, during which things would go from bad to worse. In this context, Timothy is to set himself apart by giving close attention both to his personal life and to his doctrine, thus preserving both himself and his hearers (4:11–16). Additional instructions are given regarding the care of widows (5:3–16); dealing with elders, including those who had sinned (5:17–25); the proper conduct of Christian slaves (6:1–2); and the rich (6:3–10,17–19). Timothy, on the other hand, is to guard what has been entrusted to him, as Paul's final charge makes clear (6:11–16,20–21).

2 TIMOTHY

Philip H. Towner presents the structure of 2 Timothy as follows: I. Opening Greeting (1:1–2); II. Body of the Letter (1:3–4:18); A. Call to Personal Commitment (1:3–18); B. Call to Dedication and Faithfulness (2:1–13); C. The Challenge of Opposition (2:14–26); D. Prophecy, Commitment, and Call (3:1–4:8); III. Final Instructions (4:9–18); and IV. Closing Greetings (4:19–22).[44] This structure is much to be preferred over Mounce, who rather idiosyncratically provides the following breakdown: I. Salutation (1:1–2); II. Thanksgiving (1:3–5); III. Encouragement to Timothy (1:6–2:13); IV. Instructions for Timothy and Opponents (2:14–4:8); and V. Final Words to Timothy (4:9–22).[45] The following discussion of the literary plan underlying 2 Timothy will proceed with a slightly modified version of Towner's outline.[46]

---

[44] Towner, *Letters to Timothy and Titus*, xi. Cf. Marshall, *Pastoral Epistles*, 38, whose proposal is identical.
[45] Mounce, *Pastoral Epistles*, cxxxvi.
[46] See Köstenberger, "1–2 Timothy, Titus," 566, and the following commentary for justification of this outline. The only difference between Towner and Köstenberger is that the latter keeps 2:1–26 together as a major unit (similarly, Guthrie, *Pastoral Epistles*, 132) and breaks it up into the subunits of 2:1–7,8–13, and 14–26, while Towner divides 2:1–26 into two major subunits, 2:1–13 and 2:14–26.

Overview of Structural Proposals (2 Timothy)		
Mounce	*Towner*	*Köstenberger*
1:1–2 Salutation	1:1–2 Opening	1:1–2 Opening
1:3–5 Thanksgiving	1:3–18 Call to Commitment	1:3–18 Thanksgiving, Exhortation
1:6–2:13 Encouragement	2:1–13 Call to Dedication	2:1–26 Ministry Metaphors
2:14–4:8 Opposition	2:14–26 Opposition	
	3:1–4:8 Prophecy, Call	3:1–4:8 Further Charges
4:9–22 Final Words	4:9–18 Final Instructions	4:9–18 Recent News
	4:19–22 Closing Greetings	4:19–22 Closing Greetings

Paul's second letter to Timothy opens with the customary greeting and thanksgiving (1:1–7), followed by an exhortation for Timothy not to be ashamed of Paul, who is now in prison (1:8–12). After contrasting various co-workers, Paul instructs Timothy on the nature of Christian ministry by way of three metaphors, those of the soldier, the athlete, and the farmer, each of which has important lessons to teach regarding the proper disposition of the Lord's servant (2:1–7). After stating one of the "faithful sayings" featured in the Pastorals, Paul uses three additional metaphors for Christian ministry: the workman, various instruments, and the servant (2:14–26). Additional charges, recent news, and a concluding greeting round out the letter (chaps. 3–4).

TITUS

The various proposals regarding the structure of Titus, once again, reveal a certain amount of consensus as well as differences in the details. Towner proposes the following outline: I. Opening Greeting (1:1–4); II. Body of Letter (1:5–3:11); A. Instructions to Titus (1:5–16); B. Instructions for the Church (2:1–3:11); IV. Personal Notes and Instructions (3:12–14); and V. Final Greetings and Benediction (3:15).[47] Towner's outline is similar to that of Mounce, who breaks down 1:5–16 further into 1:5–9 and 1:6–16 but keeps 3:12–15 together as a unit.[48] The structural proposal set forth below differs only slightly from these two major commentators.[49]

---

[47] Towner, *Letters to Timothy and Titus*, xii.
[48] Mounce, *Pastoral Epistles*, cxxxvi.
[49] Köstenberger, "1–2 Timothy, Titus," 603. Cf. Marshall, *Pastoral Epistles*, 24, whose proposed outline is virtually identical with that of Köstenberger.

Overview of Structural Proposals (Titus)		
Mounce	*Towner*	*Köstenberger*
1:1–4 Salutation	1:1–4 Opening	1:1–4 Opening
1:5–9 Qualifications	1:5–3:11 Body of Letter	1:5–16 Occasion for Writing
1:10–16 Problems in Crete	1:5–16 To Titus	2:1–15 Different Groups
2:1–3:11 Godly Living	2:1–3:11 To the Church	3:1–11 Doing What Is Good
3:12–15 Final Greeting	3:12–14 Personal Notes	3:12–15 Closing Comments
	3:15 Greetings	

Similar to 1 Timothy, Titus shows Paul getting straight to the point, reminding Titus why Paul left him in Crete: "to set right what was left undone and . . . to appoint elders in every town" (1:5). Also similar to Paul's first letter to Timothy, Titus is given various instructions on how to correct the enemies of the gospel while himself staying above the fray. Christians are to "adorn the teaching of God our Savior in everything" (2:10) and to devote themselves to "good work" (3:1). In keeping with the personal nature of the letter, Paul concludes with some final instructions and a closing greeting (3:12–15).

Having surveyed hermeneutical issues in the interpretation of the Pastorals, the following discussion will turn to a treatment of significant exegetical matters.

EXEGETICAL CHALLENGES

If Paul was the author of the Pastoral Epistles and his letters transcended mere ad hoc argumentation, what are some of the abiding apostolic teachings pertaining to the church in these letters? Quite clearly, Paul's pronouncements regarding church government and qualifications for church leaders must be at the top of the list. An adjudication of Paul's teaching on these issues in the Pastorals is needed all the more as the relevant passages present several major exegetical challenges, which is part of the reason why issues related to church government continue to be hotly debated and disputed today.[50]

---

[50] See the representative discussions in C. O. Brand and R. S. Norman, eds., *Perspectives on Church Government: Five Views of Church Polity* (Nashville: Broadman & Holman, 2004); and S. B. Cowan, ed., *Who Runs the Church? 4 Views on Church Government* (Counterpoints; Grand Rapids: Zondervan, 2004).

ELDERS/OVERSEERS

ONE AUTHORITATIVE OFFICE

The area of church leadership is one area where the Pastorals quite clearly set forth paradigms for the church that reach beyond their original Ephesian or Cretan context.[51] As mentioned, it has been claimed by some that the church structure found in the Pastorals reflects the second-century AD pattern of a three-tiered ecclesiastical hierarchy involving a monarchical episcopate (e.g., Ignatius of Antioch). Yet closer scrutiny reveals that the Pastorals do not in fact conform to this model but rather display a synonymous usage of the terms "overseer" (ἐπίσκοπος) and "elder" (πρεσβύτερος) as referring to one and the same office (Titus 1:5,7; cf. Acts 20:17,28; *1 Clem.* 44:1,5; Jerome, *Letter* 59).[52]

With regard to specific terminology, 1 Tim 3:1 uses the word ἐπισκοπή (cf. Acts 1:20), denoting the "office of overseer" (cf. Luke 19:44; Acts 1:20; 1 Pet 2:12), while in 3:2 ἐπίσκοπος is used, referring to the person holding such an office.[53] In the LXX, the term designates one in charge of an operation (Num 4:16); in Josephus, it denotes an "overseer" (*Ant.* 10.53; 12.254). The Qumran equivalent was the מְבַקֵּר. (1QS 6.12,20; CD 9.18–19,22; 13.6–7). Generally, πρεσβύτερος is Jewish in origin, signifying seniority, while ἐπίσκοπος is Greek, indicating a person's superintending role. Presumably overseers constituted the "board of elders" (πρεσβυτέριον) mentioned in 1 Tim 4:14.[54]

THE OFFICE OF ELDER LIMITED TO MEN

The overseer (equivalent to pastor/elder) bears ultimate responsibility for the church before God (see 1 Tim 3:15; 5:17). According to the instructions on the role of women in the previous chapter (esp. 2:12), only men are eligible for this office. In the book *Women and the Church,* edited by Andreas Köstenberger and Thomas Schreiner, the contributors have made a strong case that Paul did not permit women to serve in roles of ultimate authority and responsibility in the church on the basis of his pronouncement, "I do not permit a woman to teach or have authority over a man in the church" (1 Tim 2:12).[55] This is shown to be the most plausible understanding

---

[51] For a discussion of the different major systems of church governance, see A. J. Köstenberger, "Church Government," in *Encyclopedia of Christian Civilization* (ed. G. T. Kurian; Oxford: Blackwell, forthcoming).

[52] See the discussion under Authorship above.

[53] See Acts 20:28; Phil 1:1; Titus 1:7; 1 Pet 2:25. For πρεσβύτερος, see esp. 1 Tim 5:1,17,19; Titus 1:5; 1 Pet 5:1,5; Jas 5:14; and the book of Acts.

[54] Johnson, *Letters to Paul's Delegates,* 145.

[55] A. J. Köstenberger and T. R. Schreiner, eds., *Women in the Church: An Analysis and Application of 1 Timothy 2:9–15* (rev. ed.; Grand Rapids: Baker, 2005).

of this pivotal verse in keeping with the Ephesian background, the lexical and syntactical makeup of the verse, and exegetical and hermeneutical considerations.[56]

At the same time, it should be noted that a complementarian understanding of gender roles in the church does not depend on 1 Tim 2:12 but is based on the biblical theology of this subject throughout all of Scripture.[57] Both Jesus and Paul confirmed the husband's headship in the home, and both affirmed male leadership, Jesus by appointing twelve men as his apostles and Paul by grounding his teaching on the subject in the foundational creation narrative in the book of Genesis and by stating that elders in the church ought to be "faithful husbands," implying that only males were eligible for such a position. It is also demonstrable that the New Testament does not refer to any women serving in the position of pastor or elder in the churches planted by Paul or those under his apostolic jurisdiction.[58]

In a recent article, Philip Payne has reiterated his earlier contention that Paul in 1 Tim 2:12 forbids women only from assuming *improper* authority over men in the church.[59] Payne claims that Paul (or his amanuensis, or a pseudepigrapher) used the expression οὐδέ ("nor") in this verse essentially as a subordinating conjunction, subsuming the Greek verb αὐθεντεῖν under the head word διδάσκειν, with the resultant meaning "to teach men *by assuming* independent authority."[60] At the beginning of his article, Payne promises that he will identify "many instances" where οὐδέ "joins an *infinitive* with positive connotations to an infinitive with negative connotations."[61] However, strikingly, in none of the examples he cites on the following pages does οὐδέ link infinitives![62] At the very end of his article, Payne claims that 9 of the 102 extrabiblical parallels to 1 Tim 2:12 that I cited in a previous publication involve the use of one word with a positive and another with a negative connotation (which, if true, might allow one to construe 1 Tim 2:12 as a positive word, διδάσκειν, being

---

56 The first 1995 edition included essays by S. Baugh, S. Baldwin, A. Köstenberger, D. Gordon, T. Schreiner, R. Yarbrough, H. O. J. Brown, and an appendix by D. Doriani. The second edition featured revised essays by Baugh, Baldwin, Köstenberger, Schreiner, and Yarbrough and a new essay by D. Patterson. See also the summary of the first edition by A. J. Köstenberger, "'The Crux of the Matter': Paul's Pastoral Pronouncements Regarding Women's Roles in 1 Timothy 2:9–15," *Faith & Mission* 14/1 (Fall 1996): 24–48.

57 See A. J. Köstenberger, "Women in the Pauline Mission," in *The Gospel to the Nations: Perspectives on Paul's Mission. In Honour of Peter T. O'Brien* (ed. P. Bolt and M. Thompson; Leicester, UK/Downers Grove, IL: InterVarsity, 2000), 235–37. Contra P. B. Payne, "1 Tim 2.12 and the Use of *oude* to Combine Two Elements to Express a Single Idea," *NTS* 54 (2008): 235, who seems to suggest otherwise.

58 See Köstenberger, "Women in the Pauline Mission," 221–47.

59 P. B. Payne, "*Oude* in 1 Timothy 2:12" (unpublished paper presented at the 1988 annual meeting of the Evangelical Theological Society). See the critique of Payne in *Women in the Church*, 55–56 (retained from the first edition). Payne originally argued that the two infinitives form a hendiadys, though he no longer uses this term in his later article because of unspecified "disputes over its definition" (p. 235, n. 2).

60 See Payne, "1 Tim 2.12," 243–44. Note in this regard that Payne proposed that Paul used οὐδέ differently from Luke (see ibid., 241–42). However, it is hard to see how it is meaningful to speak of "Paul's use of *oude*" (see, e.g., p. 244: "Paul's typical use of *oude*") if the Pastorals were written by someone other than Paul (especially a pseudepigrapher), as Payne suggests as a possibility.

61 Payne, "1 Tim 2.12," 236 (emphasis added). Payne's argument in *Man and Woman, One in Christ: An Exegetical and Theological Study of Paul's Letters* (Grand Rapids: Zondervan, 2009), 356–58, proceeds along similar lines.

62 Ibid., 236–41.

modified by a negative one, αὐθεντεῖν, though still not necessarily with the second word subordinated to the first by way of hendiadys). Even if true, of course, this would still mean that the pattern of usage (positive-positive or negative-negative) I proposed would obtain over 91 percent of the time in the entire New Testament and extrabiblical Greek sources. What is more, however, even in these nine cases Payne's arguments demonstrably fall short.

(1) In 2 Cor 7:12, in the phrase neither "on account of the one who did the wrong *nor* on account of the one who was wronged," both perpetrating wrong and being victimized are viewed negatively by Paul as part of a wrong committed (two corresponding aspects of the "one single idea" Payne is affirming).

(2) In 2 Thess 3:7–8, both idleness and eating someone else's bread without paying for it are viewed negatively (Payne's discussion of this on pp. 242–43 is inadequate; clearly, in context, Paul implied that it would have been wrong for him and his associates to eat anyone's bread free of charge because doing so would have made them a "burden" to others, which clearly has a negative connotation).

(3) In Sir 18:6 (LXX), neither diminishing nor increasing God's mercies is viewed as possible or desirable; while "diminish" and "increase" are conceptual opposites, from the writer's perspective the only proper approach is to represent God's mercies accurately; hence both diminishing or increasing them is discouraged.

(4) In Diodorus Siculus, *Bib. Hist.* 3.30.2.8, both surprise and distrust express skepticism over against outright acceptance (note the escalation from surprise to distrust here).

(5) In Josephus, *Ant.* 15.165.3–4, in context, both "meddling in state affairs" and "starting a revolution" are viewed negatively. While the first term, depending on the context, is capable of having both positive and negative connotations, a negative connotation is more likely in light of the clear and consistent pattern of usage of οὐδέ elsewhere as well as other considerations.

(6) In Plutarch, *Regum et imperatorum apophthegmata* 185.A.1, both sleeping and being indolent are viewed negatively (again, there is an escalation from sleep to indolence). In the present context, the trophy of Miltiades calls for a positive response; by comparison, both sleep and indolence fall short. To adduce a passage from another of Plutarch's work which evinces a "positive view of sleep" completely misses the point, because verbal meaning is contextual rather than merely a function of lexis.

(7) In Plutarch, *Aetia Romana et Graeca* 269.D, both exact and approximate reckoning are viewed negatively in the present context (the limited skill of mathematicians).

(8) In Plutarch, *Quaestiones convivales* 711.E.3, "harming" and "getting the best of us" are both viewed negatively; both are virtual synonyms, and, certainly, wine "getting the best" of someone is not viewed positively by the writer as Payne suggests!

(9) In Plutarch, *Bruta animalia ratione uti* 990.A.11, touching is viewed negatively because it results in pain; thus both actions are viewed negatively and related to each other in terms of one action (touching) resulting in the experience of another (experiencing pain).

The difficulty with Payne's analysis of these references is his categorization of verbs as "positive" or "negative." Contrary to Payne's understanding, however, it is not the case that verbs are "positive" or "negative" by themselves.[63] Rather, verbs convey a positive or negative connotation *in context*. Thus lexical meaning by itself is inadequate to discern a given term's connotation in context. A writer's use of a given verb is to a significant extent a matter of aspect or perception and thus subjective. As shown, therefore, properly understood none of the alleged nine "problem cases" of the pattern of the usage of οὐδέ that I identified are problematic. To the contrary, they conform perfectly to this pattern, as do the other 93 of 102 instances not disputed by Payne. The pattern is always positive/positive or negative/negative, never positive/negative or vice versa.

Another difficulty pertains to Payne's contention that οὐδέ joins two expressions conveying a "single idea." This may indeed be the case (though this is an entirely different matter than whether οὐδέ joins concepts viewed positively and negatively by the writer), and I, for one, have never denied this possibility. It is important to keep in mind, however, that οὐδέ, as a coordinating conjunction, does not necessarily join two concepts to such an extent that the two actions completely merge and become indistinguishable from one another. Instead, while there may be an overlap, a certain amount of distinctness may be retained. For example, one action may result in the experience of another (e.g., touching an object leading to the experience of pain).

Therefore, to posit the presence of "one single idea" or two completely separate concepts as the only two possible alternatives is unduly disjunctive and fails to do justice to the way οὐδέ functions in Koine Greek.[64] Applied to the present case, the interpretation of 1 Tim 2:12, then, the overarching "single idea" is that women ought not to serve in authoritative church positions, whether by teaching men or by ruling

---

[63] Ibid., 251–52.

[64] Sometimes Payne's language is less precise than might be desirable, such as when he speaks of οὐδέ joining "expressions that reinforce or make more specific a single idea" (p. 236). What Payne fails to note here is that in those cases this may involve the introduction of a second, related (yet nonetheless distinct) idea. See further the discussion below.

(both functions are reserved for male elders)—two functions that are distinct yet closely related. In other words, "exercising authority" is a larger term than "teaching," since a person may exercise authority in other ways besides teaching (such as by making decisions binding on the entire church or by exercising church discipline; see also 1 Tim 5:17). Conversely, teaching is one major way in which authority is exercised in the church.

Apart from these linguistic and syntactical difficulties, Payne fails also on the level of exegesis and background.[65] With regard to background, Payne mounts an unconvincing argument that Paul sought to forbid women perpetrating false teaching in the Ephesian context. Yet this does not follow from a reading of 1 Tim 2:12 in the context of the immediately following verses. Specifically, Paul states that Adam was created first (1 Tim 2:13) and that it was not Adam who was deceived but the woman (1 Tim 2:14). This makes clear that Paul's concern is with the woman as the *victim of deception*, not as the *perpetrator of false teaching*. Nowhere in the context of 1 Tim 2:12 is Paul's point regarding Eve that she *taught Adam falsely*.

Instead, in Timothy's Ephesus there seem to have been those who told women that true spirituality consisted in refraining from engaging in their natural functions of marriage and childbearing (see, e.g., 1 Tim 2:15; 4:3; 5:14).[66] Paul's concern for women in this context was for them not to fall prey to such deception by engaging in teaching or assuming a ruling function, or by aspiring to the pastoral office (see 1 Tim 3:1–2). Instead, he wanted them to be devoted to fulfilling their domestic and familial roles. Also, if Paul's injunction in 1 Tim 2:12 was merely for women not to "assert independent authority over men," as Payne claims, why would it be the case, as he also asserts, that the present tense form of "I do not permit" in 1 Tim 2:12 "fits a *current* prohibition better than a *permanent* one"?[67] Is there ever a time when it is biblically appropriate for women to "assume independent authority over men"? It is hard to conceive of such a circumstance.

---

[65] See especially Payne's discussion on p. 247, which contains a large number of questionable assertions and logical non sequiturs, such as that Paul's statement in 1 Tim 2:13 that "Adam was formed first" "implies that woman should respect man as her source" when the verse clearly refers to Adam's prior creation, not Adam being the woman's source. Payne's discussion of affirmations of women teaching elsewhere in the Pastorals (ibid., p. 248) likewise contains assertions that fail to prove Payne's point. For example, Payne adduces the pronoun "anyone" in 1 Tim 3:1 as support for the claim that women as well as men should be allowed to serve as elders while failing to note the "faithful husband" requirement in the following verse. He proceeds to cite Timothy's instruction by his mother and grandmother (hardly relevant here, since no one disputes that mothers and grandmothers may instruct their sons or grandsons in the faith). Finally, Payne notes the injunction for older women to teach younger women in Titus 2 (likewise not relevant in a discussion of women teaching men). None of this can properly be regarded as legitimate support for the notion that women should be appointed as elders or overseers in the local church.

[66] See A. J. Köstenberger, "Ascertaining Women's God-Ordained Roles: An Interpretation of 1 Timothy 2:15," *BBR* 7 (1997): 104–11. Payne, *Man and Woman*, 417–41, maintains that according to 1 Tim 2:15 women will be saved by "the Childbirth," that is, Messiah Jesus' birth by Mary. While this is possible (though somewhat foreign to the Pauline context), a careful study of the history of interpretation of 1 Tim 2:15 reveals that this is only one of at least a half dozen common interpretations of this vexing passage, so that Payne's chosen interpretation is not nearly as compelling as he seems to suppose.

[67] Payne, "1 Tim 2.12," 243, n. 23 (emphasis added). Payne does not give support for this assertion.

For these reasons, there continues to be every reason to believe that Scripture teaches that men should serve as heads of households (e.g., Eph 5:23–24; 1 Tim 3:4–5) and as elders in the churches (1 Tim 2:12; 3:2; see also 5:17). In this way, the Bible links the authority structure in the natural family and the authority structure in the spiritual family, "God's household" (1 Tim 3:15), the church. This does not mean that women are denied significant participation in the ministry of the church. Nor is their role as wives and mothers to be disparaged or diminished in any way (see, e.g., 1 Tim 2:15). In this life, God so chose to order male-female relations in the family and the church that wives submit to husbands and the church to male elders. This neither reflects any merit on the man's part or demerit on the woman's part; such is the will of God according to Scripture.

THE "HUSBAND OF ONE WIFE" REQUIREMENT

As mentioned, the Pauline pronouncement that the role of elder or overseer is limited to men is confirmed by the qualification μιᾶς γυναικὸς ἄνδρα in 1 Tim 3:2 and Titus 1:6.[68] The exact nature of this qualification, in turn, has been subject to considerable debate. The following possibilities have been suggested: (1) disqualification of single men; (2) disqualification of divorced men; (3) disqualification of remarried widowers; (4) disqualification of polygamists; (5) disqualification of those lacking marital fidelity.[69] The first proposal is unlikely, if for no other reason that in this case Paul himself, and probably Timothy and possibly Titus as well, would have been disqualified. The second proposal, likewise, is unlikely; if so, Paul would have simply said, "not divorced."

The third view, while the most common view in patristic times, is also unlikely, because there is no good reason why widowers who remarried would have been disqualified from church leadership. Fourth, renderings such as the NIV's "husband of *but* one wife" (though note the commendable change in the TNIV to "faithful to his wife") suggest that the requirement is aimed at excluding polygamists.[70] However, polygamy was not widely practiced in the Greco-Roman world of the time.[71] S. M.

---

68 Contra Payne (ibid., 248), who claims that the word "anyone" (τις) in 1 Tim 3:1 "encompasses men and women" but gives insufficient consideration to the fact that this can hardly be said about the phrase "faithful husband" (μιᾶς γυναικὸς ἄνδρα) in the following verse. In *Man and Woman*, 459, Payne contends that the qualification for overseers to be "faithful husbands" does not presuppose that such office-holders be men, or else unmarried men would be excluded as well. But this hardly follows. More likely, Paul presupposes that overseers be male and, assuming that they were typically married, stipulates that they be faithful in their marriage relationship (see also Paul's prohibition of women teaching or having authority over men in 1 Tim 2:12). Payne (ibid., 450) also claims that nearly identical terminology used of women and overseers in 1 Timothy proves that Paul included women among those eligible to serve as elders. However, all this proves is that some of the same qualifications (such as good works, blameless character, marital faithfulness, or self-control) are applicable to both elders and women, and care should be taken not to confuse sense and reference.

69 For a discussion and adjudication of these alternatives, see A. J. Köstenberger, *God, Marriage, and Family: Rebuilding the Biblical Foundation* (Wheaton: Crossway, 2004), 259–64.

70 Cf. John Calvin, *1 & 2 Timothy & Titus* (Wheaton/Nottingham: Crossway, 1998 [1549, 1556]), 54.

71 See Mounce, *Pastoral Epistles*, 171.

Baugh, in particular, has made a convincing case for interpreting the phrase as barring men who have one or several concubines.[72] This widespread practice conflicted with biblical morals, since sexual union with a concubine constituted adultery and amounted to polygamy. Moreover, the word "but" is not in the original. For these reasons the phrase μιᾶς γυναικὸς ἄνδρα most likely represents an idiom referring to marital faithfulness.[73]

That this is the case is further confirmed by the parallel passage 1 Tim 5:9, where a widow eligible for church support is required to have been "faithful to her husband" (so even the NIV = TNIV) and where the equivalent phrase "wife of one husband" is used (cf. 1 Cor 7:2–5). In the latter instance, the phrase cannot indicate a prohibition of polyandry (being married to more than one husband at a time), since it is made of a woman bereft of her husband. Moreover, it is hardly conceivable that Paul first encouraged younger widows to get remarried and then disqualified them later on the grounds that they had, literally, been wives of more than one husband.[74]

The requirement of being, literally, an "of-one-wife-husband" may be patterned after the Roman concept of a *univira* (i.e., a "one husband"-type of wife).[75] This term denoting marital fidelity was initially applied to living women in relation to their husbands and later became an epithet given by husbands to their deceased wives (as is attested by numerous extant tombstone inscriptions).[76] The requirement of marital faithfulness for church leaders (including deacons; 1 Tim 3:12) is also consistent with the prohibition of adultery in the Decalogue (Exod 20:14 = Deut 5:18).[77]

If this interpretation is correct, divorced (and remarried) men would not necessarily be excluded from serving as overseers or deacons, especially if the divorce was biblically legitimate.[78] This would be true also if the divorce has taken place in the distant past (especially if the person was not a believer at the time) and if the man's present

[72] S. M. Baugh, "Titus," in *Zondervan Illustrated Bible Backgrounds Commentary* (ed. C. E. Arnold; Grand Rapids: Zondervan, 2002), 3:501–2.

[73] See esp. S. Page, "Marital Expectations of Church Leaders in the Pastoral Epistles," *JSNT* 50 (1993): 105–20, esp. 108–9 and 114, n. 27.

[74] Cf. P. Trummer, "Einehe nach den Pastoralbriefen," *Bib* 51 (1970): 480; apparently independently, Page, "Marital Expectations," 112; contra Fee, "Reflections on Church Order," 150, who contends that the present passage "probably prohibits remarriage of widows/widowers."

[75] Cf. M. Lightman and W. Zeisel, "Univira: An Example of Continuity and Change in Roman Society," *Church History* 46 (1977): 19–32.

[76] As the poet Catullus (first century BC) wrote, "To live content with one man is for wives an honor of honors" (111). A Roman imperial inscription reads, "She lived fifty years and was satisfied with one husband" (*CIL* 6.5162). The late-first-century BC *Laudatio Turiae* records a husband saying about his wife, "Rare are marriages, so long lasting, and ended by death, not interrupted by divorce. . . ."

[77] The present requirement contrasts with the Gnostic extremes of asceticism and sexual licentiousness. Marital fidelity was also held in high regard in the Greco-Roman world, so that this quality would commend a Christian office-holder to his pagan surroundings (cf. Page, "Marital Expectations," 117–18).

[78] Regarding the wife's marital unfaithfulness, see Matt 19:9; regarding desertion by an unbelieving wife, see 1 Cor 7:15–16; regarding remarriage subsequent to the death of one's spouse, see Rom 7:2–3. See A. J. Köstenberger, "Marriage and Family in the New Testament," in *Marriage and Family in the Biblical World* (ed. K. M. Campbell; Downers Grove, IL: InterVarsity, 2003), 256–64. See also chap. 12 in Köstenberger, *God, Marriage, and Family*.

pattern (and proven track record) is that of marital faithfulness.[79] Nevertheless, when coupled with the requirement that an overseer be "above reproach" (which includes community reputation), it may be best not to appoint divorcees to the role of overseer, especially when qualified candidates are available that did not undergo a divorce.

DEACONS

The second church office addressed in 1 Timothy 3 besides that of overseer/elder is that of deacon. Structurally, the presence of the phrase "likewise" or "in the same way" (ὡσαύτως) in 1 Tim 3:8 and 11 may suggest that qualifications are given for two other types of officeholders besides that of overseer (3:1–7). The flow of thought in 3:8–13 may indicate that one large category, that of deacon, is discussed, with Paul first addressing qualifications for male and then female office-holders, with a final verse being devoted to a concluding comment regarding male deacons and a general statement pertaining to deacons in general.

When comparing the qualifications for deacons with those for overseers, one notes the absence of terms related to teaching or ruling (most notably "able to teach," 3:2; see also 3:5b). This suggests that, in keeping with the designation "deacon" (from Gk. διάκονος, "servant") as over against "overseer," deacons are not part of that group that bears ultimate responsibility for the church.[80] At the same time, they, too, occupy a formal church office, for which they must meet certain requirements. While not part of the teaching or ruling body of the church, deacons hold important leadership roles. This is indicated by the similarity between the qualifications for overseers and deacons.[81] Although Paul does not spell out the precise realm of service for the office of deacon, one may surmise that this includes various kinds of practical helps and administration, such as benevolence, finances, or physical maintenance.[82]

According to 1 Tim 3:8, these "servants" (cf. Phil 1:1; not mentioned in Titus) "likewise" (cf. 2:9; 3:11; Titus 2:3,6) are to meet certain qualifications, whereby 1 Tim 3:8–10 and 12 relates to male and 3:11 to female "servants." The expression "their wives" in the NIV translates the Greek γυναῖκας,[83] which could also be translated "women deacons" or "deaconesses" (NIV footnote; the NASB and HCSB simply have "women," preserving the ambiguity in the original Greek). Both meanings for γυνή, "woman" (2:9,10,11,12,14) and "wife" (3:2,12; 5:9; cf. Titus 1:6),

---

[79] See Page, "Marital Expectations," 109–13.

[80] Cf. Knight, *Pastoral Epistles*, 167; contra Marshall, *Pastoral Epistles*, 485.

[81] Towner, *1–2 Timothy & Titus*, 90–91.

[82] Mounce, *Pastoral Epistles*, 207, contends that "Paul does not teach that the deacon is under the overseer . . . both overseer and deacon serve the church in different capacities." Yet overseers are in charge of the entire congregation (e.g., 5:17), which would seem to include deacons.

[83] Note that "their" is not in the original; but see the change in the NIVI to "wives" and in the TNIV to "the women" (TNIV footnote: "Probably women who are deacons").

are found in 1 Timothy; context must decide.[84] The following arguments have been advanced in favor of "women servants."[85]

(1) The absence of qualifications for overseers' wives in 1 Tim 3:1–7: all things being equal, on the assumption that 1 Tim 3:11 refers to deacons' wives, one would expect for there also to be a listing of qualifications for elders' wives earlier in the chapter, but such are not given.

(2) The phrase "in the same way" in 1 Tim 3:11 indicating an office similar to the one previously mentioned (cf. 3:8), as well as the parallel sentence structure: in 1 Tim 3:8, the phrase "in the same way" marks a transition from one office (that of elder) to another (that of deacon); by analogy, it is argued that the same phrase in 1 Tim 3:11, likewise, marks the transition from one office (male deacon) to another (female deacon).

(3) The lack of an article before "women" (γυναῖκας) in 1 Tim 3:11: without any further qualification, γυνή usually refers to "women"; if someone's "woman" (i.e., wife) is in view, this is indicated by a possessive article ("his") or in some other way ("his own," etc.); in 1 Tim 3:11, no such further qualifier is found, suggesting women servants rather than wives of deacons.

If Paul had women "servants" in mind, why did he not call them "deaconesses"? The reason may be that in his day the word διάκονος was still used for males and females alike (plus the respective article to indicate gender); it was only later that the term διακόνισσα was coined (*Apost. Const.* 8.19,20,28).[86] Thus Phoebe is identified as a διάκονος of the church at Cenchrea in Rom 16:1. Paul's mention of female "servants" coheres well with his earlier prohibition of women serving in teaching or ruling functions over men (1 Tim 2:12) and his lack of mention of women elders in 1 Tim 3:1–7.[87] Since being a "servant" (deacon) does not involve teaching or ruling, there would not seem to be a compelling theological reason why women should be kept from serving in this capacity, as long as it is kept in mind that deacon is a nonauthoritative, nonruling ecclesiastical role.

A survey of major new translations and commentaries seems to suggest that in recent years, the tide of opinion has slightly shifted toward the presence of women

---

[84] A third possibility is favored by R. M. Lewis, "The 'Women' of 1 Timothy 3:11," *BibSac* 136 (1979): 167–75, that of unmarried [single or widowed] female deacons' assistants. W. L. Liefeld, *1 & 2 Timothy/Titus* (NIVAC; Grand Rapids: Zondervan, 1999), 134, conjectures that "at first the women who served as deacons were the wives of deacons."

[85] Cf. J. H. Stiefel, "Women Deacons in 1 Timothy: A Linguistic and Literary Look at 'Women Likewise . . .' [1 Tim 3.11]," *NTS* 41 (1995): 442–57.

[86] See also the reference in Pliny the Younger, who refers to two women "called deaconesses" (*ministrae*) in Bithynia under Trajan (*Epist.* 10.96.8; c. AD 115).

[87] See the discussion above.

"servants" (deacons) in the early church. Traditionally, most major translations took the reference in 1 Tim 3:11 to be to deacons' wives, as the following list illustrates:

- KJV = NKJV: "*their* wives"
- NASB: "women"
- NIV: "their wives" (footnote: or "deaconesses")
- NRSV: "women" (footnote: or "their wives" or "women deacons")
- NLT: "their wives" (footnote: or "the women deacons")

Conversely, no major translation unequivocally affirmed in the main text a reference to women deacons in 1 Tim 3:11. In recent years, however, both the TNIV and the HCSB opted for the wording "women," perhaps marking a cautious departure from the KJV traditional rendering "*their* wives."

Also, several major recent commentaries—written by complementarian scholars, no less—affirm that the reference to Phoebe as a διάκονος in Rom 16:1 should probably be interpreted in terms of her having served in the office of deaconess.[88] The implication for church practice today is that churches could allow women to serve in the role of deaconess as long as it is kept in mind that the biblical definition of "deacon" involves serving in a nonteaching, nonruling function.

CONCLUSION

This essay has sought to provide a brief survey of major hermeneutical and exegetical challenges in interpreting the Pastoral Epistles. Major hermeneutical issues included authorship, genre and the role of background, and the Pastorals' literary integrity and structure. With regard to authorship, it was concluded that Pauline authorship continues to be preferred to alternative proposals, whether pseudonymity or allonymity.

With regard to genre and the role of background, it was argued that an ad hoc hermeneutic is too constraining and that an approach consistently distinguishing between general principle and specific application is to be favored. With regard to literary integrity, the cohesion of each of the Pastorals was noted and defended. Alternate structural proposals were noted and brief surveys of the literary plan of Paul's two letters to Timothy and his letter to Titus were provided.

Exegetically, the Pastorals were shown to reflect a two-tiered structure of church government, with a plurality of pastors/elders/overseers in charge and with deacons (most likely both male and female) fulfilling servant roles in the church. The

---

[88] See esp. T. R. Schreiner, *Romans* (BECNT; Grand Rapids: Baker, 1998), 786–87; and D. J. Moo, *The Epistle to the Romans* (NICNT; Grand Rapids: Eerdmans, 1996), 913–14. But see BDAG, 230, which calls Phoebe a "courier" (διάκονος), and the unpublished paper of T. L. Wilder, "Phoebe in Romans 16:1–2" (ETS annual meeting, 2005), who argues that Phoebe is the "letter-carrier" (διάκονος) of Romans.

"husband of one wife" requirement was shown to refer most likely to the stipulation that church leaders be faithful to their wives, stipulating marital fidelity as a core requirement for all men serving in ecclesiastical office.

While these conclusions are not the only ones possible from the New Testament data, there can be little disagreement that the Pastorals are among the most important New Testament writings for the practice of the contemporary church. The church must continue to wrestle with what Scripture teaches regarding church governance and qualifications for leadership and commit itself to abide by what it understands Scripture to teach rather operating primarily on the basis of personal preference or church tradition.[89]

What is more, it is vital for interpreters to be aware of their presuppositions and to be willing to revisit (or visit for the first time) the biblical data rather than following in the paths of one's denominational forebears. It is with the commitment to *sola Scriptura*, with the scholarly spirit of *ad fontes*, and with the dictum "In essentials, unity, in non-essentials liberty, and in all things, charity" that this modest contribution to our study and practice of the Pastoral Epistles is offered.

---

[89] See the unpublished paper by R. L. Adkisson, "Women Serving in the Church? A Biblical and Historical Look at Women Serving in the Church with Particular Attention Given to the History and Interpretation of Southern Baptists."

Chapter Two

PSEUDONYMITY, THE NEW TESTAMENT, AND THE PASTORAL EPISTLES

TERRY L. WILDER

INTRODUCTION

An old television commercial for Midas mufflers portrays a consumer at a competitor's shop asking about an exhaust system for his automobile. When the customer sees the repairman ready to install on his vehicle a muffler that does not look like the correct size, he asks, "Will that fit my car?" The installer replies, "Don't worry; we'll make it fit." The commercial is of course a modern variation of the ancient myth which tells how Procrustes would make unsuspecting travelers fit into his iron bed by stretching or cutting off their legs.

Sometimes critical scholars may be culpable of arbitrarily forcing their theories into a Procrustean bed when it comes to the study of the New Testament, especially with issues of authorship. To illustrate that this sort of thing can be done, I will take the criteria that scholars typically use to show that the Pastoral Epistles (PE) are inauthentic and apply them to Philippians—a letter generally acknowledged by everyone as authentic—to show that, using this method, even its authenticity might be questioned.[1] Such methodologies, however, can be carried too far. Thus, rather than arguing that Philippians is pseudonymous[2] I will contend that the PE

---

[1] I. H. Marshall, professor emeritus of NT at Aberdeen University, first gave me this idea. Any shortcomings in this article, however, are my own and should not be attributed to him. H. Hoehner did a similar study with Galatians. See "Did Paul Write Galatians?" in *History and Exegesis* (ed. Sang-Won [Aaron] Son; London/New York: T&T Clark, 2006), 150–169.

[2] To defend the integrity of Philippians is beyond this paper's scope. For a defense of the unity of Philippians, see G. F. Hawthorne, *Philippians* (WBC 43; Dallas: Word, 1983), xxix–xxxii; more recently, see idem, "Philippians, Letter to," in *DPL* (eds. G. F. Hawthorne, R. P. Martin, and D. G. Reid; Downer's Grove, IL: IVP, 1993), 707–13.

are genuine. Lastly, I will survey contemporary scholarship on pseudonymity and the Pastorals and draw an extended conclusion.

THE CRITERIA APPLIED TO THE PASTORALS AND TO PHILIPPIANS

Scholars who hold to the inauthenticity of the Pastorals stress that the vocabulary and style of these letters differ from the other Pauline epistles.[3] To be sure, many words found in the PE do not occur in the other Pauline writings[4]—for example, the term "godliness" (εὐσέβεια, 1 Tim 6:11). Moreover, 175 different *hapax legomena* appear in the PE that are found nowhere else in the NT[5]—for example, the terms "slave traders" (ἀνδραποδιστής, 1 Tim 1:10), "perjurers" (ἐπίορκος, 1 Tim 1:10) and "integrity" (ἀφθορία, Titus 2:7). Stylistic differences also exist between the Pastorals and the rest of the Pauline corpus—for example, several particles are absent from the PE but are present in the other Paulines.[6] Such contrasts lead many to believe that Paul did not write the PE.

But differences just as extensive can be found in Philippians. For example, consider the following words found in Philippians but nowhere else in the NT: "discernment" (αἴσθησις, 1:9); "sincerely" (ἁγνῶς, 1:17); "to frighten" (πτύρω, 1:28); "encouragement" (παραμύθιον, 2:1); "united in spirit" (σύμψυχος, 2:2); "conceit" (κενοδοξία, 2:3); "robbery" (ἁρπαγμός,[7] 2:6); "raise to the loftiest height" (ὑπερυψόω, 2:9); "under the earth" (καταχθόνιος, 2:10); "absence" (ἀπουσία, 2:12); "have courage" (εὐψυχέω, 2:19); "of like soul or mind" (ἰσόψυχος, 2:20); "genuinely" (γνησίως, 2:20); "coming near" (παραπλήσιος, 2:27); "free from anxiety" (ἄλυπος, 2:28); "risk" (παραβολεύομαι, 2:30); "mutilation" (κατατομή, 3:2); "on the eighth day" (ὀκταήμερος, 3:5); "refuse" (σκύβαλον, 3:8); "be conformed to" (συμμορφίζω, 3:10); "resurrection" (ἐξανάστασις, 3:11); "stretch out/strain" (ἐπεκτείνομαι, 3:13); "goal/mark" (σκοπός, 3:14); "differently" (ἑτέρως, 3:15); "fellow-imitator" (συμμιμητής, 3:17); "commonwealth" (πολίτευμα, 3:20); "longed for" (ἐπιπόθητος, 4:1); "yokefellow" (σύζυγος, 4:3); "lovely" (προσφιλής, 4:8); "praiseworthy" (εὔφημος, 4:8); "revive" (ἀναθάλλω, 4:10); "have no opportunity or time" (ἀκαιρέομαι, 4:10); "content" (αὐτάρκης, 4:11); "learn the secret" (μυέω, 4:12); and "receiving" (λῆμψις, 4:15).

How do we account for the fact that none of the aforementioned words are ever used elsewhere in the NT?[8] How do we explain the fact that Paul did not use any of

---

[3] This difference is usually considered the most substantial and significant objection to the Pauline authorship of the PE.

[4] D. Guthrie, *New Testament Introduction* (4th ed.; Downer's Grove, IL: IVP, 1990), 619.

[5] Ibid.

[6] Ibid.

[7] This word is extremely rare and not found even in the LXX.

[8] No doubt some would point out the fact that several of these words occur in the kenosis passage of Phil 2:5–11, which many consider to be a Christian hymn or piece that Paul may not have authored but which he nonetheless used in his letter. In other words, they would say that there is good reason to explain these terms. As someone who believes in

these words in his other letters? Using the criteria that scholars apply to the Pastorals, might not this apparent departure from Pauline style be instrumental in arguing that the authenticity of Philippians is suspect? Consistency would seem to demand it, especially for those inclined to use this criterion to argue that the Pastorals are pseudonymous.

Second, defenders of pseudonymity in the Pastorals contend that the church structure (primarily, that of overseers and deacons) in these letters is too advanced for Paul's time.[9] That is to say, the Pastorals are said to correspond to a later period when church government was more organized and controlled.[10] These scholars think the church started as "a charismatic, pneumatic organism and only later developed elders, deacons, and eventually bishops in order to combat error."[11] Opponents of authenticity often argue that the Pastoral Epistles reflect a church government of monarchial bishops.

The church government in Philippians, however, is arguably like that found in the PE. In Phil 1:1 Paul refers to both "overseers" (ἐπίσκοποι) and "deacons" (διάκονοι). This reference is significant because ἐπίσκοποι (and, for that matter, its related πρεσβύτεροι) are mentioned nowhere else in the corpus of letters attributed to Paul with the exception of the PE (e.g., 1 Tim 3:1; Titus 1:7). Further, the terms "overseers and deacons" (ἐπίσκοποι καὶ διάκονοι) do not appear joined together anywhere else in Paul's letters.[12] Though both words do occur in the PE, they are not coupled together there as they are in Philippians.[13] Consequently, one might argue in Philippians that Paul uses the terms in this way because he is speaking of administrative leaders or officers within the church who are already part of an organized structure like that found in the Pastorals. Just because "Paul" does not elaborate on these offices in Philippians as he does in the PE does not mean that a similar structure did not exist at the time of the former letter, for indeed it may have; the writer simply may have had no need to go into detail concerning these leaders in Philippians as he does in the Pastorals. And—this observation being the case—might not this issue at least raise some questions regarding the Pauline authorship of Philippians? While not necessarily a monumental observation, it nonetheless should carry some weight— especially when considered with the cumulative argument—should we be so inclined to question the authenticity of Philippians.

Philippians' authenticity, I would concur—good reason exists to explain the unique words. Surely such terms in the PE can also be explained.

9 Guthrie, *Introduction,* 615.

10 Ibid., 616.

11 As W. D. Mounce (*Pastoral Epistles* [WBC 46; Nashville: Thomas Nelson, 2000], lxxxvi) points out when discussing the view of scholars who do not believe Paul wrote 1 Tim.

12 For this point and the question as to whether or not these terms refer to one group or two, see the discussion in Hawthorne, *Philippians,* 7–8.

13 As P. T. O'Brien (*The Epistle to the Philippians* [NIGTC; Grand Rapids: Eerdmans, 1991], 46–47) correctly observes.

Those who argue against the Pauline authorship of the Pastorals usually date the false teachers opposed in these letters as later than Paul's lifetime. Thus, the nature of the opposition in the PE needs to be identified. The identity of the opponents in the Pastorals is still debated amongst scholars:[14] some say that the heresy opposed in the PE is some type of Judaism;[15] others view the opposition as Jewish-Christian opponents to the Pauline mission;[16] many say that the false teaching is a form of second-century Gnosticism;[17] still others identify the false teachers with an ascetic movement of some sort.[18] Conceding for the time being—and for the sake of argument—that the false teachers in the PE are later than Paul, we need to identify their various traits as found in the letters. Marshall provides a helpful summary when he says that the opposition consisted of the following specific characteristics: (a) their teaching was linked to Judaism (1 Tim 1:4,7; cf. 4:7; Titus 1:10,14; 3:9); (b) they encouraged asceticism (1 Tim 4:3; 5:23; 2 Tim 4:4; Titus 1:15); (c) they professed to "know" God (1 Tim 6:20; Titus 1:16); (d) they held that the resurrection was past (2 Tim 2:18); (e) connected with the latter, they may have ignored "the realities of life in the physical world" (illness and death) and claimed "some kind of special inspiration by the Spirit or other divine powers"; (f) they may have encouraged women to participate in teaching and various forms of church life (cf. 1 Tim 2); (g) they may have been Jewish-Christian in outlook and attached little importance to the Christian mission to the Gentiles (cf. 1 Tim 2:4–7; 3:16; 4:10; Titus 2:11); (h) they may have affirmed human works as the basis for God's saving grace in Christ (2 Tim 1:9; Titus 3:5); (i) they may have had a docetic understanding of Jesus (cf. 1 Tim 2:5).[19]

The nature of the opposition in Philippians is a matter of dispute just as is the makeup of the opponents in the PE. Nonetheless, the opposition described in Philippians is similar, at least in some ways, to that in the Pastorals. Assuming, for the sake of argument, that the opposition in Philippians is also later than Paul's lifetime, we find that the opponents in Philippians have some of the same characteristics as the opponents in the PE.

Like the Pastorals, the opponents in Philippians stress the law (Phil 3:2–3,6,9). Moreover, just as the PE contain a misunderstanding of the resurrection by the opposition (it is already past; cf. 2 Tim 2:18), a similar misunderstanding may be present

---

[14] The following characteristics are those provided in a summary by I. H. Marshall, in collaboration with P. H. Towner, *A Critical and Exegetical Commentary on the Pastoral Epistles* (ICC; Edinburgh: T&T Clark, 1999), 46–51.

[15] E.g., see C. Spicq, *Les Épîtres Pastorales* (4th ed.; 2 vols.; EBib; Paris: J. Gabalda, 1969), esp. 85–119.

[16] See Marshall, *Pastoral Epistles*, 47.

[17] This view enjoys the most support. E.g., see J. Roloff, *Der Erste Brief an Timotheus* (EKKNT; Zürich/Neukirchen-Vluyn: Benziger/Neukirchener, 1988), 228–38; L. Oberlinner, *Die Pastoralbriefe*. Dritte Folge. Kommentar zum Titusbrief (Band XI/2; Herders theologischer Kommentar zum NT; Freiburg: Herder, 1996), 52–73; M. Goulder, "The Pastor's Wolves: Jewish Christian Visionaries Behind the Pastoral Epistles," *NovT* 38 (1996): 242–56.

[18] E.g., see D. R. MacDonald, *The Legend and the Apostle: The Battle for Paul in Story and Canon* (Philadelphia: Westminster, 1983).

[19] Marshall, *Pastoral Epistles*, 44–46. According to Marshall, the first four characteristics (a-d) are clear while the latter five (e-i) are more disputable.

in Philippians (cf. 3:12–16). Marshall notes, "In Philippians 3 we have people who claim to be already 'perfect,' in a context where Paul talks of his own desire to attain to the resurrection."[20] If the opposition in Philippians is teaching that persons who have been circumcised and are true to the Law can become perfect, then Paul, who knows that perfection cannot be accomplished this way, warns his readers that it "comes only through Jesus Christ and at the resurrection at the last day."[21] If, on the other hand, the opponents are Gnostics, then they believed and were teaching that "perfection could be attained on earth now without waiting for, or without any need for the resurrection."[22] Might not these sorts of similarities between the opposition found in Philippians and the PE contribute to the questioning of whether the former letter is genuine?

Supporters of pseudonymity contend that the Pastorals do not emphasize characteristic Pauline doctrines like the Fatherhood of God, the believer's union with Christ, the work of the Holy Spirit, and the cross, etc.[23] Many also suggest that too much of a concern for the transmission of "sound teaching," that is, tradition (1 Tim 2:4) and the use of creeds (cf. 1 Tim 3:16; 2 Tim 1:13–14; 2:2; Titus 2:11–14, etc.) in the Pastorals reflect Christianity at the end of the first century, rather than during Paul's lifetime.[24]

Philippians likewise refers very few times to some typical Pauline themes. For example, the letter contains very few references to the Holy Spirit. Further, Paul cites in Philippians what many think to be a creedal saying or Christian hymn (cf. Phil 2:5–11),[25] which is the type of phenomenon that we see occurring in the Pastorals. Might not these observations, especially when coupled with what else we have seen thus far regarding this letter, at least raise some suspicion concerning the Pauline authorship of Philippians, should we be so inclined?

Finally, opponents of the Pauline authorship of the PE argue that these letters contain historical allusions to Paul's life that cannot be placed within the book of Acts. For example, Paul has been with Timothy and left him in Ephesus to combat false teachers while he went to Macedonia (1 Tim 1:3); similarly, he has left Titus in Crete (Titus 1:5); Paul also referred to Onesiphorus who had been seeking for him in Rome (2 Tim 1:16–17); and he is now a prisoner (2 Tim 1:8,16; cf. 4:16).

Philippians also contains historical references and details that are absent from Acts. For example, if we hold to the traditional viewpoint that Paul wrote the letter of Philippians from Rome, as most do, then we are faced with the fact that Acts con-

---

[20] Ibid., 47.
[21] Hawthorne, *Philippians*, 150.
[22] Ibid. Hawthorne does not hold this view in his commentary.
[23] Guthrie, *Introduction*, 618.
[24] Ibid., 619.
[25] See R. P. Martin, *Carmen Christi: Philippians ii 5–11 in Recent Interpretation and in the Setting of Early Christian Worship* (rev. ed.; Grand Rapids: Eerdmans, 1983).

tains no indication that Timothy was in that city with him (cf. Phil 1:1).[26] Moreover, Epaphroditus (Phil 2:25; 4:18), a person crucial to understanding the occasion of Philippians, is also not found in Acts. Further, neither Euodia and Syntyche nor their feud (Phil 4:2) is ever mentioned in Acts. Using this criterion that scholars apply to the PE, might not this similar lack of details from Philippians in Acts be used as yet another part of the cumulative argument to question the authenticity of Philippians? Consistency would seem to require it.

These findings (and perhaps others like them) obtained from the application of the criteria that scholars use to show that the PE are inauthentic might lead one—again, should one be so inclined—to say that Philippians was also not written by Paul. Interestingly, the latter conclusion is precisely the one that F. C. Baur, the leading scholar of the Tübingen school, reached many years ago.[27] Convinced by the previous studies of F. Schleiermacher on 1 Timothy[28] and J. G. Eichhorn on the other Pastorals,[29] Baur used a Hegelian dialectic to promote the view that pseudonymity existed in the NT.[30] He developed the flawed methodological principle (by which much subsequent NT scholarship was influenced) that "one canonical pseude-pigraphon leads to the possibility if not the probability of others."[31] He applied this principle first to 1 Timothy, and then to the other Pastorals. And he did not stop applying this principle as he eventually came to regard every Pauline letter—including Philippians—as pseudonymous,[32] with the exception of Galatians, Romans, and

---

[26] As Hawthorne ("Philippians," *DPL*, 710) points out in relation to the possibility of Rome as the place of the letter's origin. The provenance of Philippians is a matter of dispute primarily between two alternatives, Rome or Ephesus. For the latest article on this issue see F. S. Thielman, "Ephesus and the Literary Setting of Philippians," in *New Testament Greek and Exegesis: Essays in Honor of Gerald F. Hawthorne* (eds. A. M. Donaldson and T. B. Sailors; Grand Rapids: Eerdmans, 2003), 205–23.

[27] Baur believed that this was the case primarily because of the vocabulary and style of Philippians; he also saw Gnosticism in 2:5–11. The view that Philippians was not written by Paul was revived, with the aid of computer analysis, by A. Q. Morton and J. McLeman in their book, *Christianity in the Computer Age* (New York: Harper & Row, 1964). See also their book titled, *Paul, the Man and the Myth* (London: Hodder & Stoughton, 1966).

[28] F. Schleiermacher, *Über den Sogenannten ersten Brief des Paulus an den Timotheus* (Berlin: Realschulbuchhandlung, 1807). Schleiermacher first worked out a reasoned attack against the authenticity of 1 Timothy.

[29] J. G. Eichhorn, *Historische-kritische Einleitung in das Neue Testament* (Leipzig: Weidmanischen Buchhandlung, 1812). Eichhorn took Schleiermacher's method further and argued that Paul did not write the Pastorals.

[30] E. E. Ellis, "Pseudonymity and Canonicity of New Testament Documents," in *Worship, Theology and Ministry in the Early Church: Essays in Honour of Ralph P. Martin* (eds. M. Wilkins and T. Paige; Sheffield: Sheffield Academic Press, 1993), 212–24; 213.

[31] D. Guthrie, "The Development of the Idea of Canonical Pseudepigrapha in New Testament Criticism," in *The Authorship and Integrity of the New Testament* (ed. K. Aland; London: SPCK, 1965), 14–39; esp. 18. Convinced of the pseudonymity of 1 Timothy, Baur said that "what has happened in one case may have happened equally in several others" (F. C. Baur, *Paul, His Life and Works* [ETr. A. Menzies; 2 vols.; London: Williams and Norgate, 1875], 2:109–10). His principles appear to have achieved their logical extreme in the writings of Bruno Bauer and the Dutch skeptical school, who believed that all of the NT letters bearing Paul's name were pseudepigraphal (noted by Guthrie, "Canonical Pseudepigrapha," 21).

[32] Ellis, "Pseudonymity," 213. E.g., see F. C. Baur, "Die Christuspartei in der korinthischen Gemeinde, der Gegensatz des petrinischen und paulinischen Christentum in der ältesten Kirche . . ." *Tübinger Zeitschrift für Theologie* 5 (1831): 136–206, reprinted in *Ausgewählte Werke* (5 vols., Stuttgart: Frommann, 1963–75), 1:1–146; (cited by Ellis, "Pseudonymity," 213); see also idem, *Paul, His Life and Works* (ETr. A. Menzies; 2 vols.; London: Williams and Norgate, 1875),

1 and 2 Corinthians.[33] In my opinion, Baur, though consistent, went berserk with the methodological principle he developed, and NT scholarship has been influenced ever since by his procrustean maneuvers.

A DEFENSE OF THE AUTHENTICITY OF THE PASTORAL EPISTLES

None of what was presented above convinces me that Philippians is pseudonymous. Further, I doubt that anyone today could be persuaded that this is the case—they would think it absurd. And yet, the evidence convinces many scholars when they use this methodology to apply the same sort of criteria to the Pastorals. If not persuaded by the data found in Philippians using this method, then why the Pastorals? Instead of arguing that Philippians is pseudonymous, should not critical scholars seriously reconsider the viewpoint that the Pastorals are authentic? I think so. Next I will offer a defense of the PE's authenticity.

Scholars who put forth arguments from vocabulary and style against the authenticity of the Pastoral Epistles need seriously to reconsider that the variations in subject-matter, occasion, purpose, and addressees account for many of these differences.[34] Rather than pointing to a pseudo-author's style, the specialized vocabulary and style in the PE arguably reflects instead Paul's desire to communicate clearly to his audience.[35] The use of a secretary by Paul may also explain the presence of many words in the Pastorals. Stylistic arguments tend to be quite subjective and unimpressive. Differences exist within the other Pauline letters—not only Philippians—which are just as extensive as those between the Pastorals and the rest of the Pauline corpus.[36] Furthermore, the PE are simply too brief to determine with accuracy the writing habits of a particular author.[37]

Those who defend pseudonymity in the Pastorals with the argument that the church structure in these letters is too advanced for Paul's time need to reconsider the fact that Paul himself appointed elders at the start of his missionary work which strongly shows his concern for orderly church government (cf. Acts 14:23).[38] Other

---

1:248–49, 2:106–11; idem, *The Church History of the First Three Centuries* (2 vols.; London: Williams and Norgate, 1878–79), 1:122–31, 149–50.

[33] A. Hilgenfeld's (*Historisch-kritische Einleitung in das Neue Testament* [Leipzig: Fues, 1875] 246–47, 330–34) increase of Paul's "genuine" letters to seven (Rom, 1 & 2 Cor, Gal, Phil, 1 Thess, Phlm) later seems to have led Baur's followers to maintain a fairly fixed number of pseudepigrapha in the NT (so noted by Ellis, "Pseudonymity," 213).

[34] Ibid., 633.

[35] I think that this observation helps to account for the PE's unique vocabulary. See F. A. Tomlinson's chapter on the purpose of the PE; he elaborates more on Paul's specialized vocabulary.

[36] For examples, see Guthrie, *Introduction*, 635.

[37] T. L. Wilder, "Pseudonymity and the New Testament," *Interpreting the New Testament* (Nashville: Broadman & Holman, 2001), 296–335; 325.

[38] Guthrie, *Introduction*, 625. Though I will concede that he does not seem as concerned with church order as he is in the PE. However, there is reason for his great concern in the PE, as D. Wallace points out: "(1) In all three letters, Paul is writing to an apostolic delegate—in effect, an intermediary between himself and the leadership of the church. Thus what

biblical passages also indicate that church structure played a key part in Paul's ministry (cf. Acts 20:17–28; Phil 1:1; see also Rom 12:8; 1 Thess 5:12). Furthermore, the instructions regarding overseers in 1 Timothy and Titus simply do not reflect the monarchial church government that began to develop in the second century.[39] For example, in Titus 1:5–7 the word "overseer" is used interchangeably with "elder," and since elders are to be appointed in every town, there is no indication of a monarchial church government.

Those who defend the inauthenticity of the Pastorals with the argument that the opponents in these letters are later than Paul—whether Jewish, ascetic, Gnostic, or a combination of these—need to consider that Jewish elements (cf. Gal 2) and asceticism (cf. Rom 14) operated in Paul's time, as well as Gnosticism in its incipient form, which likely stretched back into the first century.[40] Consequently, the opposition combated in the PE does not require a date later than Paul's lifetime.

Those who support pseudonymity in the Pastorals with the contention that these letters do not emphasize characteristic Pauline doctrines need to acknowledge that standards of this nature are not accurate criteria for determining authenticity. The so-called absence of typical Pauline themes is overstated. For example, the lack of references to the Holy Spirit in the PE (found only in 1 Tim 4:1; 2 Tim 1:14; Titus 3:5) is not as big a problem as it first may seem. Other letters, such as Colossians and 2 Thessalonians, mention the Holy Spirit only once; Philippians, as seen earlier, also refers to the Spirit very few times. Moreover, the emphasis on Christian doctrine in the Pastorals does not require a later date. During his ministry, Paul stressed holding firmly to tradition (cf. 1 Cor 11:2), and often cited creedal sayings and hymns in his letters (cf. 1 Cor 15:3–5; Phil 2:6–8; Col 1:15–17, etc.).[41]

Those who oppose the Pauline authorship of the Pastoral Epistles with the argument that they contain historical allusions to Paul's life that cannot be placed within the book of Acts need to recognize that this objection suggests that only what is recorded in the book of Acts may be considered authentic. Traditionally, defenders of the authenticity of the Pastorals respond to this argument with the theory that Paul was released from his captivity in Acts 28, traveled back to the East, and was later arrested and imprisoned in Rome again. Under this view, the references to Paul in the Pastorals cannot be placed within the data of Acts because they happened at a later

---

he normally communicated in person as to church order (as he evidently must have in light of such casual references as Phil 1:1; 1 Thess 5:12, etc.), he now must put in writing. (2) In each one of the letters there are extenuating circumstances which would bring about an emphasis on church order and creedalism: (a) in 1 Timothy, the church had been infected by heretical and immoral leaders; hence, moral qualifications especially needed to be established; (b) in Titus, the church was newly planted; hence, some guidelines for selecting leaders needed to be given; (c) in 2 Timothy, Paul's death is imminent; hence, an emphasis on a fixed tradition was in order" (see http://www.bible.org/docs/soapbox/1timotl.htm; accessed November 14, 2003).

[39] Guthrie, *Introduction*, 627.
[40] Ibid., 617.
[41] Ibid., 632.

date. Those who hold to the Pauline authorship of the Pastorals also point out that the book of Acts does not record many details of Paul's life (cf. 2 Cor 11).[42] Thus, the fact that Acts does not record a second Pauline imprisonment in Rome is not unusual. If Paul had been martyred at the end of the imprisonment recorded in Acts 28, it is difficult to imagine that the author would have completed his work without mentioning this event.[43] Moreover, the fact that Paul expected to be released from prison in Philippians (1:19,25; 2:24), while he did not in the Pastorals (2 Tim 4:6–8), also suggests a subsequent Roman imprisonment. Furthermore, a social-historical study of Paul in Roman custody in Acts 28 indicates that Paul was released.[44]

External evidence from the early church attests to the Pauline authorship of the PE. Several early church leaders accepted these letters as canonical and Pauline—for example, Ignatius, Polycarp, Clement of Alexandria, Tertullian and Irenaeus.[45] Eusebius, the early church historian, said, "The epistles of Paul are fourteen, all well known and beyond doubt."[46] Those "fourteen epistles" included the Pastorals. Furthermore, the PE are listed among the Pauline letters in the Muratorian Canon. The Pauline authorship of the Pastorals was not seriously questioned until the nineteenth century.

Virtually all of the other evidence we possess from the early church is against the practice of pseudonymity.[47] The New Testament does not support the practice (see 2 Thess 2:2;[48] the Pauline signatures;[49] Rev 22:18–19[50]). Early Christian leaders

---

[42] Guthrie, *Introduction*, 622.

[43] Ibid., 624.

[44] B. Rapske, *Paul in Roman Custody* (ed. B. W. Winter; vol. 3 of *The Book of Acts in Its First-Century Setting*; Grand Rapids: Eerdmans/Carlisle: Paternoster, 1994), 191. Rapske states, "The custody in Rome as Luke reports it and the probable material basis of the deliberations leading to that custody . . . constitute a significant and highly placed Roman estimate of the trial's probable outcome, i.e., that Paul will be released."

[45] Marcion, who was fond of Paul's epistles, did not include the Pastorals in his canon of Scripture, but this is likely because he objected to some of the content in the letters.

[46] Eusebius, *Hist. eccl.* 3.3.

[47] As I have shown elsewhere in great detail; see T. L. Wilder, "Pseudonymity and the New Testament," in *Interpreting the New Testament: Essays on Methods and Issues* (ed. D. A. Black and D. S. Dockery; Nashville: B&H Academic, 2001), 296–335; and idem, *Pseudonymity, the New Testament, and Deception: An Inquiry into Intention and Reception* (Lanham, MD: University Press of America, 2004).

[48] Paul cautioned the Thessalonians that, no matter through what agency (whether "spirit, word, or letter as through us") the heresy came to them, though attributed to him and his associates, they had nothing to do with it. He would have objected to a pseudonymous letter being attributed to him which contained falsehood, wrong teaching, or inauthentic material that he did not write.

[49] Paul would have frowned upon someone using a facsimile of his signature in a pseudonymous letter which purported to be his. These greetings (1 Cor 16:21; Gal 6:11; Col 4:18; 2 Thess 3:17; Phlm 19) in Paul's own handwriting, which indicated the use of a secretary, provided a sign of his letters' authority and authenticity. See E. R. Richards, *The Secretary in the Letters of Paul* (WUNT 2.42; Tübingen: Mohr [Siebeck], 1991), 172.

[50] John warned that no one was to tamper with what he had written in Revelation by rewriting it in any way, which would subsequently give the impression that the added or subtracted words belonged to him. One can extrapolate from this interpretation to somebody writing another book and falsely attributing it to him by means of pseudonymity. John would have objected to a pseudonymous letter being attributed to him that contained falsehood, wrong teaching, or inauthentic material that he did not write. To write a pseudonymous work and attribute it to somebody is a sort of extension of tampering with an existing document. Thus, to enlarge pseudonymously an existing body of literature—for example, the Pauline corpus—by adding a few inauthentic works is to tamper with Paul's actual writings.

squarely rejected pseudonymous works as deceptive (e.g., see the responses of Serapion, bishop of Antioch [c. AD 190], who forbade use of the apocryphal *Gospel of Peter*,[51] and Asian church elders who ousted a colleague from his post for writing out of "love for Paul" the apocryphal *Acts of Paul*, which included the pseudo-apostolic letter of *3 Corinthians*.[52]). To say that the Pastorals are pseudonymous would mean that the early church was fooled by letters that it believed were authentic. True, while most of the documentary evidence dates from the second century onwards, no good reason exists to believe that the first-century church's response to pseudonymous works was any different, for large departures from the norm over a relatively short period of time are unlikely. When all is said and done, I see no compelling reason to view the PE as pseudonymous. A resort to pseudonymity is not necessary. The Pastorals, like the rest of the NT writings, may be relied upon as authentic and trustworthy.

SOME CONTEMPORARY SCHOLARSHIP ON PSEUDONYMITY AND THE PASTORAL EPISTLES

In this section, the views of some representative recent scholars on the subject of pseudonymity and the Pastoral Epistles will be highlighted. This survey will also illustrate the variety of expression on the topic.

N. Brox, who authored a commentary on the Pastorals,[53] claims that no single solution is sufficient to solve the problem of NT pseudonymity. He posits three main features to explain the phenomenon. First, he argues that the early church Fathers were more concerned with the content of writings than their authorship.[54] Second, Brox says that Christians used pseudonymity to take part in the "superior past."[55] That is to say, like others in antiquity, they admired whatever was old and believed that whatever was old was true. Thus, by using the pseudonym, writers could attribute their works to an earlier date and command such respect. Third, Brox contends that, because the idea of the "noble falsehood" pervaded antiquity, deception could be used to promote one's aims.[56] In this manner, he believes that pseudonymity was used deliberately to support the religious content of works. However, Brox too quickly discounts the documentary evidence which shows that the early church was concerned with both the content and the authorship of documents. Moreover, one struggles to see how love for antiquity could have motivated pseudepigraphers composing writings shortly after the deaths of the apostles. Furthermore, Brox imposes

---

[51] As found in Eusebius, *Hist. eccl.* 6.12,2–4.

[52] As recorded in Tertullian, *Bapt.* 17.

[53] N. Brox, *Die Pastoralbriefe* (RNT; Regensburg: Pustet, 1969). See also N. Brox, "Zu den persönliche Notizen der Pastoralbriefe," *Biblische Zeitschrift* 13 (1969): 76–94.

[54] N. Brox, *Falsche Verfasserangaben zur Erklärung der frühchristlichen Pseudepigraphie*, SBS 79 (Stuttgart: KBW, 1975): 26–36.

[55] Ibid., 52–53, 105–6.

[56] Ibid., 82–84.

the Greek idea of the noble falsehood upon writings of a primarily Jewish origin.[57] His support of a legitimate concept of deception for the NT is difficult to prove.

In encyclopedic fashion, W. Speyer has gathered and analyzed numerous ancient pseudepigrapha and literary forgeries.[58] In his study of religious pseudepigrapha, Speyer classifies these works into three distinct categories.[59] First, he discusses "genuine religious pseudepigrapha." These works were spread mainly in the Near East by the Jews, but were also known in Greece and Rome. For Speyer, such writings are not deceptive because they stem from a mythical-religious experience. In other words, the writers believed that they were possessed and inspired by a spirit (whether that of a god, spirit, or a godly wise man of the past) with the result that they did not pen their own words, but those of the one controlling them. Speyer does not place Christian pseudepigrapha into this category. Second, he explains "falsified religious pseudepigrapha." The authors of these works imitated genuine religious pseudepigrapha, used the name of one who carried authority within a religious tradition, and wrote to deceive their readers. Speyer locates most Christian pseudepigrapha within this category. Third, he evaluates "fictive religious pseudepigrapha." These works are artistic literary creations that belong to the realm of poetry and art and are not viewed as deceptive. Speyer finds none of these works in Christian literature. Speyer claims that the early Christians used forgeries "to explain, defend and spread the faith authoritatively."[60] He says that even orthodox Christians did not reject the use of the "necessary lie."[61] For example, Speyer views *3 Corinthians* as one of many counter-forgeries written to defend the church's teaching against heretics,[62] and he views the Pastoral Epistles as forgeries composed out of high moral motives serving "the development of the faith and church discipline."[63] Despite Speyer's extensive research, evidence is lacking that a pseudonymous author ever thought that he was possessed by a spirit in such a way; moreover, had these authors really undergone such mystical-religious experiences, it is difficult to imagine why they did not write in their own names.[64] Furthermore, Speyer's belief that the early church winked at forgery and used it for their own purposes is inconsistent with a people who were presumably committed to truth and moral ideals.

---

[57] Criticism noted by D. G. Meade, *Pseudonymity and Canon: An Investigation into the Relationship of Authorship and Authority in Jewish and Earliest Christian Tradition* (WUNT 2.39; Tübingen: Mohr, 1986), 12.

[58] W. Speyer, *Die literarische Fälschung im heidnischen und christlichen Altertum: Ein Versuch ihrer Deutung* (Handbuch der Altertumswissenschaft 1/2; München: Beck, 1971). See also idem, "Religiöse Pseudepigraphie und Literarische Fälschung im Altertum," in *Pseudepigraphie in der heidnischen und jüdischen-christlichen Antike* (ed. Brox; Darmstadt: Wissenschaftliche Buchgesellschaft, 1977), 195–263; and idem, "Fälschung, pseudepigraphische freie Erfindung und 'echte religiöse Pseudepigraphie,'" in *Pseudepigrapha I* (ed. K. von Fritz; Genève: O. Reverdin, 1972), 333–66, with discussion on pp. 367–72.

[59] See Speyer's summary in "Religiöse Pseudepigraphie und Literarische Fälschung," 262.

[60] Speyer, *Fälschung*, 219.

[61] Ibid., 94–95, 97.

[62] Ibid., 278–79.

[63] Ibid., 285–86, as he does also 2 Peter.

[64] Criticism noted by Meade, *Pseudonymity and Canon*, 8–9.

Especially significant amongst "later disciple"-type theories of pseudonymity is the already-cited monograph written by D. Meade, *Pseudonymity and Canon*. According to Meade, the use of the pseudonym does not indicate the literary origins of a document, but rather the authoritative tradition within which it is written. Consequently, he views the author of the Pastoral Epistles—(as he does also Ephesians, and 1 and 2 Peter)—as a later writer who was convinced of the continuity of his assertions with those of his pseudonym and who simply "reactualized" the apostles' teaching for a new generation.[65] Meade reaches this conclusion because he claims to have found such a tradition of pseudonymity in Jewish and Christian literature.

For Meade, deception only enters the scene in such works when one asks how such documents were circulated and then the idea must be radically qualified. He explains that deception can run on two levels: first, the literary origins of a book (who really wrote it?), and second, the truth or content of a work (are its ideas those of the purported author or someone else's?).[66] Meade contends that in modern practice these two levels cannot be separated and that it is their combination that causes scholars to equate deception with forgery. However, he insists that in his study of Jewish and Christian literature the two can be separated; thus the pseudonym acceptably serves to sanction the more important level of authoritative content. That is to say, authors used pseudonyms to deceive their readers, but the practice was not culpable because it acceptably promoted the content of a work. Meade gives the analogy of slavery as evidence to support his viewpoint. He says that today slavery is viewed as incompatible with the gospel, but in NT times this was not the case. Similarly, though the modern world does not accept authorial deception, Meade claims the matter was different in the first century; he argues that Christians used deceit in the fashion described by him. However, his appeal to changing moral sensitivities as justification for his views concerning deception is weak. Moreover, his dichotomy between literary origins and the content of works is extremely difficult to prove from the evidence. Furthermore, Meade assumes throughout his work that the NT contains pseudonymity and then attempts to rationalize it.

L. Donelson argues that the author of the Pastorals combines pseudepigraphy and Greco-Roman ethics in these letters to make an ethical and theological argument to his church.[67] He believes that pseudepigraphy should be considered primarily Greco-Roman and not Jewish, and makes three generalizations about it in the PE: first, the letters were written in response to heresy; second, the author used the "pedagogical lie" (i.e., he used the pseudonym to get his readers to accept the truth contained in these letters); and third, the letters appealed to the apostle and his authority to make the writer's arguments forceful and credible. Donelson clearly sees the author

---

[65] Ibid., see esp. 103–93.

[66] Ibid., 197.

[67] L. R. Donelson, *Pseudepigraphy and Ethical Argument in the Pastoral Epistles* (Tübingen: Mohr, 1986).

of the Pastorals as having intended to deceive his readers. He views pseudonymity as a dishonorable practice, and maintains that if pseudonymous writings were discovered, they were rejected and their authors condemned. Yet Donelson contends that Christians often used pseudonymity because the need for the "good lie" was so great. However, like others, Donelson unabashedly attributes deliberate deception to a people who surely would have been concerned about truth and morals.

In an article on pseudo-apostolic letters, R. Bauckham seeks to provide fresh criteria for distinguishing pseudepigraphal from authentic letters in the New Testament.[68] First, he explains the special features of the pseudepigraphal letter "by setting it within the context of a comprehensive classification of types of letters in antiquity."[69] Second, he finds, in a fairly comprehensive analysis, that ancient Jewish pseudepigraphal letters and pseudo-apostolic letters amongst the NT apocrypha conform to these types. On the basis of his study, Bauckham concludes that the Pastoral Epistles and 2 Peter[70] are probably pseudonymous, while Ephesians, James and 2 Thessalonians are only possibly so. He also finds Colossians, 1 Peter and Jude to be authentic, and suggests that Timothy wrote the Pastoral Epistles. Furthermore, Bauckham observes that "the readers of a pseudepigraphal letter cannot read it as though they were being directly addressed either by the supposed author or by the real author; they must read it as a letter written to *other* people, in the past."[71] In other words, pseudonymous letters required a distinction between the supposed addressee(s) and the real readers of a pseudepigraphal letter. Consequently, this gap had to be bridged somehow. Bauckham maintains that the author of a pseudonymous letter could bridge the gap for his readers in one of three ways. First, he could address the forebears of the real readers in a situation which has not changed up to the present. Second, he could depict the historical situation of the supposed addressees as a kind of type for the similar present situation of the actual recipients. Third, he could address the immediate hearers and future generations by means of a testament or farewell speech. However, Bauckham's work encounters a problem because it has not been determined whether pseudonymous letters ever had any actual recipients who read such works in this manner.

W. C. Wacker edited J. D. Quinn's massive collection of material on 1 and 2 Timothy for publication in a recent commentary. They contend that the Pastorals are meant only to represent Paul rather than actually be from his hand. They hold that when ancient Christians read these letters addressed to Timothy (or Titus) "they expected to hear (or overhear) a Pauline conversation in writing, to receive an icon of the apostle's soul and a convincing *characterization* that conveyed his heartfelt

68 R. J. Bauckham, "Pseudo-Apostolic Letters," *JBL* 107 (1988): 469–94.
69 Ibid., 469.
70 Bauckham (*Jude, 2 Peter* [WBC 50; Waco: Word, 1983]) believes that the pseudonym in 2 Peter is a device used by the writer to faithfully mediate the apostolic message.
71 Bauckham, "Pseudo-Apostolic Letters," 475.

personal care as well as his teaching, directives, and requests."[72] They posit that the Pastorals, circulating as a collection in the second century, or perhaps the first, "offered an authoritative message from the past, a message from a significant personality, a message containing . . . observations and instructions the significance of which was meant to transcend the setting presupposed in the text."[73] Accordingly, as 1 and 2 Timothy are from a paradigmatic apostle Paul, then Timothy and Titus are also not actual historical individuals in these letters so much as they are paradigmatic persons, with whom the current public is to identify.[74] That being the case, the places to which these letters are addressed would also have a representative function.[75] Not only does the view of Quinn and Wacker run counter to the evidence from the early church, but it also seems to encounter the same problem as that of Bauckham's work.

In his commentary, I. H. Marshall argues that the early church might easily have received the Pastoral Epistles as authoritative knowing full well that they were not written by Paul.[76] He suggests that these letters therefore be termed "allonymous" rather than pseudonymous, so that no censure attaches to their production. Marshall's case relies heavily on a comparison between the writing of the Pastoral Epistles, as he understands it, and what he sees as three plainly innocent forms of literary composition.[77] First, he notes that an author may write letters in his lifetime using a secretary to whom he delegates power to write on his behalf. Second, he points out that one may acceptably edit an authentic work after an author's death to circulate it for future generations. Third, he writes, "it is not too great a step to a situation in which somebody close to a dead person continued to write as (they thought that) he would have done."[78] Thus, for him the Pastorals lie on a continuum with these non-deceptive practices, rather than being akin to plain forgery.

Marshall argues that the Pastoral Epistles applied "fresh formulations of Pauline teaching" to deal with growing opposition in Ephesus and Crete.[79] The same author (or group which possibly included Timothy and Titus) wrote all three letters just after Paul's death, incorporating genuine Pauline material into them. Second Timothy was based on an authentic last letter of Paul to Timothy. That letter generally began to confront the opposition. Second Timothy provided the spur for the subsequent writing of 1 Timothy and Titus to deal more fully and specifically with the hostility and heresy in the two places. The epistles provided Pauline backing for Timothy, Titus,

---

[72] J. D. Quinn and W. C. Wacker, *The First and Second Letters to Timothy* (ECC; Grand Rapids: Eerdmans, 2000), 7; italics mine. See also J. D. Quinn, *The Letter to Titus* (AB; New Haven: Yale University Press, 2005).
[73] Ibid., 8–9.
[74] Ibid., 9.
[75] Ibid., 22.
[76] Marshall, *Pastoral Epistles*, 59–108.
[77] Ibid., 83–84.
[78] Ibid., 84. Marshall believes that writings in which students attributed their works to their philosophical teachers may be categorized here.
[79] Ibid., 92. For the summary presented in this paragraph, see Marshall's conclusion on p. 92.

and other church leaders to help protect their congregations from false teaching. According to Marshall, they were not deceptive in any way, as this convention was familiar to both sides. The letters only say what Paul would have said in reaction to the circumstances had he been alive.

In the end, Marshall's proposal is vulnerable to some of the same criticisms as the "fragment theory" view of the Pastorals' authorship—the idea that a pseudonymous author incorporated some genuine Pauline fragments into his letters as he wrote them.[80] The theory invites some searching questions. For example, how does one accurately determine which parts of the Pastorals rely on authentic Pauline materials and which do not? By what standard can such a judgment be made?

Any theory of pseudonymity or unauthorized allonymity in the New Testament must assume that the early Christians tolerated the practice. However, as the reader has seen, the available documentary evidence shows that the early church soundly rejected pseudo-apostolic works upon their discovery. Thus, the view that pseudepigraphic or allepigraphic writings in the names of the apostles were gladly accepted by the early church is not secure.

The foregoing discussion included some who accept and defend pseudonymity in the PE. The following review highlights some modern scholars who do not.

D. Guthrie devoted his doctoral work to the subject of pseudonymity[81] and, in a related essay, examined the disputed NT letters against the background of Jewish and noncanonical examples of pseudepigrapha.[82] Guthrie believed that one should recognize the practice of pseudepigraphy in Judaism, while being careful not to assume uncritically that a Christian writer would adopt the practice due to the absence of relevant epistolary parallels. According to Guthrie, what available evidence exists in the Christian period points to the practice of pseudepigraphy as being questionable, in the sense of being morally blameworthy. For him, such deception was difficult to reconcile with the ethos of the NT. Such conclusions no doubt carried over into Guthrie's commentary on the Pastorals.[83] In yet another article, Guthrie discussed the development of the idea of canonical pseudepigrapha and concluded,

> There is no evidence in Christian literature for the idea of a conventional literary device, by which an author as a matter of literary custom and with the full approbation of his circle of readers publishes his own productions in another's name. There was always an ulterior motive.[84]

---

80 The "fragment theory" was posited many years ago by P. N. Harrison, *The Problem of the Pastoral Epistles* (London: Oxford, 1921).

81 D. Guthrie, *Early Christian Pseudepigraphy and Its Antecedents* (unpublished Ph.D. diss., University of London, 1961).

82 D. Guthrie, "Epistolary Pseudepigraphy," in *New Testament Introduction* (4th ed., London: IVP, 1990), 1011–28.

83 This commentary has been reprinted many times and revised. See D. Guthrie, *The Pastoral Epistles: An Introduction and Commentary* (rev ed.; TNTC; Downers Grove, IL: IVP Academic, 2007).

84 D. Guthrie, "The Development of the Idea of Canonical Pseudepigrapha in New Testament Criticism," in *The Authorship and Integrity of the New Testament* (ed. K. Aland; London: SPCK, 1965), 14–39; esp. 38.

In his discussion of Paul as a letter-writer, M. Prior observes three factors that have bearing on the authorship of the Pastoral Epistles.[85] First, he draws great attention to the neglected fact that Paul wrote several letters in coauthorship with other persons. Only Romans, Ephesians and the Pastoral Epistles list Paul's name alone as the author; all the other Pauline letters mention someone else's name with Paul's.[86] Thus, Prior maintains that "the person named together with Paul had a real share in the authorship of the letters."[87] Second, he proposes that, while several of Paul's letters to churches were written with secretarial help, the Pastorals were not. Third, Prior notes that the Pastoral Epistles were written to individuals rather than to church communities. For him, these qualities account for the differences often pointed out between the Pastoral Epistles and the other Paulines. In the light of these characteristics, Prior sees no need to resort to a pseudonymous authorship in the Pastorals to resolve these variances.

In his commentary on the Pastorals, W. D. Mounce holds that the use of an amanuensis by Paul best explains the internal and external evidence as opposed to any hypothesis of fictional or fragmental authorship.[88] For Mounce, theories of post-Pauline authorship introduce too many irreconcilable problems and do not deal with the external evidence. He questions whether the critical methodology of such hypotheses is valid or instead allows conclusions that are not supported by the evidence. Helpful to his case are three excursuses treating church leaders and widows in the postapostolic church.[89] The evidence confronts the claim that the church structure found in the Pastorals is just like the developed structures in the second century.

In the introduction to his commentary, L. T. Johnson maintains that the theological biases of nineteenth-century commentators led them to conclude that many Pauline epistles were inauthentic.[90] They did so, he says, in order to preserve an "authentic Paul" that fit their ideologies. Johnson views 1 Timothy as a mandate letter to a delegate and 2 Timothy as a personal paraenetic letter. He resolves difficulties to authenticity by appealing to the role of Paul's colleagues and the use of preformed tradition. He deals with the question of style by noting that the style in the undisputed letters of Paul is not uniform. He draws attention to the methodological weakness of considering the PE as a whole rather than as separate letters. Against the claim that historical details in the PE do not fit into the narrative of Acts, he contends that the possibility cannot be excluded because we know too little of Paul's movements.

---

[85] M. Prior, *Paul the Letter-Writer and the Second Letter to Timothy* (JSNTSup 23; Sheffield: JSOT, 1989), 37–57.

[86] Ibid., 38.

[87] Ibid., 39.

[88] Mounce, *Pastoral Epistles*, cxxix.

[89] Ibid., 186–92; 207–12; 300–302.

[90] L. T. Johnson, *The First and Second Letters to Timothy* (AB; New Haven: Yale University Press, 2001).

Johnson's commentary provides a sound case for understanding 1 and 2 Timothy in the context of Paul's mission and his oversight of the congregations that he started.

In his recent commentary on 1, 2 Timothy, and Titus, P. Towner maintains that Paul authored these letters "however much or little others contributed to their messages and composition."[91] He remains open on the process of their authorship. Given the complexity of the authorial process in the Pauline corpus, he views "nothing to be gained by insisting on a particular theory" for how these letters were composed.[92] He dismisses theories of pseudonymity for these letters largely as assumptions, but with a little uneasiness finds I. H. Marshall's theory of allonymity somewhat attractive, noting that the jury continues to deliberate.

The survey in this section reveals a fairly broad range of opinion on the subject of pseudonymity and the PE. Those scholars who believe that pseudonymity exists in the PE find no ethical dilemma in this idea. They get around the ethical difficulty simply by saying that the authors of pseudonymous works were not dishonest or deceitful. Or, if they do acknowledge that such writings were deceptive, then they claim, by means of the "noble lie," that this practice of deceit was not morally culpable. Accordingly, psychological objections to the presence of pseudonymity in the PE hold no validity for defenders of the practice. Those in this group usually are also not convinced by the known responses of the early church to pseudonymity, which do not support the practice as acceptable. Most argue that early Christians were more concerned about the content of writings rather than their authorship. Leading the way as a representative of the latter belief is D. Meade, who believes that the pseudonym was an attribution of authoritative tradition, not literary origins.

Contrary to the scholars above, those who object to the presence of pseudonymity in the PE, and usually for that matter in the NT, do so for a number of reasons. Many oppose the prospect of pseudonymity on the basis of theological arguments. For them, inherent in the practice is falsehood and present in the concept of canon is truth; pseudonymity and canonicity simply do not mix. Most scholars who reject pseudonymity do so because of the ethical difficulties the idea presents. For them, the deception involved in the production of pseudonymous works simply cannot be reconciled with the NT writings, which teach truth and morality. They also argue that tremendous psychological obstacles impede the idea of a moral Christian writer who composed a pseudonymous work under a false name. Finally, these scholars also argue that the early Christian leaders who scrutinized documents would not have knowingly admitted a pseudonymous writing into the NT canon. The known attitudes of the early church towards pseudonymity favor the latter position.

---

91 P. H. Towner, *The Letters to Timothy and Titus* (NICNT; Grand Rapids: Eerdmans, 2006), 88.
92 Ibid.

CONCLUSION

Scholars should take into account several factors when studying the authorship of the PE and the subject of pseudonymity and the NT. First, they should consider the internal evidence of the New Testament writings and the external evidence of how the early church received those writings. On the one hand, renowned scholars like M. Dibelius, H. Conzelmann,[93] N. Brox,[94] P. Trummer,[95] A. T. Hanson,[96] R. J. Bauckham,[97] I. H. Marshall,[98] and R. F. Collins[99] have examined the evidence and decided that the apostle Paul did not write the Pastoral Epistles. On the other hand, well-known scholars like C. Spicq,[100] J. Jeremias,[101] D. Guthrie,[102] J. N. D. Kelly,[103] G. D. Fee,[104] G. W. Knight,[105] L. T. Johnson,[106] W. Mounce,[107] and P. H. Towner[108] have considered the identical data and decided that the apostle did write the Pastorals. These opposite conclusions might lead one to think that they were reached subjectively. It is important that scholars look honestly at the available internal and external evidence when they evaluate the practice of pseudonymity. The extant evidence on the subject clearly indicates that the early church did not accept pseudonymous writings; when discovered, such works were rejected.

Second, scholars should recognize that an ethical dilemma is created when one accepts the presence of pseudonymity in the NT. The problem here is the belief that the early church was committed to truth as a moral ideal, encouraged its members to practice it, and yet approved of deliberate deception in the production of pseudonymous writings.[109]

Third, students must realize that psychological difficulties accompany the view that pseudonymity exists in the New Testament. Is it psychologically probable that

---

[93] M. Dibelius and H. Conzelmann (*The Pastoral Epistles* [Hermeneia; Philadelphia: Fortress Press, 1972], 7) think that the writer used the apostle Paul's name and thus his authority simply as "a matter of preserving the tradition and seeing that it is applied to the current situations."

[94] Brox, *Die Pastoralbriefe*, 60–65; idem, "Zu den persönliche Notizen der Pastoralbriefe," 76–94, esp. 86.

[95] P. Trummer (*Die Paulustradition der Pastoralbriefe* [BBET 8; Frankfurt: Lang, 1978], 81–82) thinks the details in the PE are wholly fictional and invented to provide paraenetic models for how church leaders should live.

[96] A. T. Hanson (*The Pastoral Epistles* [NCB; London: Marshall, Morgan & Scott, 1982], 14–16) believes that the PE are fictional and include details that somehow preserve genuine historical tradition.

[97] Bauckham, "Pseudo-Apostolic Letters," 469–94, esp. 475.

[98] Marshall, *Pastoral Epistles*, 59–108, esp. 92.

[99] R. F. Collins, *Letters That Paul Did Not Write: The Epistle to the Hebrews and the Pauline Pseudepigrapha* (Wilmington, DE: Glazier, 1988), 88–131.

[100] C. Spicq, *Les Épîtres Pastorales* (4th ed.; 2 vols.; EBib; Paris: J. Gabalda, 1969), 157–214.

[101] J. Jeremias, *Die Briefe an Timotheus und Titus* (NTD 9; Göttingen: Vandenhoeck & Ruprecht, 1975), 1–10.

[102] D. Guthrie, *The Pastoral Epistles* (TNTC; Grand Rapids: Eerdmans/Leicester: InterVarsity Press, 1988), 11–53, esp. 48–52.

[103] J. N. D. Kelly, *A Commentary on the Pastoral Epistles* (BNTC; London: Black's, 1963), 27–34.

[104] G. D. Fee, *1 and 2 Timothy, Titus* (NIBC; Peabody, MA: Hendrickson, 1998), 23–26.

[105] G. W. Knight III, *Commentary on the Pastoral Epistles* (NIGTC; Grand Rapids: Eerdmans, 1992), 21–52.

[106] Johnson, *First and Second Letters to Timothy*, xi, 20–54, 92, 140–42.

[107] Mounce, *Pastoral Epistles*, cxviii–cxxix.

[108] Towner, *Letters to Timothy and Titus*, 9–88, esp. 86–88.

[109] Wilder, *Pseudonymity, the New Testament, and Deception*, 62–63, 78, 124.

an early Christian writer would resort to a literary practice that he knew was dishonest and would be rejected by church leaders? Such troublesome questions must be answered by those who find and accept pseudonymity anywhere in the NT.

Fourth, the importance of apostolic authorship to the early church must not be neglected. One of the criteria used by early Christians to recognize whether a writing was inspired of God and thus canonical was apostolicity, that is, whether a book had been written by an apostle or by someone under his supervision or with his approval, such as a protégé or amanuensis. Sometimes this criterion is difficult to explain and apply to canonical works such as the anonymous book of Hebrews, but it is even more difficult to do so with the idea of a canonical writing that has been authored pseudonymously.[110] On the one hand, defenders of the authenticity of the NT writings often argue that using the apostles' names in pseudonymous letters usurped their unique status and high authority for one's own unscrupulous purposes. On the other hand, supporters of pseudonymity in the NT frequently contend that the apostles' names had to be used pseudonymously to invest letters with needed authority in order to pass on apostolic tradition to a future generation, or to fight heresy with apostolic teaching. However, the existing evidence shows that such a practice was not acceptable to the early church. Also, many neglect the fact that the high authority of the apostles did not prevent others from writing in their own names or in works that are now anonymous (for example, Hebrews; *1* and *2 Clement*; *Epistle of Barnabas*; Ignatius, Polycarp). Moreover, the early church often fought heresy in letters without using apostolic pseudonyms, and, for that matter, even without using the apostles' names (for example, Jude and possibly the book of Hebrews were written against false teaching). Included among the many works written by the early church fathers in their own names against heresy are Irenaeus, *Against Heresy*; Origen, *Against Celsus*; Tertullian, *On Prescription Against Heretics*, and *Against Marcion*. Furthermore, the early Christians often transmitted the teachings of an authority figure without using pseudonymity. For example, Paul himself, when passing on the authoritative tradition of the OT to a new situation, used introductory formulae such as "It is written." Rather than writing a pseudonymous letter under an apostle's name, might not an author have written, "The apostle has said," and achieved the same result? Other examples of the transmission of authoritative teaching by the early church without using pseudonymity include: an anonymous author who began his work as "The Teaching of the Twelve Apostles" (the *Didache*); Mark, who introduces his gospel as "the beginning of the gospel of Jesus Christ"; and Luke's Acts, which gives a largely third-person narration of the teaching of the apostles.[111] Evidently, it was unnecessary to write using the apostles' names pseudonymously.

---

110 Wilder, "Pseudonymity and the New Testament," 323.
111 Ellis, "Pseudonymity," 220.

Scholars should also consider the theological and canonical ramifications if they think pseudonymity to be present in the PE. One consequence is that exegesis, and then theology, must surely be affected if we interpret a NT letter as pseudonymous because pseudonymity was not an established and nondeceptive literary convention in the early church.[112] The words of the Pastorals lose the weight of their authority if Paul does not author or authorize them but instead someone using the guise of an apostle pens them.[113] The authority that the apostle's letters assert cannot be separated from the authority of the apostle himself. The impact of pseudo-apostolicity upon exegesis is further compounded when one realizes that this demands that the letters also contain pseudo-recipients and pseudo-circumstances. So, the interpretation of a pseudo-Pauline letter, for example, must differ from one that is genuinely Pauline.[114] Consequently, the exegesis of such pseudo-Pauline letters cannot be used to form a Pauline theology.[115] Some scholars argue that the authors of pseudonymous letters do not claim apostolic authority but instead faithfully mediate the apostle's normative teaching to a new situation.[116] While this might seem to lessen the impact of pseudo-apostolicity on exegesis, surely a pseudonymous letter cannot carry as much weight as one that an apostle himself wrote or authorized.[117] Further, these scholars are still faced with the fact that such letters were deceptive and squarely rejected by the church.

The second consequence concerns the canon of Scripture itself. Should pseudonymous letters, if present in the NT, be retained in the canon? The early church clearly would have excluded such works—had they known about them. But what about the present day? Specifically, should the Pastorals be dropped from the canon if they are pseudo-apostolic letters? Amongst evangelicals the term "canon" refers to those writings which traditionally have been "recognized and accepted by the church as authoritative and inspired by God,"[118] that is, those books recognized "as an inspired message from God and the basis for Christian doctrine."[119] The word for "canon"

---

[112] D. Guthrie, "Questions of Introduction" in *New Testament Interpretation* (ed. I. H. Marshall; Carlisle: Paternoster, 1992), 105–16, esp. 112.

[113] Ibid.

[114] Ibid. To demonstrate this, Guthrie suggested comparing the commentaries of a scholar who viewed Ephesians as non-Pauline and one who understood the letter as Pauline.

[115] As S. E. Porter ("Pauline Authorship and the Pastoral Epistles: Implications for Canon," *BBR* 5 [1995]: 121–22) notes.

[116] For example, Bauckham (*Jude, 2 Peter*, 161–62) in relation to 2 Peter.

[117] Guthrie, "Questions of Introduction," 112.

[118] D. S. Dockery, *The Doctrine of the Bible* (Nashville: Convention Press, 1991), 54.

[119] Ellis, "Pseudonymity," 224. Ellis correctly notes, "This distinction is drawn between canonical and apocryphal writings." E.g., see Origen: "no one ought to use for the confirmation of doctrine any books that are outside the canonical Scriptures [*canonizatas scripturas*]," (*Commentary in Matthew 28* [on Matt 23:37–39], cited from Ellis, *The OT in Early Christianity*, 17); and Jerome: "Sicut ergo Iudith et Tobi et Macchabeorum libros legit quidem Ecclesia, sed inter canonicas scripturas non recipit, sic et haec duo volumina legat ad aedificationem plebis, non ad auctoritatem ecclesiasticorum dogmatum confirmandam" (*Prologus in Liber Salomonis*, cited in *Biblia Sacra iuxta Vulgatam Versionem*, [ed. B. Fischer; 2 vols.; Stuttgart: Bibelanstalt, 1983], 2:957); see also Ellis, *Prophecy and Hermeneutic in Early Christianity*, (Wipf & Stock, 2003), 17, 32; and B. F. Westcott, *The History of the Canon of the New Testament* (5th ed.; London: Macmillan, 1881), 12–14.

(κανών) has a wide variety of meanings,[120] but it is normally defined as a "rule or norm."[121] This term was applied to the church's rule or standard for faith and practice, and came to refer to the biblical books as "a binding norm for truth."[122]

One might argue that the Pastorals, if pseudonymous, should not be excluded from the canon because the church has accepted the works present in the NT for a few millennia. The latter argument is fair enough; at this point, however, two other variables need to come into play in regards to pseudonymity that is deceptive, namely, one's view of ethics and one's view of Scripture.

Let us first consider the question asked earlier from the standpoint of ethics. On the one hand, Scripture clearly contains the most emphatic precepts and warnings against deceit and lying[123] (e.g., Ps 101:7; Prov 14:5; Eph 4:25; Col 3:9). Moreover, the presence of the Holy Spirit, the Spirit of truth (John 14:17; 16:13), creates a background in which intentional deception would be frowned upon and thus could not flourish.

Such precepts, directives and effects like those above reflect and support a deontological view of ethics, which holds that "a right action is one whose maxim can be universalized consistently, whereas its opposite cannot be."[124] In other words, certain formal properties of the act of deception make it right or wrong, other things being equal. Thus, according to this view, if one must not deceive, then everybody must not deceive.[125]

On the other hand, one has to acknowledge that there are persons in Scripture who used deception that was mitigated by understandable priorities and circumstances: Abraham (Gen 12:13; 20:2), Isaac (Gen 26:7), Jacob (Gen 27:19), Elisha (2 Kgs 6:19), David (1 Sam 21:2) and Jehu (2 Kgs 10:18–19).[126] Though such examples of deception exist, however, the OT does not condone them. And, as we said earlier, a study of the NT terms for "deceive" or "deception" (cf. ἀπατάω and the entire ψευδ–prefixed word group) makes it difficult to demonstrate a concept of legitimate deception in the NT.[127]

Nonetheless, examples of persons who appear to believe that the use of deceit was acceptable in mitigating circumstances can also be found in post-apostolic Chris-

---

120 See the discussions by B. M. Metzger, *Canon of the New Testament* (Oxford: Clarendon, 1987), 289–91; and F. F. Bruce, *The Canon of Scripture* (Downer's Grove, IL: IVP, 1988), 17–18.
121 E. Schnabel, "History, Theology and the Biblical Canon: An Introduction to Basic Issues," *Themelios* 20/2 (Jan. 1995): 16–24, esp. 16.
122 Ibid., 19.
123 B. M. Metzger, "Literary Forgeries and Canonical Pseudepigrapha," *JBL* 91 (1972): 3–24, esp. 21.
124 K. E. Yandell, *Christianity and Philosophy* (Grand Rapids: Eerdmans/ Leicester: IVP, 1984), 172.
125 Yandell (ibid.) notes that the weakness of a deontological view of ethics is that "wrong actions may turn out to be right (or at least permissible)," or the theory may be "unacceptably obscure regarding precisely what its results amount to . . . ."
126 Metzger, "Literary Forgeries," 21.
127 Schnabel, "History, Theology and the Biblical Canon," 19; idem, "Der biblische Kanon," 59–96, 92–95. Cf. also R. Nicole ("The Biblical Concept of Truth," in *Scripture and Truth* [ed. D. A. Carson and J. D. Woodbridge; Leicester: IVP, 1983], 287–98), who studies the language of the OT and NT to show that the full biblical concept of truth consists of factuality, faithfulness and completeness.

tian circles: Clement of Alexandria (*Stromata* 7.53), Origen (*Against Celsus* 4.19), John Chrysostom (*On the Priesthood*, 1.8).[128] An analogy often used in such examples is that it is acceptable for a physician to lie to his patients for the sake of their health.[129] Such deception is considered a kind of placebo which may be good for the sick person's welfare.

This concept of the "noble lie" can also be found amongst influential people in non-Christian circles of the ancient world, for example, Plato (*Resp.* 2.376c–382b; 3.389b, 414c–e). In these examples, a lie is permissible if the goal was to heal or to save, that is, for noble aims. However, in none of the references above are pseudonymous apostolic letters ever mentioned in connection with this concept. Further, a lie is nonetheless still a lie.

Examples mentioned in the last three paragraphs reflect and support a *consequentialist* view of ethics, which holds that what makes an action right or wrong is determined by its foreseen consequences. Thus, if using intentional deception prevents some greater harm, then one is at least permitted, and possibly obliged, to deceive. The greatest weakness of such a view, however, is that unjust or wrong actions can be sanctioned as morally permissible.

Let us now consider the question posed above from the standpoint of one's view of Scripture. On the one hand, many scholars view Scripture as divine revelation, that is, as that which God has spoken—using human authors—to disclose himself.[130] Those who hold this view argue that the writings recognized as Scripture by the early church had a divine origin, that is, they were an inspired message from God.[131] Thus, in this context, deception used by a human agent in a pseudonymous work is unlikely, because a holy God, who does not deceive, speaks using the human writer of Scripture.[132]

On the other hand, many critics believe that Scripture is a human witness to or written accounts about revelation, history, or events, but is not divine revelation

---

[128] Cf. Brox, *Falsche Verfasserangaben*, 83–105; Speyer, *Die literarische Fälschung*, 94–99; and Donelson, *Pseudepigraphy and Ethical Argument*, 19.

[129] But see Galen, the second-century doctor, who complained about others who had written works in his name. Thus, at least in Galen's case, it is difficult to use this analogy to justify pseudonymous letters in this manner.

[130] Though we shall not explore how the Scriptures are inspired, they are, arguably, "concursively inspired," i.e., they are simultaneously both divine and human words. Assuming that Scripture has this dual authorship, "it is the product of God as well as of human authors" (see D. S. Dockery, *The Doctrine of the Bible* [Nashville: Convention Press, 1991], 66–71, esp. 66). Cf. also the discussion and defense of this view by D. A. Carson, "Recent Developments in the Doctrine of Scripture," *Hermeneutics, Authority, and Canon* (ed. D. A. Carson and J. D. Woodbridge; Grand Rapids: Zondervan, 1986), 5–48, esp. 45; and J. I. Packer, *Fundamentalism and the Word of God* (London: IVP, 1958), 77–84. For a concise summary of the different theories of inspiration, see M. Erickson, *Christian Theology* (3 vols.; Grand Rapids: Baker, 1983), 206–7.

[131] E.g., 2 Tim 3:16 (θεόπνευστος). For a discussion and full defense of this interpretation, see G. W. Knight III (*Commentary on the Pastoral Epistles*, NIGTC [ed. I. H. Marshall, W. W. Gasque; Grand Rapids: Eerdmans, 1992], 444–50, esp. 447) who concludes that "all Scripture has as its source God's breath and . . . this is its essential characteristic."

[132] Although, as R. D. Shaw (*The Pauline Epistles* [Edinburgh: T & T Clark, 1903], 482) pointed out, any form of literary composition that came naturally to a human author might be a proper vehicle for his message as long as there was no conscious transgression of a moral principle.

itself. The canonical writings are simply works that human authors have written about revelation. This latter hypothesis allows for a great deal of freedom on the part of the human authors of the biblical books because Scripture is not viewed as words which God spoke or authored. Accordingly, the possibility of deception by a human author in a pseudonymous work is greater in this context.

Clearly, the perspectives of scholars on Scripture and ethics will determine how they treat biblical writings and also whether or not they are able to preserve the church's traditional idea of canon with a deceptive pseudonymous letter in it. The following table lays out the various possible combinations of the views presented above in the discussion.

KEY
A = deceptive pseudonymous letter[133]
B = consequentialist view of ethics
B′ = deontological view of ethics
C = Scripture is about divine revelation and events
C′ = Scripture is divine revelation

deceptive pseudonymous letter		view of ethics		view of Scripture		canon result
A	+	B	+	C	=	canon[134]
A	+	B′	+	C	=	canon
A	+	B	+	C′	=	canon
A	+	B′	+	C′	=	no canon

Of the four possibilities above, the last combination of views does not allow one to preserve the canonical tradition described earlier. Thus, to do so one would have to change his view of (1) ethics or (2) Scripture, or (3) modify "A" by (i) arguing that pseudonymous letters were not written to deceive;[135] (ii) dropping pseudonymous letters from the canon;[136] or (iii) contending that no pseudonymous books exist in the NT.[137] One might also choose (4) to abandon the traditional concept of the

---

[133] That is, according to the findings of this study. But see the recent article of K. D. Clarke ("The Problem of Pseudonymity in Biblical Literature and Its Implications for Canon Formation," in *The Canon Debate* [ed. L. M. McDonald and J. A. Sanders; Peabody, Mass.: Hendrickson, 2002], 440–68, esp. 468), who concludes that it is difficult to respond unequivocally as to whether forgeries exist in the NT when we consider ancient standards of authorship.

[134] That is, as defined earlier in this section.

[135] Contra the conclusion reached in this study. We have already seen that many scholars believe that pseudo-apostolic works were not written to deceive their readers.

[136] E.g., as F. C. Baur suggested.

[137] As Ellis ("Pseudonymity," 224 n2) suggests. J. A. T. Robinson (*Redating the New Testament* [London: SCM, 1976], 347–48) dates all of the NT documents before 70 and contends, "Pseudonymity is invoked as if it were an accepted and

canon of Scripture described above by either (i) arguing for a different concept[138] or (ii) claiming that the traditional idea of canon is obsolete or irrelevant.[139] The point is that the traditional understanding of the biblical canon will not allow for a deceptive pseudonymous letter unless scholars make less than desirable changes in their views on ethics and revelation.

In the light of this discussion, the question posed earlier—"Should the Pastoral Epistles, if pseudo-apostolic and written with the intention to deceive, be retained in the canon?"—is provided with an answer. If scholars desire to preserve the traditional concept of canon and think, as most conservative evangelical scholars do, that the following views are those closest to the positions held by the early church: (1) apostolic pseudepigrapha were written to deceive; (2) a deontological view of ethics; (3) Scripture is divine revelation;[140] and (4) the canon of Scripture is a binding norm of truth, then they should either drop any pseudonymous letters from the canon,[141] or seriously reconsider that such pseudonymous works do not exist in the NT.[142] If Paul did not directly or indirectly write the Pastoral Epistles, then they should not be viewed as canonical. I do not think, however, that a resort to pseudonymity is necessary, neither with the Pastorals nor with the rest of the disputed NT letters.

---

acceptable way of life at a date and to an extent for which we simply have no evidence. Indeed the fact of pseudonymity is frequently just assumed: it is the explanation for it alone that is argued"; T. Zahn (*Introduction to the New Testament* [3 vols.; Edinburgh: T. & T. Clark, 1909; repr. Minneapolis: Klock, 1977], 1:160) said concerning pseudonymous Pauline writings, "Every mistake which the [pseudepigraphic] writer made . . . tended during the generation after Paul's death to make the forged letter appear in the highest degree ridiculous, at least in the Church to which it was addressed, and so absolutely to preclude its acceptance by such a Church"; others also have argued that no pseudonymous works exist in the NT. Ellis ("Pseudonymity," 224 n2) suggests that the latter theory could be true because it may be "that the Baur tradition itself is an unhistorical reconstruction based on false assumptions of 19th century scholarship."

[138] E.g., as Meade (*Pseudonymity and Canon*, 208) does. Although he believes that pseudonymous letters are deceptive (on the authorial level), concerning the canon of Scripture he says, "it is the *prophetic* model that has dominated theories of inspiration in the church almost from the very beginning. While the validity of the prophetic mode of inspiration has never been called into question, the discovery of modern criticism as to how the Bible actually came about has made this model inappropriate for the inspiration of the Bible as a whole." In other words, Meade says that the church's historic conception of canon is both "outdated and unenlightened" (criticism by J. Daryl Charles, *Literary Strategy in the Epistle of Jude* [Scranton: University of Scranton Press, 1993], 81–90, esp. 87).

[139] E.g., as M. Rist ("Pseudepigraphy and the Early Christians," 89) seems to indicate throughout his article on the subject when he says things like: "it might be noted that since no book was finally accepted into our present twenty-seven book Canon unless it was thought to have been by an apostle, or by one of their disciples, possibly about two-thirds of them are actually pseudonymous."

[140] Petr Pokorný ("Das theologische Problem der neutestamentlichen Pseudepigraphie," *EvT* 44 [1984]: 486–96, esp. 496) maintains that if one views the canon of Scripture as direct revelation from God, then he/she would have to remove pseudonymous works from the canon.

[141] As e.g., S. E. Porter ("Pauline Authorship and the Pastorals: A Response to R. W. Wall's Response," *BBR* 6 [1996]: 138; idem, "Pauline Authorship," 123) indicates. Regarding the Pastoral Epistles he maintains if they are not by Paul, then they should not be considered canonical.

[142] Though the case against the traditional authorship of some of the disputed Pauline letters is sometimes strong, several scholars today believe that no pseudonymous works exist in the NT. Scholars hold this view with good reason because (a) the greatest weakness of pseudepigraphic theories is the number of assumptions upon which they rest, and (b) recent studies focus on Paul's use of a secretary (e.g., Richards, *The Secretary in the Letters of Paul*), a co-author (e.g., Prior, *Paul the Letter-Writer*), and tradition (e.g., D. W. MacDougall, "The Authenticity of 2 Thessalonians with Special Reference to Its Use of Traditional Material" [Ph.D. thesis, University of Aberdeen, 1993]) when writing his letters. A resort to pseudonymity is not necessary.

Chapter Three

THE PURPOSE AND STEWARDSHIP THEME WITHIN THE PASTORAL EPISTLES

F. ALAN TOMLINSON

INTRODUCTION

When attempting to discover Paul's purpose for writing the Pastoral Epistles (PE), New Testament exegetes generally formulate a purpose statement from internal cues within each letter that suggest the immediate circumstance for writing. This immediate and direct approach is certainly the beginning point for discovering the purpose for writing. The appropriate question, then, having discovered this, is to ask whether the immediate occasion embodies Paul's entire purpose for writing. A. Köstenberger, recognizing the complexity of deriving the purpose from Paul's stated occasion in 1 Timothy, observes:

> Paul stated the occasion for 1 Timothy as follows: "As I urged you when I went to Macedonia, remain in Ephesus so that you may command certain people not to teach other doctrine" (1 Tim 1:3–4; see vv. 18–20). The question is whether this occasion constituted the purpose for 1 Timothy in its entirety or whether Paul had other purposes besides instructing Timothy on how to deal with these false teachers. Contrary to those who emphasize the *ad hoc* (Lat. "to this," i.e., addressed to a given circumstance only) nature of the Pastorals, it is likely that Paul's purpose was broader than merely dealing with false teachers.[1]

Köstenberger rightly observes that chaps. 1 and 4–6 focus primarily on the challenges presented by false teachers, while chaps. 2–3 center more positively on general matters

---

[1] A. Köstenberger, L. S. Kellum, and C. L. Quarles, *The Cradle, The Cross, and The Crown: An Introduction to the New Testament* (Nashville: B&H Academic, 2009), 646.

of church organization.[2] He suggests that with the phrase "first of all, then" (1 Tim 2:1) Paul introduces a central section on general organizational matters (2:1–3:13), which he concludes with a closure statement (3:14–16), emphasizing an application to the church more broadly ("But if I should be delayed, *I have written* so that you will know how people ought to act in God's household, which is the church of the living God, the pillar and foundation of the truth, 3:15). Köstenberger further points out that the solemn affirmation spoken in broad terms to the church as "the pillar and foundation of the truth" is then immediately followed by a hymn in 3:16, which identifies general core truths befitting the universal "household of God." For Köstenberger, this arrangement of the letter along with Paul's own understanding of his apostolic responsibility, employing the household metaphor to the church as a whole in previous letters (such as in Eph 2:19–20), suggests that 1 Timothy is not merely ad hoc instruction but rather has application to the "household" more broadly.

Some commentators, including Köstenberger, argue that Paul's purpose for writing had a twofold dimension: (1) an ad hoc personal dimension, namely, to instruct Timothy on how to deal with the false teachers at Ephesus; and (2) a more general dimension, to provide guidance related to a variety of issues facing not only the church at Ephesus but the church as a whole in perpetuity.[3] Most recent commentators line up with the ad hoc position. Mid-twentieth-century scholars favored the more general dimension (especially those given to a second-century dating). Given this debate with respect to the purpose of 1 Timothy and the PE generally, this chapter will examine two areas of inquiry: (1) the broader purpose of each of the PE in view of the occasion for writing as well as the various structural markers suggesting the purpose for writing within each of the PE; and (2) the controlling metaphor of estate stewardship that is "at home with" the specialized vocabulary within the epistles.

THE PURPOSE OF 1 TIMOTHY

PAUL'S PURPOSE IN VIEW OF THE OCCASION

In 1 Timothy, Paul writes special instructions to Timothy as an apostolic delegate sent on temporary assignment to Ephesus to correct and, if necessary, remove certain errant leaders within the church. Timothy, though not a pastor per se, is given instructions by Paul on "how people ought to conduct themselves in the household

---

[2] Ibid.

[3] Ibid. Cf. P. H. Towner, *The Letters to Timothy and Titus* (NICNT; Grand Rapids: Eerdmans, 2006), 70, also observes both the personal and general nature in that "the opening is designed to establish Paul's and, in this case, Timothy's authority for a church that has come to question the apostle's teaching and mission." Commenting later on the personal nature, Towner, 392, writes "this letter was first and foremost addressed to the apostolic co-worker to direct his work in Ephesus." Towner, 389, also observes that the letter was written to encourage believers to pursue appropriate behavior within the household and the church.

of God." The letter rather directly focuses on correcting errant doctrine that does not fit with the apostolic doctrinal standards.

Paul offers very little information about the specific beliefs of "those who teach contrary" (1:3). He speaks of their emphasis on myths and interminable genealogies that promote competing "speculations" (1:4). These useless speculations draw attention away from the centrality of the gospel instruction which, in the nature of the case, is "the truth" that gives rise to loving relationships within the household (1:5). He also speaks of their boast of being interpreters of law (1:8–11). The false teachers see themselves as being the guardians and protectors of a deposit of truth, namely, their interpretation of law, which they guarantee (διαβεβαιόομαι, 1:7) to be "the faith." Yet the false teachers are employing the law in an unhealthy way by promoting through it controversy and division within the house churches. They forbid marriage, and they abstain from certain foods (1 Tim 4:3)—apparently, this asceticism fits with their misuse of law.

Paul, knowing that Timothy is already well aware of the elements of false teaching which are to be fended off, merely points out the doctrinal standard with simple objective references to the gospel. D. Wallace comments on what is often overlooked in the PE with respect to Paul's perspective:

> The emphasis is more one of "belief that" than "trust in" (cf. 1 Tim 3:9; 6:20; Titus 1:13; 2:1; 2 Tim 1:14; 4:7; etc. where terms such as "the faith," "sound teaching," and "the deposit" are used). In response to this problem it should be noted that the basic reason for this kind of "objective" reference to the gospel, however, lies in the nature of these letters in contrast with the others. The other letters (excepting Philemon, of course) were written to churches, to be read aloud and apparently to function as authority as though Paul himself were there. Therefore, it was necessary for him to reiterate the truth that was to correct or stand over against their waywardness. In this case, however, the letters are written to those who themselves both know fully the content of Paul's gospel and are personally to take the place of authority in these churches that his letter had earlier done. This latter phenomenon is totally overlooked in scholarship. It is almost as if the real objection were that Paul should write such letters at all.[4]

Paul is more interested in giving Timothy guidelines to confront what is contrary to that which "the genuine faith" normally produces, namely, love for fellow "house" members (1 Tim 1:5). Contentious strife between house members does not exhibit a devotion to one another and to the δεσπότης of the household (i.e., the householder). As Paul's troubleshooter, Timothy must create an awareness within

---

4 D. B. Wallace, *1 Timothy: Introduction, Argument and Outline*; http://bible.org/series/new-testament-introductions-and-outlines (accessed July 28, 2003).

the household that controversial speculations, with their resultant divisions, do not exhibit loving household relationships.

BROADER STRUCTURAL MARKERS SUGGESTING THE PURPOSE: 1:3–7; 1:18–20; 6:20–21

Within recent scholarship, R. Van Neste has pointed out the parallels between 1 Tim 1:3–20 and 6:3–21.[5] He has demonstrated the coherence of the letter from its symmetry and literary devices, particularly with respect to 1 Tim 1:3–20 and 6:3–21. Each unit ends with a charge given to Timothy to guard the deposit with which he had been entrusted (1:18 parallels 6:20) and a section on the opponents (1:19–20 parallels 6:21). He points out the careful framing of the letter by two parallel units of thought and their corresponding exhortations:

> Therefore, the structural, syntactic, and lexical parallels between these units on the opponents cause them to cohere and support seeing 1:3–20 and 6:3–21 as an *inclusio* around the entire letter. The opponents, thus, frame the entire letter by framing both the opening [1:3–20] and closing sections [6:3–21] of the letter. This shows a significant level of care in composition. This does not look like haphazard amalgamation of disparate texts.[6]

The controlling elements that suggest the purpose are a series of separate charges to Timothy. The first charge in 1 Tim 1:3–4 forms an *inclusio* with a reiterated charge in 1 Tim 1:18–20. This frame brackets an extended directive to Timothy (1:3–20) dealing with the false teachers. The charge then in 1 Tim 1:18 also forms an *inclusio* with the climatic charge in 1 Tim 6:20. This frame surrounds the body of the letter which deals primarily with the ordering of the household. Within this parallel framing, 1 Tim 1:18–20 is the hinge that demarcates two major sections of the letter, separating the introduction/occasion (1:3–20) from the letter body (2:1–6:21). The hinge verses (1:18–20) become the key to the structure around which the letter flows.

---

[5] R. Van Neste, *Cohesion and Structure in the Pastoral Epistles* (JSNT 280; London/New York: T&T Clark, 2004); 77–145.

[6] From the essay by R. Van Neste in the present volume.

The Charge (1:3–7)	The Charge Reiterated (1:18–20 transitional hinge)	The Summary Charge (6:20–21)
Frame→ παραγγέλλω→	←Frame　　　　Frame→ →παραγγελία παρατίθημι→	←Frame ←παραθηκή
1 Timothy 1:3–7 As I urged you when I went to Macedonia, remain in Ephesus so that you may command (παραγγέλλω) certain people not to teach other doctrine [4]or to pay attention to myths and endless genealogies. These promote empty speculations rather than God's plan, which operates by faith. [5]Now the goal of our instruction is love from a pure heart, a good conscience, and a sincere faith. [6]Some have deviated from these and turned aside to fruitless discussion. [7]They want to be teachers of the law, although they don't understand what they are saying or what they are insisting on.	*1 Timothy 1:18–19* Timothy, my child, I am giving (παρατίθημι) you this instruction (παραγγελία) in keeping with the prophecies previously made about you, so that by them you may strongly engage in battle, [19]having faith and a good conscience. Some have rejected these and have suffered the shipwreck of their faith. [20]Hymenaeus and Alexander are among them, and I have delivered them to Satan, so that they may be taught not to blaspheme.	*1 Timothy 6:20–21* Timothy, guard what has been entrusted (παραθηκή) to you, avoiding irreverent, empty speech and contradictions from the "knowledge" that falsely bears that name. [21]By professing it, some people have deviated from the faith.

It seems clear from the reiterated charges that the broad contours of the letter fit with Paul's purpose for leaving Timothy at Ephesus, that is, to instruct certain people not to teach contrary to that with which they had been entrusted. The gospel deposit (6:20), the faith (1:19), the instruction par excellence (1:5) is the essence of Christian teaching centered on the gospel, and it is diametrically opposed to the empty speculation that results in endless controversies and divisions.

PAUL'S PURPOSE: 1 TIMOTHY 1:3–7; 1:18–20; 6:20–21

The initial charge by Paul to Timothy, introduced by Καθὼς παρεκάλεσά σε ("Inasmuch as I charged you"), is clear enough from context (though many translations translate it with the milder "just as I urged you"). Somewhat more difficult to understand is Paul's reason for his charge. In 1:3b–4 (all part of one sentence in Greek), Paul gives the reason for Timothy's dispatch to Ephesus:

> so that you may command certain people not to teach other doctrine or to pay attention to myths and endless genealogies. These promote empty speculations rather than God's plan, which operates by faith (1:3b–4; HCSB).

The contrastive clause "rather than God's plan, which operates by faith" can be literally rendered, "rather than [promoting] a stewardship of God in trust" (1:4). Paul assumes a verbal element to be supplied from context since the contrastive clause (beginning with "rather than," v.4) has a direct object in the accusative case with a missing verbal element. Paul will frequently leave out, for emphasis or for heightened rhetorical effect, a Greek verb. Though usually understood from the immediately preceding context, it must be supplied for meaning. In this case, it is the elliptical participle "promoting" (or "furthering"). Some translations supply this elliptical participle; for example, the NASB supplies the participle "furthering" (Gk. participle παρέχων picked up from παρέχουσιν in v. 4) in the clause, "rather than *furthering* the administration of God."

The charge actually to Timothy is to correct "certain ones" who give heed to myths and endless genealogies rather than (giving heed to the gospel instruction that *promotes/exhibits*) a stewardship in trust from God."[7]

μηδὲ προσέχειν μύθοις καὶ γενεαλογίαις ἀπεράντοις,
       αἵτινες ἐκζητήσεις παρέχουσιν
μᾶλλον ἢ
    [προσέχειν παραγγελλίαν
      ἥτις παρέχει] οἰκονομίαν θεοῦ τὴν ἐν πίστει.

The errant teaching at Ephesus does not "exhibit" (or "promote," Gk. παρέχει) "a stewardship in trust from God" (1:4). On the contrary, the opponents' myths and endless genealogies," (μύθοις καὶ γενεαλογίαις ἀπεράντοις) gives rise to contentious, competing speculations (ἐκζητήσεις, 1:4) which lead to unhealthy debates and

---

[7] The phrase with expanded ellipsis would be the following: μᾶλλον ἢ (προσέχειν παραγγελλίαν ἥτις παρέχει) οἰκονομίαν θεοῦ τὴν ἐν πίστει.

wrangling (cf. 6:4, μηδὲν ἐπιστάμενος, ἀλλὰ νοσῶν περὶ ζητήσεις καὶ λογομαχίας). Their excessive focus on such topics draws attention away from "the faith" and does not display appropriate loving relationships within the household (cf. 1:5, the goal of the παραγγελία is love).

The apostolic παραγγελία (1:5,18) for the household is the apostolic message of the gospel (cf. εὐαγγέλιον 1:11; ὁ λόγος, 1:15,18,19 [= "the faith"]). The content of the apostle's instruction is "the deposit" of the gospel which, in the nature of the case, should exhibit itself in an ordered household. In the theology of the letter, it is the deposit of "the objective faith" within the house that anticipates and initiates the mystery of a "devoted household."

The key word in the context is παραγγελία (1:5). It is assumed to be the opposite instruction to the false teaching. Within Pauline literature, it only occurs in 1 Tim 1:5,18 and in 1 Thess 4:2, in which context it is clearly Christian ethical instruction. Within Greek literature, the range of meaning varies from proclamation, announcement, instruction, command, order, charge, doctrine, or teaching. In 1 Timothy it appears to be primarily the apostolic message of the gospel with its obligation to mission and, secondarily, the apostolic charge to correct false teachers who teach contrary to apostolic teaching. This understanding is borne out in the parallel wording between the two occurrences of παραγγελία (1:5,18) which frame the introductory section (1:3–20). Other parallels to παραγγελία are the gospel (εὐαγγέλιον, with which Paul was entrusted, 1:11), the message (ὁ λόγος, which is worthy of reception by all, namely, that "Christ Jesus came into the world to save sinners," 1:15). It is also instructive to point out that "the faith" (ἡ πίστις "the faith"; identified as "the objective faith" 1:19; cf. 3:9) seems to be that "instruction" which Paul entrusted to Timothy (παρατίθεμαι σοι; 1:18).

Παραγγελία in 1 Timothy is essentially equivalent to παράδοσις, which term in the singular Paul employed in other letters when referring to the body of teaching delivered by the apostle (1 Cor 11:2; 2 Thess 2:15; 3:6). The singular "instruction" signifies the body of teaching delivered by the apostle with particular emphasis on the core truth of the gospel itself. It is the deposit (παραθηκή, 6:20); the objective faith (ἡ πίστις, 1 Tim 3:9; 4:1,6; 5:8; 6:10,21 [probably also 1:2,14; 2:7; 3:13]), the gospel, (εὐαγγέλιον, 1:11); and the word of God (4:5). This gospel instruction with its complimentary sound teaching is to be guarded and protected from the errant, idolatrous message falsely called knowledge (6:20–21).

The charge to Timothy is to instruct errant teachers not to give heed to "other, contrary teachings." The charge stated more directly would be to instruct errant teachers to give heed to the gospel "thereby, in the nature of the case, exhibiting a stewardship of God in trust" (1:3–5). They are teaching instruction that is seen to be in the category of idolatrous words (ματαιολογία, 1:6; διδασκαλίαι δαιμονίων, 4:1;

βεβήλοι κενοφωνίας, 6:20) and that emphasizes a misuse of law not in keeping with the gospel with which Paul was entrusted.

Structural Markers within 2:1—6:2 Suggesting a Broader Purpose

After the salutation and greeting (1:1–2), an extended directive to Timothy (1:3–20) commences and ends with a specific charge to Timothy (1:3–4 and 1:18–20). The later specific charge (1 Tim 1:18–20), in turn, anticipates the epistle's climatic charge (6:20–21). The two charges (1 Tim 1:18–20; 6:20–21) terminate literary units (1:3–20 and 6:3–21) which frame the letter body (2:1–6:2).

Within the letter body (2:1–6:2), Paul issues directives to the "steward" concerning conduct within the household of God (2:1–3:16); he follows this by more personal instructions to the steward with respect to various groups within his purview (4:1–6:2).

Within the first section of the letter body (2:1–3:16), the unit begins with the phrase "therefore first of all" (2:1) and ends with a terminating paragraph (3:14–16) beginning with "I am writing these things to you" (3:14). The terminating paragraph (3:14–16) explicitly states a purpose for writing the preceding directives to the steward concerning conduct within God's household (3:15). This purpose statement is broader than just correcting false teaching. Paul has given guidance to Timothy concerning "the ordering" of the household.

Throughout 2:1–3:16 there are directives issued for the ordering of the household. Beginning with the phrase "first of all" (πρῶτον πάντων, 2:1 with the rare [in the PE] inferential conjunction, "therefore," οὖν) and the reiterated verb "I urge" (παρακαλέω, 2:1; cf. 1:3), Paul issues directives to Timothy for the household in general. He mandates the initial directive for prayer with a polite yet authoritative phrase, "I urge" (παρακαλέω, 2:1). Then he continues the directives with "I want" (βούλομαι [either stated or elliptic], 2:8,9,10), stipulating instructions for the household to be applied at every meeting place ("I want men" 2:8; "likewise [I want] women" 2:9; "but [I want] what is fitting" 2:10). These directives are to Timothy who, acting as "steward over the household" (cf. 3:15), is to instruct the household on public worship in general (2:1–15).

In 3:1–16, Paul issues guidelines to Timothy with respect to qualities necessary for congregational leaders. Again, he employs authoritative directives with "it is necessary (δεῖ εἶναι, either stated or elliptic): "it is necessary that overseers be" (3:2); [it is necessary that] deacons in like manner [be]" (3:8); and "[it is necessary that] women in like manner [be]" (3:11). Paul ends the entire unit of thought (2:1–3:16) with a summarizing sentence stating his purpose:

> I am writing these things to you (sg.) in spite of the fact that I am hoping to
> come to you (sg.) quickly; yet, if I am delayed, [I am writing] in order that you

(sg.) know how it is necessary to conduct yourself (implicit sg.) in the household of God, which is the church of the living God, the pillar and foundation of the truth (1 Tim 3:14–15; my translation).

The phrase "I am writing these things" (3:14a) refers to the directives in 2:1–3:13. The elliptical "I am writing" with the qualifying phrase about delay suggests that Timothy primarily has been sent to correct errant leaders; however, if Paul is delayed (cf. 3:15a), the temporary assignment will involve a longer term of household management on Timothy's part. Timothy, as the apostolic troubleshooter, must keep in mind both proper household conduct (2:1–15) and what qualities befit congregational leaders (3:1–13). Paul assumed that errant leaders would be replaced; thus, the qualities for congregational leaders are addressed in 3:1–13.

Because Paul anticipates a possible delay in his return to Ephesus, the purpose for writing his letter (in the nature of the case) is broader than the initial purpose for sending Timothy to Ephesus, that is, correcting errant teachers. Paul's circumstances have prompted him to write to Timothy concerning matters of proper household management. Paul apparently would have dealt with these issues himself on his return. Now it seems likely that Paul's purpose for writing Timothy is broader than just dealing with the false teachers in an ad hoc situation—he is writing so that Timothy will know how it is necessary to conduct himself in the household of God. Timothy's de facto mission involves much more than just the initial charge to correct false teachers. Timothy is more than a troubleshooter; he is going to be the model and example of appropriate devotion (εὐσέβεια) for leaders within the household.[8] With this expanded mission for Timothy in view, Paul then turned to more personal instructions, charging the "steward-delegate" to expose false teachers and thus prove to be a "good servant" (4:1–7a), to be an example to the household of God with devotion to the Savior God (4:9–16), and to relate properly to the church in good order (5:2–6:2). In 6:3–21a, he returns to the initial charge to correct false teachers (cf. 1:3–20).

PAUL'S PURPOSE FOR WRITING TITUS

PAUL'S PURPOSE IN VIEW OF THE OCCASION

Apparently, after Paul's first imprisonment, Titus accompanies Paul to Crete. They minister together on the island. Shortly before Paul's departure, he issues verbal instructions to Titus to stay at Crete and install "overseers" (cf. Titus 1:7) among the newly planted house churches on the island of Crete.

---

8 "Devotion" (εὐσέβεια), though a word used frequently in the PE with a range of meanings, primarily relates to the performance of pious duties as well as obligations within a household that manifest integrity of heart, a sincere trust, and a conscientious attitude to the householder.

As Paul instructs Titus, he stays at Crete (1:5). Somewhat later Paul writes to Titus reminding him of the verbal charge "to set the remaining things in order and to appoint elders in every city" (1:5). From this reiterated written charge "to appoint elders," it is apparent that the churches have only recently been established on the island.

From where Paul writes the letter is not known. Paul apparently moves on to Ephesus, where the apostle leaves Timothy as he journeys on to Macedonia (1 Tim 1:3). Paul writes to Titus before he reaches Nicopolis (cf. Titus 3:12) on the Adriatic coast.

From the remarkable verbal similarity with 1 Timothy, it seems likely that the two letters were written about the same time.

STRUCTURAL MARKERS SUGGESTING A BROADER PURPOSE FOR TITUS: 1:11; 2:1; 3:1

Paul details more fully in this letter the instructions that he verbally related to Titus on his departure from Crete (1:5). He writes to encourage Titus as an apostolic representative to set things in order in the Cretan churches and to appoint elders/overseers in every city. The occasion of the letter is clearly given in Titus 1:5: "The reason I left you in Crete was to set right what was left undone and, as I directed you, to appoint elders in every town" (HCSB). The stated purpose has two components: (1) to set right what was left undone and (2) to appoint elders in every city.

The first component "to set right what was left undone" or "to straighten out the remaining matters" (1:5) seems to be picked up in Titus 1:11 where Paul charges that Titus "must silence" those who are teaching empty speech for profit. He follows this charge with specific instructions to component groups within the church (2:1–10). He then speaks to the theological basis for correct behavior within the household (2:11–15). The last major instruction pertains to the "setting right" of the household as a witness before the outside world (3:1–9).

The second component "to appoint elders in every city" (1:5) is picked up in the immediate context with a list of proper qualifications for elders who "as good stewards" would manage the house churches (1:5–9). The following outline suggests the broad contours of the epistle.

Outline of Titus

    I.   Introduction: salutation and occasion/purpose (1:1–5)

    II. Instructions concerning the proper qualifications for overseers who would manage the house-churches on Crete (1:6–9)

        A. Ethical qualifications for the overseer "as God's steward" (1:6–8)

           1. Above reproach with reference to his own household (1:6)

    2. Above reproach as God's steward over His household (1:7–8)
      a. Disqualifying qualities (1:7a)
      b. Possessing qualities (1:7b–8)
  B. Doctrinal qualification: fidelity to the truth and able to refute (1:9)
III. "Setting things in order" [as a good steward] with respect to inside agitators (1:10–2:15)
  A. "Setting things in order" with respect to "Judaizers" and false teachers within the church (1:10–16)
  B. "Setting things in order" within the household (2:1–10)
  C. Theological basis for household order: the return of the "owner" (2:11–15)
IV. "Setting things in order" [as a good steward] before the outside world (3:1–9)
  A. Subject to authorities (3:1–2)
  B. Our response to the "foolish" and the consequent response of our Savior (3:3–8)
 V. Final warnings (3:9–11)
  A. Avoid foolish controversies (3:9)
  B. Rules of engagement with the factious (3:10–11)
VI. Personal concerns (3:12–14)
VII. Final greeting and benediction (3:15)

PAUL'S PURPOSE FOR WRITING 2 TIMOTHY

PAUL'S PURPOSE IN VIEW OF THE OCCASION

From the particulars in the letter, an approximate scenario can be deduced. Paul apparently appears before a magistrate in a preliminary hearing at Rome (cf. 2 Tim 1:17a; 4:16–18). He realizes that he did not have long to live (4:6). Paul, consequently, summons Timothy to come to him as quickly as possible (4:9,21). Paul dispatches Tychicus to Ephesus, seemingly, as a replacement for Timothy. Of course, this scenario assumes that Timothy is still at Ephesus. Timothy's situation in 2 Timothy seems to fit with his situation at Ephesus as recorded in 1 Timothy. Both the named opponents (Hymenaeus in 1 Tim 1:20; 2 Tim 2:17; Alexander in 1 Tim 1:20; 2 Tim 4:17), and the contours of their respective heresies (cf. Hymenaeus' heresy, 2 Tim 2:17–18) are parallel. In both letters the city of Ephesus is mentioned as well as individuals specifically identified to be from the province of Asia (1 Tim 1:3; 2 Tim 4:19; cf. 2 Tim 1:15–18).

With the uncertainty as to the exact time of his demise, he wishes that Timothy comes to Rome as soon as possible to be with him one last time before he dies

(4:9,21). It is clear from the stated occasion that Paul's purpose for writing arises from his own immediate crisis—his loneliness and suffering in prison (1:4,16; 2:9; 4:13). Only Luke is with him, and he is apparently quite lonely. Consequently, Paul's direct purpose for writing is to summon his troubleshooter and co-worker, who has been sent on temporary assignment to Ephesus, to come to his side at Rome as soon as he can.

STRUCTURAL MARKERS SUGGESTING A BROADER PURPOSE FOR 2 TIMOTHY

The purpose of 2 Timothy is much broader than simply a summons to Timothy to come to Rome in order to ease Paul's loneliness. From the beginning of the letter, Paul offers advice in the way a father would advise a firstborn son. The emphasis throughout the letter is on reminding Timothy, Paul's spiritual son in the faith, to follow the role and model of "the father." Timothy is to follow the pattern established by Paul as a "loyal man of God" who did indeed guard the deposit and did entrust it to faithful men like Timothy. Timothy is to do the same (2:1–2; 4:1–2).

Second Timothy is the most personal letter within the Pauline archive. In it Paul addresses Timothy as "my beloved son." The epithet for Timothy suggests the heartfelt father-son relationship that Paul and Timothy shared (cf. Phil 2:22). Paul, as Timothy's father in the faith, would have preferred to give advice to his "son" in person (1:4). However, the exigency of his impending death compels Paul to charge Timothy, as a loyal "man of God" (i.e., steward of God), "to continue to guard the valuable deposit, the gospel" (1:14) and "to entrust it to faithful men" (2:1–2).[9] In the midst of suffering, Timothy is to persist in the proclamation of the gospel as Paul has done. If Paul should die before the arrival of Timothy at Rome, the letter itself will be Timothy's written snapshot of the faithful "father" who has dispatched the gospel in a trustworthy manner. Timothy and all those like him are to follow the pattern.

Accordingly, the purpose of 2 Timothy has two elements. The immediate purpose (the ad hoc element) is to summon Timothy to Rome where he will be placed in loyal service. The broader element is to remind "the loyal man of God" through reiterated personal charges "to guard the valuable *deposit*," the gospel, and "to entrust it to faithful men" for dispatch-ministry. These charges are based on the pattern of ministry engaged by the departing "man of God" (i.e., "steward of God").

The following outline suggests the contours of the epistle.

---

[9] "Man of God" is a term often employed in the OT as an honorific description of someone especially near to God. It is instructive that Paul only employs this term in the PE (1 Tim 6:11 and 2 Tim 3:17). It may be a direct allusion to "the house steward" imagery (cf. overseer as a good steward, Titus 1:7) as a "servant of God" in the sense of the responsible, dutiful man of the master's household: "man of so-and-so" (so the entry for ἄνθρωπος, uses 6. and 7., in H. G. Liddell and R. Scott, *Greek-English Lexicon* [9th ed. with rev. supplement; Oxford: Clarendon Press, 1996], 141, as "slave of God"; cf. "my man," Galen, *Medicus* 14.649).

Outline of 2 Timothy

I. Personal introduction: "I—my—me" (1:1–18)
    A. Letter prescript (1:1–2)
        1. Sender: the apostle . . . in keeping with the promise of life (1:1)
        2. Recipient: the beloved child (1:2a)
        3. Greeting (1:2b)
    B. Thanksgiving prompted by fond memories of Timothy (1:3–5)
    C. Personal appeal to suffer hardship for the gospel (1:6–12)
        1. Call to remembrance: the gift (1:6–7)
        2. Prohibition: don't be ashamed of the gospel (1:8a)
        3. Appeal proper: suffer hardship for the gospel (1:8b)
        4. Digression on the gospel's value: God's power demonstrated through the gospel (1:9–11a)
    D. Example of trust in God's ultimate safekeeping of his gospel—the gospel he unabashedly suffers for (1:11b–12)
    E. Summary exhortation: guard the valuable deposit [as a good steward] (1:13–14)

"guard the good deposit/treasure"
key verse 1:14

    F. Example of Onesiphorus as one who suffers hardship for the gospel (1:15–18)
        1. Negative examples: Phygelus and Hermogenes (1:15)
        2. Positive example: Onesiphorus (1:16–18)
II. Letter body: paraenesis (2:1–3: 9)
    A. Triadic paraenesis: be strong; entrust to others the gospel deposit; suffer hardship (2:1–6)
        1. Command proper (2:1–3a)

be strong-entrust-suffer hardship
key verses 2:1–3a

        2. An analogy for one who suffers hardship for the gospel: the soldier's single focus to please (2:3b–4)
        3. An analogy for one who suffers hardship for the gospel: the athlete's steadfast adherence that legitimizes (2:5)
        4. An analogy for one who suffers for the gospel: the hardworking farmer's expectation is realized (2:6)
    B. Call to remembrance: remember Christ's death and glorious resurrection (2:8–13)

1. Remembrance: Paul's motivation for enduring hardship when entrusting the gospel to others (2:8–10)
2. Affirmation in the confession/hymn we speak (2:11–13)
C. Call to mind these things (i.e., death and resurrection of Christ) when you engage false teachers within the "household" (2:14–21)
   1. Charge proper: do not wrangle with heretics (2:14)
   2. Be validated before God as a workman who understands the word (2:15)
   3. Avoid interaction with profane, idolatrous chatter—it will fan the flame of heresy (2:16–17a)
   4. Negative examples of men who engage in godless chatter (2:17b–18)
   5. Validation from the Lord: analogy from architecture—the building inscription validates the foundation (2:19)
   6. Validation from the Lord: analogy from household management (2:20–21)
      a. Two kinds of vessels/servants (2:20)
         (i) Clean silver vessels for honorable functions
         (ii) Earthenware vessels for dishonorable functions
      b. Abstain from engagement with dishonorable vessels/heretics (2:21)
   7. Flee youthful desires [i.e., arguing] yet pursue peacefully the correction of heretics (2:22–26)
      a. Command proper: flee youthful desires (2:22)
      b. Avoid disputatious people and situations (2:23)
      c. Prohibition: the slave of the lord must not be quarrelsome (2:24a)
      d. Positive exhortation: correct with gentleness knowing the devil's hold on those in error (2:24b–26)
D. Warnings not to follow the activities and teaching of the opposition, in view of the eschatological realities of the last days (3:1–9)
   1. Warning that difficult times are ahead (3:1)
   2. Characteristics of those in the midst of these difficult times (3:2–4)
      a. Lovers of selves, lovers of money (3:2)
      b. Boastful, arrogant, revilers (3:2)
      c. Disobedient to parents, ungrateful, unholy, unloving, irreconcilable (3:2–3)
      d-d΄. διάβολοι (3:3)

    c′. uncontrollable, untamed, not loving good, treacherous, reckless (3:3–4)

    b′. conceited (3:4)

    a′. lovers of evil rather than lovers of God (3:4)

   3. Contrast between outward form and inner power (3:5a)

   4. Avoid these opponents (3:5b–8)

    a. Command proper (3:5b)

    b. Actions and characteristics that identify the opponents (3:6–8)

     (i) Captivate idle women (3:6–7)

     (ii) Oppose the truth like Pharaoh's magicians, Jannes and Jambres (3:8a,b)

     (iii) Depraved mind (3:8c)

     (iv) Rejected with reference to the faith (3:8d)

   5. Their actions opposing the truth eventually will become evident to all (3:9)

III. Affirmation of Timothy's past, present, and future reliance on the gospel (3:10–4:5)

 A. Affirmation of Timothy's past faithfulness to the truth in spite of persecutions in Galatia (3:10–13)

  1. Timothy's acquaintance in Galatia with Paul's teaching, conduct, and deliverance from persecution (3:10–11)

  2. Principle for believers: persecution awaits the devout in Christ Jesus (3:12)

  3. Principle for unbelievers: their deceptive opposition will only increase (3:13)

 B. Exhortation: be faithful to the truth in the present trying circumstances (3:14–17)

  1. Exhortation proper: continue in the truth you were taught (3:14a)

  2. Reminder to Timothy of his heritage (3:14b)

  3. Reminder to Timothy of his childhood devotion to Scripture (3:15)

  4 Principle for "the man of God" (steward of God): the primacy of the God-breathed Scriptures for teaching believers and for correcting those in error (3:16–17)

 C. Solemn charge for the future: preach the gospel no matter what opposition may come your way (4:1–8)

  1. Charge proper (4:1–2b)

  2. Responsibilities: reprove, rebuke, exhort (4:2c)

3. Future defection: "professors" will turn away to false teachers who teach fables (4:3–4)
4. Charge reiterated: enduring hardship, complete your dispatching of the gospel (4:5)
5. The solemnity of the charge explained (4:6–8)
   a. Paul's end is at hand (4:6)
   b. Analogy from the games: the departure of a victor in the games (4:7–8)

IV. Personal concerns (4:9–18)
   A. Urgency for Timothy's coming: desertion or dispatch of his former companions (4:9–11a)
      1. Demas to Thessalonica (4:10a,b)
      2. Crescens to Galatia (4:10c)
      3. Titus to Dalmatia (4:10d)
      4. Luke is present (4:11a)
   B. Concluding instructions (4:11b–13)
      1. Bring Mark, one useful for dispatch-service (4:11b)
      2. Parenthesis: I have sent Tychicus to Ephesus (4:12)
      3. Bring the cloak left at Troas and the parchments (4:13)
   C. Warning about Alexander (4:14–15)
   D. Recollection of his legal hearing and a concluding deduction: the Lord's faithfulness to rescue (4:16–18)

V. Letter closing (4:19–22)
   A. Greetings (4:19–21)
   B. Benediction (4:22)

ESTATE STEWARDSHIP AS THE CONTROLLING METAPHOR WITHIN THE PASTORALS

RECENT INTERPRETATIONS

Until recently, most critical commentators recognized the importance of the concept of "household management" for the PE only in terms of a specific "recognized form" (*Gattung*) adapted and developed by the early church. These scholars identified texts, such as Eph 4:22–6:9; Col 3:18–4:1; Titus 2:2–10, as examples of a "household code" (*Haustafel*), identifying how Christians should relate to one another and to the world in view of the delay of the parousia.

In the early 1900s, Dibelius and his student Weidinger, contended that "the household code" was a Christian adaptation of ethical codes on household management borrowed from the Stoics in the second century. Christians established these routines as a way of relating to their culture in light of the delay of the parousia. R. W. Gehring admits to the deficiency of this explanation, commenting on the so-called household code in Col 3:18–4:1:

> The parallels found in the Hellenistic household management texts cannot explain the paraenetic character and content of the individual admonitions in the household codes. Among other things, this led H. von Lips to suggest that the NT domestic codes should not be categorized differently than the *oeconomica*. Instead of being recognized as a *Gattung*, the household codes are better classified as a topos. According to Lips, the domestic codes in 1 Peter, Titus, and Colossians all follow a similar pattern, which he calls a "paraenetic scheme" reflecting these areas of life: church, house, and public.[10]

Some recent German scholars understand that in the PE, the church "is characterized, even in its concrete organizational structures, by the perception of itself as a household, with 'household' understood in terms of the ancient *oikos*."[11] Here οἰκονομία and οἶκος are not understood as metaphors but as a literal characterization of how the church perceives itself in terms of household order and structure. This view seems extreme. It does not take into account Paul's purpose for writing each epistle nor does it consider how the author employs the "the topical category" of estate stewardship as a controlling metaphor in each letter. If one understands *topos* as the rubric that categorizes individual thematic elements of paraenetic material according to a central theme and that addresses particular situations within each letter, then it is best to understand the topical category of estate stewardship simply as a controlling metaphor employed by Paul to communicate to Timothy and Titus.

With respect to 1 Timothy, some recent commentators have argued that the concept οἰκονομία θεοῦ is the controlling metaphor and the theological key within the letter's opening introduction.[12] P. Towner, citing Johnson as representative of these interpreters, defines οἰκονομία θεοῦ:

> The term envisions a divinely organized pattern of life—God's ordering of reality—and the opening instruction suggests that it is apprehension of this pattern and the appropriate faith response to it that this letter will seek to explain. As Paul applies it to Christian existence, the term is expansive, encompassing the whole social, political, and religious world in much the same way

---

[10] R. W. Gehring, *House Church and Mission: The Importance of Household Structures in Early Christianity* (Peabody, MA: Hendrickson, 2004), 230; Gehring, 230n9, notes that *Gattung* is "a term used for a multiple number of texts with a common form and a common Sitz im Leben" and *topos* is "the term used to categorize individual parts of a paraenesis according to themes without these texts displaying a common form characteristic of a *Gattung*."

[11] Gehring, *House Church*, 261n181, cites representative scholars such as Michel, Lips, Luhrmann, Verner, Dassmann, Roloff, and Wagener.

[12] Towner, *Letters to Timothy and Titus*, 68, observes that "the theological perspective of 1 Timothy is shaped by the concept of *oikonomia theou* with which the letter opens." Cf. L. T. Johnson, *The Writings of the New Testament: An Interpretation* (rev. ed.; Minneapolis: Fortress, 1999), 147–54.

that the emperor would take to himself the role of the father or householder and regard the empire and its inhabitants as his household. Understood in this way, the whole of life is subject to the divine will (or is meant to be). The implications for a Christian understanding of the church in the world and mission are enormous.[13]

Towner then argues that οἰκονομία θεοῦ is the template that defines οἶκος θεοῦ, "the household/house of God (1 Tim 3:15)," in terms of a people "obedient to God's ordering." He views the people of God as a paradigm of a world obedient to God's "ordering"—a realized eschatology where the people of God are extending this reality of ordering "to more and more of the unbelieving world." The mission of God's household is to extend this reality, God's way of ordering life. This ordering is to be made known and obeyed by more and more of the unbelieving world.

Though all may not agree with Towner's "realized eschatology," Towner rightly recognizes that God's ordering of the household (οἰκονομία θεοῦ, 1 Tim 1:4), is the theological perspective that drives the argument of the letter. The sense of the phrase, however, in the PE works on two levels: (1) one sense, as Towner recognizes, specifies "the divine ordering of God's household"; and (2) the other, in a more fundamental way, denotes the "assigned responsibility" given to trustworthy servants who serve God and the household by guarding that which has been entrusted from pilferage.[14] This combined sense of stewardship is the assigned responsibility to guard the deposit of truth (i.e., the gospel, "the faith-deposit"), protecting it from pilferage as well as the delegated responsibility to bring the household into conformity with God's ordering. It seems that in 1 Tim 1:4 the two senses overlap.

PAUL'S USE OF CONTROLLING METAPHORS WITH A SPECIALIZED VOCABULARY

In many of Paul's letters, controlling metaphors, sometimes drawn from the OT, almost always involving local color, implicitly suggest theological themes. In Ephesians, Paul employs building imagery throughout the epistle to communicate the greatness of the corporate living temple that God is building. In Philippians, Paul employs civil war imagery to bring to mind a military partnership fighting on the same side for the gospel's advance. In Colossians, inheritance language speaks to those who are qualified through the gospel for an allotment in heaven. In Philemon, business metaphors suggest a "partnership" brought about by the gospel. In 1 Corinthians, slave imagery speaks to the fact that he is "your Lord in your place" and "our

---

[13] Towner, *Letters to Timothy and Titus*, 68–69.

[14] The range of meanings for οἰκονομία θεοῦ by English translations (1 Tim 1:4) demonstrate the difficulty of arriving at the sense of the word: stewardship from God, God's redemptive plan, dispensation of God, divine training, God's ordered way of life, God's plan, godly edifying, administration of God, God's work. The word οἰκονομία usually denotes either the work of a household steward (or manager) or the ordering under which he works ("stewardship," "household management").

Lord in our place" and his ownership extends to all those who call upon the name of the Lord in submission—no matter what the issue might be. In 2 Corinthians, Paul employs commendation/recommendation metaphors to speak to those who are qualified for new covenant ministry. In Galatians, slavery, inheritance and legal metaphors speak to those who legitimately are sons/heirs of Abraham. In Romans, Paul primarily employs courtroom imagery to display God's covenant faithfulness through the gospel to judge and acquit both Jews and Gentiles by means of an impartial judicial administration.

Stewardship metaphors express the controlling themes within the PE. In 1 Timothy, Paul as well as Timothy and other overseers are to "exhibit" a stewardship from God in trust. This assigned stewardship over the gospel (1:4; cf. 1:11–12) becomes the controlling metaphor of 1 Timothy. The charge actually to Timothy is to correct "certain ones" who give heed to myths and endless genealogies rather than [giving heed to the gospel instruction that promotes/exhibits] a stewardship of the gospel in trust from God. In Titus, he writes to encourage Titus as an apostolic representative to set things in order in the Cretan churches and to appoint elders/overseers/stewards in every city. In 2 Timothy, Paul charges Timothy, as a loyal "man of God" (i.e., steward of God), "to continue to guard the valuable deposit, the gospel" (1:14) and "to entrust it to faithful men" (2:1–2).

THE PROBLEM OF SPECIALIZED VOCABULARY IN THE PE

For many scholars the specialized vocabulary within the PE is an overwhelming obstacle which prevents them from recognizing Pauline authorship. It is true that the PE exhibit words, phrases, and formulaic expressions not used elsewhere in Pauline literature, such as "good conscience" (ἀγαθὴ συνείδησις), "pure heart" (καθαρὰ καρδία), "self-controlled" (σώφρων), "sound teaching" (ἡ ὑγιαίνουσα διδασκαλία), "sound words" (ὑγιαίνοντες λόγοι), modesty (σωφροσύνη), "godliness" (εὐσέβεια), to stray (ἀστοχέω), "without reproach" (ἀνεπίλημπτος), "worthy of acceptance" (ἀποδοχή), and "the account is trustworthy and worthy of all acceptance" (πιστὸς ὁ λόγος καὶ πάσης ἀποδοχῆς ἄξιος).

Sometimes synonyms are employed for more common Pauline terms: the word παραγγελία rather than παράδοσις to refer to apostolic teaching centered on the gospel and ἐπιφάνεια rather than παρουσία to refer to the return of Christ.

At other times, characteristic Pauline terminology is employed in rather uncharacteristic senses. G. Fee aptly comments that δικαιοσύνη "appears only in the sense of 'uprightness' and is a virtue to be pursued (1 Tim. 6:11; 2 Tim. 2:22), not a gift of right-standing with God."[15] L. T. Johnson cogently summarizes the problem:

---

[15] G. D. Fee, *1 and 2 Timothy, Titus* (NIBC; Peabody, MA: Hendrickson, 1988), 24.

Common Pauline terms such as "faith," Law," and "righteousness" occur, but all with slightly different nuances. "Law" appears as something that can be used "lawfully" (1 Tim 1:8); "faith" seems less an obedient response to God than the common body of conviction and commitment (Titus 1:1; 1 Tim 5:8) or, simply, a virtue (2 Tim 2:22). Righteousness does not signify a state of right relation with God but denotes a virtue in the Greek sense of "justice" (1 Tim 6:11; 2 Tim 2:22). Tradition is a deposit of truth that is to be protected (1 Tim 6:20; 2 Tim 1:12–14) rather than a process of transmission (1 Cor 11:2,23; 15:3). It must be said that each one of these elements can be found somewhere in the undisputed letters, but never in this concentrated combination. . . .

The Pauline note of conscience (συνείδησις) appears, not in terms weak and strong (cf. 1 Cor 8:7–12) but of "good" (1 Tim 1:5,19) and "pure" (1 Tim 3:9; 2 Tim 1:3) in contrast to "soiled" (Titus 1:15) and "cauterized" (1 Tim 1:10; 6:3; 2 Tim 1:13; 4:3; Titus 1:9; 2:1). Here, too, is the contrast between "healthy teaching" (1 Tim 1:10; 6:3; 2 Tim 1:13; 4:3; Titus 1:9; 2:1) and "sickness" (2 Tim 2:17; 1 Tim 4:2), expressing itself in a life of virtue (1 Tim 1:10; 3:2–4,11; 4:13; 2 Tim 2:22,24; 3:10; Titus 1:7–9; 2:7) and vice (1 Tim. 1:8–10; 2 Tim. 3:2–5; Titus 3:3).[16]

Evangelical scholars maintain that, though the PE do exhibit differences in particular word meanings, these differences are simply the result of external influences such as different situations in writing, different needs being addressed, and different audiences being addressed. C. Spicq observes:

> The Pastorals offer no characteristic that excludes their Pauline origin. The evolution of the style of the Apostle is perhaps due to the more sophisticated Greek and Roman culture, its vocabulary on subjects that he touches on for the first time, the tone of his exhortations, his age and the fact that he addresses himself to some disciples.[17]

Mounce concurs, offering an explanation typical of evangelical responses to the problem:

> That Paul uses some of his terms in different ways—and this is often exaggerated—is consistent with the historical situation and the ability of a creative genius like Paul who was not bound to say the same things always in the same ways. The passages in the PE that appear to be different from the other Pauline letters can be interpreted in ways consistent with Pauline usage. There may be a high use of traditional material, adaptation of local terminology, and the possible influence of a trusted amanuensis, but nowhere does the author of the PE say something that is necessarily contradictory to Paul's teaching.[18]

---

[16] Johnson, *Writings of the New Testament*, 428.
[17] W. D. Mounce, *Pastoral Epistles*, (WBC 46; Nashville: Thomas Nelson, 2000), cxviii, citing C. Spicq.
[18] Ibid., xcviii.

Even somewhat more problematic for some scholars is the typical Pauline terminology that has been omitted in the PE. Some important theological terms in the undisputed epistles of Paul are absent. These important omissions include "righteousness of God," "son" (of Jesus), "forgiveness," "cross," "freedom," and the flesh/Spirit dichotomy. Mounce counters that "once it is admitted that themes are 'clumped' in the Pauline letters, then it must be allowed that omissions are not necessarily significant."[19] Scholars also note that in some instances alleged theological omissions may only seem to be the case. Evangelical scholars, such as J. B. Polhill, point out that differences are more a matter of vocabulary than of true theological significance:

> Often the different flavor of the Pastorals is more a matter of vocabulary than of theological difference. For instance, some have maintained that the preexistence of Christ is never mentioned in the Pastorals. It is present, however, but in different terminology. The word epiphany is used in the Pastorals to refer to both the incarnation (2 Tim 1:10) and to the Second Coming of Christ (1 Tim 6:14; 2 Tim 4:1,8; Titus 2:13).[20]

Evangelical scholars maintain that Paul is free to use language consistent with the historical situation and his creative style. Mounce contends that most of "the unique Pauline words" within the Pastorals can be explained historically from the setting of Paul's life. He places the so-called "non-Pauline words" into various categories that can be explained within this context: (1) words related to the historical situation, (2) words related to what the opponents were doing or teaching, (3) words related to positive instruction, (4) words specifically related to issues of church leadership, (5) words employed in vice-lists, (6) words from formulaic expressions and doxologies, (7) Latinisms, (8) words addressing a rhetorical topic or using a metaphor, and (9) cognate words employing stems used elsewhere in Pauline literature.[21] Mounce then concludes his argument with the following statement:

> Of all the "non-Pauline" words Harrison identified, only eight-three have not been explained on the basis of these influences. Spicq says that there are only about forty words in the PE that are unusual to biblical texts. Therefore, one must wonder if any weight is to be given to stylistic arguments that do not take into consideration the expressed occasion and purpose of the PE. It seems that there is no necessary relationship between *hapax legomena* and authorship within the limited context of the biblical text.[22]

---

[19] Ibid., xc.

[20] J. B. Polhill, *Paul and His Letters* (Nashville: Broadman & Holman, 1999), 401.

[21] Mounce, *Pastoral Epistles*, civ–cx.

[22] Ibid., cxii–cxiii.

AN EXTENDED TOPICAL GROUPING SUGGESTED BY A SPECIALIZED VOCABULARY MATRIX

Paul certainly is capable of employing specialized vocabulary. For example, within 1 Cor 3:9b–17, Paul employs more than 10 different words, phrases, or clauses from construction contracts, words actually found elsewhere in 1 Corinthians and in Paul, yet in this context with new connotative meaning related to construction activities or processes (e.g., μίσθ- stems in construction contracts; cf. *IG* 22 244 col. 1, line 55).

In other epistles, Paul regularly employs Greek words which "carry" a metaphor and are pregnant with meaning. In Ephesians, πλήρωμα uniquely is employed as a synonym for ἐκκλησία and σῶμα. Paul apparently chose this synonym for the "church" (which is also identified as the "corporate body," Eph 1:23) because he wants to make the connection later in the letter that the church is to be filled with all the "planned fullness" which God is able to construct (τῷ δὲ δυναμένῳ ὑπὲρ πάντα ποιῆσαι, Eph 3:19–20). The Greek word πλήρωμα is a term employed in construction contracts for the material components of a structure. Paul is quite creative in his word use—he may employ a word with an entirely new and rare sense ("faith" in the sense of "assigned responsibility," "assigned trust" in Rom 12:3,6) or simply coin new words.

Specialized vocabulary is sometimes more a reflection of trying to communicate with clarity to an audience rather than any stereotypical function of an author's style. In 1 Corinthians, Paul employs more than 75 words and phrases drawn from slavery. In Ephesians, there are more than 80 words employed regularly in construction texts—some even semitechnical in meaning (e.g., πλήρωμα in 3:20 and ποιέω in 3:21). In Philippians, a very specialized military vocabulary of more than 70 words occurs throughout the context (e.g., σύζυγος, fellow-soldier, fellow-comrade; συναθλέω, contend together). Some of the vocabulary in Philippians is unique, fitting the audience he addresses—those who live in a veterans' colony. Paul will never again employ the military idiom "to work out the deliverance of yourselves" (Phil 2:12).

W. Mounce, commenting on the specialized vocabulary in the PE, classifies a set of *hapax legomena* employed in the PE under the rubric "topical groups." "He observes that "often words occur in groups and are addressing a topic or using a metaphor."[23] He then takes note of a glossary of words in the PE drawn from such areas as athletic training, military life, and pastoral life among others.[24]

In the PE as well as the undisputed Pauline epistles one can demonstrate Paul's use of extended metaphor from everyday life (or allusions from the first-century setting) by identifying "extended allusion" (or "background-metaphors") from a matrix of terms and concepts within a sentence, paragraph, or book that fit with a specific

---

[23] Ibid., cix.
[24] Ibid., cix–cx.

language glossary (e.g., military terms, slavery terms, construction terms, stewardship terms, etc.). This "language glossary" is our equivalent of shoptalk—various jargon, such as "computerese," "Wall-Streetese," or "businessese." The cohesion of this jargon within the macro-context is marked by its "fit" within the overall synthetic argument of the book or letter. Terms within the glossary matrix must then cohere by their "fit-ness" (cohesion) with the micro-text. This cohesion requires that each term within its own immediate context cohere at phrase level, sentence level, paragraph level, and unit level.

Extended background-metaphors coherently fit within their immediate biblical context: the vehicle of the metaphor (the concrete background element) fits with the tenor of the metaphor (the theological point being presented). Paul regularly employs topical groupings of words from everyday life that seem to fit his occasion and purpose for writing. He employs an extended metaphor with a particular glossary matrix to carry his synthetic argument.

Within the PE this glossary matrix appears to be terms from estate stewardship or from household management. Though his key themes, purposes, and occasions for writing are different in each letter of the PE, Paul seems to draw from the same trough—exhortations and directives drawn from household management. Paul probably borrows these controlling metaphors from Jesus' parables concerning faithful or dutiful service within the Messiah's household. This idea will be explored in the next section.

TOPICAL GROUPING OF ESTATE STEWARDSHIP TERMS IN LUKE AND MATTHEW

In the NT, the primary image of faithful stewardship is drawn primarily from the Lucan parables on "the call to faithful stewardship" (Luke 12:35–48) and "the parable of the clever steward" (Luke 16:1–13). Imagery may also be drawn from the Matthean parables: "The faithful and unfaithful slave over the household" (Matt 24:45–51; the one who is ἐπὶ τῆς οἰκετείας αὐτοῦ; Matt 24:45) and "the parable of the entrusted possessions" (Matt 25:14–30). In each of the scenarios, service in the master's house and in his absence concludes with a call to accountability (λόγος or some other related phrase of accountability) when the master comes.[25] The faithful steward (ὁ πιστὸς οἰκονόμος; see e.g., Luke 12:42) is the one to be put in a leadership position over the other servants within the household. The steward is to be from among those who serve in dutiful readiness like men expectantly awaiting their own master (ἀνθρώποις προσδεχομένοις τὸν κύριον ἑαυτῶν, Luke 12:36).[26] The

---

[25] The scenario, however, in Luke 16 is slightly different: the master, an absentee landlord, summons the steward to the master's primary residence to give an accounting (cf. Luke 16:1–2; esp. οὗτος διεβλήθη αὐτῷ and φωνήσας αὐτὸν εἶπεν αὐτῷ· τί τοῦτο ἀκούω περὶ σοῦ;).

[26] The term ἄνθρωπος is a common term referring to slaves generally and especially those within the household.

steward (οἰκονόμος Luke 12:42; 16:3), who is selected from among the house slaves (ἄνθρωποι, Luke 12:36), is always called to give "an accounting of the 'account'"[27]

From Luke 12, key terms (or phrases) identified with stewardship include the following: διακονέω (v. 37 in a word play), οἰκοδεσπότης (v. 39), ἕτοιμοι (v. 40), ὁ πιστὸς οἰκονόμος (v. 42), ἐν ἡμέρα (v. 46), οἱ ἄπιστοι (v. 46), ποιήσας πρὸς τὸ θέλημα αὐτοῦ (v. 47), πολὺ ζητηθήσεται (v. 48), and παρατίθημι (v. 48, "much was entrusted," παρέθεντο πολύ).

From Luke 16, key terms from stewardship include: οἰκονόμος (v. 1), ἀπόδος τὸν λόγον τῆς οἰκονομίας σου (v. 2), οὐ γὰρ δύνη ἔτι οἰκονομεῖν (v. 2), ὁ κύριός μου ἀφαιρεῖται τὴν οἰκονομίαν ἀπ᾽ ἐμοῦ (v. 3), μετασταθῶ ἐκ τῆς οἰκονομίας (v. 4), Ὁ πιστὸς (v. 10), and πιστεύσει (v. 11, τίς ὑμῖν πιστεύσει "who will entrust to you . . . ").

From Matthew 24, the phrases include: ὁ πιστὸς δοῦλος καὶ φρόνιμος (v. 45), κατέστησεν ὁ κύριος (v. 45), ἐπὶ τῆς οἰκετείας αὐτοῦ (v. 45), ἐπὶ πᾶσιν τοῖς ὑπάρχουσιν αὐτοῦ καταστήσει αὐτόν (v. 47), ἐὰν δὲ εἴπῃ ὁ κακὸς δοῦλος ἐκεῖνος ἐν τῇ καρδίᾳ αὐτοῦ (v. 48), and καὶ διχοτομήσει αὐτὸν καὶ τὸ μέρος αὐτοῦ μετὰ τῶν ὑποκριτῶν θήσει (v. 51).

From Matthew 25, important phrases include: Ὥσπερ γὰρ ἄνθρωπος ἀποδημῶν ἐκάλεσεν τοὺς ἰδίους δούλους καὶ παρέδωκεν αὐτοῖς τὰ ὑπάρχοντα αὐτοῦ (v. 14), μετὰ δὲ πολὺν χρόνον ἔρχεται ὁ κύριος τῶν δούλων ἐκείνων καὶ συναίρει λόγον μετ᾽ αὐτῶν (v. 19), μοι παρέδωκας (v. 20), δοῦλε ἀγαθὲ καὶ πιστέ (v. 21), ἧς πιστός (v. 21), μοι παρέδωκας (v. 22), δοῦλε ἀγαθὲ καὶ πιστέ (v. 23), πονηρὲ δοῦλε καὶ ὀκνηρέ (v. 26), and τὸν ἀχρεῖον δοῦλον (v. 30).

Some of the key terms and phrases within the stewardship parables are the same terms (or close synonyms) that are employed by Paul in the PE. Paul, when addressing the need for faithful service by leaders, will usually employ terms associated with estate stewardship or household management. When he excoriates the unfaithful because of untrustworthy service, he again employs terms associated with household management.

The employment of household management terms seems to be an obvious choice by Paul to communicate to the faithful servants, as well as to the untrustworthy, at Ephesus and Crete. What a powerful metaphor to address a variety of issues within the PE while "the master is away"!

ESTATE STEWARDSHIP IN THE ROMAN WORLD

Paul views himself as a "sent one" with derived authority from God to adjudicate matters of church life. In an adaptation of ancient memoranda, he writes a personal

[27] This accounting is called a λόγος (cf. ἀπόδος τὸν λόγον τῆς οἰκονομίας σού οὐ γὰρ δύνη ἔτι οἰκονομεῖν, Luke 16:2; συναίρει λόγον μετ᾽ αὐτῶν, Matt 25:19) or some other related phrase implying accountability (cf. Luke 12:44,46).

75

(though public) letter to Timothy, mandating personal instructions to Timothy which also include authoritative instruction for the whole community. The letter, with its mix of third-person plural imperatives addressed to the Christian community and its more private second-person singular imperatives addressed to Timothy, may be reflective of other contemporary communication with specific mandates from one in authority to one in a subordinate position of trust.[28] In the public arena, such letters would include informal letters of advice from a ruler "to specific individual representatives, carrying instructions for the delegate to execute."[29] In the private arena, it is assumed that these letters would consist of dispatched instructions from a property owner to bailiffs, agents, or stewards with responsibility over the administration of various household estates, each with their own managers.

During the three-hundred-year period prior to the writing of 1 Timothy, philosophical treatises on household management were published. One text, *De re rustica*, written by Lucius Iunius Columella in AD 60–65, includes a concluding section on estate management describing the duties of the steward (Book 11) and the steward's wife (Book 12). This work, contemporaneous with Paul, is one of many famous texts on household management.

In the Roman empire of the first century, absentee landlords dominate the landscape. The empire itself is carved up into large tracts owned by a comparatively few wealthy individuals. By the middle of the Republican period, most farms are either worked by tenants working on rented land or by slaves laboring on large estates.[30] Wealthy landowners live in the city and visit their farm estates only occasionally. Farm workers, who might be free persons or slaves, work the land, and a manager or overseer manages the farming operations. If the landowner possesses multiple household estates, individual stewards would be responsible for each estate household. From their large *domus*, estate owners would annually dispatch agents to their various landed estates throughout the empire. These landed estates represented the extended household of the master. As agents of the master, these stewards would inspect and certify the local accounts and report on the managing of the household.

Corruption by stewards on these distant estates was rampant. Columella observes the dishonesty and carelessness of slave stewards whose account books are fraudulent (Columella, *De re rustica* 1.7.6–7):

> On far off estates, to which visits by the owner are not easy. . . . Slaves damage grain land very seriously. They rent out oxen; they do not feed them or the other animals well. . . . They record the sowing of far more seed than they have

28 Towner, *Letters to Timothy and Titus*, 35.
29 Johnson, *Writings of the New Testament*, 439. Johnson cites P. Teub. 703 as an example.
30 J. Shelton, *As the Romans Did: A Sourcebook in Roman Social History* (2nd ed.; New York: Oxford University Press, 1998), 7.

actually sown. . . . They lessen the total amount [of harvested seed] by outright dishonesty or by carelessness. They themselves even steal it, and they certainly do not guard against theft by others. And they don't even record the amount of grain honestly in their account book. The result is that both overseer and slaves commit crimes, and the land quite often gets a bad reputation.[31]

Estate-householders (or their chief stewards) often arrived without warning at the estate in order to check on accounts before they could be doctored. Cato (*De agricultura*, 2) writes concerning the master's unannounced arrival at one of his estates and the subsequent accounting:

When he has learned how the farm is being looked after, what work is being done, and what has not been done, he should summon his slave-foreman the next day and ask how much work has been completed. . . . Look over his account books for ready cash, grain, fodder supplies, wine, oil—what has been sold, what payments have been collected, how much is left, and what remains to be sold.[32]

Stewardship texts often address the appointing of steward overseers who are engaged in the common work so that they may be a ready example for others to imitate. Varro, *De re rustica*, 1.17.3, offers the qualities of a good steward overseer:

It is very important that the overseer be experienced . . . for he must not only give orders but also perform the work, so that the other slaves may imitate him and understand that he has been made their overseer for good reason—he is superior to them in knowledge. However, overseers should not be allowed to force obedience with whips rather than with words, if words can achieve the same result.[33]

Paul apparently views himself as the "chief steward" of the household, having sent Timothy and Titus on temporary assignments as his delegated agents to check on the household churches. Timothy is to correct the leadership at Ephesus, and Titus is to appoint elders in the new churches on the island of Crete. Apparently Paul viewed his responsibility for these churches as like that of a chief steward overseeing scattered household estates.

KEY PHRASES FROM HOUSEHOLD MANAGEMENT IN THE PE

It seems likely, given Paul's use of controlling metaphors in his letters and his penchant for establishing themes and purposes within each letter's introduction (salutation, thanksgiving, or intercessory prayers), that one should be able to find this

---

[31] Translation from Shelton, *As the Romans Did*, 156.
[32] Ibid., 170.
[33] Ibid., 172.

pattern within the PE. Paul probably employs these controlling metaphors to communicate to an audience that is for the most part functionally illiterate.[34]

Terms from household management (the primary glossary matrix) find their way into the PE at major seams: letter openings, closings, topic shifts, emphatic charges/exhortations, and formulaic closures. This glossary matrix, however, does not suggest a monolithic understanding of some standard "stewardese." Meaning always derives from context and takes on a variety of nuances depending on that context. One should be reminded of L. T. Johnson's advice:

> The household theme . . . is prevalent in Paul but takes on a variety of forms
> and nuances depending on the community Paul addresses. Even appeals to
> the character of the language itself provide ambiguous evidence. These let-
> ters [PE] do have a more Greek and less "biblical" mode of presentation. Yet,
> before drawing conclusions, it is good to remember that the "biblical" style
> of Paul in Galatians and Romans is no more natural than his "Greek" style in
> 1 Thessalonians or Philippians. His style is affected by his subject matter, his
> audience. . . .[35]

Terms from the glossary matrix are especially prominent within the letter introductions and letter seams where Paul usually presignals his theme and purpose for writing. Within 1 Timothy, the seams (1:3–7; 1:18–20; 3:14–16; and 6:20–21) are the letter's "joints" around which the outline is constructed. Important allusions to estate stewardship are embedded prominently within these seams (as well as running throughout the letter). A few terms are actually jargon from stewardship texts (e.g.. "a stewardship . . . in trust," "hold fast the deposit"). Other terms find a very prominent place within estate stewardship but are not technical terms unique to estate stewardship (e.g., εὐσέβεια, equivalent to the Latin *pietas*, denoting duty, devotion, piety toward the head of the house, as well as to other household members, and the words πίστις or παραθήκη, denoting the deposit to be guarded or protected). Sometimes terms and phrases are employed within other social contexts (religious, business, military, etc.), yet also have a prominent place within the language of estate stewardship texts (e.g., "I entrust to you").

Certain terms and phrases at important "seams" within 1 Timothy suggest allusions to estate stewardship. The first seam, following the letter salutation and greeting, initiates the letter introduction by stating Paul's purpose for dispatching Timothy. The occasion of the letter (1:3–5) establishes the theme: "not to give attention to myths and to endless genealogies which promote speculations [about the gospel] rather than [to pay attention to the gospel instruction that exhibits] a

[34] W. V. Harris, *Ancient Literacy* (Harvard: Belknap, 1989), 267, estimates below 15% literacy in the Roman empire in the first century AD. Of course with respect to the PE, Timothy and Titus, the primary readers, are obviously literate, but the vast majority of those within the respective churches would not be.

[35] Johnson, *Writings of the New Testament*, 428.

78

stewardship of God in trust" ([παρέχει] οἰκονομίαν θεοῦ τὴν ἐν πίστει, 1:4; see above discussion).

The phrase "a stewardship of God in trust" (οἰκονομίαν θεοῦ τὴν ἐν πίστει; 1 Tim 1:4) probably includes a wordplay on the phrase ἐν πίστει—the word-play being understood in context as "a stewardship of God *in trust* (ἐν πίστει)" as well as "a stewardship from God *with respect to the [objective] faith* (ἐν πίστει)." The article in the Greek construction is a function marker connecting the modifying prepositional phrase ἐν πίστει to its head-noun οἰκονομία. The prepositional phrase most naturally fits the head-noun in the sense of reference, being translated "with reference to 'the faith.'"[36] The stewardship in trust is the stewardship that God has entrusted with reference to the faith-deposit.[37] Paul employs colorful words from estate stewardship that speak of an entrusted deposit (πίστις). He identifies the entrustment given him as the gospel (1 Tim 1:11), as the truth (2:7, the neuter relative refers to vv. 5–6, which is the "truth" of 2:4).

The second major seam (1:18–20 which serves as a transition to the letter body) also includes imagery from entrustment language. He identifies the entrustment given Timothy as "the instruction" (ἡ παραγγελία, 1:18). This is "the instruction" that Paul personally entrusted to Timothy (1:5; cf. 1 Tim 1:18) and that others, who do not possess faith and a good conscience, have suffered shipwreck concerning "the faith" (1:20).

The third major seam (2:14–16, which serves as a transition between two major sections of the letter body, 2:1–13 and 3:1–6:2) again includes a metaphor from estate stewardship: "in order that you may know how it is necessary to conduct yourself in the household of God."

The fourth major seam is the summary exhortation for the entire letter which closes the letter body and it again includes entrustment language from estate stewardship: "guard the deposit" (6:20). The objective faith, the gospel, is the entrusted deposit (cf. 6:21; the deposit is equated with "the faith" and is an antithesis to that "which is falsely called knowledge").

Not only do the seams suggest allusions to estate stewardship, but also formulaic expressions found within 1 Timothy (as well as the PE) call to mind allusions to estate stewardship. One such formulaic expression is the phrase "the 'account' [of the gospel] is trustworthy and worthy of all reception," 1:15. It seems a distinct possibility that the formulaic expression may well allude to the gospel deposit. Paul has been entrusted the steward's account (λόγος; i.e., the word) and has kept it from pilferage

---

[36] "The faith" understood as "the objective faith" or "the content of the faith" is a distinct possibility. The omission of the article within prepositional phrases is normal—even when the object of the preposition is definite in sense. Within prepositional phrases, the article usually is not necessary for specificity.

[37] In Greek, "entrustment" language regularly employs πίστις for "that which is entrusted." This πίστις can refer to various "entrustments": a charge entrusted (e.g., "having received the entrusted charge by the demos to himself" παραλαβὼν τὴν ἐ[γ]χειρισθεῖσαν ἑαυτ[ῶι πί]στιν ὑπὸ τοῦ δήμου, *IG* 22 1028.72), an office of responsibility given (e.g., Polybius 5.41.2), or a deposit entrusted.

(1 Tim 1:15a, cf. 1:15b; 4:9–10). Paul then reminds Timothy that he has entrusted to him "the instruction" that has not been adulterated or pilfered (1:18). Timothy, unlike those who teach contrary, actually does possess faith and a good conscience necessary for a loyal man of God who is entrusted with the gospel account (1:19; cf. 2 Timothy's serving with a good conscience). Timothy observes his obligations in accordance with a good conscience (maintaining loyalty and a good conscience in his household duty).

Other possible words and phrases alluding to estate stewardship from 1 Timothy include: "show yourself an example," 4:12; "prescribe these things well," 5:7; "I solemnly charge you," 5:21; "man of" 6:11; and "I charge you . . . keep the instruction," 6:13–14.

In 2 Timothy, with the end near, Paul wrote to Timothy, as a loyal "man of God" (i.e., a steward of God), "to guard the valuable deposit, the gospel" and "to entrust it to faithful men." This deposit is the very same gospel with which Paul was entrusted (1:11; cf. 1:10). "Man of God" is a term employed in the OT often as an honorific description of someone especially near to God. It is instructive that Paul only employs this term in the PE (1 Tim 6:11 and 2 Tim 3:17). It may be a direct allusion to "the house steward" imagery (cf. overseer as a good steward, Titus 1:7), referring to a "servant of God" in the sense of the responsible, dutiful man of the master's household, a "man of so-and-so" (so the entry in Liddell and Scott as "slave of God"; cf. "my man" Galen, *Medicus* 14.649).[38]

Terms and phrases possibly alluding to estate stewardship from 2 Timothy include: "Guard the deposit which has been entrusted to you" (1:14); "entrust to faithful men" (2:2); "present yourself approved as a workman who does not need to be ashamed" (2:15); "useful to the master" (2:21); "the Lord's slave" (2:24); "man of God" (3:17; man of "so-and-so," steward of "so-and-so"); "I solemnly charge" (4:1); and "Be prepared" [to dispatch a duty] (4:2).

Terms and phrases from estate stewardship in Titus are drawn from the metaphor of a steward setting in order the household (1:5). Paul details more fully in this letter the instructions he verbally related to Titus on his departure from Crete (1:5). Phrases from estate stewardship include: "according to a common faith" (1:4); "the proclamation entrusted to me" (1:3); "I left you behind that you would set in order" (1:5); "Overseer . . . as God's steward" (1:7); "who overturn whole households" (1:11); "speak what is fitting for healthy teaching" (2:1); "showing all good faith" (2:10); "a people for his own good possession" (2:14); "ready for every good deed" (3:1); "this is a trustworthy statement" (3:8); and "unprofitable and worthless" (3:9).

38 See ἄνθρωπος, 6. and 7., in Liddell and Scott, *Greek-English Lexicon*, 141.

CORRESPONDENCES BETWEEN HOUSEHOLD MANAGEMENT AND THE "MANAGEMENT" OF THE CHURCH

From the texts of the PE, R. Gehring has compiled lexical correspondences between the terms employed in estate stewardship and those employed in "management" of the church.[39] He identifies correspondences between terms employed in exhortations addressed in the PE to the private Christian households and the same terms employed in paraenesis to the church as a whole. He identifies these in four broad categories:

1. Terminological Inferences to Parallels between House and Church
   a. Paul employs the parallel use of προΐστημι in one's own house and in the church (cf. 1 Tim 3:4–5,12 with 5:17).
   b. Slaves are admonished not to disrespect (καταπρονέω) their masters (1 Tim 6:2), and the same is expected from the church in relation to the authorities (μηδείς καταφρονείτω, 1 Tim 4:12; μηδείς περιφρονείτω, Titus 2:15).
2. Correspondence between Assertions about House and Family and Assertions about Church Organizational Structures[40]
   a. Virtue and vice catalogs (1 Tim 1:9–10; 2:2; 6:4–6; 2 Tim 2:21; 3:2–4; Titus 1:10–12; 2:12; 3:1–3)
   b. Duty codes (qualifications and behavior of office holders: 1 Tim 1:12; 3:2–4;8–10; 4:12; 5:1–5,17; 2 Tim 2:2,24; Titus 1:5–6,7–8; 2:7)
   c. Instructions regarding the behavior of individual groups (1 Tim 2:8–10; 3:4,11; 5:11–13; 6:1–2,17–18; Titus 1:6; 2:2–6,9–10)
3. Correspondence between the Designation for Duties within the Church Leadership and Duties within the Household
   a. Manage, direct (1 Tim 3:5; 5:17)
   b. Care for (1 Tim. 3:5)
   c. Command (1 Tim. 1:3; 4:11; 5:7; 6:13,18)
   d. Rebuke (Titus 3:15)
   e. Terms for teaching and training (2 Tim 3:16; Titus 2:11–12)
4. Correspondence between Duties of the Householder and Duties of the Individual Church Members to Submit to the Head of the Household (1 Tim 2:11–12; 4:11–16; 2 Tim 2:14; 3:7,14,16–17; Titus 3:14)

From these parallels, it seems likely that some of the key terms within the PE were chosen for their connection to estate stewardship or household management.

---

[39] Gehring, *House Church and Mission*, 261–62.
[40] Lips cited by Gehring, *House Church and Mission*, 261n183.

This correspondence of parallel ideas and language suggests that other so-called specialized language in the PE may have been employed for its communicative effect with respect to the metaphor of estate stewardship.

CONCLUSION

This chapter looked at the purpose of each of the PE in view of the stated occasion as well as any broader purposes for writing suggested by the various structural markers within each of the PE. In 1 Timothy, because Paul anticipates a possible delay in his return to Ephesus (cf. 1 Tim 3:15), it was suggested that the purpose for writing the epistle, in the nature of the case, is broader than the initial purpose for sending Timothy to Ephesus to correct errant teachers (1 Tim 1:3). Paul's circumstances have prompted him to write to Timothy concerning matters of proper household management. Paul apparently would have dealt with these issues himself on his return. Now it seems likely that Paul's purpose for writing Timothy is broader than just dealing with the false teachers in an ad hoc situation—he is writing so that Timothy will know how it is necessary to conduct himself in the household of God.

Timothy's de facto mission involves much more than just the initial charge to correct false teachers. Timothy is more than a troubleshooter; he is going to be the model and example of appropriate devotion (εὐσέβεια) for leaders within the household. With this expanded mission for Timothy in view, Paul issues directives to the "steward" concerning conduct within the household of God (2:1–3:16); he follows this by more personal instructions to him with respect to various groups within his purview (4:1–6:2). These personal instructions charge the steward-delegate to expose false teachers and thus prove to be a "good servant" (4:1–7a), to be an example to the household of God with devotion to the Savior God (4:9–16), and to relate properly to the church in good order (5:2–6:2). In 6:3–21a, he returns to the initial charge to correct false teachers (cf. 1:3–20).

The purpose for writing the letter to Titus relates to the setting in order of God's household (including the appointment of overseers in the recently planted churches on Crete). He writes to encourage Titus as an apostolic representative to set things in order in the Cretan churches and to appoint elders/overseers in every city. The occasion of the letter is clearly given in Titus 1:5: "The reason I left you in Crete was to set right what was left undone and, as I directed you, to appoint elders in every town" (HCSB).

The stated purpose has two components: (1) to set right what was left undone and (2) to appoint elders in every city. The first component "to set right what was left undone" or "to straighten out the remaining matters" (1:5) seems to be picked up in Titus 1:10–12, where Paul charges that Titus "must silence" those who are teaching empty speech for profit. He follows this charge with specific instructions to component groups within the church (2:1–10). He then speaks to the theological basis for correct behavior within the household (2:11–15). The last major instruction pertains to the "setting right" of the household as a witness before the outside world (3:1–9). The second component "to appoint elders in every city" (1:5) is picked up in the immediate context with a list of proper qualifications for elders who "as good stewards" would manage the house-churches (1:5–9).

It has been suggested that the purpose of 2 Timothy has two elements. The immediate purpose (the ad hoc element) is to summon Timothy to Rome where he will be placed in loyal service. The broader element is to remind "the loyal man of God" through reiterated personal charges "to guard the valuable deposit," the gospel, and "to entrust it to faithful men" for dispatch-ministry. These charges are based on the pattern of ministry engaged by the departing "man of God" (i.e., "steward of God").

The second major section of the chapter explored the controlling metaphor of estate stewardship. Within this section, we surveyed commentators who acknowledge the household language as a central element to understanding the PE. We briefly surveyed recent German scholars who understood the language not as metaphors but as a literal characterization of how the church perceives itself in terms of household order and structure. We also looked at two recent American commentators who have argued that the concept of οἰκονομία θεοῦ is the controlling theme within the PE.

Following this brief survey, we then looked at Paul's general practice of employing controlling metaphors (with a specialized vocabulary) to establish controlling themes within his letters. We next looked at the so-called "problem of specialized vocabulary" within the PE—suggesting that some of the specialized vocabulary may be a topical grouping of estate stewardship terms to carry his synthetic argument in the PE.

It was then suggested that Paul probably borrows these stewardship metaphors from Jesus' parables concerning faithful or dutiful service within the Messiah's household (Matt 24:45–51, 25:14–30; Luke 12:35–48, 16:1–13).

After looking at the stewardship terms in Jesus' parables, we took a brief look at estate stewardship in the Roman world. I posited that Paul apparently views himself like a chief steward overseeing scattered household estates. He sends out Timothy and Titus on temporary assignments as his delegated agents to check on the household churches. Timothy is to correct the leadership at Ephesus and Titus to appoint elders in the new churches on the island of Crete.

The next section looked at key terms from estate stewardship in the PE. The final section dealt with internal correspondences within the letters between terms employed in exhortation to the private Christian households and the same terms employed in paraenesis to the church as a whole. It was noted that from these internal parallels it seems likely that some of the key terms within the PE were chosen for their connection to estate stewardship (or household management).

Chapter Four

COHESION AND STRUCTURE IN
THE PASTORAL EPISTLES

RAY VAN NESTE

THE PROBLEM WITH THE PASTORALS

In many respects the Pastoral Epistles have been the "ugly ducklings" of NT scholarship, or at least of Pauline studies. For various reasons, the Pastorals have been singled out for abuse and negative analysis.[1] A. T. Hanson's 1982 commentary is a key exemplar of this assessment with his condescending attitude toward these three letters. Of the author (whom he assumes is not Paul) Hanson writes, "He does not have any doctrine of his own, but makes use of whatever comes to him in the sources which he uses."[2] Hanson notes that Paul also used preformed materials but says Paul integrated these pieces into his own argument. Hanson continues:

> Not so with the Pastorals. Here the material is simply presented with its implied christology and no attempt is made to work it into a consistent doctrine. The consequence is that we find several different ways of expressing the significance of Christ in the Pastorals, not all consistent with each other.[3]

---

[1] E. Tamez explicitly states that 1 Timothy must be read in a way different from other biblical texts because otherwise we will end up with interpretations which would be "uncomfortable" for more democratic, egalitarian settings. She says we must be able "to dissent from certain affirmations of the text that contradict the gospel itself. To be able to understand historically and culturally why something is affirmed and to have the freedom to not accept its declarations because, paradoxically, it goes against the will of God in solidarity with the excluded, should be a new step in the communitarian biblical hermeneutics" (*Struggles for Power in Early Christianity: A Study of the First Letter to Timothy* [Orbis Books, 2007], xix–xx).

[2] A. T. Hanson, *The Pastoral Epistles* (Grand Rapids: Eerdmans, 1982), 38–39.

[3] Ibid.

A few more quotes help illustrate the overall assessment of these letters.

> There seems to be nothing very distinctive about Titus, unless it be the nega-
> tive feature that it has no Pauline transposition and no scriptural *midrash*.
> This is why one is led to suspect that Titus was written last of all and that the
> author was beginning to run short of material.[4]

> He [the author of the PE] is no profound theologian.[5]

> The author of the Pastorals could not do much at the intellectual level, but he
> could and did help to strengthen the institution [the church].[6]

Hanson does concede that the author of the Pastorals is "less moralistic, less unfortunately ambitious in his use of Scripture" than Clement of Rome;[7] but, lest this be
too positive, Hanson goes on to state: "there is little evidence that the author of the
Pastorals would himself be very competent if he were ever to be required to prove or
defend the Christian tradition from Scripture."[8] While Hanson is a key representative of this view, the view is not limited to him or his era. In a recent essay German
scholar, G. Häfner, wrote, "it seems clear that the author of these letters is no expert
in Scripture-based reasoning."[9]

These criticisms are wide ranging, covering various issues, but they typically
are rooted in a negative assessment of the way in which the letters are written. An
overall negative assessment of the letters' theology is attached to the significant
stream of modern scholarship that argues (and sometimes assumes) the Pastoral
Epistles lack any significant, careful order or structure. Scholars in this stream argue
that these letters are composed of various literary forms which have been combined
in a less-than-artistic form. J. Reed refers to the "abusive estimation that the PE
are, to put it bluntly, incoherent."[10] This can be illustrated by a few representative
quotes:

> There is no sustained thought beyond the limits of the separate paragraphs;
> from paragraph to paragraph—and sometimes even within paragraphs (e.g.,
> 1 Tim 2:8ff)—the topic changes without preparation and sometimes appar-
> ently without motive.[11]

---

[4] Ibid., 47.

[5] Ibid., 50.

[6] Ibid.

[7] Ibid.

[8] Ibid., 51.

[9] G. Häfner, "Deuteronomy in the Pastoral Epistles," in *Deuteronomy in the New Testament* (ed. S. Moyise and M. J. Menken; London: T&T Clark, 2007), 137.

[10] J. T. Reed, "To Timothy or Not? A Discourse Analysis of 1 Timothy," in *Biblical Greek Language and Linguistics: Open Questions in Current Research* (ed. S. E. Porter and D. A. Carson; JSNTSS 80; Sheffield: JSOT Press, 1993), 91.

[11] B. S. Easton, *The Pastoral Epistles* (London: SCM Press, 1948), 14.

> There is a lack of studied order, some subjects being treated more than once in the same letter without apparent premeditation. . . . These letters are, therefore, far removed from literary exercises.[12]

> In this sort of writing, however, there is no need to labor to discover logical order or subtle lines of thought supposed to provide coherence.[13]

> The Pastorals are made up of a miscellaneous collection of material. They have no unifying theme; there is no development of thought.[14]

Not only is the theology generally seen to be a collection of traditions, but it is also usually treated as a fairly arbitrary, inconsistent, unthought-out amalgam with little coherence.[15]

> Organization and development of thought are expected from an author, but the Pastorals are characterized by a remarkable lack of both.[16]

> The letters have no driving concern, no consistent focus of interest; instead they read like an anthology of traditions, many arranged mechanically together by topic, some simply juxtaposed.[17]

As the quotes above show, this negative view of the Pastorals is found among supporters of Pauline authorship (e.g., Guthrie) as well as those who argue against Pauline authorship (e.g., Hanson). Although much work has been done affirming a more positive reading of the Pastorals, this negative view persists.[18] This negative view of the coherence of the letters has profound implications for how one reads the letters and understands their message or theology.

A MORE POSITIVE READING

The consensus negative view began to be seriously challenged in the 1970s with J. Thurén's article, which argued for a coherent structure in 1 Tim 6:3–21 and R. Karris' unpublished (though often cited) dissertation, which examined possible relations

---

12 D. Guthrie, *The Pastoral Epistles* (2nd ed.; Grand Rapids: Eerdmans, 1990), 18.

13 F. D. Gealy and M. P. Noyes, "The First and Second Epistles to Timothy and the Epistle to Titus," in vol. II of The Interpreter's Bible, (ed. G. A. Buttrick; Nashville: Abingdon Press, 1955), 457, in discussion of 1 Tim 6:17–19.

14 A. T. Hanson, *The Pastoral Epistles*, 42.

15 F. Young, *The Theology of the Pastoral Letters* (Cambridge: Cambridge University Press, 1994), 47. Young here is describing a typical approach but is not commending the approach.

16 D. Miller, *The Pastoral Letters as Composite Documents* (SNTSMS 93; Cambridge: Cambridge University Press, 1997), 139.

17 Ibid., 138. See similar statements, pp. 9, 11, 13, 17, 59–60, 80, 82, 86, 91, 100, 101, 129, 130, 132, 135, 139.

18 For a very recent example, see Häfner, "Deuteronomy in the Pastoral Epistles," 136–51.

between the various traditional materials within the Pastoral Epistles.[19] The floodgates opened in the 1980s with the appearance of four monographs that dealt with the coherence of the Pastorals.[20] D. C. Verner argued that the use of household codes in the Pastorals revealed a clear and consistent social setting for all three letters and that the letters united around the purpose statement of 1 Tim 3:14–16.[21] L. R. Donelson argued that Aristotelian ethical logic provided the way to understand the connections between the various units within the Pastorals.[22] B. Fiore found coherence in the use of personal example in the Pastorals on parallel with their use in the Socratic epistles.[23] P. H. Towner demonstrated the coherence of the theological message of the letters, with the message of salvation at its core.[24] While these studies differed from each other and received their critiques, the overall coherence of the Pastorals was widely accepted. Indeed, writing after the completion of his monograph, Donelson stated:

> There is a change of mood in scholarship on the Pastoral Epistles. No longer do scholars simply assume, as they did for several generations, that these letters are awkward combinations of diverse literary forms.[25]

Towner, in 1995, could write of a new consensus marked by, among other things, the fact that "the PE are recognised as presenting a coherent theological and ethical argument to a real church or churches somewhere in time."[26] This consensus has been affirmed and furthered in articles by P. Bush, J. T. Reed and R. J. Gibson on the structure of 1 Timothy[27]; articles by C. J. Classen and E. Wendland on the structure

---

[19] J. Thurén, "Die Struktur der Schlußparänese 1. Tim. 6,3–21," *TZ* 26 (1970): 241–53; R. J. Karris, "The Function and Sitz im Leben of the Parenetic Elements in the Pastoral Epistles" (Ph.D. diss., Harvard University, 1971).

[20] G. Fee's commentary (*1 and 2 Timothy, Titus* [Peabody, MA: Hendrickson, 1988]) should also probably be mentioned as he devoted significant space to arguing for a real-life situation that pulled together the different parts of each letter.

[21] D. C. Verner, *The Household of God, The Social World of the Pastoral Epistles* (SBLDS 71; Chico, CA: Scholars Press, 1983).

[22] L. Donelson, *Pseudepigraphy and Ethical Argument in the Pastoral Epistles* (HUT 22; Tübingen: Mohr, 1986).

[23] B. Fiore, *The Function of Personal Example in the Socratic and Pastoral Epistles* (Analecta Biblica 105; Rome: Biblical Institute Press, 1986).

[24] P. H. Towner, *The Goal of Our Instruction, The Structure of Theology and Ethics in the Pastoral Epistles* (JSNTSS 34; Sheffield: JSOT Press, 1989).

[25] L. R. Donelson, "The Structure of Ethical Argument in the Pastorals," *BTB* 18 (1988): 108.

[26] P. H. Towner, "Pauline Theology or Pauline Tradition in the Pastoral Epistles: The Question of Method," *TynBul* 46 (1995): 288.

[27] P. Bush, "A Note on the Structure of 1 Timothy," *NTS* 36 (1990): 152–56; J. T. Reed, "Cohesive Ties in 1 Timothy: In Defense of the Epistle's Unity," *Neotestamentica* 26 (1992): 192–213; "Discourse Features in New Testament Letters, with Special Reference to the Structure of 1 Timothy," *Journal of Translation and Textlinguistics* 6 (1993): 228–52; "To Timothy or Not? A Discourse Analysis of 1 Timothy," in *Biblical Greek Language and Linguistics* (ed. S. E. Porter and D. A. Carson; JSNTS 80; Sheffield: JSOT Press, 1993), 90–118; R. J. Gibson, "The Literary Coherence of 1 Timothy," *RTR* 55 (1996): 53–66.

of Titus[28]; Genade's recent dissertation providing a rhetorical analysis of Titus[29]; and the significant interest in the structure of the letters in the commentaries by Roloff,[30] Quinn,[31] Mounce[32] and especially Marshall, who gives more attention specifically to structure than any previous commentary.[33] Also, more recent theses and monographs have further pursued theological coherence in the Pastoral Epistles.[34] Thus, Marshall can state:

> There is a growing body of evidence that the Pastoral Epistles are not a conglomerate of miscellaneous ideas roughly thrown together with no clear plan, purpose or structure. On the contrary, they demonstrate signs of a coherent structure and of theological competence.[35]

While this more positive opinion of the Pastorals advances, however, not all have been convinced. Indeed, in a review of Marshall's commentary, C. K. Barrett indicated that he remains unconvinced of the level of coherence for which Marshall argues.[36] Furthermore, in 1997 Cambridge University Press published J. D. Miller's *The Pastoral Letters as Composite Documents*, probably the most thoroughgoing argument to date for incoherence in the Pastorals.[37]

---

28 C. J. Classen, "A Rhetorical Reading of the Epistle to Titus," in *The Rhetorical Analysis of Scripture: Essays from the 1995 London Conference* (ed. S. E. Porter and T. H. Olbricht; JSNTSS 146; Sheffield: Sheffield Academic Press, 1997), 427–44; E. R. Wendland, "'Let No One Disregard You!' (Titus 2:15): Church Discipline and the Construction of Discourse in a Personal, 'Pastoral' Epistle," in *Discourse Analysis and the New Testament* (ed. S. E. Porter and J. T. Reed; JSNTSS 170; Sheffield: Sheffield Academic Press, 1999), 334–51.

29 A. A. Genade, "A Text-Centered Rhetorical Analysis of Paul's Letter to Titus" (Ph.D. diss., University of the Free State, 2007).

30 J. Roloff, *Der Erste Brief an Timotheus* (Zürich/Neukirchen-Vlyun: Benziger/Neukirchener, 1988).

31 J. D. Quinn, *The Letter to Titus* (New York: Doubleday, 1990), 5–6, and often in discussion of various passages (e.g., p. 83); J. D. Quinn and W. C. Wacker, *The First and Second Letters to Timothy* (Grand Rapids, MI/Cambridge, UK: Eerdmans, 2000), throughout commentary in discussion of several passages.

32 W. D. Mounce, *Pastoral Epistles* (Nashville: Thomas Nelson, 2000), cxxxvi, and often in discussion of various passages.

33 I. H. Marshall, *The Pastoral Epistles* (ICC; Edinburgh: T&T Clark, 1999). In his review of Marshall's commentary (*JTS* 52 [2001]), C. K. Barrett says Marshall's section on genre and structure "may well be regarded as the most original part of the commentary" (825).

34 E.g., A. Lau, *Manifest in the Flesh: The Epiphany Christology of the Pastoral Epistles* (WUNT 2.86; Tübingen: Mohr/Siebeck, 1996); H. Stettler, *Die Christologie der Pastoralbriefe* (WUNT 2.105; Tübingen: Mohr/Siebeck, 1998); G. Couser, "God and Christian Existence in 1 and 2 Timothy and Titus" (Ph.D. thesis, University of Aberdeen, 1992); C. Hetzler, "Our Savior and King: Theology Proper in 1 Timothy" (Ph.D. thesis, Southern Baptist Theological Seminary, 2008); M. Yarbrough, "Paul's Utilization of Preformed Traditions in 1 Timothy: An Evaluation of the Apostle's Literary, Rhetorical, and Theological Tactics to Combat Counter-Mission Doctrine" (Ph.D. diss., Dallas Theological Seminary, 2008).

35 I. H. Marshall, "The Christology of Luke-Acts and the Pastoral Epistles," in *Crossing Boundaries: Essays in Biblical Interpretation in Honor of Michael D. Goulder* (ed. S. E. Porter et al.; Leiden: Brill, 1994), 171.

36 C. K. Barrett, review of I. H. Marshall, *A Critical and Exegetical Commentary on the Pastoral Epistles*, in *JTS* 52 (2001): 825. Barrett writes, "It may be that he is sometimes too ready to defend the logical argument of the epistles." This is not a stark criticism but is evidence that the opinion of cohesiveness has not yet gained full acceptance.

37 Miller, *Composite Documents*, cited earlier. My own *Cohesion and Structure in the Pastoral Epistles* (London: T&T Clark, 2005) is a comprehensive response to Miller.

So coherence is gaining ground but has not won the day. Let's turn now to a summary of some key examples of coherent, careful writing and reasoning in the Pastoral Epistles.

APPROACH

Any approach to the question of coherence/incoherence must take seriously how those in the original audience would have read/heard texts. This may be a statement of the obvious, but far too often arguments for incoherence are based on anachronistic readings. Three areas will be examined here:[38]

1. Awareness of literary forms
2. Symmetry
3. Transitional Devices

In each category I will take up a few texts as examples. Since I have dealt more thoroughly with Titus in previous articles,[39] I will focus here on 1–2 Timothy.

AWARENESS OF LITERARY FORMS

This is the area where failure to appreciate texts in their own setting is most apparent. Certain portions of the Pastoral Epistles are criticized as being deficient— and thus probably sloppily inserted—without proper awareness of literary forms in ancient letter writing.

LISTS

For example, we can look at the vice list in 1 Tim 1:9–10. Miller and Hanson both criticize the general proviso that concludes the vice list (καὶ εἴ τι . . . ἀντίκειται) as out of place following a list of such serious offenses. Hanson even dubs it "a rather lame ending."[40] However, similar clauses are used to conclude such lists in the accepted Paulines (e.g., Rom 13:9; Gal 5:21).[41] More importantly, J. T. Fitzgerald, in a study of catalogues or lists in the ancient world, found that "many end with a formula of abbreviation ('and the like') or a collective reference ('and all the others')."[42] Thus, even if the proviso may seem "lame" to modern readers, there is no basis for seeing

---

[38] Semantic chains are not considered here but have been dealt with in my *Cohesion and Structure in the Pastoral Epistles*, cf. 16–17.

[39] "Structure and Cohesion in Titus," *BT* 53 (2002): 118–33; "The Message of Titus: An Overview," *SBJT* 7 (2003): 18–30.

[40] Miller, *Composite Documents*, 63; Hanson, *Pastoral Epistles*, 59.

[41] So also J. H. Bernard, *Pastoral Epistles* (Kessinger Publishing, 2009), 28; G. W. Knight III, *Commentary on the Pastoral Epistles* (NIGTC; Grand Rapids: Eerdmans, 1992), 88; Quinn and Wacker, *Letters to Timothy*, 102. Hanson, *Pastoral Epistles*, concedes this.

[42] J. T. Fitzgerald, "The Catalogue in Ancient Greek Literature," in *The Rhetorical Analysis of Scripture, Essays from the 1995 London Conference* (ed. S. E. Porter and T. H. Olbricht; Sheffield: Sheffield Academic Press, 1997), 288.

here a shift to a disparate source, because this was a common way to end such lists in the ancient world.

THANKSGIVING

Quinn and Wacker criticize the placement of the thanksgiving in 1 Timothy, writing, "here in First Timothy it appears dislocated, from the point of view of the normal positioning of the thanksgiving prayer in the ancient epistolary genre as well as in other letters of Paul."[43] While it is true that the placement of the thanksgiving is unusual in comparison with the other letters attributed to Paul, Quinn and Wacker are simply wrong in stating that its position is somehow abnormal in comparison with the use of thanksgivings in ancient epistolary literature in general. Two recent articles (by P. Arzt and J. T. Reed) provide the most extensive treatment of thanksgivings in the papyri to date.[44] Both articles conclude, with copious examples, that thanksgivings in the papyri letters are not confined to the introduction of letters but occur in various places with a wide range of uses. Arzt concludes:

> There are no formal "introductory thanksgivings" in the proemia of letters contemporaneous with the Pauline and other New Testament letters; hence any reconstruction of such an "introductory thanksgiving" shatters on the lack of evidence.[45]

Although Reed contests several points of Arzt's argument, he agrees that thanksgivings should not be referred to as "introductory" since they can be found in the openings, bodies and closings of Hellenistic letters.[46]

> It is clear from the papyri that thanksgiving was not a matter to be limited to either the opening or the closing sections. . . . In other words, an epistolary thanksgiving *formula* may appear in various locations within the discourse.[47]

Thus, the placement of the thanksgiving in 1 Timothy, while different from other NT letters, is not abnormal in comparison with ancient letters in general. There is, then, nothing amiss concerning the location of 1:12–17.

---

43 Quinn and Wacker, *Letters to Timothy*, 122. This idea appears to be what motivated the view mentioned by Moffatt that 1:12–17 have been accidentally misplaced and originally came between 1:2 and 1:3 (James Moffatt, *An Introduction to the Literature of the New Testament* [rev. 3rd ed.; Edinburgh: T&T Clark], 402).

44 P. Arzt, "The 'Epistolary Introductory Thanksgiving' in the Papyri and in Paul," *Nov T* 36 (1994): 29–46; J. T. Reed, "Are Paul's Thanksgivings 'Epistolary'?" *JSNT* 61 (1996): 87–99. Arzt describes his article as "a more extensive examination of papyrus letters than has been undertaken previously, so far as I am aware." Reed, who writes in response to Arzt, affirms this appraisal while advancing yet more evidence himself.

45 Arzt, "'Epistolary Introductory Thanksgiving,'" 44.

46 Reed, "Are Paul's Thanksgivings 'Epistolary'?" 87, 89, 99. One example is P. Oxy 1.113.13. Reed, 87, also notes that expressions of thanksgiving also occur in the opening, body, and closing of Pauline letters.

47 Ibid., 96.

These examples of lists and thanksgivings illustrate the fact that to appreciate the coherence and flow of ancient letters we need a good awareness of ancient writing, lest we by default judge writings from a previous time and culture by the standards of our own different time and culture.

REPETITION AND SYMMETRY

Repetition of key words or concepts and symmetrical arrangement of arguments are commonly recognized methods of producing a cohesive, coherent argument. Klaus Berger has noted that the most common and most important form of textual connection is repetition.[48] Furthermore, J. T. Reed has shown that the form of rhetoric that most impacted epistolary theorists and letter writers in the Greco-Roman world was the area referred to as "style," which incorporated repetition, parallelism, and chiasm.[49] Indeed, the rhetorical use of symmetrical patterns has been demonstrated in the letters of Seneca, Pliny, and Cicero[50] and in other Greco-Roman literature.[51] Add to this the reality of an oral culture in the first-century world, and one really ought to *expect* to find significant verbal repetitions and symmetrical patterns in New Testament letters.[52] Indeed, H. I. Marrou has argued that basic education in Roman times included learning the alphabet not only backward and forward but also "both ways at once, ΑΩ, ΒΨ, ΓΧ . . . ΜΝ."[53] This supports the suggestion that people in that time could naturally think in chiastic patterns.[54] It is, then, not unreasonable to look for intentional symmetry in letters from the Greco-Roman era.

There are many examples of such symmetrical arrangement in the Pastoral Epistles.[55] Here I will provide one example at a paragraph level and one at the level of the entire discourse (letter).

---

[48] K. Berger, *Exegese des Neuen Testament* (Heidelberg: Quelle & Meyer, 1977), 13, "Das wichtigste und vielseitigste Mittel der Textverknüpfung ist die *Wiederholung.*" E. Wendland has even suggested a form of structural analysis based on repetition alone in "Cohesion in Colossians: A Structural-Thematic Outline," *Notes on Translation* 6 (1992): 28–62.

[49] J. T. Reed, *A Discourse Analysis of Philippians: Method and Rhetoric in the Debate over Literary Integrity* (Library of New Testament Studies; London: Sheffield Academic Press, 1997), 450–51. See also S. Porter, "The Theoretical Justification for Application of Rhetorical Categories to Pauline Epistolary Literature," in *Rhetoric and the New Testament: Essays from the 1992 Heidelberg Conference* (ed. S. E. Porter and T. H. Olbricht; Sheffield: JSOT Press, 1993), 100–22.

[50] R. B. Steele, "Chiasmus in the Epistles of Cicero, Seneca, Pliny and Fronto," in *Studies in Honor of Basil L. Gildersleeve* (Baltimore: Johns Hopkins Press, 1902), 339–52.

[51] J. D. Harvey, *Listening to the Text: Oral Patterning in Paul's Letters* (Grand Rapids: Baker, 1998), 61–96.

[52] Cf. C. W. Davis, *Oral Biblical Criticism: The Influence of the Principles of Orality on the Literary Structure of Paul's Epistle to the Philippians* (Sheffield: Sheffield Academic Press, 1999); P. J. Achtemeier, "*Omne Verbum Sonat*: The New Testament and the Oral Environment of Late Western Antiquity," *JBL* 109 (1990): 3–27.

[53] Marrou, *A History of Education in Antiquity* (New York: Sheed and Ward, 1956), 151 (see also 269–70).

[54] Cf. A. Stock, "Chiastic Awareness and Education in Antiquity," *BTB* 14 (1984): 23–27.

[55] Further examples can be found in Van Neste, *Cohesion and Structure in the Pastoral Epistles*, JSNTSup 280 (London/New York: T&T Clark International, 2004). An example of symmetrical arrangement for the whole of the letter to Titus can be found in Van Neste, "Structure and Cohesion in Titus," *BT* 53 (2002): 118–33.

2 TIMOTHY 1:6–12 (A PARAGRAPH EXAMPLE)

This passage has often been critiqued as failing to cohere. For example, Miller writes:

> One looks in vain for any sustained development of thought; the material is constantly disrupted by changing subject matter, variations in literary style, and the presence of seemingly unnecessary expressions. In short it reads poorly as a literary unit.[56]

Specifically, Miller argues that these verses are made up of the following independent bits: 6,7,8, 9–10,11,12a,12b.[57] There is not space here to examine the unit as a whole, but examination of the verbal repetition alone demonstrates significant cohesion.

Lexical and thematic repetition show that 1:12 is strongly connected with the preceding material. First, v. 12 mirrors v. 8 with Paul serving as the example for Timothy. The two key verbs in v. 8 and v. 12 are related (lexically and semantically) and occur in chiastic order. Timothy is urged not to be ashamed (ἐπαισχύνομαι) but to "suffer with" Paul (συγκακοπαθέω) for the gospel, and Paul suffers (πάσχω) in his role of proclaiming the gospel and is not ashamed (ἐπαισχύνομαι).[58] Thus, v. 12 returns to Paul specifically to portray him as already doing what he urges Timothy to do. Verse 12 is then still connected logically with the exhortation in v. 8, serving as further grounds for the exhortation. The parallelism also envelops the doctrinal statement in vv. 9–11, further affirming the inclusion of these verses. There is then no basis for Miller's division between v. 12b and the preceding material. Further, just as the charges to Timothy in v. 6 and v. 8 are grounded in a statement about God and his power (δύναμις), so Paul's statement about his experience is grounded in a statement about God with particular reference to his power (δυνατός). These three occurrences of the δυν- root are the only occurrences in 2 Timothy 1. This binds v. 12 not only with the exhortation in v. 8, which it supports, but also with v. 6. Verse 12 is further connected with v. 6 by its repetition of δι᾽ ἣν αἰτίαν, which only occurs in these two places in the letter.[59] The symmetry and lexical repetition can be set out as follows:

---

[56] Miller, *Composite Documents*, 100.

[57] Miller, *Composite Documents*, connects v. 12b with vv. 13–14. I argue that vv. 13–14 are also part of this section, though here I have only focused on vv. 6–12 (see my *Cohesion and Structure*, 148–58).

[58] See M. Wolter, *Die Pastoralbriefe als Paulustradition* (Göttingen: Vandenhoeck und Ruprecht, 1988), 216. Quinn and Wacker, *Letters to Timothy*, 602, and Johnson, *Letters to Paul's Delegates*, 52, also note the verbal repetitions between v. 8 and v. 12.

[59] Quinn and Wacker, *Letters to Timothy*, 602, also suggest the lexical repetitions between v. 12 and vv. 6,8 indicate an "inclusion."

v. 6 δι' ἣν αἰτίαν

οὐ γὰρ ἔδωκεν ἡμῖν ὁ <mark>θεὸς</mark> πνεῦμα . . . <mark>δυνάμεως</mark>

v. 8 οὖν

(A) μὴ <mark>ἐπαισχυνθῇς</mark> τὸ μαρτύριον τοῦ κυρίου ἡμῶν μηδὲ ἐμὲ τὸν δέσμιον αὐτοῦ

(B) ἀλλὰ <mark>συγκακοπάθησον</mark> τῷ εὐαγγελίῳ κατὰ <mark>δύναμιν</mark> <mark>θεοῦ</mark>

vv. 9–10 statement of gospel closing with τοῦ εὐαγγελίου

v. 11 Paul's appointment

v. 12 δι' ἣν αἰτίαν

(B′) καὶ ταῦτα <mark>πάσχω</mark>

(A′) ἀλλ' οὐκ <mark>ἐπαισχύνομαι</mark>

οἶδα γὰρ <mark>ᾧ</mark> . . . ὅτι <mark>δυνατός</mark> ἐστιν

This layout shows the numerous lexical and thematic connections within vv. 6–12. This unit coheres as two similar exhortations to service grounded in God with reference to his power. Verse 12 specifically connects with v. 8, reiterating its main verbs while presenting Paul as the example for Timothy to follow. These kinds of connections suggest careful, deliberate composition and help us in following the train of thought.

1 TIMOTHY 1 AND 6 (AN EXAMPLE OVER AN ENTIRE LETTER)

There are many different connections throughout 1 Timothy. One commonly noticed connection is the parallel between chaps. 1 and 6. I will summarize the previous discussion on these parallels and add to the discussion, demonstrating how this binds the letter together.

J. Thurén first put forward the argument that parallels between 1:3–20 and 6:3–21 suggest an inclusio.[60] Thurén noted four parallels between chaps. 1 and 6: (1) a grace wish (1:2; 6:21); (2) a warning about those who are straying from the faith (1:5–6; 6:20–21); (3) a doxology (1:17; 6:15–16); and (4) an exhortation to Timothy to remember his ordination and to fight the good fight (1:18–20; 6:11–12).[61] The last parallel actually has three significant pieces: the reference to Timothy, the reference to ordination, and the phrase "fight the good fight." While it may be noted that the repetition of the grace wish is not very helpful, since this regularly occurs at the opening and closing of every letter in the Pauline corpus, the other parallels are striking. These parallels have then been expanded upon by others, perhaps most notably Bush, Roloff, Oberlinner, and Couser.[62]

---

[60] J. Thurén, "Die Struktur der Schlußparänese 1.Tim.6,3–21," *TZ* 26 (1970): 241–53.

[61] Ibid., 242–43.

[62] P. G. Bush, "A Note on the Structure of 1 Timothy," *NTS* 36 (1990): 152–56; J. Roloff, *Der Erste Brief an Timotheus* (Zürich/Neukirchen-Vluyn: Benziger/Neukirchener, 1988); L. Oberlinner, *Die Pastoralbriefe. Erste Folge. Kommentar zum Ersten Timotheusbrief* (Freiburg: Herder, 1994); G. A. Couser, "God and Christian Experience in the Pastoral

There are also similarities in the exhortations to Timothy. Foremost, Roloff has noted that each of these sections remains almost entirely on the level of communication directly from Paul to Timothy, or as he calls it, "sender recipient communication."[63] Related to this, the vocative Τιμόθεε occurs in 1:18 and 6:20 and nowhere else in the letter. Though Bush was wrong to say these were the only occurrences of vocative address in the letter, the other occurrence is also found within these sections (6:11). "Deposit" language is found in both 1:18 (Ταύτην τὴν παραγγελίαν παρατίθεμαι σοι) and 6:20 (τὴν παραθήκην φύλαξον), where Timothy is seen as the recipient of a message or task from Paul.[64]

There are also similarities in the discussions of the opponents. For example, both sections open with reference to ἑτροδιδασκαλέω (1:3; 6:3). Dibelius-Conzelmann also noted that in both sections those who teach wrongly are characterized as ignorant (μηδὲν ἐπιστάμενος, 6:4; μὴ νοοῦντες, 1:7),[65] and Oberlinner noted they are associated with disputes using similar words (ἐκζήτησις, 1:4; ζήτησις, 6:4).[66] Oberlinner also noted the presence of vice lists in both 1:9–10 and 6:4.[67] Then, Roloff expanded on Thurén's recognition of a warning about those straying from the faith in 1:5–6 and 6:20–21 by noting that the statements employ almost identical vocabulary.[68] Different scholars have noted a continuity in that there are warnings about those straying from the faith, though interestingly they have connected different passages. Thurén connected 1:5–6 and 6:20–21. Bush connected 1:19 and 6:21. Roloff connected 1:19 and 6:11. The differences here may point to an area in which the understanding of the parallel between these sections can be enhanced.

Little has been made of the fact that both 1:3–20 and 6:3–21 both open and close with a discussion of the opponents, forming parallel inclusios around these sections. This means there are within these sections four discrete discussions of the opponents, and this is why different scholars have made different connections regarding the warnings about opponents. In fact there is a high degree of similarity between all four units. The following table presents the parallels within these units.

Epistles: Toward *Theological Method and Meaning*," *NovT* 42 (2000): 279–82. Couser, 281–82, further expounds the connections between the doxologies already noted by Thurén and concludes, "It is apparent that the author intended 1:17 and 6:15–16 to be seen in relationship to one another both on the conceptual and functional level."

63 Roloff, *Timotheus*, 49: "Wie das Proömium, so bleibt auch der ausführliche Sclußabschnitt fast ganz auf der Ebene der Absender-Empfänger-Kommunikation, mit Ausnahme der kontextbedingten Abschweifung 6,17–19."

64 Bush, "Note on Structure of 1 Timothy," 153; Roloff, *Timotheus*, 49; Oberlinner, *Timotheusbrief*, 309. However, Couser, "God and Christian Experience in the Pastoral Epistles," 272n47, disputes this connection since the charge in 1:18 is simply the task at Ephesus while the "trust" in 6:20 refers to the Christian message more broadly. This is a valid critique, but the use of similar language and the picture of Timothy as the recipient of Paul may still create a significant link.

65 M. Dibelius and H. Conzelmann (*The Pastoral Epistles* [Hermeneia; Philadelphia: Fortress Press, 1972], 83.

66 Oberlinner, *Timotheusbrief*, 270.

67 Ibid.

68 Roloff, *Timotheus*, 327.

1:3–7	1:18–20	6:3–10	6:20–21
ὧν τινες ἀστοχήσαντες	ἥν τινες ἀπωσάμενοι	ἧς τινες … ἀπεπλανήθησαν	ἥν τινες … ἠστόχησαν
ὧν refers to πίστις (among other things)	ἥν refers to πίστις (among other things)	ἀπὸ τῆς πίστεως	περὶ τὴν πίστιν
ἐξετράπησαν	-----	-----	ἐκτρεπόμενος
προσέχειν myths & genealogies	-----	ὀρεγόμενοι wealth	ἐπαγγελλόμενοι falsely called knowledge
ματαιολογίαν	-----	λογομαχίας (λογ- root)	κενοφωνίας
ἐκζητήσεις	-----	ζητήσεις	-----
συνειδήσεως ἀγαθῆς	ἀγαθὴν συνείδησιν	depraved νοῦν	-----
Produces negative: παρέχουσιν specula- tion	-----	Produces negative: ἐξ ὧν γίνεται envy, strife, etc.	-----
-----	shipwreck, handed over to Satan	ruin and destruction pierced with pains	-----
μὴ νοοῦντες	[need to be taught]	μηδὲν ἐπιστάμενος ἀνοήτους	falsely called knowledge
θέλοντες	-----	βουλόμενοί ἐπιθυμίας	-----
-----	taught not βλασφημεῖν	result in βλασφημίαι	-----
τις ἑτεροδιδασκαλεῖν	-----	τις ἑτεροδιδασκαλεῖ	-----

This table incorporates the parallels previously noted by scholars while including some further observations. Perhaps most importantly, it lays out clearly the great
similarity in the way each unit refers to "certain ones" who turn away from the faith.
These parallels make significant connections between units. First, the verb ἐκτρέπω
occurs only twice in the letter, in the first and last units on the opponents (1:6 6:20).
In both instances it refers to the teaching of the opponents, though different nuances
of meaning of the verb are used in the two places ("stray after" in 1:6, and "avoid" in
6:20). Interestingly, another parallel is that the object of ἐκτρέπω in both instances

refs to foolish talk (ματαιολογία, 1:6; κενοφωνία, 6:20). These two words are practically synonyms. They occur as adjacent listings in Louw and Nida, both under the subdomain of "Foolish Talk."[69] Marshall also says that according to Hesychius and Suidas these words were synonyms.[70] A third parallel is the statement that the opponents' teaching produces negative results. This occurs in 1:4 where the opponents teaching gives rise to (παρέχω) speculation as opposed to God's work and in 6:4 where in reference to the opponents' speculations it says out of this comes (ἐξ ὧν γίνεται) strife, envy, blasphemies, evil suspicions, etc. In each instance this is connected with the speculations of the opponents. Fourth, in 1:7 as in 6:9–10 some of the problems with the opponents are presented as "desires" for the wrong things (θέλω, 1:7; βούλομαι, ἐπιθυμία, ὀρέγω, 6:9–10). In both 1:3–7 and 6:3–10, the unit closes with these wrong desires and they provide the contrast from which the following unit develops. Lastly, there may be a connection between βλασφημέω in 1:20 and βλασφημία in 6:4, though the word does also occur in 1:13 and 6:1.[71]

Therefore, the structural, syntactic, and lexical parallels between these units regarding the opponents cause them to cohere and support seeing 1:3–20 and 6:3–21 as an inclusio around the entire letter. The opponents, thus, frame the entire letter by framing both the opening and closing sections of the letter. This shows a significant level of care in composition. This does not look like haphazard amalgamation of disparate texts.

TRANSITIONAL DEVICES

"Linkage, or repetition of what was just said as a means of getting started on the next part, provides cohesion within paragraphs in some languages and between paragraphs in others."[72] In other words it is common in a new unit (or sentence) to repeat, or in some way to link back to, information from a previous unit (or sentence). A. Vanhoye pioneered the work in differentiating devices of such linkage in his work on Hebrews.[73] Vanhoye discussed "hook words," referring to a pattern in which an expression or word inserted at the end of one unit (but not common earlier in the unit) is taken up again at the beginning of the next unit (but is not common in the rest of the unit). It is important that words that serve as "hooks" are not common elsewhere in the units connected. This suggests the author has intentionally placed them at the end of one unit to prepare for the next one. Vanhoye's work was

---

69 See J. P. Louw and E. A. Nida et al., *Greek-English Lexicon of the New Testament: Based on Semantic Domains* (2 vols.; 2nd ed.; New York: United Bible Societies, 1989), 33.374–33.381, for the subdomain of "Foolish Talk" under the domain "Communication." Ματαιολογία is 33.377 and κενοφωνία is 33.376.

70 Marshall, *Pastoral Epistles*, 677n135.

71 More on connections between 1 Timothy 1 and 1 Timothy 6 can be found in Van Neste, *Cohesion and Structure*, 77–145.

72 J. Grimes, *The Thread of Discourse* (The Hague: Mouton, 1975), 259.

73 A. Vanhoye, *La Structure Littéraire de L'Épitre aux Hébreux* (2nd ed.; Paris: Desclée de Brouwer, 1976); *Structure and Message of the Epistle to the Hebrews* (Rome: Editrice Pontificio Instituto Biblico, 1989).

subsequently developed by H. V. D. Parunak[74] and, more recently, G. H. Guthrie.[75] From these works we can glean several useful devices, in addition to the "hook word" already mentioned.

First, there may be "hooked keywords."[76] This could occur when a term that is prominent in one unit (hence "keyword") is repeated at the beginning of the next unit (but is not a keyword in the second unit) or when a hook word occurs at the end of one unit and then becomes a keyword in the following unit.[77] Second, there is the "hinge,"[78] in which one unit of text serves as a transitional element between the units on either side of it. The preceding unit connects to the hinge which then connects to the following unit. It may be difficult to determine whether the "hinge" should be considered part of the preceding or following unit since it connects strongly to both and thus creates a transition. Similarly, Guthrie identified the transitional effect of "overlapping constituents" in which a passage is used simultaneously as the conclusion of one unit and the introduction to the following unit.[79]

What is common in these transitional devices is the intermingling of prominent words or phrases at the extremities of two units in order to create a connection. Recently B. W. Longenecker has provided some historical basis for these linguistic ideas when he demonstrated that creating this sort of connection between units was encouraged at least by Lucian of Samosata, the second-century rhetorician (c. AD 125–80).[80] As Longenecker notes, Lucian in his *How to Write History* encourages the achieving of "clarity . . . by the interweaving of subjects" (τὸ σαφές . . . τῇ συμπεριπλοκῇ τῶν πραγμάτων). This sounds quite similar to several of the transition devices just mentioned. This is even clearer in the advice Lucian gives about linking separate sections in a narrative:

> Though all parts must be independently perfected, when the first is complete the second will be brought into essential connection with it, and attached like one link of a chain to another; there must be no possibility of separating them;

[74] H. V. D. Parunak, "Transitional Techniques in the Bible," *JBL* 102 (1983): 525–48.

[75] G. H. Guthrie, *The Structure of Hebrews: A Text-Linguistic Analysis* (Leiden: Brill, 1994); "Cohesion Shifts and Stitches in Philippians," in *Discourse Analysis and Other Topics in Biblical Greek* (ed. S. E. Porter and D. A. Carson; Sheffield: Sheffield Academic Press, 1995), 36–59.

[76] Guthrie, *Structure of Hebrews*, 100–102; Parunak, "Transitional Techniques," 532–40. Parunak calls this device "linked keyword."

[77] Guthrie also refers to the possibility of a combination of these two sorts of hooked keywords (*Structure of Hebrews*, 100–102).

[78] Parunak, "Transitional Techniques," 540–46; Guthrie, *Structure of Hebrews*, 105–11. Guthrie refers to this device as an "intermediary transition." Guthrie's term is more precise, but Parunak's term will be used since it is probably recognizable to most and is more manageable.

[79] Guthrie, *Structure of Hebrews*, 102–104.

[80] B. W. Longenecker, "'Linked Like a Chain': Rev 22.6–9 in Light of an Ancient Transition Technique," *NTS* 47 (2001): 105–117.

no mere bundle of parallel threads; the first is not simply to be next to the second, but part of it, *their extremities intermingling.*[81]

As Longenecker notes, there is no indication that Lucian thought of his advice as novel; rather, he sets out what seems to him to be normal practice. This combined with the occurrences deduced by Guthrie in Hebrews and by Parunak in various portions of the Bible suggest that this was a common technique in the ancient world.[82]

Transitional devices like these occur commonly in the Pastoral Epistles.[83] Here I will focus on transitional devices in 1 Timothy 1 and 1 Timothy 6 since these sections were discussed above. I will also include a brief look at a variation of these transitional devices found in 2 Timothy.

1 TIMOTHY 1

The first three paragraphs in 1 Timothy 1 provide an interesting display of transitional devices. Though some find these transitional devices awkward in their connections, these devices show the train of thought from one paragraph to the next.

1:3–7 and 1:8–11   Between 1:3–7 and 1:8–11 scholars commonly note a connection concerning the use of the Law.[84] This argument can be enhanced, though, since "Law" provides not simply a common theme but a hooked keyword. Verse 7 stands out from the rest of its paragraph by introducing new information.[85] The key new point introduced in 1:7 is that the opponents desire to be "Law teachers" (νομοδιδάσκαλοι). There has been no previous mention of the Law. Verses 8–11 then opens with three occurrences of "Law" vocabulary (νόμος, v. 8; νομίμως, v. 8; νόμος, v. 9).[86] These are the only occurrences in the entire letter of νόμος vocabulary. Thus, there is a clear and strong connection formed as 1:7 closes the discussion of the opponents by introducing the topic (teaching of the Law) which will be further developed in the following unit.

Additionally, there is another hook. Verse 7 describes the opponents as not knowing what they try to teach (μὴ νοοῦντες), that is, the Law. This is the first occurrence of noetic vocabulary in the letter. In contrast (δέ), 1:8–9 state that Paul and those with him ("we") do know (οἴδαμεν, v. 8; εἰδώς, v. 9) how the Law is properly

---

[81] Translation by H. W. Fowler and F. G. Fowler, *The Works of Lucian* (Oxford: Clarendon, 1905), 2:133 (italics added). The Greek text reads: καὶ τὸ πρῶτον ἐξεργασάμενος ἐπάξει τὸ δεύτερον ἐχόμενον αὐτοῦ καὶ ἁλύσεως τρόπον συνηρμοσμένον ὡς μὴ διακεκόφθαι μηδὲ διηγήσεις πολλὰς εἶναι ἀλλήλαις παρακειμένας ἀλλ' ἀεὶ τῷ πρώτῳ τὸ δεύτερον μὴ γειτνιᾶν μόνον, ἀλλὰ καὶ κοινωνεῖν καὶ ἀνακεκρᾶσθαι κατὰ τὰ ἄκρα.

[82] Longenecker also cites Quintilian, *Institutio oratoria*, 9.4.129, but Quintilian's statements are not as clear.

[83] Numerous other examples can be found throughout Van Neste, *Cohesion and Structure*.

[84] Miller, *Composite Documents*, 61, however, disputes any connection, writing, "It is difficult to identify any clear development of thought between 1:7 and that which follows."

[85] See also Marshall, *Pastoral Epistles*, 372.

[86] Quinn and Wacker, *Letters to Timothy*, 91, also note a connection of "repeated *m* sounds" from 1:7. However, the value of such repetitions (including not only initial sounds but any sounds within any word) is uncertain.

used.[87] This suggests that 1:8–11 follows 1:3–7 logically, providing the corrective to the opponents' false understanding of the Law. Thus, these two hooks provide clear cohesion between these two units.

Verses 8–11 also close with a similar idea to that which opened 1:3–7. Verse 10 refers to that which is contrary to sound doctrine (εἴ τι ἕτερον τῇ ὑγιαινούσῃ διδασκαλίᾳ ἀντίκειται), and 1:3 refers to those who teach contrary (ἑτεροδιδασκαλεῖν). Both the wording and the idea are very similar, and surely the same group is in mind. Thus, following the vice list, 1:10b serves to bring the discussion back to the idea of those who are not in accord with Pauline teaching, suggesting 1:8–11 was composed in light of 1:3–7.

1:8–11 and 1:12–17   The connection between 1:8–11 and 1:12–17 is even more contested. The topic does change between the two paragraphs, but 1:11 introduces new information that prepares for vv. 12–17. Shifts contained in v. 11 serve as "hooks" preparing the way for 1:12–17. Four such shifts are of particular interest here. First, εὐαγγέλιον occurs in 1:11 for the first (and only) time in the letter. Though this word coheres with the previous mentions of proper teaching, it introduces a more specific reference to the saving message. Secondly, the idea of Paul being entrusted with a special ministry ("the gospel") occurs in 1:11 for the first time in the body of the letter.[88] Third, the mention of Paul's receiving a ministry uses the verb πιστεύω, the only occurrence of the πιστ- root in 1:8–11. Fourth, the mention of Paul being entrusted with the gospel (ὃ ἐπιστεύθην ἐγώ) brings Paul back to the forefront with the only occurrence of a first-person-singular referent in 1:8–11, and indeed the first such occurrence since 1:3. Each of these new elements become major components of 1:12–17 showing that 1:11 was deliberately constructed to introduce 1:12–17. First, vv. 12–17 spell out the message of the εὐαγγέλιον by rehearsing Paul's conversion replete with a discussion of Christ's salvific intent and the use of common words associated with the gospel such as χάρις, πίστις, σῴζω, ζωή, αἰώνιος, and Χριστός Ἰησοῦς.[89] Second, while 1:12–17 discusses Paul's conversion, it begins by explicitly referring to his being strengthened and placed in ministry (v. 12), a clear connection with Paul being entrusted with the gospel in 1:11. Third, the πιστ- root, which occurred in 1:8–11 only at the end of v. 11, becomes a keyword in 1:12–17, occurring five times (πίστον, v. 12; ἀπιστίᾳ, v. 13; πίστεως, v. 14; πίστος, v. 15; πιστεύειν, v. 16).[90] Fourth, although in 1:8–11 a first-person singular referent occurred only in 1:11, 1:12–17 begins with a first-person verb (ἔχω) and first-person referents occur a

---

[87] Cf. L. T. Johnson, *The First and Second Letters to Timothy* (AB 35A; New York: Doubleday, 2001), 167, "The contrast with the ignorance of the would-be teachers is deliberate and emphatic." The contrast is also noted by Quinn and Wacker, *Letters to Timothy*, 91; J. M. Bassler, *1 Timothy, 2 Timothy, Titus* (ANTC; Nashville: Abingdon Press, 1996), 40. These, however, do not note how the positioning of the words creates a hooking device.

[88] Knight, *Pastoral Epistles*, 92, writes, "V. 11 with its assertion that the gospel was entrusted to Paul provides the setting for vv. 12–17." Cf. Barrett, *Pastoral Epistles*, 44.

[89] Johnson, *Letters to Timothy*, 183, also suggests vv. 12–17 expound the "healthy teaching" of vv. 10–11.

[90] See also Mounce, *Pastoral Epistles*, 47, 50.

total of seven times in 1:12–17, one of the densest collections of first-person referents in the letter.[91] Indeed, after occurring in 1:11, the pronoun ἐγώ, occurs only four more times in the letter, three of which are in 1:12–17 (vv. 12,15,16).[92] That these four elements (lexical, semantic, and deictic) are introduced in 1:11 and carry on through 1:12–17 argues strongly that these two units were intended to be contiguous and that they were written in light of each other.[93] The transition then is clearly signaled and not unexpected.

In addition to these hooks, the two units seem to have parallel closings. Both units close with their only mention of θεός (1:11,17) and in both instances "glory" (δόξα) is associated with God along with other honorific modifiers.[94] The only other occurrence of δόξα in the entire letter is 3:16. Verse 11 seems to be a "mini-doxology" preparing a way for the proper doxology in 1:17. The presence and number of these connections directly contradicts Miller's assertion that 1:12–17 has only a "loose tie" to its context and, therefore, was probably just inserted as a preformed block of material.[95]

1 TIMOTHY 6

6:1–2 and 6:3–10   Miller says 6:3–5 "returns abruptly to the subject of false teachers" and is "unmotivated by what precedes."[96] However, a number of scholars have noted that 6:2c (Ταῦτα δίδασκε καὶ παρακάλει) serves as a transition linking 6:3–5 with what precedes.[97] Verse 2c can be labeled a "hinge" and stands apart both from what precedes and what follows as its second-person singular imperatives are not found in the units on either side of it. Ταῦτα, though, connects with the previous material as a summarizing statement.[98] It then provides the foil for 6:3–5. Timothy is to teach (διδάσκω) these things, but there are others who "teach otherwise" (ἑτεροδιδασκαλέω).[99] By summing up the previous material in terms of teaching (esp. with the use of διδάσκω), a transition is created for addressing those who do not teach these things. This begins a series of switching contrasts that runs through 6:3–10.[100] Thus, the return to false teachers in 6:3–5 is neither "abrupt" nor "unmotivated by what precedes."

---

91 1:12, ἔχω, με; 1:13, ἠλεήθην, ἐποίησα; 1:15, εἰμι ἐγώ; 1:16, ἠλεήθην, ἐμοί. The two words in 1:15 are considered one occurrence since they function together.

92 The other occurrence is 2:7.

93 Marshall, *Pastoral Epistles*, 361, also notes this "hook" and the one in 1:7 and agrees (in note 1) that it appears that these hooks were "deliberately introduced to prepare for what follows."

94 Mounce, *Pastoral Epistles*, 59, briefly notes some of this parallel.

95 Miller, *Composite Documents*, 65.

96 Ibid., 89.

97 Cf. Marshall, *Pastoral Epistles*, 634, "Verse 2b is transitional, summing up the previous material and stressing the need to teach it. At the same time, it provides the positive statement to which the activity of the opponents forms a contrast." See also Mounce, *Pastoral Epistles*, 335; Barrett, *Pastoral Epistles*, 83.

98 Marshall, *Pastoral Epistles*, 637, "Despite the minority opinion that it refers forwards (Scott, 72f.), ταῦτα must refer backwards." So also, e.g., Johnson, *Letters to Timothy*, 291; Mounce, *Pastoral Epistles*, 336; Oberlinner, *Timotheusbrief*, 267–68; Roloff, *Timotheus*, 325.

99 So also Roloff, *Timotheus*, 326; Marshall, *Pastoral Epistles*, 638.

100 The fact that 6:2c is so well suited to this function as a hinge critically damages R. Falconer's position that 6:2c is

Furthermore, there are some connections between 6:1–2b and 6:3–10 beyond the hinge in 6:2c. First, in a very general sense, 6:3–10 continues the concern with groups within the church, since presumably the opponents were within the church. Whereas 6:1–2 (and previous verses) had been concerned with those due proper honor, 6:3–10 switches to those not due honor. Whereas 6:1–2 (and previous verses) had been concerned with proper behavior, the opponents are marked by improper behavior. More specifically, there are at least two significant lexical connections between 6:1–2 and 6:3–10. The behavior of the slaves is to be motivated by a desire that the name of God and the teaching (διδασκαλία) not be slandered (βλασφημέω). However, the opponents fail to hold to godly teaching (διδασκαλία, v. 3), and their disputings produce slander (βλασφημία; v. 4) among other things.[101]

6:3–10 and 6:11–16   This connection is among the most doubted in the letter. Miller claims there is "no logical connection" with the preceding material.[102] Dibelius-Conzelmann represent a common view when they suggest vv. 11–16 appear to be an intrusion between v. 10 and v. 17.[103] Some have even suggested vv. 11–16 may be a later editorial insertion.[104]

However, there are a number of linguistic connections between these two units. First, as in the last unit, the connection is primarily one of contrast.[105] A sharp contrast is denoted by Σὺ δέ in v. 11. Having discussed the improper motives of the false teachers, Paul urges Timothy not to be like them. Both vv. 8–10 and vv. 11–12 give the sense of striving after something, but while some have yearned for riches (βούλομαι, v. 9; ὀρέγω, v. 10), Timothy is to flee this and pursue (διώκω) virtues. Whereas the greed of the opponents would lead to destruction (ὄλθερος, ἀπώλεια; v. 9), the virtues urged on Timothy would allow him to take hold of eternal life (v. 12).[106] Also, whereas vv. 3–10 open with a vice list, vv. 11–16 opens with a virtue list.[107] Secondly, there is a structural parallel between 6:2b and 6:11a. Both sentences begin with a second-person singular imperative with ταῦτα, and neither ταῦτα nor imperatives nor any second-person referent occurs between. In both sentences, the imperative serves as a link with previous material (affirming in 6:2b, contrasting in 6:11a) and provides a foil for what follows. Thus v. 11 serves as a hinge, with 11a ("flee these things") restating (in contrast) the previous material as a foil and 11b ("but pursue righteousness," etc.)

---

an insertion (*The Pastoral Epistles* [Oxford: Oxford University Press, 1937], 152).

[101] There may also be a contrast between the thought of rendering benefit to another (εὐεργεσία) in 6:2 and the greed of 6:9–10.

[102] Miller, *Composite Documents*, 91.

[103] Dibelius-Conzelmann, *Pastoral Epistles*, 87. So also K. Läger, *Die Christologie der Pastoralbriefe* (Hamburger Theologische Studien 12; Munster: Lit, 1996), 55; Easton, *Pastoral Epistles*, 165; J. L. Houlden's description of them as a "triptych," (*The Pastoral Epistles: 1 and 2 Timothy, Titus* [PNTC; London: SCM Press, 1976], 100.

[104] E.g., N. Brox, *Die Pastoralbriefe* (Regensburg: Verlag Friedrich Pustet, 1969), 212. Falconer, *Pastoral Epistles*, 156, suggests at least part of v. 11 is an editorial addition.

[105] Cf. Roloff, *Timotheus*, 340, "Der Abschnitt [6:11–16] hat die Funktion einer Antithese zu VV3–10."

[106] The desires of the opponents are even called "harmful" (βλαβερός).

[107] So also Roloff, *Timotheus*, 341.

moving (by means of another contrast) to the new material. This is a thoroughly logical and common transitional device. Involved in this hinge are contrasting references
to "faith." Πίστις occurs three times in these two units, once at the close of 6:3–10
(v. 10) and twice at the beginning of 6:11–16 (vv. 11,12). Whereas the opponents
wander away from the faith (v. 10), Timothy is to pursue "faith" (v. 11) and fight the
good fight of "faith" (v. 11). Lastly, εὐσέβεια appears to function as a hooked keyword
connecting the two units. The word occurs three times in vv. 3–10 and is an important
point. It then recurs in v. 11, the beginning of the next unit. Timothy is to flee the
vices of the opponents as described in vv. 3–10 but to pursue εὐσέβεια, which has been
clarified in contrast to the opponents in vv. 3–10.

Thus, 6:11–16 is significantly connected to 6:3–10 in ways that suggest 6:11–16
have been intentionally shaped to follow 6:3–10.

6:11–16 and 6:17–19   The connection between these two units has been hotly
contested as well, since many scholars have assumed that vv. 17–19 should follow on
from v. 10. Thus, Miller says this section abruptly returns to the theme of 6:6–10 and
"breaks any thread of continuity between 6:16 and 6:20."[108] For this reason, some
have regarded vv. 17–19 as a later addition[109] or have attributed it to a pause in dic-
tation.[110] It is true that the doxology in the preceding verses creates a sense of closure
so that v. 17 seems like a fresh start, but there are several indicators of continuity
between 6:11–16 and 17–19.

First, 6:17 continues the second-person singular address that is common in the previous unit. Additionally, vv. 17–19 are presented as an exhortation to Timothy built on
an imperative, just as vv. 11–14. There are also a number of lexical connections between
the two units. First, παραγγέλλω occurs in v. 13 and v. 17. It is the last main verb of vv.
11–16 and the first main verb of vv. 17–19. As Paul exhorted Timothy, so Timothy is
to exhort those who are rich.[111] The shift from calling Timothy to personal faithfulness
to calling him to exhort others to faithfulness has occurred often in this letter. Secondly,
almost the exact phrase is used to call both Timothy and the rich to take hold of life
(ἐπιλαβοῦ τῆς αἰωνίου ζωῆς, v. 12; ἐπιλάβωνται τῆς ὄντως ζωῆς, v. 19). This is similar
to the use of παραγγέλλω, in that what Timothy receives personally as exhortation from
Paul, he then passes on to others. Third, αἰών and αἰώνιος occur in vv. 12,16, and 17.
Verses 11–16 is concerned with taking hold of "eternal" life (v. 12) and with the one who
has "eternal" power (v. 16). Verses 17–19 then open by referring to those who are rich

[108] Miller, *Composite Documents*, 93. Similarly, Dibelius-Conzelmann, *Pastoral Epistles*, 91; W. Lock, *The Pastoral Epistles* (Edinburgh: T & T Clark, 1924), 73; Easton, *Pastoral Epistles*, 169–70. According to Quinn and Wacker (*Letters to Timothy*, 550), Käsemann in *Essays on New Testament Themes*, trans. W. J. Montague, SBT 41 [Philadelphia: Fortress, 1964], 112) called the abrupt transition "brutal."

[109] Easton, *Pastoral Epistles*, 170; Falconer, *Pastoral Epistles*, 158; Gealy, "Epistles to Timothy and the Epistle to Titus," 456–57. Gealy also mentions A. von Harnack, *Der Chronologie der altchristlichen Litteratur bis Eusebius* (Leipzig: J. C. Hinrichs, 1897), 1:482, as a proponent of this view.

[110] C. Spicq, *Les Épîtres Pastorales* (*EBib*; 4th ed.; Paris: J. Gabalda, 1969), 575.

[111] Cf. Oberlinner, *Timotheusbrief*, 303.

"in this present age." The use of the same root in contrasting ways suggests a contrast is being made between the two units. This serves to lessen the significance of the riches that these people have, because those riches are only for this present age, whereas there is life that is eternal and comes from the God who has eternal power. Lastly, the exhortation in v. 17 for the rich to hope in God with the implication that God is more reliable than riches works well following the exalted doxology of vv. 15–16.

These links between 6:11–16 and 6:17–19 suggest that, although there is a significant shift between these two units, there is sufficient continuity to hold them together and there seems to be some deliberate play on words between the two units.

6:17–19 and 6:20–21   Some scholars have found very little connection between these two units. For example, Easton and Falconer suggest vv. 20–21 may be another later addition,[112] and Miller suggests vv. 20–21 are the original ending of a short letter into which the preceding material was incorporated.[113] However, there are some significant continuities between the two units. First, both units begin with a second-person singular imperative and have no other imperative in the rest of the unit. Accordingly, there is a continuity in genre as both units are exhortations to Timothy concerning his role in the church.[114] The units also have contrasting endings with the rich laying for themselves a good foundation for the future and taking hold of true life and the opponents straying from the faith. As Timothy is to exhort the rich to shun evil and to prepare well for eternity, so Timothy is to shun evil knowing that it will not lead to life but rather to the destruction of faith.

2 TIMOTHY 1:15–18

Lastly, one example from 2 Timothy 1 demonstrates an interesting variation on these transitional devices. Verses 15–18 appears to be out of place between 1:6–14 and 2:1–13 since they contains no imperatives, are not explicit exhortation, and shift to an interest in third parties rather than Timothy specifically. However, 1:15–18 appears to be crafted in such a way as to connect the two units as perhaps an illustrative pause.[115] Verses 15–18 stand out from the other two units in that they have only two second-person referents; however, these two second-person verbs are placed as the very first and very last words of the unit, thus connecting to the second-person address on either side.

1:6–14		1:15–18			2:1–13
2nd person		2s	3rd person	2s	2nd person

By introducing and concluding 1:15–18 with references to Timothy, the author connects this "report" on "others" to the admonitions to Timothy.

---

[112] Easton, *Pastoral Epistles*, 170; Falconer, *Pastoral Epistles*, 160.

[113] Miller, *Composite Documents*, 94–95.

[114] The shift from opponents to Timothy is common in this letter and has just happened above in 6:11.

[115] Marshall, *Pastoral Epistles*, 36, notes "1.15–18 . . . appears to act as a bridge between the preceding and following units," though he does not refer to the connective function of the personal referents.

Verses 15–18 also fit within the exhortations as an example that was common in ancient exhortatory discourse, as was noted earlier.[116] The eschatological perspective of the other two units is found in 1:15–18 as well as the concern for the Lord's verdict "on that day" (1:18). The ideas of abandonment and shame (1:15,16) cohere with the theme of faithful endurance, and the thread of Paul's imprisonment runs through this unit as well as the other two (δέσμιος, 1:8; ἅλυσις, 1:16; δεσμός, 2:9).

This argumentation contradicts the view of Dibelius-Conzelmann, Barrett, Lohfink[117] and others who argue that 2:1 begins the actual paraenesis of the letter with chap 1 being introductory. These views fail to account for the significant cohesion between 1:6–14 and 2:1–13. For example Dibelius-Conzelmann write, "After 'Paul' has introduced himself as an example in the first section [1:3–14], the next section of 2 Timothy presents the actual parenesis (extending to 2 Tim 4:8)."[118] In fact, however, 1:6–14 is as paraenetic as 2:1–13, and Paul still functions as an example in 2:9–10. There is then a significant unity between these units.

These examples demonstrate the various ways transitional devices are used to connect one paragraph to the next. In each case they also suggest careful composition and deliberate argumentation.

CONCLUSION AND IMPLICATIONS

In this brief survey I have attempted to summarize the position of those who argue that the Pastoral Epistles lack coherent structure and flow of thought. I have not attempted to respond to this critique comprehensively,[119] but have sought to give a few examples of different ways in which we see significant levels of connection across these texts. The examples given here and many others demonstrate that these three letters function well as first-century letters.

The implications of this are basic but important. In spite of arguments to the contrary, we should read these three letters as coherent documents with a reasonable flow of thought. We should interpret each paragraph in light of its connection to the rest of the letter rather than abstracting a unit from the rest of the letter and speculating about its "original setting." The connection between one unit and another may not always be clear (as is the case in any other human discourse), but there is insufficient ground for then deciding there is no connection to be found. Rather, we must work further to understand the flow of thought and to understand the connections intended by the author. And, since a coherent flow of thought can be demonstrated in these letters, there is a basis for doing theological investigation in these texts.

---

[116] Cf. Fiore, *The Function of Personal Example*, 26–163; Donelson, *Pseudepigraphy*, 94.
[117] G. Lohfink, "Paulinische Theologie in der Rezeption der Pastoralbriefe," in *Paulus in den neutestamentlichen Spätschriften: Zur Paulusrezeptionim Neuen Testament* (Freiburg: Herder, 1981), 89–91. Wolter, *Pastoralbrief als Paulustradition*, 215–16, esp. interacts with and counters Lohfink.
[118] Dibelius-Conzelmann, *Pastoral Epistles*, 107.
[119] A thorough response is my goal in *Cohesion and Structure in the Pastoral Epistles*.

Chapter Five

THE SOVEREIGN SAVIOR OF
1 AND 2 TIMOTHY AND TITUS

GREG A. COUSER

A former beloved college professor liked to refer to Paul's letters to Timothy and Titus as "A Manual for Pastors." These were books preeminently about ecclesiology and, in particular, the role of leadership in the church. Someone would need to go elsewhere in Paul for a discussion of the more foundational themes of God and his saving work in Christ. For a variety of different reasons, modern scholarship has largely taken a similarly dismissive approach to issues other than ecclesiology in these letters (in particular, tracing the ways the post-Pauline church developed). Many have done so because they were convinced that 1 and 2 Timothy and Titus are not only literary ruses (pseudepigraphic letters), but the unknown author was no real theologian in his own right.[1] Even for more conservative scholars, their theology came to contribute little to the shape and content of a Pauline theology predominantly constructed from the "undisputed letters"—Romans, 1 and 2 Corinthians, Galatians, Philippians, 1 Thessalonians, and Philemon.[2]

The tide has definitely begun to turn. Recent works have begun to recognize, and probe, the theological depth and creativity of these letters.[3] This study will attempt

---

[1] As a representative sample of many, see W. Schenk, "Die Briefe an Timotheus I und II und an Titus (Pastoralbriefe) in der neueren Forschung (1945–85)," *ANRW* II 25.4: 3404–38, and A. T. Hanson, *The Pastoral Epistles* (NCBC; London: Marshall, Morgan & Scott, 1982), 2–51.

[2] E.g., Ben Witherington (*The Paul Quest: The Renewed Search for the Jew from Tarsus* [Downers Grove: InterVarsity, 1998], 280), although cautioning against leaving the disputed Paulines completely out of the discussion, goes on to say that "our primary source for discerning Paul's theology must be the Pauline letters themselves, and especially the capital or undisputed Paulines which have more theological substance than the Pastoral Epistles."

[3] J. Bassler, "A Plethora of Epiphanies: Christology in the Pastoral Epistles," *PSB* 7 (1996): 310–25; F. Young, *The Theology of the Pastoral Letters* (Cambridge: Cambridge University Press, 1994); L. Donelson, *Pseudepigraphy and Ethical Argument in the Pastoral Epistles* (Tübingen: Mohr-Siebeck, 1986); P. Towner, *The Goal of Our Instruction: The Structure of Theology and Ethics in the Pastoral Epistles* (JSNTSup 34; Sheffield: JSOT Press, 1989).

to extend that discussion by focusing on the doctrine of God in 1 and 2 Timothy and Titus (hereafter, *theo*logy). While it has been frequently noted that the way God is addressed is markedly unique, few have attempted a comprehensive discussion of the content and function of the statements about God in these letters.[4] The following discussion attempts to lay out the main contours of the *theo*logy as well as to highlight some of the more incidental statements that nonetheless contribute to a full understanding of the God of Timothy and Titus.

GUIDING FRAMEWORK

Given the important ramifications for the study to follow,[5] it is important to note that the following study proceeds on the basis of the documents' literary self-presentation.[6] This is to say that the apostle Paul is assumed to be the author of 1 and 2 Timothy and Titus.[7] Each represents an individual piece of correspondence directed toward particular occasions in the life of the church at Ephesus and Crete. The recipients are Timothy and Titus, the apostolic delegates known from Paul's own correspondence to have accompanied and assisted him in his ministry.[8] The methodological significance of this standpoint is twofold. First, this calls for a treatment of each letter on its own in order to discuss its *theo*logy in light of the circumstances presented by that letter.[9] Paul's theologizing is done within the context of the oc-

---

[4] For a recent attempt, see J. Fitzmyer, "The Savior God," in *The Forgotten God: Perspectives in Biblical Theology* (ed. A. Das and F. Matera; Louisville: Westminster John Knox, 2002), 181–96. With a view to 1 Tim only, see J. Sumney, "'God our Savior': The Fundamental Operational Theological Assertion of 1 Timothy," *HBT* 21 (1999): 105–23; L. Johnson, "Oikonomia Theou: The Theological Voice of 1 Timothy from the Perspective of Pauline Authorship," *HBT* 21 (1999): 87–104; and M. Mitchell, "'Speaking of God as He was Able': A Response to Luke Timothy Johnson and Jerry L. Sumney," *HBT* 21 (1999): 124–29.

[5] See S. Porter, "Pauline Authorship and the Pastoral Epistles," *BBR* 5 (1995): 120–23.

[6] This phrase, and related approach, is taken from L. T. Johnson *(Letters to Paul's Delegates: 1 Timothy, 2 Timothy, Titus* [Valley Forge, PA: Trinity Press, 1996], 21–33) and stands over against the increasing common approach of "double-pseudepigraphy," i.e., where both the author and recipients are literary fictions (e.g., D. Meade, *Pseudonymity and Canon* [WUNT 39; Tübingen: Mohr-Siebeck, 1986], 127, and R. Collins, *1 & 2 Timothy and Titus: A Commentary* [NTL; Louisville: John Knox Press, 2002], 10).

[7] For the various options possible for "authorship," see esp. P. Towner's introductory discussion in *The Letters to Timothy and Titus* (Grand Rapids: Eerdmans, 2006), 83–89. See also M. Prior, *Paul the Letter Writer and the Second Letter to Timothy* (JSNTSup 23; Sheffield: JSOT, 1989), and E. R. Richards, *The Secretary in the Letters of Paul* (WUNT 2/42; Tübingen: Mohr-Siebeck, 1991).

[8] Space prohibits a full defense of Pauline authorship as the most *historically* plausible and convincing explanation for the production, content, and canonical status of these letters. For a thorough defense, as well as a nearly complete bibliography on the issue of the authenticity of these letters, see W. Mounce, *Pastoral Epistles* (WBC 46; Nashville: Thomas Nelson, 2000), lxxxiii–cxxix. For a concise overview of the issues with penetrating insights, see S. Porter, "Pauline Authorship," 105–23, and "Pauline Authorship and the Pastoral Epistles: A Response to R. W. Wall's Response," *BBR* 6 (1996): 133–38.

[9] This approach stands over against pseudonymous approaches that require a literary unity that sees the letters as a "minicorpus," allowing the interpreter to "speak of the theological system of the corpus as a whole" (Bassler, "Epiphanies," 311; cf. Towner, "Pauline Theology or Pauline Tradition in the Pastoral Epistles," *TynBul* 46 [1995]: 301–303).

casion.[10] Second, we assume that the *theo*logical material is most properly informed and nuanced with reference to Paul's earlier teaching on these subjects. Thus, in the following studies we will only attempt to surface and synthesize the *theo*logical contributions of each letter in its own right. We will not offer a composite theology of a discrete corpus under the assumption of its literary integrity and pseudonymous character.

1 TIMOTHY: THE SOVEREIGN GOD AND HIS CREATION

First Timothy portrays a church under attack by an opposition arising from within the ranks of the established church leadership.[11] Timothy needs to silence their spiritually unhealthy teaching and to steer the church back onto the path to spiritual well-being.[12] As developed elsewhere,[13] it seems most plausible to view the heresy as a combination of the views of P. Towner and R. Kidd.[14] Kidd speaks to the false teachers' motivation and means of ascent. The language of the "office codes" (1 Tim 3:1–13; Titus 1:6–9) and the wealthy status of the antagonists (6:9,17) suggest that church leaders had primarily come from the ranks of local elites.[15] Operating with a largely secular understanding of leadership (the *quid pro quo* patronage system), one shared by a significant portion of the Ephesian church, these men rose to places of prominence in the community. Sadly, these were values largely incongruent with those needed for church leadership—the qualities of a life of "godliness" (εὐσέβεια).[16] Towner's work makes sense of the letter's coherent and sophisticated theological response to their teaching and its effects. He relates the sustained emphasis on soteriology to the false teaching and suggests that the antagonists were proposing an "overrealized eschatology." Seeing the resurrection as past (cf. 2 Tim 2:18), these men were suggesting that salvation can be largely realized in the "now"

---

[10] The particulars of the occasion of each letter gave rise to his particular way of referring to God's person and acts. This is not to say that Paul's understanding of God somehow arose in its substance out of the situations addressed. But it is to say that in each letter, as elsewhere, Paul's "foundational convictions" are expressed in "concrete, contingent forms of application" (B. Corley, "Biblical Theology of the New Testament" in *Foundations for Biblical Interpretation* [ed. D. Dockery et. al.; Nashville: Broadman and Holman, 1994], 556; cf. Towner, *Letters*, 88–89). Though J. Aageson adopts this same approach (*Paul, the Pastoral Epistles, and the Early Church* [Library of Pauline Studies; Peabody, MA: Hendrickson, 2008]), his reading overplays the distinctiveness of the individual letters and underplays their theological commonality.

[11] G. Fee (*1 and 2 Timothy and Titus* [NIBC 13; Peabody, MA: Hendrickson, 1988], 7–8) makes this case succinctly and convincingly (see also Towner, *Goal*, 28–33).

[12] On the medical imagery employed, see A. J. Malherbe, "Medical Imagery in the Pastoral Epistles," in *Texts and Testaments: Critical Essays on the Bible and Early Church Fathers* (San Antonio: Trinity University Press, 1980), 19–35.

[13] G. Couser, "God and Christian Existence in the Pastoral Epistles: Toward *Theo*logical Method and Meaning," *NovT* 42 (2000): 267–71.

[14] Towner, *Goal*, 21–45; R. Kidd, *Wealth and Beneficence in the Pastoral Epistles: A "Bourgeois" Form of Early Christianity?* (SBLDS 122; Atlanta: Scholars Press, 1990), 91–98.

[15] Kidd, *Beneficence*, 91.

[16] Ibid., 98.

---

on the spiritual plane.[17] The weight of expectation had been shifted from the future to the present. A central effect of this shift resulted in illegitimately putting God's saving work over against his present purposes in creation (cf. 1 Tim 2:13–15; 4:3–5; 5:3,14). Thus, the heresy is centered on God—in particular, on the character and implications of his saving acts in Christ for his "household" (3:15) in the present. God and how he saves are under discussion.

This distortion of God's saving acts can explain the way God and his acts are described throughout the letter as well as the relationship these statements sustain to the household instructions. Indeed, the nature of this relationship between the *theo*logy and household material is crucial for a full apprehension of Paul's *theo*logy. With an ABABA structure, Paul recapitulates and develops particular emphases as he transitions back and forth between sections directly and indirectly related to Timothy's assignment, that is, "the command" (1:3–4,18; 4:11; 6:13).[18] The theologically rich "A" sections create a progressively developed literary and theological (a theology to be proclaimed and embodied by Timothy) context surrounding the household material.[19] Then, in 2:1–7 Paul clarifies the relationship between the "A" and "B" sections grammatically.[20] The οὖν in 2:1 presents the following household material as an inference of what precedes.[21] Thus, when he recapitulates and extends the theological substructure driving Timothy's ministry laid out in 1:3–20 (which is found in the "A" sections generally) in 2:3–7, Paul exemplifies the type of theological reflection that likely lays behind his household code material altogether.[22]

With that structure in mind, what *theo*logy emerges in Paul's response to this situation? From the opening designation of God as the "Savior" and Jesus as "our hope" in his salutation (1:1), Paul's initial "A" section sets a *theo*logical trajectory from the perspective of soteriology. He draws on a common LXX pairing of God as Savior and

---

[17] Towner, *Goal*, 32. For helpful insights on the issue of overrealized eschatology generally, see A. Thiselton, "Luther and Barth on 1 Corinthians 15: Six Theses for Theology in Relation to Recent Interpretation," in *The Bible, the Reformation and the Church* (ed. W. P. Stephens; JSNTSup 105; Sheffield: Sheffield Academic, 1995), 258–89.

[18] The "A" sections (1:3–20; 3:14–4:16; 6:2b–21) address Timothy's task at Ephesus in light of his opponents' teaching and his and Paul's common understanding of God's saving work in Christ. In the "B" sections (2:1–3:13; 5:1–6:2a) Paul speaks indirectly to Timothy and more directly to the congregation in that he expresses the content and mode of the corrective teaching Timothy is to convey to the various segments of the community (see G. Couser, "Theological Method," 262–83, and, essentially, R. Van Neste, *Cohesion and Structure in the Pastoral Epistles* [JSNTSup 280; T & T Clark International: New York, 2004]). F. Thielman suggests that this interplay fits the literary *modus operandi* of a "letter of official mandate." As such, the letter served both as a "reminder to the subordinate of his duties and as a public commission for this subordinate" (*Theology of the New Testament* [Grand Rapids: Zondervan, 2005], 414).

[19] On "household codes" see P. Towner, "Households and Household Codes," *DPL*, 417–19.

[20] In particular, this contrasts sharply with the anacolutha at the resumption of the household material at 5:1 (cf. Couser, "Theological Method," 276).

[21] Contra J. Heckert who argues for a continuative οὖν here (*Discourse Function of Conjoiners in the Pastoral Epistles* [Dallas: SIL, 1996], 98–99). Heckert's conclusion is hampered by his failure to see chap 1 as an integrated whole bound tightly together by an *inclusio* (note, e.g., the reference to Timothy's charge in v. 3, παραγγείλῃς, and v. 18, παραγγελίαν). There is no need to resume a topic Paul never left (so also Fee, *1 and 2 Timothy*, 61).

[22] In addition, the πρῶτον πάντων of 2:1 suggests that this is the first in a series as well as first in importance (see I. H. Marshall, *The Pastoral Epistles* [ICC; T & T Clark International: New York, 1999], 418–19). This reinforces the paradigmatic quality of 2:1–7.

source of hope, with the hope based in the saving acts upon which the title, Savior, is predicated.[23] Yet now, in light of the ministry of Christ, this hope has come to concrete expression in him (cf. Titus 2:13).[24] Paul has drawn upon a recognized OT pairing of concepts to freshly express his well-known pattern of God effecting salvation in Christ (cf. 2 Cor 5:18–19). Moreover, Paul asserts that his apostolic mission derives from the joint "command" of God and Christ. This phrase, κατ᾽ ἐπιταγὴν, conveys both the notion of an individual command as well as a general decree.[25] Thus, this phrase likely involves Paul's personal sending. Yet, the use of descriptors in Paul's other salutations as well as the express references to his call elsewhere in 1 Tim (1:12,16; 2:7; cf. 2 Tim 1:11) argue for a broader reference to the command as well. This broader sense seems especially likely given the close relationship between this phrase and an early kerygmatic summary in Titus 1:2 and Rom 16:26,[26] the once hidden/now revealed structure so common throughout Paul's letters.[27] W. Lock took from the link to Rom 16 that the thought behind the phrase is the King of the Ages (cf. 1:17) revealing the message of salvation and calling for obedience.[28] In addition, it suggests the common commitment of God and Christ to the plan and its outworking, an emphasis that will appear repeatedly throughout this letter (cf. 1:11–17; 2:5; 3:15–16; 4:6, 10; 5:4–5, 11,21; 6:13–15). This is consistent with Paul's regular por-

---

[23] See Pss 61(62):5–8; 64:5; 24(25):5; 26(27):9,13; Mic 7:7; and Isa 62:11 (cf. Jdt 9:11 and Pss. Sol. 8:31–33). The LXX backdrop is strongly suggested by the preoccupation of the antagonists with the Law (1:7–8; cf. Titus 3:9) and the nature of Paul's condemnation of them ("they do not know what they are talking about or what they so confidently affirm," 1:7b). Both point to the central role that the OT Scriptures played in the controversy enveloping the Ephesian community. Donelson (*Pseudepigraphy*, 126) suggests that the false teachers, with their interest in "genealogies" and "myths," might have been "puzzling out the difficulties in Paul with a detailed and aggressive hermeneutic of the OT" (cf. S. Westerholm, "The Law and the 'Just Man' [1 Tim. 1:3–11]," *ST* 36 [1982]: 81).

[24] Since the "hope of glory" (Rom 5:2) had been virtually concretized in the person of Christ by Paul (Col 1:27; cf. Phil 3:20; 1 Thess 1:10) and since within his letters the "Day of the Lord Yahweh" could also become the "Day of the Lord Christ" (L. Kreitzer, *Jesus and God in Paul's Eschatology* [JSNTSup 19; Sheffield: JSOT, 1987], 112–25), it is not difficult to see how a reading of the OT in light of the ministry of Christ would prompt a rendering of the OT savior-concept in terms of Christ as "the Hope."

[25] See G. Delling ("Επιταγὴν," *TDNT* 8:8, 37) for the general sense and G. H. R. Horsley ("κατ᾽ ἐπιταγὴν," *New Docs* [1982], 86, 90) for the individual sense.

[26] Whether or not this passage can be attributed to Paul, the option that seems most plausible (see I. H. Marshall, "Romans 16:25–27: An Apt Conclusion," in *Romans and the People of God* [ed. S. Soderland and N. T. Wright; Grand Rapids: Eerdmans, 1999], 170–84; T. Schreiner, *Romans* [ECNT 6; Grand Rapids: Baker, 1998], 810–18; and L. W. Hurtado, "The Doxology at the End of Romans," in *New Testament Textual Criticism: Its Significance for Exegesis* [Oxford: Clarendon, 1981], 185–99), it nonetheless still bears witness to the relationship of this phrase to this kerygmatic schema within Pauline circles.

[27] Nils Dahl refers to these summaries as variations of an early "schema" ("Formgeschichtliche Beobachtungen zur Christus Verkündigung in der Gemeindepredigt" in *NT Studien für Rudolf Bultmann* [BZNW 21; Berlin: Töpelmann, 1954], 4–5). Dahl cites 2 Tim 1:9–11 and Titus 1:1–3 as examples (p. 5). However, in utilizing the term "schema," caution must be urged in referring to such passages as variations on a distinct form-critical unit. These passages are schematic only in that they represent concise references to the decisive historical implementation of God's hidden, age-old plan of salvation in the Christ event, the foundational event in Paul generally, using a variety of appropriate traditional terms and phrases (cf. M. Bockmuehl, *Revelation and Mystery* [WUNT 2/39; Tübingen: Mohr, 1990], 208–10). Marshall refers to these summaries in terms of the "once/now structure" and sees a close relationship with Rom 16:25–27 ("Apt," 180–83).

[28] W. Lock, *A Critical and Exegetical Commentary on the Pastoral Epistles* (ICC; Edinburgh: T & T Clark, 1924), 5.

trayal of Christ as a willing participant in God's saving purposes (cf. 2:6; Titus 2:14; Gal 1:4; 2:20; Eph 5:2,25). Bringing these insights together, what appears *in nuce* in this opening salutation is the thought of a divine salvation plan that has Christ at its core; it is a plan that looks to the future for its consummation, and it is mediated to the present via the proclamation of appointed messengers. This is subsequently fleshed out as the theological backdrop and warrant for Timothy's call and for the attitudes and behaviors commended to the community in light of the heresy's impact.

However, before continuing to flesh out the main soteriological thrust in his *theo*logy, the reference to God as "Father" warrants a few comments. Certainly it is no surprise to find God referred to as "Father" here (cf. 2 Tim 1:2; Titus 1:4). Yet, in light of the variation in the prayer wish itself[29] and Paul's emphasis throughout on the maintenance and authoritative role of tradition,[30] there is no reason to assume this reference is merely formulaic. It seems more probable that this traditional and, for Paul,[31] theologically loaded designation stands alongside this less prominent formulation of God as "Savior" to color and inform the latter in terms of the former. The "Savior" is the "God and Father" who is the source of the believers' spiritual life and the one who pours out his love upon them.[32]

Following his opening salutation, Paul continues his soteriological focus as he initially restates the prophetic charge that governs Timothy's ministry at Ephesus (1:3,18).[33] The divine source of this charge intimates what will be explicit later on (cf. 4:10,16), that Timothy's particular service at Ephesus falls under the command of the Savior (via Christ, 4:6) in order to facilitate God's saving purposes there (cf. 6:11, where Timothy is a "man of God"). From the outset, Trinitarian conceptions lie near the surface. Each member of the Godhead is involved in implementing this saving plan of God, the Savior/Father. Unsurprisingly, Timothy's charge at Ephesus is to stand over against those who are opposing the οἰκονομίαν θεοῦ (1:3–4) and, at the same time, redirect the church back toward the life of "love" (1:5). Fee has rightly

---

[29] Paul varies between wishing "grace and peace" (Rom 1:7; Phil 1:2; Titus 1:4; etc.), his most frequent pairing in opening prayer wishes, to wishing "grace, mercy, and peace" (1:2; cf. 2 Tim 2:2).

[30] From the use of "trustworthy sayings" (1:15; 3:1; 4:9) to explicit calls to guard what has been entrusted (4:15–16; 6:14), Paul points to the importance of maintaining tradition. Thus, though he may rearticulate his theology to meet the exigencies of a given occasion, it would go against Paul's presentation of himself here (and in his other letters) to think that these new forms stood over against the conceptual bounds of the old (cf. A. Lau, *Manifest in the Flesh: The Epiphany Christology of the Pastoral Epistles* [WUNT 2.86; Tübingen: Mohr-Siebeck, 1996], 178–79, 222, 263, and E. Ellis, "Traditions in the Pastoral Epistles" in *Early Jewish and Christian Exegesis* [ed. C. Evans & W. Stinespring; Atlanta: Scholars Press, 1987], 237–53).

[31] God as Father "forms a basic assumption behind all that the apostle writes. . . . Moreover, it is frequently reflected in the course of the discussions, whether doctrinal or practical. Indeed there is no concept of God which dominates the theology of Paul more than this" (D. Guthrie and R. P. Martin, "God," *DPL*, 357).

[32] Ibid.

[33] G. Delling (*Worship in the New Testament* [trans. Percy Scott; London: Darton, Longman and Todd, 1962], 40), in light of the continued existence of prophecy in the church (Did. 11:7–12; 13:1,3–4,6; 15:1–2) and the plural of προφητείας, maintains that "prophetic revelation" is the "instrumentality" through which Timothy received his commission, not "through an act of ecclesiastical bureaucracy." See also M. Haykin, "The Fading Vision? The Spirit and Freedom in the Pastoral Epistles," *EQ* 57 (1985): 294–97.

emphasized the importance of these opening statements for understanding the occasion and purpose of the letter.[34] In particular, this phrase introduces the reader to one of the most important *theo*logical statements in the letter and thus calls for close scrutiny.[35]

What exactly does Paul refer to by οἰκονομίαν θεοῦ? Renderings of this phrase tend to run along two lines. The first understands this phrase essentially in terms of the secondary variant, οἰκοδομήν, as moral exhortation for the Christian.[36] The second understands οἰκονομία with a salvation-historical emphasis along the lines of Eph 1:10; 3:9, namely, God's arrangement for the redemption of mankind.[37] However, both seem to come into play here such that a clear distinction seems unwarranted. While the character of the opening salutation leans heavily toward the latter significance, the immediately following context both confirms this and seems to incorporate the former as well. As intimated above, 1:3–20 is a tightly constructed literary unit bound together by an *inclusio* framework.[38] In 1:3–11 the antagonists are moving the community away from the truth. With misplaced confidence (1:7b), they were using the OT law in a manner incongruent with its nature as law (1:8), that is, contrary to the intent of God who "laid it down."[39] This identifies them with those who stand over against the gospel (1:9–10), the content of which is the "glory of blessed God" (v. 11).[40] Moreover, what is more pertinent for defining οἰκονομίαν θεοῦ is that Paul clearly implies that, in failing to govern their teaching by the norm of the gospel, their law-based teaching is unhealthy. Thus, to teach contrary to this gospel is to fail to promote lifestyles and behaviors consistent with the οἰκονομίαν

---

[34] This steers away from seeing 3:15 as the central purpose statement of the letter, i.e., church order as the antidote for the heresy. On the prevalence of this view, see Towner, "Pauline Theology," 290–300.

[35] D. Verner's study, *The Household of God: The Social World of the Pastoral Epistles* (SBLDS 71; Chico, CA: Scholars Press, 1983), rightly points to the importance of this phrase as an aspect of the author's interest in the household motif generally. As indicators of this interest, note also 3:5,15 as well as the use of so-called "household codes" (e.g. 2:8–15; 6:1–2; on this whole issue, see Towner, *Goal*, 169–99, and Kidd, *Beneficence*, 75–93). However, Verner's study fails to convince in arguing that the Greco-Roman notion of the household, with all of its attendant notions of class and social distinctions, functions to transform the church into the mold of the secular household (83–107). For further critique of Verner, see note 58 below and esp. Kidd, *Beneficence*, 157–58.

[36] Hanson, *Pastoral*, 57; D. Guthrie, *The Pastoral Epistles* (TNTC 14; Grand Rapids: Eerdmans, 1986), 58; RSV, "divine training"; cf. M. Dibelius and H. Conzelmann, *The Pastoral Epistles* (ET; Hermeneia: Philadelphia: Fortress, 1972), 17.

[37] See Donelson, *Pseudepigraphy*, 133; Young, *Theology*, 55; and Fee, *1 and 2 Timothy*, 42, 48, 92.

[38] The use of παραγγέλλω and its forms (1:3,4,18) ties this section tightly together. This is confirmed by the position and consequent anaphoric force of the ταύτην in 1:18a.

[39] There is a rich vein of *theo*logy embedded here regarding God and Scripture, something made more explicit elsewhere (2 Tim 3:15–16). God has given the Mosaic Law. That Law only finds its "goodness" for the believer when its reading is governed by the "sound teaching." This teaching is "sound" only in so far as it is normed against the "gospel," the record of God's saving acts in Christ entrusted to Paul. Thus God revealed his will in the Mosaic Law, his intent governs its use, and given the role of the "gospel" as the norming norm, his subsequent acts in Christ reorient the reading of that Law among his people—something not happening among Paul's antagonists (see G. Couser, "Using the Law Lawfully: A Short Study on Paul and the Law in 1 Timothy," *MJT* 2 [2003]: 43–52).

[40] J. Kelly, *The Pastoral Epistles* (1960; repr., Peabody: Hendrickson, 1988), 51; J. Roloff, *Die Erste Brief an Timotheus* [EKK 15; Zürich: Benziger, 1988], 79–80; and C. Spicq, *Le Épîtres Pastorales* (Paris: Gabala, 1947), 337.

θεοῦ. This suggests that the gospel stands in relationship to the οἰκονομίαν θεοῦ as the theological core. The subsequent teaching directed to believers intends to flesh out the manner of life consistent with God's saving plan as expressed in the gospel, that is, they specify the "household rules" if you will.[41] Thus, the gospel and the associated direction for God's household are both dimensions of the οἰκονομίαν θεοῦ.

Paul's connection of the "gospel" with "the blessed God" in 1:11 utilizes a concept of God that brings the salvation-historical dimension of οἰκονομίαν θεοῦ to the fore. In Hellenistic usage a "blessed" (μακάριος) deity was an aloof one.[42] However, in 1 Tim 6:15 and Titus 2:13, μακάριος is intimately related to God's saving acts through Christ. "The blessed and only sovereign" is the one who "will make manifest" the consummation of the present time of salvation in the epiphany of Christ (1 Tim 6:15a; cf. 2 Tim 4:1).[43] This event is fittingly described in Titus 2:13 as the "blessed hope." Here in 1 Tim 1:11 it is the "*glory* of the blessed God" that is the content of the gospel. This is a "glory" centered on the past inbreaking of Christ "into the world to save sinners" (v. 15; cf. Titus 2:11; 3:4),[44] an event elsewhere referred to as the "epiphany of our Savior, Jesus Christ" (2 Tim 1:10; cf. 2 Cor 4:6). And, it is an event, given the direction of the doxology in 1:17 and its head title, "King over the Ages," which is understood to fall under the "blessed" God's governance (see below). Thus, by "blessed" Paul draws on the overtones of God's freedom even as he consistently tethers this freedom to his redemptive work in Christ. God's freedom to do as he wishes does not detach him from the world. Rather, his own "good pleasure" (cf. Eph 1:5,9) is to intervene redemptively in the world in Christ.

The salvation-historical conception of οἰκονομίαν θεοῦ remains front and center when Paul testifies in 1:12–17. The whole testimony elaborates on v. 11, specifically, on the nature of the gospel and how God entrusted it to Paul. Paul testifies that God had shown him mercy,[45] the wonder of which is highlighted by the brutal portrait Paul paints of his pre-Christian past. Moreover, Paul asserts that God's saving work extends to his incorporation by Christ into the ongoing prosecution of that work.

---

[41] Both Towner (*Goal*, 125–26) and H. von Lips (*Glaube, Gemeinde, Amt. Zum Verstandis der Ordination in den Pastoralbriefen* [FRLANT 122; Göttingen: Vandenhoeck & Ruprecht, 1979], 30) point to the distinction between "teaching" and the "gospel." See also Couser, "Using Law Lawfully," 50–51.

[42] B. S. Easton, *The Pastoral Epistles* (London: SCM Press, 1948), 179–80.

[43] Lau convincingly argues that Paul's use of the epiphany terminology (ἐπιφάνεια, 1 Tim 6:14; 2 Tim 1:10; 4:1,8; Titus 2:13; ἐπιφαίνω, Titus 2:11; 3:4; cf. ἐπιφανής, 2 Thess 2:8) represents a contemporization of the "*incarnation and pre-existence found in the Pauline Son of God christology*" (italics his; *Manifest*, 263). Paul's use hearkens back to Hellenistic Jewish circles where this terminology comes to express OT theophanic conceptions of a visible, helping intervention of God for his people (Ibid, 182–88, 223; cf. Towner, *Letters*, 416–18). His choice of these terms (along with, e.g., μακάριος) may be due to their culturally driven currency in Ephesus and, with Titus, their firm attachment to his response to the looming Ephesian threat (cf. Couser, "God and Christian Existence in 1 and 2 Timothy and Titus" [Ph.D. diss., Aberdeen University, 1992], 246–60; R. Oster, "The Ephesian Artemis as an Opponent of Early Christianity," *JAC* 19 [1976]: 39–40; R. Oster, "Holy Days in Honour of Artemis," *NDIEC* [1987]: 81).

[44] "The kerygmatic formula of 1 Tim. 1:15 is no mere formal citation. . . . It serves as the linchpin of the entire section." (Lau, *Manifest*, 71).

[45] The passive here (1:13; cf. 1:16), as commonly in Paul, emphasizes God's initiative (cf. Roloff, *Timotheus*, 94).

This makes him a showcase of Christ's boundless patience for the benefit of all those yet to believe unto eternal life (1:16). Finally, Paul ends with a soaring doxology stressing the transcendent sovereignty of God (v. 17), returning to and elaborating on what was latent in the "blessed" of v. 11. Interestingly, Paul directs his doxology to God after testifying to the "trustworthy" character of a saying which highlights Christ's initiative (v. 15), something already intimated in the joint nature of κατ' ἐπιταγὴν (1:1). Yet, the doxology implies, especially with its head title, "King of the Ages," that Christ's mission still falls within God's sovereign governance. Indeed, given its background and context, the title can hardly just refer to God's eternality.[46] "Eternal" is associated with God's rule in the OT.[47] Moreover, this title resonates with the language of prayer in the pre-Christian Hellenistic synagogue.[48] This connection likely occurred because this title delineated God's relationship to the world which justified the very act of prayer.[49] The sense here seems to be close to O. Knoch's view of it, summarized by Marshall, as a reference to "the scope of God's rule, i.e., over the unending series of future ages, or possibly over the periods of salvation history."[50] This sense of the doxology's head title also suggests that the remaining epithets might be more about God's redemptive activity in the world than his essence. This seems especially likely since this doxology is mirrored and expanded in 1 Tim 6:15–16 in decidedly relational terms.[51] There, "King over the ages" finds its counterpart in "the blessed and only Sovereign, the King of kings, and the Lord of lords." God is unique in that he has no superior. Again, not so much of an emphasis on his character as a statement on his relationship to the power structures of the cosmos. The "immortality" of God in 1:17 is in 6:16 something singularly under God's control.[52] Given the contextual emphasis on "life" as the focus of Timothy's labors (6:12), as something sourced in God (v. 13a), as the substance of Christ's witness (v. 13b), and

---

[46] J. Barr points to the common use of the plural of αἰών in titles carrying the significant of "forever" (*Biblical Words for Time* [SBT 33; London: SCM, 1969], 70, 80. Thus R. Deichgräber renders the phrase "the eternal-timeless king" (*Gotteshymnus und Christushymnus in der frühen Christenheit* [SUNT 5; Göttingen: Vandenhoeck & Ruprecht, 1967], 92–93).

[47] In the OT, God is the "Eternal God" (Gen 21:33; Isa 40:28; cf. Ps 90:2) so that that which pertains to him, being rooted in his own existence, has the same everlasting quality (e.g., glory, Ps 104:31; truth, Ps 117:2; kindness, Isa 54:8; his love, Jer 31:3). Likewise, this quality is naturally and firmly attached to his sovereign rule, encompassing his chosen people (Judg 8:23; Ps 47:7; Isa 8:7;), all nations (Ps 47:8–9), and all gods (Ps 97; Jer 10:10–11;). Thus, it is natural that, since his rule is unending (Exod 15:18; Pss 10:16; 29:10; 66:7; 93:1–2; 146:10), he should be designated as "Eternal King" (Jer 10:10).

[48] Kelly, *Pastoral*, 55; N. Brox, *Die Pastoralbriefe* (RNT; Regensburg: Verlag Friedrich Pustet, 1969), 116; and V. Hasler, *Die Briefe an Timotheus und Titus* (Zürich: Theologischer Verlag, 1978), 17.

[49] Speaking of the general understanding of later Judaism concerning God's relationship to the world, E. Stauffer states: "Israel may pray to this Protector in all its needs. There is no situation over which He is not the Lord. For He is Lord of all elements of the world and the forces of destiny. The people of God is not subject to fortune; it is subject to the Lord of heaven and earth" ("Θεός," *TDNT* 3:115).

[50] Marshall, *Pastoral Epistles*, 405.

[51] Couser, "*Theo*logical Method," 280–82. It has long been recognized that 6:15–16 presents God in more traditional Jewish terms (Fee, *1 and 2 Timothy*, 152–54; Hanson, *Pastoral*, 62, 112).

[52] He is "the only one who possesses ἀθανασίαν" (a near synonym to ἀφθάρτος in 1:17).

as the alternative pursuit for the materialistic rich (v. 19),[53] coupled with the association of "immortality" with the promised "life" God brings to light in the gospel in 2 Tim 1:10 (cf. 1:1), the force of 6:16 seems to clearly fall on the side of that which God *bestows* in his saving acts in Christ when apprehended by faith (cf. 1 Tim 2:4; 4:8–10).[54] Even in the context of 1:17, the "immortal" God is the one who "had mercy" on Paul to the end that Christ could hold him forth as a "pattern for those about to believe on him (Christ) for eternal life" (v. 16). Even when Paul refers to God as "invisible," in light of 6:16, it suggests an emphasis on his inaccessibility in order to place his redemptive oversight beyond human manipulation and influence.[55] Again, this is a statement about how God relates to the world. Finally, the singularity of God in the μόνῳ of 1:17 is also heightened throughout the doxological passage of 6:15–16. He alone is the ruler of rulers, he alone possesses immortality, and he dwells in a place he alone can access. What emerges here is the classic Jewish use of μόνος to make an absolute claim for God's sovereignty.[56] In both passages, these paeans to God serve to describe the one who sovereignly rules over the decisive saving interventions of Christ, past (1:15) and future (6:14). Moreover, as 6:15 makes clear, his involvement is not deistically conceived as if he has put this plan in motion only to watch its outworking from afar. The Sovereign God brings about this decisive saving event not only at his own time but also by his own direct action.[57] In sum, 1:12–17 records Paul's praise to the redemptive sovereign as he reflects on God's merciful saving plan implemented in Christ and proclaimed through appointed agents—the οἰκονομίαν θεοῦ. The God so merciful to Paul is the "King *over* the Ages," the unchallenged sovereign who is at work in Christ dispensing life in a manner and at a time he alone has determined.

Consequently, when Paul returns to Timothy's charge at the end of 1 Tim 1, he encourages him to hold fast to the truths represented in Paul's testimony as well as warns him of the dangers represented by the erring brothers. Sadly and ironically (cf. 1:7b), they are standing alongside the *pre*-Christian Paul as blasphemers (cf. 1:13a,20). However, unlike Paul (1:13b), they are *knowingly* "turning away from" the truth in misrepresenting the essence of God's saving work in Christ as expressed in the gospel (1:6,19). They are acting as if they can rewrite God's saving arrangement and, with their attempted rewrite, are wreaking havoc on the members of God's

---

53 For "eternal (genuine) life" as the central focus here, see Couser, "*Theo*logical Method," 276–77, esp. n. 59.

54 The fact that Paul elsewhere describes the resurrected believer with the language of immortality (1 Cor 15:53–54) indicates that "the Christian hope is nothing less than participation in God's unique self-generating life" (Towner, *Letters*, 421).

55 In the OT God hides himself from man's gaze for to see him is to die (Exod 3:6; 33:20,23; Judg 13:22; 1 Kgs 19:13; Isa 6:5). This makes God's dwelling "unapproachable" (Exod 19:16–22; Ps 104:2; cf. Ezek 1:26–2:1 and for the "light" of God's presence).

56 Fitzmyer, "Savior God," 182–83.

57 Towner, *Letters*, 420 (cf. also Marshall, *Pastoral*, 666). For God's involvement in Christ's future advent, see Matt 24:36; Mark 13:32; Acts 1:7; 1 Thess 4:14,16; 2 Thess 1:6–7.

"household" (the "church," 3:15).[58] Left to their own creative speculations, battles over theological esoterica consume their gatherings (1:4,6; 2:8) and the "ship" of their faith (and those "on board" with them)[59] has run off course and crashed up on the rocks (1:19; cf. 6:21). The gospel with its ethical implications for God's "household" and his οἰκονομία has been displaced.

What we find then is that the οἰκονομίαν θεοῦ refers to God's arrangement for the redemption of mankind with its attendant ethical implications. Paul prepares for this in the salutation and decisively confirms it with a testimony that rearticulates the saving work of God in Christ in a way that stresses its fixed character. This saving arrangement falls under the auspices of the consummately sovereign Savior God, the singular "King over the Ages" who is inaccessible (and so beyond human machinations) and who alone bestows immortality/life. God alone has set the parameters of his saving plan, with the past and future epiphanies of Christ providing the crucial salvation-historical framework (1:15; 6:14). It is he, through Christ via the prophetic Spirit (1:18; cf. 4:14), who entrusts the proclamation of his saving acts to his appointed messengers. When it is internalized by God's people, it promotes a life of "love" (1:5). Paul meets the antagonist's challenge to that arrangement by asserting its unassailable character. It is here, in framing the battle as a battle for or against God's οἰκονομίαν, that the battle lines are drawn in terms of both *theo*logy and its ethical implications.

This conception of οἰκονομίαν θεοῦ as God's "household rules" is validated by its reemergence in the middle "A" section (3:14–4:16), even as it is extended and clarified. As mentioned above, though he is careful to control and clarify this vague expression by his more characteristic (and distinctive) ἐκκλησία θεοῦ, he brings the thought of God's household rules forward and thereby sustains that emphasis by referring to the Ephesian believers as "God's household" (3:15; cf. 3:5). More precisely, they are those who belong to God (θεοῦ) and among whom God manifests his presence (ζῶντος),[60] a presence which thrusts ethical demands on them with regard

---

58 The relative, ἥτις, is feminine by attraction to ἐκκλησία. Attraction "occurs when the focus of the discourse is on the predicate nom.: the dominant gender reveals the dominant idea of the passage" (D. Wallace, *Greek Grammar Beyond the Basics* [Grand Rapids: Zondervan, 1996], 338; cf. also Roloff, *Erste Briefe*, 199). Thus, grammatically, and by the extensive elaboration on ἐκκλησία in the following phrase, "belonging to the living God, a support and pillar of the truth," ἐκκλησία stands as the controlling metaphor for Paul's use of the preceding οἴκῳ θεοῦ, a relatively ambiguous notion (cf. C. K. Barrett, *The Pastoral Epistles* [NCB; Oxford: Clarendon, 1963], 63). Also, the designation of the ἐκκλησία as τοῦ θεοῦ occurs almost exclusively in Paul (e.g., Rom 16:16; 1 Cor 10:32; 11:16,22; 12:28; Gal 1:13; 1 Thess 2:14; 1 Tim 3:5), with Acts 20:28 being the only exception. Even there, Luke shows a close affinity to Pauline conceptions (cf. K. Schmidt, " Ἐκκλησία," *TDNT* 3:506–507).

59 Paul implies that some "women" are behaving in the assemblies in a manner inconsistent with "respect for God" (2:10) and that some young widows' behavior is promoting misrepresentations of the church by its opponents (5:14) and that certain slaves are bringing God's name into disrepute by their attitudes toward their masters (6:1–2).

60 See Num 14:28 and Josh 3:10 where "living God" is used to emphasize God's presence with his people. For this sense here, cf. L. Oberlinner, *Die Pastoralbriefe. Erste Folge. Kommentar zum Ersten Timotheusbrief* (Herders theologischer Kommentar zum NT Band XI/2; Freiburg: Herder, 1994), 157; M. J. Goodwin, "The Pauline Background of the Living God as Interpretive Context for 1 Timothy 4.10," *JSNT* 61 (1996): 65–85.

to the "truth." Suspicions that temple conceptions lie close at hand are confirmed by the temple imagery with which the further description of the church as a "supporting pillar of the truth" is laden.[61] The immanence of God emerges powerfully here. The people of God are the dwelling place of God, his temple. Not only is his house, his people, structured by his household rules, but the "householder" is active in their midst. He holds them accountable even as it is his very presence that graciously constitutes them as his people and enables them to embrace their identity and calling (4:10; cf. 2 Tim 2:20–21). Also, as for Paul in 1:15, the revealed truth they are to buttress is centered on God's helping intervention in Christ (v. 16).

Indeed, as we consider God's relationship to his οἰκονομίαν, this is a good place to develop two prominent threads emphasizing God's immanence that run through the letter. First, Paul regularly reminds Timothy, and the readers through Timothy, that God's household lives "in the sight of God" (2:3; 5:4,21; 6:13; cf. 2 Tim 2:14; 4:1).[62] Each occurrence of this ἐνώπιον formulation asserts that the divine imprimatur drives the conduct enjoined. And on those occasions where Paul directs an adjuration toward Timothy (5:21; 6:13), an even more immediate involvement of God is emphasized. God is present as a witness at the declarations and, in accordance with the different ways God is referred to in these adjurations,[63] he will stay involved up until the end of the age in monitoring (5:21) and enabling (6:13) Timothy with respect to the behavior enjoined.[64] Second, God's ongoing presence and provision likely stands behind Paul's repeated reference to believers as those who "hope in God." Believers rightly related to God have placed their hope in him by virtue of their faith in Christ and persist in doing so (4:10; 5:4; 6:17; cf. 1:1; Titus 2:15). This hope refers to both the present and future existence of the community and its members. The God of this hope is active in the world along with Christ, appointing servants who embrace and declare Christ as "the hope" (1:1). It is because God is actively giving believers the "now-and-to-come" life he promised (4:8; cf. 2 Tim 1:1) that Paul finds the motivation he needs for arduous labor in his service (4:10)—the type of service that

---

61 On the combination of household/temple imagery here, see Mounce, *Pastoral*, 220–21; Marshall, *Pastoral Epistles*, 508; Towner, "Households," 417–19. Elsewhere in Paul see 1 Cor 3:9; 4:1; 9:17; Gal 6:10 for household imagery; 1 Cor 3:16–17 and 6:19 for temple imagery; and Eph 2:19 for a combination of both in the same passage (cf. B. Gärtner, *The Temple and the Community in Qumran and the New Testament* [SNTSMS 1; Cambridge: Cambridge University Press, 1965], 60–66).

62 For a full treatment of this formulation, see Couser, "Christian Existence," 48–75.

63 On this formulation, see G. Stählin, "Zum Gebrauch von Beteuerungsformeln im Neuen Testament," *NovT* 5/6 (1962/63): 115–43, esp. 125n7.

64 The choice of "God, Christ Jesus and the elect angels" in 5:21 conveys the conception of the final assize in contemporary parlance (cf. Matt 16:27; 24:30–31,36; 25:31–34; Mark 8:38; 1 Thess 3:13; 4:16; 2 Thess 1:6–8; Rev 3:5; for the OT theophanic backdrop see T. F. Glasson, *The Second Advent: The Origin of the New Testament Doctrine* [London: Epworth, 1947], 176). On the other hand, the reference to God as the one who "gives life to and sustains the life of everything" in 6:13 (see below) stresses his positive disposition toward, and the resources available through him for, Timothy's call to "keep the commandment spotless," i.e., to "lay hold of eternal life" (for the relationship between these phrases, see Couser, "*Theological Method*," 276–77). Moreover, this sustaining God is the one who will close the present age at the "appearance of Christ" (6:15). God's presence and sustenance encompass the whole of the present age.

promotes God's saving work in and through his servants (v. 16). In contrast, those whom Paul and Timothy oppose are those who, duped by Satan (4:2; 5:15; cf. 2 Tim 2:25–26; 3:8), "wander away from the truth" (1:6), "abandon the faith" (4:1), "have wandered from the faith" (6:10,21; cf. 2 Tim 1:15; 2:18; 4:4,16), and "put their hope in wealth" (6:17; cf. 4:10). "Genuine" widows steadfastly look to God for what they need (5:5). They are utterly dependent on God and are committed to the purposes and priorities of God in their widowhood (vv. 9–10)—unlike the destructive young widows who have turned aside after "Satan" (5:6,15; cf. 2 Tim 3:6–7). God, on behalf of the genuine widow, calls his people to care for the needs of those who are utterly dependent on him, whether those responsible are immediate family members (5:4,16) or the household of God generally (5:9). Lastly, the rich are only properly oriented to their wealth, with the hope of finding "genuine life," when they approach their riches from a posture of ongoing dependence on God (6:17). He alone is their real security for life now and to come. They can rest from their striving since God provides "every good thing" for their "enjoyment." Moreover, his own example of a lavish generosity toward his people for their blessing provides the life-giving ethic to guide the rich in the use of their resources (6:18–19).

We now need to return to 1 Tim 3:16 to pick up a second key *theo*logical concept that stands alongside the household imagery. There, Paul characterized the revealed truth ("mystery") of God's saving intervention in Christ as that which pertains to "godliness" (εὐσέβεια).[65] Though this is its first appearance in the "A" sections, it was already introduced by Paul in a near hendiadys with σεμνότης in 2:2.[66] Yet, he robustly develops the concept in chap. 4. There, we find that it is this manner of life that "holds (God's) promise of the now-and-to-come life" (4:8). This life should be emphatically affirmed (v. 9) for it is grounded in a settled hope in the "living God, who is the Savior of all who believe" (v. 10). The one who is living a "godly" life is living in a manner consistent with what is entailed in God's saving acts in Christ proclaimed in the gospel. Thus, Paul exhorts Timothy to "command these truths and teach them" (v. 11) by both proclaiming and embodying them (vv. 12–15). It is this manner of life that promotes the fullest realization of God's saving work in Timothy's life and in the lives of those to whom he ministers in Ephesus (v. 16). Now when we back up to Paul's aforementioned use of the εὐσέβεια concept in 2:2, it is not surprising to find it functioning as the norm governing the "quiet and tranquil

---

[65] 1 and 2 Tim and Titus have the largest concentration of the εὐσέβεια word-group in the NT.

[66] Σεμνότητι (and σεμνός), though less frequent than the εὐσέβεια word-group, do figure into Paul's description of the believer's life on several occasions (cf. 1 Tim 3:4,8,11; Titus 2:2,7). In 1 Tim where the church is the "household or family of God" and "its members are a priestly congregation," C. Spicq argues that σεμνότητι signifies a "mode of existence defined by piety and worship, marked by the seriousness, gravity, decency that are fitting in God's presence" ("σεμνός, σεμνότης," *TLNT* 3:245). Similar to εὐσέβεια, it embodies the type of demeanor and bearing, with its consequent effects upon others, true of one who has grasped the grandeur and significance of God's saving acts in Christ. Yet, the development and prominence of εὐσέβεια suggests that σεμνός / σεμνότης constitute a conceptual subset of the former, i.e., these terms stand in a hyponymous semantic relationship with εὐσέβεια.

life." This "life" is a "godly" life since it results from a submission to the Savior God and his redemptive purposes (as spelled out in vv. 3–7), a submission referred to metonymically in Paul's call to prayer.[67] Thus, the integration of *theo*logy and life that we saw more explicitly in chap. 4 is initially brought to expression in the theological reasoning in vv. 3–7. Consequently, Paul can use εὐσέβεια in the final "A" section as shorthand for the life properly oriented to God in Christ and that which forms the antithesis of the antagonists (6:3,5,6,11).[68] Most likely through the mediation of Hellenistic Judaism,[69] the term brings together both a correct knowledge of God and the behavior that is consistent with that knowledge, and all of this is a possibility because of God's intervention in Christ.[70] In one term Paul welds together theology and ethics and provides a label for the manner of life shaped by and promoting the οἰκονομίαν θεοῦ.

As the paradigmatic portion of the household material altogether, 2:1–7 is then the foundational move in Paul's attempt to restructure God's household so that the various segments would fill the roles demanded by the saving purposes (i.e., that they live in εὐσεβείᾳ). Within 2:1–7 Paul extends and clarifies the *theo*logical substructure even as he represents this section as an inference of chap. 1. The emphasis running through the passage is the universality of the scope of the "prayers" of 2:1 and, as we will see below, their *theo*logical priority and soteriological focus. Thus, the redemptive sovereignty developed over 1:11–17 reappears here with additional elaboration. Not only are the prayers to be made "on behalf of *all* people" and "*all* those in authority" but the theological rationale provided in vv. 3–7 substantiates this scope even as it emphasizes their priority.[71] In vv. 3–4 Paul begins by asserting the inference he has drawn from his reflection on the nature of God and the nature of Christ's and his own ministry in vv. 5–7. Paul concludes that God must desire all to be saved (an "all" which is later qualified as all "who believe," 4:10).[72] It is "God, the Savior," he who desires "all to be saved and come to the knowledge of the truth," who finds the

---

[67] The pleonastic focus on prayer here is comparable to Jesus' statement in Mark 11:17. It amounts to a call to be driven by the priorities of God in that it is an activity that preeminently signifies a humble dependence upon and submission to God.

[68] Εὐσέβεια becomes "a shorthand expression for the quality of life demanded of the members of God's house" (Couser, "Theological Method," 274). It functions to describe the manner of life that is nothing less than "true Christianity" (Marshall, *Pastoral Epistles*, 142–43).

[69] J. Quinn, *The Letter to Titus* (AB 35; New York: Doubleday, 1990), 282–91.

[70] Towner, *Goal*, 150; cf. Mounce, *Pastoral*, 83; G. W. Knight, *The Pastoral Epistles: A Commentary on the Greek Text* (NIGTC: Grand Rapids: Eerdmans), 117.

[71] The τοῦτο beginning v. 3 most likely envisions the whole of vv. 1–2. The use of the near demonstrative to refer to a previous statement as a whole is relatively common in 1 Tim (cf. 1:9; 4:16; 5:3). Each of these occurrences make it highly unlikely that the τοῦτο in 2:3 has v. 2 only, or even primarily, in view (against Collins, *Timothy and Titus*, 59).

[72] First Timothy 4:10 recalls 2:1–7, and with μάλιστα πιστῶν draws out the ἡμῶν (2:3), which normally accompanies σωτήρ, whether used of God or Christ (cf. 1:1; 2 Tim 1:10; Titus 1:3,4; 2:10,13; 3:4,6). Μάλιστα carries the sense of "namely," "to be precise" (T. C. Skeat, "Especially the Parchments: A Note on 2 Tim. 4:13," *JTS* 30 [1979]: 173–77; I. H. Marshall, "Universal Grace and Atonement in the Pastoral Epistles" in *The Grace of God, The Will of Man* [ed. Clark Pinnock; Grand Rapids: Eerdmans, 1989], 55; cf. Fitzmyer, "Savior God," 188). The precise relationship between God's willing and man's believing for salvation is not addressed directly in 1 Tim (cf. 2 Tim 1:9; 2:10; Titus 1:1; 3:5). At the

exhortation of vv. 1–2 "acceptable."[73] Paul's conclusion concerning God's will is first a corollary of the fact that "God is one" (εἷς θεός). Paul appears to be drawing here on the sense developed more explicitly in his earlier writings. In Rom 3:29–30 (cf. Gal 3:20; Eph 4:4–6), Paul argues from the singularity of God to the conclusion that salvation was open to Jew *and* Gentile.[74] This is made clear by the next plank in Paul's argument where he reflects on the saving work of Christ in a way that directly connects to and informs the εἷς θεός formula. First, with the repetition of "one" in conjunction with the mediatorial role of Christ, Paul makes explicit what is implicit in the εἷς θεός formula. Not only are God and Christ united in their "oneness," with decided overtones of deity with regard to Christ,[75] but that "oneness" is explicated in terms of Christ giving himself "as a ransom for *all* people." That which was implied in 1:11–17 and mirrored in the paean of 6:15–16, God's absolute claim of sovereignty over all matters of redemption, comes to the surface here in terms of the more characteristic εἷς θεός. Paul further connects the work of Christ with God by specifying that this "testimony" of Christ, this self-giving ransom for *all*,[76] occurred at "God's own right time" (καιροῖς ἰδίοις). This is a phrase used elsewhere (1 Tim 6:15; Titus 1:3) to designate the event to which it refers as divinely determined and, as such, as proceeding from God's salvation plan.[77] Moreover, in each use it is employed by Paul to directly or indirectly link the past and future epiphanies of Christ to the saving plan of God.[78] Thus, the character of Christ and especially the nature and the timing of the work of Christ add additional support to the universal scope of God's saving will and its priority (even as God's governance of the redemptive sphere is emphasized

same time, the very limitation of God's status as savior to believers suggests that, while God may indiscriminately make provision for the salvation of all in Christ, he cannot be claimed as savior by those who do not believe (cf. 1 Tim 1:16).

[73] "To be saved and come to the knowledge of the truth" is a phrase that gives the ultimate end of God's salvific work first and then provides the immediate end that leads to the former. The cognitive side of conversion, the hearing and grasping of the "truth," the gospel message (1 Tim 2:7a; 4:3; 2 Tim 2:25), is most likely emphasized in light of the departure from the truth on the behalf of the antagonists (cf. 1 Tim 6:5). See Mounce (*Pastoral*, 86), citing C. J. Ellicott, *The Pastoral Epistles of St Paul* (3rd ed.; London: Longman, 1864), 28. This stands contrary to G. Kretschmar's contention that the phrase "to come to the knowledge of the truth" indicates that teaching has displaced faith such that salvation becomes a matter of attainment. Faith becomes something learned in the household ("Der paulinische Glaube in den Pastoralbriefe," in *Glaube im Neuen Testament* [ed. F. Hahn and H. Klein; Neukirchen: Neukirchener, 1982], 115–240). Kretschmar fails to note the polemical slant of this wording and neglects the clear place of faith throughout these letters (cf. 1 Tim 1:16; 3:16; Titus 3:8), not to mention the strong emphasis on salvation by grace apart from works (2 Tim 1:9; Titus 3:5; cf. I. H. Marshall, "Salvation, Grace and Works in the Later Writings in the Pauline Corpus," *NTS* 42 [1996]: 352–54).

[74] See Towner, *Goal*, 50–51.

[75] See Fee, *1 and 2 Timothy*, 68, and I. H. Marshall, "The Development of the Concept of Redemption in the New Testament" in *Jesus the Saviour: Studies in New Testament Theology* (Downers Grove: InterVarsity, 1990), 166.

[76] That the referent of τόν μαρτύριον is the phrase, "the one who gave himself as a ransom for all" (v. 6a), see Couser, "'The Testimony about the Lord,' 'Borne by the Lord,' or Both?: An Insight into Paul and Jesus in the Pastoral Epistles," *TynBul* 55 [2004]: 301–304; Kelly, *Pastoral*, 64; and N. Brox, *Pastoralbriefe*, 129.

[77] See Roloff, *Erste Briefe*, 123–24; Fee, *1 and 2 Timothy*, 66; Kelly, *Pastoral*, 64; E. F. Scott, *The Pastoral Epistles* (London: Hodder & Stoughton, 1948), 22; Dibelius, *Pastoral*, 43, 131; O. Cullmann, *Christ and Time* (trans. F. V. Filson; London: SCM, 1951), 39–43; A. J. Malherbe, "'In Season and Out of Season': 2 Timothy 4:2," *JBL* 103/2 (1984): 243; G. Delling, "Καιρός," *TDNT* 3:460–61.

[78] Its link to the epiphany/appearance of Christ is indisputable in the case of 1 Tim 6:15. On Titus 1:3, see below.

further). The final plank in Paul's argument appears in the depiction of his own call, which rounds out this passage.[79] The relative, ὅ (v. 7a), which has the testimony (τόν μαρτύριον) as its referent, specifies that "for which" (εἰς ὅ) Paul has been appointed by God (noting the divine passive, ἐτέθην). It is this "testimony," the self-giving of Christ as a ransom for *all* men, that Paul is to proclaim as a preacher, apostle, and teacher. Moreover, not only is his message universal in scope but the very subjects of his work as a preacher, apostle, and teacher are "the Gentiles" (ἐθνῶν; cf. 2 Tim 4:17).[80]

Now, as Paul begins his targeted exhortations to the community through Timothy in 2:8, Paul has made it clear that God's saving plan and associated ethical implications are to structure and motivate the operations of his household, corporately and individually. They are to live ἐν εὐσεβείᾳ. There is no hint that the instructions to follow are driven by some accommodationist ethic designed to help the church just "get along in the world" by re-envisioning God and his purposes in order to remove tension points between the church and the surrounding culture. The "culture" made possible and demanded by God's saving acts in Christ, like the saving glory of God driving Paul's interface with various cultures in 1 Cor 9:19–23; 10:31–11:1, is driving Paul's structuring of God's people in Ephesus. It may or may not reflect contemporary values and perspectives. But even if it does, it does so because that is what is demanded in order to appropriately experience for oneself (cf. 2:15; 4:8–10,16; 5:14–15) as well as manifest in and for the world (cf. 2:8; 3:7; 6:1–2) God's saving purposes. His unequivocal assertion that nothing has changed in God's saving work, even though the antagonists claim otherwise, just further emphasizes *theo*logy as the decisive shaping force in the life of the community. As Paul's gospel declares, God's saving acts in Christ have and will take place at God's "own right time." God's redemptive purposes are secure for he is the unassailable, incomparable sovereign, the ruler who alone exercises redemptive governance over the world. He has acted in Christ to inaugurate his saving intervention and will yet act in Christ to consummate it. Moreover, he has mediated that deliverance secured by Christ to the world through appointed messengers for the blessing of its inhabitants. To know what God is up to and what that means for the life of the church in this "time in between the times" of God's saving interventions in Christ is what it means to "lay hold of eternal (genuine) life" now (cf. 6:12,19). For Paul, God's transcendence is emphasized in order to undergird and reinforce his *redemptive* governance without diminishing his immanence.

Alongside this emphasis on God's redemptive governance is a significant *theo*logical strain focused on God as Creator (1 Tim. 2:13–15; 4:3–5; 5:1,3–15; 6:13).

---

79 For a convincing description of the function of 2:7, see Fee, *1 and 2 Timothy*, 67 (against Towner, *Goal*, 205).

80 Undoubtedly Paul is referring to his unique call as the "apostle to the Gentiles" (Rom. 15:15–16; Gal 2:8) in order to emphasize that his very own calling, i.e., being a Jewish believer called to take the message of God's saving acts in Christ to the Gentiles, verifies the universal scope of God's saving will.

This emphasis combats a dualism arising from the overrealized eschatology of the antagonists. Paul condemns the ascetic tendencies of the antagonists, the emancipatory tendencies among certain women, and the breakdown of the family by asserting that participation in God's saving work does not render the institutions and provisions of the created order irrelevant or passé. Over against the antagonists' contempt of creation, Paul asserts that "every created thing is good" (4:4a; cf. 1 Cor 9:25–26). The good creation is intended by God for the blessing of his household.[81] In fact, the somewhat unusual designation of God as the one "who gives life to all things" (6:13) may be intended by Paul to assert that life in all of its forms, physical and spiritual, not only has its source and sustenance in God but also can find its proper integration in those rightly related to the Creator as Savior.[82] The provisions and structures in creation are for the flourishing of God's people (cf. 6:17) when they are "received with thanksgiving"—as gifts from God whose goodness is experienced when his gifts are humbly embraced and appropriated toward the end for which he created them (cf. Rom 14:6). Thus, the woman who takes up the sphere for which she has been "formed" (2:11–14) will experience the fullness of her salvation when this embrace is accompanied by the other disciplines necessary for any believer to further their commitment to Christ (2:15).[83] In doing so, she will maximize her own potential as an "actor" within the performance of God's redemptive drama being played out in and through the gathered community of God's people. So also, when children take up their responsibility toward their aged parents (5:4,16) by embracing the created order enforced in the fifth command of the Decalogue (5:3),[84] this is "acceptable in God's sight." This upholds the created order so that their life does not constitute a denial of the faith (v. 8). Additionally, should young widows abandon their creation-nullifying denial of marriage, the personal (v. 11) and corporate destruction (vv. 12–13) would likely cease and they would provide no hindrance to God's saving purposes in the culture around them (v. 14b). To participate in God's saving work is to be able to perceive that the elements of God's created order (specifically, the functional division between the genders within the community, the institutions of marriage and family, and the material provisions) are set in place by God, respectively, for the spiritual protection, social enrichment, and physical sustenance of the believer. This gospel-centered hermeneutic is something decidedly absent in the confident, yet incompetent,

---

[81] I.e., "those who believe and have come to know the truth," v. 4:3b. Marshall (*Pastoral*, 229, 375), in his excursus "Goodness and Good Works in the Pastoral Epistles," demonstrates that something is good in the Pastorals primarily because it is something "ordained or approved by God." Marshall (227) argues that καλός develops a technical sense "to refer to something specifically Christian," e.g., "the good teaching" (1 Tim 4:6b), "the good warfare" (1:18), "the good fight of faith" (6:12a), "the good confession" (6:12b).

[82] See J. Jeremias, *Die Briefe an Timotheus und Titus* (NTD 9; Göttingen: Vandenhoeck & Ruprecht, 1963), 46, and Hasler, *Timotheus und Titus*, 50.

[83] "In a somewhat awkward manner, Paul is saying that a woman's salvation and the practical outworking of that salvation . . . do not consist in altering her church role. Rather, she is to accept her God-given role, one of the specific functions being the bearing of children (synecdoche)" (Mounce, *Pastoral*, 146).

[84] B. Winter, "Providentia for the Widows of 1 Timothy 5:3–16," *TynBul* 39 (1988): 92, 98.

OT-based pronouncement of the antagonists (cf. 1:6–7). Their misperception of the times placed the creation purposes of God in opposition to his redemptive purposes. Paul can conscience no such disparity in God's acts. The creation purposes of God this side of the new heavens and earth stand in a complementary relationship to his redemptive purposes in Christ.

The eschatologically driven emancipatory impulse is also evident among slaves (6:1–2).[85] Yet Paul does not turn to creation to address this issue. God's purposes in creation provide no *theo*logical resources as they do for issues related to male/female relationships in the church, the institutions of marriage and family, and material provision. The problem here does not consist in an attack against something established by God for life this side of the eschaton. Paul already signaled this when he grouped "slave-traders," those who treat humans as nothing more than commodities to be captured, bought and sold, with those who the law condemns (1:10). Thus, as he addresses believing slaves enslaved to unbelieving masters in 6:1, his guidance is offered under the assumption of the injustice and inhumanity of their condition—their "yoke" is a given. At the same time, this also suggests that whatever the contours of the relationship between believing masters and their believing slaves may have been in 6:2, it does not fall under the category of 1:10. It is the behavior and attitudes of the believing slaves that concerns Paul, not those of their brother-masters. Thus, he addresses these scenarios in a manner analogous to 1 Cor 7:20–24, where he appeals to God's saving purposes in order to shape the response of believing Jews, Gentiles, and slaves to their circumstances.[86] It is this sense that parallels Paul's rationale behind his advice to slaves with unbelieving masters in 1 Tim 6:1b and those with believing masters in v. 2b. For slaves with unbelieving masters, he encourages them to be careful not to act toward their masters in a way that would misrepresent God's character, his "name," and the teaching that spells out the implications of that character for his household. Given the *theo*logical substructure of the book as a whole, Paul is urging them to model their service after the same type of undeserving honor on display in God's saving acts in Christ. As Paul experienced, the Savior God he encountered in Christ is the God whose glory was on display in Christ's astounding patience with the "worst" of sinners—"a blasphemer, persecutor, and violent man" (1:11–17). Moreover, Christ willingly cooperated with God's saving will. "He came into the world to save" such "sinners" (1:15). He is "the one who gave himself" in order to pay "the price of manumission" for "all" those enslaved to sin (2:6). Thus, if

---

86 In the context Paul urges believers married to unbelievers to stay committed to their marriages to further God's saving purposes within their family (vv. 14–16). He supports this by an appeal to providence. God "called" to them where they are, intending all along that they would redemptively engage that sphere (vv. 17,20,24). By analogy, Jews should not abandon their fellow Jews, Gentiles should not abandon their fellow Gentiles, and slaves should not abandon the sphere of relationships surrounding their enslavement. Even though Paul likely encourages slaves to gain their freedom if they can (v. 21b), given the context, the goal is not primarily civil freedom. Paul encourages slaves to respond to their situation with an eye toward maximizing its potential for furthering God's saving purposes in and through them there.

the slave is to represent God in his slavery, he will accord honor to the dishonorable as he patiently endures hardship and abuse for the sake of his master's salvation.[87] For believing slaves with believing masters, the (most likely rich) masters mentioned here were apparently manifesting a God-centered ethic toward their slaves.[88] Thus, they were not rebuked for misrepresenting God, because their relationship to their slaves reflected God's lavish generosity toward his people for their flourishing.[89] So when Paul refers to the masters as "brothers" who are "faithful" and "beloved" in that they "undertake benevolence," it seems that the masters behaved as brothers toward their slaves.[90] Consequently, they were committed to their flourishing—functioning like the head of a household and no longer as a master over property.[91]

Space demands that we summarize our *theo*logical findings for 1 Timothy. This *theo*logy arises in response to the nature of the heresy plaguing the church. The problem revolves around how God saves. In the face of a blasphemous distortion of God's redemptive program, Paul responds with an emphasis on God's sovereignty in order to stress the fixed, unalterable character of his saving will. In particular, his unchallenged sovereignty is most closely tied to the saving interventions of Christ, his epiphanies. He is the only one who determines when the key saving interventions of Christ occur, whether in the past or the future. At the same time, God works in cooperation with Christ and the Spirit toward the implementation and proclamation of his saving acts in Christ. His mercy is on display not only in those who believe on Christ unto eternal life, but also in Christ's empowering of his servants by the agency of the Spirit to proclaim the glory of God in the gospel. The Trinitarian conceptions evident here avoid any subordinationism while they reflect a functional ordering. Moreover, even though he is the unchallenged King over the Ages, he does not govern from afar through surrogates (whether divine or human) or by virtue of some impersonal process which he has set in motion. He is the present and future hope of the widow. He is present among his people for their blessings and guidance. He stands as a witness during Paul's adjurations to Timothy, providing resources and accountability for the behavior enjoined. In addition, his role as Creator is asserted and brought into relationship with his redemptive governance in order to combat a type

---

[87] One can clearly hear echoes of Jesus' teaching concerning loving one's enemies (Matt 5:38–48; Luke 6:27–36; cf. 1 Tim 6:3).

[88] As Kidd, it seems most plausible to render the difficult phrase in v. 2b (πιστοί . . . ἀντιλαβανόμενοι) as "for faithful and beloved are the ones (the masters) who undertake benevolence" (*Beneficence*, 140–56, esp. 156).

[89] This ethic is spelled out in 6:17–19, where it is grounded in God's lavish generosity ("who richly supplies us with all things to enjoy"). Throughout 1 Tim the lavish benevolence of God is on display in the salvation he provides through the Christ-event (1:11–17; 2:3–7; 4:10; and 6:14–16; cf. Titus 3:4–5) preeminently and, secondarily, in his rich provision for all in creation (4:3–5).

[90] What comes to mind here is Paul's advice to Philemon to reenvision his relationship to Onesimus in a manner demanded by the love of God in Christ, which Philemon had experienced (vv. 4–6,9). Paul wanted Philemon to treat Onesimus the slave as a "dear brother" or, in other words, as he would treat Paul himself (v. 17).

[91] In any event, this would be a manner significantly different from the dehumanization on display in the slave-trading castigated in 1:10. Indeed, this type of deference toward their slaves may add an additional explanation for the readiness of the slaves to despise these masters in the first place.

of eschatological dualism that essentially puts God at odds with himself. A proper understanding of God's redemptive purposes will positively dispose the believer toward the gender roles, institutions, and material provisions that God has created for their protection and flourishing. God has set out his household rules, the saving purposes in Christ with their implications for his people, for the flourishing of his people.

2 TIMOTHY: STANDING ON THE PROMISES OF GOD

Second Timothy narrows the conversation dramatically to Paul and Timothy against the backdrop of a seemingly intensifying struggle. This is a much more private conversation. Paul writes to his "dear son" in the faith (1:2)[92] in a time of dire crisis. There are no "household" or "office" codes intended for third parties. Appeals draw on the depth of familiarity between Paul and Timothy, as borne out by Paul's "longing" and Timothy's "tears." Paul speaks intimately of Timothy's extended family by name (1:5–6). He knows what that family meant to Timothy in terms of his spiritual heritage (3:15). He draws on those familial bonds and loyalties to strengthen Timothy's ongoing resolve. He can encourage Timothy's already impressive loyalty to the message they have in common by appealing to the bonds forged between them as they shared life together in the cause of the gospel (3:10–11,14). Paul recalls their hardships in the trenches to remind Timothy of the inevitability of suffering for those following Christ (3:13). That which the Spirit prophecies about these "last days" is all too true (cp. 3:1–9; 4:3–4 with 1 Tim 4:1–5). Consequently, Timothy should not be surprised that he is facing a massive defection from the gospel (1:15) and that Paul is facing what appears to him to be certain martyrdom (4:6)—and all but alone at that (4:9,16)! "Father" and "son" are drawn even closer together as they apparently find themselves among the few "who have longed" (and continue to long) "for his (Christ's) appearing" (4:10).

Beginning with the enigmatic κατ᾽ ἐπαγγελίαν ζωῆς (1:1) right through to Paul's confident assertion in 4:18, "the Lord will rescue me . . . and bring me safely into his heavenly kingdom," a stress on the certainty of the saving purposes of God (in Christ) lies at the heart of 2 Timothy much like it does in 1 Timothy. Indeed, one of the central theological tenets thought to be lurking behind the problems in 1 Timothy is clearly expressed in this letter. Hymenaeus and Philetus are challenging the essential pattern of God's salvation plan as proclaimed by Paul and, now, by Timothy. They claim that the "resurrection is already past" (2:18; cf. 2:8). In particular, as suggested for 1 Timothy, it seems that the challenge lies in a shift of the weight of expectation for the believer from the future to the present. In some sense, most likely on the spiritual plane, the believer has largely arrived at that which "resurrection"

---

[92] Note the change in tone from the more polemical "genuine son" of 1 Tim 1:4 (cf. Titus 1:4).

entails in Paul's theology—the consummation of salvation. The effect of this "soteriological disordering" has led the antagonists into a toxic lifestyle ("a form of godliness devoid of power," 3:5) which is ravaging Ephesus and its environs (1:15,18; 3:6; 4:10). Consequently, 2 Timothy repeatedly, unequivocally affirms that Paul's gospel, which Timothy himself has "been convinced of" (3:15), possesses the divine imprimatur (cf. 1:9–11). Moreover, being empowered by God (1:8), it cannot be hindered by the current heresy from providing for the salvation of God's chosen. God's word cannot be bound (2:9). The foundation of his household cannot be shaken (2:19). In the end, all will be judged—the living and the dead—by this God and Christ at his consummative coming (4:1). Thus, the persistent preaching of his unaltered word is imperative, whether the audience wants to hear it or not (4:2–5).

As expected, Paul's *theo*logy begins to emerge nearly as soon as he puts ink to parchment. Paul begins the letter with a common reference to the source of his apostolic ministry, "God's will." This phrase portrays Paul's call as both gracious/undeserved in nature and as an obligation from God. Throughout 1 and 2 Timothy and Titus and his writings generally, Paul conceives of his apostolic appointment as one of service to the gospel (1:8,11; 4:17; cf. 1 Tim 1:1; Titus 1:3; 2 Cor 3:6–7), originating in God's mercy (cf. 1 Tim 1:13,16; 2 Cor 4:1; 1 Cor 7:25).[93] However, with the addition of κατ᾽ ἐπαγγελίαν ζωῆς (1:1) Paul narrows the focus of this more innocuous phrase and immediately gives a soteriological cast to the letter. The promise here is certainly God's. This is an alternative way to refer to God's saving "purpose" (cf. 1:9) in order to stress God's act of commitment to that plan as well as the positive nature of its outcome for those who embrace it by faith. Thus, consistently throughout 1 and 2 Timothy and Titus, that which God promises is "life" ("life now and to come," 1 Tim 4:8; "eternal life," Titus 1:2). Elsewhere in this letter Paul presents the "gospel" as the expression of this plan/promise (1:8–10; 2:8–10; cf. the near synonym "proclamation" in 4:18). As such, although the κατ᾽ may very well carry the common dual significance of a "standard" according to which one acts and a "cause" that motivates one to act, the general tone of the phrase and the role of this thought elsewhere in these letters seems to place the emphasis on "cause," "basis."[94] Thus, from the outset Paul pointedly alludes to the eschatological focus motivating his apostolic labors (cf. 1 Tim 4:10). Indeed this thought reemerges conceptually in 2:10. There Paul "endures" all this hardship in order that those "chosen by God" might receive "the salvation which is in Christ with eternal glory," a phrase synonymous with the "promise of life." For Paul, the "life" provided by God in Christ to those who believe invades and transforms the "now," while still looking to the future,

---

[93] See the treatment of this phrase with particular reference to the Corinthian correspondence in V. Furnish, "Der 'Wille Gottes' in paulinischer Sicht," in *Jesu Rede von Gott und ihre Nachgeschichte im frühen Christentum* (ed. D. Koch et al.; Gütersloh: Gerd Mohn, 1989), 209–11.

[94] The meaning "in accordance with" can also disappear entirely, so that κατά means simply "because of, as a result of, on the basis of" (BDAG, 512–13; cf. Rom 5:2; Gal 2:2; 1 Tim 5:21; and 2 Tim 1:9).

that time "to come," for its full realization ("immortality," 1:10; "eternal glory," 2:10; "will deliver me into his heavenly kingdom," 4:18).[95] Consequently, throughout the letter Paul repeatedly speaks of the future consummation as that which motivates him (cf. 1:12; 2:11–13,15; 4:1,8,18). Conversely, while Paul "longs for his [Christ's] appearing" (4:8), Demas has deserted him because he "longs for the present age" (v. 10). In sum, echoing our findings for 1 Timothy, the thought of God's saving plan in Christ emerges *in nuce* in this opening salutation.[96] Paul echoes the note of expectation found in 1 Tim 1:1, "Christ Jesus, our hope," though here it is expressed in less formal terms with a greater emphasis on what Paul himself has realized. At the same time, "promise," as such, forcibly casts this conflict in terms of a challenge to God's (and Christ's, cf. 1:8; 2:13; 4:17–18) power and loyalty (1:12). A challenge to this pattern can be nothing other than a challenge to God's credibility.

That God is active in keeping his promise leads Paul to an outburst of thanksgiving[97] as he opens his introductory thanksgiving period. Given the severity of the crisis and the close relationship between Paul and Timothy, the joy and relief expressed here is understandable. Yet this is no mere exclamation; Paul "gives thanks" because he sees Timothy's persistence as a concrete demonstration of the faithfulness and power of God. That Timothy has not been swept away by the near tsunami of defections from the gospel can be attributed to nothing other than the power of God's Spirit (vv. 6–7).[98] With the mention of the "Spirit," Paul has introduced the final member of the Godhead, demonstrating the same Trinitarian conceptions evident in 1 Timothy. God sets the overall trajectory, the will/promise/plan (cf. 1:1,9); Christ sends out appointed servants (1:1); and the Spirit enables and empowers toward the end for which they were appointed by Christ in the will of God. God's enabling through the Spirit as an outworking of his faithfulness to his saving promises relieves and encourages Paul. Once again, God is actively involved in the lives of his servants toward the accomplishment of his saving purposes in and through them.

The present form of λατρεύω[99] deserves emphasis. Throughout the letter Paul sees his present condition as a result of and a venue for rendering service and devotion to God. His imprisonment has resulted from his service to God in the proclamation of the gospel (2:9). It is that same service that makes him persevere in the face of the hardships found there. Though he is in fetters, God's Word is not constrained by his

---

95 See Fitzmeyer, "The Savior God," 188.

96 Marshall, *Pastoral*, 685; Van Neste, *Cohesion*, 216.

97 Χάριν ἔχω τῷ Θεῷ (cf. Rom 6:17; 7:25; 1 Cor 15:57; 2 Cor 2:14; 8:16; 9:15) probably serves to distinguish the thanksgiving that occurred as he wrote the letter from that which occurred in his regular prayer times, something he refers to in the ὡς clause of v. 3b (R. Gebauer, *Das Gebet bei Paulus* [Monographien und Studienbuchen; Giessen: Brunnen, 1989], 137; cf. Deichgräber, *Gotteshymnus*, 44).

98 See Haykin, "Fading Vision," 298. Cf. also J. Quinn, "The Holy Spirit in the Pastoral Epistles," in *Sin, Salvation, and the Spirit* (ed. D. Durken; Collegeville, MN: Liturgical Press, 1979), 359–60, and R. Fung, "Charismatic Ministry versus Organized Ministry? An Examination of an Alleged Antithesis," *EQ* 52 (1980): 206–10.

99 In both the LXX and NT as a whole, λατρεύω never depicts homage rendered between men but always of that service offered by man to the divine (cf. Rom 1:9,25; Phil 3:3; H. Stathmann, "Λατρεύω," *TDNT* 4:62–63).

circumstances. For this reason he continues to persevere in his service so that God's chosen might receive salvation (2:10). What Paul speaks of later in his admonition to "join (with me) in suffering for the advance of the gospel" (1:8; cf. 2:3)[100] and elsewhere as his "partnership" with the gospel (Phil 1:5,7,27–30; 4:3; and 1 Cor 9:23), that is, of partnering with God who is working out his saving purposes proclaimed in the gospel, lies close at hand here. What surfaces is a view of God who actively furthers his saving purposes in the world by working in and through his servants. God has given Timothy an enablement by his Spirit toward the faithful accomplishment of his task at Ephesus, a task centered on the protection and promotion of the gospel (1:9–10).[101] Consequently, Paul urges Timothy to fulfill his present commission to serve God's saving purposes at Ephesus by being a "workman" who can stand "approved" before God in the end (2:15). He must live a life "pleasing" to the "master" who established the household of God's people (see below), with a particular emphasis on removing any taint of the antagonists' "gangrenous" influence (2:21). He must engage those who oppose carefully and compassionately, all the while understanding that change will come about only if "God grants them repentance" (2:24). The effectiveness of his reclamation work among those who oppose is dependent upon God's intervention for its redemptive success (cf. 2 Cor 3:5). Indeed, Paul's adjurations[102] not to get distracted as he battles the antagonists (2:14) and to faithfully proclaim the word of God's salvation (4:1–2) not only point to God as an assenting witness to their delivery but, clearly in the latter adjuration, remind Timothy that God will monitor the nature of his compliance and will hold him accountable in the end. And, should Timothy run his divinely appointed "course" as Paul has (4:7), when he stands before the future assize with Christ as the presiding judge (1:18; 4:1,8,18), the judge will enable him (like Onesiphorus) to find "mercy before the Lord" God (παρὰ κυρίου, 1:18).[103] Finally, the adoption of λατρεύω and its forms in the NT is in line with the general assumption by the early Christian community of Jewish expressions of devotion to God in order to claim that the worship of God in Christ was the legitimate continuation of that devotion. This gives Paul's identification of God salvation-historical overtones especially since he goes on to say that his service carries forward

---

[100] Towner (*Letters*, 465; cf. Kelly, *Pastoral*, 161; Marshall, *Pastoral*, 703–4) takes συγκακοπαθέω, a term apparently coined by Paul, to imply that Paul is urging Timothy to join *him* in suffering for the sake of the gospel. D. R. Hall ("Fellow-Workers with the Gospel," *ExpTim* 85 [1973/74]: 119–20; cf. RSV, NEB, TEV) takes it as an encouragement to suffer "alongside" the *gospel*, where there is a near personification of the gospel as an agent in the outworking of the plan which forms its substance. In either case, a dense figure occurs here where the suffering enjoined is in service of the furtherance of God's saving purposes as proclaimed in the "gospel," either as a partner directly with God or indirectly through partnering with Paul.

[101] On the chiastic structure of 2 Tim 1:6–14, which has the twice-referred-to "gospel" at its core (vv. 9–10), see Couser, "Testimony," 314–15.

[102] On this ἐνώπιον . . . form, see p. 116 above.

[103] Though unusual in 2 Tim it is widely accepted that God is the referent of this second "Lord" here (see Fee, *1 and 2 Timothy*, 238). The picture emerges of the Lord Jesus interceding before the Lord God on behalf of the believer at the eschatological assize to secure blessing from God as warranted by the believer's earthly service (cf. Heb 4:16).

in an unbroken stream the service rendered to God by his Jewish forbearers.[104] As he affirms in 2:8, the Christ at the center of God's saving purposes (1:9–10) is none other than the one who "descended from David."

Alongside the enablement and encouragement the Spirit supplies, Timothy should take courage from God's expressed commitment to the maintenance and stability of his people. That which God has founded, the people of God,[105] is secure (2 Tim 2:19). In a manner reminiscent of the mix of household/church/temple imagery in 1 Tim 3:15, God is depicted as the "master" of his "household," the people of God. God marks his people with a "seal," designating them as authentically his and, particularly in this context, falling under his care (cf. Rom 4:11; 1 Cor 9:2; 2 Cor 1:22; Eph 1:13).[106] His "seal," which is metaphorically "placed" on his people, amounts to statements that reveal God's disposition toward them as well as their disposition toward him. His household consists of those he brought into relationship with himself, those he chose (cf. 1:9; 2:10).[107] On the flip side, and as a result of his gracious choosing, those whom he has "known" are those who "name his name," the language of prayer reminiscent of the emphasis of 1 Tim 2:1–2, and "turn away from wickedness." As such they are "vessels of honor" who purify themselves from the influence of the antagonists so that they are prepared for an unlimited sphere of service (2:21). What Paul does here is an illustration of what he will encourage Timothy to do in 3:15–16, drawing our attention to God's revelation of himself in the Scriptures for the guidance and enablement of his people. Paul has drawn on the resources in the God-given (θεόπνευστος)[108] Scriptures for Timothy's profit (v. 15). He has provided him with some of the "wisdom" necessary to appropriate that which is his in Christ for the furtherance of his God-given task at Ephesus. Reading the Scriptures through a Christocentric lens provides resources for furthering God's saving purposes in Christ in and through his people. As a result, in 2:21 and in 3:17 the end result is that "the one who names God's name"/"the man of God" is "prepared/equipped for every good work."

The nature of the promise that God has made, the word to which he is committed so that, energized by his power, it cannot be thwarted, is primarily elaborated

---

[104] "The apostle, by his conversion to Christianity, did not interrupt his connection with the λατρεύειν of his ancestors, because it was a necessary condition of the new faith to honor the God of revelation whom the Jews served" (J. E. Huther, *Critical and Exegetical Handbook to the Epistles to Timothy and Titus* [Meyer's Commentary on the New Testament 9; trans. D. Hunter; 1884; repr., Peabody, Mass: Hendrickson, 1983], 203–4).

[105] With the similarity to 1 Tim 3:15, the true church is most likely that which God securely founds (Towner, *Letters*, 531–32).

[106] Marshall, *Pastoral Epistles*, 756.

[107] The first quotation is clearly taken from Num 16:5 with the second very likely summarizing the thrust of the OT narrative in Numbers, using a combination of phrases drawn from various OT texts (cf. LXX Isa 26:13 with Num 16:26–27; Towner, *Letters*, 536–37). The sense of "know" here is clearly Hebraic and carries the notion of "recognize someone as belonging to him, choose" (R. Bultmann, "Γινώσκω," *TDNT* 1:706).

[108] See P. Wolfe, "The Place and Use of Scripture in the Pastoral Epistles" (Ph.D. diss., Aberdeen University, 1990), 133–39.

in 1:9–10 (with a more limited elaboration in 2:8). Fee refers to such passages as places where Paul succinctly expresses the heart of the gospel, "salvation in Christ." As is true elsewhere in Paul, the "form" and "imagery" expressing the content are predicated almost altogether on either "1) the aspect of the *human predicament* from which God is saving his people, or 2) the *nature of the error* that he perceives his gospel as standing in opposition to."[109] Notably, Paul sets off 1:9–10 within his opening thanksgiving period by constructing a chiastic structure in 1:6–14 that puts the twice-referred-to "gospel" (1:8,10) at its core. This is an understandable emphasis given what has been suggested above, namely, that the letter revolves around the preservation and propagation of the promise/word of God in the face of a withering attack against it. It is here that Paul sets out the substance of that promise in terms of the "gospel." This gives a clear referent to the repeated calls throughout the letter for Timothy to faithfully support and propagate God's word. What Paul's service is facilitating and what Timothy has been enabled to protect and promote is laid out here with additional elaboration in 2:8.

This concise summary of God's saving acts in Christ flows out of the phrase, κατὰ δύναμιν θεοῦ (v. 8). The sense of the phrase is tied to how we see vv. 9–10. Timothy is being encouraged to endure hardship in his task because the power "according to" which he labors is the very power of God on display in the Christ-event. At the same time, the delineation of this power in the apostolic summary of the gospel also serves to spell out the message which is the medium of God's saving power in the present age. The power of God is operative through this message toward the creation of a genuinely "godly" life. This is unlike the antagonists' "word," which led to a progressively lifeless form of "godliness" because it was not true to God's acts in Christ (1:17–18). The power of God was not operative in and through it (3:5–7). What God's power accomplished is first spelled out in two attributive participles. The combination of the two probably suggests that the first, "who saved us," refers to salvation in a general sense while the second, "called us," refers to the individual application of that salvation. This reflects the interplay between God's general purposes and the implementation of those purposes within time. There is no detachment here on God's part. The God who provides salvation is the God who calls individuals to a way of life that is set apart to him.[110] In addition, God does not act in response to human effort. Rather, his saving acts are based in "his own purpose" and, consequently, are extensions of his "grace"—a grace coming to concrete expression in Christ (1:10; cf. Titus 2:11,14) and appropriated by faith (2 Tim 1:5,13; 3:15). The gracious nature

---

[109] G. Fee, "Toward a Theology of 2 Timothy—from a Pauline Perspective," *SBL Seminar Papers, 1997* (SBLSP 36; Chico, CA: Scholars, 1997), 737–38 (italics his). The concept underlying this process in Paul is encapsulated in the term Paul uses in 1:13, ὑποτύπωσιν (E. Lee, "Words Denoting 'Pattern' in the New Testament," *NTS* 8 [1961/62]: 172).

[110] This sense comes powerfully to the fore when Paul depicts God's people as a household established and governed by God. The one who pleases the master is the one who "departs from unrighteousness," "cleanses himself of the influence of the antagonists," "has been set apart," and "pursues righteousness . . . along with all of those who call upon the Lord out of a clean heart" (2:19–22). Note also that the "scriptures" which "make one wise unto salvation" are "holy" (3:15).

of his saving work is further emphasized when Paul notes that God determined to give this grace in Christ before time began. Together, these thoughts suggest that God is the one who freely initiates salvation, that its outworking in history is determined by him, and, being a matter of grace, that it is wholly dependent upon him for its realization. In v. 10 Paul moves on to the manner in which God brought this premundane plan to fruition in the present age ("now"). He brought his purpose to light in the gracious helping intervention of Christ Jesus, fittingly described as "our Savior." The nature of that intervention consists in delivering those who claim him as Savior from the tyranny of death through his death as well as unveiling eternal life through his resurrection. As in 1 Timothy, the past Christ-event stands at the inauguration of God's saving intervention in the present age. At the same time, its decisive role centers this moment within the outworking of God's plan. This Christ-event was planned and anticipated in the ages preceding ("as my ancestors did," 1:3; "before time began," 1:8; "from the seed of David," 2:8) and yet looks forward in that it is the life of the end—eschatological life—that has broken into the present in Christ. As such, it looks forward to the future helping intervention of Christ for its full realization (4:1–2; cf. 1 Tim 4:8). Finally, with the phrase "through the gospel unto which I was appointed as a preacher" (2 Tim 1:11b–12), Paul explains that God's saving purposes include the mediation of this saving work to the present via appointed messengers. In this once/now schema, Paul once again emphasizes God's redemptive governance, a prominent emphasis in 1 Timothy as well. Salvation and its outworking are solely in God's hands, from its premundane origins to its decisive manifestation in the Christ-event, to its mediation in the present through appointed messengers, to its experience by believers and, finally, by implication, to its full realization at the end of the age. Salvation is firmly settled in and solely determined by the counsel of God. Consequently, Paul chiastically emphasizes the need to embrace humiliation and suffering in identifying with Christ (1:8,12) to protect, keep, guard this life-giving word (vv. 9–10) by the enabling of God's Spirit (vv. 6–7,14).[111]

In 2:8 Paul recalls 1:9–10 even as he singles out and thus emphasizes two crucial elements. By referring to Christ's resurrection in the passive, Paul casts it as an event brought about by God, as in 1:10. It is singled out from the other events and put out of chronological order most likely because a distorted understanding of the resurrection lay at the center of the gangrenous teaching of the antagonists (2:17–18). The phrase that follows, "descended from the line of David," apparently serves to wed this event to salvation-history. It situates this theological datum within the "plan" of God.[112] It provides a reminder of the interpretive context in which the former must be understood if the "elect" are to "receive salvation in Christ Jesus with eternal glory" through Paul's and Timothy's proclamation (2:10). It is this word alone, because it

---

[111] See Couser, "Testimony," 314–15.
[112] See Fee, *1 and 2 Timothy*, 246.

is "God's," which possesses an unstoppable dynamism. Unlike the "word" of the antagonist, to borrow from Isaiah (55:11), this word "will not return void." This phrase draws us back to the "power of God" on display in the implementation of his saving purposes in 1:9–10. It also evokes the thoughts there of the settled and solely determined nature of those purposes.

Consequently, though Paul's theological response in 2 Timothy resonates with that of 1 Timothy, the theological language narrowly focuses on the needs of Timothy in light of the worsening situation. The difficulty of Timothy's situation, compounded by the gravity of Paul's, pares down Paul's concerns to what is crucial, to what is the irreducible, indispensible core. That which is peripheral recedes to the background. As Timothy "fights the good fight" it is crucial to know what theological ground cannot be surrendered if God's saving purposes are to be furthered in and through him. Furthermore, in such a dire situation, Paul reminds Timothy of how God (along with Christ and the Holy Spirit) works out his redemptive plan by enabling those entrusted with its dissemination. As a result, the theological concerns focus on the core truths of the gospel, though selected and expressed in light of the particularities of the current situation. Additionally, Paul seems to depict God as intensely personal and the roles of Christ and the Spirit are more prominent than what we find in 1 Timothy. Concerning God in particular, he is the God who promises and so enables, stands by, and equips his servant so that his intentions for his chosen will come to fruition. This all culminates with God's assessment of his servant over against what was expected of him in the outworking of that promise.

TITUS: THE SAVIOR AND HIS CHOSEN

Similar to 1 Timothy, this letter authorizes and advises a trusted co-worker who is on an assignment from Paul. Titus was left in Crete "to straighten out what was left unfinished" in this apparently new missionary outpost (1:5a). The lack of leadership is the first "loose end" that needs Titus's attention. Though the qualifications for leadership nearly replicate those in 1 Timothy, their fullness evokes the dynamics of a new institution. The body of the letter, like 1 Timothy, goes on to speak to the church through Paul's delegate to instruct the community on the manner of life consistent with their status as God the Savior's "elect"/family (cf. 1:1; 2:1,5,8,10,14; 3:5,8). Chapter 2 breaks the community down into its various segments while chapter 3 speaks to the community as a whole. Echoing 1 Timothy, Paul intersperses his instructions with intense periods of theological reflection (1:1–4; 2:11–15; 3:3–8). These provide the framework out of which the instruction arises, not to mention its warrant and motivation.

The depiction of God also resonates strongly with that of 1 Timothy in particular but also that of 2 Timothy. At the same time, the *theo*logical language has a greater breadth here. The similarities seem to arise because the Ephesian/Asian heresy is still in view. Paul describes the threat that concerns him with language and concepts employed in 1 and 2 Timothy.[113] There is a Jewish, law-based flavor to the antagonists in each case. Yet differences emerge. Ephesus is an established community unlike Crete. Moreover, the degree to which the respective communities have been affected by the false teaching appears to differ.[114] The tone of Titus lacks the urgency of the Ephesian situation—few second-person imperatives, no vocative appeals, no call to endurance, only one ταῦτα imperative (2:15; cf. 1 Tim 4:6,11,15; 5:7,21; 6:2,11), and no solemn ἐνώπιον adjurations (cf. 1 Tim 5:21; 6:13; 2 Tim 2:14; 4:1).[115] The instructions have a theoretical air, suggesting more of a defensive preparation than an offensive assault.[116] Titus gives the impression that Paul is writing with the specter of the disastrous impact of the Ephesian antagonists before his mind's eye. Their inroads into the leadership structure there and throughout Asia pointed to the real danger they might pose to the fledgling community at Crete. Unsurprisingly, his first instructions center on getting capable, theologically grounded leaders (1:9–11). However, the softer tone, the more general nature of the instruction and Paul's incorporation of a wider range of theological resources may suggest a more treatise-type approach in hopes of both grounding the fledgling community of believers and preventing the type of situation already operative in Ephesus and Asia more generally. What stridency we find arises from the potential threat and, maybe more so, the challenge posed by the Cretans' cultural heritage (or lack thereof, 1:12).[117]

The *theo*logy from the perspective of soteriology that we found in 1 Timothy runs through the introduction and succeeding theological passages. Right from the beginning, the letter digs into *theo*logy with a view to the threat on the horizon and the needs of fledgling believers in a culture that suffers from a significant moral deficit. Paul begins by identifying himself as "a servant of God." He is most likely drawing on the significance of this title in OT prophetic contexts (LXX 4 Kgs 9:7; Ezek 38:17; Amos 3:7).[118] He places himself in a long line of those chosen by God to proclaim God's message. It implies what is more clearly affirmed when he says that it was "by command of God our Savior" that he was "entrusted" with "his word," the

---

[113] The antagonists disrupt the community with Jewish/law-based "myths" (1 Tim 1:4,7; Titus 1:10,14) and "genealogies" (1 Tim 1:4; Titus 3:9). They manifest a powerless life of empty profession (2 Tim 3:5; Titus 1:16). They are driven by "gain" (1 Tim 6:5–6; Titus 1:11) and overturn households through their influence (1 Tim 5:13; 2 Tim 3:6; Titus 1:11). See Towner, *Goal*, 31, 44; Kelly, *Pastoral*, 237; and Jeremias, *Briefe*, 71.

[114] For the common nature of the heresy threatening both communities, see Towner, *Goal*, 21–45. On the difference of approach between 1 and 2 Timothy and Titus, the latter being more apotropaic in nature, see Fee, *1 and 2 Timothy*, 11, and S. Caulley, "Fighting the Good Fight: The Pastoral Epistles in Canonical-Critical Perspective," *SBL Seminar Papers, 1987* (SBLSP 26; Atlanta: Scholars Press, 1987), 561.

[115] See Fee, *1 and 2 Timothy*, 11.

[116] See Caulley, "Fighting the Good Fight," 561.

[117] On Cretan culture, see B. Winter, *Roman Wives, Roman Widows: The Appearance of New Women and the Pauline Communities* (Grand Rapids: Eerdmans, 2003), 149–50.

[118] G. Sass, "Zur Beteutung von *doulos* bei Paulus," *ZNW* 40 (1941): 31.

gospel (v. 3). The two phrases governed by κατά spell out the nature of the divine commission from God through Christ ("apostle of Jesus Christ"). First, Paul presents his purpose to be the promotion of ongoing belief among those whom God has chosen (cf. Rom 8:33; Col 3:12). Paul's designation of believers as those "chosen by God" also appropriates OT language[119] and, as there, "lays stress on the sense of God's choice of the Church and of its duty to carry His Truth to the world."[120] Indeed, this term implies what is made more explicit in the second phrase, which gives the content and end toward which their faith is to be directed, "the truth that promotes godliness." Paul presents himself as one who has been commissioned by God through Christ to strengthen the faith of God's chosen. Something is accomplished through teaching the truth that leads to a life that appropriately manifests God and his saving purposes in the world.

Echoing 1 Tim 4:8 and 2 Tim 1:11, Paul goes on to specify the core content of that "truth" (yet another concise reference to the "once/now" schema) even as he further anchors his commission in God's saving purposes. The whole endeavor is founded on his eager expectation of realizing (in himself and the rest of the "chosen") the Savior God's promise of "eternal life." This is the unalterable, certain reality since it arises from the premundane (and, thus, free) promise of the God who can do nothing other than stay true to his word.[121] Once again, there are echoes here of what we found in 1 Timothy, where Paul strongly emphasized the unalterable saving purposes of God over against the blasphemous rewriting of those purposes by the Ephesian antagonists. Indeed, God's nature has been decisively confirmed because it has been "manifested." At the same time, in affirming God's truthfulness, Paul makes an abrupt shift grammatically as well as conceptually to more directly connect the message of the schema with the message he proclaims.[122] Just as the promised life is elsewhere the outworking of God's plan made manifest in the Christ-event (2 Tim 1:9–10; cf. 1 Tim 3:16), so the gospel and its proclamation are made manifest at God's own right time (καίροις ἰδίοις). The manifestation of this "word in preaching" is as much a part of God's "command" as the "life" realized by those who believe the message and the decisive Christ-event, which made the offer of life possible in the first place (1 Tim 2:6; cf. 6:15). Paul's proclamation of the gospel is yet another demonstration of God's commitment to his premundane promise of life in Christ. And since Paul was "entrusted by command of God, our Savior" (cf. 1 Tim 1:1,11;

---

[119] See esp. Exod 19:4–6; Ps 104(105):6,43; Isa 43:20–21; 45:4; 65:9,15,22(23); Tob 8:15; Sir 46:1; 47:22; Wis 3:9; 4:15.

[120] Lock, *Pastoral*, 125.

[121] Given the prophetic overtones of "servant" in 1:1, note the importance of the veracity/faithfulness of God in OT prophetic contexts (e.g., Num 23:19; Isa 44:24–28; Ezek 12:24–25; cf. Quinn, *Letter to Titus*, 55.

[122] Grammatically, anacoluthon occurs with the shift of objects between "promised" and "made manifest." Whereas the grammar would suggest that the "promised life" would be the object of both verbs, Paul replaces it with "his word" following "made manifest." Conceptually, from what Paul does elsewhere in this letter, we would expect Christ to be the object of φανηρόω here.

2:7; 2 Tim 1:11), a phrase which speaks of both a broad notion of God's saving plan as well as the particular demand made on Paul within that plan, Paul further situates his ministry within the overarching saving purposes of God. As God's servant, he carries out his prophetic role for the furtherance of God's saving work, the growth of the God's chosen. Fittingly, he carries out his service "based on the hope of eternal life," a sure ground (and if the looming threat is the overrealized eschatology infecting Ephesus, a necessary point of orientation) since the God who cannot lie has freely bound himself to bring it about.

Paul's second piece of extended *theo*logical reflection occurs in Titus 2:11–15. It is introduced as the theological basis for the preceding paraenesis (2:1–10) and as the amplification of the "teaching" variously referred to in vv. 1,5,7,10.[123] He builds on his opening reference to believers as "God's chosen" by drawing on a complex of related OT concepts associated primarily with the Exodus, as mediated through Hellenistic Judaism, to reinforce his paraenetic aims. Paul asserts that "the grace of God" was on display in his saving intervention in Christ (v. 14a; cf. Titus 3:6–7).[124] As such, to assert that it was God's grace that appeared is not an expression calculated to guard God's transcendence but to characterize the intervention according to its essential character.[125] Particularly reminiscent of 1 Tim 2:4–7, this intervention had the whole of humanity in view though, as 3:8 makes clear, only those who believe can enter into its saving benefits. Moreover, it is the nature of this saving intervention in terms of its constitutive effects upon those who enter into it by faith that are crucial for the current context. Those who truly "know God," unlike the antagonists looming on the horizon (1:16), understand that this intervention in Christ has freed them to be a people for his own possession who as such are obligated to promote his purposes in the world, i.e., are "zealous for good works" (v. 14; cf. discussion on 1:1 above). This amounts to an elaboration on the aim of Paul's servanthood from 1:1 and also fits well into the complex of motifs associated with Exodus imagery. A central aim in God's deliverance of the nation of Israel from bondage was that this people would tell forth his praises and serve as the vehicle through whom his absolute sovereignty would be demonstrated before the watching world, an aim taken up repeatedly in the OT. Their redemption by Yahweh meant that God had graciously chosen the

---

123 See Towner, *Goal*, 94, 289n182; Brox, *Pastoralbriefe*, 297; and Lock, *Pastoral*, 143.

124 That 2:11 should be understood in terms of v. 14a is supported by the close parallel in 2 Tim 1:9–10 where there, as here, God's "grace" is what comes to expression at the "ἐπιφάνεια of our savior, Christ Jesus." Additionally, it is the nature of Christ's redemptive work in v. 14 that explains why the helping intervention of God's grace instructs the believer "to deny ungodliness and worldly desires and to live sensibly, righteously and godly in the present age" (v. 12).

125 Against S. Mott ("Greek Ethics and Christian Conversion: The Philonic Background of Titus 2:10–13 and 3:3–7," *NovT* 20 [1978]: 46, see also p. 40), who contends that Titus evidences a dependence upon the "philosophically attuned Judaism represented by Philo." Note also the OT/LXX examples of the near personification of divine attributes in contexts where his intervention in the world are under discussion (Ps 39[40]:11; 56[57]:3; 93[94]:18). Outside of Titus, see Rom 2:4 where it is the χρηστὸν of God that "leads" men to "repentance" and, esp., 1 Cor 1:30 where Christ is the one who "became wisdom ('righteousness,' 'sanctification,' 'redemption') from God."

Jewish nation to be his very own people and committed himself to be their God.[126] Thus OT authors generally refer to (Exod 20:2; Lev 19:36; Num 15:40; Deut 10:21) or recount in detail the acts of Yahweh that constitute the Exodus (Deut 11:1–8; 29:2–9; cf. 6:20–25; Ps 77[78]:5–55) as the basis for God's demand that the people of Israel devote themselves to Yahweh exclusively and keep his commands unreservedly.[127] To mention the fact of God's deliverance of Israel from Egyptian bondage was to remind Israel of the covenant obligations that God has to them and they to God. Paul appropriates this complex of images to locate his paraenesis within God's saving purposes in Christ and, as such, to give it a binding force. The manner of life he urges upon the various segments of God's people is an outgrowth of the saving intervention of God in Christ so that to live otherwise is to misrepresent God and, thus, to hinder his saving purposes in and through his people.

Whereas 2:11–14 focuses on structuring the believers at Crete from within with a view to the impact of their corporate existence on God's saving purposes in the world, Paul's *theo*logical reflection in 3:3–8 looks at the manner of direct engagement warranted by the nature of God's saving acts in Christ.[128] Paul appeals to the pattern of God's saving work alongside an appeal to their sense of empathy (v. 3), to orient their interaction with the broader society and its structures. Similar to 2:11, God's saving intervention is first characterized as a manifestation of his "kindness and love of mankind" and then subsequently explained in terms of the Christ-event (v. 6).[129] At the same time it extends beyond chap. 2 in that Paul goes on to spell out how the benefits of God's mercy in Christ are mediated to those who believe in Christ through the regenerative work of the Spirit.[130] Additionally, Paul describes salvation in terms of "justification," its legal, positional aspect, in a manner akin to Rom 10:10.[131] Thus, to reflect on their entrapped, misanthropic past should not only help them see why

---

[126] See D. Daube, *The Exodus Pattern in the Bible* (London: Faber & Faber, 1963), 12–13.

[127] See G. Delling, "Partizipiale Gottesprädikationen in den Briefen des Neuen Testaments," *ST* 27 (1963): 15–18, and W. C. Kaiser, "The Theology of the OT," in *Introductory Articles* (ed. F. Gaebelein; vol. 1 of *Expositor's Bible Commentary*; Grand Rapids: Zondervan, 1979), 295–96.

[128] As in 1:1–4 and 2:11–14, there is a particular emphasis on the acts of God in 3:1–8. God is the Savior who acts for man's salvation in Christ; he is the subject of each active verb (ἐπιφαίνω, v. 4; σῴζω, v. 5; ἐκχέω, v. 6) except one (ποιέω), and the expressed or unexpressed agent of both passive verb forms (δικαιόω and γίνομαι, v. 7). The aorist tense of the verbs speaks of the present deliverance from the perspective of God's redemptive history (Barrett, *Pastoral*, 144).

[129] Paul appropriates for the gospel a combination of terms used in "Hellenism and Hellenistic Judaism to describe the highest virtues of both deities and human rulers" (Fee, *1 and 2 Timothy*, 203; Cf. Dibelius, *Pastoral*, 143–46). However, polemical aims seem to be absent. Paul primarily does so to characterize God's intervention in Christ in this way to serve his paraenetic aims. The "kindness and love of mankind" form a pointed contrast to the pre-Christian conduct of the Cretans (v. 3) and aptly undergird the universal character of the Christian mission, which surfaces in the "every man" of v. 2 and the generic "men" in v. 8 (cf. 1 Tim 2:4; 4:10; Titus 2:11).

[130] Paul characteristically correlates the notions of justification, Spirit baptism, and inheritance here (cf. 1 Cor 6:10–11; Gal 3:24–29). Note especially the parallels to the 1 Corinthians passage. Both are marked by an absence of the role of faith; both refer to the agency of the Spirit in an event involving baptism; both are Trinitarian; and both depict conversion as a single act with various aspects (cf. J. Dunn, *Baptism in the Holy Spirit* (SBT 15; London: SCM, 1970), 167, and I. H. Marshall, "Faith and Works in the Pastoral Epistles," *SNTU-A* 9 [1984], 207–208).

[131] See Dunn, *Baptism*, 167; Towner, *Goal*, 114; Barrett, *Pastoral*, 143–44.

God's intervention had to be unconditional (i.e., detached from the merits of the objects of his mercy), but it also sets before them the way of the people of God in the world. A resonance with the OT motifs surrounding the Exodus also lies close to the surface here. The command to love the sojourner is empathetically motivated by reminding the Israelites (God's people whose status is totally dependent on God's initiating choice; Deut 7:6–8; 9:4–6) of their own experience as sojourners in Egypt. Moreover, God's love for the sojourner, a love they experienced during their sojourn in Egypt, provides the pattern for redeemed Israel's approach to the sojourner (Deut 10:18–19; cf. 5:15; 15:15; 24:18,22; Exod 22:21; 23:9; and Lev 19:33–34). According to J. McConville, "the whole concept of the behaviour of Israelite man towards his fellow-man is explicated by the analogy of the behaviour of Yahweh towards his people."[132] Similarly, as those whom God has set apart for himself so that they might represent him and his purposes in the world, this necessitates that they manifest the same valuing of people, generosity of spirit, and active good will toward their society and its structures (vv. 1–2,8) that is on display in God's merciful intervention in Christ. Here we have the pattern for mission, whereas in 2:11–14 we might think of Paul instructing the community in order that it might be an appropriate platform from which the mission to the world can be undertaken.

What we meet in Titus is a conception of God very similar to what we have found elsewhere in 1 Timothy in particular, but also in 2 Timothy. God has freely made a premundane determination to redemptively intervene in Christ. Yet here Paul more directly emphasizes that this determination also embraces the very proclamation of his saving acts through his appointed messengers by making the proclamation something that occurs at God's "own right time." Moreover, he more fully intimates how the benefits of God's saving intervention in Christ are mediated to those who believe through the regenerative work of the Spirit. As such, he more fully explicates the Trinitarian nature of salvation alongside his already well-established depiction of God and Christ working in tandem. Their roles are distinct yet bound by the same purpose so that he can depict the work of Christ in terms of God's grace and designate both as Savior. The eschatological "life" promised by God, actualized in the Christ-event, and mediated through the Spirit to those who believe has as its end the constitution of a people to represent and further, in their communal life and in their engagement with the wider world, God's saving purposes in Christ.

---

[132] J. McConville, *Law and Theology in Deuteronomy* (JSOT 33; Sheffield: JSOT, 1984), 37.

Chapter Six

THE MYSTERY OF GODLINESS IS GREAT: CHRISTOLOGY IN THE PASTORAL EPISTLES

DANIEL L. AKIN

He was manifested in the flesh,
justified in the Spirit,
seen by angels,
preached among the Gentiles,
believed on in the world,
taken up in glory. (1 Tim 3:16 HCSB)

The Christology of the epistles of First and Second Timothy and Titus is embedded in occasional letters written by Paul to his faithful associates in the ministry of the gospel. The Christology in these letters emerges against the backdrop of concerns related to false teaching and proper ecclesiology. Once more we discover that there are some benefits in false teaching! However, Christology is not just related to these concerns, as our inductive analysis will reveal. Issues of theology proper, Trinitarianism, soteriology, and eschatology will also interact with the Christology of the Pastorals.

Various methods have been pursued in studying the Christology of these three letters. Each has merit in its own right.[1] For our purposes we will examine the Christology of the Pastorals as follows: (1) we will work through each book individually and inductively, and (2) we will note common themes and emphases in the three letters with summary and concluding observations based upon what we have discovered.

---

[1] In particular one should note G. Fee, *Pauline Christology: An Exegetical-Theological Study* (Peabody: Hendrickson, 2007), 418–47; A. Lau, *Manifest in the Flesh: The Epiphany Christology of the Pastoral Epistles* (Tubingen: Mohr-Siebeck, 1996); and P. Towner, "Christology in the Letters to Timothy and Titus" in R. N. Longenecker, *Contours of Christology in the New Testament* (Grand Rapids: Eerdmans, 2005), 219–44. See Fee, *Pauline Christology*, 419n1, for an extensive listing of specialized studies. He notes more than 12.

Our goal is to allow the Pastorals to speak unhindered by external constraints as much as possible. In other words, if we were to come across these three letters and only these three letters written by a man named Paul, what would we discover concerning his thoughts about Jesus Christ?

It should be noted that this author affirms the Pauline authorship of the Pastorals, though he suspects the hand of Dr. Luke assisted in the composition of the letters. I also believe the chronological order of the letters to be 1 Timothy, Titus, then 2 Timothy. This will not greatly affect our investigation. It will, however, be the order by which we will conduct our study.

THE CHRISTOLOGY OF 1 TIMOTHY

Paul begins 1 Timothy with a threefold reference to Jesus Christ. He identifies himself as "an apostle of Christ Jesus" and notes that "the Lord Jesus Christ [is] our hope" (1:1). He affirms in v. 2 that "grace, mercy, and peace" flow equally from both "God our Father and Jesus Christ our Lord." The Lordship of Jesus Christ appears to be a particularly important theme in this letter as he is so designated in 1:1,2,12; 5:21; and 6:3. That the Lord Jesus Christ is placed on equal status with God the Father as the dispenser of grace, mercy, and peace certainly implies an equality of deity while maintaining a distinction in person. Implications for Trinitarian reflection are not developed since there is no mention of the Spirit.[2]

Following the salutation in 1:1–2, Paul moves to warn Timothy and the Ephesians (1:3) of the dangers of false doctrine (1:3–11). There is nothing of an overt christological nature in these verses, though the connection of "sound doctrine" (1:10) to "the glorious gospel of the blessed God" (1:11) prepares us for significant christological content in the next paragraph (1:12–17). In v. 12 Paul further develops the theme of his apostleship mentioned in 1:1 by pointing out that "Christ Jesus our Lord" (cf. 1:2) enabled him and counted him faithful, putting him in the ministry, that is, the ministry of the glorious gospel "that was entrusted to me" (1:11 HCSB). He notes that "the grace of our Lord was exceedingly abundant, with faith and love which are in Christ Jesus" (1:14).[3] Paul then introduces the first of five faithful sayings in the Pastorals (1:15; 3:1; 4:9; 2 Tim. 2:11, Titus 3:8): "Christ Jesus came into this world to save sinners, of whom I am chief."[4]

This "explosive confession" bears important theological weight. First, Messiah Jesus came. There is a clear implication of our Lord's preexistence. Second, he "came into the world to save sinners." Here Paul fills in the content of the "glorious gospel" in 1:11 (cf. 1 Cor 15:3–4). Third, we observe a gentle wedding of Christ's person and

---

[2] The Holy Spirit is only referenced in 3:16; 4:1.

[3] It cannot be too strongly emphasized that to ascribe such blessings and gifts to any human person would sound nonsensical. Only one who is himself divine can be the exceedingly abundant giver of grace, faith, and love.

[4] The phrase "This is a faithful saying" is unique to the Pastorals.

work in this declaration. Fourth, as the chief of sinners, Paul's salvation was a demonstration of mercy and for the purpose of providing a pattern of how Jesus Christ saves sinners unto everlasting life. It would not be difficult to conclude that only one who is himself eternal can impart eternal or everlasting life. Such a salvation ushers in an outburst of worship in 1:17: "to the King eternal, immortal, invisible, to God who alone is wise, be honor and glory forever and ever. Amen." There is a beautiful harmony that exists within the Godhead in the great redemptive drama of the Bible.

Chapter 2 begins with a strong christological note, again wedding the person and work of Christ but with a different and complementary emphasis. God our Savior[5] desires that we pray for all men because he desires that all people "be saved and come to the knowledge of the truth" (2:3 to 4). This salvation contains a universal invitation but has an exclusive avenue as 2:5–6 make clear. With echoes of the *Shema* (Deut 6:4–6) resounding in the background, Paul develops further aspects of the glorious gospel of Christ Jesus who came into the world to save sinners. The oneness of God dictates the oneness of his plan of salvation. That oneness is powerfully declared in that there is one mediator, one go-between between God and man, "the Man Christ Jesus" (cf. John 14:6; Acts 4:12). Emphases here fall heavily on the humanity of Christ and his identification with sinful man (cf. Heb 2:14–18). Jesus Christ is not an angel or an apparent human. He is truly and genuinely human just as we are, apart from sin (2 Cor 5:21; Heb 4:15). Perhaps a denial of Jesus' real humanity was a component of the unsound doctrines of 1:3–4 and the blasphemies of Hymenaeus and Alexander in 1:18–20. A second emphasis that zeroes in on the work of Christ appears in v. 6: He "gave Himself a ransom for all." Once again Christology and soteriology are wedded (cf. 1:15). "Ransom for all" affirms a universal aspect of the atonement and draws upon Old Testament themes found in Exodus and Isaiah 53. Jesus spoke in very similar terms (Paul's inspiration or source here?!) in Mark 10:45 where he unites the suffering servant of Isaiah 53 to the Son of Man in Daniel 7 and redefines the kind of Messiah he would be. Paul will allude to the theme of redemption once more in the Pastorals in Titus 2:14. Jesus paid a price so that condemned sinners might be saved and set free from bondage and slavery to sin. One should not miss the import of the phrase, "He gave Himself." This is the language of substitution. Of this glorious gospel Paul was appointed a preacher, apostle and teacher (2:7). The Lord who saves is the Lord who appoints (cf. 1:1).

There is little direct or explicit christological content in 2:8–3:13. However, the reality of Jesus Christ's Lordship certainly inspired Paul's instruction on the proper behavior of men (2:8) and women (2:9–15) and the spiritual qualifications of overseers (3:1–7) and deacons (3:8–13).

---

[5] Both God the Father and God the Son are called "Savior" in the Pastorals, often in close connection with one another (Titus 1:3–4; 2:10,13; 3:4,6). God is designated as "Savior" in 1 Tim 1:1; 2:3; 4:10; Titus 1:3; 2:10; 3:4. Jesus is called "Savior" in Titus 1:4; 2:13; 3:6; 2 Tim 1:10. Paul does not use the title of "Savior" for Jesus in 1 Timothy. See Towner, "Christology," 222–23.

First Timothy 3:14–16 appears to encapsulate the purpose of this letter. It is the fulcrum of the epistle in more ways than one. It is captured in the phrase "that you may know how you ought to conduct yourself in the house of God, which is the church of the living God, the pillar and ground of the truth" (3:15). Somewhat surprisingly following this statement, we are introduced to one of the great christological confessions in all of Scripture (3:16). Its rhythmic and poetic nature would lend support to the idea that it was an early Christian hymn, telling in concise and summary fashion the story of Jesus Christ. In six bold and striking statements, Paul depicts the career of Jesus. First, there is an emphatic declaration of the incarnation and another intimation of deity: "He was manifested in the flesh" (cf. John 1:14). Jesus came from another place and existence, making his entrance into our world and revealing himself "in flesh" (ἐν σαρκί). This was a real manifestation of a real man in real flesh (cf. 2:5). Second, "He was justified [or vindicated] in the Spirit." This language would seem to point to his resurrection from the dead (cf. Rom. 1:4; 1 Pet 3:18). Fee says it this way, "through resurrection and exaltation he has now entered the realm of our final eschatological existence, the realm of the Spirit."[6] Third, he was "seen by angels." Resurrected and exalted as "Lord," the angels were privileged to celebrate his victory over (1) sin (1:15) and (2) deceiving spirits and doctrines of demons (4:1). Fourth, he is "proclaimed among the nations" (ESV) and, fifth, he is "believed on in the world." Jesus and his saving and redeeming work provide the content of the glorious gospel that we proclaim and call sinners to believe. This constitutes the mystery of godliness in terms of human responsibility, both for the church (we proclaim it) and humanity (they must believe it). Jesus is the gospel, and it is this One we must proclaim and call the world to believe on that they might receive everlasting life (1:16). Such a response on the part of sinners can rightly be demanded because this Jesus has, sixthly, been "received up in glory," a reference to our Lord's climatic exaltation (cf. Phil 2:9–11).[7] The comments of Towner are especially insightful at this point: "In preaching, the church takes up its role in continuing the revelation of God's plan. Christ's human life, death and resurrection fulfill God's plan to save the nations, and the plan has already begun to achieve universal success. Christology, therefore, leads to missiology."[8]

Chapter 4 constitutes a strong word concerning false teachers (4:1–5) and the call to faithful ministry in the face of this challenge (4:6–16). The only direct reference to Jesus Christ is in 4:6, where we are told we will be "a good minister of Jesus Christ" if we instruct in good doctrine (cf. 4:13).

---

[6] Fee, *Pauline Christology*, 433.

[7] Many students of the Pastorals, perhaps most, see the sixth and final line as a second reference to the Ascension (the first being line 3). However, if the hymn is giving us a broad chronological portrayal of the career of the Christ, then our Lord's ultimate exaltation is the better interpretation of the final line. Such an understanding fits well the natural progression of the prior five lines of the hymn.

[8] Towner, "Christology," 232.

Chapter 5 contains only two references to Christ in the context of proper behavior in the local community of believers. We are to act wisely and appropriately toward older and younger family members in the faith (5:1–2). This especially is to be the case with widows (5:3–16), the younger of whom may betray vows they made to the Lord "when their passions draw them away from Christ" (5:11 ESV). In addition, when it comes to disciplining sinning elders (5:17–20) or other practical matters of the faith (5:22–25), we are charged "before God and the Lord Jesus Christ and the elect angels," to do so "without prejudice, doing nothing with partiality." There is a heavenly court that observes all our activities.

Chapter 6 begins in the same line of argument as the end of chapter 5. Slaves are called upon to honor their masters (6:1–2) as a matter of proper Christian deportment. Paul then moves once more to address the danger of false teachers, noting that they teach "a different doctrine" that "does not agree with the sound or wholesome words of our Lord Jesus Christ [full majestic title] and the teaching that accords with godliness" (6:3 ESV). This train of thought continues through the end of the chapter (v. 21) with a significant christological interlude appearing in 6:13–16. Once again Paul stresses the humanity of Jesus Christ by pointing to the moment in history when he "witnessed the good confession before Pontius Pilate" (6:13). This confession becomes the basis and example for the believer's own good confession (6:12–14). There then appears a new christological element in the four major christological texts in 1 Timothy (e.g., 1:15; 2:3–6; 3:16; 6:13–16), an element that brings Christology and eschatology together. Previously there has been a focus on our Lord's first coming via incarnation. Now Paul introduces the idea of a second epiphany as the basis for his ethical challenge: "that you keep this commandment [maintain a good confession] without spot, blameless until our Lord Jesus Christ's appearing" (ἐπιφανείας). This appearing "He will manifest in His own time" (v. 15). As was the case in 1:15–17, Paul concludes this pericope with a note of doxological praise rooted in "absolute monotheism."[9] For whatever reason Paul senses the need to nail down the real humanity of Jesus within the context of Christian monotheism. Fee is quite helpful in striking a biblical balance at this point: "However we are to understand Paul's understanding of the ontological relationship between God and Christ, Father and Son, he will not let the reality of Christ's genuine deity overrule his basic, absolute monotheism—precisely the issue in any Pauline Christology."[10]

THE CHRISTOLOGY OF TITUS

Titus is a short, three-chapter, forty-six-verse letter to a trusted and courageous associate of Paul's. Some fondly refer to him as Paul's "spiritual hit-man" because of

---

[9] Fee, *Pauline Christology*, 435.
[10] Ibid.

his propensity to send Titus to deal with difficult situations (e.g., Corinth). His assignment on Crete (1:5) is no exception.

This letter is remarkable when it comes to its Christology because of the scarcity of references. There are only four (1:1,4; 2:13–14; 3:6). However, though limited in verbiage, there are very important matters addressed in each.

In his greeting (1:1–4) Paul once more refers to himself as an apostle of Jesus Christ (1:1), something he does in each of the Pastorals. He also calls himself "a slave of God" (HCSB). There is, however, a striking absence here and throughout the remainder of the letter: there is not a single reference to Jesus as "Lord" (κύριος). This is utterly unique as this is the only Pauline epistle not to use this particular title for Jesus. We should not make more of this observation than we ought, but it is certainly a point of interest. Paul concludes his salutation by again noting that he is the blessed recipient of "grace and peace from God the Father and Christ Jesus our Savior." Several christological observations are worth noting.

First, it is usually Paul's habit to call himself a slave or servant (δοῦλος) of Jesus Christ (e.g., Rom 1:1; Gal 1:10; Phil 1:1). In fact, this is the only time in all of his letters that he refers to himself as a slave of God. Fee, however, gets to the heart of what we should make of this when he writes, "The Christological point, of course, is that elsewhere Paul says the same thing about his relationship to Christ. Thus, at the beginning of this letter we find the same kind of *easy interchange* [emphasis mine] between God and Christ that one meets throughout the corpus, only this time it is God the Father assuming the role ordinarily attributed to Christ."[11]

Second, Paul again places on equal standing the Father and the Son ("Christ Jesus our Savior") as the source of "grace and peace." The use of a single preposition "from" (ἀπό) with a compound object "God the Father and Christ Jesus our Savior" only heightens the importance of the statement. Paul, by the way, follows this same pattern in both 1 and 2 Timothy. What we receive from the Father we equally receive from Christ Jesus.

Third, and perhaps most significantly, Christ Jesus is given the title "Savior" (σωτήρ) in v. 4. A number of crucial observations are warranted here. Jesus will also be identified as Savior in 2:13 and 3:6. In addition, the Father is also designated as Savior in 1:3 and 3:4. In other words, in the closest proximity God and Christ Jesus (1:3,4) and God and Jesus Christ (3:4,6) are identified as our Savior. Once more the interchange is made in an unpretentious, matter-of-fact, noncontroversial manner. It is quite normal and natural for Paul to ascribe Saviorhood to God or Jesus. Paul sees

---

[11] Fee, *Pauline Christology*, 438. I. H. Marshall notes, "one effect of the designation is to bring out the parallel with the OT servants of God, which some see as the author's main intention." *The Pastoral Epistles* (ICC; New York: T&T Clark, 1999), 117.

no conflict and he feels no tension. To know Jesus as Savior is to know God as Savior and vice versa.[12]

One does not find a single christological reference in 1:5–2:10. It is noted that a faithful overseer is God's manager or steward (1:7) and that there are those who "profess to know God, but they deny Him by their works" (1:16). Exhortations to various groups within the church (2:1–10) conclude with the charge that we are to "adorn the teaching of God our Savior in everything" (2:10).

Paul then moves to pen one of two great soteriological texts in Titus and, for that matter, in all of Scripture (2:11–14 and 3:4–8). In 2:11–14 Paul begins with a note of "grace," pointing out that it has appeared providing salvation for all people (v. 11). This salvation instructs us "to deny godlessness and worldly lust and to live in a sensible, righteous, and godly way in the present age" (v. 12). We are to live in this realm of God's grace "while we wait for the blessed hope and the appearing of the glory of our great God and Savior, Jesus Christ" (v. 13). "He gave Himself for us to redeem us . . . and to cleanse for Himself a special people" (v. 14).

We again see a close connection between Christology and soteriology. God's grace has appeared, bringing salvation to all. This speaks of a universal provision, not universalism. In the incarnation of the Son of God (v. 11) the grace of God was manifested (ἐπεφάνη). This manifestation has major implications for our sanctification "in the present age" (v. 12). What follows in v. 13 is both startling and highly debatable. Living a life in concert with the grace of God in salvation that previously appeared, we now wait with expectation for a second and future appearing (ἐπιφάνειαν) described by Paul as "the blessed hope and the appearing of the glory of our God and Savior, Jesus Christ." There is much here to note as well as to attempt to unravel.

First, there is an epiphany bracket, or framework, that informs our Christology and unites it to eschatology in the context of soteriology. The One who has appeared in history (v. 11) will appear again in history (v. 13). Second, his future epiphany is described as a blessed hope and the appearing of the glory or a "glorious appearing." This sets it in some contrast to the first epiphany, one of shame, humiliation, and suffering (see v. 14 and the phrase "He gave Himself," a short-hand for the shame and humiliation of the crucifixion). Third, and most controversial in terms of its exact meaning, this second epiphany will be "the appearing of our great God and Savior, Jesus Christ." This particular phrase has been variously understood in one of three

---

[12] Towner, "Christology," 222–23, notes that "'Savior' (*sōtēr*) was already a well-known appellation of Yahweh in the Septuagint, where the exodus was the archetypal salvation event." He also notes, that the title of Savior is applied to Jesus in the later Pauline corpus (Eph 5:23; Phil 3:20; 2 Tim 1:10; Titus 1:4, 2:13, 3:6). He also thinks the use of "'Savior' in the Roman imperial cult for the deified emperor delayed application of the term to Christ. It may finally have been used of Christ (1) because of an increased drawing of meaning from their biblical tradition by believers in Christ and (2) in response to the escalating influence of the stories, symbols, and expectations of the imperial religion on the church and culture. Given this environment of Old Testament rootage and the use of 'Savior' language for Hellenistic kings, heroes, and gods, we should not imagine that Christians simply co-opted such politically loaded language as a matter of convenience. Rather, the title seems to have been chosen deliberately to make a point."

different ways, with outstanding New Testament scholars lining up behind each option: (1) one person is in view, Jesus Christ, and we have a clear and overt affirmation of his deity; (2) two persons are in view, and the text should be understood as a reference to the great God and our Savior Jesus Christ; (3) two persons are in view, and the sense is "the glory of God is manifested in Jesus Christ."

This is one of those texts where dogmatic certainty is clearly out of bounds. Massive amounts of ink have been spilt defending each of these perspectives.[13] However, it seems option 1 as noted above is the better understanding of the text and that along with at least Rom 9:5, and probably more, it is a direct declaration of the deity of Jesus Christ. It is the most natural reading of the text. It is also the most difficult theologically. In other words, if Paul did not want to ascribe divinity to Jesus, he easily could have written the verse differently. Knight summarizes well the compelling arguments for this perspective:

> In its favor is, first, that the "appearance" in the NT always refers to one person, Christ, not two. Second, the hope of the Christian elsewhere in Paul is centered in Christ and his return. Third, the joining of two nouns by καί with one article, as here, usually designates one thing or person (see BDF §276.3; Robertson, *Grammar,* 786; idem, "Greek Article"). Fourth, the words "God and Savior" (θεοῦ καί σωτῆρος) are found together as a title designating one person in the Greek usage of the period (see the literature cited in MHT I, 84; Robertson, *Grammar,* 786; BAGD s.v. σωτῆρ). Fifth, the following verse, v. 14, carries on the thought of this verse by referring back to it with the words ὅς ἔδωκεν ἑαυτόν, as if only one person, Christ, were in view (so Lock).[14]

Knight ends his analysis by saying:

> This verse concludes with the name Ἰησοῦ Χριστοῦ in apposition to the preceding designation, "our great God and Savior," thereby indicating precisely who it is of whom Paul has been writing. This is one of the infrequent, but important, occasions where Jesus is specifically designated θεός, "God." The others are arguably Rom. 9:5; Jn. 1:1; 1:18 (according to some manuscripts); 20:28; Heb. 1:8ff.; 2 Pet 1:1; and possibly 1 Jn. 5:20. The use of θεός makes explicit what is implicit elsewhere in the NT, where Jesus is said to have the attributes of God, to do the work of God, and to receive the worship and allegiance due only to God. These references are infrequent, probably because the NT usually designates the Father as "God" and Jesus as "Lord" (cf., e.g., the Trinitarian blessing in 2 Cor. 13:14 and Paul's argument for monotheism in

13 See, e.g., Fee, *Pauline Christology,* 440–48; M. Harris, *Jesus as God: The New Testament Use of Theos in Reference to Jesus* (Grand Rapids: Baker, 1992), 173–85; P. Towner, *The Letters To Timothy and Titus* (NICNT Grand Rapids: Eerdmans, 2006), 750–58; and G. Knight, *The Pastoral Epistles* (Grand Rapids: Eerdmans, 1992), 321–26. Each is fair and thorough in examining the issue, identifying the various teams (!), and laying out the playing field fairly and with balance.
14 Knight, *Pastoral Epistles,* 323.

1 Cor. 8:4–6, where he writes of "one God, the Father," and "one Lord, Jesus Christ" [v. 6].[15]

Chapter 3 begins by explaining further what it means "to live in a sensible, righteous and godly way in the present age" (2:12), to live as those who have been redeemed (cf. 1 Tim 2:6) "from all lawlessness . . . eager to do good works." It means being "submissive to rulers and authorities" (3:1), avoiding slander and fighting, being kind and gentle to all people (3:2). After all, if Jesus has shown kindness to all in bringing salvation (2:11), how can we who know him as Savior do less? Furthermore, before trusting Christ as Savior, "we too were once foolish, disobedient, deceived, captives of various passions and pleasures, living in malice and envy, hateful, detesting one another" (3:3). However, that all changed "when the goodness and love for man appeared from God our Savior" (3:4). It should be noted that this is the third of three "appearings" in Titus: (1) the grace of God (2:11), (2) the glory of God (2:13), (3) the goodness of God (3:4). This goodness has its source in God our Savior (fifth of its six uses in Titus). It has mankind as its object. Titus 3:5 is perhaps the most important verse in the Bible on the doctrine of regeneration,[16] the new birth experienced by those who repent of their sin and put their trust completely and exclusively in Jesus Christ. Paul begins by telling us how regeneration did not happen: "Not by works of righteousness that we had done, but according to mercy He saved us." How? "By the washing of regeneration and renewing of the Holy Spirit." Regeneration consists

---

[15] Ibid., 326. Interestingly Towner makes a spirited defense for Titus 2:13 as a single reference to Jesus Christ and his deity in "Christology in the Letters to Timothy and Titus," 236–37, but backs away from that view in his commentary (*The Letters to Timothy and Titus*, 750–58), arguing instead for the third perspective listed above, that Jesus Christ is best identified with "the glory of God." His earlier argument, which complements that of Knight, and which I find more compelling is as follows: "But does 2:13 refer to the epiphany of one person ('of our great God and Savior, Jesus Christ') or two ('of our great God and of our savior Jesus Christ')? The rarity of divine appellations for Christ in the New Testament perhaps favors the latter. But Paul may have committed himself to the former in Rom 9:5 (cf. 2 Pet 1:1), and Col 1:19 pursues a similar line. And a number of other factors favor a single christological reference: (1) 'God and Savior' was a widely used title that generally referred to a single deity; (2) a single definite article governs the two titles 'God and Savior'; (3) 'epiphany' is used only of Christ in these letters; and (4) a future coming of the Father in association with the End is unprecedented. It seems most reasonable, therefore, that the reference here is to the future 'epiphany' of 'our God and Savior, Jesus Christ.'

The theme of Christ's sharing of the status of Savior in 1:3–4, which is present also in the pairing of 2:10 and 13, invites this extraordinary climax. But this sharing between God and Jesus Christ, together with the divine transfer of their activities, reaches critical mass here in 2:11–14. We are familiar with the statement that describes the Savior as the one 'who gave himself for us' (cf. 1 Tim 2:6; Gal 1:4; Eph 5:2). But the intertextual echoes in the purpose statements of 2:14—which recall statements in Exod 19:5; Deut 7:6; 14:2; and Ezek 37:23—suggest that Christ is here understood to have done the work of Yahweh in producing a unique 'people for his own possession.' And this christological development, which urges a refinement of monotheism, is easily accommodated in the epiphany concept, which is used of Christ as the appearance of God in both human history and the future *parousia* (cf. Lau, *Manifest in Flesh*).

Christology in 2:11–14, therefore, sharply challenges the Cretan lie and its corollary tale of Zeus's rise from humanity to deity. Human salvation is equated with the epiphany of Jesus Christ, who was already before his manifestation God and Savior. True civilized culture emerges from Christ's first historical appearance (vv. 11–12) and will be completed in the future epiphany of the divine Savior (vv. 13–14)." For a more recent yet similar argument, see R. M. Bowman Jr., "Jesus Christ, God Manifest: Titus 2:13 Revisited," *JETS* 51 (December 2008): 733–52.

[16] Of course, Jesus and his encounter with Nicodemus in John 3 is also crucial to our understanding of this doctrine.

negatively of a cleansing and positively of a renewing, both brought about by the Holy Spirit. This is the first and only mention of the Holy Spirit in Titus. Regeneration washes us, makes us clean through the new birth. The imagery of washing has nothing to do with baptism, for it is the Holy Spirit who is washing us, not externally but internally. The picture looks back to Ezek 36:25–27, where the prophet writes, "Then I will sprinkle clean water on you, and you shall be clean; I will cleanse you from all your filthiness and from all your idols. I will give you a new heart and put a new Spirit within you; I will take the heart of stone out of your flesh and give you a heart of flesh. I will put My Spirit within you and cause you to walk in My statutes, and you will keep My judgments and do them" (NKJV). It complements Eph 5:26, which speaks of our being cleansed by the washing of water by the Word.

God is generous when he gives us his Spirit. He has poured him out on us "abundantly (generously, richly) through Jesus Christ our Savior" (cf. 3:4). Paul is probably looking back to Pentecost and the coming of the Spirit in Acts 2. However, what God did then for the believers gathered in the Upper Room he does for every believer in regeneration. His Spirit comes to be *with* them and *in* them in abundance. Justified, we are declared righteous. By virtue of the imputed righteousness of Christ we stand before God just as if we had never sinned and just as if we had always obeyed God perfectly. We are not made justified. We are declared justified. How did we receive this legal acquittal, this forensic standing of righteousness before God? Paul now adds a fourth motive as to why our great God saved us. It was his *kindness* that moved him to save us (v. 4). It was his *love* that moved him to save us (v. 4). It was his *mercy* that moved him to save us (v. 5). Now it is his *grace* that moved him to save us (v. 7). Having saved us, regenerated us, and justified us, he now comforts us with a word about our future. We are heirs with the hope of eternal life. As a united work of our Triune God, the Father (vv. 4–5), the Son (v. 6), and the Holy Spirit (v. 5), our inheritance is a signed, sealed, and settled issue. Once more Paul has wed soteriology to Christology to eschatology, this time in the context of Trinitarianism. In particular, Jesus made possible our regeneration through the Spirit, he is our justification, and he is the ground of our hope of eternal life, all being the result of the kindness and love of God our Savior for all men. Such a great salvation is more than enough motivation to avoid dissension (3:9–11) and to maintain good works (3:12–15).

THE CHRISTOLOGY OF 2 TIMOTHY

Second Timothy is Paul's benedictory address, his final letter. He writes while imprisoned (1:16), but circumstances are significantly different than when he penned what are traditionally called the "prison epistles" of Ephesians, Philippians, Colossians, and Philemon. Those letters were written while he was under house arrest with limited freedom and access (Acts 28:30–31; Eph 3:1; 6:21–24; Phil 1:7,12–13;

4:21–23; Col 4:3,7–18; Phlm 1,9,23–25). Second Timothy is completely different. Paul is now all alone except for Luke (4:11), and he appears to see his execution as imminent (4:6–8). Tradition says he was incarcerated in the Mamertine Prison, though we cannot be certain this is the case.[17] As Paul's final words to a "true" (1 Tim 1:2) and "beloved son" (2 Tim 1:2), the words of this letter are grave and important. As an older man at the end of his life, Paul is reflective and intimate in the details he shares. He hurts concerning the defection of those who once labored for the gospel at his side (1:15,17–18; 4:10,11,16), but he also rejoices in the faithfulness and usefulness of others (1:5,16; 4:10–13,19–21).

Paul begins by noting once more that he is "an apostle of Jesus Christ" and this "by God's will; for the promise of life in Christ Jesus" (1:1 HCSB). Paul has been sent on assignment to represent Jesus the Christ in accordance with the will of God with the promise of life (eternal life), which is found only in Christ Jesus (note the double use of Jesus Christ/Christ Jesus in v. 1). For a third time Paul rejoices in the fact that Christian graces (here "grace, mercy, and peace" as in 1 Tim 1:2; Titus 1:4 mentions only "grace and peace") flow equally "from (ἀπό) God the Father and Christ Jesus our Lord."[18] Equality with the Father, Lordship, and the source of life are all ascribed to Jesus in the greeting.

Paul proceeds to a note of thanksgiving for Timothy's faith and heritage (1:3–6), urging him "to keep ablaze the gift of God" in him, serving God with courage, strength, love, and sound judgment (1:7). He challenges him not to be ashamed of the Lord or himself (Paul) but rather to share in suffering for the gospel (1:8). Paul then introduces the first major christological text in the epistle, emphasizing the fact that through the gospel God "has saved us and called us with a holy calling" and that he has done so "according to His own purpose and grace," all of which was "given to us in Christ Jesus before time began" (1:9). That which began in eternity past "has now been made evident through the appearing of our Savior Christ Jesus, who has abolished death and has brought life (cf. 1:1) and immortality to light through the gospel" (1:10). For all of this Paul preaches and suffers, but with no shame, for he knows the One in whom he has believed and is confident of his ability to keep safe all that Paul has committed to him until "that Day," the day of eschatological consummation at the return of Christ (1:11–12). A number of observations can be gleaned from this text.

First, there is an affirmation of Christ's preexistence in 1:9. God's gospel of salvation already existed, having been given to Christ Jesus before time ever began.

---

[17] J. Polhill, *Paul & His Letters* (Nashville: B&H Academic, 1999), 427. Polhill is doubtful concerning the traditional place of imprisonment. On the Mamertine Prison, see M. Webb, *The Churches and Catacombs of Early Christian Rome: A Comprehensive Guide* (Sussex Academic Press, 2002).

[18] Fee, *Pauline Christology*, 449, notes that Christ is mentioned by name or title 29 times in this epistle. It is more than twice the number of times that God is referenced.

Second, this great salvation reached a historic moment at the appearing of our Savior Jesus Christ. The incarnation, clearly in view here, was not the beginning of Messiah's existence. The incarnation was his manifestation in space and time, his humble entrance into the flow of history.

Third, one facet of the gospel's power to save is that our Savior has abolished death on the one hand and brought life and immortality on the other. By his appearing, Jesus Christ brought life and immortality to light through the gospel even though it had been given to him before time began. Though lacking an overt reference, it seems clear that Paul is saying that the means whereby Jesus Christ abolished death and brought eternal life is his bodily resurrection. The fact that he rose and remains alive is the ground or basis for his giving us the gift of life eternal.

Fourth, once more soteriology (emerging out of Christology) is wed to eschatology. The life made possible by the appearing of the Savior is immortal life, eternal life. Further, it is a life entrusted to Christ, who is able to guard it until the eschatological day of salvation's completion. Our future is secure and made possible by the work of Jesus Christ promised before time began but made manifest in history in incarnation and resurrection. The Christology here is high and precise.

Paul concludes chap. 1 (1:13–18) by charging Timothy to "hold on to the pattern of sound teaching," the kind of teaching he has just received in 1:8–12 as well as the teaching he had heard verbally from Paul. Such teaching transpired in the environment of "faith and love that are in Christ Jesus." Then, at the end of the chapter, in v. 18, Paul writes a most remarkable statement. He asks "the Lord" (κύριος), most certainly a reference to Jesus, to grant to Onesiphorous "mercy from the Lord (κύριος) on that day," the day of eschatological judgment. What is remarkable is that the latter use of Lord (κύριος) is almost certainly a reference to God the Father. Thus in the same verse Paul applies the title of "Lord" both to Jesus and to the Father.

Chapter 2 begins with a call to be strong in the realm of grace that is found in Christ Jesus. Paul summons Timothy to do the work of a teacher (2:1–2), soldier (2:3–4), athlete (2:5), and farmer (2:6–7). Of interest is the description of the believer as a soldier of Jesus Christ (v. 4). He points out that it is Christ who enlisted us as his soldier. Jesus is now our commander-in-chief, and our single ambition is to "please Him." Paul says think on these things, "For the Lord (κύριος) will give you understanding in everything." Paul may be referencing the LXX version of Prov 2:6. Though apparently insignificant on the surface, Fee points out, "It does reflect a common Pauline feature: where the apostle cites, alludes to, or echoes an OT κύριος = Yahweh text, the 'Lord' for him is Jesus Christ. Thus we have yet another instance in the corpus where a divine action attributed to God in the OT has for Paul now become the prerogative of Christ as well."[19] Other texts that reflect this pattern include 2:19,22,24; 4:14,16–18.

[19] Fee, *Pauline Christology*, 455.

Building on this fourfold calling, Paul moves into the second important christological text in 2:8–13. Paul highlights two particular truths that draw attention to our Lord's earthly existence: (1) He is risen from the dead, and (2) He descended from David. This is according to what Paul calls "my gospel" (2:8). Again the insights of Fee are helpful:

> Here especially the Christological concerns that dominated 1 Timothy—the reality of Christ's incarnation and thus of his earthly life—are spelled out in striking detail. This emphasis begins with the single instance in this letter of the reversed order of the combined name: "Remember *Jesus Christ*," which here puts emphasis on Jesus' earthly life, as the two qualifiers that follow make clear. In keeping with the emphasis in the preceding narrative, Paul mentions Jesus' resurrection as the matter of first importance; but by referring to his Davidic descent as well, Paul also puts emphasis on Jesus' being the Jewish Messiah.[20]

Paul says it is for this gospel that he suffers as an evildoer (2:9) and endures for the elect "that they, may obtain salvation, which is in Christ Jesus, with eternal glory" (2:10). Eschatological hope is again a motivation for faithfulness and perseverance. Indeed in the fifth and final "trustworthy saying" in the Pauline corpus (2:11–13), Paul develops the theme of endurance with a word of encouragement and a word of warning: "If we have died with Him [1:10], we will also live with Him [2:8]; if we endure [2:10], we will also reign with Him [2:10]; if we deny Him [1:15; 2:16–18; 3:1–9], He will also deny us [3:9], if we are faithless [4:3,9,14], He remains faithful [4:17], for He cannot deny Himself [4:18]." This text draws on individual themes found throughout the book as noted after each phrase, and yet the emphasis falls not so much on the believer's endurance as on the faithfulness of Jesus Christ. As God is faithful, he is faithful, for he is the Lord!

Chapter 2 concludes with a contrasting of faithful and unfaithful workers in 2:14–26, preparing the way for Paul's warning of the apostasy that will characterize the last days (3:1–9). A comparative analysis can provide clarity and perspective on this extended section that contains only scattered christological references. Each is noted by an (*) in the following chart.

---

[20] Ibid., 453.

The Faithful Worker	The Unfaithful Worker
Recalls sound teaching (2:1–2,14); is a diligent worker approved by God who rightly divides the word of truth (2:15).	Fights over unprofitable words that ruin the hearers (2:14).
*Affirms God's solid foundation (Isa 28:16); is confident that "*The Lord* knows who are His" (Num 16:5); "names the *name of the Lord*" (Isa 26:13); turns away from unrighteousness (2:19).	Engages in irreverent, empty speech that produces godlessness and spreads like gangrene (2:16–17).
*Purifies himself for usefulness to the *Master* (2:20–21).	*Deviates from the truth, denies the [future bodily] *resurrection* and ruins the faith of those who follow their false teaching (2:17–18).
Flees from youthful passions and pursues righteousness from a pure heart (2:22); is gentle, able to teach and patient, desiring that God will grant repentance to those captured by the devil (2:24–26).	Gets involved in foolish and ignorant disputes that breed quarrels (2:23). Needs repentance (2:25). Foolish in his thinking and trapped by the devil to do his will (2:26).
*Sees himself as the *Lord's slave* or servant (a title given to Moses, the servant of Yahweh, 2:24).	Precursor to the gross evil and corruption of the last days (3:1–9).

Summarizing this section, we see Paul applying Old Testament texts about Yahweh to Jesus. He is now the Lord and Master, and we are his servants or slaves. Paul could only make such declarations about one who is himself God. We could scarcely imagine him calling us to give such allegiance and devotion to any human person, no matter their status or accomplishments. Only one who is God can command and expect such unreserved commitment. Subtly, though obviously once we dive into the text, a high Christology is present once again.

Second Timothy 3:10–4:5 hangs together well as a unit. The focus is twofold: (1) the man of God and (2) the Word of God. In terms of Christology, Paul reminds Timothy that the Lord rescued him from various persecutions in the ministry of the gospel (3:11), but that he must not forget that "all those who want to live a godly life in Christ Jesus will be persecuted" (3:12). As this was our Lord's experience, we should expect nothing different.

He reminds Timothy that it is "the Holy Scriptures which are able to make you wise for salvation," a salvation that is "through faith which is in Christ Jesus" (3:15 NKJV). These scriptures are "God-breathed" (3:16) and "profitable for teaching, for rebuking, for correcting, for training in righteousness so that the man of God may be complete, equipped for every good work" (3:16–17 HCSB). Such a sacred text and its faithful proclamation constitute a sacred assignment and receive a sacred charge, a charge given "before God and Christ Jesus, who is going to judge the living and the dead, by His appearing and His kingdom" (4:1). Here the prerogatives of deity are clearly and plainly ascribed to Jesus. As God judges the saved and lost, so Jesus judges as well. As we anticipate the coming kingdom of God, we are informed that this kingdom is also Christ's kingdom as well. In the period prior to his appearing and kingdom, we "preach the word" (4:2 NKJV) and "do the work of an evangelist" (4:5), an evangelist of King Jesus, Israel's Messiah, who will come again, judge the world, and establish his kingdom for all to see.

Paul concludes his final letter (4:6–22) with some of the most tender and heartbreaking words in all of Scripture. From a human perspective, death is imminent (4:7) and only Luke is with him (4:11). Yet he is confident that "in the future, there is reserved for me the crown of righteousness, which the Lord, the righteous Judge [4:1], will give me on that day, and not only to me, but to all who have loved His appearing" (4:8 HCSB). Once more the divine prerogative of eschatological judge is given to Jesus. Furthermore, though no one stood with him at his first defense (4:16), the Lord did, and "strengthened me" (4:17). In fact Paul is confident that "The Lord will rescue me from every evil work and will bring me safely into His heavenly kingdom." To such confident expectation there can only be one response: "To Him be the glory forever and ever! Amen" (4:18). Elsewhere Paul said it like this, "For me, living is Christ and dying is gain" (Phil 1:21). Thus he can conclude his last letter with these final words, "The Lord be with your spirit. Grace be with you!" (4:22). The book closes on a note of faith and confidence in the One Paul once vigorously opposed, but now knows as Lord, the Lord who will be with him when all others forsake him, the Lord who will safely bring him into the heavenly kingdom, the Lord that Paul, in easy and comfortable terms, acknowledges as his God in title, person, and work.

SUMMARY OBSERVATIONS

Our inductive analysis of the Pastorals has yielded much christological fruit. A high Christology has emerged with remarkable simplicity within the natural ebb and flow of the books. To say it another way, what we discover in terms of Christology is the normal and natural air that Paul and the first-century church breathed. The following highlights our investigation:

(1) Paul was comfortable in ascribing divine attributes, titles, and prerogatives to Jesus. He is the Lord (κύριος = Yahweh) and he is God (Titus 2:13). He is the object of doxology (worship) and prayer (2 Tim 1:16,18; 4:22). He is the heavenly King (1 Tim 3:16) and eschatological Judge (2 Tim 2:12; 4:1,8,18). He is the source of life (2 Tim 1:1) and the One who with the Father equally bestows the graces of the Christian faith on needy believers (1 Tim 1:2; 2 Tim 1:2; Titus 1:4).

(2) The divine nature of Christ is comfortably set alongside his true and genuine humanity. He is "the man Christ Jesus" (1 Tim 2:5) who was "manifested in the flesh" (1 Tim 3:16). He was of the seed of David (2 Tim 2:8) "who gave a good confession before Pontius Pilate" (1 Tim 6:13).

(3) As to his work, he is the Savior (see footnote 5) who saves (1 Tim 1:15; 2 Tim 1:9), mediates (1 Tim 2:5), ransoms (1 Tim 2:6), keeps and delivers (2 Tim 1:12; 4:17–18), redeems (Titus 2:14), purifies (Titus 2:14), justifies (Titus 3:7), and gives eternal life (Titus 3:7).[21]

(4) In the context of eschatology, he has come (2 Tim 1:10; Titus 2:11; 3:4) and he will come again (1 Tim 6:14; 2 Tim 4:1,8; Titus 2:13). In other words, there is a twofold or two-stage-epiphany Christology in the Pastorals. Towner, in this context says, "I prefer to regard the epiphany/Savior framework of the Pastorals as a christological feature that links these three letters loosely into a distinctive cluster."[22]

(5) As the risen, ascended, and coming-again Lord, the Lordship of Jesus Christ undergirds and permeates the entire Pastoral corpus. The extended sections dealing with practical church matters and personal ethics have the shadow of Christ's Lordship cast over them. Because Christ Jesus is Lord, we should trust him and obey him, serve him and work for him (e.g., Titus 2:11–14). We have a divine Savior who, though preexistent, became incarnate on our behalf. He is the seed of David (Messiah) long anticipated and now revealed. As the exalted and coming-again Lord, he has the right to demand our worship, prayers, and obedience. He stands by us and strengthens us in the moments of greatest trial and difficulty (2 Tim 4:17). Therefore "Let everyone who names the name of Christ depart from iniquity . . . but pursue righteousness, faith, love, peace with those who call on the Lord out of a pure heart" (2 Tim 2:19,22 NKJV).

21 For a concise and helpful summary on salvation, see W. Mounce, *Pastoral Epistles* (WBC; Nashville: Nelson, 2000), cxxxii–cxxxv.

22 Towner, "Christology," 244; see also pp. 223–26. Towner further notes, "Recent scholars have spoken of an 'epiphany Christology' in the Pastoral Epistles, though there is wide variation among their interpretations" (223). His summation: "(1) God's grace *has appeared* in the epiphany of his Son; (2) it is *being revealed* in and through the church's proclamation of the gospel; and (3) it *will be revealed* finally and ultimately in the future epiphany of the Lord" (225). Marshall also has an excursus on "Christology and the concept of epiphany" (287–96).

Chapter Seven

THE FUNCTION OF SALVATION IN THE LETTERS TO TIMOTHY AND TITUS

GEORGE M. WIELAND

The language and ideas of salvation are pervasive in the Pastoral Epistles. Particularly notable is the high incidence of salvation terms, namely, "save" (σῴζω), "Savior" (σωτήρ), "salvation" (σωτηρία), and its related adverb, "soterially"/"bringing salvation" (σωτήριος). The material commended as a "faithful word" (πιστὸς ὁ λόγος), another distinctive of these letters, often has salvation as its theme.[1] This evident interest in salvation has been interpreted in widely varying ways. Some find in these letters numerous elements of a fully Pauline soteriology,[2] whereas others discover indications of a departure from Paul's gospel. M. Dibelius and H. Conzelman describe a shrinking of the expectation of the parousia, leading to a reinterpretation of salvation as realized in the present age in a peaceful life of "good citizenship" (*christliche Bürgerlichkeit*).[3] J. Roloff discerns a lessening of eschatological urgency and charismatic vitality, giving way to a more subdued training in the way of salvation within

---

[1] See I. H. Marshall, "'Sometimes Only Orthodox'—Is There More to the Pastoral Epistles?" *Epworth Review* 20 (1993): 12–24; F. Young, *The Theology of the Pastoral Letters* (Cambridge: Cambridge University Press, 1994), 55; C. Spicq, *Les Épîtres Pastorales* (2 vols.; 4th ed.; Paris: Gabalda, 1966), 257. On the "faithful words," see R. A. Campbell, "Identifying the Faithful Sayings in the PE," *JSNT* 54 (1994): 73–86. There have been few studies of salvation as a theme in the PE, but see A. Klöpper, "Zur Soteriologie der Pastoralbriefe (Tit. 3:4–7; 2 Tim 1:9–11; Tit. 2:11–14)." *ZWT* 47 (1904): 57–88; P. H. Towner, *The Goal of Our Instruction: The Structure of Theology and Ethics in the Pastoral Epistles* (JSNTSup 34; Sheffield: Sheffield Academic Press, 1989), 75–119; J. D. Quinn, "Salvation in the PE," in *The Letter to Titus* (New York: Doubleday, 1990), 304–15; I. H. Marshall, "Salvation in the Pastoral Epistles," in *Frühes Christentum* (ed. H. Lichtenberger; vol. 3 of *Geschichte-Tradition-Reflexion*, ed. H. Cancik, H. Lichtenberger, and P. Schäfer; Tübingen: J. C. B. Mohr, 1996), 449–69; J. Sumney, "'God Our Savior': The Theology of 1 Timothy," *Lexington Theological Quarterly* 33 (1998): 151–61; and G. M. Wieland, *The Significance of Salvation: A Study of Salvation Language in the Pastoral Epistles* (Milton Keynes: Paternoster, 2006).

[2] G. D. Fee, *1 and 2 Timothy, Titus* (NIBC 13; Peabody, Mass.: Hendrickson, 1988), 15–17; cf. Marshall, "Salvation in the Pastoral Epistles," 467.

[3] M. Dibelius and H. Conzelmann, *A Commentary on the Pastoral Epistles* (trans. P. Buttolph and A. Yarbo; Hermeneia; Philadelphia: Fortress, 1972), 9–10.

the instruction and worship of the church.[4] The role of Paul himself has been highlighted as the normative transmitter of the teaching that guaranteed salvation.[5] For K. Läger, the "Paulology" in the PE eclipses even their Christology.[6]

Others look beyond the Pauline tradition, tracing the soteriological ideas in the PE to the wider Hellenistic environment. S. C. Mott has described affinities between the PE and Greek ideals of ethical deliverance, mediated through Hellenistic Judaism.[7] V. Hasler finds the key to the soteriology of the PE in a non-Pauline revelation schema drawn from Greek religion with ideas of a benevolent deity whose will to save is manifested in an epiphany.[8] L. R. Donelson attributes to a pseudonymous author the construction of a quite novel salvation schema designed to concentrate power in the hands of a leadership group,[9] achieved by the use of elaborate rhetorical strategies to persuade readers that salvation is available only through the cultivation of certain virtues, which salvation is in turn dependent on baptism by the hand of particular leaders and submission to the teaching of those leaders.[10]

This extreme diversity of readings is due in part to a high degree of selectivity in the discussion of the evidence. At one end of the spectrum we find H. Merkel championing what he understands to be a Pauline doctrine of justification by faith, but at the cost of dismissing inconvenient evidence (1 Tim 2:15; 4:16) as un-Pauline,[11] and at the other, Dibelius and Conzelmann devaluing as part of a "formulaic entity" the note of future hope in Titus 3:7 that is in tension with their "Christian citizenship" interpretation.[12] Donelson simply passes over without comment the distinctly Pauline affirmations about God saving "not by works of righteousness that we had done, but according to His mercy" and people being "justified by His grace" (Titus 3:5,7), although they appear at the heart of what he takes to be the key text for his system, Titus 3:4–7.[13] This is remarkable given his recognition of logical coherence in the argument of the PE.[14] An adequate explanation of salvation in these letters must

---

[4] J. Roloff, *Der erste Brief an Timotheus* (EKKNT 15; Zurich: Benziger, 1988). Spicq, who regards the PE as authentically Pauline, understands the church to be a "saving institution" within which salvation is available (*Les Épîtres Pastorales*, 257–64).

[5] See M. Wolter, *Die Pastoralbriefe als Paulustradition* (FRLANT 146; Göttingen: Vandenhoeck & Ruprecht, 1988), 269–70.

[6] K. Läger, *Die Christologie der Pastoralbriefe* (HTS 12; Münster: Lit, 1996), 177.

[7] S. C. Mott, "Greek Ethics and Christian Conversion: The Philonic Background of Titus 2:10–14 and 3:3–7," *NovT* 20 (1978): 22–48; cf. Quinn, *Titus*, 315.

[8] V. Hasler, *Die Briefe an Timotheus und Titus (Pastoralbriefe)* (ZBKNT 12; Zürich: Theologischer, 1978), 8–9.

[9] L. R. Donelson, *Pseudepigraphy and Ethical Argument in the Pastoral Epistles* (HUT 22; Tübingen: J. C. B. Mohr, 1986).

[10] Ibid., 153.

[11] H. Merkel, *Die Pastoralbriefe* (NTD 9.1; Göttingen: Vandenhoeck & Ruprecht, 1991), 15, 40.

[12] Dibelius-Conzelmann, *Pastoral Epistles*, 150.

[13] Donelson, *Pseudepigraphy*, 138–39, 143.

[14] On this coherence, see also B. Fiore, *The Function of Personal Example in the Socratic and Pastoral Epistles* (AnBib 105; Rome: Biblical Institute, 1986); Towner, *Goal*, who shows the integration of theological and ethical material; and R. Van Neste, *Cohesion and Structure in the Pastoral Epistles* (JSNTSup 280; London: T&T Clark, 2004) who demonstrates logical cohesion in each of the three PE separately. On treating the three as discrete letters rather than one corpus, see W.

take into account all the relevant material and understand it in terms of each letter's purpose.

Such a task would be too ambitious for this essay, but a start may be made by considering briefly each of the occurrences of the explicit salvation language (σῴζω, etc.) in each of the PE. Since these are letters of guidance and encouragement to colleagues involved in ministry and mission, we may ask how the references to salvation serve the letters' paraenetic goals. This approach will help to bring into view the conceptual framework within which the paraenesis would be effective. It also takes seriously the differing occasions of the three letters and will allow distinctive emphases appropriate to each set of circumstances to emerge.[15]

1 TIMOTHY

This letter's stated concern is the activity of certain teachers within the community (1 Tim 1:3–11). They are characterized by a fascination with the esoteric, including speculative interpretations of the OT, and ascetic demands (e.g., 1 Tim 1:6–10; 4:1–4; 6:20–21).[16]

1:1

> *Paul, an apostle of Christ Jesus according to the command of God our Savior and of Christ Jesus, our hope.*

Salvation appears in this opening sentence of 1 Timothy in the ascription of the title "Savior" (σωτήρ) to God. "Father" is the first mentioned predicate of God in every NT letter of Paul apart from here and Titus 1:1–3, perhaps signaling a particular interest in these letters in God's saving function. The pairing of "God our Savior" with "Christ Jesus, our hope" (ἐλπίς) is interesting. The only biblical precedent for combining the predicates "Savior" and "hope" is Ps 64:6 LXX (Ps 65:5 MT), where the God who is "our Savior" is also "the hope of all the ends of the earth and of the farthest seas" (NIV). It would be appropriate in a missionary letter to pick up this universalizing impulse, and indeed to focus it christologically. In 1 Timothy Christian ministers (1 Tim 4:8–10), widows (1 Tim 5:5), and the rich (1 Tim 6:17) are all urged to put their hope in God, relying on him for both the present life and the life to come. Both spheres fall within the scope of God's saving activity. The letter's introduction presents Paul's apostleship, and by extension the roles of Timothy and the local teachers, as of soteriological significance in that they derive from the will of the Savior God.

A. Richards, *Difference and Distance in Post-Pauline Christianity: An Epistolary Analysis of the Pastorals* (SBL 44; New York: Peter Lang, 2002); cf. L.T. Johnson, *The First and Second Letters to Timothy* (AB 35a; New York: Doubleday, 2001), 82.

[15] See Wieland, *Significance of Salvation*, for the exegetical discussion that yields the conclusions reported here.

[16] Fee reads the entire letter in the light of 1:3. See Fee, *1 and 2 Timothy, Titus*, 7–10.

1:15–16

This saying is trustworthy and deserving of full acceptance: "Christ Jesus came into the world to save sinners"—and I am the worst of them. [16]But I received mercy because of this, so that in me, the worst [of them], Christ Jesus might demonstrate the utmost patience as an example to those who would believe in Him for eternal life.

In this passage Paul is presented as the erstwhile opponent who now serves Christ.[17] While ministry is the primary thought (with a glance at opponents who may yet become faithful servants), the larger theme of salvation is also treated. The turning of Paul from the status of enemy to that of servant illustrates the assertion that it is specifically sinners who are the objects of Christ's saving work. This highlights the soteriological conviction that saving is due not to human deserving but to the divine attributes of mercy, grace, and patience. This saving is inextricably bound up with Christ and his coming into the world, which has brought the possibility of salvation. The outcome of saving is eternal life, appropriated by believing in Christ, which seems to imply trusting him for that outcome on the basis of the message about him. A conversion, a coming to believe with resultant transformation of life, is in view. Within such a framework the proclamation of the message is significant, and Paul's effectiveness as a missionary is heightened by the encapsulation in his own history of the saving that he proclaims.

2:1–7

First of all, then, I urge that petitions, prayers, intercessions, and thanksgivings be made for everyone, [2]for kings and all those who are in authority, so that we may lead a tranquil and quiet life in all godliness and dignity. [3]This is good, and it pleases God our Savior, [4]who wants everyone to be saved and to come to the knowledge of the truth.

[5]For there is one God
and one mediator between God and man,
a man, Christ Jesus,
[6]who gave Himself—a ransom for all,
a testimony at the proper time.

[7]For this I was appointed a herald, an apostle (I am telling the truth; I am not lying), and a teacher of the Gentiles in faith and truth.

Again, God is both "our" Savior and the God whose salvation is to be declared to the world. The peaceful life for which prayer is offered in this passage is not the content of salvation but an environment in which salvation may be extended to people through their hearing and coming to acknowledge the message about Christ. A

---

17 See M. Wolter, "Paulus, der bekehrte Gottesfeind. Zum Verständnis von 1.Tim. 1:13," *NovT* 31 (1989): 48–66.

universalizing tendency is again apparent in the insistence that God's will to save and Christ's self-giving are directed toward all, strengthened, perhaps intentionally, by the phrasing of the *Hingabemotiv* identifying "all" rather than "many" as the potential beneficiaries of Christ's self-giving (1 Tim 2:6; cf. Mark 10:45).[18] Christ's role in the provision of salvation is mediatorial, carrying OT priestly and sacrificial overtones. The missionary activity of bearing testimony is of vital importance in making salvation available, and within a salvation-historical framework, the present age is the time of the eschatological witness to the nations which constitutes Paul's calling.

2:15

> *But she will be saved through childbearing, if she continues in faith, love, and holiness, with good sense.*

This puzzling statement concludes a haggadic excursus in support of paraenesis to Christian women.[19] The shift from singular ("she will be saved") to plural ("if they continue") corresponds to the transition from an allusion to the promise of victory over the serpent for the woman's seed, begun to be realized through Eve's childbearing (Gen 3:15–16), to a statement of the means whereby all women—and men—may enter into salvation, by a faith that perseveres and shows itself in love and holiness. Eve's childbearing therefore contributes to the history of salvation. This has the practical effect of affirming motherhood as a sphere within which salvation may be realized, countering tendencies to exclude women from salvation. The statement in 2:15 is identified as a "faithful word" (1 Tim 3:1), which recalls listeners from the enticing notions of false teachers to the trustworthy way of salvation.

4:10

> *In fact, we labor and strive for this, because we have put our hope in the living God, who is the Savior of everyone, especially of those who believe.*

In its context in 1 Timothy 4, this statement about God the Savior illuminates several aspects of salvation. The source of salvation is God, the one true living God whom Israel knew but who is Savior not only for Israel but for all people.[20] This Savior God bestows benefits here and now, in a good creation to be enjoyed, in the

---

[18] See P. H. Towner, *The Letters to Timothy and Titus* (NICNT; Grand Rapids: Eerdmans, 2006), 183–84.

[19] To the range of possible interpretations described by I. H. Marshall, *The Pastoral Epistles* (ICC; Edinburgh: T&T Clark, 1999), 467–70, may be added the proposal of K. L. Waters Sr., that the "childbearing" is an allegory for the cultivation of saving virtues (K. L. Waters Sr., "Saved Through Childbearing: Virtues as Children in 1 Timothy 2:11–15," *JBL* 123 [2004]: 703–35). By extensive examples from Greek philosophy and Hellenistic Judaism, Waters shows that children could be a metaphor for virtues, and that producing virtues could be represented as generating or giving birth to children (though not specifically with the term τεκνογονία used in 1 Tim 2:15). Although such an allegorical reading might be possible, it remains to be seen whether interpreters will judge it more plausible than other equally possible proposed solutions.

[20] See M. J. Goodwin, "The Pauline Background of the Living God as Interpretive Context for 1 Timothy 4.10," *JSNT* 61 (1996): 65–85.

rewards of godly living and in provision for his servants in the fulfilment of their mission. Nevertheless, the greatest benefit and goal of salvation remains, namely, eschatological life, related to the life of God himself. It is received by faith, conceived as an attitude of trust and hope in God allied to the acceptance of a body of teaching about Christ and the living out of its behavioral implications. It is assumed that such faith and life belong within the church, the community of Christian believers, which relates to God in a manner analogous to Israel in the OT. The nature of God and the promise of salvation provide motivation for the continuing work of mission.

4:16

> *Be conscientious about yourself and your teaching; persevere in these things, for by doing this you will save both yourself and your hearers.*

The exhortation in 4:16 posits a close connection between the activity of the Christian minister and the realization of God's saving purpose. Since salvation is linked to faith, one who teaches the Christian faith becomes an agent of God's saving.

2 TIMOTHY

This letter, highly personal in tone, urges costly persistence in the work of mission and ministry in threatening circumstances marked by opposition within the community and persecution from the state. Paul himself is in prison and death seems imminent.

1:8–10

> *So don't be ashamed of the testimony about our Lord, or of me His prisoner. Instead, share in suffering for the gospel, relying on the power of God,*
> *⁹who has saved us and called us with a holy calling,*
> *not according to our works, but according to His own purpose and grace,*
> *which was given to us in Christ Jesus before time began.*
> *¹⁰This has now been made evident*
> *through the appearing of our Savior Christ Jesus, who has abolished death*
> *and has brought life and immortality to light through the gospel.*

This passage expresses a concept of salvation in relation to which highly developed theological, eschatological, christological, and missiological aspects may be discerned. Salvation is the act of God (who saves and calls), and it is grounded in the character and purpose of God. It is set within a "kairological" schema which extends from before time (2 Tim 1:9) through the present age (2 Tim 1:10) and on into a future of indestructible life, which is the focus of the gift of salvation. Salvation is therefore experienced as both already and not yet, living as God's holy people now while anticipating the eschatological gift of life. The concept of salvation is thoroughly christological; although God saves, Christ is the "Savior," and even the pretemporal saving purpose and grace of God have been given "in Christ" before his coming into the world. God's gift of life is revealed epiphanically in Christ, either in his incarnation or possibly more specifically in his resurrection.[21] Human witness participates in the divine disclosure as, through the gospel entrusted to Paul and thence to Timothy, salvation is extended to those who will yet be saved. It is, however, God who continues to guard the gospel and guarantee its ultimate success.

2:8–10

> *Keep in mind Jesus Christ, risen from the dead, descended from David, according to my gospel. [9]For this I suffer, to the point of being bound like a criminal; but God's message is not bound. [10]This is why I endure all things for the elect: so that they also may obtain salvation, which is in Christ Jesus, with eternal glory.*

This paraenetic passage, urging the acceptance of suffering in the cause of the gospel, establishes a link between costly ministry and the effecting of God's saving purpose. As in the Lukan tradition of Pauline preaching, the primary datum of the gospel is the resurrection of Jesus, which confirms his messianic identity.[22] The "of the seed of David" reference, allusions to God's purpose implicit in his "word" (λόγος) that is "not bound," and the description of those who will be saved as "the elect" are all consistent with a salvation-historical framework. Christ's suffering, however, also serves an exemplary purpose, as does the endurance of Paul himself. There are overtones of the martyrological tradition of Hellenistic Judaism (particularly in 2 and 4 Maccabees), coloring the characterization of Paul's ministry. The salvation statement in 2 Tim 2:8–10 leads into an exhortation to would-be servants of the gospel to identify with Christ in his death and suffering, life and reign (2 Tim 2:11–13). The prospect of an apocalyptic final judgement issuing in eternal life with Christ motivates to eschatological endurance and continuing faithfulness, but, somewhat in tension with that, the final word is of confidence in Christ's faithfulness specifically in the fulfilment of his saving purpose.

3:14–15

> *But as for you, continue in what you have learned and firmly believed, knowing those from whom you learned, [15]and that from childhood you have known the sacred Scriptures, which are able to instruct you for salvation through faith in Christ Jesus.*

The attribution of salvific power to the OT Scriptures is to be understood in terms of two emphases of this letter, the soteriological outcome of ministry rightly

---

[21] On the significance of Paul's vision of the risen Christ for his understanding of the gospel and his mission, see A. F. Segal, "Paul's Thinking about the Resurrection in Its Jewish Context," *NTS* 44 (1998): 400–419.

[22] See I. H. Marshall, "The Christology of the Pastoral Epistles," *SNTU* 13 (1988): 157–77, 166–67.

exercised and the continuity between the faith of Judaism and the Christian gospel. The OT directs those taught by it to faith in Christ and a life of righteousness, and hence to salvation.

4:16–18

At my first defense, no one came to my assistance, but everyone deserted me. May it not be counted against them. [17]But the Lord stood with me and strengthened me, so that the proclamation might be fully made through me, and all the Gentiles might hear. So I was rescued from the lion's mouth. [18]The Lord will rescue me from every evil work and will bring me safely into His heavenly kingdom. To Him be the glory forever and ever! Amen.

The past rescue (ῥύομαι, v. 17b), the first of the two savings to which this passage testifies, illustrates the conviction that runs through 2 Timothy that, in fulfillment of God's saving purpose, he will ensure that his message reaches its destination, specifically, the Gentile world. To that end God has preserved and empowered his messenger. The presentation alludes to the OT and intertestamental theme of God's vindication of his servants, though they suffer at the hands of human authorities. The language hints at an apocalyptic context, suggesting a kairologically significant end-time setting for Paul's witness. The second anticipated saving (σῴζω, v. 18a) envisages an eschatological vindication issuing in acceptance into the eternal heavenly kingdom that Christ will establish at his coming.

TITUS

This missionary letter has in view an early stage in the establishing of Christian witness in the inhospitable environment of pagan Crete, further complicated by a Judaizing opposition. At various points, formulations of salvation teaching seem to be particularly shaped for contextual engagement with religious and social realities on Roman Crete.[23]

1:1–4

Paul, a slave of God, and an apostle of Jesus Christ for the faith of God's elect and the knowledge of the truth that leads to godliness, [2]in the hope of eternal life that God, who cannot lie, promised before time began, [3]and has in His own time revealed His message in the proclamation that I was entrusted with by the command of God our Savior:
[4]To Titus, my true child in our common faith.
Grace and peace from God the Father and Christ Jesus our Savior.

---

[23] For a detailed investigation of the missionary approach of this letter to its specific environment, see G. M. Wieland, "Roman Crete and the Letter to Titus," *NTS* 55 (2009): 338–354.

This rich opening to the letter establishes both God and Christ and, by derivation, the ministries of Paul and Titus, as soterial in character. Christian salvation, whose content is eternal life, represents the fulfillment of God's eternal purpose expressed in OT promises by "the undeceiving God" (ὁ ἀψευδὴς θεός, Titus 1:2), who is implicitly contrasted with Zeus, the "father of Crete" but notorious as a deceiver. The present age is the time set for the manifesting of this salvation. Those who embrace the hope, hold to the faith, and cultivate a godly life in accordance with the apostolic teaching are God's elect, to whom accrue the status and blessings of the OT people of God.

2:11–14

> For the grace of God has appeared, with salvation for all people, [12]instructing us to deny godlessness and worldly lusts and to live in a sensible, righteous, and godly way in the present age, [13]while we wait for the blessed hope and the appearing of the glory of our great God and Savior, Jesus Christ. [14]He gave Himself for us to redeem us from all lawlessness and to cleanse for Himself a special people, eager to do good works.

The understanding of salvation that emerges from this unit seems at first glance to be something of a hybrid. Concepts such as epiphany and the virtues (Titus 2:11–13) are evocative of the Hellenistic environment, whereas the closing statement draws on familiar Jewish categories of redemption, lawlessness, purification, the special people, and zeal (Titus 2:14). The reference to Christ (Titus 2:13–14) joins the two parts, and it is the understanding of the Christ event that enables Paul both to relate it soteriologically to the Jewish faith tradition and to open it up in missional engagement with the ideals of the Hellenistic world. For this new community of faith in its mission context, a sense of identity is thus created that is specifically Christocentric but connected backward to the heritage of biblical faith and outward to the Greek world.

Salvation is presented as awaiting completion when Jesus appears as the Divine Savior,[24] but in this present world, God's grace, which is soterial in its intent, effects moral transformation in individuals, thus creating a community after the OT pattern of a people purified and devoted to God. The doing good that results commends the teaching about God and salvation, in line with the missionary interest evident in the insistence that this salvific grace is revealed for all people. While the transfer from *Unheil* to *Heil* may be depicted as a process effected by the training operation of God's grace, it is also understood forensically as the accomplished outcome of Christ's sacrificial self-giving, which deals with the consequences of "lawlessness" (ἀνομία) and establishes his ownership of the redeemed people.

---

[24] See M. J. Harris, "Our Great God and Savior (Titus 2:13)," in *Jesus as God: The New Testament Use of Theos in Reference to Jesus* (Grand Rapids: Baker, 1992), 173–85.

3:4–7

> But when the goodness and love for man
> appeared from God our Savior,
> [5]He saved us —
> not by works of righteousness that we had done,
> but according to His mercy,
> through the washing of regeneration
> and renewal by the Holy Spirit.
> [6]This [Spirit] He poured out on us abundantly
> through Jesus Christ our Savior,
> [7]so that having been justified by His grace,
> we may become heirs with the hope of eternal life.

In this paraenetically motivated section, a rich fund of salvation material is utilized to persuade readers that the outcome of God's saving in those who have embraced the Christian message should be good lives that benefit others. Salvation is beyond human achievement.[25] It is God's work, due to his essential goodness, effected through the self-giving of Christ and the influence of the Spirit. The Trinity is glimpsed as a partnership in the saving enterprise. Again, both God and Jesus Christ are "our Savior." From the divine perspective, salvation has already been achieved, but for the recipient it involves a distinct point of change associated with coming to faith in God in response to the Christian message, a cleansing and generating of new life by the Spirit, and a continuing renewal of life also by the Spirit. The effect is to create a righteous condition, qualifying the beneficiaries for eternal life. This condition is visible now in behavior that contrasts with their former lives outside this salvation.

SALVATION IN THE THREE LETTERS

SHARED FRAMEWORK, DISTINCTIVE PRESENTATIONS

Common to the three letters are the prominence of salvation language, signs of engagement with the Hellenistic environment, and the incorporation of traditional materials relating to salvation. The various parts make sense within a coherent conceptual framework. Salvation begins in the pretemporal decision of God, attested by the OT Scriptures; it is effected through the historic Christ event and the continuing ministry of the gospel, by which people come to a knowledge of the truth. Transformation of life, under the training of grace, is evident in those who await the final realization of salvation upon Christ's appearing in glory and the entry into eternal

---

[25] B. Witherington III comments, "Here we have Paul's message clothed in a more Hellenistic fashion" (*Letters and Homilies for Hellenized Christians: A Socio-Historical Commentary on Titus, 1–2 Timothy and 1–3 John* [LHHC 1; Downers Grove, IL: InterVarsity, 2006], 158).

life. Salvation has been graciously manifested and is potentially for all, and therefore prayer should be offered for all; costly witness must be maintained and healthy teaching transmitted. Paul's message is the authentic gospel. and his successors must be faithful to it. Within this shared framework each letter presents aspects of salvation in a way that serves its particular missional and paraenetic purpose.

First Timothy, adopting a stance over against opponents who devalue the present material world and limit access to salvation, presents God as the beneficent Savior of all through his providential ordering of the created world, who is also executing a plan of eschatological salvation for all who believe in Christ. The gospel must not be perverted by a futile asceticism nor obscured by useless esoteric speculation. Believers are to be taught to enjoy God's good provision in this world while living generously and praying and working that all may come to a saving knowledge of the truth.

In 2 Timothy the tone is one of personal paraenesis, urging the faithful exercise of ministry in the face of opposition. The present age is a time of opposition for witnesses to the gospel, hardship for Christ's servants, and persecution for all who want to live godly lives. The focus of hope in this context is eschatological, immortal life in Christ's heavenly kingdom. The call is to faithfulness in ministry, by which God carries forward his saving purpose for others. For the ministers themselves the prospect of their own eternal salvation encourages perseverance.

The presentation of salvation in Titus is characterized by creative missional engagement with a particular Hellenistic context. Points of contact are found in the worlds of religion and popular philosophy that open the way for explications of the promise of God our Savior, the work and future appearing of Christ our Savior, and the present evidence of salvation through grace-trained and Spirit-infused lives that carry the goodness of God into households, communities, and society at large.

THE BENEFITS OF SALVATION

All three letters envisage a final salvation comprising a future eternal life, together with present experiences of God's saving. It is in relation to the latter that they are most diverse. In 1 Timothy, the faith in God that will bring entry into the life to come also enhances the enjoyment of much in the present life, as it is recognized and received with gratitude as the gift of a benevolent God. Titus also promises present benefit, in the ethical transformation which is the existential dimension of the cleansing that is central to God's saving intervention. In 2 Timothy, however, the focus is firmly on the hope of future salvation, and present experiences of God's saving are primarily in the context of preserving and enabling for the fulfillment of ministry in a hostile environment.

GOD AND CHRIST IN RELATION TO SALVATION

Each of the three letters exhibits its own distinctive emphases in its presentation of God and Christ in relation to salvation. First Timothy speaks of "God our Savior" in a manner reminiscent of the OT but extends the scope of his saving beyond Israel to all, for whom he is the universal benefactor. It is also God's desire that all should attain eschatological salvation, but this is specifically in and through Christ, made available though his incarnation and priestly mediation, and realized at his return. In Christ grace and mercy are received by all who make him the object of their faith. In 2 Timothy God is revealed as the instigator and guarantor of eternal life, which depends upon his mercy and grace and is coming to fruition as his eternal saving purpose unfolds. Central to that purpose is Christ, locus of the pretemporal gift of grace, Davidic Messiah and Savior by virtue of his victory over death, which has opened the way to immortality for those who are identified with him. The risen Christ will return as eschatological judge with the authority to bestow life in his kingdom, and meantime his gracious and empowering presence is experienced by those who are on the way to eternal life. Titus claims "God our Savior" for the Christian community, for whom God and Christ, who is also "our God and Savior," are closely identified. Salvation will be consummated with the epiphany of Christ the Divine Savior. Nonetheless, there are functional specificities in the roles of God and Christ in relation to salvation. To God is ascribed the pretemporal promise of eternal life and the grace and mercy to which it is due, and it is achieved through Christ's historic self-giving to redeem and his channeling of cleansing and renewal by the Holy Spirit.

While there are differences of emphasis and detail, then, all three letters regard the historic Christ-event as crucial to the provision of eschatological salvation, assume Christ's continuing gracious influence in the present age, and envisage a future manifestation of Christ that will usher in final salvation. There is greater diversity in the presentations of God in relation to salvation, with 1 Timothy universalizing Israel's Savior God, 2 Timothy stressing God's eternal saving purpose realized in Christ, and Titus claiming God as the Savior specifically of the Christian community.

PAUL AND SALVATION

With varying emphases, the three letters all present Paul as exercising a soteriologically significant ministry, specifically as one through whom the message of God's saving purpose and its realization through Christ is made known. His ministry has its source in God's commissioning and is related to the outcome of eternal life (1 Tim 1:1; 2 Tim 1:1; Titus 1:1–3). First Timothy stresses Paul's calling as a teacher of the Gentiles and understands Paul's ministry as part of the eschatological witness to the nations that belongs to the end times. Second Timothy refers Paul's ministry to the eternal purpose of God, on which grounds its success is assured. At the same time it has a martyrological character in that he must suffer for the sake of it and persevere in faithfulness, and through doing so he contributes to the salvation of others. In Titus Paul is the authorized proclaimer of the message of God's salvation who can declare what must be taught in the missionary congregations, and again this ministry is located at a divinely appointed and therefore soteriologically significant time. The differing emphases are in accord with the special interests of each letter, but all agree that Paul is a channel of God's revelation of his saving intent and means. Each letter also recognizes that other people—Timothy, Titus, and those whom they will teach and appoint—also participate in the making known of what God has revealed, and the emphasis lies on the authoritative content of the message rather than the leadership status and authority of Paul.

THOSE WHO ARE SAVED

All three PE present salvation as the possession of those who accept and hold to the message of God's saving through Christ as proclaimed by Paul and other faithful messengers. All understand such faith to include right belief together with life choices and behavior consistent with an orientation of life toward the final salvation anticipated. Again, however, each has its own distinctive emphases. First Timothy is concerned to stress, against exclusivist interpretations, that there is the possibility of salvation for "all," specifically including sinners, Gentiles, and women. Urging perseverance in costly ministry, 2 Timothy highlights the outcome of salvation for faithful servants of Christ and those who benefit from their ministry (including Gentiles). There is a confidence that as they come to faith God's eternal saving purpose is unfolding. In Titus it is "we," the Christian community in a missionary context, who have been saved through accepting the health-giving teaching of the Pauline missionaries and learning to live distinctively as God's people.

KEY TERMS

All three letters make use of the terms σωτήρ ("savior"), ἐπιφάνεια ("appearing"), and εὐσέβεια ("piety," "godliness"), and various cognate terms. Here also may be discerned both general similarities and distinctive features.

In 1 Timothy it is God who is σωτήρ (1:1; 2:3; 4:10), the OT "God our Savior" who is also the Savior of all. There seems to be an intention to universalize the concept over against any exclusivistic tendency. Titus is distinctive in another way, applying the predicate "our Savior" to both God and Christ (1:3,4; 2:10,13; 3:4,6). The latter is identified as the agent through whom God's saving is realized. In the sole occurrence of the term in 2 Timothy, it is Christ who is σωτήρ (1:10), and through his epiphany God's saving grace was revealed and its outcome, life, and immortality, brought to light. Although the term is common to the three letters, therefore, it is used in distinctive ways in each.

The term ἐπιφάνεια is used once in 1 Timothy (6:14), where it signifies the future appearing of Christ. The incarnation of Christ is described in the phrase "manifested in the flesh" (3:15), but the verb here is the much more common φανερόω. Second Timothy has three instances of ἐπιφάνεια. Twice the reference is to the future appearing of Christ and once to the historic Christ-event as an appearing through which God's saving grace and the life and immortality that are its outcome were revealed (1:9–10). In Titus the noun depicts Christ's future appearing (2:13), whereas the verb (ἐπιφαίνω) describes the manifesting of God's saving grace (2:11) and of his goodness and love for people (3:4). While the Christ-event is doubtless the key element in the making known of these aspects of God's nature and purpose, it is not entirely clear that the intention is to describe the incarnation per se as an epiphany. Even in 2 Tim 1:10, where the noun is used in relation to Christ, the focus seems to be not so much on Christ's coming into the world as on his resurrection, the basis for the claim that he had "abolished death and brought immortality and life to light through the gospel." These observations weigh against the view that there is a developed and consistent two-epiphany schema that imposes a uniform content on epiphany terms across the letters.[26] It is preferable to allow that these letters have found epiphany language useful in more than one way in the communication of aspects of their soteriological schemas.

First Timothy presents εὐσέβεια in a very positive light as that which brings eschatological gain as well as temporal benefit (4:8; 6:6). Although "our" εὐσέβεια is determined by specific christological beliefs (3:16), the term principally represents a religiously shaped way of living. As such it is the practical goal of the apostolic teaching (6:3) and should be cultivated by all believers (2:2) and in particular by teachers such as Timothy (4:7). It is possible for false teachers to pursue it for the wrong motives (6:5). In contrast to 1 Timothy, the noun εὐσέβεια appears only once in Titus, where it is again an envisaged outcome of true teaching (1:1), but the idea recurs in the use of the adverbial form εὐσεβῶς to indicate an aspect of the mode of living produced by the training (παιδεία) of grace (2:12). The references in 2 Timothy strike a different tone. False teachers can present an appearance of εὐσέβεια but deny its power (3:5), and far from being a way to benefit in this life, those who want to live εὐσεβῶς will have to suffer persecution (3:12).

---

[26] See, e.g., A. Lau, *Manifest in Flesh: The Epiphany Christology of the Pastoral Epistles* (WUNT 2.86; Tübingen: J. C. B. Mohr, 1996), and H. Stettler, *Die Christologie der Pastoralbriefe* (WUNT 2.105; Tübingen: J. C. B. Mohr, 1998).

IMPLICATIONS FOR UNDERSTANDING THE PE

THE INDIVIDUAL COHERENCE AND DISTINCTIVENESS OF THE THREE PE

First, the general point may be made that the observations above weigh against the notion that the soteriological material in the PE is inserted haphazardly and with little reflection. In all three, the use made of salvation concepts lends effective support to the paraenesis and the distinctive features of each presentation of salvation are in accord with the general character and paraenetic goals of each letter in question. This adds to the growing body of evidence for the internal rhetorical and theological coherence of each of these letters.[27]

On the other hand, the results of this study challenge the assumption that the three are most adequately understood as a single three-part work.[28] The three letters do exhibit aspects of a shared soteriological perspective, but this is also shared more widely within the NT. There is sufficient specificity about the application of soteriological material in each letter to support the view that each represents a distinct response to a particular occasion. Even terms commonly taken to be characteristic of the PE as a group are found to be utilized in different ways in the three letters. Clearly there are implications here for the study of the PE. If each of these letters offers its own distinctive soteriological presentation, it must be asked whether each may not also have a unique contribution to make in other areas. The voice of each should be heard. Those interpretations of the PE that treat its themes by formulating syntheses of relevant material in the three letters and on that basis describing a single perspective or set of concerns suffer from a confusion of voices and a flattening of the distinctive profiles of each of the letters.[29]

THE SOTERIOLOGICAL PERSPECTIVE(S) OF THE PE

Our survey of salvation material challenges certain widely held perceptions of the soteriology of the PE, such as that the eschatological horizon has receded and the focus is now on "good citizenship" in the present age, that the presentation of salvation in the PE is designed to bolster the power of a leadership group, that the PE elevate Paul to a privileged place as the only authorized bearer of the saving message, and more generally that the theology of salvation found in the PE represents a decline or departure from Pauline soteriology.

---

[27] In agreement with, e.g., Fiore, *Personal Example;* Towner, *Goal;* M. Harding, *Tradition and Rhetoric in the Pastoral Epistles* (SBL 3; New York: Peter Lang, 1998); K. D. Tollefson, "Titus: Epistle of Religious Revitalization," *BTB* 30 (2000): 145–57; and against J. D. Miller, *The Pastoral Letters as Composite Documents* (SNTSMS 93; Cambridge: Cambridge University Press, 1997).

[28] Supporting the tentative suggestion by Johnson, *1 & 2 Timothy*, 82.

[29] See, e.g., Richards, *Difference and Distance.*

In 1990 J. L. Houlden wrote, "Certain views have become almost *de rigeur* in the recent study of the Pastoral Epistles," among which he lists church life marked by institutionalization, salvation seen as something achieved in the past through Christ and appropriated through baptism, and that the PE represent "bourgeois Christianity," a desire to live respectably and comfortably but not provocatively in the world.[30] He was in effect testifying to the influence that Dibelius and Conzelmann's *christliche Bürgerlichkeit* interpretation continued to hold in PE scholarship at that time.[31] This approach has, however, come under increasing strain in recent years.[32] While it is true that 1 Timothy and Titus demonstrate an interest in Christian existence in the world (the observation is less valid for 2 Timothy), the explanation of this concern in terms of a soteriological perspective that lacks any real future dimension must be disputed. This view fails to appreciate that there is in 1 Timothy a recognition both of the general "saving" benefits that God in his universal benefactor role provides for the world and of the particular hope of eternal life that is made available through Christ. The latter hope focuses upon a future appearing of Christ, and although the present life is not disparaged, it is the anticipated future that is the "life that is real" (6:19). It is of Titus that it would be most valid to claim that the consciousness of salvation serves as the presupposition of an attitude of good citizenship (2:14; 3:1–5), but even here salvation is not complete until the coming of Christ in glory and the inheriting of eternal life. Moreover, the overt defensive or missionary concern must also be taken into account in explaining the behavioral exhortations. In 2 Timothy the more negative appraisal of the "last days" is the ground against which the figure of eschatological salvation is the more sharply delineated. In none of the PE has the prospect of future salvation disappeared. It remains a persuasive and powerful consideration that each letter is able to deploy rhetorically. The *christliche Bürgerlichkeit* perspective misses the mark most completely in relation to 2 Timothy, where salvation's eschatological horizon dominates.

Donelson's reading of the PE attempts to trace a sophisticated soteriological schema deliberately constructed as an ideological stratagem designed to place power in the hands of cultic leaders. According to this plan, "it is solely by way of virtue that God saves."[33] Jesus' saving consists in teaching the way of virtue and rewarding virtue at the final judgment.[34] This teaching has been handed down by Paul and taken

[30] J. L. Houlden, review of P. H. Towner, *The Goal of Our Instruction*, *ExpT* 101 (1990): 312–13.

[31] See Dibelius-Conzelmann, *Pastoral Epistles*, 10. This approach still surfaces in general surveys, e.g., in the description of the PE in D. L. Barr, *New Testament Story: An Introduction* (2nd ed.; Belmont: Wadsworth Publishing Company, 1995), 171–72: "Attention to the present has eclipsed concern for the future kingdom. Church as organization is replacing church as family. The desire to be well thought of by those outside has eroded freedom."

[32] See R. Schwarz, *Bürgerliches Christentum im Neuen Testament?* (Klosterneuburg: OKB, 1983); Towner, *Goal*; R. M. Kidd, *Wealth and Beneficence in the Pastoral Epistles: A "Bourgeois" Form of Early Christianity?* (SBLDS 122; Atlanta: Scholars Press, 1990).

[33] Donelson, *Pseudepigraphy*, 140; cf. 153, "quiet virtues constitute the sole means of salvation."

[34] Ibid., 139: "Thus Jesus saves, because virtues save."

over by cultic leaders, so that, "the effective power of Jesus' epiphany is mediated to believers by way of cultic leaders."[35] It is the spirit who enables the performance of those virtuous deeds which will save, but this too works in the interests of the leaders since, "Part of God's management of this plan is the restriction of access to the spirit to the cultic act of baptism. . . . In order to possess this spirit, one must appear before the church leaders and become subject to them."[36] Despite Donelson's complaint that earlier interpreters had erred by trying to construct the author's theological system from statements plucked from their contexts in the PE, his own discussion of the evidence suffers from a high degree of selectivity of another sort. He privileges those passages that extol the virtuous life but sets aside or simply ignores other statements (e.g., Titus 3:5a and 2 Tim 1:9) that explicitly deny that people are saved because of meritorious accomplishment. The assertion that to be baptized involves entering into subjection to the church leaders, an important part of Donelson's system, is not in the text at all, but must be assumed on the basis of his reconstruction of the situation and purpose of the PE in the context of a second-century ecclesiastical power struggle. The recognition of a missionary setting on Crete permits a more satisfactory reading of Titus, including the reference to washing and the Spirit (Titus 3:4–7), in terms of contextual engagement.[37]

K. Läger proposed that in the PE it is "Paulology" rather than Christology that comes to the fore.[38] She sees in the PE a "symbiotic unity" of Paul with his message of the saving work of Christ. Paul—and only Paul!—is the mediator of the message, and message and messenger are integrated to such an extent that Paul himself becomes an essential element in the message of salvation. This overstates the case. Certainly in each of these letters the message of salvation is expressly that which was entrusted to Paul. It is not, however, the person of Paul but the message and its faithful ministry that are the means by which salvation is mediated. Paul is presented as the authorized bearer of the former (1 Tim 1:11; 2:7; 2 Tim 1:11,13; 2:2,8; Titus 1:3) and the primary exemplar for the latter (in 1 Tim 1:1,12–16; and especially in 2 Tim 1:1,11–12; 2:8–10; 3:10–11; 4:6–18; this is not such a major emphasis in Titus, although it might be suggested in 1:1). The first is in keeping with the polemical aim of refuting opponents, and the second supports the paraenetic goal of encouraging faithful ministry. To suggest, therefore, that the foundational axiom for this author is, *extra Paulum nostrum nulla salus*,[39] is to misrepresent him. He would perhaps rather affirm, *extra evangelium nostrum* (which we learned from Paul) *nulla salus*. Läger is correct, however, to stress the very significant place that each of these letters affords

[35] Ibid., 142.
[36] Ibid., 143.
[37] See discussion of this passage in Wieland, "Roman Crete and the Letter to Titus," 349–51.
[38] Läger, *Christologie*, especially in the sections on "Soteriologie, Christologie und 'Paulologie,'" 175–80, and "Die soteriologische Funktion des Paulus," 128–30.
[39] Ibid., 177.

169

to the transmission of the message of salvation. The three letters share a conviction that faithful teaching of the authentic message issues in salvation and to that extent participates in the salvation process.

A decline from the Paul of the undisputed letters is commonly estimated on the grounds of the absence from the PE of certain themes held to be central to Paul's understanding of the gospel. It is true that none of the letters provide a comprehensive exposition of Pauline soteriology, but it could be argued that neither is this found in most of the undisputed letters of Paul.[40] The presence of certain themes and emphases instead of others underscores the occasionality of these letters and reminds the interpreter that the author has selected material and themes to support particular paraenetic or polemical objectives.[41] With this in mind, it would be methodologically unsafe to argue from the absence of particular features or themes in any of these short letters that their author must have no place for them in his soteriology. Furthermore, there is considerable agreement with the earlier Paul on those aspects of salvation that each of the PE does reveal. As well as specific points of correspondence, the recognition of the coherence of thought of each letter requires that those elements in each that would be generally admitted to be Pauline in character must be acknowledged to be integral to the thought of the letter writer, rather than merely stray pieces of Pauline tradition inserted but not necessarily understood. Considering each letter separately allows each to stand independently alongside the Pauline corpus, and in the case of two out of the three, the effect has been to lessen the distance relative to that which is sensed between Paul and a synthesis of the three PE.

For 2 Timothy standing alone, the distance seems very slight. Here is a concept of salvation that stretches from God's pretemporal purpose and grace to eschatological saving and reward, that focuses upon Jesus Christ, Messiah and Lord, who in his death and resurrection destroyed death and opened the kingdom of heaven, and that calls the elect to identify themselves with Christ in his death and, by his grace and Spirit, maintain their witness until they are finally saved into his heavenly kingdom. The short letter of Titus, while employing some novel language, also moves from pretemporal promise to eschatological glory, finding the source of salvation in God's grace and mercy, its achievement in Christ's self-giving to redeem and the giving of new life by the Spirit. Again, when considered independently of the other PE, the language of "justified by grace" resonates with that of Paul and is not contradicted by the practical emphasis on good works as the proper way of life of the community whose behavior is intended to authenticate its message. Of the three, it is 1 Timothy

---

[40] Johnson makes the valid point that the picture is distorted by reading not only the PE but also the undisputed letters of Paul as "composite constructs" (*1 & 2 Timothy*, 82).

[41] The same pertains, of course, to the *Hauptbriefe*. As W. D. Mounce remarks, "A quick look at the acknowledged Pauline letters shows that frequently a theme that is common in one book is of considerably less significance in another, or is totally omitted" (*The Pastoral Epistles* [WBC 46; Dallas: Word, 2000], lxxxix, with a table of examples and further discussion on pp. xc–xci).

with its exposition of the general providence of God and the corresponding call to godliness (εὐσέβεια) that strikes the reader as the most distant from the undisputed Pauline letters. Yet even here the insistence that "everything created by God is good" (1 Tim 4:4) sits comfortably, as Dunn recognizes, with "Paul's essentially Jewish conception of a cosmos which was created good," in which "nothing is unclean in itself" (Rom 14:14).[42] In addition, 1 Timothy, in agreement with Paul, speaks of a particular saving for eternal life that has been made possible by Christ's coming to save sinners, which involved his incarnation and self-giving as a ransom, and is received by those who put their faith in him.

CONCLUSIONS

The study of salvation language in the PE confirms the importance of salvation as a theme in each of these letters. Not only is salvation language prevalent, but in all three letters the concept of salvation plays a vital role in relation to the letter's purpose. The three share a soteriological outlook that exhibits to varying degrees a salvation-historical framework, in which salvation has its origin in the purpose of God, is implemented through the historic Christ-event, continues to be realized existentially through the proclamation of the message of salvation and a response of faith, and will reach its consummation in the gift of eternal life at Christ's return. They agree that this salvation is universally available but is received by those who believe the gospel and orient their lives to its eschatological promise and present ethical demands.

Within this broad outline, however, each of the three letters makes its own use of soteriological concepts to address particular concerns and advance specific interests. In 1 Timothy the presentation has a polemical edge, responding to heterodox teaching of an exclusivist, ascetic character that has gained a foothold in the church; Paul counters this false teaching by stressing the universality of the scope of salvation, insisting that the Savior God of Israel is the one God and Savior of all, celebrating his benevolent provision of a good creation while pointing beyond the present age to a future of even greater worth for those who respond in faith to the message about Christ which is to be preached to all. The concern in 2 Timothy is paraenetic, urging the exercise of faithful, costly ministry in the face of harsh opposition that may even extend to physical death. In this context it is not the enjoyment of salvation here and now but the prospect of eschatological reward that is emphasized, together with the promise of grace and empowerment for faithfulness and the assurance that God himself is watching over his saving purpose and will fulfill it, whatever may happen to his servants in the present age. For Titus, the establishment of missionary congregations calls for the nurturing of a clear sense of Christian identity and community. This is found in the appropriation of OT soteriological categories for the

---

[42] J. D. G. Dunn, *The Theology of Paul the Apostle* (Grand Rapids: Eerdmans, 1998), 39.

Christian believers and an emphasis on the present ethical transformation that marks out these believers from both the general society of which they were once part and rival teachers and their followers. In this missionary context bold steps are taken to express salvation concepts originating in Judaism in terms accessible to a non-Jewish Hellenistic audience.

In three distinct ways, then, the two letters to Timothy and the letter to Titus address challenges facing the church and its mission by setting their various situations within a soteriological framework that—insofar as it can be uncovered from what is affirmed, expounded, or seems to be assumed—is consistent in outline with that of the earlier Pauline letters. It is this framework that makes the paraenesis effective, as readers are urged on the basis of soteriological convictions to resist inward-looking, restrictive tendencies within the church and hold to a gospel universal in scope (1 Timothy), to continue faithful in the ministry of the gospel despite opposition and apparent setbacks (2 Timothy), and to nurture missionary communities whose lifestyle would serve as a demonstration of the saving efficacy of the message of God's grace (Titus). The particular emphases and form of each presentation are thus explicable in terms of three separate situations with their distinct pastoral and missiological challenges.

Chapter Eight

ECCLESIOLOGY IN THE PASTORAL EPISTLES

BENJAMIN L. MERKLE

Although the Greek word ἐκκλησία ("church," "congregation," or "assembly") occurs only three times in the Pastoral Epistles (1 Tim 3:5,15; 5:16), it is a dominant theme that runs throughout these epistles.[1] In 1 Tim 3:15 Paul states that the reason he is writing to Timothy and the congregation at Ephesus is so that they "will know how people ought to act in God's household, which is the church of the living God, the pillar and foundation of the truth." Thus, it could be argued that the church is at the very center of Paul's message in 1 Timothy and perhaps also in 2 Timothy and Titus.[2] For example, in 1 Timothy Paul urges Timothy to fight against false teachers who have entered the church (1:3–20), exhorts the congregation to pray for their government leaders (2:1–8), encourages women to dress appropriately and not teach or exercise authority over men in the worship services (2:9–15), supplies various qualifications needed for church officers (overseers, 3:1–7; deacons, 3:8–13), quotes a common creed (3:16), warns of false teachers (4:1–5), reminds Timothy not to neglect his responsibilities of teaching and reading the Scriptures (4:6–16), instructs the congregation on appropriate behavior among various age groups (5:1–2), provides the qualifications needed for widows to receive aid from the church (5:3–16), teaches the congregation concerning the payment, removal, and appointment of elders (5:17–25), and gives instruction against trusting in riches while charging Timothy to remain faithful to his calling (6:2–21).[3]

---

[1] Ἐκκλησία appears 59 times in the rest of the Pauline corpus.

[2] Regarding 1 Timothy, G. W. Knight comments, "Since the whole letter is about the church, it would be inappropriate to restrict the description of the church in it to the three occurrences of ἐκκλησία" (*The Pastoral Epistles* [NIGTC; Grand Rapids: Eerdmans; Carlisle: Paternoster, 1992], 180–81). Similarly, R. W. Gehring maintains that the concept of the church is "the main topic in the Pastorals" (*House Church and Mission: The Importance of Household Structures in Early Christianity* [Peabody, Mass.: Hendrickson, 2004], 260).

[3] In Titus Paul writes concerning the appointing and qualifications of elders/overseers (1:5–9), the teaching of the true gospel in the church (2:1,7–8,15; 3:1–2), and warns about false teachers and false teachings (1:10–16; 3:9–11). Although 2 Timothy is the most personal of the Pastoral Epistles, we also find many elements related to ecclesiology in

At first glance it appears that 1 Tim 3:5 ("church of God") and 1 Tim 3:15 ("church of the living God") refer to the universal church, whereas 1 Tim 5:16 ("the church should not be burdened" by widows who can be helped by others) refers to the local church. It could be argued, however, that all three uses refer to the local church. First Timothy 3:4 indicates that in order for someone to be qualified to serve as an overseer in the church, he must manage his household well and have his children under control. Verse 5 then draws a parallel between leading the family and leading the church ("If anyone does not know how to manage his own household, how will he take care of God's church [ἐκκλησία θεοῦ]?"). Although Paul sometimes refers to the church in its universal capacity (such as in the letters of Ephesians and Colossians), most of his references refer to the local community of believers. In the case of 1 Tim 3:5, it is best to understand the usage as referring to the local church based on the context.[4] Paul indicates that the work of the overseer is to take care of the church or household of God. Therefore, because Paul's reference to ἐκκλησία is tied to the work of the overseer whose duty it is to care for the local congregation of believers, it is likely that it refers to the local church. Likewise, although in 1 Tim 3:15 Paul speaks about "the church of the living God [ἐκκλησία θεοῦ ζῶντος]" (and not "the church at Ephesus"), it is apparent that he is not thinking of the universal church but of the local church.[5] We know this because Paul's stated purpose in writing this epistle was so that the Ephesian Christians would know how to conduct themselves in God's household. Thus, Paul is not thinking abstractly about the universal church but concretely about how Christians are to behave in their local assembly.

Paul uses many metaphors to describe the church. Perhaps the most common images are the church as the people of God, the body or bride of Christ, and the temple of the Holy Spirit.[6] The metaphor that is mostly used in the Pastoral Epistles, however, is that of the family or household. For example, in 1 Tim 3:5 and 12 a person qualified to be an overseer or deacon must know how to manage his household well before he is fit to hold an office in the church. An overseer is also said to be God's steward or manager (Titus 1:7)—one who manages the affairs of God's household or family. In 1 Tim 3:15 Paul explicitly calls the church the "household of God." The attitude toward different age groups in the church is likened to familial relationships (1 Tim 5:1–2). The church is to care for widows who are truly in need because they

---

this letter. Paul mentions the need to train church leaders (2:2), the need to teach and preach apostolic doctrine (1:13–14; 2:2,14–15,24–25; 3:14–16; 4:1–2), and the need to rebuke false teachers (2:14,16–18,23; 3:1–9; 4:3–4).

[4] So P. H. Towner, *The Letters to Timothy and Titus* (NICNT; Grand Rapids: Eerdmans, 2006), 256; A. D. Clarke, *A Pauline Theology of Church Leadership* (LNTS 362; London: T&T Clark, 2008), 59. Although Paul is referring to the local church, he is not referring to a specific local church but is speaking general terms. This usage is revealed by the anarthrous use of the term ἐκκλησία (so W. D. Mounce, *Pastoral Epistles* [WBC 46; Nashville: Nelson, 2000], 180).

[5] So Mounce, *Pastoral Epistles*, 220–21 (cf. Towner, *Timothy and Titus*, 256).

[6] See D. L. Akin, ed., *A Theology for the Church* (Nashville: B&H, 2007), 772–75; W. Grudem, *Systematic Theology: An Introduction to Biblical Doctrine* (Leicester: InterVarsity; Grand Rapids: Zondervan, 1994), 858–59; M. J. Erickson, *Christian Theology* (2nd ed.; Grand Rapids: Baker, 1998), 1044–51.

are part of the spiritual family (1 Tim 5:3–16). The metaphor of a house containing honorable and dishonorable vessels is used to encourage Timothy (2 Tim 2:20–21). Finally, Paul refers to Timothy and Titus as sons (1 Tim 1:2,18; 2 Tim 1:2; 2:1; Titus 1:4).

In recent years the metaphor of household or οἶκος has become a dominating grid in which the Pastoral Epistles, and especially the leadership structure of the church, has been interpreted.[7] For example, Verner argues that the author of the Pastorals assumes that church leaders come from a high social standing.[8] He bases this argument on 1 Tim 3:12, where it is said that deacons must not only manage their children but also manage "their own households." He claims that this language indicates that the author is not only referring to wives and children but also slaves, which would indicate that the house owner comes from a high social strata.[9] Verner suggests that society not only influenced the form of church leadership (leaders were chosen based on their position in society) but also influenced the motivation for some to assume positions of leadership. He states:

> The author appears to speak for his church in regarding office in the church as socially prestigious in the same way that citizens of Greek cities and members of associations regarded office holding (1 Tim 3:1,13). One undertook offices as a socially prominent member of one's community in order to fulfill one's civic duties. The social rewards were increased recognition and further enhanced social standing.[10]

Following the lead of Verner, Campbell likewise insists that sociological factors contributed to the development of the leadership structure of the Christian churches. He writes, "The evidence is consistent with the idea that Paul allowed local leadership to emerge in accordance with local realities of power and patronage."[11] Campbell posits that the household, and not the synagogue, is the key to understanding the development of the early church. He maintains that the house churches of the New Testament were not simply buildings but were "extended families with built-in authority patterns of their own."[12] Because the earliest churches met in homes, Paul was dependent on finding someone with a house large enough for meetings. The homeowner, then, would naturally be respected and viewed as the leader of the church.[13]

---

[7] See, for example, D. C. Verner, *The Household of God: The Social World of the Pastoral Epistles* (SBLDS 71; Chico, CA: Scholars Press, 1983); J. Roloff, *Der erste Brief an Timotheus* (EKKNT 15; Zurich: Benzigen; Neukirchen-Vluyn: Neukirchener, 1988), 169–89; R. A. Campbell, *The Elders: Seniority within Earliest Christianity* (SNTIW; Edinburgh: T&T Clark, 1994); Gehring, *House Church*, 260.

[8] Verner, *Household of God*, 152, 159.

[9] Ibid., 133–34, 152, 180.

[10] Ibid., 160 (also see p. 183).

[11] Campbell, *Elders*, 104.

[12] Ibid., 118.

[13] Ibid., 126–31, 196–205. Campbell maintains that the leader of the house church may be given the title "overseer" but not "elder." Only when the overseers of various house churches assembled together could they collectively be called

Campbell concludes: "If the earliest Christians met in homes, then they also had leaders at the household level, leaders provided by the household structure itself."[14]

Gehring holds to a similar position as Campbell, though he offers a few distinctions.[15] He argues that the household (οἶκος) language of the Pastorals clearly signifies a house church setting for local congregations. These congregations would have met in private houses belonging to wealthy members of the congregation. He suggests that the household imagery is not only to be understood metaphorically but also concretely, including its leadership structure. He notes, "Viewed in this way, 'house or family of God' becomes the model for responsible behavior as well as for church order and leadership structures, and thus the central, all-guiding image for the self-understanding and organization of the church."[16] God is viewed as the head (δεσπότης) who appoints an overseer (ἐπίσκοπος) as a house administrator (οἰκονόμος). Because of their position in society, it would have been natural for homeowners to assume leadership positions in the church that met in their homes. "Consequently, it was quite natural that household patterns impressed themselves upon the social reality of the congregation."[17] With Campbell, Gehring concludes that the singular form of overseer in the Pastoral Epistles is evidence that a single leader is envisioned as the leader of the house church. Moreover, he claims that the push for a single leader was caused by the very concept of the church as the house of God. He writes, "The metaphorical use of the expression 'house of God' as the description of the church led to the notion of one single overseer as congregational leader (first as the leader of a house church, then as the leader of the whole church at that location)."[18]

There are several problems with these types of reconstructions. First, such reconstructions are highly speculative. They place great emphasis on claims that are difficult to prove. For example, how do we know that Paul is writing the Pastoral Epistles to encourage overseers at the house level to become overseers at the city level (as Campbell suggests)? There are many other plausible explanations why Paul uses the singular form of the title "overseer" (see below). Second, why should we assume that the household language is based on society and not on the broader theological idea that God is father and that those who trust in Christ are his children and thus part of his family? Third, is the author of the Pastorals really encouraging wealthy homeowners to assume positions of leadership in the church for their own personal

---

"elders." The Pastoral Epistles were written to encourage house-church leaders to step up and become "overseers" at the city level.

[14] Ibid., 153.

[15] Gehring, *House Church*, 278–81, notes at least two problems that he has with Campbell's historical reconstruction. First, Gehring doubts that leaders of house churches were called overseers in the primitive church in Jerusalem. Second, Gehring affirms that the title "elders" is a designation of an office (and not merely a title of honor)—at least in the church in Jerusalem and in the Pastoral Epistles.

[16] Ibid., 261.

[17] Ibid., 298.

[18] Ibid.

gain (for "increased recognition" and "enhanced social standing") as Verner suggests? This does not sound like the type of servant leadership that we find in the teaching of Jesus (Matt 20:25–28; Mark 10:42–45; Luke 22:25–27). Finally, the household metaphor is used in other places in Paul's writings—it is not unique to the Pastoral Epistles. Mounce aptly warns, "The metaphor of the house is relatively minor in the PE and cannot bear the weight placed on it by Verner and others. . . . The metaphor is not a dominating force in the thought of the author and is not used to enforce a rigid structure on the Ephesian and Cretan churches."[19]

Many other items could be discussed under the large banner of ecclesiology (e.g., the role of women, false teachers/teachings, the role of prayer, Scripture reading, or preaching/teaching, etc.). We will, however, focus our attention on the concept of office, including specifics about the two offices of elder/overseer and deacon. But first we will discuss the broader concept of organized ministries in Paul's letters to churches in order to demonstrate that there is continuity in the organizational structure with that found in the Pastoral Epistles.

ORGANIZED MINISTRIES IN PAUL'S LETTERS TO CHURCHES

For more than a century and a half, theologians and historians have vigorously disputed the organizational structure of the earliest Christian communities. With the advent of biblical criticism, the discovery and availability of new sources, and the freedom to challenge the status quo, scholars began to posit new theories related to the development of ecclesiastical structures in the primitive church. It was assumed that because the books of the New Testament could be accurately dated, the comparison of later New Testament documents with earlier ones demonstrated a historical and theological evolution. A reconstruction of the early church was then proposed based on the relevant data. This reconstruction usually stated that the earliest congregations had no officers or formal ecclesiastical organization. The church was led by the free movements of the Spirit and not by static legal codes. The church's embracing of such formal structures (early catholicism) eventually led to its downfall in later centuries. This new view began in Germany but soon spread to England and eventually to the United States. Among Protestant scholars it came to be the "consensus" view.[20]

This "new consensus" viewed the hierarchical structure of the early church as a later addition and even a corruption. The earliest churches had no such fixed law but were led by the direct influence of the Spirit. Jesus had no office and warned his disciples not to seek the power of rank, as is typical among the heathen rulers. Furthermore, when comparing the authentic writings of Paul (Romans, 1 and 2 Corinthians,

---

[19] Mounce, *Pastoral Epistles*, 221.

[20] Proponents of the new consensus include R. Rothe, F. C. Baur, A. Ritschl, E. Hatch, R. Sohm, W. Lowrie, A. von Harnack, R. Bultmann, H. von Campenhausen, E. Schweizer, and E. Käsemann.

Galatians, Philippians, and 1 Thessalonians) with the later (pseudonymous) Pauline Epistles (Ephesians, Colossians, 2 Thessalonians, 1 and 2 Timothy, and Titus), there is a marked difference in organizational structure. The community is no longer led by divinely appointed apostles, prophets, teachers, and other gifted charismatics, but is now led by humanly appointed church officials. The functional, fluid references to those who serve (e.g., co-worker, servant, or overseer) now give way to official, permanent roles. More than any other New Testament writings, the Pastoral Epistles demonstrate the most advanced institutionalization of the church. Church offices are firmly established and those elected to the office receive the *charismata* of the Spirit through human mediation. This institutionalization is further developed in the writings of Clement and Ignatius. Within a century, the authority of the church was thus transferred from the Spirit-endowed charismatics to institutional officers.[21]

Although the above position offers some important correctives (such as affirming the priesthood of all believers and thereby rejecting a rigid clergy-laity distinction), this view has its problems.[22] For example, it is unjustifiable to elevate the organizational structure of the Corinthian church as if Paul were writing a manual of church polity. Paul's letters were occasional and address specific congregational concerns. Also, it is circular reasoning to argue that the Pastoral Epistles are late (i.e., second-century) documents because they contain elements of authoritative church offices and at the same time to argue that because the Pastoral Epistles are late documents, the church offices which they mention must be of late origin. Furthermore, the highly organized nature of the Qumran community, which was sensitive to the Spirit's presence and their being "the community of the end time," raises serious questions as to the probability that the early church, which likewise thought of itself as being "the community of the end time" and possessing the Spirit, should be a charismatic anarchy.[23]

Although it is true that the organizational structure in the Pastoral Epistles appears to be more advanced than the early Pauline epistles, indicating that there is some organizational development found in the New Testament, all of Paul's letters to churches contain elements of organized ministries. Some have noted that the New Testament—especially Paul's early writings—seems to have purposely avoided the technical conception of office.[24] The omission of such technical terms such as

21 For a more complete treatment of the office-charisma debate, see B. L. Merkle, *The Elder and Overseer: One Office in the Early Church* (SBL 57; New York: Peter Lang, 2003), 67–89.

22 Recent scholars who reject the "new consensus" include H. Ridderbos, H. A. Lombard, and R. Y. K. Fung.

23 E. E. Ellis also notes that "at Qumran a ministry of the prophetic spirit, not unlike that of the pneumatics in the Pauline community, existed within a highly structured religious community" (*Pauline Theology: Ministry and Society* [Grand Rapids: Eerdmans, 1989], 89).

24 For example, E. Käsemann states that "the New Testament seems of set purpose to have avoided the technical conception of office which could have been expressed by such words as λειτουργία, τιμή, and ἀρχή" ("Ministry and Community in the New Testament," trans. W . J. Montague, in *Essays on New Testament Themes* [SBT 41; Philadelphia: Fortress, 1964], 63). Käsemann's assessment, however, is not completely accurate because the terms he names were not likely to be used for an ecclesiastical office by the earliest church. The term λειτουργία occurs six times in the New Testament

λειτουργία, τιμή, and ἀρχή is not proof that the *concept* of office, or more broadly, organized ministry, does not exist. There is evidence that Paul established and endorsed organized ministries and offices in the churches with which he had contact.[25] That is, in every one of the churches to which he writes, Paul affirms organized ministries or offices in the church.

For example, in Rom 16:1–2 Phoebe is called a διάκονος of the church in Cenchreae, which can signify that she was more than merely a "servant" but actually held the office of "deacon." In 1 Cor 16:15–16 Paul exhorts the congregation to submit themselves to the leadership of Stephanas and his household because they devoted themselves to serving the church. In Gal 6:6 Paul commands those who receive teaching to support those who provide the teaching. In Eph 4:11 Paul indicates that Jesus has given the church gifts that include the offices of apostle, prophet, evangelist, and pastor-teacher. In Phil 1:1 Paul greets the entire congregation but also specifically mentions the "overseers" (ἐπίσκοποι) and "deacons" (διακόνοι). In Colossians Paul identifies Epaphras (1:7; 4:12) and Archippus (4:17) as leaders in the church. Finally, in 1 Thess 5:12–13 Paul encourages the congregation to recognize (or respect) and to esteem very highly the leaders in the church because of their hard work of leading and admonishing.[26] Although some of these references do not constitute fully developed offices, Paul clearly affirmed organized ministries in his congregations.[27]

---

but is never used as the title of an office-holder (Luke 1:23; 2 Cor 9:12; Phil 2:17,30; Heb 8:6; 9:21; cf. λειτουργός which occurs in Rom 13:6; 15:16; Phil 2:25; Heb 1:7; 8:2). It usually refers to the service one performs to God. In the Septuagint it is often used for the ceremonial service performed by the priest. Only later did λειτουργία come to be used as a technical term for a church office (e.g., *1 Clem.* 44:2,3,6). Therefore, one would not expect this term to be used as an official designation in the early church. The second term, τιμή, is also an unlikely term to be used for a New Testament church office. This term is primarily used to signify (1) price, value or (2) honor, reverence. Under the second meaning it can take on the added quality of "place of honor" or "(honorable) office," although it is used as such only once in the New Testament. In Heb 5:4 it refers to the high priest's (official) dignity, a dignity which now belongs only to Christ. As a result, when this term is used with a more technical sense, it is reserved for the honor of Christ alone. The last term, ἀρχή, can be used to signify a "ruler" or "authority." In the Septuagint and the New Testament, the term is used to refer to government officials, religious officials, the rule of angels and demons, and the rule of Christ. Again, it is questionable whether this term is an appropriate title for a servant-leader in the church (cf. Mark 10:42–44). Christ alone is the ἀρχή of the Church. Küng makes a similar assessment. He states that the New Testament avoided such terms as ἀρχή and τιμή, because "despite the varieties of area they cover, they have one common factor: all express a relationship of rulers and ruled. And it is precisely this which makes them unusable" (H. Küng, *The Church* [trans. R. and R. Ockenden, New York: Sheed & Ward, 1967], 389). It appears that the nature of the New Testament ministry demanded other terms for those selected to be the leaders of the church.

[25] The following elements are often considered to be constitutive for office: (1) permanency, (2) recognition by others (possibly by a title); (3) authority or dignity; (4) payment; and (5) appointment (probably including the laying on of hands). Of course, all these elements do not have to be present. For example, one can serve in an official capacity without receiving payment or without having been officially appointed. When those elements are present, however, it adds to the seriousness and solemnity of the position. The first three elements (permanence, recognition, and authority) may be regarded as representing the essential qualities of "office" and are naturally bound up with one another (see U. Brockhaus, *Charisma und Amt: Die paulinische Charismenlehre auf dem Hintergrund der frühchristlichen Gemeindefunktionen* [Wuppertal: R. Brockaus, 1972], 24n106, 25n123; B. Holmberg, *Paul and Power: The Structure of Authority in the Primitive Church as Reflected in the Pauline Epistles* [Philadelphia: Fortress, 1980], 109–12).

[26] For a more complete treatment of these verses, see Merkle, *Elder and Overseer*, 94–113.

[27] It should be noted, however, that Paul is more interested in service than he is with any office. For example, Holmberg states, "The general impression we get when reading Paul's letters is that the local offices were rather unimportant. . . .

THE OFFICE OF ELDER/OVERSEER

In the Pastoral Epistles, Paul mentions several terms that denote church offices: overseer (1 Tim 3:1–2; Titus 1:7), elder (1 Tim 4:14; 5:17,19; Titus 1:5), and deacon (1 Tim 3:8,12). "Evangelist" is mentioned in 2 Tim 4:5 (as well as Acts 21:8 and Eph 4:11) but is not normally considered a *church* office. Those who hold this title are given the task of ministering outside the church as they seek to evangelize unbelievers (Acts 21:8) or are those who accompanied the apostles or were sent on special tasks (2 Tim 4:5). Some also suggest that there was a formal order of widows. Although the care of widows does seem to reflect a rather organized and official "order," one should not be surprised that widows are singled out because special provisions were made for them from the very beginning of the church (see Acts 6:1–6). Paul, however, might be regarded as essentially teaching against the institutionalization of providing for widows by restricting those who receive aid.[28]

If we do not consider "evangelist" and the "order of widows" as church offices, we are left with three terms to discuss: elder, overseer, and deacon. After we discuss the relationship between the terms elder and overseer, we shall consider the office of deacon and finally address the role that Timothy and Titus have in their respective churches.

THE RELATIONSHIP BETWEEN THE TERMS "ELDER" AND "OVERSEER"

Many scholars of the nineteenth century assumed the terms "elder" and "overseer" to be synonymous. J. B. Lightfoot, for example, confidently states, "It is a fact now generally recognised by theologians of all shades of opinion, that in the language of the New Testament the same officer in the Church is called indifferently 'bishop' (*episkopos*) and 'elder' or 'presbyter' (*presbuteros*)."[29] This position was also common among the early fathers. In the early fifth century, Jerome commented, "Indeed with

---

even if the apostle seems to appreciate them" (*Paul and Power*, 112). Some reasons for this phenomenon are (1) Paul's own authority was still preeminent; (2) the presence of prophets and teachers limited the need for other leaders; (3) the young churches were not in a position to be self-governed; and (4) Paul normally addressed his letters to whole congregations, not simply the leadership. It is the one who *teaches* the word who receives some sort of compensation (Gal 6:6). It is those who *labor*, *lead*, and *admonish* who are to be respected *because of their work* (1 Thess 5:12). The church is to be subject to those who *devote themselves to ministry* (1 Cor 16:15–16). Epaphras is called a faithful *servant* who has *labored earnestly* for the gospel (Col 1:7; 4:12). Archippus is exhorted to fulfill his *ministry* (Col 4:17). Although at times Paul more specifically speaks of office (Rom 16:1–2; Eph 4:11; Phil 1:1), his main concern is that the gospel is advanced. Yet, for that advancement to take place, it is often necessary that others recognize and respect those in leadership positions.

28 Knight states, "Essentially what Paul is doing is correcting the tendency toward institutionalization by restricting the care for widows to widows over 60 years of age who have no family members to care for them and who are spiritually qualified for any special service the church may ask of them. This approach, which emphasizes the family and curtails institutionalization while affirming the need for the family and the church to care for widows, is certainly moving in the opposite direction from that which developed later in the church" (*Pastoral Epistles*, 31). Also see Mounce, *Pastoral Epistles*, lxxxvii.

29 J. B. Lightfoot, *St. Paul's Epistle to the Philippians* (London: Macmillan, 1881), 95. Similarly, E. Hatch writes, "The admissions of both mediaeval and modern writers of almost all schools of theological opinion have practically removed

the ancients these names were synonymous, one alluding to the office, the other to the age of the clergy."[30] In more recent times, however, the majority view has shifted. Many have challenged this former consensus and are offering alternative positions.

At least seven reasons have caused the traditional view to be challenged. First, in the Pastoral Epistles "overseer" is always in the singular whereas "the elders" is always in the plural (except in 1 Tim 5:19). The use of the singular in 1 Tim 3:2 is especially noticeable against the plural "deacons" used in 1 Tim 3:8. Second, in both 1 Tim 3:2 and Titus 1:7, "the overseer" (τὸν ἐπίσκοπον) contains the definite article, which perhaps indicates the elevation of one overseer above the elders.[31] Third, teaching is the responsibility of all overseers (1 Tim 3:2; Titus 1:9), but apparently only some of the elders have this responsibility (1 Tim 5:17). Fourth, where the overseer and deacons are mentioned the elders are not, and where the elders are mentioned the overseer and deacons are not. This usage shows that the terms are not really used interchangeably because they are not used in the same contexts. Fifth, one would not expect two distinct terms to refer to the same office. Sixth, the development of the monarchical bishop in the second century suggests an incipient form can already be found in the New Testament (especially the Pastoral Epistles). Although few would argue that the overseer in the Pastoral Epistles is to be equated with the monarchical bishop, many do identify the beginning development of such a system. Seventh, because the Pastoral Epistles are addressed to individuals and not churches, some argue that Timothy and Titus are intended to portray prototypes of the monarchical bishop.

Based on these (and other) reasons, scholars have proposed a number of alternate views concerning the relationship between the terms "elder" and "overseer." There are at least four recent positions that have garnered some support.[32]

(1) The term "elder" is never a title of an office but is only a designation for age or honor. Although the overseers would routinely be chosen from among the elders, the elders as such were simply those who were respected as the older members of the community.[33]

---

this from the list of disputed questions" (*The Organization of the Early Christian Churches* [The 1880 Bampton Lectures; New York: Lenox Hill, 1881; reprint, 1972], 39n31).

[30] Jerome, *Letter* 69.3 (*NPNF2*; 6:143). Lightfoot further notes, "But, though more full than other writers, [Jerome] is hardly more explicit. Of his predecessors the Ambrosian Hilary had discerned the same truth. Of his contemporaries and successors, Chrysostom, Pelagius, Theodore of Mopsuestia, Theodoret, all acknowledge it. Thus in every one of the extant commentaries on the epistles containing the crucial passages, whether Greek or Latin, before the close of the fifth century, this identity is affirmed" (*Philippians*, 99).

[31] For example, Campenhausen states, "In the Pastoral Epistles the 'bishop' is always spoken of in the singular. The simplest explanation of this fact is that monarchical episcopacy is by now the prevailing system, and that the one bishop has already become the head of the presbyterate" (H. Campenhausen, *Ecclesiastical Authority and Spiritual Power in the Church of the First Three Centuries* [trans. J. A. Baker; Stanford: Stanford University Press, 1969], 107).

[32] For a more complete survey of these views, see Merkle, *Elder and Overseer*, 4–21.

[33] Those who hold this view include R. Sohm, M. R. Vincent, W. Lowrie, A. von Harnack, J. Jeremias, R. A. Campbell, and A. E. Harvey.

(2) Overseers are a special type of elder. That is, they are elders who also perform the special functions of preaching and teaching (1 Tim 5:17). Although the term "elder" is a title of an office-holder, those who held this office were limited in their duties. Thus, this position maintains that the overseers are a subset of specialized elders who have the added responsibilities of preaching and teaching. There is still a plurality of overseers in each church, ruling out the idea of a monarchical bishop.[34]

(3) The overseer is above, but still identified with, the elders. Each church had one overseer who was the president of the elders. The overseer, however, is still identified with the council of the elders, being selected from their ranks to preside over them and the church.[35]

(4) The overseer is above, but not identified with, the elders. The overseer is the monarchical bishop, with sole, supreme authority.[36]

EVIDENCE THAT THE TERMS "ELDER" AND "OVERSEER" DENOTE THE SAME OFFICE

All of the above positions deny that the terms "elder" and "overseer" are equated in the Pastoral Epistles. Although each view has some strengths that need to be taken into account, they all have difficulties that cannot be overcome. For example, to claim that elder is never a title of an office-holder in the Pastoral Epistles goes against the evidence. This can be demonstrated by the term's official use in the Old Testament, early Judaism, and the Greco-Roman sources.[37] Also, in the New Testament itself, the term is clearly used for an office-holder (see Acts 14:23; Titus 1:5–7). It is also insufficient to claim that the ecclesiology in the Pastoral Epistles is so advanced that the overseer is an office above that of the elder. As we have already seen, much of the organizational structure found in the Pastorals can be traced back to Paul's early letters.

The view that elder and overseer are used interchangeably in the Pastoral Epistles (and the New Testament) is best able to account for all the New Testament data.[38] The following discussion demonstrates that in the Pastoral Epistles the terms "elder" and "overseer" refer to the same office.[39] There are three texts we will examine in detail

---

[34] Those who hold this view include H. von Soden, C. von Weizsäcker, P. Carrington, P. Benoit, J. N. D. Kelly, G. Bornkamm, H. W. Beyer, M. Goguel, O. Pfleiderer, G. Holtz, N. Brox, L. Goppelt, M. Dibelius and H. Conzelmann, K. Kertelge, J. P. Meier, J. G. Sobosan, L. Floor, S. G. Wilson, R. E. Brown, and G. Fee.

[35] Those who hold this view include F. C. Baur, W. Lock, A. M. Farrer, C. K. Barrett, P. Grelot, J. Gnilka, C. Spicq, W. Schmithals, F. Hahn, H. von Lips, E. Lohse, J. Roloff, K. Giles, H. Merkel, and L. T. Johnson.

[36] There is some variation within this view. Some affirm a monarchical bishop (E. Käsemann, H. von Campenhausen, and A. T. Hanson). Others maintain that the overseer has not yet reached the point where he could rightly be called a monarchical bishop (G. G. Blum and H. W. Bartsch). Still others state that the concept of a monarchical bishop is the author's ideal but not the actual state of affairs in the churches to which he was writing (L. Oberlinner and B. S. Easton).

[37] For an overview of the background of the terms "elder" and "overseer," see Merkle, *Elder and Overseer*, 23–65.

[38] Those who hold this view include J. B. Lightfoot, C. Gore, E. Hatch, E. F. Scott, W. Michaelis, R. Bultmann, H. Schlier, E. Schweizer, M. M. Bourke, P. Burke, H. Ridderbos, J. Rohde, R. Schwarz, G. Schöllgen, E. E. Ellis, D. A. Carson and D. J. Moo, G. Knight, J. Ysebaert, D. Mappes, and W. D. Mounce.

[39] Although most who hold this position see elder and overseer as completely interchangeable, Fee maintains that it is possible that the term "elders" covers both overseers and deacons (G. Fee, *1 and 2 Timothy, Titus*, NIBC [Peabody,

because they mention the terms elder and/or overseer: Titus 1:5–9; 1 Tim 3:1–7 and 1 Tim 5:17–25. Because Titus represents an ecclesiastic structure less developed than that of 1 Timothy, we will discuss Paul's letter to Titus first.

TITUS 1:5–7

Although there are many questions that could be asked of this text, we will focus our attention on the relationship between the terms "elder" and "overseer." From a *prima facie* reading of this text, it appears as if the author uses the terms to refer to the same office ("appoint elders . . . for an overseer"). Yet, many point out that such a reading is simplistic because πρεσβύτερος occurs in the plural whereas ἐπίσκοπος is in the singular.[40] There are, however, compelling reasons for equating the offices of elder and overseer in Titus 1:5–7.

(1) The connective γάρ in v. 7 suggests that Paul is referring to the same office. If the overseer represents a separate office, then the use of γάρ is obscure. The elders are to be blameless meeting certain qualifications for (γάρ) as overseers they are God's stewards.[41]

(2) Because the switch to the singular actually takes place in v. 6 with the use of the singular indefinite pronoun τις, one should not be surprised by the continuation of the singular in v. 7 with the use of ἐπίσκοπος.

(3) It is more natural to list the requirements in the singular because every elder/overseer must individually meet the qualifications. The singular form is therefore a generic singular, referring to anyone who would meet the qualifications listed.[42]

(4) It is not uncommon for Paul to alternate between singular and plural generic nouns, particularly within the Pastoral Epistles.[43] Based on this pattern found in the

---

Mass.: Hendrickson, 1984], 22, 78, 128. This view is also held by D. Powell, "Ordo Presbyterii," *JTS* 26 [1975]: 306). Although it is true that the terms were somewhat flexible, this view is not likely because the New Testament often uses elders and overseers interchangeably but never elders and deacons. Mounce rightly notes that "it would be confusing to join two distinct groups [i.e., overseers and deacons] under the same title without some contextual indication" (Mounce, *Pastoral Epistles*, 308).

[40] According to R. A. Campbell, the shift from the plural "elders" to the singular "overseer" refers to the appointment of "monepiskopoi," leaders over the churches at the city level (κατὰ πόλιν). Why then are those appointed first called "elders" (πρεσβύτεροι)? Campbell states that it is either because that is the group from which they come, or because πρεσβύτεροι is a collective term of honour no less suitable for a number of leaders of town churches than of house churches. The writer then refers to the ἐπίσκοπος in the singular because it is the recognition of a single overseer with which he is concerned (Campbell, *Elders*, 244).

[41] Mounce states that γάρ "ties the discussion together and argues against the suggestion that the overseers are distinct from the elders" (*Pastoral Epistles*, 390).

[42] So Fee, *1 and 2 Timothy, Titus*, 84; D. Guthrie, *The Pastoral Epistles* (rev. ed.; TNTC 14; Leicester, England: Inter-Varsity; Grand Rapids: Eerdmans, 1990), 32–33; J. N. D. Kelly, *A Commentary on the Pastoral Epistles* (BNTC; London: Adam & Charles Black, 1963), 13, 231; Knight, *Pastoral Epistles*, 176, 291; T. D. Lea and H. P. Griffin, *1, 2 Timothy, Titus* (NAC 34; Nashville: Broadman, 1992), 283; I. H. Marshall, *A Critical and Exegetical Commentary on the Pastoral Epistles*, in collaboration with P. H. Towner (ICC; Edinburgh: T&T Clark, 1999), 160, 178; Mounce, *Pastoral Epistles*, 163, 390; P. H. Towner, *The Goal of Our Instruction: The Structure of Theology and Ethics in the Pastoral Epistles* (JSNTSup 34; Sheffield: JSOT, 1989), 225.

[43] For example, in 1 Tim 2:8 Paul addresses the men (τοὺς ἄνδρας) but then speaks of the singular man (ἀνδρός) in v. 12. Again, in 1 Tim 2:9 Paul exhorts the women (γυναῖκας) to adorn themselves in modest apparel, but in v. 11 he says,

Pastoral Epistles, one should not be surprised to find the author first referring to the "elders" (plural) and then to the "overseer" (singular).

(5) In both classical and biblical Greek, καθίστημι is used with the meaning of appointing someone to office—the office being in the accusative case. For example, Luke 12:14 states, "Who appointed Me a judge or arbitrator over you?" (τίς με κατέστησεν κριτὴν ἢ μεριστὴν ἐφ᾽ ὑμᾶς;). Another example is found in 1 Macc 3:55: "And after this Judas appointed leaders [κατέστησεν ἡγουμένους] over the people."[44] In each case, the office to which the appointment is made is clearly set forth with the office being in the accusative case. Therefore, if Titus 1:5 is to be understood as meaning that Titus was to appoint elderly men to be office holders, the verb "to appoint" would require an additional accusative construction specifying to what office the elderly men are to be appointed. Because the term "elder" (πρεσβυτέρους) is the only accusative in the text, those who fail to see elder as an office, in essence, argue that Paul is commanding Titus to appoint some to be older men.[45]

(6) The author of the Pastoral Epistles may have been using a preformed piece of tradition similar to virtue lists found in the Hellenistic world.[46] If the tradition contained the singular "overseer," then it would be more natural to adjust the text to

---

"A woman [γυνή] should learn in silence." In 1 Tim 2:15 this principle is again illustrated. Paul concludes his discussion on the role of women by stating that "she will be saved [σωθήσεται] through childbearing if they continue [μείνωσιν] in faith, love, and holiness, with self-control." In the same sentence Paul switches from the singular to the plural. This same pattern is also found in 1 Tim 5. In v. 1 Paul commands Timothy not to rebuke an older man (πρεσβυτέρῳ) but to exhort him as a father (πατέρα) and the younger men (νεωτέρους) as brothers (ἀδελφούς). Furthermore, in vv. 3 and 4 of the same chapter, Paul reminds the church, "Support widows [χήρας] who are genuinely widows" and then goes on to say, "But if any widow [χήρα] has children or grandchildren. . . ." In v. 11 he switches back to the plural when he speaks of the "younger widows" (νεωτέρας). It should be noted that this passage concerning widows is particularly important because, like Titus 1, this passage also deals with qualifications for a particular position. Finally, 1 Tim 5:17 states that elders (πρεσβύτεροι) who rule well are worthy of double honor. Yet, in v. 19 we are told that the church should not receive an accusation against "an elder" (πρεσβύτερου). Verse 20 then speaks of "those who sin" (τοὺς ἁμαρτάνας), which most agree refers to the elders.

44 Cf. Matt 24:45: "Who then is the faithful and wise slave whom his master appointed [κατέστησεν] over his household." Also see Exod 2:14; 1 Macc 10:20; 4 Macc 4:16; Acts 7:10,27,35; Heb 5:1; *1 Clem.* 42:5; 43:1.

45 Harvey appeals to *1 Clem.* 42:4 which states that the apostles "appointed their firstfruits . . . to be bishops and deacons" (καθίστανον τὰς ἀπαρχὰς αὐτῶν . . . εἰς ἐπισκόπους καὶ διακόνους). "Firstfruit" is an expression in 1 Cor 16:15 meaning "first converts." Because no one can be *appointed* a first convert, A. E. Harvey argues that the passage obviously means that the apostles appointed their first converts to hold particular offices ("Elders," *JTS* 25 [1974]: 329). Thus, Harvey translates Titus 1:5, "Appoint (to positions of responsibility) those of your elders (i.e., elder members) who have such and such a character: for the bishop must be . . ." (ibid., 331). The problem with comparing *1 Clem.* 42:4 to Titus 1:5 is that the former does not leave open the question as to what office the first converts were appointed. The text goes on to say that they appointed their firstfruits "to be overseers and deacons." The nature of the appointment is clarified by the phrase εἰς ἐπισκόπους καὶ διακόνους. If Titus 1:5 stated that Titus was to appoint elders "to be overseers" (εἰς ἐπισκόπους), then Harvey's comparison would be valid (C. H. Roberts also notes that you would expect the text not simply to read πρεσβύτερος but ἐκ τῶν πρεσβυτέρων ["Elders: A Note," *JTS* 26 (1975): 404]). Such a comparison, however, is misleading because we are not told to which office the elders are appointed. It is therefore not grammatically justifiable to claim the text means that elders (i.e., older or honored men) were appointed to the office of overseer.

46 See E. E. Ellis, "Traditions in the Pastoral Epistles," in *Early Jewish and Christian Exegesis* (ed. C. Evans and W. F. Stinespring; Atlanta: Scholars Press, 1987), 237–53; idem, *The Making of the New Testament Documents* [BIS 39; Leiden: Brill, 1999], 406–25. There appears to be a general consensus that the lists in 1 Tim 3 and Titus 1 are based on preformed traditions.

fit the tradition than vice-versa.[47] The fact that the lists of Titus 1 and 1 Timothy 3 are so similar supports this conclusion.[48]

If preformed traditions are being used, why are the lists of qualifications not identical? For example, why does the list in 1 Timothy include "not . . . a new convert" (μὴ νεόφυτον, 3:6) whereas Titus omits it? This omission may have been a necessary modification due to the early stage of development of the Cretan churches. Relatively new converts would then be needed in leadership of the younger churches.

(7) It appears that the church in Crete was a relatively young church based on the following comparisons of Titus 1 with 1 Timothy 3:[49] (a) Titus omits the qualification of not being a new convert. (b) Titus gives no qualifications for deacons.[50] (c) Timothy is never told to appoint elders because they already existed. Apparently, Paul was with Titus in Crete but had to leave before he could appoint elders (cf. Acts 14:23). (d) Because there is no discussion of the removal of a bad elder in Titus as there is in 1 Tim 5:17–25, this possibly indicates that they did not yet have elders. (e) There is no order of widows mentioned in Titus (cf. 1 Tim 5:3–16). Consequently, if the churches in Crete were relatively young, how likely is it that these churches were dealing with the developed concept of a monarchical bishop?[51]

(8) Finally, there are similar cases where an author switches from elder to overseer in the New Testament, demonstrating that the words are used interchangeably. In Acts 20 Paul sends for the Ephesian elders to exhort them in their work (Acts 20:17). He charges them to take heed of themselves and of all the flock because the

---

[47] Cf. the singular πρεσβύτερος of 1 Tim 5:1 and the singular widow of 1 Tim 5:9.

[48] For example, the qualifications begin in a strikingly similar fashion: δεῖ γὰρ τὸν ἐπίσκοπον ἀνέγκλητον εἶναι (Titus 1:7); δεῖ οὖν τὸν ἐπίσκοπον ἀνεπίληπτον εἶναι (1 Tim 3:2). The different particles used can be explained on the basis of context, while the adjectives ἀνέγκλητον and ἀνεπίληπτον are mere synonyms. The same requirement is also at the head of each list: μιᾶς γυναικὸς ἀνήρ (Titus 1:6); μιᾶς γυναικὸς ἄνδρα (1 Tim 3:2). Furthermore, the elements in the following lists are generally comparable. The use of a preformed office code may also explain why the author of Titus uses the definite article (τὸν ἐπίσκοπον). J. P. Meier comments, "It may be, of course, that the singular in vs. 7 is also due to the fact that the author is here quoting a set list of requirements, a list in which *ton episkopon* is firmly embedded" ("Presbyteros in the Pastoral Epistles," *CBQ* 35 [1973]: 338). Mappes also notes, "The articular, singular construction of τὸν ἐπίσκοπον might be interpreted to mean a single overseer in a church, but because Paul has not changed subjects, the context requires that τὸν ἐπίσκοπον represents the group of πρεσβύτεροι" (D. Mappes, "The New Testament Elder, Overseer, and Pastor," *BSac* 154 [1997]: 166–67).

[49] So P. Carrington, *The First Christian Century* (vol. 1 of *The Early Christian Church*; Cambridge: Cambridge University Press, 1957), 269; L. T. Johnson, *Letters to Paul's Delegates: 1 Timothy, 2 Timothy, Titus* (Valley Forge, PA: Trinity Press International, 1996), 223; Kelly, *Pastoral Epistles*, 78; Lea-Griffin, *1, 2 Timothy, Titus*, 278n11; Marshall, *Pastoral Epistles*, 146; Meier, "Presbyteros in the Pastoral Epistles," 337; Mounce, *Pastoral Epistles*, 385–86; Towner, *Goal of Our Instruction*, 233. Meier states that in relation to 1 Timothy, "One gets the impression when reading Tit[us] that a much more primitive state of ecclesiastical affairs is being described" ("Presbyteros in the Pastoral Epistles," 337). Against this view, H. Merklein argues that the church at Crete was more advanced than the Ephesian church (*Das kirchliche Amt nach dem Epheserbrief* [SANT 33; Munich: Kösel, 1973], 390).

[50] Knight agrees, "Tit[us] 1:5 suggests that the church in Crete had been established only a short time and was still virtually unorganized. In such a situation, only the initial rank of officers is prescribed, i.e., the bishops/presbyters, while 1 Tim 3 refers to both bishops and deacons" (*Pastoral Epistles*, 175). Also see Marshall, *Pastoral Epistles*, 488.

[51] So Guthrie, *Pastoral Epistles*, 36–37. Later he notes, "It is also surprising that he left the distinction between elders and bishops so ambiguous, if by the time of writing there was no possibility of the terms being used for the same office, as they are in the Pastorals" (ibid., 38).

Holy Spirit has made them "overseers [ἐπισκόπους], to shepherd the church of God" (Acts 20:28). First, Luke records that Paul calls them elders, but then has Paul referring to them as overseers ("he sent to Ephesus and called for the elders . . . the Holy Spirit has appointed you as overseers"). Another example of the close connection between elder and overseer is found in 1 Pet 5:1–2, which states, "The elders who are among you I exhort . . . shepherd the flock of God which is among you, serving as overseers [ἐπισκοποῦτες]" (NKJV). Although the verb form is used (ἐπισκοπέω), this text demonstrates that the duties of an elder involved exercising oversight over the church. It is therefore reasonable to maintain that πρεσβύτερος and ἐπίσκοπος refer to the same office in Titus 1.[52]

1 TIMOTHY 3:1–7; 5:17–25

As with the Titus 1 text, the focus of this section will not be to exegete the verses under discussion but to expand on those items that shed light on the nature of the relationship between elder and overseer. That is, we will demonstrate that the terms "elder" and "overseer" refer to the same office in this epistle. Similar to the arguments made with respect to Titus 1:5–7, it is often maintained that references to "the overseer" in 1 Tim 3:1–2 and references to "the elders" in 1 Tim 5:17 represent two distinct offices. There is, however, significant evidence that Paul uses the two terms to refer to the same office.

(1) It is probable that the singular form (τὸν ἐπίσκοπον) in 1 Tim 3:2 is a generic singular. Fee comments, "[the εἴ τις] clause in v. 1, which has led to the singular in this verse, is a nonlimiting, or generalizing, conditional sentence. It recurs in 1 Tim 5:8 and 6:3, and in both cases—esp. 6:3—refers to a group of more than one."[53] The context of 1 Tim 2:8–3:16 also argues against the monadic view because the singular generic noun is often used (e.g., 1 Tim 2:11–12). Furthermore, the argument that "overseer" always appears in the singular in the Pastoral Epistles is a weak argument because it only occurs three times, and in precisely the same context (cf. 1 Tim 3:1,2; Titus 1:7).

The argument that the singular τὸν ἐπίσκοπον cannot be generic because the following reference to deacons (διακόνους) in v. 8 is plural is not as weighty as might first appear. Towner rightly notes that the absence of either a δεῖ . . . εἶναι (1 Tim 3:2; Titus 1:7) or a conditional εἴ τις (Titus 1:6; cf. 1 Tim 3:1) introductory formula, "and the disruptive insertion of v. 11 (qualifications pertaining to deaconesses or deacons' wives) give the impression that the deacon code was added on the spur of

---

52 H. W. Beyer rightly states, "The qualifications of presbyters here are like those of the bishops in 1 Tm. 3:2ff. In fact, there is an alteration of terms in Tt. 1:7, where we suddenly have ἐπίσκοπος instead of πρεσβύτερος. This is another proof that the two terms originally referred to the same thing" ("ἐπίσκοπος," *TDNT* 2:617). Also see *1 Clem.* 42–44.

53 Fee, *1 and 2 Timothy, Titus*, 84. Mounce likewise comments, "In 1 Timothy it appears that since there is only one office of overseer (with many fulfilling the role), Paul begins 3:1–7 with the generic singular . . . and to stay consistent continues with singular forms" (*Pastoral Epistles*, 163).

the moment, perhaps being modeled on the longer-standing bishop code."[54] In addition, as we have seen earlier, the author of the Pastorals often shifts from the generic singular to the plural.

(2) If overseer and elder represent two separate offices, it is strange that Paul never mentions the qualifications of elders in 1 Timothy, especially because the character of the one who is to fill the office of elder is so important. For example, in 1 Tim 5:22 Paul cautions Timothy not to lay hands (i.e., appoint) anyone to the position of an elder hastily because that position is to be filled only by qualified individuals (cf. 4:14; 2 Tim 1:6). If elder is a distinct office from overseer, it would seem that qualifications would be clearly stated for such an important position.[55]

(3) Nowhere are the three offices (elder, overseer, and deacon) mentioned together, which suggests that a three-tiered ecclesiastical system is foreign to the Pastoral Epistles. The letters of Ignatius, on the other hand, make a clear distinction between the monarchical bishop and the presbytery. That is, in Ignatius for the first time we see a three-tiered ecclesiastical system with a bishop, a presbytery (or elders), and deacons. For example, Ignatius exhorts his readers:

> Be eager to do everything in godly harmony, the bishop presiding in the place of God and the presbyters in the place of the council of the apostles and the deacons, who are most dear to me, having been entrusted with the service of Jesus Christ. (*Magn.* 6:1)[56]

For Ignatius, the overseer is clearly distinct from the council of elders and is the sole head of the city-church. Such a distinction, however, is nowhere found in the Pastoral Epistles.

(4) The fact that qualifications are given and not duties also argues against seeing this epistle in the context of a later, more developed system with a monarchical bishop. The only exception is that the overseer should be "an able teacher." But as Mounce states, "An ability to teach and an exemplary character do not point to developments beyond the Pauline churches."[57]

(5) The interchangeable usage of "elder" and "overseer" in some writings of the postapostolic era is further evidence that the terms represented the same office in the apostolic era. For example, *1 Clement*, written at the end of the first century AD, uses

---

[54] Towner, *Goal of Our Instruction*, 227.

[55] In the context Paul warns that patience is necessary because Timothy is in danger of sharing in the sins of others. Verses 24–25 add that the sins of some are not readily apparent, and therefore it is sometimes difficult to immediately know if one is qualified for an office. Patience is needed to let the negative qualities surface before hastily appointing someone to office. This admonition to Timothy is similar to 1 Tim 3:6 (which states that overseers must not be recent converts) and to 3:10 (which commands the candidates for the office of deacon to undergo a period of testing in order confirm their character).

[56] All quotations from Ignatius are from J. B. Lightfoot, J. R. Harmer, and M. W. Holmes, eds., *The Apostolic Fathers: Greek Text and English Translations of Their Writings* (2nd ed.; Grand Rapids: Baker, 1992). Also see Ign. *Eph.* 2:2; 4:1; Ign. *Magn.* 2:1; 13:1; Ign. *Trall.* 2:2–3; 7:2; Ign. *Phld.* 4:1; 7:1; Ign. *Smyrn.* 8:1; 12:2; Ign. *Pol.* 6:1.

[57] Mounce, *Pastoral Epistles*, 154.

the terms elder and overseer interchangeably.[58] In *1 Clem.* 44:4–5, the author mentions how it is wrong to depose πρεσβύτεροι from the ἐπισκοπή. It is interesting that in this passage the "office of overseer" is in the singular while the "elders" who fill that office are in the plural (cf. Titus 1:5–7).[59] This is evidence that in Corinth (the letter's destination) and Rome (the letter's provenance) the churches had no monarchical bishop.[60]

(6) The fact that elders and overseers are said to have the same function in the church (i.e., ruling/leading and teaching) also suggests that the two terms refer to the same office. First Timothy 3:4–5 states that an *overseer* must know how to manage (προΐστημι) his own household before he is fit to take care of (ἐπιμελέομαι) the church (cf. Rom 12:8; 1 Thess 5:12). Likewise, 1 Tim 5:17 speaks of *elders* who rule (προΐστημι) well, indicating that all elders are involved in ruling or leading the church.[61]

In a similar manner, both are also given the duty of teaching the congregation. In 1 Tim 3:2 every *overseer* must be "an able teacher" in order to be qualified, and in Titus 1:9 an *overseer* must "be able both to encourage with sound teaching and to refute those who contradict it." Likewise, *elders* who rule well should be considered worthy of double honor, "especially those who work hard at preaching and teaching" (1 Tim 5:17). Because elders and overseers are given the same tasks of ruling/leading and teaching, they should be viewed as representing the same office.

(7) It is argued that because an overseer must be "an able teacher" (διδακτικόν, 1 Tim 3:2; cf. Titus 1:9) and only some elders "work hard at preaching and teaching" (1 Tim 5:17), this suggests that only those elders who taught were designated with the title "overseer." This interpretation, however, fails to acknowledge that among those

---

[58] E. G. Jay also maintains that "for [Clement] the word ἐπίσκοπος is clearly a synonym for πρεσβύτερος. He gives no hint in the letter of a claim to a higher status. . . . His letter gives us no reason to suppose that either in Rome or in Corinth in the last decade of the first century the presbyters as a corporate body did not exercise ἐπισκοπή, the oversight of the affairs of their churches in general, with responsibility for discipline, instruction, and the administration of the sacraments. Monepiscopacy . . . was not established there on the eve of the second century" ("From Presbyter-Bishops to Bishops and Presbyters," *SecCent* 1 [1981]: 136; also see B. E. Bowe, *A Church in Crisis: Ecclesiology and Paraenesis in Clement of Rome* [HDR 23; Minneapolis: Fortress, 1988], 149). Jay also asserts that the monepiscopacy is not found in the *Didache*, Polycarp, and Hermas (ibid., 128, 142–43; also see P. Burke, "The Monarchical Episcopate at the End of the First Century," *JES* 7 [1970]: 499–518). Cf. *Did.* 15:1 (ἐπίσκοποι and διάκονοι); Pol. *Phil.* 5:3 (πρεσβύτεροι and διάκονοι); Herm. *Vis.* 3.5.1 (ἀπόστολοι and ἐπίσκοποι and διδάσκαλοι and διάκονοι).

[59] Elsewhere Clement speaks of ἐπίσκοποι and διάκονοι without mentioning πρεσβύτεροι (*1 Clem.* 42:4–5).

[60] Campbell suggests that the church at Corinth did have a monarchical bishop and that Clement knew of this development, but because he did not approve of the rise of one person over the other leaders, Clement writes to have the overseers/elders reinstated. Campbell states, "Clement wants to preserve the identification of elders and overseers that he knows belongs to the time of the apostles . . . but some unnamed person has sought to promote his own episcopacy at the expense of the other house-church ἐπίσκοποι" (*Elders*, 214). Such a reconstruction is highly speculative and questionable because it reinterprets the basic thrust of the entire letter based on someone (a self-promoted bishop) who is never mentioned. Furthermore, Clement charges the entire congregation (you plural), not one person, for removing the elders from their leadership positions (*1 Clem.* 44:6).

[61] J. D. Quinn and W. C. Wacker state that "a *presbyter* is here defined in terms of his *proïstanai*, and this in turn was precisely the term that 1 Tim 3:4–5 used to illustrate the relationship of the *episkopos* to the church" (*The First and Second Letters to Timothy*, [ECC; Grand Rapids: Eerdmans, 2000], 459).

who hold the same office, there is likely to be some who are more gifted in particular areas, such as teaching.[62] Also, if 1 Tim 3:2–7 and Titus 1:7–9 represent preformed traditional codes, "then it is conceivable that requirements related to function were meant to be typical, that is, generally related to the office, but not necessarily to be carried out by every office-holder, at least not in the sense of 1 Tim 5.17."[63] As a rule every candidate for this office was to have some abilities in teaching.[64]

Mounce states that the phrase καλῶς προεστῶτες (1 Tim 5:17) could be interpreted the following ways while still addressing only one office: (a) "While asserting that all elders are able to teach, Paul could have based the division on those currently teaching and those who were not. Perhaps . . . [some] overseers would have had to vary the amount of time spent specifically on teaching because of other responsibilities, and this admonition would address those actively teaching."[65] (b) This phrase "could apply to gifted teachers who were currently leading in other ways (while still allowing for one-on-one teaching, both with the opponents and the other members of the church), and 'laboring hard at preaching and teaching' could apply to those currently teaching the church as a whole."[66] (c) "The division could be based on those who were able to teach and those who were especially gifted to teach, dividing the elders on the basis of ability and giftedness and assuming that the more gifted did more of the corporate instruction."[67]

Furthermore, there is also the possibility of translating μάλιστα as "namely" or "that is" instead of "especially."[68] In this case Paul is not making a distinction between those who rule well and those who, in addition to ruling well, also preach and teach. Rather, those who rule well are precisely those who teach and preach (i.e., Paul is

---

[62] Mappes comments, "While all elder-overseer-pastors must be able to teach (1 Tim 3:2) and exhort and refute with sound doctrine (Titus 1:9), they may not all have the spiritual gifts of teaching and exhorting (Rom. 12:7)" ("New Testament Elder," 174).

[63] Towner, *Goal of Our Instruction*, 226.

[64] M. Dibelius and H. Conzelmann assert that διδακτικός ("skillful in teaching," 1 Tim 3:2) "does not prove that the bishop had already assumed, as his regular duty, the office of teaching . . . but only that some capability in this regard was desired" (*The Pastoral Epistles* [trans. P. Buttolph and A. Yarbro; Hermeneia; Philadelphia: Fortress, 1972], 53).

[65] Mounce, *Pastoral Epistles*, 308. This is the position of Kelly, *Pastoral Epistles*, 124–25, and Quinn-Wacker, *First and Second Letters to Timothy*, 459. Quinn-Wacker write, "The point here is that some (and they are relatively few, one would surmise, because of the doubling of the honorarium) have obviously devoted all their time to this service and have done it well" (ibid.).

[66] Mounce, *Pastoral Epistles*, 308.

[67] Ibid. This is the position of E. F. Scott, *The Pastoral Epistles* (MNTC; New York: Harper, 1936), 64–65; C. K. Barrett, *The Pastoral Epistles in the English Bible* (Oxford: Clarendon, 1963), 79; Mappes, "New Testament Elder," 174; and G. W. Knight, who writes, "Although all elders are to be able to teach (1 Tim 3:2) and thus to instruct the people of God and to communicate with those who oppose biblical teaching (Tit 1:9ff.), the 1 Timothy 5:17 passage recognizes that among the elders, all of whom are to be able to teach, there are those so gifted by God with the ability to teach the Word that they are called by God to give their life in such a calling or occupation and deserve therefore to be remunerated for such a calling and occupation" ("Two Offices [Elders/Bishops and Deacons] and Two Orders of Elders [Preaching/Teaching Elders and Ruling Elders]: A New Testament Study," *Presbyterion* 11 [1985]: 6).

[68] See T. C. Skeat, who convincingly argues that μάλιστα is often best translated as "namely" ("'Especially the Parchments': A Note on 2 Timothy IV. 13," *JTS* 30 [1979]: 173–77). Those who follow this interpretation include Marshall, *Pastoral Epistles*, 612; and Towner, *1–2 Timothy & Titus*, 125.

stating that the elders rule well *by* their teaching and preaching). This interpretation seems to fit the author's stress on the importance of teaching and a threefold division of elders is hard to imagine.[69]

(8) The reason two terms are given for the same office could be explained by the general use of the terms: elder is more a description of character whereas overseer is more a description of function.[70] It appears that originally various congregations preferred one term over the other. The Jewish congregations apparently favored the term πρεσβύτερος, while the Gentile congregations favored the term ἐπίσκοπος. Over time these two terms came to be used in the same congregations and could be used interchangeably because they referred to the leaders of the congregation. It is likely that both terms remained due to the important connotations each term carried. The term πρεσβύτερος conveyed the idea of a wise, mature leader who was honored and respected by those of the community. The term ἐπίσκοπος spoke more to the work of the individual whose duty it was to provide "oversight" to the congregation. The term conveyed the idea of protection and supervision over those under their care.[71]

THE OFFICE OF DEACON[72]

Surprisingly, the Greek term διάκονος only occurs three or four times as a designation of an office-holder (Rom 16:1[?]; Phil 1:1; 1 Tim 3:8,12). The first occurrence is in Rom 16:1, where Phoebe is called a διάκονος "of the church in Cenchreae." This particular reference is debated as to whether Paul is using the term διάκονος as a general term for "servant" or as a more technical term for a "deacon" (i.e., a church officer). Most English Bible versions choose the more neutral term "servant," but the RSV renders it "deaconess" and the NRSV renders it "deacon." The second occur-

---

69 Yet even with this interpretation a distinction can be made between two types of elders. If "ruling well" is defined by "working hard at preaching and teaching," then a distinction can still be made between those who rule well (i.e., preach and teach) and those who do not rule well (i.e., do not preach and teach). For example, Knight states that it is likely that Paul "is speaking of a subgroup of the 'overseers' that consists of those who are *especially* gifted by God to teach, as opposed to other overseers, who must all 'be *able* to teach'" (*Pastoral Epistles*, 233). But it is also possible that Paul is speaking generally of all the elders and is not intending to distinguish a subgroup (So P. H. Towner, *1–2 Timothy & Titus* [IVPNTC 14; Downers Grove, IL: InterVarsity, 1994], 125). Regardless of how this difficult verse is interpreted, it in no way demands one to see two offices involved. At most, the text indicates a distinction of function within one particular office.

70 P. Schaff states that "the terms PRESBYTER (or Elder) and BISHOP (or Overseer, Superintendent) denote in the New Testament one and the same office, with this difference . . . that the one signifies the dignity, the other the duty" (*Apostolic Christianity* [vol. 1 of *History of the Christian Church*; 3rd rev. ed.; Peabody, Mass.: Hendrickson, 1996; originally published in 1858], 491–92). C. K. Barrett states, "It is broadly speaking true that the one designation describes ministers from a sociological, the other from a theological angle" (*A Critical and Exegetical Commentary on the Acts* [ICC; Edinburgh: T&T Clark, 1998], 2:975).

71 The term "pastor" (or "shepherd")—only found in Eph 4:11 as a title of an office in the church—also represents the same office as elder/overseer for at least two reasons. First, elders/overseers are given the same tasks of shepherding and teaching (cf. with Acts 20:17,28; Eph 4:11; 1 Tim 3:2; 5:17; Titus 1:9; 1 Pet 5:1–3). Second, if the office of "pastor" is distinct from the elder/overseer, what are the qualifications needed for those who hold this office? Paul provides the qualifications for the elder/overseer but never for the pastor. Perhaps the reason for this omission is because in giving the qualifications for the elder/overseer, he is giving the qualifications for those who can also be called "pastor."

72 This section is an adaptation of my earlier work, *40 Questions about Elders and Deacons* (Grand Rapids: Kregel, 2008), 227–32, 238–48.

rence of διάκονος as a reference to a church office is found in Paul's opening greeting in his letter to the Philippians. He addresses "all the saints in Christ Jesus who are in Philippi, including the overseers and deacons" (Phil 1:1). This is the only place where Paul greets church officers in the salutation of his letters and is perhaps the clearest indication of a distinction between church members and church leaders in Paul's early writings.

The final two occurrences of διάκονος as a reference to a church office are found in 1 Timothy 3 where Paul lists the requirements needed for "deacons." It is striking that Paul does not explain the duties of this office, which suggests that the Ephesian church already had experience with deacons. Paul simply lists the qualifications and assumes the church will use these officers in the appropriate manner. Because Paul does not list any of the duties deacons should perform, it is likely that the early church understood the Seven chosen in Acts 6 to be a model for their own ministry.[73] That is, as deacons they were responsible for caring for the physical needs of the congregation and doing whatever was needed so that the elders could focus on their work of teaching and shepherding.

The New Testament does not provide much information concerning the role of deacons. The requirements given in 1 Tim 3:8–12 focus on the deacon's character and family life. There are, however, some clues as to the function of deacons when their requirements are compared with those of the elders. Although many of the qualifications are the same or very similar, there are some notable differences.

Perhaps the most noticeable distinction between elders and deacons is that deacons do not need to be "an able teacher" (1 Tim 3:2; cf. 5:17). Deacons are called to "hold" to the faith with a clear conscience, but they are not called to "teach" that faith (1 Tim 3:9). This suggests that the deacons do not have an official teaching role in the church. D. A. Carson rightly comments, "Deacons were responsible to serve the church in a variety of subsidiary roles, but enjoyed no church-recognized teaching authority akin to that of elders."[74] This does not mean that deacons cannot teach in any capacity, but simply that they are not called to teach or preach as a matter of responsibility related to their office as deacon.

Like elders, deacons must manage their house and children well (1 Tim 3:4,12). But when referring to deacons, Paul omits the section where he compares managing one's household to taking care of God's church (1 Tim 3:5). The reason for this

---

[73] Cf. Clarke who states, "The popular association with the temporary difficulties associated with the Jerusalem church in Acts 6.1–6 is an unhelpful background that has led many to hold that the duties of deacons were practical or administrative" (*Pauline Theology*, 76).

[74] D. A. Carson, "Church, Authority in the," *Evangelical Dictionary of Theology* (ed. W. E. Elwell; Grand Rapids: Baker, 1984), 229. Grudem likewise states, "It is significant that nowhere in the New Testament do deacons have ruling authority over the church as the elders do, nor are deacons ever required to be able to teach Scripture or sound doctrine" (W. Grudem, *Systematic Theology: An Introduction to Biblical Doctrine* [Leicester: InterVarsity Press/Grand Rapids: Eerdmans, 1994], 920).

omission is most likely due to the fact that deacons are not given a ruling or leading position in the church—a function that belongs to the elders.

Other differences provide us with less information. Some maintain that the omission for deacons to be gentle and not quarrelsome (1 Tim 3:3) may indicate that the elders were often put in situations that required such characteristics. Knight, for example, suggests that this omission "may reflect the fact that the deacon is not in the role of one who must give oversight and direction, as well as discipline, in sometimes difficult situations that make such qualifications imperative."[75]

Although Paul indicates that a person must be tested before he can hold the office of deacon (1 Tim 3:10), the requirement that he cannot be a new convert is not included. Paul notes that if an elder is a recent convert "he might become conceited" (1 Tim 3:6). One implication concerning this distinction could be that those who hold the office of elder—because they possess leadership over the church—are more susceptible to pride. On the contrary, it is not as likely for a deacon—someone who is in more of a servant role—to fall into this same sin.

The fact that Paul includes the character of a deacon's wife might also reveal an important distinction (1 Tim 3:11).[76] Because the role of a deacon is focused toward serving and not leading, a wife could easily be involved. The wife of an elder would be more limited because Paul forbids women "to teach or to have authority over a man" (1 Tim 2:12). Finally, the title "overseer" (1 Tim 3:2) implies general oversight over the spiritual well-being of the congregation, whereas the title "deacon" implies one who has a service-oriented ministry.

Having discussed some distinctions between elders and deacons, we have yet to specify the precise duties of deacons. We have already indicated that deacons are not responsible to teach or lead the congregation. They are not the spiritual leaders of the church. Instead, the deacons provide leadership over the service-oriented functions of the church. The Bible, however, does not clearly indicate the function of deacons. But based on the pattern established in Acts 6 with the apostles and the Seven, it seems best to view the deacons as servants who do whatever is necessary to allow the elders to accomplish their God-given calling of shepherding and teaching the church.[77] Just as the apostles delegated administrative responsibilities to the Seven, so the elders are to delegate responsibilities to the deacons so that the elders can focus their efforts elsewhere.[78]

---

[75] Knight, *Pastoral Epistles*, 167.

[76] If indeed this text refers to the wives of deacons and not to women deacons.

[77] The role of the Seven should not be compared too closely with the role of the deacons because Steven was also a miracle-worker (Acts 6:8) and preacher (6:8–10) and Philip was an evangelist (Acts 21:8).

[78] P. Newton rightly concludes, "In the servant role, deacons take care of those mundane and temporal matters of church life so that elders are freed to concentrate upon spiritual matters. Deacons provide much needed wisdom and energy to the ample physical needs in the church, often using such provision as opportunities to minister as well to the spiritual needs of others" (*Elders in Congregational Life: Rediscovering the Biblical Model for Church Leadership* [Grand Rapids: Kregel, 2005], 41).

There are some clues as to the function of deacons based on the requirements in 1 Timothy 3. Grudem offers some possibilities:

> [Deacons] seem to have had some responsibility in caring for the finances of the church, since they had to be people who were "not greedy for gain" (v. 8). They perhaps had some administrative responsibilities in other activities of the church as well, because they were to manage their children and their households well (v. 12). They may also have ministered to the physical needs of those in the church or community who needed help [Acts 6]. . . . Moreover, if verse 11 speaks of their wives (as I think it does), then it would also be likely that they were involved in some house-to-house visitation and counseling, because the wives are to be "no slanderers."[79]

We must note, however, that some of the requirements could have been given to counter the characteristics of false teachers and were not so much directed toward their duties. Mounce maintains that the requirements listed suggest that a deacon would have substantial contact with people: not be double-tongued; a dignified wife; faithful in marriage; a well-managed family.[80] Again, although such a conclusion is possible, it cannot be given too much weight.

There are a number of factors in Scripture that indicate that the office of deacon is, in one sense, a lesser office than that of the eldership. First, the function of the deacons is to provide support for the elders so that they can continue their work without being distracted by other matters. Just as the apostles appointed seven men to take care of the task of overseeing the physical needs of the congregation in the daily distribution of food (Acts 6:1–6), so the deacons are needed so that the elders can attend to the spiritual needs of the congregation. The title "deacon" also suggests one who has a secondary role as one who comes beside and assists others.

Second, the office of deacon is mentioned after the office of elder/overseer. There are two examples in the New Testament. In Phil 1:1, Paul not only greets the entire congregation (as was his normal practice), but he also greets the "overseers and deacons." Later, when Paul lists the needed qualifications for overseers and deacons in 1 Timothy 3, the qualifications for overseers are listed first. Although such ordering does not necessarily indicate order of priority, it at least may emphasize the importance of those who teach and lead the church.

Third, references to the office of deacon are far less frequent than references to the office of elder. Although the general use of the Greek term διάκονος occurs quite frequently, the more specific use of the term as a reference of an office-holder is only found three or four times in the New Testament (Rom 16:1[?]; Phil 1:1;

---

79 Grudem, *Systematic Theology*, 919.
80 Mounce, *Pastoral Epistles*, 195.

1 Tim 3:8,12). On the other hand, the terms "elder" and "overseer" as a reference to an office-holder occur more than 20 times.[81]

Fourth, elders were appointed to new churches before deacons were. The early church in Jerusalem had elders before they had deacons—assuming the Seven appointed in Acts 6 could not technically be considered "deacons." During Paul's first missionary journey, he and Barnabas appointed elders in the church of Asia Minor (Acts 14:23). Yet nowhere does Luke indicate that deacons were appointed. Although this omission does not prove that deacons did not exist in the churches at that time, the fact that they are not mentioned indicates that they were not as important to the progress of the gospel according to Luke. Later, Paul commands Titus to appoint elders in every city on the island of Crete (Titus 1:5) but says nothing of deacons. If deacons were as important to the life of the church, it would seem that he would have also included instructions to appoint deacons and included the needed qualifications as he did in 1 Timothy.

It should be noted that the office of deacon is also distinct from that of the elder/overseer in at least two ways. First, the office of deacon is not a lower office in the sense that one must become a deacon before he can serve as an elder. These offices are distinguished by their function in the church and the gifts of the individual. Similar, yet distinct, qualifications are given for elders and for deacons. Paul does not indicate in his qualifications for elders that one must have first been a deacon. As a matter of fact, his comment that an elder must not be a recent convert (1 Tim 3:6) would make little sense if he expected a person to be a deacon before he could move up to the position of an elder. Furthermore, it is likely that many churches did not have deacons at the beginning of their existence. Second, deacons are also distinct from elders in the sense that they are not merely the personal assistants of the elders but are called to serve the church (cf. the Seven in Acts 6 who were enlisted to serve the church, not the apostles).

THE ROLE OF TIMOTHY AND TITUS

There are at least two ways in which the roles of Timothy and Titus have been misunderstood. First, there are some who see Timothy and Titus not as the real recipients of the letters but as merely representing the monarchical bishop, who is the real recipient. Thus, the authority of the overseer or bishop is found in the position represented by "Timothy" or "Titus." One argument in favor of this position is that in Titus 1:9 the overseer is expected to be able "to refute" (ἐλέγχειν) those who contradict. Yet in 1 Tim 5:20 "Timothy" is told to "rebuke" (ἔλεγχε) those who sin in the presence of all. Because the overseer has the task of rebuking, it is then concluded

---

[81] Elder: Acts 11:30; 14:23; 15:2,4,6,22,23; 16:4; 20:17; 21:18; 1 Tim 5:17,19; Titus 1:5; Jas 5:14; 1 Pet 5:1,5; 2 John 1; 3 John 1. Overseer: Acts 20:28; Phil 1:1; 1 Tim 3:2; Titus 1:7.

that the addressee of 1 Timothy is an overseer or bishop who has the sole authority to rebuke those who sin.

The theory that Timothy and Titus actually represent the monarchical bishop is based on a number of questionable assumptions.[82] First, one has to assume that Paul did not author the letters but that a later disciple wrote under Paul's name. Second, one has to assume that the author is not writing to Timothy and Titus but is simply using the guise of those names to address the monarchical bishop. Third, one has to assume that the authority given to "Timothy" and "Titus" is actually meant for the monarchical bishop. In the end nothing is as it appears, but everything is reinterpreted within a speculative reconstruction—none of which can be proven. It is best to see Timothy and Titus as Paul's apostolic delegates with temporary authority given to them by Paul in order to see that the churches under Paul's authority remain faithful to the gospel of Christ.[83]

Furthermore, in Ignatius, the authority given to the bishop as the sole leader of the church is above that given even to Timothy and Titus. In his letter to the Smyrnaeans, Ignatius writes:

> You must all follow the bishop, as Jesus Christ followed the Father. . . . Let no one do anything that has to do with the church without the bishop. Only that Eucharist which is under the authority of the bishop (or whomever he himself designates) is to be considered valid. Wherever the bishop appears, there let the congregation be. . . . It is not permissible either to baptize or to hold a love feast without the bishop. But whatever he approves is also pleasing to God, in order that everything you do may be trustworthy and valid. . . . It is good to acknowledge God and the bishop. The one who honors the bishop has been honored by God; the one who does anything without the bishop's knowledge serves the devil. (*Smyrn.* 8:1–9:1)

Elsewhere we read, "For all those who belong to God and Jesus Christ are with the bishop" (*Phil.* 3:2) and that the bishop is to be regarded "as the Lord himself" (*Eph.* 6:1).[84] Nowhere in the Pastorals is obedience to Timothy or Titus equated with obedience to God. The emphasis in the Pastorals is clearly on obedience to the true gospel as taught by Timothy and Titus, not to an office-bearer. After comparing the Pastoral Epistles with Ignatius, Mounce comments, "The similarities are so superficial, and the differences so extreme, that this becomes one of the strongest arguments

---

[82] For a modern variation on this position, see W. A. Richards, *Difference and Distance in Post-Pauline Christianity: An Epistolary Analysis of the Pastorals* (SBL 44; New York: Peter Lang, 2002).

[83] Mounce rightly states, "Timothy and Titus are never pictured as the bishops of the Ephesian and Cretan churches (neither the title nor the function is ever applied to them). They are apostolic delegates, exercising Paul's authority over the churches, standing outside the formal structure of the church" (*Pastoral Epistles*, 187; also see Towner, *Timothy and Titus*, 242).

[84] For the bishop's authority, also see Ign. *Eph.* 2:1–2; 4:1; 5:3; 6:1; Ign. *Magn.* 2:1; 3:1 6:1; Ign. *Trall.* 2:1–2; 3:1; 13:2; Ign. *Phld.* 3:2; Ign. *Pol.* 6:1.

that the PE are not from the second century and in fact reflect a much earlier stage of the church's institutional development."[85]

Another mistake is to view Timothy and Titus as the elders or pastors of the churches in Ephesus or Crete.[86] Although it is true that they often performed the same functions or duties that are expected of elders or pastors,[87] it would be wrong to assume that the authority Timothy and Titus possessed is the same authority that should be given to elders or pastors. The reason for this distinction is because Timothy and Titus were not merely elders but also had the additional authority of being Paul's apostolic delegates.[88]

There are at least three reasons that compel us to make a distinction between the roles of Timothy and Titus and the role of the elder or overseer. First, both Timothy and Titus held a temporary position. Timothy was one of Paul's most faithful and trusted missionary companions.[89] He was sent as Paul's apostolic delegate to protect the church in Ephesus from false teachings and give the church proper guidelines for who should lead the church and how the church should function (1 Tim 1:3–4). His role was temporary. Once the church was healthy enough to function without him, he would return to Paul and continue his traveling ministry with the apostle. At the end of 2 Timothy, Paul instructs his beloved friend, "Make every effort to come to me soon" (2 Tim 4:9). Timothy's task at Ephesus was specific and once his task was

---

[85] Mounce, *Pastoral Epistles*, 186. Johnson similarly comments, "The elements of church order found in 1 Timothy and Titus are far closer to that in the undisputed letters of Paul than to the ecclesiastical structure found in the letters of Ignatius of Antioch (*Letters to Paul's Delegates*, 16). Later he adds, "1 Timothy lacks entirely the elaborate theological legitimation found in Ignatius" (ibid., 174; also see, idem, "Paul's Ecclesiology," in *The Cambridge Companion to St. Paul* [Cambridge: Cambridge University Press, 2003], 210). Against this view, J. W. Aageson claims, "Ignatius does not mark a break with the ecclesiology of 1 Timothy and Titus but a continuation and extension of it. In that line of development the Pastorals, based on their theological and structural patterns, are positioned closer to Ignatius than to Paul" (*Paul, the Pastoral Epistles, and the Early Church* [Peabody, Mass.: Hendrickson, 2008], 138.

[86] This section is an adaptation of my earlier work, *40 Questions about Elders and Deacons* (Grand Rapids: Kregel, 2008), 101–05.

[87] For example, elders are responsible for teaching and preaching the word of God (Eph 4:11; 1 Thess 5:12; 1 Tim 3:2; 5:17; Titus 1:9). Likewise, this responsibility is given to Timothy and Titus (1 Tim 1:3; 4:11; 6:2; 2 Tim 2:2; Titus 2:1,7,15; 3:1).

[88] Mounce rightly acknowledges the uniqueness of their position: "Timothy and Titus stand outside the church structure. They are not bishops or elders, and are not members of the local church. They are itinerant, apostolic delegates sent with Paul's authority to deal with local problems, just as they do in Acts. Timothy and Titus are never told to rely on their institutional position in the local church for authority; rather they rely on the authority of Paul and the gospel" (*Pastoral Epistles*, lxxxviii). For others who hold that Timothy and Titus did not hold any office in the church but were sent as Paul's apostolic delegates with temporary authority, see Knight, *Pastoral Epistles*, 29; Kelly, *Pastoral Epistles*, 13–14; Guthrie, *Pastoral Epistles*, 38–39.

[89] He joined Paul on his second missionary journey and became a nearly constant companion of the apostle. Very early in their relationship Paul found that he could trust Timothy with the task of finishing what he himself could not. For example, Timothy was left behind in Berea after Paul was encouraged by the local believers to flee the city (Acts 17:14). Later, Timothy became Paul's emissary to Thessalonica to help strengthen their faith (1 Thess 3:2–3). Then Paul sent Timothy, along with Erastus, to Macedonia while Paul himself remained in Asia (Acts 19:22). Timothy was also chosen by Paul to travel to Corinth so that he could remind them of Paul's ways in Christ (1 Cor 4:17). During his first Roman imprisonment, Paul made plans to send Timothy to Philippi, although there is no clear indication elsewhere in Scripture that he actually traveled there during this time (Phil 2:19). Finally, in 1 Timothy we read that Paul urges Timothy to remain at Ephesus in order to combat the false teaching that had infiltrated the church (1 Tim 1:3–4).

completed, he would move to another ministry under the leadership and authority of Paul.

The same is true for Titus who was also one of Paul's trusted associates.[90] Paul left Titus behind in Crete in order to finish the work that Paul himself was unable to complete. Titus' work, however, did not end in Crete. When his work in Crete was finished, or at least things were stable, Paul wanted Titus to meet him at Nicopolis (Titus 3:12). Finally, according to 2 Tim 4:10, Titus went to Dalmatia. As with Timothy, Titus' role in the churches in Crete was temporary. As Paul's apostolic delegate, he was left behind to establish the churches. Once they were sufficiently established, Titus moved on to another ministry under the leadership of Paul.

A second reason Timothy and Titus should not be regarded merely as elders or overseers is because it was their task to appoint elders in the churches. The authority to appoint elders is more authority than any one elder possesses. In Acts, Paul and Barnabas appointed elders in many churches in Asia Minor. As an apostle, Paul had the authority to publicly appoint these leaders to a recognized office. Timothy and Titus are also able to appoint elders, not because they themselves are elders, but because they have the greater authority of being Paul's apostolic delegates. For instance, Paul warns Timothy, "Don't be too quick to lay hands on anyone, and don't share in the sins of others" (1 Tim 5:22). As one with authority over the church, Timothy must be cautious of laying his hands (i.e., appointing) anyone to the office of elder who is not truly qualified.

Titus was also given the task of appointing elders. Paul writes, "The reason I left you in Crete was to set right what was left undone and, as I directed you, to appoint elders in every town" (Titus 1:5). According to Acts 14:23, it was Paul's custom to appoint elders in the churches. Paul's quick and unexpected departure forced him to assign this important responsibility to Titus. Titus was not an elder but was to appoint elders. His authority over the churches was temporary because no elders existed. Once elders were appointed and the church was firmly established, Titus would be free to leave the direction of the church in the hands of the elders.

The third reason Timothy and Titus should not be viewed as elders is that a single leadership position with the authority they possessed is not found in the New Testament. It is clear that they possess authority that is higher than that of the elders. The churches were normally led by a group of elders who collectively lead the

---

[90] He was born to Greek parents and became an early traveling companion of Paul (Gal 2:1,3). Although never mentioned in the book of Acts, he accompanied Paul and Barnabas to the church in Jerusalem during the so-called "Jerusalem Council" (Acts 15). Titus became instrumental in helping Paul deal with the problems in the Corinthian church. Following his first canonical letter to the Corinthians, Paul made an emergency visit to Corinth, but he was not well-received. As a result, he wrote a harsh letter to the Corinthians and sent Titus to deliver it (2 Cor 12:18). Titus apparently returned to Paul with good news; when Paul later penned 2 Corinthians, he again sent his "partner and co-worker" as the messenger (2 Cor 8:23). Several years later, after being released from his first Roman imprisonment, Paul made a visit to the island of Crete. For some unknown reason, however, Paul was forced to leave Crete prematurely.

church.[91] But in the case of the churches in Ephesus and Crete, Timothy and Titus stand above the congregation carrying with them the commission and authority of the apostle Paul.

CONCLUSION

Not only is the church at the center of God's mission; it is also the center of Paul's words to Timothy and Titus. Paul's main purpose in writing these letters (at least 1 Timothy) is so that Christians will know how "to act in God's household, which is the church of the living God, the pillar and foundation of the truth" (1 Tim 3:15). Although there is some development in organizational structure between Paul's earlier writing and the Pastoral Epistles, it is unfair to characterize the latter as representing a radical institutionalization of the ministry. The Pastorals provide us with crucial information concerning the offices of elder or overseer and deacon—offices that are also depicted in Paul's earlier writings. There was no monarchical bishop when the Pastorals were written. Instead, the terms "elder" and "overseer" (or bishop) were used interchangeably to represent the same office. Although deacons are not the primary leaders in the church, they are needed because they allow the elders/overseers to focus on their main task of shepherding and teaching the congregation. The qualifications given for deacons are very similar to that of the overseers as both lists focus on the character of the individual. The main difference is that deacons do not have a teaching role because they do not need to be "an able teacher" (1 Tim 3:2). Although it is true that in one sense the office of deacon is a lower office than that of the elder/overseer, it is also a distinct office so that those who become elders do not need to first serve as deacons. Finally, Timothy and Titus should not be viewed as representing the monarchical bishop who is the real recipient of the letters, and neither should they be viewed merely as elders/overseers. They are Paul's apostolic delegates who serve the church not as bishops nor as overseers but with the authority of the apostle Paul himself.

---

[91] Elders: Acts 11:30; 14:23; 15:2,4,6,22,23; 16:4; 20:17; 21:18; 1 Tim 5:17; Titus 1:5; Jas 5:14; 1 Pet 5:1,5; overseers: Acts 20:28; Phil 1:1; deacons: Phil 1:1; 1 Tim 3:8,12; leaders (with no specific title given): 1 Cor 16:15–16; 1 Thess 5:12; Heb 13:7,17,24.

Chapter Nine

THE SAGACIOUS USE OF SCRIPTURE

B. PAUL WOLFE

Paul concludes his writing ministry with a strong affirmation of the character and usefulness of Scripture (2 Tim 3:15–17). This is no surprise. In Rom 15:4 and 1 Cor 10:11 he makes similar remarks about Scripture, though nothing quite as comprehensive. Perhaps more significantly, he previously exhibited a deep and explicit interaction with Scripture for his theological and ethical argumentation and pastoral exhortations. His convictions regarding Scripture can be seen by the way he uses Scripture. Paul's use of Scripture has been the subject of tremendous analysis, though seldom have the Pastoral Epistles (PE) been given their due focus.[1] Does Paul live up to his own standards and exhortations in these final letters? Does the pattern within the PE reflect his commitments articulated and reflected elsewhere? What role does Scripture play in a period of transition from the first generation to the second generation of leadership? Given the substantive presence of tradition within these letters, does Paul simply repeat prior uses of Scripture, or is there any evidence of fresh and continuing interaction with Scripture?

Many of the citations of and allusions to Scripture within the PE are also found elsewhere within the Pauline corpus or within Jewish or Christian tradition. Thus, a few scholars have attempted to make the case that the PE reflect second generation dependence on Paul or other sources, rather than directly engaging the Scriptures—a preMarcion Marcionism, if you will.[2] Two points should be noted here. First, it is

---

[1] As exceptions to the rule, see A. T. Hanson, "The Use of the Old Testament in the Pastoral Epistles," *IBS* 3 (1981): 203–19; idem, *The Living Utterances of God* (London: Darton, Longman and Todd, 1983), 131–40; P. H. Towner, "1–2 Timothy and Titus," in *Commentary on the New Testament Use of the Old Testament* (ed. G. K. Beale and D. A. Carson; Grand Rapids: Baker, 2007), 891–918; and my "The Place and Use of Scripture in the Pastoral Epistles," (Ph.D. diss., University of Aberdeen, 1990).

[2] A. E. Barnett, *Paul Becomes a Literary Influence* (Chicago: University of Chicago, 1941); A. T. Hanson, *The Pastoral Epistles* (London: Marshall, Morgan and Scott, 1982); idem, "The Use of the Old Testament in the Pastoral Epistles"; P. Trummer, *Die Paulustradition der Pastoralbriefe* (Frankfurt am Main: Lang, 1978); idem, "Corpus Paulinum–Corpus Pastorale: Zur Ortung der Paulustradition in den Pastoralbriefen," in *Paulus in den Neutestamentlichen Spätschriften: Zur Paulusrezeption im Neuen Testament* (ed. K. Kertelge; Freiburg: Herder, 1981), 122–45; C. M. Nielsen, "Scripture in the

not insignificant that the OT appears more frequently and explicitly in the PE than in Ephesians, Philippians, Colossians, and 1 and 2 Thessalonians. Second, as will become evident, there are distinct indications of a unique use of Scripture within the PE and thus no need to posit the work of a merely stodgy traditionalist.

Towner is precisely right that "in theory no part of a NT text is off limits for an OT allusion, echo, or resonance to occur."[3] The NT is so firmly and thoroughly seated upon the OT that virtually every utterance within it is at least implicitly engaged with the OT at some level. In the following pages we will examine closely several instances of the explicit use of Scripture in the PE. We will briefly consider a few other possible occurrences of Scripture before concluding the study. A close look at Paul's use of Scripture in the PE reveals that he truly believes his admonition to Timothy that the Scriptures lead to wisdom and salvation as they are read through faith in Christ Jesus (2 Tim 3:15).

Two passages in the PE have an introductory formula (IF) that signals an explicit citation, namely, 1 Tim 5:18 and 2 Tim 2:19. Both passages are remarkable, though in different respects. We will deal with these two texts first, followed by a brief examination of 1 Tim 2:12–15; 5:19–25; 2 Tim 4:16–18; Titus 2:14; and 1 Tim 5:18b. We reserve 5:18b until last. The use of Scripture there is so striking. We conclude the study with a few brief comments regarding other PE texts that have been linked with OT texts in one way or another, though unjustifiably in our view.

1 TIMOTHY 5:18A

The IF in 1 Tim 5:18 reads, "For the Scripture says," a common way of introducing a citation from Scripture. Paul employs the same IF in Rom 4:3; 9:17; 10:11; 11:2; and Gal 4:30. The IF is followed by a quotation from Deut 25:4 to support the injunction regarding ministerial support: "You must not muzzle an ox that is threshing grain." Other than the order, the wording is the same as the LXX. Not only does this saying also occur in 1 Cor 9:9; it shows up several times in the Talmud as well. Especially relevant are the examples from tractates *Bava Metzi'a* and *Gittin*. In both of these, Deut 25:4 is used to support a worker's right to eat of the food that falls while the work is being done. Hanson regarded the Mosaic directive as a standard prooftext in dealing with questions of remuneration of workers.[4] The saying has taken on the life of a proverb and was put to use in various contexts.

Both the IF and the wording of the citation in 1 Cor 9:9 differ from 1 Timothy, making exclusive dependence upon 1 Corinthians unlikely. Regardless of how

Pastoral Epistles," *PRS* 7 (1980): 4–23; against which see my "Scripture in the Pastoral Epistles: PreMarcion Marcionism?" *PRS* 16 (1989): 5–16.

3 Towner, "1–2 Timothy and Titus," 891. Towner's study is quite helpful and insightful, though it does in my judgment have a couple of significant gaps, most notably 1 Tim 5:19–25.

4 Hanson, *The Pastoral Epistles*, 102; idem, *Studies in Paul's Technique and Theology* (London: SPCK, 1974), 166.

widespread and proverbial the saying had become, the IF in both 1 Cor 9:9 and 1 Tim 5:18 point to an authoritative *written* source. Given that 1 Tim 5:18 accords with the saying in Deuteronomy and not 1 Corinthians, it is likely that is the source.

Paul has drawn here upon the Scriptures, more particularly the law of Moses, to adduce an ethical authority by way of analogy. This reflects his conviction that "All Scripture is . . . profitable for teaching" (2 Tim 3:16), even though "the law is not meant for a righteous person" (1 Tim 1:9). We will return to 5:18 near the end of the essay to examine the second saying.

2 TIMOTHY 2:19

This verse is composed of an unusual two-part introductory formula and two apparent citations, the first of which can be confidently ascribed to Num 16:5. The "solid foundation" appears to refer to the church in general,[5] as opposed to the local church in Ephesus,[6] Christ and the apostles,[7] or any other more limited entity.[8] The two sayings that follow refer to Israel in their original context, but are concerned with the church in Paul's application here. The first saying assures the faithful that they will not be forgotten. The second saying reminds them of the incumbent moral obligation upon those who claim to be the Lord's people. These scriptural references then give hope and correction in the face of disturbing and misleading false doctrine. The "seal" is a metaphor reflecting the seriousness and authenticity of the foundation drawn from the truthfulness of the following citations.[9]

It is generally concluded that both sayings that follow have their origin in the OT. There is, however, much less certainty concerning the source of the second saying. The first saying ("The Lord knows those who are His") is based upon Num 16:5 as the following comparison makes clear:

LXX Num 16:5 =   ἔγνω ὁ θεὸς τοὺς ὄντας αὐτοῦ
2 Tim 2:19a =   ἔγνω κύριος τοὺς ὄντας αὐτοῦ

Hanson emphasizes the aspect of revolt in both contexts, the rebellion of Korah in Numbers, and the actions of Hymenaeus and Philetus in 1 Timothy.[10] Revolt is not the only idea that has given rise to the quotations; it is also the content of the false

---

[5] Towner, "1–2 Timothy and Titus," 904, suggests that the foundation imagery recalls Isa 28:16.

[6] J. N. D. Kelly, *A Commentary on the Pastoral Epistles* (Grand Rapids: Baker, 1981), 186.

[7] W. Lock, *The Pastoral Epistles* (Edinburgh: T & T Clark, 1924), 100.

[8] Hanson, *The Pastoral Epistles*, 137; M. Dibelius and H. Conzelmann, *The Pastoral Epistles* (Philadelphia: Fortress, 1972), 112.

[9] The seal imagery within the passage has led some scholars to conclude the sayings were drawn from baptismal liturgy. This interpretation is no more likely here than in Eph 1:13 and 4:30. For a cogent argument against the liturgical interpretation, see M. Barth, *Ephesians: Introduction, Translation, and Commentary on Chapters 1–3* (New York: Doubleday and Company, 1974), 135–39.

[10] A. T. Hanson, *Studies in the Pastoral Epistles* (London: SPCK, 1968), 35–36.

teaching. There is an antithesis within the passage (μέντοι, "nevertheless") aimed at the false teaching of the opponents concerning the resurrection. They have claimed that it has already taken place. Paul utilizes this saying about the Lord's knowledge of his people to reassure those who may be disturbed by this teaching.

The doctrinal deviation of Hymenaeus and Philetus leads directly to moral deviation. Paul employs a passage of Scripture to correct the doctrinal error of the opponents and cut off the influence of their moral deviation. The recipients can be sure the resurrection has not taken place. God has not forgotten them, and they are still accountable to him.

The source of the second saying is not so readily identified, even if its general theological import is. The saying, which reads ἀποστήτω ἀπὸ ἀδικίας πᾶς ὁ ὀνομάζων τὸ ὄνομα κυρίου ("Everyone who names the name of the Lord must turn away from unrighteousness"), has affinities with several passages of Scripture. It has been, in one way or another, connected with Lev 24:16; Num 16:26; Josh 23:7; Pss 6:8; 34:14; Prov 3:7; Isa 26:13; 52:11.

There is minimal similarity with Isa 26:13. The connection with Ps 34:14 and Prov 3:7 involves sentiment only and provides no concrete help toward determining a source. Joshua 23:7 speaks of naming the names of gods, but this refers to false gods, and the verbal similarities with the verse are rather unimpressive. The Greek of Lev 24:16 provides an almost exact parallel with the second half of the saying: ὀνομάζων δὲ τὸ ὄνομα κυρίου. As noted by Hanson,[11] if the saying was originally drawn from this verse, then there is a certain amount of irony involved, for in the context of Leviticus 24, ὀνομάζω is used in the sense of blasphemy, which is of course forbidden. The connection between these two passages is peripheral at best regarding the idea of departing from iniquity.

Psalm 6:8 (LXX 6:9) uses an imperatival form of the same verb (ἀφίστημι, "turn away") and is likewise concerned with iniquity. However, the two passages use different nouns for iniquity. More importantly, in the Psalm it is the workers of iniquity who are commanded to depart from the righteous one, whereas in 2 Timothy the righteous are commanded to depart from iniquity.

Isaiah 52:11 contains a prophetic command to the people of God to depart from Babylon and in so doing to keep themselves free from anything unclean, i.e., iniquity. The command is stated by using the same verb for "turn away" as in 2 Tim 2:19. In addition, Isa 52:11 is the only text considered thus far that has an explicit connection with both aspects of 2 Tim 2:19. Verse 11 itself has an implicit relationship with naming the name of the Lord when it directs the command to "you who carry the vessels of the LORD," but v. 6 makes it explicit: "My people will know My name." While this Isaianic prophecy does not correspond exactly to 2 Tim 2:19b, nonetheless, it could have been influential in forming the Timothy saying.

---

[11] Ibid., 138; Hanson, *Utterances*, 137.

Perhaps the most likely origin is to be found by turning back to the story of the rebellion of Korah and his associates in Numbers 16. In v. 26 Moses commands the people to "Get away now from the tents of these wicked men. Don't touch anything that belongs to them." Here is the clear and pervasive idea of turning away from wickedness. This is to be done by the Lord's people, the ones whom he knows are his (v. 5), which corresponds to "naming the name of the Lord." Recall that Num 16:5 was cited in 2 Tim 2:19a. The contexts of Numbers 16 and 2 Timothy 2 have striking similarities. Paul could have been drawing on Numbers 16 from memory, or the Christian expression of Numbers 16 may have already become traditional in this form, hence the unusual IF. In any case, it is reasonable, though not certain, that this is a good example of Dodd's thesis that NT citations of the OT were pointers to the broader OT context.[12]

The strong connection with the story of Korah's rebellion in Numbers 16 could indicate a common Jewish and Christian tradition. Bauckham suggests there was a well-established tradition that used Cain, Balaam, and Korah as "typical" sinners, insubordinates, and heretics.[13] With reference to Korah, the material in Numbers 16 is supplemented in Jewish tradition, for example, in Sir. 45:18–19, Pseudo-Philo, *Bib. Ant.* 16:1, *Midr. Num.* 18:2–4, and the comments in *Tg Ps.-J.* on Num 16:2. Jude 11 and *1 Clem.* 51:3–4 reflect these traditions. In light of the many times the story of Korah is used in this way and the "allusive character of the reference in 2 Tim 2:19," Bauckham regards this as pointing to a "well-established tradition."[14] He could well be right.

The passage also has connections with Matt 7:23 and Luke 13:27, though the dominical sayings command a departure by evildoers from the speaker, whereas in 2 Timothy the righteous are commanded to depart from evil. The parallels are more pronounced in the Lucan version.

All the above factors converge to indicate an established tradition that asserts the incompatibility of God's people and evil, often incorporating OT characters as negative examples. That Paul links these two sayings in 2 Tim 2:19, one of which is certainly drawn originally from the OT, without in some way identifying either of them as Scripture (as he does in 1 Tim 5:18, where he also links two sayings), could be the final indication that Paul is here utilizing well-known tradition. The unusual introductory formula, coupled with the terse, mnemonic character of the sayings, also adds to the likelihood of this conclusion.

Paul's use of the OT in this passage then is not immediate but secondary. It has come to him mediated through Jewish and Christian tradition. This does not indicate that he was unaware of the OT heritage of the sayings. The implication is instead that

---

[12] C. H. Dodd, *According to the Scriptures* (London: Nisbet, 1953).
[13] R. J. Bauckham, *Jude, 2 Peter* (Waco, TX: Word, 1983), 78–83.
[14] Ibid., 83.

he approved of this traditional use of the OT and has here employed it for his own purposes.

This passage is an excellent example of the intimate connection within these epistles between right believing and right living. The first saying addresses the doctrinal issue, and the second sets forth the practical imperative based upon the doctrinal indicative. The passage also indicates sensitivity to the context of the OT. The two sayings together represent an appropriation of the entire story in Numbers 16, and not mere prooftexting.

1 TIMOTHY 2:12–15

A very clear reference to the OT story of Adam and Eve is found in 1 Tim 2:13–14. In the context of this passage, Paul is setting forth principles and rules for community behavior, apparently with regard to public worship. As he gives instructions for the women, he states that they are not to teach or to have authority over men in the church (vv. 11–12). In order to buttress this controversial statement (at least to modern ears), Paul turns to Scripture and makes use of the creation/fall account in Genesis 2–3.

Paul gives two justifications for his instructions regarding women. The priority of Adam in creation indicates his headship; Eve then was presumably to submit to him. Paul wished to preserve what he saw as the natural order of things. Second, Eve's guilt was the result of being deceived, while Adam's was not. Paul views the creation account and its principal figures as historical and representational. Adam and Eve and their respective relationship as portrayed by Scripture serve as the paradigm, positively and negatively.

Paul has turned to Scripture for support of his injunction concerning church order. Whether Paul sees the relationship of Adam and Eve as the prototype for all other male-female relationships or views their experience as exemplary, it is significant that he applies his understanding of this account to the church. In this sense, Paul's interpretations are only implied in the original scriptural account. But even given the implied nature of Paul's interpretation, it was to him nonetheless "a matter of course and unimpeachable," and the impression is given that he most probably would not see the matter any other way.[15]

Paul's appropriation of the Adam-Eve narrative was certainly in line with a well-established tradition. Appropriate examples prior to the PE include Sir. 25:24; Philo,

---

[15] Dibelius and Conzelmann, *Pastoral Epistles*, 47. The evidence is not compelling that the use of ἐξαπατάω by Paul betrays the fact that he is dependent on and influenced by the tradition that the serpent seduced Eve in the garden. In support of this view, see Hanson, *Studies in the Pastoral Epistles*, 76; Dibelius and Conzelmann, *Pastoral Epistles*, 47–48; C. C. Kroeger, "Ancient Heresies and a Strange Greek Verb," *RefJ* 29 (1979): 14. Against this view see my "The Place and Use of Scripture in the Pastoral Epistles" (Ph.D. diss., Aberdeen University, 1990).

QG 1.33–47; and 1 Cor 11:8–12; 14:34.[16] The last example is expressed in a pattern very much like 1 Timothy, further suggesting the traditional nature of the account. The pattern is "silence in the church—submission—OT."[17] The Corinthian phrase "as even the law says" (14:34) is instructive since the law says no such thing explicitly, indicative of a traditional understanding of the Genesis account. Ellis argues that the traditional nature of the passage in 1 Timothy can be assumed because the saying is governed by πιστὸς ὁ λόγος.[18] This would establish more firmly the preformed traditional nature of the statement. However, it seems more likely that the faithful saying formula governs what follows it.[19]

In spite of the traditional background, Paul's use of the narrative here is distinctive. The correlations between Genesis and 1 Timothy are conceptual and structural. The following chart indicates the concepts in play on the left and the structural consistency of the two texts.[20]

	Genesis	**1 Timothy**
Distinctive Roles	2:18,20	2:12,15
Creation	2:21–25	2:13
Fall	3:1–7	2:14
Curse	3:16 (23–24)	2:15
Redemption	3:15	2:15

The distinctiveness of the roles is reflected in Genesis by Adam's exercise of authority, though he is in need of a "helper," followed by the subsequent creation of Eve to fill that role. The transgression of Eve, followed by Adam's, results in the curse. The curse is not the last word or end of the story; there is a hope of redemption. The argument, based as it is on chronological priority in creation and fall, and a one-sided emphasis on the sin of Eve, does not sit well with modern Western ears. Paul regards it as quite sufficient and faithful to Scripture.

Perhaps the most subtle aspect of the text is the comment in 1 Tim 2:15 that "she will be saved through childbearing, if she continues in faith, love, and holiness, with good sense."[21] The reference to childbearing is a metonymy used to refer to the curse within the Genesis narrative. Recall the curse upon Eve: "I will intensify your

[16] See Towner, "1–2 Timothy and Titus," 896–97, for discussion of the traditions behind this use of Genesis.

[17] D. Moo, "I Timothy 2:11–15: Meaning and Significance," *TrinJ* 1(1980): 64.

[18] E. E. Ellis, "Traditions in the Pastoral Epistles," in *Early Jewish and Christian Exegesis: Studies in Memory of William Hugh Brownlee* (ed. C. A. Evans; Decatur, GA: Scholars Press, 1987), 239.

[19] See G. W. Knight III, *The Faithful Sayings in the Pastoral Letters* (Grand Rapids: Baker, 1979), 50–54.

[20] Towner sees only three parallels within the two passages ("1–2 Timothy and Titus," 894–95). See his discussion for a more detailed description of the verbal similarities between the respective texts.

[21] This translation (HCSB) obscures part of the difficulty by maintaining a singular verb throughout v. 15, when in fact Paul switches from a singular "she" at the beginning to the plural "they" in the second half.

labor pains; you will bear children in anguish" (Gen 3:16). The reference to salvation through childbearing, combined with the virtues mentioned, functions similarly in order to recall God's promise to Eve; the seed of Eve will strike the head of the serpent and evil will be requited. The women of Ephesus, just like Eve, have a divinely ordained role which involves both constraint and promise, just like Eve. A rebellion against the constraint is antithetical to the life of "faith, love, and holiness," and antithetical to the submission called for in v. 11.[22] The concluding reference to "good sense" brings the passage full circle back to the same virtue mentioned in v. 9.[23]

The context of 1 Timothy 3 is concerned with ecclesiastical integrity. Paul's theological framework reflects a close relationship between creation and the church, as indicated in at least 1 Timothy 4:3–5, Romans 1, Ephesian 3 and Colossians 1. This closeness is taken to a new level here in 1 Timothy 2. It is not unreasonable to suppose that Paul here is addressing a particular problem or set of problems with his proscriptions. It is another matter entirely, though, to suppose that we know the precise nature of the problem(s) since Paul does not say.[24] Apparently the problems involved at least women, overrealized eschatology, and domestic issues (in addition to 2:9–15, see 1 Tim 3:4–5; 4:3–4; 5:13–14; 2 Tim 2:18; 3:6). Perhaps the most we can say with certainty is that in this passage and its immediate context, Paul is addressing the dissensions of men (v. 8) and the immodesty of women, both in dress (vv. 9–10) and behavior (vv. 11–15), and he regards the OT text as sufficient to address the latter without extensive elaboration. His use of the Genesis narrative displays sensitivity to the context of the original text. He is not prooftexting but attempting to engage the text and its implications in a manner faithful to both the original text and the continuing purposes of God in salvation history. The created order has not been replaced or suspended by the breaking in of the kingdom of God.

One of Hanson's categories regarding the use of Scripture in the PE is the author's use of an OT text to provide structure for his own narrative.[25] In spite of Hanson's neglect of it, this passage seems to be a good example of exactly that. On the basis of the use of Scripture in this and the two former passages, one might get the impression that Paul *only* uses the OT as he receives it through tradition. The following passage serves to dispel that impression.

---

22 The submission of v. 11 is as much if not more to God and his Word as it is to men.

23 T. R. Schreiner, "An Interpretation of 1 Timothy 2:9–15: A Dialogue with Scholarship," in *Women in the Church: A Fresh Analysis of 1 Timothy 2:9–15* (eds. A. J. Köstenberger, T. R. Schreiner, and H. S. Baldwin; Grand Rapids: Baker, 1995), 151.

24 See especially Köstenberger, Schreiner and Baldwin, eds., *Women in the Church.*

25 Hanson, "The Use of the Old Testament in the Pastoral Epistles," 210–14.

1 TIMOTHY 5:19-25

This passage also may reflect influence from tradition, but without doubt it evinces Paul's personal imprint with regard to the use of the OT. In what is a certain allusion to the OT, he states that a charge against an elder should not be entertained "except on the evidence of two or three witnesses" (v. 19). This principle is found in Deut 17:6 and 19:15. This principle is also in 2 Cor 13:1. The application here is more restricted, concerned as it is with the role of elders.

While the OT background of v. 19 is acknowledged by virtually all commentators, the Deuteronomic influence is more extensive than just this singular verse. It has been convincingly argued by J. W. Fuller that the influence of Deut 19:15–20 can be detected also in 1 Tim 5:20–25.[26] There are four parallel concerns within Timothy and Deuteronomy: (1) concern about justice; (2) the desired effect of the judgment, that is, to produce fear in the onlookers; (3) warnings against demonstrating pity or partiality in judgment; and (4) the presence of a triadic higher court in each passage, that is, the Lord, priests, and judges in Deuteronomy, and in 1 Timothy, God, Christ Jesus, and the elect angels. Fuller concludes "there is more than just a casual dependence of 1 Tim 5:19–21 upon Deut 19:15–20."[27]

Again Paul is using the OT in a manner reflected in the tradition of the wider church. This is evident in that the text is also employed in Matt 18:16, and the principle referred to in John 8:17 and Heb 10:28, all in addition to the already mentioned reference in 2 Cor 13:1.[28]

Paul's exposition and application here is unique. The writer to the Hebrews comes closest to Paul in his use of this principle. All four of the above factors are implied in the passage (Heb 10:26–31), with an element resembling the triadic higher court being rather more explicit (v. 29) but short of what Paul says. The Matthean account has a central concern for justice and a public rebuke but no mention of fear in the onlookers as the desired result of the rebuke. The other factors are absent from Matthew. The appearance in 2 Corinthians is accompanied by a concern for fear in the community members, but this is more closely aligned with the apostolic pronouncements and action than with the enactment of the principle of witnesses enshrined in Deuteronomy. The Johannine reference has the least in common with what is in the PE.

In light of the widespread use of the principle of witnesses, it might be suggested that the present passage is not evidence of Paul going directly to the OT himself. On the basis of a "*tauta* formula," Ellis views this passage as an example of preformed tradition.[29] The passage, though, cannot be so easily pigeon-holed. Ellis limits the

---

[26] "Of Elders and Triads in 1 Timothy 5.19–25," *NTS* 29 (1983): 258–63.

[27] Ibid., 260.

[28] This principle possibly lies behind several other NT passages. See H. van Vliet, *No Single Testimony: A Study on the Adoption of the Law of Deut. 19:15 Par. into the New Testament* (Utrecht: Dukkerij Kemink en Zoon, 1958), 2–5.

[29] Ellis, "Traditions in the Pastoral Epistles," 243–45.

supposed preformed statement to vv. 19–20. But vv. 19–21 surely should be seen as a unit based on the ideas and pattern of an identifiable OT background. None of the other uses of the witness principle explicitly incorporate the same number of parallelisms as does 1 Timothy. It stands on its own both in the extent to which it follows the passage in Deuteronomy and in terms of its application.

This passage thus represents Paul's own initiative in using the OT. Striking is the analogous relationship between the Lord, priests, and the judges of Deuteronomy, and God, Christ Jesus, and the elect angels in Timothy. In both passages, the particulars of the trio were selected because they were already connected with judgment. In the context of the early church, priests and judges obviously did not play a part in the same way as they did in the nation of Israel. Thus Paul substituted Christ Jesus and the elect angels, both of which were connected with eschatological judgment. The continuity of the two passages is seen in that both present a heavenly or divinely ordained triad that indicates that justice is the concern of God and his order of things and therefore should be the concern of his people. Just as the testimony of two or three witnesses is required on the human level, so also will those who make judgments on that level be judged on a higher level.

H. van Vliet demonstrated that the legal principle enshrined in Deut 19:15 was not an integral part of the Greek and Roman societies in the first century AD. It was thus not on the basis of familiar contemporary practices that it found frequent expression in the church. Instead, its roots tap directly into Jewish conceptions of justice. This principle is pervasive in the OT, valid in all relationships throughout it. "It is not only a law of evidence, to be used in the court, it is a part of the O. T. way of life, asking for a brotherly dealing also with transgressors, it is part also of God's way of revealing Himself and of dealing with His people. . . . The adoption of this rule into the N. T. means the adoption of an essential part of the message of the Old Testament."[30]

This distinctive example of Paul's personal use of the OT demonstrates his presuppositions as to the authority and usefulness of the OT. He writes under the conviction that this aspect of the essential message of the OT is for the church. In doing so, he has again applied the OT in an analogical fashion. If the principles were applied to the common person, then by analogy how much more applicable to the leaders of God's people?

2 TIMOTHY 4:16–18

Hanson detects four examples of a structural use of Scripture in the PE: 1 Tim 1:14–16 = Exod 34:6; 1 Tim 2:3–5 = Isa 45:21–22; 2 Tim 3:11 = Ps 34:19; and

---

[30] van Vliet, *No Single Testimony*, 63, 73.

2 Tim 4:16–18 = Ps 22.[31] We will deal with 1 Tim 2:3–5 below. Of the other three, two (1 Tim 1:14–16 and 2 Tim 3:11) have such coincidental "parallels" and tenuous support as to cast serious doubt upon Paul having purposefully modeled his statements on the respective OT passages.

Such is not the case, however, with the fourth passage. Second Timothy 4:16–18 has striking resemblances to Ps 22 (LXX Ps 21). Hanson asserts four similarities between these passages: (1) the desertion of the subject or speaker, 2 Tim 4:16 and Ps 22:2; (2) the inclusion of people from all nations, 2 Tim 4:17 and Ps 22:28; (3) deliverance of the subject or speaker from the lion's mouth, 2 Tim 4:17 and Ps 22:22; and (4) deliverance from evil or evildoers, 2 Tim 4:18 and Ps 22:17.[32]

There are differences in the order of the two narratives, and the description is much more tightly packed in 2 Timothy. There is not exact modeling of the one on the other. Furthermore, the fourth of Hanson's comparisons seems misplaced. It seems more appropriate to compare 2 Tim 4:18 with Ps 22:9 or 22:21. All this being said, though, there are substantial and informative similarities between the two passages.

In my earlier work I concluded that it is doubtful that Paul meant the parallels to extend beyond the surface resemblances.[33] In other words, Paul's employment of the Psalm was not intended to identify himself with the sufferer in the Psalm, and thus, so I said then, the contribution of this passage to an understanding of his approach to the OT is negligible. I was wrong about that.

The emphasis on suffering in 2 Timothy (see 1:8,12,15; 2:3,9–10; 3:11–12,14), and Paul's self-understanding, which is so tightly woven around the person and work of Christ that it is only natural for him to identify himself with the sufferer in the Psalm (see Col 1:24; Phil 3:4b–11 compared with Phil 2:6–11), make it difficult to see Paul's description of his own suffering here as a coincidental brush with the OT. This passage then does provide a window into Paul's approach to reading the OT. Therein he finds the right lens through which to view his own life, and the defining patterns by which to judge his own circumstances. Paul's prayer in v. 16 for the forgiveness of those who deserted him strengthens the christological flavor of Paul's mind-set and his use of the OT in this passage.[34]

The glaring omission in Hanson's overview (and my own earlier thinking) is the intentional and pregnant connections Paul makes between himself and the messianic sufferer in the Psalm. Paul's life and circumstances represent a subordinate fulfillment of the Psalm. Towner's superb study concludes thusly: "Paul's suffering,

---

[31] Hanson, "The Use of the Old Testament in the Pastoral Epistles," 210–14.

[32] Ibid., 213–14.

[33] Wolfe, "The Place and Use of Scripture in the Pastoral Epistles," 65.

[34] Subsequent to changing my own mind regarding this passage, I discovered Towner's similar approach to the text ("1–2 Timothy and Titus," 909–13). He provides the most thorough and helpful discussion of Paul's use of the OT within this passage.

the abandonment he experienced, and his impending death all fit the Jesus mold. Yet his experience in no way supersedes that of Jesus; rather, it is the complementary outworking of one who has taken to himself the cruciform character and behavior of the Lord."[35]

TITUS 2:14

Within Titus 2:14 there is a reference to a dominical saying, and there are echoes of the OT. Most probably, given Paul's emphasis throughout the PE, the dominical saying holds the central place within this verse, but the OT echoes are very closely related.

The passage reflects the saying of Jesus in Mark 10:45b and Matt 20:28b. A hint of the saying also appears in 1 Tim 2:6. Paul adds interpretive comments in both places, more substantially so in Titus where the language is reflective of the OT. That Ps 130:8 (LXX 129:8) is behind this text is commonly acknowledged. The idea of redemption from iniquity is central to both passages, and Paul uses the same terms for sin/lawlessness (ἀνομία) and redemption (λυτρόω) as are in the Psalm, whereas in 1 Tim 2:6 the term ἀντίλυτρον is used, and in 2 Tim 2:19 ἀδικία is used instead of ἀνομία as here. It is not insignificant, however, that Paul has replaced the psalmist's "Israel" with "us," a strong hint at the NT development of the idea of redemption and the understanding of the church as the unique people of God drawn from all nations (1 Tim 2:4; 4:10).

The latter half of the verse reflects other OT texts. Towner sees Ezek 37:23, coupled with similar wording in 36:25–27, behind the cleansing imagery.[36] The OT is saturated with the idea of Israel as a "special people." Exodus 19:5 is close to Titus 2:14 in wording; closer still is Deut 14:2 (see also Deut 26:18 and 2 Sam 7:23–24). Deuteronomy 4:20 and 7:6 explicitly link the uniqueness of Israel to the Exodus. Ezekiel 36:25–33 links the uniqueness of Israel with their spiritual cleansing,[37] in a manner anticipating the new covenant. In Titus, Paul seems to have pulled together all of these threads; the messianic act, deliverance, and cleansing are all employed here as Paul's articulation of the gospel and its implications. Paul has expressed himself here in distinctive OT concepts and terminology.

The cue for Paul to establish this theological construct from the OT is surely from Jesus himself. It is widely acknowledged that the saying in Mark 10:45 reflects in some measure the suffering servant of Isaiah 53.[38] Paul turns to the Scriptures in

---

35 Ibid., 912–13.
36 Towner, "1–2 Timothy and Titus," 914.
37 Ibid., 915.
38 See V. Taylor, *The Gospel According to St. Mark* (London: MacMillan, 1959), 445–46; W. L. Lane, *The Gospel According to Mark* (Grand Rapids: Eerdmans, 1974), 383–84; J. R. Edwards, *The Gospel according to Mark* (Grand Rapids: Eerdmans, 2002), 327–28; against this view see M. D. Hooker, *The Gospel According to Saint Mark* (Peabody: Hendrickson, 1991), 248–49.

order to interpret what the Son of Man came to do. In doing so he is following the example of his Lord. In addition, as noted above, Paul has changed the words of the psalmist to reflect the distinctly Christian view that the church is the object of God's redemptive actions. Furthermore, the reflexive ἑαυτῷ points back to Jesus Christ and adds a distinctly christocentric stamp to this OT concept. It is not only through Jesus Christ giving himself that this redemptive cleansing has been secured, but it is also for himself that it has been accomplished. The church constitutes the people purified for God's (Jesus Christ's!) own possession. It is thus to the gospel that Paul turns in order to correctly understand the Scriptures, and to the Scriptures he turns to interpret the gospel. Jesus set this pattern.

The deep connection between Paul's theology and OT teaching is emerging in a dialectical relationship. This passage is a good example of the sort of reciprocal correlation between Scripture and tradition that pervades these epistles. Paul has demonstrated a concern to anchor the church's faith and self-understanding in the Scriptures. God has done in the church what he promised through the psalmist to do for Israel.

1 TIMOTHY 5:18B

As already seen above, 1 Tim 5:18 begins with a very common IF followed by a quotation of Deut. 25:4. Following these two elements is a dominical saying ("The laborer is worthy of his wages") that is found in Luke 10:7 and similarly in Matt 10:10 and to which Paul refers in 1 Cor. 9:14. The two sayings in 1 Tim 5:18 are separated only by καί ("and"). This immediately raises a question. Does Paul actually intend here to equate a NT writing with the OT as Scripture? There is the possibility that the IF refers only to the first saying. If this is the case, then the second saying is simply epexegetical, tacked on for confirmation or explanation. The other option is that the IF governs the second quotation as well and that it, too, is regarded as Scripture by the author.

The rationale for the first view, that is, that only the initial saying is governed by the IF and thus called Scripture, is summed up rather well by Fee: "the term *Scripture* meant *only* the OT for Christians until the end of the second century."[39] The IF governs only the first saying; otherwise the statement of the author becomes an anachronism.[40] The source of the saying in question could not have been called Scripture here, because Scripture could not have included a dominical saying *at this*

---

[39] G. D. Fee, *1 and 2 Timothy, Titus* (NIBC; Peabody, MA: Hendrickson, 1998), 134 (emphasis original).

[40] A. E. Harvey ("'The Workman Is Worthy of His Hire: Fortunes of a Proverb in the Early Church," *NovT* 24 [1982]: 212), though not adopting the "first saying only" view, nonetheless gives succinct expression to why its advocates do. He states: "Now of course the O.T. does not contain this text; and it is hardly conceivable that the author of the Pastorals would have referred to any existing record of the sayings of Jesus as 'Scripture.'" Harvey concluded that the author has mistakenly called the second saying Scripture as well because he thought it came from the OT.

time. Because Scripture could not have included such a saying at this time, the author is not referring to the second saying as Scripture. Since indications that the emerging NT writings were being viewed as Scripture are rare, if not absent, before Marcion, then such an attitude did not exist.[41]

I wish to argue, instead, that there is nothing in the text to support the perspective above and everything to oppose it. The perspective above is based on extratextual historical paradigms that fly in the face of this text in particular. The dominical saying as well as the saying from the Torah has been drawn from a source that the author has consciously referred to as Scripture. "The two sayings are clearly coordinate. If the first is 'scripture,' so is the second."[42] What follows the verb has been marked as Scripture. The force of the καί does not render the verse "the Scripture says . . . and this is supported by . . . "; instead, we should understand "the Scripture says this *and* this." My contention is that Paul has quoted Luke 10:7 as Scripture. I wish to offer seven arguments in support of this straightforward reading of the text.

(1) There are in fact other passages in the NT where the same construction, IF + Scripture + καί + Scripture, is found. Mark 7:10; Acts 1:20; and Heb 1:8–10 all offer parallels. In each one, καί is used in a normal conjunctive sense in order to join two coordinate clauses that are also scriptural quotations. This is exactly the case in the present passage. Questions regarding the coordinate nature of the construction and whether the IF governs one or both of the quotations are not even issues in any of these parallel examples. Neither should they be in 1 Tim 5:18.

(2) Within the PE themselves there is a parallel that has been ignored by scholars. As we have already seen above, in 2 Tim 2:19 Paul introduces two quotations, separated only by καί and preceded by an IF. No one suggests that the second quotation in 2 Tim 2:19 has a different status from the first. It is recognized that the normal interpretation of such a construction would not posit any discrepancy between the sayings.[43]

(3) It is of significance to note that the second saying is sandwiched between definite cases of scriptural indebtedness. The first saying is clearly a quotation of Deut 25:4. As we have seen above, immediately following the second saying of v. 18, vv. 19–25 contain strong allusions to Deuteronomy 19. This entire section about elders, 5:17–25, is saturated with Scripture. The second saying in v. 18 is consonant with that pattern.

(4) Besides being the only sayings in the PE introduced with a typical introductory formula for introducing *scriptural* quotations, the sayings in v. 18 are also the

---

41 Of course, 2 Pet 3:16 is important here, especially considering recent scholarship dating 2 Peter between AD 80–90. See Bauckham, *Jude, 2 Peter*, 157–58.

42 W. Hendriksen, *I & II Timothy and Titus* (London: Banner of Truth Trust, 1959), 181.

43 C. Spicq (*Les Épîtres Pastorales* [Paris: Librairie Lecoffre, 1969], 238) has noted the analogous relationship of 2 Tim 2:19 to 1 Tim 5:18, but only in the sense of both linking OT sayings and apostolic sayings. This also is relevant to our point but is actually noting a different aspect of the parallel. We are pointing out the analogous construction, i.e., how the verses are put together; he noted the analogous content, i.e., what was used to put the verses together.

only exact quotations in the PE. When the dominical saying of 5:18b is compared with the three previous uses of the same saying, one will see that it is an exact parallel to Luke 10:7 in contrast with the other two instances. 1 Corinthians 9:14 is no quotation at all, but is a paraphrase of or a reference to a command of the Lord. Matthew 10:10; Luke 10:7; and 1 Tim 5:18 compare as follows.

Matt 10:10 ἄξιος γὰρ ὁ ἐργάτης τῆς τροφῆς αὐτοῦ.
Luke 10:7   ἄξιος γὰρ ὁ ἐργάτης τοῦ μισθοῦ αὐτοῦ.
1 Tim 5:18 ἄξιος ὁ ἐργάτης τοῦ μισθοῦ αὐτου.

First Timothy 5:18 does omit γὰρ ("for"), but this omission is more likely to confirm the role of the quotation as Scripture. If Paul intended the quotation to be epexegetical, then γὰρ would have been the most likely way to indicate that, just as it did in the dominical usage. Instead, he omitted γὰρ and simply connected the two sayings with καί. First Timothy 5:18 appears to be an direct citation of Luke 10:7. This adds credence to the view that the IF governs both sayings. This is an astonishing—indeed, even unbelievable—thing to many.[44]

(5) It is widely recognized that there are several similarities with Luke in the PE that were likely more than coincidence. It has been argued that the similarities with the Lucan works were so extensive and striking that common authorship must be seriously entertained.[45] Other scholars, less enamored with the similarities than Wilson but nonetheless recognizing their indisputable presence, have adopted the view that Luke was the amanuensis for the writing of these epistles.[46] These considerations show that 1 Tim 5:18 is not an isolated point of contact between the PE and Luke.

(6) The teaching and actions of Jesus represented and manifested a new kind of authority. This is both in contrast to and fulfillment of the Torah and the other canonical writings. This new authority, based on the Christian acknowledgment of Jesus as Lord, made it inevitable that his words and teaching were received as authoritative from the start, and, as von Campenhausen notes, the idea and scope of the "canon" should therefore be reevaluated.[47] In this context it is only natural that an emphasis on the teaching of Jesus as authoritative, yea, even canonical, would develop quickly.

---

[44] Harvey, "Workman Is Worthy," 209–21, argued that the saying in question was probably a common proverb, readily recognized as such, and not regarded as Scripture. The multiple attestation of the saying (Matt 10:10; Luke 10:7; 1 Cor 15:24; *Did.* 13:2) adds credence to its identity as a common proverb. However, these texts do not reflect a cavalier reference to some unknown philosopher/teacher whose words outlived their creator. Even if the saying had come into existence before Jesus used it, it was still *his* use that was important for the writers of the NT. Harvey suggests that the author of the PE mistakenly—but pardonably—thought the "proverb" came from the OT. In this way Harvey acknowledged what the text itself indicates, namely, that the second saying has the same status as the first, without violating his presupposition as to the inconceivability of a saying's source or gospel being regarded as Scripture at this time.

[45] S. G. Wilson, *Luke and the Pastoral Epistles* (London: SPCK, 1979). In his review of Wilson's book (*JSNT* 10 [1981]: 69–74), I. H. Marshall adequately refuted Wilson's thesis; see also Hanson, *The Pastoral Epistles*, 8–9.

[46] E.g., C. F. D. Moule, "The Problem of the Pastoral Epistles: A Reappraisal," *BJRL* 47 (1965): 430–52.

[47] H. von Campenhausen, *The Formation of the Christian Bible* (Philadelphia: Fortress, 1977), 1–2.

The PE emphatically reflect this attitude. In 1 Tim 6:3–4 the author says: "If any one teaches otherwise and does not agree with the sound words of our Lord Jesus Christ and the teaching which accords with godliness, he is puffed up with conceit, he knows nothing." A close look at 1:3,10–11 reveals striking similarities with 6:3. The concern in both passages is with those who teach "other doctrine" (the verb ἑτεροδιδασκαλέω is used in 1:3 and the noun ἑτεροδιδασκαλία in 6:3, the only NT occurrences of these terms, followed in each case by similar statements about "sound teaching" in 1:10 and 6:3):

1:10   "whatever else is contrary to the sound teaching"
6:3   "does not agree with the sound teaching"

This is all then concluded with:

1:11   "based on the glorious gospel of the blessed God"
6:3   "the teaching that promotes godliness"

Moreover, 6:3 is a specific reference to "words of the Lord Jesus Christ" in contrast to "other doctrine." The author is fully aware of and uses specific teaching of the Lord (1 Tim 2:6; Titus 2:14). There is a "canon-consciousness" here with respect to Jesus' teaching. This attitude toward the teaching of Jesus that permeates the PE adds credence to the view that 5:18b is also regarded by Paul as Scripture.[48]

(7) The dominical tradition and the Pauline tradition are combined with the broader received tradition. The gospel, and the teaching connected with it, is designated as the commandment or charge (1 Tim 1:5,18; 6:14). Paul uses terms such as παραγγελία ("instruction," always in connection with apostolic or divine authority; in the synoptics it is found only on the lips of Jesus) and "*the* faith" (1 Tim 3:9; 4:1,6; 5:8; 6:10,21; Titus 1:13). With this view of the gospel and the church's teaching, it is hardly surprising for Paul to refer to it as a deposit (παραθήκη, 1 Tim 6:20; 2 Tim 1:12,14), that which has been entrusted (παρατίθημι, 1 Tim 1:18; 2 Tim 2:2, and the passive of πιστεύω, 1 Tim 1:11; Titus 1:3).

The responsibility of Timothy is twofold. Just as Paul had "fought the good fight" and "finished the race" (2 Tim 4:7), Timothy is exhorted to do likewise. In sum, he is charged (παραγγέλλω) to "keep the commandment unstained and free from reproach" (1 Tim 6:14 ESV). The initial exhortation is obviously aimed at the moral life of Timothy; he is to keep his personal life above reproach. But "the commandment" is the teaching per se, the gospel and its ramifications. Timothy is given the

---

48 R. Saarinen (*The Pastoral Epistles with Philemon and Jude* [Brazos Theological Commentary on the Bible; Grand Rapids: Brazos Press, 2008], 93) states, "The theological interpretation here can follow the plain meaning, which regards the words of Jesus as scripture." This view, he says, is assumed in 1 Tim 4:13, on which he comments, "we find here a first step toward the canonization of Christian texts" (84).

responsibility of upholding and preserving the faith, the tradition that corresponds to the truth (1 Tim 2:4; 3:15; 4:3; 2 Tim 2:15,25; 3:8; 4:4; Titus 1:1,14).

In keeping with this initial responsibility, there is a second one. In order to insure the continued preservation of the received tradition, Timothy is to "entrust [it] to faithful men who will be able to teach others also" (2 Tim 2:2 ESV). Just as Paul has entrusted it to him, he is to do the same with others. This dual responsibility is very clear in 2 Timothy where the charge to guard the deposit (1:13–14) is closely followed by the charge to pass it on (2:2). Titus is instructed similarly (Titus 1:9).

The assumption underlying all this is that the tradition is identifiable and must remain intact; it serves as the objective expression of the church's subjective faith. The author is stressing that the former must remain clear and constant in order for the latter not to be misplaced. The dominical and apostolic traditions have become authoritative in themselves. Even the law is subservient to this new tradition (1 Tim 1:8–11).

The author often ascribes to the tradition the same features and purpose that he explicitly ascribes to Scripture. In 2 Tim 3:15–17, he speaks of Scripture as being able to make one wise unto salvation and able to give guidance in a godly life. These are the exact same things that he says of the apostolic tradition (1 Tim 2:4; 4:16; 2 Tim 1:10–11; 2:9–10; Titus 1:1–2).

Likewise the so-called faithful sayings represent what is possibly a non-Pauline tradition that the author uses in an authoritative manner. Running throughout the PE is a motif of standardization, or "canon-consciousness." Every indication within the PE affirms that Paul wrote with the presupposition that the apostolic tradition is the norm for the church and amounted to an extension of the scope of Scripture.

This motif is presented by a family or cluster of associated terms and concepts, occurs with striking frequency, occurs within a somewhat unlikely or avoidable context (letters to close personal co-workers), occurs in significant contexts (in the salutations and the concluding remarks and in the personal exhortations to Timothy and Titus), and is presented clearly and coherently with the related terms and concepts.[49]

The early church was surprisingly slow to take the implications of the gospel to their logical end with regard to the Christian Scriptures.[50] Paul anticipated the logical development that would soon ensue, had perceived the need for this development even in his own time (the need was due to the proliferation of distortions of the gospel by various opponents), and had consciously made a move in this direction. In this respect he was truly ahead of his time. This fact, however, should not lead us to deny the presence of such an attitude. History has been replete with men and women whose ideas were ahead of their time. Besides, there is further NT support in 2 Pet 3:16 indicating the development of this attitude. The tradition is authoritative. The

---

[49] W. Freedman, "The Literary Motif: A Definition and Evaluation," *Novel* 4 (1970): 123–31.
[50] D. A. Hagner, *The Use of the Old and New Testaments in Clement of Rome* (Leiden: Brill, 1973), 340.

tradition must be preserved. The tradition is canonical. The tradition is becoming scriptural. These seem to be Paul's working presuppositions.

If the faithful sayings (1 Tim 1:15; 3:1; 4:9; 2 Tim 2:11; Titus 3:8) had been recorded in writing, instead of saying "πιστὸς ὁ λόγος" ("this saying is trustworthy"), Paul might well have said "γέγραπται" ("it is written") or "λέγει γὰρ ἡ γραφή" ("for the Scripture says"). This brings us back to where we started because, in a sense, this is exactly what has happened in 1 Tim 5:18. As noted earlier, the saying of the Lord in this verse is also alluded to by Paul in 1 Cor 9:14, yet there he does not refer to it as Scripture. Some years later in 1 Timothy, it is quoted as Scripture.[51] In the PE we have what is probably the earliest extant literary reference to a NT document as Scripture. If the second saying of 1 Tim 5:18 were in fact found in the OT, no one would hesitate acknowledging the obvious, that is, the coordinate nature of the verse and the specific OT reference from which the quotation was drawn.

FINAL CONSIDERATIONS

A few other passages within the PE have been linked in one way or another with the OT. Whatever connections are here are more subtle and varied, and probably mediated through tradition, though perhaps no less important for Paul.

Any echo of Isa 45:21–22[52] or Job 9:32–33[53] within 1 Tim 2:3–6 is so faint as to be unhelpful. Verse 6 is acknowledged by virtually all commentators to be a reminiscence of the dominical saying in Mark 10:45. Yet Paul has not made the explicit connection between the ransom and iniquity that appears in Titus 2:14. Instead, the dominical saying has largely retained its traditional character. The dependence here is on Christian tradition, so much so that the passage ends by Paul noting that his calling is specifically for the purpose of proclaiming just that, namely, Christian tradition.

First Timothy 6:1 ("so that God's name and His teaching will not be blasphemed") and Titus 2:5 ("so that God's message will not be slandered") reflect common OT language and priority. As Paul expresses his concern about how the church is viewed by outsiders, his thoughts spill out in a manner consistent with the Scriptures, primarily exemplified by Isa 52:5. This sort of expression is also widely manifest in Christian traditions (Rom 2:24; Jas 2:7; 2 Pet 2:2; *1 Clem*: 47:7; *2 Clem*: 13:2; Ignatius, *Trall.* 8:2; Polycarp, *Phil* 10:3; Justin, *Dial* 17:2). In Titus the principle is expressed positively. Proper behavior can "adorn the doctrine of God" (2:10 ESV) as

---

51 Spicq (*Épitres*, 238–39) also emphasizes the closeness of 2 Tim 2:19b with Luke 13:27 as further indicating the connection of the OT with apostolic writings, with the latter being used in the same manner as the former, and enjoying the same authoritative status.

52 Hanson, "The Use of the Old Testament in the Pastoral Epistles," 212.

53 Hanson, *Studies in the Pastoral Epistles*, 56–62.

well discredit it. Both negatively and positively, tradition rooted in the OT has served Paul in calling the members of the community of faith to a life of godliness.

First Timothy 6:15 contains titles common in ancient Jewish literature[54] and found elsewhere in the NT in Rev 17:14 and 19:16.[55] The basic ascription had most probably become such a commonly used title that its use without further elaboration would not elicit any particular OT passage. This is not to say Paul was unaware of its OT background; such unawareness is completely implausible.

The just recompense of God, the principle applied in 2 Tim 4:14 to Alexander the coppersmith, is found throughout the OT. The clearest examples are Ps 62:14b (LXX 61:13), Ps 28:4 (LXX 27:4), and Prov 24:12. The principle is also evident in other parts of the NT: Rom 2:6 (an explicit quotation of Prov 24:12), Matt 25:31–46; John 5:28–29; 2 Cor 11:15; 1 Pet 1:17; Rev 2:23; 16:6; 20:13. One might say that this principle was a staple of early Christian paraenesis, permeating as it does everything from the Gospels to the Apocalypse. Paul then is not likely drawing from the OT but is expressing himself in traditional OT language.

Second Timothy 3:8 also is an example of Paul's use of tradition, which has deep roots within the OT. A widespread and multifaceted apocryphal tradition grew up around the accounts described in Exodus 7–14. Two of Pharaoh's magicians came to be named in the legend as Jannes and Jambres.[56] The tradition ultimately became significant enough to spawn a book, *The Book of Jannes and Jambres*. Origen comments that the reference in 2 Tim 3:8 is dependent on this book. Ambrosiaster makes a similar statement. It is reasonable to assume that Paul was not unaware that this tradition was ultimately based on the OT, but it was the tradition to which he was here indebted.

CONCLUSION

What picture has emerged regarding the use of Scripture in the PE? Paul was dependent on tradition for many of the connections to the OT within these three epistles, but he did not restrict himself to traditional expressions or exegesis. These letters demonstrate interpretive work and applications not paralleled elsewhere in the NT. There is a constant weaving together of OT language and principles, the teaching of Jesus, and Christian tradition. One could reasonably say that these letters reflect

---

[54] Portions of the titles or very similar phrases appear in Deut 9:26; 10:17; Ezra 7:12; Esth 4:17; Ps 135:2–3; Ezek 26:7; Dan 2:37,47; 4:37; 2 Macc 13:4; 3 Macc 2:2; 5:35; 1 Enoch 9:4; 63:4; 84:2.

[55] G. K. Beale ("The Origin of the Title 'King of Kings and Lord of Lords' in Revelation 17.14," *NTS* 31 [1985]: 618–20) argues convincingly that the origin of the title for John lies in Dan 4:37. The factors that establish this in Revelation are not present in 1 Timothy.

[56] See A. Pietersma and R. T. Lutz, "Jannes and Jambres," in *The Old Testament Pseudepigrapha* (ed. J. H. Charlesworth; Garden City: Doubleday and Company, 1985), 2:427–30; M. McNamara, *The New Testament and the Palestinian Targum to the Pentateuch* (Rome: Pontifical Biblical Institute, 1966), 82–96; L. L. Grabbe, "The Jannes/Jambres Tradition in Targum Pseudo-Jonathan and Its Date," *JBL* 98 (1979): 393–401.

the work of a mature biblical theologian, at home in the text of Scripture and using it subtly and powerfully to make proclamation, to correct doctrinal error and ethical deviation, and to provide guidance for the church in transition. In doing so, Paul sets a final example for his co-workers and the churches to pay close attention to the Word and handle it carefully.

There is in the PE no deeply engaging theological argumentation involving the Scriptures, as one finds, for example, in Romans or Hebrews. One gets the impression that all this has already been worked out. Doctrinal controversies are present (e.g., 2 Tim 2:19), and to the Scriptures Paul appeals to correct these, but for the most part Paul's use of Scripture here is practically oriented. The Scriptures provide guidelines for leadership and public worship and ethical exhortation. The opponents are insubordinate and unethical. Accordingly, the uses of Scripture are for practical purposes. There is no fulfillment motif running through the use of Scripture in these epistles. The use of the OT in Titus 2:14 certainly implies the idea of fulfillment, but it is something of an exception. Most remarkable is the quotation of a Gospel as Scripture (the implications of which are significant). Given Paul's comments regarding Scripture in 2 Tim 3:15–17, and similar comments regarding *the* teaching of Jesus and *the* received tradition, this development in inscripturation is not as incredible conceptually as it *seems* historically.

Chapter Ten

THE ETHICS OF THE PASTORAL EPISTLES

THORVALD B. MADSEN II

INTRODUCTION

The Pastoral Epistles contain two types of statements related to proper conduct. Some of them capture various aspects of the Christian worldview, declaring what God is like and what he has done for particular groups of people—Paul, Timothy, the church, and so forth. Others state or imply what the affected person's duties are, given that same set of facts. In this sense, the Pastoral Epistles dwell on the *basis* for Christian conduct, as opposed to merely drawing boundaries for action. They tell us what really matters in this life and why. They also describe the ideal "Pauline" Christian, naming the virtues he would have and the vices he would shun—in summary detail, of course, but with enough content to stimulate careful reflection. Therefore, the Pastoral Epistles should not be forgotten as we negotiate the challenges of modern Christian discipleship, even if they lack the overt drama of Paul's other letters.[1] Twenty-first-century problems are new, but not entirely so—not new enough to keep the Pastoral Epistles from addressing them with apostolic authority.

Consider a few choices that confront us today. What are the primary duties of the modern church leader? Which tasks can be left to others or completed at one's leisure? Who should be in charge? What traits and abilities should he have? What stance should Christians take with respect to their culture? Should they be iconoclasts? Conformists? What impact does the gospel have on the traditional roles of society? How can we show compassion freely but also wisely? How can the church identify its enemies and deal appropriately (even redemptively) with them? These are modern questions but also timeless ones. We still want to know what Paul would say

---

[1] One says "overt" here because all sorts of currents are flowing beneath the calm surface of the Pastoral Epistles, rather like some local churches any of us might know.

and do, and he touches on each of these topics in the Pastoral Epistles, giving practical responses based on first principles. One hopes that a survey of the moral teaching found here will highlight their continued relevance.

Our approach to this subject will follow a two-part outline. In the first instance, we will consider the "logic" of ethics in the Pastoral Epistles, asking an established question from the study of other Pauline epistles—especially Romans, 1 and 2 Corinthians, Galatians, Philippians, Colossians, and 1 Thessalonians. Is the structure of ethics in the Pastoral Epistles "indicative and imperative," that is, "gift and task" as described in some detail below? An answer given here will uncover Paul's general approach to ethics in the Pastoral Epistles compared with his other letters. It would be a surprise to find an entirely different paradigm at work here, though that is possible *a priori*. Secondly, we will examine the actual commands given to Timothy and Titus and others, from general rules down to concrete exhortations, paying special attention to the various groups addressed in these letters (deacons, women, servants, etc.).

THE LOGIC OF MORALITY IN THE PASTORAL EPISTLES

Scripture defines the moral ideal for all persons, whoever they are, because its moral perspective is not relativistic. Murder, idolatry, fornication, and lying are not wrong for some and right for others. The biblical virtues are good traits for everyone to have, whatever their circumstances. Nevertheless, most of the Bible's moral teaching has a target audience *in essence*, or logically, not just from a practical standpoint. Consequently, the structure of its exhortations tends to be, "You shall do X [or doing X is *urgent* for you], either (a) "because you belong to God in a special way" or (b) "because God has done this special thing for you." The target audience of the OT is Israel; in the NT, the audience is the church. However, both testaments adopt the same template—one that has been called "indicative and imperative" or "gift and task," because of how closely the two sides may resemble one another.[2] Following the imperative would make the audience "become what it already is" somehow, and therein lies the familiar tension.

Indeed, one can find examples where the *prima facie* difference between the audience's identity and obligation is a mere change of grammatical mood. Thus, holiness (the fact or "indicative") requires holiness (the duty or "imperative"). Righteousness (gift) calls for righteousness (task). Spiritual people (indicative) must become

---

2 On this topic, see R. Bultmann, "Das Problem der Ethik bei Paulus," *ZNW* 23 (1924): 123. The entire essay is also translated by C. Stenchke and appears as "The Problem of Ethics in Paul," in *Understanding Paul's Ethics* (ed. B. S. Rosner; Carlisle: Paternoster, 1995), 195–216. Cf. also B. Rosner, *Paul, Scripture, and Ethics* (Leiden: Brill, 1994), 86–87; W. Schrage, *The Ethics of the New Testament* (trans. D. Green; Philadelphia: Fortress, 1988), 167–72; and T. B. Madsen, "Indicative and Imperative in Paul and Ancient Judaism: A Comparative Study" (Ph.D. diss., University of Aberdeen, 1998).

spiritually guided (imperative). In light of these parallels, some have suggested that one of the two dimensions—gift or task—must be less "real" than the other and included only on pragmatic or provisional grounds. God's people are not really sanctified, justified, indwelled by the Spirit, and so forth, but no harm done: a bit of constructive self-deception is a good thing, if it motivates proper behavior. Or perhaps the Bible's moral exhortations jump-start a process that renders them obsolete over time, especially in the shadow of Christ's imminent return. Either way, the indicative is taken to contradict the imperative, so that a fair dose of "spin" is needed to harmonize the related theological constructs.

As it happens, however, no apologies are necessary: gift and task stand together because God has not chosen to accomplish all aspects of redemption immediately. Rather, the indicative (God's temporally and/or logically prior act for us) covers a series of changes that take effect at different times and in various degrees—some now, some later; some fully, some partially; some having God himself as their efficient cause, others operating through the means of Christian ministry, empowered by the Spirit. God's people retain a basis for thanksgiving and assurance, while sensing an inescapable dependence upon him for ultimate victory. The two sides do not contradict one another; on the contrary, they belong together, and their linkage creates this distinctive style of moral exhortation found in the OT and NT. In the NT, some good examples can be found in 1 and 2 Peter, which base the responsibility of obedience, especially through the trials of persecution, on the church's given identity as "aliens and strangers."[3] Note, for example, the transition in 1 Peter 1 from the "gift" described in vv. 3–12 to the moral exhortations that follow in vv. 13–16. The subsequent text, vv. 17–24, manifests a complex intermingling of these two dimensions, as we see also in 2:9–12.

But nowhere does this pattern appear more frequently than in the letters of Paul. Believers have died to sin and must therefore resist its waning influence (Romans 6). As people overtaken by the Spirit, they must put aside the mind-set of the flesh (Rom 8:1–17). They live by the Spirit and, for that reason, are obliged to walk by the Spirit (Gal 5:25). The church, as an unleavened batch of dough, ought to "clean out the old leaven" of disobedience (1 Cor 5:7). Even at the macro-level, Paul's letters tend to proceed from new life to new living, as per their theological and ethical sections (so, e.g., Romans 1–11; 12–16; Galatians 1–4; 5–6; Ephesians 1–3; 4–6). This feature of Paul's major epistles is widely recognized. One thinks of it as *the* Pauline paraenetic style, if any style is. This sheds its own light on his entire moral perspective: the apostle presses for behavioral change only because he believes that his audience differs supernaturally from everyone else. Therefore, our study of ethics in the Pastoral Epistles might usefully begin with a diagnostic question: does the moral teaching found here follow this same "indicative and imperative" or "gift and task" structure?

---

3 All translations of the biblical text are taken from the New American Standard Version unless otherwise indicated.

THE GIFT AND TASK OF GODLINESS

The answer to our question should be "yes," if taken in moderation. Some examples would be uncontroversial, such as Titus 3:1–7. In this text, Paul tells Timothy, "Remind them to be subject to rulers, to authorities, to be obedient, to be ready for every good deed, to malign no one, to be peaceable, gentle, showing every consideration for all men" (vv. 1–2). Then he gives the basis of their duty, expressed in the standard "indicative" form (vv. 3–7):

> For we also once were foolish ourselves, disobedient, deceived, enslaved to various lusts and pleasures, spending our life in malice and envy, hateful, hating one another. But when the kindness of God our Savior and *His* love for mankind appeared, He saved us, not on the basis of deeds which we have done in righteousness, but according to His mercy, by the washing of regeneration and renewing by the Holy Spirit, whom He poured out upon us richly through Jesus Christ our Savior, so that being justified by His grace we would be made heirs according to *the* hope of eternal life.

The gift of salvation precedes and grounds the tasks given in vv. 1–2, providing a paradigm case of the Pauline hortatory style.

The previous text, Titus 2:1–14, follows the same template. In this case, Paul has commands for older men (v. 2), older women (v. 3), younger women (vv. 4–5), younger men (v. 6), Timothy himself (vv. 7–8), and slaves (vv. 9–10). Then, as a basis for their assigned duties, Paul describes the great change that has occurred, one that defines the church as a new people (vv. 11–14):

> For the grace of God has appeared, bringing salvation to all men, instructing us to deny ungodliness and worldly desires and to live sensibly, righteously and godly in the present age, looking for the blessed hope and the appearing of the glory of our great God and Savior, Christ Jesus, who gave Himself for us to redeem us from every lawless deed, and to purify for Himself a people for His own possession, zealous for good deeds.

The "indicative" of new life in Christ, as these verses capture it, logically precedes and forms the basis of the "imperative" given above. This passage, like the previous one, matches our expectations exactly because (a) it links gift and task inferentially; and (b) the former describes the church's new identity or situation. We even have the familiar, *prima facie* tensions in play. Since the believers of Crete are washed, regenerated, spiritually renewed, and justified (Titus 3:3–7, "indicative"), they must assume the justified and reborn lifestyle (Titus 3:1–2). Since they have been redeemed "from every lawless deed" and have become "a people for His own possession" (Titus 2:14; cf. Exod 19:5), they must "deny ungodliness" and "live sensibly, righteously and godly in the present age" (Titus 2:12). At the very least, therefore, we can say that Titus manifests the Pauline "gift and task" framework.

A final case comes from 1 Tim 3:14–15 and its surrounding context. This passage supports both the preceding exhortations and those that follow because it features a central metaphor—if not *the* controlling metaphor—informing the entire letter.[4] The church is the "household of God," which needs to function in ways that please the "living God." To that end, Paul gives instructions (cf. 1:1–3:13 and 4:1–6:10) meant to protect the church's status as the "pillar and support of the truth," the last term being defined by its congruence with the christological summary of v. 16. The indicative lends urgency to the task of discovering how to please God, as conditioned by each person's niche in the church and society. One could not find a better illustration of gift-and-task paraenesis.

THE GIFT AND TASK OF STEWARDSHIP

The standard "indicative and imperative" template would have the church as its target audience, rather than any narrower category of Christians, and to that extent, the following examples stretch the normal boundaries of the paradigm as defined by, say, Titus 2:1–14; 3:1–7; Rom 6:1–14; and Col 3:1–17. Nevertheless, Paul does construe his own apostleship and the leading roles of the church as "gifts" or "indicatives" in the relevant sense. God entrusts certain people with a stewardship over his household and empowers them to serve as he desires. They differ from ordinary Christians, and their supernatural identity within the church, as a transforming "indicative," requires a superadded commitment to ministry, endurance, and godliness (imperative).

In 1 Timothy 1, for example, Paul describes his own position as (a) a stewardship given to him by God and (b) one having moral implications. His greeting points to his unique position and authority in standard terms, "Paul, an apostle of Christ Jesus according to the commandment of God our Savior, and of Christ Jesus." (v. 1), and the remainder of this chapter invests v. 1 with immediate, practical significance. Verse 4 contrasts the myths and genealogies of the false teachers, which promote "speculations," with sound teaching, which leads to stewardship of the gospel, a responsibility discharged as a trust from God. Further down, in vv. 11–12, Paul says that he has been "entrusted" (ἐπιστεύθην) with the gospel and also "strengthened" to carry out his responsibilities (v. 12a), having been appointed to serve (v. 12b). Taken together, these verses construe Paul's apostleship as an assigned and empowered stewardship of the gospel, and this gift yields the task of defending the gospel both immediately and through delegates such as Timothy. In 1:18–19, the latter's own status become the basis of moral exhortation. Verse 18 reminds Timothy of "prophetic utterances" that indicated a calling to leadership and also applies the latter with a charge to "fight

---

[4] Cf. the essay by F. A. Tomlinson in the present volume.

the good fight," this being a metaphorical summary of his difficult assignment in Ephesus.

First Timothy 4:11–15 offers a good example of "gift and task" instruction, this time having Timothy as its direct recipient. Paul tells the latter to command and teach the doctrines and practices of his letter, giving balanced attention to matters of character and job performance. "In speech, conduct, love, faith *and* purity," Timothy must "show [himself] an example of those who believe" (v. 12). Verse 13 then takes up the performance aspects of Timothy's calling: "Until I come, give attention to the *public* reading *of Scripture*, to exhortation and teaching." These exhortations rest on the gift given to Timothy "by prophetic utterance" with the laying on of hands (v. 14). A similar inference occurs in 6:11–16, where Timothy is the "man of God" (v. 11a) whose identity as such informs the behavior expected of him in vv. 11b–16, though other Christians would fall under the same heading in a broader sense.

Paul's second letter to Timothy dwells on the gift and task of ministry, with special reference to the reality of suffering and the need to endure it. In 1:6, for example, he tells Timothy to "kindle afresh the gift of God which is in [him] through the laying on [Paul's] hands." This gift is the Holy Spirit himself, whose influence on each Christian produces abilities to meet various challenges of the new life, especially those of gospel witness in the face of hardship. The Spirit would produce in Timothy "power" or courage, "love," and "self-control" (v. 7), the first of them being a quality which Timothy probably struggled with at crucial points in his ministry, especially when opposed by false teachers and moral deviants. In 1:14, Paul enjoins Timothy to "guard" what has been entrusted to him (imperative) by the power of the indwelling Holy Spirit (indicative).

Thus the logic of morality in the Pastoral Epistles can be regarded as "indicative and imperative" at the (a) macro- and (b) micro-levels, that is, when Paul addresses (a) the entire church, as a new people, or (b) considers the duties of some particular gifted and called Christian. Even the same tensions arise here, as in Paul's major epistles, especially when the "gift" applies to someone like Timothy. He has the Spirit of "power and love and self-control," but he does not manifest these virtues automatically, as we might have expected. On the contrary, Paul's language suggests ongoing concern about Timothy's boldness in witness, and thus he encourages him to be freshly shaped by the Spirit's influence. The one side undercuts the other only to the extent that we adopt an un-Pauline, all-or-nothing view of the Christian life and readiness for ministry. The larger result here is that the Pastoral Epistles connect "is" and "ought," or fact and value, in ways that track closely and deeply with the major epistles. The life that pleases God begins with his own redemptive acts and follows as a response to them. We do what we are, and our lives are an outworking of several definitive and irreversible changes secured by the cross and effected individually by the Spirit.

THE CONTENT OF MORALITY IN
THE PASTORAL EPISTLES

This section considers the content of morality in the Pastoral Epistles, observing the particular commands given to various subgroups. Paul addresses Timothy and Titus, overseers and deacons, women and men, children and slaves—that is, all sorts of people. But the largest gap in these letters exists between the duties of leaders and the duties of everyone else, not in terms of content but emphasis, and we can see why, given the controversies that caused Paul to write. The problem in Ephesus and Crete is that several would-be apostles—or, at any rate, several aspiring VIPs—have risen up with eccentric doctrines and practices that efface the gospel and factionalize the churches.[5] Consequently, Paul's moral teaching concentrates on the values and objectives of leadership and the perversions to which they are commonly subject, and our own survey will reflect this approach. Section A considers the duties of those who lead, while section B surveys the duties of everyone else.

THE DUTIES OF THOSE WHO LEAD

Timothy and Titus are neither pastors of local churches nor apostles. They stand between Paul and local congregations and therefore hold positions that do not exist today, if only because no apostles are around to create them.[6] The latter can no longer send out representatives like Timothy and Titus, and no one today is "called" in that exact sense. At the same time, the Pastoral Epistles look forward to a time when the tasks of leadership will fall to others, operating under the authority of these letters and the rest of Scripture (cf. 2 Tim 3:16). Consequently, we shall not consider as separate categories (a) the duties of Timothy and Titus, on the one hand, and (b) the duties of everyone else who leads, on the other. For our purposes, it will suffice to examine them collectively, taking Timothy and Titus to be examples for others to follow.

PROTECT THE GOSPEL MESSAGE

Within three verses of 1 Timothy, Paul gives one of the main reasons why his "son" in the faith (v. 18) must remain in Ephesus. Certain men are teaching false doctrines, and Timothy has to confront them. Paul knows that this assignment will be difficult for someone as young as Timothy (4:12), but Timothy has no choice and has been equipped by God to do so (1:18; 4:14). False doctrine threatens the very existence of the church by obscuring its distinctive identity and the gospel itself. Consequently, Timothy must oppose local heretics and appoint elders who will join

---

[5] For a concise discussion of the opposition in Ephesus and Crete, see I. H. Marshall, in collaboration with P. H. Towner, *A Critical and Exegetical Commentary on the Pastoral Epistles* (ICC; Edinburgh: T & T Clark, 1999), 40–51.

[6] Cf. J. N. D. Kelly, *A Commentary on the Pastoral Epistles* (HNTC; New York: Harper and Row, 1963), 14: "The impression left . . . is that [Timothy and Titus] are the Apostle's personal emissaries, with an *ad hoc*, temporary mandate."

225

him in this struggle. The same challenge confronts Titus (1:5–11). False teaching has come to Crete, and he needs to answer it with the help of reliable overseers. Thus, both letters envision a two-sided teaching ministry involving offense and defense: the overseer must conserve the gospel entrusted to him and directly refute heresy.

Surprisingly, however, Paul does not dissect the heresy of Ephesus and Crete, giving Timothy and Titus ammunition for their rebuttals.[7] Rather, he treats it impatiently, as if details would dignify it.[8] Nevertheless, some conclusions here are safer than others. We should note, for example, Paul's innuendo that only an especially wicked person would accept and teach these things, someone whose conscience has been "seared" or damaged by contrary loyalties (1 Tim 4:2; cf. Titus 1:14–15). His opponents are not innocently confused or mistaken; they have consciously embraced "doctrines of demons" (v. 1). We also know that they claimed an incorporeal resurrection for themselves at the very least (2 Tim 2:18) and spun elaborate yarns from the OT (1 Tim 1:4,7; Titus 1:14; 3:9). All this had the following practical result: now one had to live—in carefully selective ways—as if the eschaton had arrived, abstaining from marriage and certain foods (1 Tim 4:3).[9] Taken as a whole, these doctrines set up a caste system of high and low achievers, measured against a finished salvation to be accessed through ascetic habits and special learning.[10]

Paul's warnings thus compare strongly to what Jesus says about false prophets in Matt 7:15–20: they do what they do because of who they are. Heresies trace back to character defects, which soon become visible, as fruit reveals the tree. In some cases, the false teaching rationalizes wickedness that has already taken hold, such as the confirmed thug who learns to call his crimes "jihad." Or perhaps the heresy conjures misbehavior out of thin, ideological air. Either way, both Jesus and Paul commend to us the same diagnostic tool: watch what the false prophets do, not just what they say. This practice exposes their idols and final objectives, and it lets one anticipate who will accept what they say. The false prophet might covet the wealth aimed at esoteric gurus (e.g., 2 Tim 3:1–5), and his marks would include, say, "weak women weighed down with sins" (2 Tim 3:6).

---

[7] We are assuming that the false teaching in both places is approximately the same (so, e.g., Marshall, *Pastoral Epistles*, 41; G. Knight, *The Pastoral Epistles: A Commentary on the Greek Text* [NIGTC; Grand Rapids: Paternoster, 1992], 11–12.), though we need not postulate complete agreement, especially if one could not have summarized it neatly.

[8] Cf. W. D. Mounce, *Pastoral Epistles* (WBC 46; Nashville: Thomas Nelson, 2000), xcvii: "the Ephesian error was not a well-formulated theological position that could be described and criticized. It was a loose association of ideas permeated with sinful behavior. This lack of content and coherence made it impossible for Paul to evaluate the heresy systematically, as he did in other situations."

[9] One says "carefully selective" here because their asceticism had convenient limits, that is, it stopped at the luxuries for which they craved more money.

[10] Cf. P. Towner, *The Letters to Timothy and Titus* (NICNT; Grand Rapids: Eerdmans, 2006), 567: "For whatever reasons, they found Paul's gospel insufficient or uncomfortable, probably because it did not affirm them as they wished to be affirmed. . . . Perhaps because of its stress on equality or universality, those who insecurities depended instead on affirmation of their uniqueness tended to resort to interpretations that underlined limitations and reinforced boundaries."

PREACH THE WORD

Paul charges Timothy and Titus to teach sound doctrine and practice constantly, even without the immediate pressure of opposing heresy. The same duty applies to the overseer, who must be "able to teach" and, if need be, refute error (1 Tim 3:2; Titus 1:9). One summary of this ongoing task appears in 2 Tim 4:1–2, where Paul charges Timothy to "preach the Word" at all times, under all conditions, assuming these will often be unfavorable. Likewise, 1 Tim 4:11–14 concentrates on the teaching ministry of leadership: "Command and teach these things," and then, "devote yourself to the public reading of Scripture, to preaching and to teaching" (NIV). Diligence in this regard opens doors for conversion and makes established believers less vulnerable to false teaching. The same task of instruction would apply to overseers following Timothy and Titus and who, in their own case, base their authority on the revealed truths of Scripture. The impression given by Titus 2:1–15, for example, is that all kinds of people will need instruction all of the time. Consequently, the leadership of the church must concentrate heavily on its teaching ministry.[11]

ENDURE HARDSHIP

Paul suffered much as an evangelist and teacher, sometimes by accident, though usually by the design of his enemies. In 2 Cor 11:25–27, he "boasts" of shipwrecks, excessive labors, sleeplessness, and hunger, none of which follow necessarily from persecution. However, his troubles usually arose in conflict with anti-Christian forces, and he prepares Timothy and Titus for similar trials, not to mention the overseers of local churches. They will inherit his mantle of "teaching, conduct, purpose, faith, patience, love, perseverance, persecutions, *and* sufferings" because "all who desire to live godly in Christ Jesus will be persecuted" (2 Tim 3:10–12). Just as Paul himself has endured "everything for the sake of the elect" (2 Tim 2:10 NIV), they will have to preach the word and correct false teaching, come what may. To that extent, their lives will contrast sharply with Paul's opponents, who desire entourages and material wealth (cf. 1 Tim 3:5; 6:5–10; Titus 1:10). Through their conduct and character, Paul and his co-workers will try to be at peace with everyone, not giving unnecessary offense, but this teaching assumes that the preacher will face opposition. It cannot finally be avoided because the gospel contradicts the pluralistic impulse in religion and the relaxed moral standards seen in some dimensions of ancient Mediterranean culture.

LIVE CIRCUMSPECTLY

Paul's instructions to Timothy and Titus, and then to all who lead, strongly emphasize the need for admirable Christian character, defined with reference to the

---

[11] Cf. M. Dever, "The Doctrine of the Church," in *A Theology for the Church* (ed. D. L. Akin; Nashville: B&H Academic, 2007), 802: "All of the qualifications listed here [regarding the elder] are applicable for all Christians, except one—the ability to teach."

circumspect or proverbial virtues. Good leaders for Ephesus and Crete will be careful and considerate. They know which hills to die on and pursue their goals with gentleness and respect. They do not crave wealth or the limelight but go about their business in a quiet, workmanlike way. Timothy and Titus should appoint elders who devote themselves to learning and who remain available to wise counsel. The candidates must enjoy the respect of their wives, children, and peers, as demonstrated by the peace of their households and other relationships. If they are maligned, the accusations must come only from bad people. To the general public and the saints, they will be "above reproach" (1 Tim 3:2).

Paul certainly would not restrict these virtues to the church's leadership, as though two standards were in play—one set for the leaders, another for the regular folks.[12] Everyone ought to be this way in the ideal case. However, he exhorts the overseers and deacons with special urgency, given their higher profile within the church and society. They live "on screen," so to speak, causing their words, actions, and example to have multiplied effects. Thus, an overseer's virtue becomes an example for ordinary believers, and it would make the gospel winsome to outsiders (so, e.g., 1 Tim 4:12). On the other hand, an angry, selfishly ambitious man will harm the church in an equal and opposite way. Therefore, the Pastoral Epistles strongly emphasize the overseer's need for outstanding Christian character and conduct.

More than 20 virtues of an overseer appear in the Pastoral Epistles, half of which apply to the deacons as well. This overlap is not surprising, of course, since: (a) Paul uses general terms, and (b) they mainly describe common Christian decency.[13] But we should note in passing how they correct the vices of Paul's opponents. If the false teachers do evil for the sake of money, Paul will stress the need for contentment among the elders. If pride leads to heresy and factionalism, the elder must devote himself to the plain, unglamorous work of orthodox churchmanship. In some ways, perhaps, the businesslike tone of these letters has a defensive effect, drying the church's clay before creative geniuses can reshape it for wealth and acclaim. Overall, the ideal second-generation leader is a mature, sensible, well-mannered servant, along the lines traced below.

LOVE

At several points in these letters, Paul tells Timothy or Titus to excel in love, giving this virtue a prominent place in his exhortations. To be sure, he never expressly defines love in the Pastoral Epistles, as per 1 Corinthians 13, but we get the general

---

12 So, e.g., Marshall, *Pastoral Epistles*, 472.

13 Cf. D. Guthrie, *The Pastoral Epistles* (TNTC 14; Grand Rapids: Eerdmans, 1990), 91: "It is surprising that the required standards, particularly the negative ones (*e.g.*, *not given to much wine, not quarrelsome*), do not lead us to suppose that the usual aspirant for office was of particularly high quality, since no exceptional virtues are demanded. Yet this in itself accurately reflects the earliest state of the Christian church, when the majority of converts probably came from a background of low moral ideals."

idea of it from the contexts where it appears. Love is, for example, one of the major changes brought about in Paul's own conversion: "the grace of our Lord was more than abundant" in his case, yielding "the faith and love which are *found* in Christ Jesus" (1 Tim 1:14). At one time, he persecuted the church as an insolent and violent man (1 Tim 1:13), but now all things are new, with special reference to love. Love is also one of three qualities engendered by the Spirit given to Timothy (2 Tim 1:6–7) and the one said to be absent in his opponents. Thus we can see more clearly how Paul would define "love" by examining his indictment of the bad actors in Ephesus and Crete, since their ministry rests upon and stimulates the contrary vices.

In 1 Tim 1:5, their ideas generate vain discussions that set aside "love from a pure heart and a good conscience and a sincere faith." In 1 Tim 6:4–5, Paul says that their controversies produce "envy, strife, abusive language, evil suspicions, and constant friction between men of depraved mind." Love would contrast with all of these vices, whatever else it does, and Paul's remarks in 1 Tim 1:5 and 6:4–5 corroborate our hypothesis. The Christian leader must habitually sacrifice his own interests and well-being for the sake of those under his care. He will give up rights when necessary and appreciate that he cannot serve Christ without serving his people, as opposed to using them for supposedly higher purposes. Given its connection to service, love would encompass all the other virtues named in the Pastoral Epistles, though we should highlight a few others for clarifying emphasis.

HUMILITY

In his major epistles, Paul construes humility as a foundational virtue. At least we might surmise that he does so, based on how much "leveling" occurs therein. He forbids boasting unless it has the work of Christ as its ground (1 Cor 1:31). He describes the message of the cross as a trap set for the "wise man" and "debater of this age," a device through which God shames the wise and strong. One has two options: (a) save face by rejecting the shame of the cross or (b) be saved by the crucified Messiah and Lord. One cannot do both (1 Cor 1:20–29). The cross forces that "either/or" decision and excludes the proud man from the sphere of grace. In Romans and Ephesians, Paul lays the groundwork for Christian unity by reminding his readers that no one must "think more highly of himself than he ought to think" (Rom 12:3) and that all Christians are once-dead people now made alive by grace alone (Eph 2:1–10). The major epistles regard pride as the source of much trouble, especially opposition to Paul's message of the cross.

Not surprisingly, therefore, the Pastoral Epistles contain several warnings for leaders (and would-be leaders) against pride or being "puffed up," and they expressly forbid the overseer to be such a person. In Titus 1:7, Paul says that he must not be "arrogant" or "quick tempered," the former often causing the latter. He may not be a new convert, according to 1 Tim 3:6, because early promotion could make him "conceited" and easy prey for the devil.[14] Later on Paul associates false teaching with hubris: his opponents are "conceited" and have an ungodly taste for combat (1 Tim 6:2–5). They should not be allowed to lead. Likewise, in 2 Tim 3:1–17, Paul warns that false teachers will arise in these times and that their errors stem from debased character. They are "lovers of self," "boastful," and "arrogant" (v. 2). In v. 4 he calls them "conceited" once more. Therefore, overseers may not be chosen from those who admire themselves and feel entitled to special indulgences from lesser mortals, because this attitude makes them turn away from serving God's people and toward false doctrines.

GENTLENESS

The overseer must have a light touch in dealing with others, given how much time he spends with difficult people attempting to train them in righteousness. He must not be "pugnacious" but "gentle" and "peaceable" (1 Tim 3:3). Aggressive persons might accomplish much in secular concerns, but Paul sees them as liability to the church. Angry men who relish confrontation are not fit to "convince, rebuke, and exhort" weak and needy Christians, as Timothy must do (2 Tim 4:2 NKJV). One detects a similar danger in 2 Corinthians 11, where Paul's opponents have exalted themselves and have become self-promoting narcissists and bullies (v. 20), having rejected his own example of "weakness," "fear," and "much trembling," that is, an example of patent humility (1 Cor 2:3).[15] The temptation to fight fire with fire is, of course, a strong one, given the provocations Timothy will face; he will have no trouble seeing how transparently egoistic and corrupt his opponents are, and they themselves will know this quite well also. All the evidence will seem to favor lashing out, adopting ungodly methods for Christian purposes. Nevertheless, Paul tells Timothy to demonstrate extraordinary "patience" in such circumstances (2 Tim 4:3–4). "The Lord's bond-servant must not be quarrelsome, but be kind to all . . . patient when wronged, with gentleness correcting those who are in opposition" (2 Tim 2:24–25).

CONTENTMENT

Christian leadership provides many opportunities for dishonest gain. Laymen tend to see their leaders as conduits of divine grace, and some of the former will pay handsomely for supernatural favors. Others may hope to gain immunity from moral censure by keeping their pastor (or others of Christian influence) in jewels. Accordingly, Paul treats "money-plus-ministry" as an especially dangerous combination and warns Timothy strongly about it. The candidate overseer must not be a "lover of

---

14 The term τυφωθείς could suggest the danger of becoming dazzled or blinded by power so that the neophyte acts foolishly (so Marshall, *Pastoral Epistles*, 482); however, Paul would also be concerned about pride in this context, given the arrogance of his enemies (cf. BDAG, "τυφόω," 1021).

15 Cf. D. Garland, *2 Corinthians* (NAC 29; Nashville: Broadman & Holman, 1999), 488.

money" (1 Tim 3:3 NIV). Likewise, Timothy should reject deacons if they are greedy for gain (μὴ αἰσχροκερδεῖς, v. 8). Paul even connects the love of money with heresy: in 1 Tim 6:5, he blames the false teachers for thinking (wrongly) that "godliness" should be rewarded with "gain," as though new doctrines access new revenue streams. Thus he reminds Timothy that only godliness combined with contentment leads to gain, the latter being understood eschatologically, not temporally (vv. 6–8). At the very least, contentment protects the Christian leader from falling into traps set by the love of money (vv. 9–10).

CHASTITY

Paul says that the overseer must be μιᾶς γυναικὸς ἄνδρα (1 Tim 3:2). Literally, he must be a "one-woman" man, but the phrase is unclear on its own, and Paul does not go on to explain what it requires. So v. 2 has stimulated much debate, and two solutions have emerged as primary: (a) the phrase μιᾶς γυναικὸς ἄνδρα means "faithful husband," as opposed to a man who, whether married or not, "sleeps around"; or (b) it requires sexual fidelity *plus* the absence of any prior marriages ending in divorce, to say nothing of forbidding polygamy. Since option (b) wrings more content out of μιᾶς γυναικὸς ἄνδρα than (a), option (b) carries the heavier burden of proof, and there are some reasons to doubt whether this burden can be met. For one thing, if the NT elsewhere permits divorce under certain narrow conditions (adultery and abandonment), then the stronger readings of v. 2 would not retract those exceptions. We also should avoid interpretations that set up two standards of morality (vs. ability) in the Pastoral Epistles, that is, a high one for the overseer and a low one for the layman. Finally, the basic difficulty in reading μιᾶς γυναικὸς ἄνδρα along the lines of (b) above is that Paul could have just said "not divorced" had this been what he meant.[16] We have moved quickly here, of course, but option (a) seems to be more natural to this context, where general habits and virtues are at issue.[17]

The overseer must be faithful or abstinent, as the case may be. He is careful around young women, treating them with "all purity" or "with absolute purity" (1 Tim 5:2). He does not flirt with anyone or risk putting himself in compromising situations. Our modern experience with fallen pastors allows us to understand Paul's emphasis here.[18] Finally, while the phrase μιᾶς γυναικὸς ἄνδρα concentrates on marital faithfulness, its narrower focus as such does not permit the church to disregard altogether a candidate's history of divorce, if he has one. Multiple divorces would be

[16] Cf. J. J. Davis, *Evangelical Ethics* (3rd ed.; Phillipsburg, N.J.: P&R, 2004), 112: "If the Apostle had specifically intended to bar divorced persons from leadership positions in the church, he could have made his point clearly and unambiguously by writing *me apolelumenon* ('not divorced'), rather than *mias gunaikas andra*."

[17] So, e.g., A. J. Köstenberger, with D. W. Jones, *God, Marriage, and Family: Rebuilding the Biblical Foundation* (Wheaton: Crossway, 2004), 259–69; Towner, *Timothy and Titus*, 250–251; Mounce, *Pastoral Epistles*, 173, 185; Knight, *Pastoral Epistles*, 158–59.

[18] Cf. Marshall, *Pastoral Epistles*, 574: "Explicit mention of the need for this attitude suggests that there may have been a problem in the church for a young leader."

a "red flag" surely, as would a divorce that occurred precipitously or on grounds that were not biblical. Local congregations also need to consider whether the overseer, if divorced, would still be "above reproach" in the eyes of his own community. All things considered, the answer to this question might be "yes," especially in North America, but that judgment has to be reached on a case-by-case basis. Divorce is not the unforgivable sin, but it can be a significant handicap in some ministry settings.

THE DUTIES OF THOSE WHO FOLLOW

The Pastoral Epistles also contain exhortations for those who serve under the authority of overseers.[19] As an expedient, we will put deacons under this category as well as laymen, while acknowledging that the former could easily have been assigned some areas of stewardship and subordinate leadership. Indeed, our basic purpose in distinguishing leaders from followers thus far is simply to acknowledge (a) that the Pastoral Epistles are written directly to Timothy and Titus; and (b) that the two of them, along with Paul himself, function as examples set for leaders who will succeed them in the oversight of churches, including the oversight of deacons associated with each one. We do not have two levels of virtue, then, but two levels of urgency in pursuit of them, plus two categories of service. With this caveat in place, we may consider the duties assigned to followers, concentrating on instructions directed to various subgroups of the church such as deacons, women, slaves, and widows. Finally, since the instructions given to overseers and deacons would largely cover men as such, we will not discuss the latter's responsibilities separately.

DEACONS

The Pastoral Epistles do not offer a job description for deacons, telling us exactly what they are supposed to do. We gather, of course, that they occupied discernable and highly visible offices within the church compared to the ordinary layman, and that they were likely to have had designated areas of responsibility that addressed physical needs and logistics.[20] These inferences follow from Paul's teaching in 1 Tim 3:8–13, which suggests on its face that not all men would qualify as deacons. For example, deacons must follow the overseers in being sober-minded, honest, temperate, and content, doing these things for the same reasons (v. 8). They also had to affirm orthodox doctrine, "holding to the mystery of the faith with a clear conscience" (v. 9), because of their higher profile and influence on the direction of the local church. Some administrative responsibility is also suggested by the requirement that they manage their own children and households well (v. 12), with this activity provid-

---

[19] Or more precisely in the Pastoral Epistles, "under the authority of Paul, Timothy, Titus, and overseers," but this nuance does not affect the presentation offered here.

[20] So Dever, "The Doctrine of the Church," 798–800, who depends heavily on Acts 6 to give content to the deacon's actual responsibilities.

ing evidence of supervisory ability. Finally, Paul requires them to be μιᾶς γυναικὸς ἄνδρες, "one-wife men," which means what it does in v. 2. In general, our discussion of the overseer's duties covers the deacons by implication.

WOMEN

Paul's teaching on the qualifications of elders and deacons is controversial, because its says "No" more often than we wish to hear. Most men are not "overseer material," based on what he says in 1 Timothy 3. Indeed, most men would not be "deacon material" either, and this result offends the modern sensibility that requires us to affirm everyone's dreams and subjective callings. But the debate intensifies when we see what Paul says about the ministry of women because he says "No" to them *even more often*, though never capriciously. There are some roles in the church that women may not assume, whatever their apparent gifts. Sometimes they must keep silent and let the men speak, even if they have learned a lot and could run circles around their pastors, deacons, and husbands. For Paul, "can" does not imply "may," given the specific roles assigned to men and women by God in the very act of creation. These days one could clear a room just by reading 1 Tim 2:11–15, but this text fits into a larger, coherent view of male-female relationships.[21]

In v. 13 Paul gives a motive clause that explains the hard teaching in v. 12. The command is, "But I do not allow a woman to teach or exercise authority over a man, but to remain quiet" (v. 12). Then comes the reason: "it was Adam who was first created, *and* then Eve" (v. 13). To make an obvious point, God did not create men and women simultaneously. On the contrary, they appear in sequence; from this fact, Paul draws a *prescriptive* conclusion: their order of creation indicates how God expects wives and husbands to relate. Eve has the same dignity before God as Adam does, but Adam is in charge. As v. 14 implies, things went terribly wrong when the two of them experimented with this order.[22] This view is "complementarian," therefore, because it holds in tension two exegetical results, that is, (a) Adam and Eve—therefore all wives and husbands—need each other, the one offering strengths that the other does not have; and (b) husbands are the servant-leaders of their wives (cf. Eph 5:21–33). But if the apostle's view is complementarian (versus "egalitarian"), as we have argued, then we should expect the woman of Pauline virtue to be well-informed and discerning but also modest, cooperative, and deferential to the male leadership of the home and church. And this, unsurprisingly, is just what we do find in the Pastoral Epistles.

---

[21] Contra, e.g., D. Scholer, "2 Timothy 2:9–15 and the Place of Women in the Church's Ministry," in *A Feminist Companion to the Deutero-Pauline Epistles* (ed. A.-J. Levine; London: T & T Clark International, 2003), 98–121, who regards this teaching as an entirely ad hoc and occasional response to local first-century conditions in Ephesus.

[22] Paul need not be taken here to suggest that women are more gullible than men. The danger is, rather, that *both* men and women are weakened in their judgment when they trade places.

For Paul, male leadership begins in the home and extends to the church. The one implies the other, even from a practical standpoint.[23] If women could serve as the pastors of local churches, they would exercise headship over their own husbands, which Paul forbids (cf. Titus 2:5). Likewise, this arrangement sends a mixed signal even in cases where an *unmarried* woman is the senior pastor. If women may oversee churches, why should they not oversee households and husbands? Against these possibilities, Paul's view is quite consistent: men are to lead households and churches, taking particular responsibility for the secure transmission of doctrine and practice. He also forbids women to disrupt the worship services by attending them in sexually enticing or costly attire (1 Tim 2:9) and by challenging the authority of the one who teaches (v. 11). Paul obliges the women to learn in a quiet, low-key way, as opposed to assuming control with unsolicited remarks and arguments. Insoluble, pointless disputes threaten to hinder the prayers of both men and women because of their distracting and antisocial effects (cf. vv. 1–2,8).[24]

On the positive side, Paul allows women to support the church's work administratively and teach other women. In fact, when writing to Titus, he *requires* mature women to teach the novices, encouraging them "to love their husbands, to love their children, *to be* sensible, pure, workers at home, kind, being subject to their own husbands" (Titus 2:4–5). These virtues protect the church's reputation and public witness (v. 5b). Likewise, 1 Tim 3:8–13 presupposes that certain women will have servant responsibilities, even if they are not called "deacons." Perhaps these women in v. 11 are the deacons' own wives; it would help, in that case, if they were "dignified, not malicious gossips, but temperate, faithful in all things." But some of them might just be highly active, and therefore highly visible, servants in their own right. Either way, Paul does not sideline women altogether from ministry, and thus he regulates their conduct along with the other subgroups.

WIDOWS

The early church tried to assist women who could not care for themselves, specifically widows having no marital prospects. First Timothy 5:9 refers to their being "enlisted," which implies some kind of ongoing benevolence program. Perhaps these widows were expected to serve as they were able, but Paul does not give them assigned tasks, as if they were an "order" along Roman Catholic lines. They did what they did voluntarily, or so we assume, and this fact—if it is a fact—accounts for Paul's strictness about who gets help. It seems that he understood what we also know from

---

23 So, e.g., V. Poythress, "The Church as Family: Why Male Leadership in the Family Requires Male Leadership in the Church," in *Recovering Biblical Manhood and Womanhood* (ed. W. Grudem and J. Piper; Wheaton: Crossway, 1991), 237–38.

24 For a thorough discussion of this text and its application, see D. Moo, "What Does It Mean Not to Teach or Have Authority Over Men?" in *Recovering Biblical Manhood and Womanhood* (ed. W. Grudem and J. Piper; Wheaton: Crossway, 1991), 179–93.

modern experience with entitlement programs: *One gets what he pays for,* including dependency (some legitimate, some otherwise). So Paul sets the bar high to avoid abuses of the church's generosity.

For a start, Paul requires assisted widows to be at least 60 years of age (v. 9) and to have no relatives (e.g., children and grandchildren) who might otherwise care for them (v. 4). Furthermore, he describes the character that they need to have demonstrated (even before they became widows), and these remarks shed light on his general ideal for the Christian woman. "Genuine widows" (v. 3) should be constant in prayer, which this group would be almost reflexively, given their constant need (1 Tim 5:5; cf. Eph 6:18). They must not devote themselves to "wanton pleasure" (v. 6), especially in settings where others have nothing. Their lifestyles will indicate how needy they really are. "Good works" for such women—indeed, for all women—include marital faithfulness (v. 9), caring for children, and hospitality (v. 10), the last two giving evidence of compassion and diligence.

Paul also requires the widows to have "washed the saints' feet" (v. 10), which would include the literal act itself (cf. John 13:14), plus other menial tasks of its kind.[25] This tendency shows the exact kind of humility and love that would set Christians apart from narcissistic pagans (or it ought to do so). The developing picture, then, is of an exceptionally compassionate, self-forgetful, and energetic co-worker—a rare type, of course, but Paul's aim is to ensure that this sort of woman gets help, if anyone does. The church's resources must not be depleted by perfectly capable or marriageable women, or by wantons, to the detriment of widows who have served the Lord faithfully all of their lives. Unworthy candidates, in contrast, include women who have lived for themselves, shunning the menial or unglamorous tasks of service (v. 6).

The church's resources were limited back then, as they are now, and people have always been drawn to easy money, some getting it by allowing others to support their indigent relatives. Consequently, Paul requires even the godliest widow to be cared for by her own family members in the first instance before she is handed off to the church. He tells families to "practice piety" (εὐσεβεῖν) toward their own relatives because "this is acceptable in the sight of God" (1 Tim 5:4). After this command, a dire warning follows: if someone neglects a needy parent or relative, "he has denied the faith and is worse than an unbeliever" (v. 8). Professing Christians would know better, and their acts of neglect bring shame on the church (cf. v. 7).

Young widows would be denied enrollment on the same basis. They should try to remarry and not become wards of the church if they have options. But Paul adds two further rationales for tough love in their case, and both of them track with major concerns of the Pastoral Epistles. First, he implies that idleness is the friend of misbehavior: it lets the wantons do their worst full-time, according to the process described

---

[25] The "saints" would not be a priestly class of some sort but Christians generally, both men and women.

235

in 1 Tim 5:13. Without the press of daily labor, they might "go around from house to house," turning themselves into "gossips and busybodies." They involve themselves inappropriately in other people's business and, in some cases, might even become "superspreaders" of theological disease, given the number of households that they could visit in their spare time (cf. 2 Tim 3:6). "Kept" men would go wrong in similar ways, one assumes, but Paul's teaching addresses the more common arrangement.

In v. 11 Paul says that the church should not enroll younger widows, because some of them will later wish to marry, having felt "sensual desires in disregard of Christ," and if they actually marry, they will have "set aside their previous pledge" (v. 12). On the other hand, in v. 14 Paul encourages younger widows to get married, as if their doing so were ideal. Thus, we need to explain why marriage is wrong in the first case but right in the second one, and two main strategies for doing so have been suggested. Perhaps v. 12 blames the young widows for a lack of follow-through. They "married" the church, so to speak, and thus got enrolled; but now Handsome Christian has come along, and they are looking for loopholes. Thus, if they were to marry, they would be breaking their vows of chastity and service, and that is why marriage would be wrong for them but not for a widow who has made no such promise (v. 14). However, we would do better to interpret v. 12 in the light of v. 8, where πίστις also occurs and refers, in that case, not to a "pledge" but to the faith as such—what Christians believe and preach. If we understand πίστις thusly in v. 12, the risk of enrolling young widows becomes all-too-familiar, that is, lovesick apostasy made worse by the wandering widow's semicustodial relationship to the church.

This latter view has several advantages. In the first place, it applies a contextual definition to πίστις: "the faith" is, after all, what Timothy and Titus must guard as something entrusted to them. Secondly, interpreting πίστις as such gets us out of postulating an "order" of widows in the early church (i.e., single women living in the latter's employ and charged with specific duties); and we should indeed want out, one supposes, since we lack strong, independent evidence for such a theory. Thirdly, this view allows us to negotiate v. 14 without incident: here Paul actively steers young widows toward the domestic life of marriage, childbearing, and so on, which makes perfect sense provided that vv. 11–12 do not construe marriage as a step down from a higher vocation, and they would not according to this second view. Verses 11–12 seek to avoid tying restless and unproven young widows to the church economically, for when some of them get options, even disgraceful ones (as per the sense of ὅταν γὰρ καταστρηνιάσωσιν τοῦ Χριστοῦ in v. 11), they leave. We can expect these instructions to offend some modern readers, given (a) Paul's "take" on troubles with young widows and (b) our own egalitarian tropisms. But the key word here is "certain," not "all," and Paul's teaching must by its very nature address common tendencies.

SERVANTS

In 1 Tim 6:1–2, Paul devotes a few words to Christian slaves, especially the ones serving converted masters, for some of them might draw unhealthy conclusions from his ecclesiology. The apostle says elsewhere that, in Christ, "there is neither Jew nor Greek, there is neither slave nor free man, there is neither male nor female" (Gal 3:28). Yet he does not want believers of the first century to become social revolutionaries so that conversion seems to put chips on shoulders everywhere, if it does anything. This pattern of behavior would harm the gospel witness and contradict the teaching of Christ who encouraged a "rendering under Caesar" as appropriate. Therefore, Paul tells slaves to "regard their own masters as worthy of all honor" lest the church's reputation suffer (v. 1). Likewise, the servants of Christian masters ought to consider their obligations as a built-in, ongoing opportunity to wash the saints' feet and love their brothers in Christ (v. 2). These instructions find their mark with special force, given Paul's diagnosis of the false teachers in the following vv. 3–5. One way to describe the latter's problem is that they lack just the kind of humility that slaves must show toward their own masters.

CONCLUDING REFLECTIONS

As we conclude, two observations would seem to be in order. First, let me make a comment regarding the authorship of the Pastoral Epistles. Many NT scholars deny that Paul wrote the Pastoral Epistles, directly or otherwise, perhaps by dictating them to an scribe or commissioning someone else to ghostwrite them with a view to his own authoritative vetting.[26] On the contrary, these letters result from a procedure called "pseudonymity" or "allonymity," whereby an author stamps his own work with greater authority or cachet by attributing it to recognized literary figure, someone like the apostle Paul.[27] Accordingly, these letters made the canonical "cut" because the early church either (a) mistakenly attributed them to Paul himself or (b) played along with the actual writer's harmless literary convention.[28] Perhaps some mixture of these

---

[26] As a modern example of this last arrangement, one might consider A. Flew's most recent book, *There Is a God: How the World's Most Notorious Atheist Changed His Mind* (New York: HarperCollins, 2007), which ultra-Darwinist critics have suspected is de facto pseudonymous, with Flew being supposedly too old at 84 to do competent philosophical work. Certainly the style of this book differs substantially from, say, his *God and Philosophy* (2nd ed.; Amherst: Prometheus, 2005), but Flew himself accounts for the difference: he is indeed 84, as reported, and thus gave Roy Abraham Varghese substantial liberty to express in writing what he (Flew) wanted to say. A phrase on the title page of the later work, "with Roy Abraham Varghese," removes all doubt about collaborative influences.

[27] I. H. Marshall has proposed the use of "allonymous" as an alternative to "pseudonymous" in these cases, so as not to prejudge whether the author of these letters has, in borrowing Paul's name, behaved unethically (*Pastoral Epistles*, 84). In his own commentary on the Pastorals, Towner (Marshall's collaborator on the ICC commentary) tilts cautiously toward Pauline authorship (*Timothy and Titus*, 88).

[28] The phrase "*transparent* fiction" is used by R. Bauckham in reference to 2 Peter, but it also seems to capture what the Pastoral Epistles would be, according to option (b) above. Cf. R. Bauckham, *Jude, 2 Peter* (WBC 50; Waco: Word, 1983), 134; and T. L. Wilder, *Pseudonymity, the New Testament, and Deception* (Lanham: University Press of America, 2004), for a critique of same.

factors let them clear customs. Either cause would have the same end, however: these letters are not what they seem to be prima facie.

One reason given for doubting the Pauline authorship of the Pastoral Epistles concerns their basic view of the Christian life and its obligations, compared with the others. Consider the major epistles first, as a baseline. In these letters (e.g., Romans, 1 and 2 Corinthians, Galatians, Philippians), believers live constantly in the shadow of the cross and Christ's imminent return. His death, burial, and resurrection have, considered as one event, transformed the church's existence, such that her people now constitute a new humanity, living in the world but no longer "of" it. The cross has rescued us from the guilt and power of sin, and the Holy Spirit presently indwells the body of Christ as an edifying presence, producing love for the family of God, boldness in witness, and endurance in suffering. By the same token, Paul tends to judge misbehavior looking through cruciform lenses. Why do people teach false doctrines and divide the church into competing factions? They do so because they have not died to self in Christ but are honor-seeking egoists, being more interested in public appearances than the glory of Christ. These are powerful, arresting themes that emphasize radical obedience, and they reinforce Paul's vigorous, often-polemical style.

In contrast, so the theory goes, the Pastoral Epistles lack theological vitality and embrace conventional standards of virtue. Their author teaches as one of the scribes rather than as an apostle, standing on his own authority and having the confidence to make fresh applications of a deeply understood theological "indicative."[29] He is cautious and dispassionate. He takes a special interest in church polity, among other things, and is not interesting—not half as much as Paul can be in rhetorical overdrive. Likewise, it is suggested, discipleship in the Pastoral Epistles is a fairly soft ride. No zeal for unity and selfless love here, but rather some peace and quiet, Lord willing, as the church makes its home in the world (1 Tim 2:1–2). Martin Dibelius summarizes this policy of cultural détente, saying that it aims for *christliche Bürgerlichkeit*, or "good Christian citizenship," founded on sound doctrine and with less emphasis on present, supernatural experience and eschatological urgency.[30] The major epistles wrestle creatively with practical theology and theological practice, always linking the "indicative" of new life in Christ to the "imperative" of radical, new living. In the Pastoral Epistles, one sees a bit of indicative and lots of imperative, but the tone is prudential and derivative, being heavily footnoted with "trustworthy" sayings. Or so we are given to understand.

In this study, however, we have been more impressed with the similarities between the two sets of letters rather than their differences. The Pastoral Epistles manifest a unique style and tone, to be sure, but their core "logic" and content agree with the major epistles. This author adopts the Pauline method, tracing his exhortations

---

29 So, e.g., A. T. Hanson, *Studies in the Pastoral Epistles* (London: SPCK, 1968), 110–11.
30 M. Dibelius and H. Conzelmann, *The Pastoral Epistles* (Hermeneia; Philadelphia: Fortress, 1972), 39–40.

back to supernatural changes wrought by God in Christ. He applauds similar virtues and actions, that is, the ones that would conserve the unity of the church and its gospel witness. These letters differ from the others in "atmosphere," but even that change makes sense: Paul has adopted a controlling metaphor, the "household of God," which by its very nature would call for businesslike paraenesis and a cooler, dispassionate tone. The time had come to strengthen the church by (a) locking in essential doctrines and (b) raising up temperamentally conservative leaders. The Pastoral Epistles would do both of these things. To this extent, at any rate, they have enough "Paul" in them to be his own letters.[31]

Secondly, we might notice the cost that these letters attach to being a Christian, especially for someone who leads. That is, the Pastoral Epistles imply that ministry entails almost constant struggle against false doctrines, false disciples, and cavalier disobedience. Ambitious and abusive men will gain power in the churches and foment discord. The saints will stop loving one another as alliances replace friendships and trusted co-workers "go native" in the critical hour. Believers in every place and of every kind will eventually suffer, because the gospel offends people and threatens their impious agendas. We have an unflattering, uncompromising, and intrusive story to tell, even though it ends well (for some) and contains wonderful promises. Accordingly, the aspiring country-club Christian gets no encouragement from these letters, to say nothing of the others. Their recipients did not live in an analgesic world, and Paul assumes that hardly any Christian would. We can try to avoid suffering where possible, but never at the cost of disobedience. Therefore, we just have to endure sometimes, keeping the faith while others swerve out of line.

Peter's epistles hold the same perspectives in tension. On the one hand, his readers must sojourn as admirable and unproblematic neighbors, living excellent lives, so that unbelievers will glorify God "on the day of visitation" (1 Pet 2:12). They should submit to the authorities, some of whom are sent "for the punishment of evildoers and the praise of those who do right" (v. 14). The call to harmony in 1 Pet 3:8–9 is addressed implicitly to "Whoever would love life and see good days" (v. 10 NIV), as if peace were a realistic goal for "aliens and strangers" (2:11). On the other hand, Peter assumes that Christians will suffer anyway, painting their lives black and blue all over. The essential paradox appears in 1 Pet 3:13–14. Things are looking up when he asks, "Who is there to harm you if you prove zealous for what is good?" (v. 13). Then comes the qualification: "But even if you should suffer for the sake of righteousness, you are blessed" (v. 14). Likewise, in the Pastoral Epistles, one does his best to fit in, knowing that he cannot finally and always succeed.

The overseer, especially, gets a fair dose of reality from Paul, as if to steel him against discouragement. On the one hand, he must display virtues that anyone ought

---

[31] For a detailed critique of this view and overall treatment of ethics in the Pastoral Epistles, the ideal starting point is P. Towner, *The Goal of Our Instruction* (JSNTSup 34; Sheffield: Sheffield Academic, 1989).

to admire, always protecting his reputation with outsiders. Nevertheless, he also tells Timothy that ministry requires plain, unvarnished endurance—the ability to hold on when things go sour, as they inevitably will. The faithful steward presses on in spite of hardship and danger, loving prisoners for the gospel (like Paul), even when chained. Indeed, "all who desire to live godly in Christ Jesus will be persecuted" (2 Tim 3:12).[32] No one escapes it for long, and highly visible members of the church—people like Paul, Timothy, and the overseers who follow them—will suffer disproportionately, no matter how kind, gentle, and respectable they might be. These themes line up exactly with what Paul says elsewhere about following Christ, with the Corinthian correspondence being a prime example. We have a charge to keep, guarding a trust given to us. The task will seldom be easy, but it will always be wonderful.

---

[32] Concerning the stress placed on suffering in 2 Timothy compared with 1 Timothy and Titus, see Marshall, *Pastoral Epistles*, 39–40.

Chapter Eleven

MISSION IN THE PASTORAL EPISTLES

CHIAO EK HO

The study of "mission" is an overlooked area in New Testament studies,[1] and the Pastoral Epistles themselves have been an overlooked corpus in Pauline studies until recently. Ever since D. N. Bardot (for Titus), then Paul Anton dubbed these letters "the Pastoral Epistles" in the mid-eighteenth century, this nomenclature has remained with these documents. The focus on these letters as pastoral letters written to instruct pastoral coworkers has the unfortunate effect of overlooking their usefulness as documents with a distinct missionary outlook and theology. Note Raymond Brown's remarks on the Pastorals: "Paul's interests are now no longer primarily missionary but pastoral; he is concerned with tending the existing flock. Of course, such an interest is not lacking in his early letters, but appropriately these three letters have been dubbed 'Pastoral' par excellence."[2]

In large part, the reading of the Pastoral Epistles (hereafter PE) as primarily pastoral in orientation can be traced to the critical assumptions of the authorship of these writings. The majority reading of the PE in critical scholarship sees these letters as pseudepigraphs written to perpetuate the Pauline tradition (*Paulustradition*) or the Pauline gospel. In this view, the authority of Paul as apostle was invoked to confer legitimacy on these documents with the primary purpose of safeguarding the teachings of Paul.[3] The PE are thus read as second-century "early catholic" documents,

---

[1] Note the remark by A. J. Köstenberger and P. T. O'Brien: "Mission has thus far been one of the step-children of New Testament theology. Rarely has this significant biblical theme been given its due in the overall discipline" (*Salvation to the Ends of the Earth: A Biblical Theology of Mission* [Downers Grove, IL: InterVarsity, 2001], 19).

[2] R. E. Brown, *Churches the Apostles Left Behind* (London: Geoffrey Chapman, 1979), 31.

[3] The situations that purportedly gave rise to this include: (1) the emergence of a new generation needing guidance to confront contemporary challenges (so N. Brox, *Die Pastoralbriefe* [RNT 7/2; Regensburg: Friedrich Pustet, 1969], 63; F. Young, *The Theology of the Pastoral Letters* [New Testament Theology; Cambridge: Cambridge University Press, 1994], 22–23; M. Y. MacDonald, *The Pauline Churches: A Social-Historical Study of Institutionalization in the Pauline and Deutero-Pauline Writings* [SNTSMS 57; Cambridge: Cambridge University Press, 1988], 159–234); (2) a need to rehabilitate Paul by conservative Paulinists in the face of misrepresentation of Paul's teachings by radical opponents (so, e.g., D. R. MacDonald, *The Legend and the Apostle: The Battle for Paul in Story and Canon* [Philadelphia: Westminster Press,

241

written when the parousia was no longer imminent. The church was then thought to be characterized by consolidation and domestication rather than proselytization and mission. R. Bultmann's comments are typical of this critical viewpoint, who says that the PE "show that to a large extent Christians are preparing for a rather long duration of this world and that the Christian faith, losing its eschatological tension, is becoming a Christian-bourgeois piety."[4] Seen this way, the church's existence has been famously described as *christliche Bürgerlichkeit*[5] by Martin Dibelius in his influential commentary. Howard Kee, in summing up his study of Christian origins, makes this comment concerning the PE: "The community behind these documents is the early-second-century equivalent of a middle-to-upper-class organization, worries about its reputation, the tightness of its hierarchy, the purity of its doctrine, and the stability of its enterprise throughout succeeding generations (2 Tim 1:5)."[6]

Commentators who see the PE as authentic Pauline letters also tend to emphasize their preoccupation with false teaching, church organization, and ethical concerns of their representative communities.[7] To be sure, there are many internal issues being addressed in the PE. But reading the Pastorals one-dimensionally—as inward-looking documents solely preoccupied with intracommunity issues—invites the question: whatever happened to the Christian mission during the time of the Pastorals? We know that the Christian communities did grow steadily, if not spectacularly, by the turn of the first century AD.[8] R. MacMullen, for one, estimates that Christianity was the dominant religion in some little towns or districts by the turn of the second century AD.[9] There is certainly evidence within the Pastorals that the perception of outsiders toward the communities addressed was important (e.g., 1 Tim 3:7; 5:14; 6:1; Titus 2:5,9–10; 3:2,8). In this chapter, we will demonstrate that the background and setting of the PE—for all its focus on countering false teachers

1983]); and (3) a desire to maintain the integrity of the Pauline gospel for future generations (so J. Roloff, *Die erste Brief An Timotheus* [EKK 15; Zurich: Benziger Verlag, 1988], 42; C. K. Barrett, *Pastoral Epistles* [NCB; Oxford: Clarendon Press, 1963], 32–34).

[4] R. Bultmann, *Theology of the New Testament* (2 vols.; New York: Scribner's, 1951–1955), 2:114, 183, 186.

[5] This approximates the idea of "good citizenship," the notion of living with the appearance of respectability by conforming to the ethos of the wider world; M. Dibelius and H. Conzelmann, *The Pastoral Epistles* (Hermeneia; Philadelphia: Fortress Press, 1972), 8–10.

[6] H. C. Kee, *Christian Origins in Sociological Perspective* (London: SCM, 1980), 119.

[7] E.g., see the respective commentaries of C. Spicq (*Les Épîtres Pastorales* [4th ed.; 2 vols.; EBib; Paris: J. Gabalda, 1969]), J. Jeremias (*Briefe an Timotheus und Titus* [NTD 9; Göttingen: Vandenhoeck & Ruprecht, 1975]), and J. N. D. Kelly (*A Commentary on the Pastoral Epistles* [BNTC; London: Black's, 1963]). But the recent major treatments by I. H. Marshall (*A Critical and Exegetical Commentary on the Pastoral Epistles* [ICC; Edinburgh: T&T Clark, 1999]), and P. H. Towner (*The Letters to Timothy and Titus* [NICNT; Grand Rapids: Eerdmans, 2006]) are exceptions—the missionary character of the PE features prominently in their respective commentaries.

[8] See, e.g., Pliny the Younger's complaint to Trajan in AD 110 about the emptying of temples and the poor sale of the meat of sacrificed animals owing to the aggressive expansion of the repulsive "superstition" (*Letters* 10.96.9–10).

[9] Cf. R. MacMullen, *Christianizing the Roman Empire (AD 100–400)* (New Haven: Yale University Press, 1984), 32, esp. n. 26. Also L. Goppelt, commenting on the forces that gave form to the church in postapostolic times, remarks that "the Pastorals took for granted that such men [evangelists] would continue the missionary and pastoral work after the apostles had left the scene" (*Apostolic and Post-Apostolic Times* [London: A. & C. Black, 1970], 191. For a useful and thorough recent work, see E. J. Schnabel, *Early Christian Mission* (2 vols.; Downers Grove, IL: InterVarsity, 2004).

and church management—remains essentially missionary in character. The theology and ethics of the PE are strongly undergirded by "gospel" idioms and kerygmatic texts throughout. More significantly, the ethical posture of the Pastorals is not defensive and merely inward-looking as some commentators have suggested but is also outward-looking and missionary in orientation. Lastly, the portrait of Paul, far from stylized and hagiographical (see below), also suggests that these documents are intentionally missionary in outlook.

TITUS

The context of the letter to Titus is the Mediterranean island of Crete, known for its warring cities, piracy, wild pagan worship, and immoral practices. Lying was apparently regarded as acceptable in Cretan culture; thus the coining of the term κρητίζω (from the island's name, Crete [Κρήτη]), which means "to play the Cretan," that is, "to lie."[10] There were a significant number of Jews on the island, some of whom had been present on the day of Pentecost and had presumably become Christians (cf. Acts 2:11).[11] At any rate, Paul was concerned that the young Cretan church become established and continue with the mission. Like any young church, there was still much scope for missionary activities, whether in the ongoing preaching of the gospel or the establishment of the nascent communities through pastoral care and instruction. Thus we see Paul directing Titus to put leadership in place and complete what remained of the Pauline mission (Titus 1:5).

TITUS 1:1–4

The opening salutation of Paul describes his role as an apostle "to further the faith of God's elect and their knowledge of the truth which accords with godliness, in hope of eternal life . . . through the preaching with which I have been entrusted by command of God our Savior" (RSV). This is a most striking statement of mission in the letter to Titus. Paul indicates here that his role as an apostle is to preach God's word for the purpose of (κατά) establishing the faith of God's chosen people and increasing their "knowledge of the truth that is in accordance with godliness."[12] This underscores the purpose of Paul's commission, which is to strengthen the faith of the elect. There is no exegetical or theological reason why "the elect" may not be taken proleptically; if so, it would stress the evangelistic goal of Paul's apostolic commission, that is, to convert and establish the faith of those whom God has already chosen. This

---

[10] Cf. Towner, *The Letters to Timothy and Titus*, 670. Paul probably used the saying "Cretans are always liars" (Titus 1:12) to contrast the cultural reputation of Cretans as liars with his earlier thought of "God who never lies" (Titus 1:2).

[11] For a historical reconstruction of the situation in Crete, see Towner, *Letters to Timothy and Titus*, 670–71, 694–712; W. D. Mounce, *Pastoral Epistles* (WBC; Nashville: Thomas Nelson, 2000), lix–lxii, 394–404.

[12] Although the preposition κατά can be variously translated, it is best understood as introducing the goal or purpose of Paul's apostleship; for a detailed discussion on this, see Marshall, *Pastoral Epistles*, 119–20.

is further substantiated and strengthened by the statements immediately following. I. H. Marshall thus correctly observes: "As a missionary, an apostle is concerned with both of these, with developing faith and knowledge and with helping believers to become godly."[13]

Further, the gospel that Paul was to preach is characterized as the fulfillment of God's promise of "eternal life"—surely the goal of any missionary endeavor. The means of realizing this promise is through the "preaching" (κήρυγμα) of the gospel entrusted to Paul by "God our Savior." There is much stress on Paul's role as a missionary and the gospel he proclaims. One can argue that this lengthy self-description serves almost as an exordium, a prologue to the whole letter. Note that the key words in this prescript anticipate the themes of the letter: "faith" (πίστις, 1:1,4,13; 2:2,10; 3:15); "godliness" (εὐσέβεια, 1:1; 2:12); "hope" (ἐλπίς, 1:2; 2:13; 3:7); "eternal life" (ζωῆς αἰωνίου, 1:2; 3:7); "salvation" (σωτήρ/σώζω/σωτήριος, 1:3,4; 2:10,11,13; 3:4,5,6); and the concept of divine appearance (φανερόω, 1:3; ἐπιφάνεια, 2:13; and ἐπιφαίνω, 2:11; 3:4). If so, the whole letter to Titus is framed by Paul's missionary calling and the centrality of the gospel that he preaches.[14]

The description of "God our Savior" (v. 3) is a characteristic description of God in the PE (cf. Titus 2:10; 3:4; 1 Tim 1:1; 2:3; 4:10). This accentuates the saving role of God as deliverer and protector, a theme repeated frequently in the OT.[15] But this designation is also applied to Jesus (v. 4). Towner is correct to note that the title of "Savior," when applied to Jesus, is distinctly different from its use in mystery religions or the ruler cult; the primary thought behind the title of "Savior" in the NT is a deliverance of people from their sins (see Titus 1:4; 2:13; 3:6; cf. 2 Tim 1:10).[16] Moreover, the references to "God our Savior" in the respective contexts of Titus 1:3; 2:10; and 3:4 (cf. 1 Tim 2:3; 4:10) depict God as the initiator of the plan of salvation whereas the use of "Christ our Savior" in Titus 2:13 and 3:6 reflects Christ as the redemptive agent of salvation. There is reference to the initial appearance of Christ that effects salvation through the Christ event (Titus 3:6); there is also a reference to the truth that Jesus Christ must appear yet again (Titus 2:13).

The theology of mission intimated here is a rich one and parallels the teachings in the acknowledged Paulines: God is the initiator of mission and Jesus Christ is the agent of his redemptive plan. There is a historical and a future perspective in the message of the gospel; we proclaim the saving work of Christ as a historical event and hold up Christ's future appearing and the promise of eternal life as the hope of every believer.

---

13 I. H. Marshall, *New Testament Theology: Many Witnesses, One Gospel* (Downers Grove: InterVarsity, 2004), 399.

14 So Towner, *Letters to Timothy and Titus*, 662–63; Marshall, *Pastoral Epistles*, 111–12.

15 E.g., Deut 32:15; 1 Sam 10:19; Ps 24:5; Isa 12:2; Mic 7:7; Hab 3:18; 1 Macc 4.30; Bar 4.22.

16 P. H. Towner, *The Goal of Our Instruction: The Structure of Theology and Ethics in the Pastoral Epistles* (JSNTSup 34; Sheffield: JSOT Press, 1989), 76.

THE "GOOD WITNESS" MOTIF

The exhortation to "good works" in its various forms (ἔργον ἀγαθόν/καλὰ ἔργα) is a motif that permeates the PE. The concept of "good work/deeds" occurs 14 times in these letters: ἔργον ἀγαθόν in 1 Tim 2:10; 5:10; 2 Tim 2:21; 3:17; Titus 1:16; 3:1; καλὰ ἔργα in 1 Tim 3:1; 5:10,25; 6:18; Titus 2:7,14; 3:8,14).[17] In Titus 1:16 and 3:1, ἔργον ἀγαθόν appears in the singular and is preceded by πᾶς, giving a generalizing sense of this being a habitual activity.[18]

The expression "every good work" (NKJV) in Titus 1:16 is used in reference to the false teachers in Crete (cf. 1:10–16), highlighting the incongruence between their profession of faith and their observable conduct. There is a gap between the two in reality, and Paul depicts these false teachers as "detestable, disobedient, and unfit for any good work" (NRSV). By contrast, Titus was to teach what is consistent with sound doctrine and the accompanying conduct that should follow genuine faith (cf. 2:1–10). It is noteworthy that Paul should use the expression "unfit [ἀδόκιμος] for any good work" to characterize the heretics, giving the sense that their behavior is below the requisite standard when put to the test; it is hence useless, worthless, and to be rejected.

Perhaps inherent is the notion that authentic Christian faith should demonstrate a lifestyle that witnesses positively for furthering the gospel. This is particularly suggestive in Titus 2:10, where Paul urges that Christian slaves live counter-culturally "so that they may be an ornament [κοσμέω] to the doctrine of God our Savior" (NRSV). It has often been noted that the ancient cultural perception of slaves was stereotypical and negative.[19] As a class (but not necessarily as individuals), slaves were often loathed for their petty vices and treated with suspicion. In ancient literature, slaves were often caricatured as "insolent"[20] and inclined to "pilfer."[21] Paul's admonition to believing slaves to not "talk back" (ἀντιλέγω; this conveys the idea of insolence) or "pilfer" (νοσφίζομαι) but instead to be "submissive in everything," "pleasing," and "showing all good faith" is thus highly significant. When such behavior is lived out, believers would certainly stand out in contemporary society.[22] This admonition evidently was given with the non-Christian masters in mind since "masters" are not mentioned in the *Haustafeln* in Titus (unlike Paul's letter to Timothy; cf. 1 Tim 6:2). In his

---

[17] Although καλός has the nuanced meaning of "attractiveness" in comparison with ἀγαθός, both ἔργον ἀγαθόν and καλὰ ἔργα should be understood as synonymous concepts; for discussion, see Marshall, *Pastoral Epistles*, 227–29.

[18] So Marshall, *Pastoral Epistles*, 228.

[19] See, e.g., T. Wiedemann, *Greek and Roman Slavery* (Baltimore: John Hopkins University Press, 1981); K. R. Bradley, *Slaves and Slavery in Rome* (New York: Cambridge University Press, 1994).

[20] See Seneca's description of the responses of slaves: "too loud a reply, too rebellious a look, a muttering of something that I do not quite hear," resulting in Seneca's ears being offended (*Ira*, 3.24.2).

[21] See, e.g., Xenophon, *Mem.* 2.1.16; Pliny the Elder, *Nat.* 33.6.26–27; *Avot* 2.8.

[22] J. Murphy-O'Connor rightly comments: "The comportment of a slave who was utterly devoted and scrupulously honest could not fail to provoke wonder that turned to attentive respect when the source of this miraculous change was claimed to be the gospel" ("Community and Apostolate: Reflections on 1 Timothy 2:1–7," *TBT* 67 [1973]: 1263).

comments here, J. D. Quinn correctly notes: "The purpose for this thoroughgoing, verifiable reliability is missionary in character."[23] We also note that the use of κοσμέω is striking and underscores the concern for the gospel to be attractive to outsiders. This certainly is the sense of the word as used in 1 Pet 3:5; the thrust of the ethical instruction in 1 Pet 3:1–6 is patently evangelistically motivated. The context of Titus 2:10 is similarly evangelistically motivated as it is grounded in a powerful statement of the gospel (cf. 2:11–14).

Such positive witness to the gospel is also evident in the use of the expression "every good work" in Titus 3:1. The paraenesis to live in a socially acceptable manner was directed with outsiders in view ("to all people," πρὸς πάντας ἀνθρώπους; 3:2) and motivated by the redemptive work of "God our Savior" (cf. 3:3–7). Titus was also exhorted to be a "model of good deeds" (2:7 RSV), to be "zealous for good deeds" (2:14 RSV), and to teach believers to "devote themselves to good works" (3:8,14 NRSV). These instructions, coupled with the concern for "respectability" in the eyes of nonbelievers (Titus 1:7; 2:5,8; cf. 1 Tim 3:2,7; 5:7,14; 6:1), give the paraenesis in Titus 2:2–3:2 a strong missionary orientation.[24] Negatively, proper conduct is imperative so that the "word of God" (= gospel) will not be maligned (2:5) or believers put in a position of reproach (2:8); positively, the believers' godly conduct would "adorn" and commend the "teaching of God our Savior" (= gospel) to others (2:10).

TITUS 2:11–14 AND 3:4–7

The most striking aspect of an underlying missionary outlook in Titus is that the ethical teaching within Titus 2:2–3:2 is grounded on the Christ event. Titus 2:11–14 and 3:4–7 are two doctrinally loaded texts that are purportedly adopted from traditional creeds.[25] It is an open question whether the author adopted such traditions in a wholesale manner or adapted the traditional material. The latter is more likely, and we see the author skillfully weaving such traditional material seamlessly into his paraenesis.[26]

In Titus 2:11–14, the "grace of God" has "appeared" to save "the whole of humanity" (πᾶσιν ἀνθρώποις). This indicates that the intended scope of the saving grace of God is to be universal. The process through which the salvation is made effectual is by "training" or "educating" (παιδεύω) believers. They are trained to (a) deny ungodliness and worldly passions, and (b) live self-controlled, upright, and godly lives in this present age. What is significant for our present purpose is to note that this "appearance" of the "grace of God" has a salvation-historical perspective;

---

23 J. D. Quinn, *The Letter to Titus* (AB 35: New York: Doubleday, 1990), 149.

24 See Towner's comment on the concern for respectability in Titus 2:5: "This theme acquires more of a missionary slant in the NT as the concern for witness to outsiders develops (cf. 1 Tim 6:1; 1 Thess 4:12; 1 Pet 2:11–12). The fear is that unbelievers might trace the unconventional (and especially promiscuous) behavior of young women to the Christian gospel they have embraced and the God in whom this message originated" (*Letters to Timothy and Titus*, 728–29).

25 For a full discussion of this, see Marshall, *Pastoral Epistles*, 263–66.

26 So Towner, *Letters to Timothy and Titus*, 744–45.

it is a reference to the pivotal historical event of Jesus' first advent and the work of atonement that he came to do. This is suggested by the use of "appear" (ἐπιφαίνω) and the phrase "in the present age" (ἐν τῷ νῦν αἰῶνι).[27] There is also the "blessed hope" of the future consummation, the "manifestation" (ἐπιφάνεια) of the "glory of our great God and Savior, Jesus Christ." This is exalted language of the climatic event of Christ's parousia, but the focus is still on Jesus as the Savior (σωτήρ) who gave himself for us so as to redeem us from all iniquity (v. 14). This is the heart of the kerygma, the focus of the Pauline gospel. The witness motif is clear: believers are to deny ungodliness and worldly passions, live sober, upright, and godly lives (v. 12), and be zealous for good deeds (v. 14). In sum, believers are not only the happy beneficiaries of the redemptive work of Christ, but they are to live out the message of the gospel and commend it to others.

Titus 3:4–7 is another strong affirmation of the gospel as the basis of Christian behavior: salvation is wholly God's initiative, according to his "goodness" (χρηστότης, v. 4), "love for people" (φιλανθρωπία, v. 4), and "mercy" (ἔλεος, v. 5) that is independent of human righteousness; the redemptive work of Christ is viewed especially from the standpoint of the regenerating work of the Holy Spirit (3:6). Contextually, there is a shift of focus beginning from Titus 3:1; the instructions in Titus 2:1–10 are addressed to various groups within the church, whereas Titus 3:1–11 is directed to the whole church community. Specifically, believers are to live in subjection to civil authorities and be ready for every good work (3:1), to avoid malice and contention, and show meekness and courtesy to "all people" (3:2). Although "all people" is a reference to people in general, it is the nonbelieving world that is primarily in view here.[28] This is evident from the immediate reference to the preconversion lives of the readers (3:3). The orientation towards outsiders would mean that the exhortations to "readiness for good work/deeds" (3:1,8) and civility toward others (3:2) have a missionary dimension; such benign acts were to be performed from the viewpoint of gratitude toward God (3:3–7) and with the hope that outsiders would become believers. Marshall correctly notes that such an outgoing "attitude may lead to the conversion of unbelievers" and "would move the thrust of the text beyond the level of *christliche Bürgerlichkeit*."[29]

Titus concludes with a list of missionary concerns (Titus 3:12–14). It is noteworthy that within such a short letter, Titus contains such powerful statements of the gospel as 2:11–14 and 3:4–7. The "good witness" motif is also particularly pronounced in this letter. Its prescript is unsurpassed among the letters in the Pauline corpus for its explicit purpose statement on mission. The setting of the letter suggests an environment ripe for missionary endeavor as it is largely pagan. Indeed, the Cretan

---

[27] Cf. G.W. Knight III, *Pastoral Epistles* (NIGTC; Carlisle: Paternoster, 1992), 318–19.

[28] Cf. Knight, *Pastoral Epistles*, 331, 334.

[29] Marshall, *Pastoral Epistles*, 299.

church serves as a prototype of the thousands of fledgling Christian communities that need ongoing missionary care at any point in the history of the church, even today.

1 TIMOTHY

The first letter of Paul to Timothy has similar concerns as his letter to Titus: it was written to counter the threat of heresy to the Pauline mission (cf. 1 Tim 1:3–11) and to organize and regulate the conduct of the believing community (cf. 1 Tim 3:14–15). Unlike Titus, Paul was writing to an established church at Ephesus, a church mired in heresy when it should have been establishing the gospel and sending out missionaries to propagate it. Although the challenge posed by the false teachers and church organization[30] are *prima facie* concerns, there is an underlying missionary outlook in its theology and instruction to Timothy.

HERESY AND MISSIONS

Countering heresy and missions are not mutually exclusive endeavors. Managing and countering heresies are part of the continuing care of believing communities by the church planter and his associates. Warning and protecting believing communities against the insidious teachings of heretics have been a part of the apostle Paul's mandate as "Apostle to the Gentiles" (Acts 20:17–35; Gal 1:6–24; Phil 3:2,18–19; Col 2:8–23;). Protecting the believing community from harmful and opposing teachings does not necessarily imply that the orthodox community is defensive, adopting an inward-looking posture. Note Ben Witherington's comments:

> If 1 and 2 Timothy are concerned with Christians in a cosmopolitan city like Ephesus, where there was a wide variety of religious influences and forms of syncretism, then it is not surprising that from a pragmatic point of view a clear and conservative policy about theological and ethical matters was necessary. Christianity wanted to be a good witness to those who might be drawn to the faith, but at the same time wanted to protect the new church from slipping into familiar pagan ways or a syncretistic compromise of the faith. This meant (1) being morally exemplary citizens, and (2) attacking any heresy or immorality that might compromise the witness to the city as well as the harmony of the community.[31]

Broadly speaking, prophylactic instruction could be seen as being motivated by mission since it is the flip side of the same coin, that is, keeping proselytes within the fold. Paul was clearly concerned to protect the flock (e.g., 1 Tim 4:6; 2 Tim 2:14; Titus 2:1). The argument of 1 Tim 1:3–16 suggests that the criticism of the heretics

---

[30] This includes the selection and placement of respectable and reliable leaders, care of widows, and the conduct of elders.
[31] B. Witherington III, *Women in the Earliest Churches* (Cambridge: Cambridge University Press, 1988), 118.

(vv. 3–10) was closely related to the nature of the gospel in the conversion experience of Paul (vv. 12–16). The efficacy of the "glorious gospel," as exemplified by the apostle Paul's ministry, forms a vivid contrast to the practices of the false teachers. This suggests that part of the responsibilities of a minister of the gospel include active opposition to heretical teachings and practices when present.

A related question is this: how did the problem with the false teachers hinder the missionary enterprise in the PE? The greatest danger of heresy in the early Christian communities was that it perverted the gospel. It not only undermined the faith of the converts but also hindered the evangelistic efforts of the church. Through presenting another/different (ἑτεροδιδασκαλεῖν) gospel (cf. 1 Tim 1:3), false teachers would have confused interested unbelievers, engendered skepticism, and stifled interest in the gospel. Besides, they would have created pernicious schisms within the church and drained energy and resources away from the evangelistic efforts of the community. The resulting effect was a divided church having lost its appeal to outsiders (cf. 1 Tim 3:7; Titus 2:10). This is evident from the observation that the opponents did not display an interest to further the Pauline mission but were interested only in esoteric speculations and stirring up controversies (1 Tim 1:4,6–7). It could well be that Paul, by not engaging them in the specifics of their doctrine (except in passing; cf. 1 Tim 4:3–5), was demonstrating that he refused to be drawn into their futile and divisive discussions and controversies; instead, he was more interested to safeguard the Pauline mission and to extend its mission.

1 TIMOTHY 1:12–17

It is instructive that Paul should reflect on his commission in these verses immediately following the section on heresy. Faithfulness to the gospel and the false teachers continue to occupy his thoughts (cf. 1:18–20). This again reiterates our observation of the correlation between mission and heresy noted above, albeit a negative one.

Paul's account of his commission was set off by the thought of the "glorious gospel" with which he has been entrusted (v. 11). He has been called to safeguard and propagate the gospel (v. 11), and this led to his reflections on the source of his strength and his gratitude to God for appointing him (vv. 12–14). Paul was especially grateful for his commission since he was cognizant of his past as a "blasphemer," "persecutor," and "man of violence" (v. 13 NRSV). John Collins has convincingly argued that Paul's appointment "to his service" (εἰς διακονίαν, v. 12) is not to be understood as an appointment to some vague service of Christ; it is "an appointment 'to mission,' that is, to the sacred mission of going forth with the gospel." He supports this assertion by noting that contextually the gospel was being entrusted to Paul (v. 11), strength was given to him for the task (v. 12), and he was being considered faithful (v. 12)—the *sine qua non* of a minister charged with a message; it is on these grounds that Paul argued for the authenticity of his claim to the mission in Corinth (2 Cor 11:23; cf. Rom 11:13 and Acts 21:19).[32]

First Timothy 1:12–17 is also theocentric in emphasis:[33] although Paul's conversion is held out as an example/prototype (ὑποτύπωσις), the point of the passage is to emphasize the richness of God's patience and mercy and not Paul's preconversion past.[34] Paul describes the nature of God's "grace" (χάρις) as "super-abounding" (ὑπερπλεονάζω) and that which works itself out experientially in a life of "faith and love that are in Christ Jesus" (v. 14).[35] God's grace is expressed climactically as a "trustworthy saying": Christ Jesus came into the world to save sinners (v. 15). This characteristic formula in the PE must be seen to be more than a citation; it emphasizes the veracity of the saying and gives it a mark of orthodox approval and acceptance in the Pauline community.[36] Several aspects of Paul's missionary theology can be gleaned here in 1 Tim 1:12–17: (1) Grace is viewed not just from the standpoint of salvation through God's power but also linked to active service (v. 12) and the efficacy of the gospel (vv. 14–16); (2) Jesus Christ is the agent and the focal point of the redemptive mission of God (v. 15); (3) salvation is viewed as undeserved mercy, superabundant grace, and effected by belief in Christ;[37] and (4) the scope and object of Christ's redemptive work is sinful humanity (v. 15).

1 TIMOTHY 2:1–7

This section directs attention away from the false teachers to positive instruction concerning prayer in the believing community. In v. 1 the point of departure for this exhortation is that prayer in its various forms was to be offered on behalf of "all people" (πάντων ἀνθρώπων). Those in authority were singled out for prayer as they were responsible for creating peaceful conditions conducive for quiet and godly existence (v. 2). Prayer for all (people) is "good" (καλός) and "pleasing" (ἀπόδεκτος) to God, echoing Old Testament legal and cultic language (e.g., Deut 6:18; Lev 1:3). What is more significant is that God our Savior "desires for all [πάντας ἀνθρώπους] to be saved and to come to the knowledge of the truth" (vv. 3–4). The use of "all"

---

[32] J. N. Collins, *Diakonia: Re-interpreting the Ancient Sources* (Oxford: Oxford University Press, 1990), 215.

[33] See the doxology in v. 17 that rounds up this section.

[34] Contra Dibelius-Conzelmann, *Pastoral Epistles*, 26; and Roloff, *Die erste Brief*, 85, who suggest that the pseudonymous author of the PE had incorporated the tradition of "faithful" Paul (cf. 1 Cor 7:25b) into the Pauline anamnesis here in 1 Tim 1:12–17.

[35] The connection between the two qualities "faith" and "love" and the preceding "grace of our Lord" is loose and not altogether clear; nevertheless, their use elsewhere as twin qualities (2 Tim 1:13) or in a list with others (1 Tim 2:15; 4:12; 6:11; 2 Tim 2:22; 3:10) indicates that they are to be understood at an existential and practical level, that is, the experience of God's saving grace produces a life characterized by faith and love; cf. Towner, *Letters to Timothy and Titus*, 141–43.

[36] See, e.g., G. W. Knight III, *The Faithful Sayings in the Pastoral Letters* (Kampen: Kok, 1968); Marshall, *Pastoral Epistles*, 326–30; Towner, *Letters to Timothy and Titus*, 143–45.

[37] Note how the thought of Paul being "entrusted" with the gospel flows into his self-testimony; the "hook word" πιστεύω (v. 11) introduces a whole series of words from the πίστις word-group: πιστός (v. 12), πίστεως (v. 14), πιστός (v. 15), πιστεύειν (v. 16). Also, there is a concentration of gospel-related terminology in this short section: "Christ" (4x), "sinner" (2x), "mercy" (2x), "grace," "patience," "unbelief," "faith," and "love."

(πᾶς) is intentional and emphasizes the universality of the salvation offered by God. The theological perspective being emphasized here is that God is a missionary God who wants all people everywhere to be saved.

Further, God's will to save people is theologically rooted in the truth that "there is one God; there is also one mediator between God and humankind, Christ Jesus, himself human, who gave himself a ransom for all" (vv. 5–6a NRSV). The adjective "one" (εἷς)—describing God and Christ Jesus, the human mediator—stands in striking contrast with the four references to "all" (πᾶς) people.[38] The point of this contrast is to highlight the Pauline teaching that though salvation is universally accessible, it can only be appropriated by the one redemptive act of Christ Jesus, God's chosen mediator between him and sinful humanity. Christ Jesus came as the human mediator to give his life a "ransom for all" (cf. Mark 10:45), suggesting that it was an intentional, voluntary, and sacrificial act on his part. The contrast between "one" (εἷς) and "all" (πᾶς) indicates that the universality of salvation is held in tension by the exclusiveness of the cross in Paul's soteriology.[39]

Paul ends this section by linking his mission as herald, apostle, and teacher of the Gentiles (v. 7) to the theological and christological statements of the gospel (vv. 4–6). This linkage to his apostolate shows that Paul's exhortation to his churches is never far from the gospel he proclaims or his consciousness of himself as a missionary to the Gentiles. Besides, his solemn vow "I am telling the truth, I am not lying" in v. 7 suggests that the false teachers were challenging his apostleship. Paul thus asserts his authority over them by calling attention to his appointment as "preacher," "apostle," and "teacher of the Gentiles" to proclaim the truth of the gospel.[40] These observations of 1 Tim 2:1–7 go against the influential interpretation by Dibelius and others. Dibelius' reading of the exhortation to pray for all and for those in authority stems from his notion that a secularized ethical code (*christliche Bürgerlichkeit*) is present, that is, the need for a quiet and peaceful existence in the light of the disappointment of the church over the alleged delay of the parousia. To the contrary, we have demonstrated instead that Paul's admonition for prayer in 1 Tim 2:1–7 stems from his exigencies as a missionary and is grounded upon his theological conviction of the God who saves and who desires for all people to come to a knowledge of the truth through Christ Jesus.

---

[38] The word πᾶς actually occurs six times in 1 Tim 2:1–7, but only four of them are used with reference to people; see vv. 1,2,4 and 6; cf. "first of all" (πρῶτον πάντων) in v. 1 and "in every way" (ἐν πάσῃ) in v. 3.

[39] For a helpful treatment of soteriology in the PE, see G. M. Wieland, *The Significance of Salvation: A Study of Salvation Language in the Pastoral Epistles* (PBM; Milton Keynes: Paternoster, 2006).

[40] Note that v. 7 is a purpose clause introduced by "for this I was appointed" (εἰς ὃ ἐτέθην ἐγώ); cf. 2 Tim 1:11 where the same clause is used.

CHURCH ORGANIZATION

Like prophylactic instructions to protect fledgling congregations against heretics, instructions regarding congregational management and organization constitute a part of the continuing responsibilities of any missionary or church planter. If we are right in pointing to an underlying missionary outlook in Paul's instructions against the false teachers, there is similarly a missionary concern in his instructions concerning the selection of elders and deacons in the congregation.

1 TIMOTHY 3:1–13

It is commonly noted that the list of leadership criteria found in 1 Tim 3:1–13 (cf. Titus 1:5–9) primarily concerns the character traits of potential leaders and not so much specific duties and abilities (the relevant gifts and abilities are probably assumed to be present). Even then, most of the qualities are general ethical virtues valued in Greco-Roman society and are in themselves not particularly Christian. With the exception of such attributes as "not a new convert" (v. 6), being able to "care for God's church" (v. 5), and to "hold to the mystery of the faith" (v. 9), the rest of the positive and negative traits are found in typical lists of virtues and vices.[41] They are also qualities expected in every believer and especially in leaders who were to be role models of such behavior.[42] The convergence of the leadership traits prescribed in 1 Tim 3:1–7 with the values of the wider society stem from an underlying concern for credibility and respectability vis-à-vis those outside the church. This is evidenced by the presence and position of δεῖ ("it is necessary") at the head of the list in 1 Tim 3:2, suggesting the importance of what is to follow: τὸν ἐπίσκοπον ἀνεπίλημπτον εἶναι ("for the overseer is to be above reproach," 1 Tim 3:2).[43] The word δεῖ is again used to emphasize the injunction in 1 Tim 3:7: μαρτυρίαν καλὴν ἔχειν ἀπὸ τῶν ἔξωθεν ("must have a good witness to outsiders"). The concern for the leader's blameless behavior and good standing is reiterated in the so-called "deacon's code" (1 Tim 3:10,13).

The qualifications for an overseer were probably not meant to be exhaustive but served to give a picture of a respectable and benign patriarch who was worthy of leadership; yet the whole text (vv. 3–7) is directed toward and culminates in the concern for the overseer's reputation with those outside the church (v. 7). Some of these same virtues are prescribed more generally in other contexts; see, e.g., "temperate" and "sensible" as a requirement for all older believers (cf. Titus 2:2) and "gentle" and "not quarrelsome" as a requirement for all believers (cf. Titus 3:2). A person

---

41 Cf. Marshall, *Pastoral Epistles*, 147.

42 So Towner, *Letters to Timothy and Titus*, 241.

43 Cf. Titus 1:7: "It is necessary (δεῖ) for the overseer to be beyond reproach (ἀνέγκλητος)"; the different predicate adjective ἀνέγκλητος used here (as compared with ἀνεπίλημπτον in 1 Tim 3:2) conveys a synonymous idea since the two terms share a common semantic domain.

who possesses such qualities would have, for the most part, enjoyed a good reputation with others; there would not be a need to point this out unless this particular characteristic, namely, that of having a good witness to outsiders, was intended to be accented by the author. The leader's good standing with outsiders is to protect him from falling into "reproach" (ὀνειδισμός) and the "snare" (παγίς) of the devil. What the "reproach" and "snare" refer to is unclear, but they evidently point to the condemnation and loss of credibility as a result of some spiritual and/or moral failure of the leader. *Second Clement* suggests such a possibility when the lifestyle of leaders is not commensurate with their teaching:

> For when the heathen hear from our mouth the oracles of God, they wonder at their beauty and greatness; afterwards, when they find out that our deeds are unworthy of our words which we speak, they turn from their wonder to blasphemy, saying that it is a myth and delusion. (*2 Clem.* 13.3)[44]

In his study on the motives behind the desire to make a good impression on outsiders, W. C. van Unnik concludes that it was to (1) protect the honor of God's name and (2) win the heathen (i.e., the motive is missionary).[45] Similarly, J. Roloff sees a connection between the "good testimony" of the church (as represented by its leaders) and the effectiveness to the church's mission.[46]

M. Davies, however, suggests that offended outsiders may potentially create difficulties for the Christians by treating them with contempt, ignoring them, or highlighting their existence to the local governor and drawing attention to their perceived disloyalty for not participating in Greco-Roman worship.[47] F. Young, in commenting on the early Christians in the world, similarly remarks: "Those who produced and read these letters reveal themselves as deeply aware of their unconventionality and their marginalization in relation to wider society. All the more reason, then, not to appear unnecessarily threatening to the established order!"[48] But this is surely too negative and defensive a posture to take concerning Paul's instruction on leadership. From our study, we have seen that although the context for such instruction may be an actual or anticipated leadership crisis brought about by the false teachers or erring elders, it is more than the safety of the community that is in view. There is a missionary impetus that should not be overlooked.

---

[44] The terms "blasphemy" (βλασφημία) and "reproach" (ὀνειδισμός) share the same semantic domain; cf. J. P. Louw and E. A. Nida et al., *Greek-English Lexicon of the New Testament: Based on Semantic Domains* (2 vols.; 2nd ed.; New York: United Bible Societies, 1989), 1:433–34.

[45] W. C. van Unnik, "Die Rücksicht auf die Reaktion der Nicht-Christen als Motiv in der altchristlichen Paränese," in *Judentum, Urchristentum, Kirche: Festschrift für Joachim Jeremias* (ed. W. Eltester; *ZNW* 26; Berlin: Akademie, 1964), 221–34.

[46] Roloff, *Der erste Brief*, 161–62.

[47] M. Davies, *The Pastoral Epistles* (NTG; Sheffield: Sheffield Academic Press, 1996), 78.

[48] Young, *Pastoral Letters*, 40.

1 TIMOTHY 3:14-16

This section explains Paul's purpose for writing 1 Timothy: he wanted to instruct Timothy (and the church) on how they ought to conduct themselves and on his anticipated delay in returning to them. It continues with the underlying theme of mission from 1 Tim 2:1, calling on the congregation to pray for the salvation of all people (2:1–8), instructing the women to behave responsibly in worship (2:9–15), and emphasizing the need to select leaders of good standing for the sake of the gospel (3:1–13).

A key metaphor of the church in 1 Timothy is the "household of God" (οἶκος θεοῦ; 1 Tim 3:15). This is an apt metaphor considering the instruction to choose wise managers of households in the selection of leaders for the church (vv. 4–5,12). Though the term "household" (οἶκος) is used as a theological concept for the church in 1 Tim 3:15, it also reflects the social reality of the Christian communities reflected in the PE (early Christians met in homes). The background is likely to be the Greco-Roman household, with its related ideas of the *paterfamilias* and lines of authority, conduct, and mutual responsibilities within the household. The household is a significant focal point of the interlocking webs of relationships, an arena where evangelism and missionary activities often took place.[49] Halvor Moxnes encapsulates the first-century AD situation well: "It was this urban context, with the institution of the household within a system of patronage and structures of personal authority, which provided the setting for the first Christians and which circumscribed their possibilities for social behavior. This was also an arena of interaction between Christians and pagans."[50]

From depicting the church as "God's household," Paul goes on to elaborate that it is "the church of the living God." The force of the epithet "living God" (θεοῦ ζῶντος) is unclear; it may serve to emphasize the nature of God as true and living in contrast to the lifeless idols of the heathen (Acts 14:15; 1 Thess 1:9; cf. Ps 83:3 LXX), or stress the presence of God among his people (Rom 9:26; 2 Cor 3:3; 6:16; cf. Num 14:28; Josh 3:10).[51] But since a similar expression is used in 1 Tim 4:10, it is better to take our understanding from there. We note that Paul there is using the language and motifs typical of his mission: (1) the clause "toil and strive" is reminiscent of Paul's missionary endeavor (cf. Col 1:29); (2) the expression "living God" is characteristic of Paul's missionary preaching, especially when he mentions the conversion of believers by the "living God" in relation to their pagan past (e.g., 2 Cor 3:3; 1 Thess 1:9b; cf. Acts 14:15); and (3) God is described as "the Savior of all people, namely

---

[49] See C. E. Ho, "Do the Work of an Evangelist: The Missionary Outlook of the Pastoral Epistles" (Ph.D. diss., University of Aberdeen, 2000), 61–82.

[50] H. Moxnes, "What Is Family? Problems in Constructing Early Christian Families," in *Constructing Early Christian Families: Families as Social Reality and Metaphor* (ed. H. Moxnes; London: Routledge, 1997), 26.

[51] Cf. Marshall, *Pastoral Epistles*, 509.

[μάλιστα],[52] of those who believe." It is thus better to read the epithet "living God" in 3:15 with reference to the saving intention of God, underscoring the missionary character of Yahweh. Believers are thus the "gathered community" (ἐκκλησία) of this living, missionary God.

Paul also depicts the church as "the pillar [στῦλος] and bulwark (ἑδραίωμα) of the truth" (NRSV). The term στῦλος is primarily used in architecture for a pillar providing support (e.g., Exod 13:21,22; Deut 31:15 LXX); but it is also used figuratively to describe key leaders of the early church (cf. Gal 2:9) and the saints who endure through the last tribulation (Rev 3:12). Here in 1 Tim 3:15, the term could refer to a freestanding column denoting a lofty sign (*Zeichen*) rather than a supporting structure.[53] The complementary term ἑδραίωμα is a New Testament *hapax legomenon*; its cognate ἑδρασμα means "foundation" (e.g., LXX 3 Kg 8:13) and suggests ideas of firmness, stability, and permanence.[54] These two terms could well be a hendiadys, in which case the phrase στῦλος καί ἑδραίωμα τῆς ἀληθείας could be translated as "the foundational pillar of truth." This suggests a picture of the church not just as a place where truth resides but also as a sort of freestanding column of truth for all to see and come to in their search for God. This is a striking depiction of the missionary purpose of the church in the PE.

The climax of 1 Tim 3:14–16 is the Christ hymn in v. 16. There is much discussion on the structure and tradition history of this hymn.[55] Although the specific meaning of parts of the hymn are debated (especially of lines 2, 3, and 6), its overall message is clear. It is a call to confess the "mystery of godliness," essentially an affirmation of the truth of Christ's humanity and the universal salvation that he brings. The Christ hymn fleshes out this "mystery," revealing what was previously secret: Jesus appeared in human history in the flesh and has been vindicated and exalted in heaven and on earth; moreover, he has become an object of proclamation and belief. What is noteworthy for our purpose is that the proclamation of the Christ event (line 4) and the positive response to the gospel (line 5) are seen to be equally emphasized along with the traditional facts of the gospel (that is, his incarnation, resurrection, and ascension). This "mystery" is thus a comprehensive historical and theological statement of the Christ event with a strong missionary component. It is to be owned and confessed by the believers at Ephesus. Towner correctly notes that this would invariably be "a subversive echo of the city's bold claim, 'Great is Artemis of the Ephesians' (Acts

---

[52] Although μάλιστα is commonly translated as "especially," it is more natural in this context to translate it as "namely" or "more precisely"; see T. C. Skeat, "'Especially the Parchments': A Note on 2 Tim 4:13," *JTS* 30 (1979): 173–77.

[53] Roloff, *Der erste Brief*, 200–201; A. T. Hanson, *The Pastoral Epistles* (Grand Rapids: Eerdmans, 1982), 83; against L. Oberlinner, *Die Pastoralbriefe. Zweite Folge. Kommentar zum Zweiten Timotheusbrief* (HTKNT 11/2; Freiburg: Herder, 1995), 1:159. Roloff's conclusion is based on his understanding of τῆς ἀληθείας as a qualitative genitive that describes truth as intrinsic to the στῦλος and ἑδραίωμα; the church is thus seen not as a part of an edifice that supports the truth but as a witnessing and solid institution (*Gründung*) that has itself been determined by the truth.

[54] Cf. E. Stauffer, "ἑδραῖος," *TDNT* 2:363–64.

[55] Cf. the detailed discussion in Marshall, *Pastoral Epistles*, 497–504.

19:28,34; cf. 19:27,35)."[56] He goes on to remark that this would "hijack the pagan rhetoric to rewrite this bit of the local religious story in terms of the gospel-promise of a new mode of existence, in Christ."[57]

SUMMARY

It can be surmised that had it not been for the immediate concerns with the false teachings and congregational management—all valid as part of the continuing care of any missionary and church planter—active evangelism perhaps would have been highlighted more in this letter. Even then, an underlying missionary outlook is evident in the texts we have examined: the frequent use of christological and soteriological statements and their close proximity to some of the key instructions to Timothy; the suggestive metaphors of the church for missions; and the proclamation and belief in the humanity, vindication, and exaltation of Christ in the Christ hymn (1 Tim 3:16). We can therefore conclude that the motif of missions in 1 Timothy is an essential and emphatic one.

2 TIMOTHY

The second letter to Timothy is the final letter of the apostle Paul in the NT canon. It is the most personal of the PE, and Paul is consciously handing over the baton of the gospel to Timothy. As such, there is an intense concern for the gospel being properly transmitted with its integrity kept intact. There are also many personal elements therein, which has led some commentators to describe 2 Timothy as being a "last testament" of Paul.[58] Those who see it as testamentary literature invariably conclude that it is pseudepigraphical and that it approaches the level of hagiography. R. F. Collins, for one, suggests that the images of Paul as "apostle, ecclesial authority and model Christian" are traces or expressions of an "emerging Pauline hagiography"; they represent "a first sketch of Paul, saint of the Christian church."[59] But by far the most influential perspective of critical scholarship sees Paul as the guarantor of the apostolic tradition, the one upon whom the succession of the gospel and the church depends.[60] Their underlying assumption is that teaching, order, and instruction in the post-Pauline church come from Paul alone; the gospel is "his gospel" and his authority is absolute. The portrait of Paul thus lends credibility and authenticity to

---

[56] Towner, *Letters to Timothy and Titus*, 227.

[57] Ibid., 227.

[58] See, e.g., M. Wolter, *Die Pastoralbriefe als Paulustradition* (FRLANT 146; Göttingen: Vandenhoeck & Ruprecht, 1988), 222–41.

[59] R. F. Collins, "The Image of Paul in the Pastorals," *LTP* 31 (1975): 147–73.

[60] For those who take this view, though with varying expressions and nuanced understandings, see Dibelius-Conzelmann, *Pastoral Epistles*, 9; K. Wegenast, *Das Verständis der Tradition bei Paulus und in den Deuteropaulinien* (WNANT 8; Neukirchen: Neukirchener, 1962), 143–50; Brox, *Die Pastoralbriefe*, 72; Roloff, *Der erste Brief*, 94–96; and Wolter, *Die Pastoralbriefe als Paulustradition*, 27–29.

the message in the PE and becomes "integral to their argument."[61] Such a portrait of Paul also purportedly guarantees the continuity of the apostolic tradition after Paul's demise.[62]

The corollary of the above viewpoints is to paint a portrait of a highly authoritative Paul whose influence is unsurpassed. In our opinion, such assessments of the Paul in the Pastorals exaggerate his authority and influence in these letters vis-à-vis those in the acknowledged Paulines.[63] The evidence adduced for the view of Paul as an overwhelmingly authoritative apostle include the manner with which he silences his detractors; instead of using reasoned logic to refute his opponents, Paul in the PE is seen to stamp his authority and summarily dismiss his opponents with polemic.[64] But one can argue against this view that his acknowledged letters too are very harsh (e.g., see Rom 16:17–18; 2 Cor 11:13–15; Gal 5:12; 6:13; Phil 3:2,18–19).[65] One can also point to instances in the PE where Paul uses reasoned logic to clarify theological instruction (e.g., 1 Tim 1:8; 4:3–5,7–8; 6:5–10; 2 Tim 1:8–12; 2:7,14; and Titus 1:15). It is patently difficult to formulate conclusions on the portrait of Paul that are based on criteria as nebulous as authorial "tone," whether authoritative or otherwise. One may detect varying tones within the same letter, corresponding to the author's intention to persuade, warn, correct, comfort, or instruct, as the case may be (e.g., gentle when persuading; harsh when rebuking; didactic when instructing, etc.). It is thus unhelpful to generalize and to characterize the portrait of Paul in the PE as particularly authoritative. Besides, it can also be argued that prophylactic letters need to be somewhat authoritative if it is to be efficacious.

What about the other description of the portrait of Paul as the beginning of hagiography? The language used to depict Paul in the PE is qualitatively different from that used to describe Paul in hagiographical literature. For example, Clement of Rome hails Paul as "the greatest example of endurance" (*1 Clem.* 5.7); Polycarp describes him as "the blessed and glorious Paul" (*Phil.* 3.2); and the apocryphal *Acts of Paul* portray Paul as a global missionary performing fantastic miracles. Even A.T. Hanson, who reads the PE as pseudonymous writings, makes the same observation: "We can say with confidence that the atmosphere of the Pastorals is totally unlike that of the later apocryphal stories of Paul."[66] By contrast, Paul in the PE is presented at times as weak, lonely, and needy (e.g., 2 Tim 1:15–18; 4:9–11). Further, some

---

[61] Young, *Pastoral Letters*, 123.

[62] J. C. Beker, *Heirs of Paul: Paul's Legacy in the New Testament and in the Church Today* (Edinburgh: T & T Clark, 1992), 37.

[63] In certain Jewish-Christian circles, Paul was regarded with sustained suspicion (e.g., Origen, *Cels.* 5.65; Irenaeus, *Haer.* 1.26.2; 3.15.1) and even outright hostility (e.g., the pseudo-Clementines); cf. W. Bauer, *Orthodoxy and Heresy in Earliest Christianity* (London: SCM Press, 1971), 241–85.

[64] Cf. Beker, *Heirs*, 39–41; Davies, *Pastoral Epistles*, 91–93.

[65] So L. T. Johnson, *The Writings of the New Testament: An Interpretation* (rev. ed.; Philadelphia: Fortress, 1999), 426; indeed, G. D. Fee remarks that the emphasis on Paul's authority in the Pastorals is "mild" in comparison with that in Galatians and 2 Corinthians (*1 & 2 Timothy, Titus* [NIBC; Peabody, Mass.: Hendrickson, 1984], 30n23).

[66] Hanson, *The Pastoral Epistles*, 16.

aspects of Paul's characterizations seem rather inappropriate, if indeed the Pauline portrait is intended to be hagiographical.[67]

In short, the portrait of Paul in the PE is authoritative, but he cannot be seen to be more authoritative than the Paul in his acknowledged writings. To see Paul's portrait in the Pastorals as "emerging Pauline hagiography" is straining the evidence, to say the least. It is not inconceivable that those who argue from the position of pseudonymity often draw conclusions which tend to reinforce their assumptions of authorship. We propose, instead, to present Paul as a missionary paradigm, an exemplar who inspires mission-consciousness in the readers of 2 Timothy.[68] Such a reading sees 2 Timothy as a personal *paraenetic-protreptic* letter, and recent advocates of this perspective include L. T. Johnson and P. H. Towner.[69]

2 TIMOTHY 1:1,11

Paul introduces himself in 2 Timothy as "an apostle of Christ Jesus by the will of God according to the promise of the life which is in Christ Jesus" (2 Tim 1:1 RSV). "Apostle" is a technical term in the NT for the authorized representative of Christ (or the churches) who engages in some delegated tasks, usually in relation to missionary work.[70] The description of Paul as an "apostle of Christ Jesus" and the qualifying prepositional phrase "by the will of God" emphasize the choice and authority of Paul as Christ's personal representative of the gospel (cf. 1 Cor 1:1; 2 Cor 1:1). The second prepositional phrase "according to the promise of the life in Christ Jesus" can be variously translated, depending on how one understands the preposition κατά: (1) "according to" (NIV) or "in conformity with" as a standard of measure or (2) "for the sake of" as a part of the purpose clause (NRSV). The proximity and linkage to Paul as "apostle" in the salutation and the broader context of the letters, which gives a missionary mandate to Paul's co-workers, favors the second interpretation. The prepositional phrase thus translated highlights the purpose of Paul's apostleship, which is to proclaim "the promise of life in Christ Jesus," that is, the gospel.[71] In

---

[67] Paul speaks about how he suffers "shame" as a "prisoner" (2 Tim 1:8) and about his "suffering and wearing fetters like a criminal" (2 Tim 2:9); this is not typical language for hagiography. Cf. also his admission that he was formerly a "blasphemer, persecutor, and violent man" (1 Tim 1:13) and his view of himself as the "foremost of sinners" (1 Tim 1:15).

[68] The appeal to the example of an individual has a long tradition in Greco-Roman moral exhortation; cf. A.J. Malherbe, *Moral Exhortation: A Greco-Roman Sourcebook* (Philadelphia: Westminster Press, 1986), esp. 34–40 and 135–38; B. Fiore, *The Function of Personal Example in the Socratic and Pastoral Epistles* (Rome: Biblical Institute Press, 1986); and B. Dodd, *Paul's Paradigmatic "I": Personal Strategy as Literary Strategy* (JSNTSup 177; Sheffield: Sheffield Academic Press, 1999).

[69] Cf. L. T. Johnson, *Letters to Paul's Delegates: 1 Timothy, 2 Timothy, Titus* (Valley Forge, PA: Trinity Press International, 1996), 37–41; Towner, *Letters to Timothy and Titus*, 35–36, 79.

[70] For a survey of the wide-ranging literature on the concept of "apostle," see F. H. Agnew, "The Origin of the New Testament Apostolic-Concept: A Review of Research," *JBL* 105 (1986): 75–96.

[71] So, e.g., J. N. D. Kelly, *The Pastoral Epistles* (HNTC; New York: Harper and Row, 1963), 153; Towner, *Letters to Timothy and Titus*, 441–42.

other words, Paul's mission as an apostle is to announce God's promise of eternal life through union with Christ.

Paul is also characterized as "preacher" (κῆρυξ), "apostle" (ἀπόστολος), and "teacher" (διδάσκαλος) in 2 Tim 1:11 (cf. 1 Tim 2:7). The use of herald/preacher is uncommon in the NT (occurs only 3x; 1 Tim 2:7; 2 Tim 1:11; and 2 Pet 2:5)[72] and is strikingly absent from the lists of specific functions in the church (cf. 1 Cor 12:28–30; Rom 12:6–8; and Eph 4:11). What is noteworthy is that κῆρυξ puts the accent on proclamation to groups of people, thus attaching an outward, evangelistic horizon to the notion behind this particular term. Why the threefold characterization of Paul as "preacher," "apostle," and "teacher"? Collins suggests that the author "consciously intended to multiply the epithets applied to Paul so as to convey the idea that Paul has the fullness of the apostolate."[73] Again, the notion behind this is to suggest that the threefold description does not have any specific role except to paint a picture of Paul with undisputed and unparalleled authority. But the respective contexts of 1 Tim 2:7 and 2 Tim 1:11 suggest that this threefold description of Paul must be understood in connection with Paul's apostolic mission. First Timothy 2:7 comes at the end of one of the most important christological and missiological passages in the NT, giving the purpose of Paul's appointment as "preacher," "apostle," and "teacher"; it underscores Paul's mission to bear testimony to the universal redemptive work of Christ (see above). Second Timothy 1:11, on the other hand, affirms Paul's own role in the gospel, which is at the heart of his admonition to Timothy, that is, to be unashamed of the gospel and willing to suffer for it. Unlike Collins, we thus conclude that Paul is deliberately and comprehensively depicted as "preacher," "apostle," and "teacher" to emphasize the depth and scope of his mission (cf. *1 Clem* 5:7); it is as if Paul is to be held up as the epitome of all that a missionary can be for those who follow after.

2 TIMOTHY 1:8–12; 2:8–10; 4:6–8

The portrait of Paul in these texts is that of a suffering missionary and willing martyr. Suffering for the sake of the gospel was for Paul an integral part of his apostolic identity (2 Tim 1:11–12; 2:8–10);[74] it is often linked to his ministry, especially the ongoing proclamation of the gospel.[75] Of the three Pastoral letters, the theme of suffering is the most pronounced in 2 Timothy.[76] This letter depicts Paul as a persecuted apostle, suffering for the faith (cf. 2 Tim 1:8–12; 2:3–13; 3:10–12; 4:5–8), as well as an abandoned prisoner, conscious of his impending martyrdom (2 Tim 4:6).

---

[72] Note, however, that its cognate verb κηρύσσειν (to preach/herald/proclaim) is a common NT word and occurs 17x in the Pauline corpus alone, including 1 Tim 3:16 and 2 Tim 4:12.

[73] Collins, "Image of Paul," 154.

[74] Cf. 1 Cor 4:9–13; 2 Cor 4:7–12; 11:23ff.; Gal 4:13; 6:17; 1 Thess 2:1–2.

[75] Cf. Rom 8:17; 2 Cor 4:7–15; Phil 1:12, 29; 1 Thess 1:6; 2:14; 3:4.

[76] There are only three oblique references to some form of hardship and suffering in 1 Timothy: 1 Tim 1:18 and 6:12 contain instructions to Timothy to "fight the good fight," and 1 Tim 4:10 suggests some form of hardship in striving after godliness. The theme of suffering and martyrdom is conspicuously absent in Titus.

In 2 Tim 1:8–12, Paul instructs Timothy to emulate him in suffering for the sake of the gospel; in the course of his mission, Timothy was to take his share of suffering and not be ashamed of the "testimony of the Lord" or of Paul in his imprisonment. The link between "shame"/"suffering" and the gospel is reminiscent of Rom 1:16. Paul here is alluding to the shame associated with the gospel concerning Jesus, the scandalous message of identifying with a crucified messiah. Paul describes this message elsewhere as a "stumbling block to Jews" and "folly to Gentiles" (cf. 1 Cor 1:23). Besides the message, being identified with its authorized messenger also brings shame since Paul is now imprisoned as a criminal, ostracized (2 Tim 1:15), with few friends (2 Tim 4:11,16), and on the brink of execution as an enemy of the empire (2 Tim 4:6). Paul's position, coupled with Timothy's own circumstances at Ephesus, made it needful for Paul to reiterate his admonition to Timothy to be unashamed (vv. 8,12; cf. 2 Tim 1:16). In a manner typical of the PE, Paul supports his appeal to Timothy with a semi-creedal formulation of the gospel (vv. 9–10).

One pertinent question for our study is whether the portrait of Paul as sufferer and martyr is merely a stylized one. If so, one would expect the characterization of Paul's suffering to be akin to those of suffering sages found in popular Greco-Roman moral philosophy. Such presentations of Paul's suffering in 1 Cor 4:8–13; 2 Cor 4:7–12; 6:3–10; 11:23–29 are thought to parallel so-called "catalogues of suffering" (περίστασις lists) found in Stoic and Cynic philosophy (e.g., Plutarch *Mor.* 326D–333C; 361E–362A; Epictetus *Diss.* 2.19.12–32; 4.7.13–15; Seneca *Ep. Mor.* 85.26–27).[77] However, evidence for such "catalogues of suffering" is absent from the PE.[78] Upon examination, it is clear that 2 Tim 1:8–12 is distinctly different from the "catalogues of suffering" of Greco-Roman philosophers: such catalogues typically focus on the individual to vindicate perceived weaknesses and/or prove this person's character and perseverance in the midst of suffering; by contrast, the thrust of 2 Tim 1:8–12 demonstrates the resilience and progress of the gospel in the face of opposition. The focus is not so much on Paul as it is on the gospel; whether it is Paul or Timothy, those involved in proclaiming the gospel will suffer since gospel ministry and suffering go together. It is this gospel for which Paul experiences suffering unashamedly, and it is ultimately not Paul but God who will safeguard its integrity until "that day," probably a reference to the parousia (cf. v. 12).

The strong linkage between the preaching of the gospel and the theme of suffering is reinforced in 2 Tim 2:8–10. Paul makes it clear that it is the gospel for which (ἐν ᾧ)[79] he is suffering and imprisoned ("wearing fetters like a criminal"; cf. v. 9).

---

[77] Cf. R. Bultmann, *Primitive Christianity in Its Contemporary Setting* (New York: World, 1956), 135–45; J. T. Fitzgerald, *Cracks in an Earthen Vessel: An Examination of the Catalogues of Hardships in the Corinthian Correspondence* (Atlanta: Scholars, 1988).

[78] The one passage that remotely resembles a "catalogue of suffering" is 2 Tim 3:10–12; even here the list contains mainly qualities of character rather than a listing of instances of hardship or suffering.

[79] The relative pronoun ᾧ refers back to the gospel as its antecedent while ἐν is properly translated as a causal preposition meaning "for" (so RSV, NASB, NIV).

But he is quick to add that "the word of God is not fettered." Paul continues in v. 10: "Therefore I endure everything for the sake of the elect" for the purpose that "they might obtain salvation in Christ with its eternal glory." Missions then is the *raison d'être* of Paul's willingness to suffer and endure hardships in the PE. Toward the end of 2 Timothy, Paul announces his impending martyrdom. He is now "on the point of being sacrificed" and realizes that "his departure is at hand" (4:6). There is no sense of regret since he has "fought the good fight," "finished the race," and "kept the faith" (4:7 NRSV). On the contrary, he eagerly anticipates the eschatological prize from the righteous judge, the Lord himself (4:8). Paul thus draws attention to himself as a paradigm for Timothy and the Ephesian believers so that they might emulate him in his suffering for the gospel. By its vivid and realistic portrayal of Paul's sufferings and martyrdom for the sake of the gospel, 2 Timothy presents Paul not as a missionary stylized from tradition but as a true-to-life missionary, an exemplar who inspires mission-consciousness in the readers.

2 TIMOTHY 4:1–5,9–18

In 2 Timothy, which is the last known letter of Paul, Paul is understandably concerned to pass the baton of the gospel to his trusted followers (cf. 2 Tim 1:13–14; 2:1–2; 3:14–17). The missionary heart of Paul is clearly seen from such concerns and from his last instructions to Timothy. Although staring execution and death in the face, Paul continues to be concerned about the missionary enterprise and the welfare of his band of co-workers.

Paul charged Timothy to "preach the Word" (κήρυξον τὸν λόγον); he is "to be ready" (ἐφίστημι) whether it is convenient or not ("in season and out of season"), to "convince" (ἐλέγχω), "rebuke" (ἐπιτιμάω), "encourage" (παρακαλέω) with unfailing patience and careful instruction (4:2). The question that arises is this: did Paul direct Timothy merely to instruct a congregation who needed the Word of God preached to them, perhaps with the false teachings in view? If so, the contents of Timothy's preaching were strictly intended for the believers and would be void of any evangelistic word.[80] But Paul's call for Timothy to "do the work of an evangelist" suggests otherwise (4:5). Paul uses four imperatives to communicate Timothy's responsibility as a minister of the Word: Timothy is to be "sober" (νήφω) at all times, "endure suffering" (κακοπαθέω), do the work of an "evangelist" (εὐαγγελιστής),[81] and to fulfill his "ministry" (διακονία). It is instructive that Paul should single out Timothy's role as an evangelist in his final letter to him. If nothing else, it suggests that preaching the gospel lies at the heart of Paul's concern for the church.

---

[80] So Oberlinner, *Pastoralbriefe*, 2:155.

[81] Although εὐαγγελιστής is thought by some to refer to an ecclesiastical office, recent commentators place more stress on its function in leadership and preaching; cf. A. Campbell, "Do the Work of an Evangelist," *EQ* 64 (1992): 117–29.

Like Titus 3:12–14, Paul appears extremely concerned with developments on the mission field in 2 Tim 4:9–18:[82] He wanted Timothy to come to him as soon as possible (2 Tim 4:9) and for Titus to meet him at Nicopolis (Titus 3:12). He requested for Mark to be brought to him for he saw usefulness in him for service (2 Tim 4:11). He was sending Tychicus to Ephesus (2 Tim 4:12); Crescens and Titus have left/been sent to Galatia and Dalmatia respectively (2 Tim 4:10);[83] Demas was reported to have deserted Paul as he "loved this present world";[84] he was replacing Titus with Artemas or Tychicus (Titus 3:12). Paul also asked for his "scrolls and parchments" (2 Tim 4:13), presumably to study and write his missionary letters. M. Prior has argued extensively that Paul was assembling another team for missionary work.[85] Admittedly, these brief notes will not allow us to reconstruct the historical situation with a high degree of certainty; however, they do suggest a picture of an apostle still very much in the forefront of missionary work.

Paul also recalls in 2 Tim 4:17 how at his pretrial hearing ("first defense") the Lord "stood by" and "strengthened" him so that through him the proclamation may be completed and that "all the nations" (πάντα τὰ ἔθνη; cf. 1 Tim 2:7; 3:16) might hear the gospel.[86] The expression πάντα τὰ ἔθνη occurs frequently as a missionary formula in the NT (cf. Matt 24:14; 25:32; 28:19; Mark 11:17; 13:10; Luke 24:47; Acts 14:16; 15:17).[87] It is a Pauline concept pregnant with meaning, summing up in a single phrase the universal scope of God's salvation plan from the promise of Abraham (Gen 18:18; 22:18; 26:4) to its fuller unveiling in the Psalms and the Prophets (cf. Ps 67:2–5; Isa 66:18; Ezek 38:16; Hag 2:7). In describing his own mission in these terms, Paul gives evidence that he saw his own ministry as the outworking of the OT promises of God to the nations (cf. Rom 1:5; 15:11; 16:26; Gal 3:28). It is thus highly significant for our study that Paul reflected this in the *personalia* of 2 Tim 4:17.

---

82 The *personalia* of 2 Tim 4:9–18 is often held up as the "final court of appeal" for defenders of Pauline authorship; conversely, those who subscribe to the pseudonymous authorship in the PE view such personal details as a deliberate attempt on the part of the author to create verisimilitude (cf. L. R. Donelson, *Pseudepigraphy and Ethical Argument in the Pastoral Epistles* (Tübingen: Mohr, 1986), 23). One wonders, however, why there is a need to create so many elaborate details if such a portrait was meant simply to lend authority to the writings.

83 Kelly suggests that Crescens and Titus have both been sent (*Pastoral Epistles*, 213).

84 Kelly paints the scenario that this "desertion" was not apostasy but a desire for ease and comfort, coupled with a disinclination to share Paul's privations (*Pastoral Epistles*, 212); he further suggests that Demas went there for missionary work, as it was in a region where a more friendly reception could be expected (p. 213).

85 M. Prior, *Paul the Letter-Writer and the Second Letter to Timothy* (JSNTSup 23; Sheffield: Shefield Academic Press, 1989), esp. 104–12. Prior interprets Paul's desire to see Timothy (2 Tim 1:4) and the urgency of his request to meet up (2 Tim 4:9,21) as evidence of Paul's missionary zeal and intention for further mission. Attractive though this suggestion is, we cannot totally agree with Prior's reading of 2 Tim 4:6–8 arguing for the release of Paul from incarceration and death (pp. 98–103).

86 Though there is some discussion arguing for the expression πάντα τὰ ἔθνη to be a reference to "Gentiles," there is no reason why Jews should be excluded; thus it is better to translate it as "all the nations"; cf. Towner, *Letters to Timothy and Titus*, 643.

87 See F. Hahn for the significance of πάντα τὰ ἔθνη as a missionary formula (*Mission in the New Testament* [London: SCM, 1965], 71).

In summary, the self-presentation of Paul in 2 Timothy is the familiar picture of him as apostle, preacher, and teacher. What is most striking in this letter is the poignant description of him as a suffering missionary, willing and ready to die a martyr's death. In this farewell letter to Timothy, we sense Paul's deep concern to pass on the gospel baton to "faithful men" and his preoccupation with matters big and small on the mission field. Second Timothy underscores our contention that the portrait of Paul in the PE, far from being stylized and hagiographical, is personal and true to life. It serves as a worthy missionary paradigm for Timothy and the church throughout the ages.

MISSIONARY OUTLOOK OF THE PASTORALS

Bringing the strands of our study together, it is perhaps helpful to conclude that there is a distinct, underlying missionary outlook in the PE. We have been using this expression and here is a good place to flesh it out further. When we speak of "missionary outlook," we are referring to the mission-thought framework of the author that informs his response to the specific situations being addressed; in other words, can we discern an underlying concern for the work of missions even as Paul addresses the various matters in these letters?[88] To be sure, all New Testament documents are missionary documents; they are written by missionaries for the church (for missionary colleagues in the case of the PE) to advance the work of missions. But are these documents written with an additional outward glance toward missions to those outside the church, or merely preoccupied with intracommunity needs and insiders in view? So when we speak of an underlying missionary outlook, we are referring to the overarching framework of thought that has missions at its centre, somewhat akin to a "theological center" referred to by some.[89]

Such a missionary outlook does not conflict with the issues that are being addressed in the PE, whether it is church management or the opposition of false teachers. This mission-thought framework of the author of the PE may even inform what he addresses in these letters (e.g., Paul in addressing the false teachings may be cognizant of the work of missions being undermined). Ascertaining the theological outlook, whether missionary or otherwise, is particularly important for the PE as the Pauline authorship of these letters remains disputed. If nothing else, knowing the theological outlook will enable us to determine what sort of person is behind the writing of the PE.

---

[88] We often hear the expression "Such and such a person is essentially a missionary at heart"; this means that missions is a high priority in this person's life and decisions filter through from such a missionary orientation.

[89] Many posit a "theological center" in Paul; see, e.g., J. C. Beker, *Paul the Apostle: the Triumph of God in Life and Thought* (Edinburgh: T & T Clark, 1980); and N. A. Dahl, *Studies in Paul: Theology for Early Christian Mission* (Minneapolis: Augsburg, 1977). But see D. A. Carson, "New Testament Theology," *DLNT,* 796–814, where he asserts that "the pursuit of the centre is chimerical" (p. 810).

Missionary Context: Separate Backgrounds and Settings

In introducing a study on NT mission, William J. Larkin Jr. remarks: "The New Testament is a missionary document, containing preaching (the Gospels), model mission history (Acts), and letters written primarily by missionaries while on mission." Larkin goes on to point out that "the documents themselves, more often than not, are aimed at encouraging these Christians in mission."[90] This is certainly true of the PE. The backgrounds and settings of these letters give evidence that they were birthed in the exigencies of the Pauline mission. Titus was written to a nascent congregation where evangelism and mission were still very much in the forefront. The letters of 1 Timothy and Titus contain much instruction to enable Paul's missionary co-workers to accomplish their roles on the mission field. Second Timothy was written to safeguard the Pauline mission for the next generation of leaders. Indeed, the major concern with heresy and church organization has been observed to be not incompatible with missions. Though mission is a common concern in all three letters, the setting for each letter is not entirely the same. Titus was written to a relatively young congregation (Crete) as compared with the letters to Timothy (Ephesus). Whereas 1 Timothy and Titus are full of instructions for their respective congregations, 2 Timothy is more personal and preoccupied with Timothy's situation and the need to entrust the gospel to trusted co-workers in view of Paul's impending demise. As such, these three letters should be read separately and not as composite letters, as suggested by some commentators.[91]

Missionary Posture: Ethics of Engagement

Since ethical conduct is often the most visible dimension of the church to outsiders, the ethical instruction of the PE is critical to an understanding of the missionary impetus in the PE. There are many practical instructions addressed to diverse groups in these letters: women and widows, slaves, the rich. *Haustafel*-type material can be seen from 1 Tim 2:1–15; 5:1–2; 6:1–2,17–19; Titus 2:1–10.[92] For our study, it is relevant to ask if such texts are motivated by merely an interest in self-preservation or are ultimately evangelistically motivated. Both could be at work since these are not necessarily mutually exclusive.

Even from our brief study above, we have already seen that the perception of outsiders toward the communities addressed in these letters was important (e.g., 1 Tim 3:7; 5:14; 6:1; Titus 2:5,9–10; 3:2,8). There is a recurring concern for behavior to be

---

90 W. J. Larkin Jr. and J. F. Williams, eds., *Mission in the New Testament: An Evangelical Approach* (Maryknoll, New York: Orbis Books, 1998), 1.

91 E.g., see Young's insistence that "the three letters belong together, because only together do they make sense," (*Pastoral Letters*, 142), or J. L. Houlden's description of them as a "triptych" (*The Pastoral Epistles: 1 and 2 Timothy, Titus* [PNTC; London: SCM Press, 1976], 19).

92 Cf. Towner, *Goal of Our Instruction*, 169–222.

"beyond reproach" (cf. 1 Tim 3:2; 5:7,14; Titus 1:7) and not leave room for outsiders/opponents to slander members of the community or denigrate its doctrines (cf. 1 Tim 6:1; Titus 2:8). The "good witness" motif is prominent in these letters. This has been seen to be inextricably bound to the gospel. In other words, the PE teaches that authentic Christian faith should reflect a lifestyle that witnesses positively for furthering the gospel. This goes against the reading of M. Davies, F. Young, and others who posit a "defensive-conformist" ethics in the PE, or Dibelius-Conzelmann's characterization of the household code as an "accommodation to secular ethics."[93]

From our study, it is more correct to speak of "apologetic-missionary" ethics in the PE. P. H. Towner stands out among recent commentators as having made the strongest case for this position. In his study on theology and ethics in the PE, he argues against the view that the paraenesis to slaves and widows is purely defensive-apologetic; he notes that the proclamation of the gospel is central to the theology of the author even though the controlling motive of the household code in the NT may not be uniformly that of mission. He concludes that the *Haustafel* ethic in the PE goes beyond stressing respectability of lifestyle (to ensure peaceful coexistence with the world) and enables the church to enjoy a meaningful, redemptive interface with the observing world.[94]

Further, it has often been noted that the PE adopt Hellenistic ethical language such as "godliness" (εὐσέβεια), "self-control" (σώφρων/σωφροσύνη), "respectability" (σεμνότης), and "sobriety" (νηφάλιος).[95] From this, many modern commentators draw the conclusion that the PE are pseudonymous and that the writer is deliberately espousing conformity to secular ethics. But Paul could simply be adapting as an experienced missionary, reshaping the ethical jargon, and infusing them with Christian meaning.[96] In other words, Paul contextualizes his Christian teachings in the PE (both ethics and theology) through leveraging terms that have contemporary currency; his intent is to speak effectively and meaningfully to hearers in a Hellenistic milieu. In Marshall's words, they "provided a contact point with pagan society."[97] In short, the missionary posture in the PE is one of engagement with the culture.

---

[93] By "defensive-conformist" ethics, we refer to ethical behavior motivated by the need to conform to the expectations of society out of fear of reprisals or persecution; it is an essentially defensive posture that does not leave room for missionary engagement in any form. On the other hand, the description "accommodation to secular ethics" refers to the ethics of good citizenship posited by Dibelius and is coined by Towner to describe this ("Household Code," *DLNT*, 516).

[94] Towner, *Goal of Our Instruction*, 169–99, esp. 177–78 and 189.

[95] Paul similarly borrows from the wider culture for several of his theological concepts that are unique to the PE, such as "epiphany" (ἐπιφάνεια) christology.

[96] So Towner, *Letters to Timothy and Titus*, 169–71.

[97] Marshall, *Pastoral Epistles*, 144.

MISSIONARY MESSAGE: THE CENTRALITY OF THE SAVING GOSPEL

The importance of the redemptive gospel is underscored throughout the PE from the numerous kergymatic texts and related terminology and metaphors. Interestingly, the term "gospel" (εὐαγγέλιον) occurs only four times in the PE (1 Tim 1:11; 2 Tim 1:8,10; 2:8); the paucity of its occurrence, however, belies the centrality of the notion of the gospel in these letters. Gospel-related terminology and metaphors are found embedded everywhere, including "the deposit" (παραθήκη; cf. 1 Tim 6:20; 2 Tim 1:12,14), "the word" (ὁ λόγος), "the teaching" (ἡ διδασκαλία),[98] "the proclamation" (τὸ κήρυγμα), "the truth" (ἡ ἀλήθεια) or "knowledge of the truth" (ἐπίγνωσις ἀληθείας), "the testimony" (τὸ μαρτύριον; 1 Tim 2:6; 2 Tim 1:8) or "testimony of our Lord" (τὸ μαρτύριον τοῦ κυρίου ἡμῶν; 2 Tim 1:8), and "the mystery of faith" (τὸ μυστήριον τῆς πίστεως; 1 Tim 3:9). These terms and metaphors may have been formulated to some extent with the false teachings in view, but they provide us with a definition of the gospel as Paul understands it in these letters. Coupled with the kerygmatic statements, they provide us with content and meaning for the faith and beliefs of the believers and those who would come to faith through them.

The prevalence of kerygmatic statements is characteristic of the PE. Even from a cursory examination of some of them above, we can delineate important theological themes: (1) God is the source of grace and initiator of salvation (1 Tim 1:12–17; 2:3–5; 2 Tim 1:8–10; Titus 3:4–7);[99] (2) Jesus Christ is the agent and focal point of the redemptive mission of God (1 Tim 1:15; 2:5; 2 Tim 1:10; Titus 2:13–14); (3) salvation is a work of grace (viewed as underserved mercy) and effected by belief and faith in Christ (1 Tim 1:14; 2 Tim 1:9; Titus 2:11; 3:5–7); (4) the scope and object of Christ's redemptive work is sinful humanity (1 Tim 1:15; 2:4; 2 Tim 2:8; Titus 2:13–14); and (5) salvation is universally accessible (1 Tim 2:4; 2 Tim 2:10; Titus 2:11). These themes follow closely with Paul's theology of salvation. Note Marshall's conclusion: "Whether or not the author knew the Pauline Epistles or even composed them, the fact remains that the Pastoral Epistles are confessedly a statement of Pauline teaching and are basically in harmony with his theology."[100]

MISSIONARY PARADIGM: PORTRAIT OF PAUL AS MISSIONARY PAR EXCELLENCE

Far from being "static and dogmatic" on the way to being a legend,[101] the Paul we meet in the PE is much more a true-to-life missionary who is passionate about the

---

[98] Note especially how διδασκαλία is being characterized in the PE; it is qualified by "good" ("good doctrine," καλῆς διδασκαλίας; 1 Tim 4:6), "godliness" ("the teaching which accords with godliness," τῇ κατ᾽ εὐσέβειαν διδασκαλίᾳ; 1 Tim 6:3), and "sound" ("sound doctrine," ὑγιαίνουσα διδασκαλία; 1 Tim 1:10; 2 Tim 4:3; Titus 1:9; 2:1).

[99] This is closely identified with the designation of God as savior; cf. 1 Tim 1:1; 2:3; 4:10; Titus 1:3; 2:10; 3:4.

[100] Cf. Marshall, *New Testament Theology,* 407–09.

[101] For this characterization of Paul in the PE, see Beker, *Heirs of Paul,* 40.

gospel being preached and kept complete and unadulterated for future generations. His portrait in the PE is that of an earnest and exemplary missionary, willing to suffer and die for the gospel, not the stylized portrait of the legendary Paul that some commentators make him out to be. The portrait of Paul as apostle, preacher, and teacher fully engaged in missionary endeavors is evident. The letters show that not only was Paul a missionary, but he was a missionary par excellence. In these letters he will certainly remain as a missionary paradigm worthy of emulation by all.

CONCLUSION

From our examination of the letters in the PE, we have seen how these letters articulate an underlying missionary outlook and a theology of mission *à la* Paul. The "bourgeois-Christian" ethical outlook postulated by Dibelius has again been exposed as weak and unhelpful as an historical interpretive construct. Reading these documents as mission-oriented documents, as we propose, better approximates the historical reality of the growing church in Ephesus and Crete in the first century AD. The examination of the language and kerygmatic statements gives us cause to conclude that the theology of the PE is close to that of the historical Paul in emphasis and substance. Part of the theological and ethical idiom may have been nuanced to more effectively speak to readers in a different setting who were facing their own set of challenges, but the theology and ethical language on the whole remain close to those of the historical Paul. This in itself does not prove that the PE were written by Paul. What our study has shown, however, is that the PE were written by someone close to Paul who shares his mission-thought structure and missionary heartbeat, if not written by Paul himself. With the missionary character of these letters, it is perhaps time to read these letters as individual letters in their own right (instead of reading them as composite letters, as insisted by some) and rethink the nomenclature of these letters as "Pastoral Epistles."

Chapter Twelve

THE PASTORAL EPISTLES IN RECENT STUDY

I. HOWARD MARSHALL

INTRODUCTION

For this closing chapter[1] I was asked to provide a general overview of scholarship on the Pastoral Epistles since the turn of the century[2] that will act as a general guide to the area. It has been prepared independently of the preceding, focused essays and is not intended to summarize or comment upon them. In view of the continuing debate over the authorship of these letters, I shall use the term "the Pastor" as a means of referring to "the person who composed these letters," whether the scholars whose work I am describing identify the author either as Paul in his capacity as the presumed author or as some other (possibly unidentified) person (or persons).[3] The survey falls into two parts. The first, briefer part is an annotated catalogue of commentaries on the Epistles, and the second, major part examines special areas of interest and lists

---

[1] At the request of the editors this chapter incorporates material from my article "The Pastoral Epistles in (Very) Recent Study," *MJT* 2.1 (Fall 2003): 3–37 (cf. also "Some Recent Commentaries on the Pastoral Epistles," *ExpT* 117:4 [2005–2006], 140–43). It contains material based on reviews published in various journals: L. T. Johnson, *The First and Second Letters to Timothy: A New Translation with Introduction and Commentary*, in *BibInt* 10:1 (2002): 100–102; J. M. Holmes, *Text in a Whirlwind: A Critique of Four Exegetical Devices at 1 Timothy 2.9–15*, in *Evangel* 20:2 (Summer 2002): 60–61; H. Stettler, *Die Christologie der Pastoralbriefe*, in *EuroJTh* 8:2 (1999): 186–88; R. F. Collins, *1 & 2 Timothy and Titus: A Commentary*, in *BBR* 14:1 (2004): 136–37; W. A. Richards, *Difference and Distance in Post-Pauline Christianity: An Epistolary Analysis of the Pastorals*, in *Evangel* 21.3 (Autumn 2003): 94–95; L. K. Pietersen, *The Polemic of the Pastorals*, in *JTS*, n.s., 56:2 (October 2005), 594–596; H.-W. Neudorfer, *Der erste Brief des Paulus an Timotheus*, in *EuroJTh* 15:1 (2006), 76–77; J. W. Aageson, *Paul, the Pastoral Epistles, and the Early Church*, in *Themelios* 33:3 (December 2008), 85–87 (online). In what follows commentaries are referred to simply by the author's name and other works by author's name and short title; for full details see the bibliography at the end of the article.

[2] For earlier surveys see I. H. Marshall, "Prospects for the Pastoral Epistles," in *Doing Theology for the People of God: Studies in Honor of J. I. Packer* (ed. D. Lewis and A. McGrath; Downers Grove: IVP, 1996), 137–55; idem, "Recent Study of the Pastoral Epistles," *Themelios* 23:1 (1997): 3–29; M. Harding, *What Are They Saying About the Pastoral Epistles?* (New York, Paulist, 2001); J. Herzer, "Abschied von Konsens" (surveys Oberlinner, Quinn and Wacker, Johnson, and Weiser).

[3] I include here the possibilities that the letters are not all by the same author or that a team of persons were involved. The context will make it clear what the reference is.

some of the questions that are currently on the table for further consideration. It concludes with a listing of recent contributions to the study of the letters. The scope is deliberately wider than the theology of the letters so that a broader context may be provided for study.

PART I: COMMENTARIES

After a lengthy period during which little attention was paid to the letters by commentators, a flurry of major publications has appeared in commentary form.[4] The rough starting point for our survey is 1999, the year in which my own commentary on the Epistles (International Critical Commentary) was published, followed soon after by the Word Biblical Commentary by W. D. Mounce (2000). Already in 1990 J. D. Quinn's work on Titus had been published posthumously in the Anchor Bible, and it was known that his massive collection of material on 1 and 2 Timothy was being edited for publication by W. C. Wacker. However, when it did appear, it was in a new series, the Eerdmans Critical Commentary (2000). The Anchor Bible publishers had evidently decided not to use Quinn's material, and a fresh treatment was provided by L. T. Johnson (2001). The second volume of three to be devoted to the Pastorals in the Evangelisch-Katholischer Kommentar, that on 2 Timothy by A. Weiser, appeared in 2003.[5] Finally, in the heavyweight category came P. H. Towner's contribution to the New International Commentary (Eerdmans, 2006).

The middleweight category is represented by a new series, The New Testament Library (Westminster John Knox), which was inaugurated with the volume on the Pastoral Epistles by R. F. Collins (2002). Here also belong the earlier NIV Application Commentary from W. L. Liefeld (1999), B. Witherington III's section in his Letters and Homilies for Hellenized Christians (2006), the volume in Sacra Pagina by B. Fiore (2007), and the inaugural volume on 1 Timothy in the Historisch-Theologische Auslegung by H.-W. Neudorfer (2004), together with the theological exposition by R. Saarinen in the Brazos Theological Commentary on the Bible (2008) and the applicatory commentary by G. T. Montague in the Catholic Commentary on Scared Scripture. Patristic comments will be found in P. Gorday, and most recently we have J. Twomey's history of interpretation.[6]

In the lightweight category (in terms of size, not of quality of contents) we have the contribution to the *New Interpreter's Bible* from J. D. G. Dunn (2000) and A. Köstenberger's treatment in the revised edition of *The Expositor's Bible Commentary:* (2006). Two recent one-volume commentaries contain succinct treatments, that in

---

[4] Herzer, "Abschied," 1267, says that at least 15 new commentaries have appeared since 1990. He reviews a representative group consisting of Quinn, Quinn and Wacker, Johnson, and Weiser.

[5] The commentary on 1 Timothy by J. Roloff (1988) falls outside our period. The volume on Titus has yet to appear.

[6] Prophecy is no part of my role here, but we can expect further commentaries in the not-too-distant future from A. J. Malherbe (Hermeneia), S. E. Porter (Baker), R. Wall (Two Horizons), and T. L. Wilder (Mentor).

The Oxford Bible Commentary by C. Drury (2001) and that in *Eerdmans Commentary on the Bible* by P. Perkins (2003).

I now comment briefly on commentaries in the first two of these categories, dealing with format and general issues and not with details of exegesis.[7]

W. D. MOUNCE

Mounce's commentary follows the established pattern of the Word series in which it stands. It is geared to the Greek text, but Greek-less readers who are prepared to learn the Greek alphabet will be able to cope with most of it. The lengthy introduction is organized around the topic of authorship. Mounce's distinctive is that he defends a theory of authorship by Paul himself with the aid of an amanuensis over against all theories that the letters are post-Pauline. The theology of the letters gets only five pages, but some aspects of it are briefly mentioned in summarizing the response to the heresy combated in the letters and the alleged theological differences from Paul. There is no overall discussion of the structure of the letters, but the introductions to each section of the commentary deal specifically with "Form/Structure/Setting." Each section also offers translation, textual notes, detailed exegetical comments, and a final "Explanation" which is supposed to deal with the passage's "relevance to the ongoing biblical revelation" but is sometimes more of a summary of the exegesis. This commentary offers careful exegesis, interacting with other commentaries and reference works but not to any great extent with periodical literature (despite the extensive listings of it). There are five excursuses, three of them dealing with church leaders and widows in the postapostolic church (valuable in showing that the Pastoral Epistles do not come close to the developed systems found in the second century) but none on specifically theological issues.[8] The approach reflects the Reformed and conservative theological stance of the author, especially with regard to the place of women in the church. The "Explanation" of 1 Tim 2:8–15 is concerned simply to stress that worth is not determined by role (and therefore a woman's worth is not lessened if she is not allowed to exercise authority over men and teach them),

---

[7] A volume that is not a commentary but is intended to be a helpful reference book for students is Reuter, *Synopse*, a synopsis which presents the Greek text of the Pastoral Epistles with parallels from the rest of the Pauline corpus arranged in parallel columns (like a Gospel Synopsis). The working hypothesis is that the Pastoral Epistles are pseudonymous and the author(s) had access to a collection of Pauline epistles. The synopsis is then a tool for study in making comparisons between the Pastoral Epistles and the other letters and is usable whatever one's critical assumptions for that purpose. Full indexes enable the reader to know what parallels exist to each verse in the Pastoral Epistles and also what verses in the corpus have parallels in the Pastoral Epistles. The parallels are assigned to three categories, apparently in terms of relative closeness, but unfortunately the system is not explained for the reader (as presumably it was in the first volume of the series to which this volume belongs). The compiler transgresses on the side of inclusion of all remotely possible parallels, and the resemblances are underlined with great precision. I'm not sure how useful it all is, but it has its helpful points, such as placing together texts containing ἐπιφάνεια and its virtual synonym παρουσία.

[8] Mounce is not alone in this curious omission. Lacking from several of these commentaries is the attempt to express the characteristic theology of the letter(s). Any discussion in the introductory material tends to be concerned with possible similarities to and differences from the acknowledged letters of Paul and their relevance to the question of authorship.

but questions regarding the applicability of Paul's teaching in the modern world are not raised.

J. D. QUINN AND W. C. WACKER

Regrettably the magnificent resource provided by Quinn and Wacker on 1 and 2 Timothy is very unfriendly to the reader. The body of the commentary has only two different running heads: "Notes and Comments on First Timothy" and "Notes and Comments on Second Timothy," so there is nothing to tell the reader what is the subject matter on any given page (apart from consulting the list of contents). Following the pattern of the Anchor Bible (for which it was originally destined), the commentary on each section of text consists of a translation followed by "Notes" and "Comments." The Notes are evidently concerned with points of detail; the Comments are more in the nature of a running commentary. But Wacker was apparently faced with a task of almost insuperable difficulty in that what he inherited was a continuous exposition (with masses of added annotations) with no indication of how the material was to be divided up, and for half the commentary he himself had to create the Notes. The rationale for apportioning material between Notes and Comments is not clear, and the reader has a hard struggle with material split up in this way. If you open at random almost any page of the commentary, you do not know what chapter and verse is being discussed, and whether what is before you is Note or Comment. Nor is there any introductory material on matters pertaining to a pericope as a whole. The commentary rambles on from one point to another, leaving the reader bewildered and overwhelmed. This is tragic because there is a wealth of useful comment here, particularly on the usage of the words in ancient literature. There is also a lot of unnecessary detail, as when the contents of a concordance are unfolded regardless of whether the information is relevant. All this is to say that this is a reference book that will be indispensable to the advanced student, but it is virtually unusable by the majority of us. It is a great pity that this book could not have been better edited and typeset. Fortunately, Quinn's own earlier work on Titus in the Anchor Bible is less opaque, but it too suffers from the same tendencies that appear to be in part due to the peculiar format of the series.[9]

L. T. JOHNSON

The volume on 1 and 2 Timothy that did appear in the Anchor Bible Commentary follows its familiar format: for each pericope there are provided a translation, "notes" on matters of detail (textual, linguistic, and exegetical), and a "comment" on the section as a whole. Alongside a general introduction there are short introductions

---

[9] M. Prior, "Revisiting," is essentially an appreciation of Quinn's work, commending its detailed study of the texts but expressing reservations toward its overall hypothesis that the letters were intended to rehabilitate Paul at a later date. Prior reaffirms his view of the authenticity of 2 Timothy (but not of 1 Tim and Titus).

to each of 1 and 2 Timothy, reflecting the author's conviction that the Pastoral Epistles should each be studied in their own right with due regard to their individuality. The author includes a useful history of the interpretation of the two letters (although he does not use this much in the actual commentary). He provides much lexicographical material on the vocabulary of the letters (particularly listing the parallels in Hellenistic moral writers). He eschews virtually all reference to other commentators and does not enter into interaction with them on controversial points of exegesis. This is a weakness in that there are places where the arguments in favor of other interpretations are not sufficiently stated and answered.[10]

Johnson reads the letters on the hypothesis of Pauline authorship and seeks to demonstrate the greater likelihood of this reading that is shared by at least 27 twentieth-century commentaries. As with Titus, 1 and 2 Timothy are letters to one of Paul's "delegates." First Timothy takes the form of a "mandate" in which Timothy is given his instructions for his work in Ephesus in the form of a letter that is also meant to be read by the congregation.[11] Second Timothy is a personal paraenetic letter meant primarily for encouragement in a difficult situation. The genre of the letters can explain why Timothy is given instruction concerning matters about which he might be presumed to be already well informed.

Difficulties in the way of authenticity are resolved by appeal to the role of Paul's colleagues and the use of traditions.[12] The question of style is sidestepped by claiming that the style in the acknowledged letters is not uniform. Attention is drawn to the methodological weakness of considering the Pastoral Epistles as a whole rather than as separate letters (although this point rather underrates the degree of common style and content in the Pastoral Epistles when compared with the acknowledged letters of Paul). We know too little of Paul's movements to be able to exclude the possibility of the Pastoral Epistles fitting into his career as narrated in Acts. Johnson's reading of the letters provides a solid case for understanding them consistently in the context of Paul's own mission and superintendence of the congregations that he founded.

---

10 I am not sure what is the rationale for including discussion of a mass of textual variants which have no claim to originality or of providing a host of references to the usage of Greek words in Classical and Hellenistic writers (which the average user of the commentary may not be able to access), helpful though it may be to be reminded once and for all that the New Testament writers share much of the vocabulary and ideas of the Hellenistic world.

Johnson published his shorter commentary, *Letters to Paul's Delegates* (Valley Forge: TPI, 1996), before this major work. The reader, pressed for time and/or not wanting the technical details, will find all the essential exegetical material for the author's actual interpretation of the two letters in this smaller volume together with the added bonus of his interpretation of Titus.

11 Johnson makes use of PTebt 703 as an example of a "mandate" in establishing the genre of 1 Timothy. Here he follows the suggestion of C. Spicq. However, his argument has been subjected to a detailed critique by Mitchell, "P Tebt 703." Briefly, she argues that this third-century BC papyrus is not a letter but a memorandum and that it does not establish the existence of a genre of "*mandata principis* letters" to which 1 Timothy belongs, and further that Johnston's claim that this supports the authenticity of it as a letter of Paul is flawed. But Johnson's argument is not tied to his use of this papyrus.

12 Some acknowledgment and evaluation of E. E. Ellis's work on this point would have been apposite.

Time and again the exegesis confirms the plausibility of placing the letters within this general period rather than much later.

Johnson's arguments against the alternative hypothesis of late pseudonymous composition are well rehearsed. Both Mounce and he make important observations on the questions of vocabulary and style, but neither in my view really faces up to the cumulative effect of a distinctive style of writing, rhetoric, and theologizing.[13]

A. WEISER

A. Weiser on 2 Timothy comes in the Evangelisch-Katholischer Kommentar zum Neuen Testament, an ecumenical effort that demonstrates that, when it comes to biblical scholarship, Roman Catholic and Protestant scholars stand close together in their approaches. This volume thus forms a companion to the major work on 1 Timothy by J. Roloff (1988); we still await Titus in the series. This is a full-scale critical volume with a 43-page introduction and a 270-page commentary with detailed analysis, explanation, and summary for each section, along with fuller notes on key terms and excurses. The author confesses to his ambivalence over the thoughtlessness of the author over many problems of church life and his contrasting transformations of traditional material to create an important contribution to the world of his day and the continuing influence of his picture of Paul (vii). The letter is taken to be pseudonymous, with a brief discussion of the arguments for and against, and then the exegesis is conducted on this level; it is assumed that the personal details in chap. 4 are based on statements in 1 Corinthians and Philippians and are generally not historical (there are said to be too many tensions between the various statements to enable us to harmonize them with one another and other sources for Paul's career).

The Roman Catholic angle of interest emerges in the discussion of 2 Tim 1:18 which, it is argued (rightly!), is not an example of prayer for the dead. But the appended *Wirkungsgeschichte* notes that it has been so seen in the history of both Catholic and Protestant (especially Lutheran) exegesis, and the author is in danger of arguing that the prayer could be used for the dead as well as for the living (on the basis of the biblical hope of resurrection and entry into God's kingdom), and this gives some kind of justification for the practice on the grounds that "the exclusion of the dead from prayer clashes with the Pastoral Epistles in view of this confession" (the reference is to 2 Tim 1:10).[14]

Weiser is not happy with the way the Pastor deals with opponents: his onesidedness is to be regretted, and the positions of his opponents need to be taken more seriously to gain better insight into their understanding (208).[15]

---

[13] See the critical discussion by Herzer, "Abschied."
[14] Weiser, *Zweite Brief*, 142n112, citing L. Oberlinner.
[15] Ibid., 208.

In his interpretation of 2 Tim 3:16 he translates: "Every Scripture is, in virtue of its being given by God, also useful . . . in fitting the Christian leader for the good work of caring for the congregation." There is a lengthy excursus on the *Wirkungsgeschichte;* it is claimed that in the early centuries the text was not cited in discussions of the nature of Scripture and that a rather watered-down version of inspiration is now common to Catholics, Protestants, and Orthodox, although Weiser recognizes the widespread influence of fundamentalist positions that reject historical-critical study and embrace total freedom from error in Scripture.

I. H. MARSHALL

My own work[16] in the International Critical Commentary with its approximately 900 pages is very similar in scale and manner of treatment to that by Mounce. The 100-page Introduction inevitably focuses on the questions of authorship and situation, but it also discusses the genre and structure of the letters in some detail and the character of the theology. The difficulties in accepting direct Pauline authorship are acknowledged, and an acceptable alternative is sought in the hypothesis of allonymity, that is, the letters are put together on the basis of Pauline materials and traditions by a later compiler without any intention to deceive the audience (by contrast with theories of pseudonymity which regard the letters as later attempts to deceive the audience). In each section of the commentary there is a general discussion of the pericope as a whole, followed by text-critical notes and then verse-by-verse exegesis that aims to cover all questions and sources of information that can illuminate the meaning of the text; significant theological, ethical, and ecclesiological themes are discussed at greater length in 11 excursuses. There is considerable interaction with other scholarly literature on the letters, and possibly some danger of overcitation of other scholars. The commentary is possibly unique in treating the letters in the order Titus, 1 Timothy, and 2 Timothy; this is not necessarily the order of composition (on my hypothesis 2 Timothy may have been the earliest written), but it aims to bring Titus out of the shadow of its bigger brother and allow it to speak for itself.[17] One or two subsequent writers have referred to me as a defender of a theory of pseudonymity; it was precisely to avoid this insinuation that I used the term allonymity and defined what I understood by it. Of course, the theory is open to criticism and may be thought to be untenable, but that is a different matter. One conservative observer has commented that my exegesis is at times flawed by my theory of authorship; I strenuously reject this somewhat tendentious assessment because (a) it simply assumes that my theory of authorship is wrong, and (b) I do not think that at any

---

16 Included because the editors requested it.
17 Since I first wrote this sentence, B. Witherington has followed my example, but this is because he thinks that Titus is the earliest of the three letters.

significant point my exegesis is incompatible with a more conservative hypothesis regarding authorship.

P. H. TOWNER

Probably the most important work from the "conservative" side is the mature and definitive expression of a lifetime of study by P. H. Towner.[18] As regards format, this is a full-length technical contribution to the New International Commentary on the New Testament. The style of this series relegates all technical discussion involving Greek to footnotes, leaving a text that is straightforward and problem-free for the reader who lacks the language. Each section of the commentary contains a short overview followed by a verse-by-verse running exegesis that includes occasional expository comments.

Towner wants to say farewell to the term "Pastoral Epistles." He recognizes that the three letters do form an identifiable, distinctive group within the Pauline corpus in that they are all written to co-workers rather than to congregations (88–89). He is prepared with Johnson to think of them as a cluster rather than as a corpus. He wants to explore their distinctiveness, reading them each in their individual contexts, then as bearing some relation to one another, then as part of the wider Pauline corpus, and so on. Care is taken to treat the three letters as individual compositions, each with its own distinctive purpose rather than assuming that they can be treated as three parts of what is essentially one tripartite composition.

The question of authorship is left "open" but with a decided bias toward some form of Pauline authorship. The various arguments for a late dating of the letters fall short of proof and nothing in the setting forces a separation from Paul. He admits that it is not possible on present evidence to prove Pauline authorship. However, the letters fit into the shift from the first to the second missionary generation and reflect a different facet of Paul's mission: here Paul is dealing with his co-workers.

Towner toys very briefly with the idea that Paul's earlier letters, which name cosenders, were joint efforts, but the Pastorals, which do not do so, are Paul's own work (87), and this may account for the change in style. He himself refers to this as merely a possibility, and he would be wise not to accept it. For those who adopt this proposal face the unlikely consequence that the theological depth and versatility that we undoubtedly find in the earlier letters when compared with the more pedestrian presentation in the Pastorals has to be attributed to Paul's coauthors, whereas Paul himself is responsible for the less exciting material in the latter.

He attacks the "majority" view that argues for a setting in second-century, third-to-fourth generation Christianity, adjusting to life in the secular world. On this view

---

[18] The main lines of Towner's interpretation should already be familiar to many readers from his doctoral monograph on the theology of the letters and his contribution to the IVP New Testament Commentary series, but the sheer size of this volume (over 900 pp.) means that there is much more in this impressive volume.

there is a real, coherent theological agenda, which includes maintaining the Pauline tradition but interpreting it to fit a new situation. This has been done by creating further documents purporting to be from Paul, which reinterpret what he said in his earlier writings, and in particular to refute the appeal to Paul by the writer's opponents on such specific matters as the status of slaves and women, in both cases stressing subordination over against any attempts to covet leadership roles and equality with other believers.

Towner disputes the appeal to the practice of pseudonymity. He claims that this flourished in intertestamental Judaism and Greco-Roman philosophical schools rather than early Christianity. Early Christians decisively rejected fakes that were shown to be such, including Pauline imitations. The time gap between the original authors (like Paul) and their imitators were very short compared with other examples (figures from the primeval past; earlier philosophers).

The majority view is forced to explain all the specific allusions as fictive and to devise motives for their invention and find points in the traditions that triggered off the inventions.[19] Towner argues that there is no need to attempt reconciliation with the known facts about Paul's life simply because the record is too fragmentary. He wants to remain open on how exactly the letters were composed.

Regarding style, Towner questions whether there was one Pauline "style" into which all the authentic material can be fitted. Rather, there was input from colleagues and a mixture of styles (diatribe, midrash, and so on; compare the very different amounts and manners of use of the OT). As Johnson argues, the unusual vocabulary tends to cluster in passages dealing with topics like the heresy and church order not covered in the authentic letters.

The pseudonymity theory is said to require the assumption of a corpus of letters to be read as such. Against this view is cited the odd character of Titus whose role in a corpus is problematic. Further 1 Clement and Ignatius suggest that the apostolic age is over and make the production of further apostolic letters very difficult. Polycarp's acceptance and Marcion's rejection alike speak for an earlier date of composition.

Towner devotes an extensive discussion to the theology of the letters. He identifies the overarching themes as being:

- Salvation (epiphany, salvation, work of Christ);
- The Pauline gospel and mission;
- The Holy Spirit (quite brief);
- The Christian life;

---

[19] It is a great pity that he was not able to include an assessment of the work of A. Merz (cf. Towner, 19–20; see further below) which develops a case for understanding the letters as providing a fictitious self-presentation by Paul through fictitious self-references. One has to ask which approach makes better sense of the material and leaves fewer loose ends. It seems possible to offer this kind of explanation of almost anything in the letters, but the question is not whether such explanations can be made to appear plausible but whether the text demands them.

- Church and leadership;
- The authority and use of Scripture.

The christological center is found in the use of the terms Savior and epiphany. But there are trajectories of christology in the three letters. First Timothy stresses the humanity of the Savior, who is the template and pattern for his people. Titus stresses the Co-Savior, the elevated Christ who is alongside God and whose epiphany challenges Cretan culture. Second Timothy stresses his suffering and vindication as a paradigm for his suffering followers.

This type of analysis in terms of unity and diverse trajectories is then perceived in a broader context. First Timothy stresses the ordering of God: his "economy" and the church as his household. Titus is more concerned with the God who does not lie over against the cultural deception of Crete. Finally 2 Timothy is concerned with suffering and succession.

In this way Towner offers a coherent and defensible analysis of what is going on in the letters if they are seen in the context of the end of Paul's life and missionary work.

R. F. COLLINS

Collins's commentary is the first volume to appear in The New Testament Library, published by Westminster John Knox. There are short introductions to the corpus of letters and then to each of them separately. Each section of commentary begins with a brief introduction followed by the author's own translation, notes on major textual variants, and then detailed verse-by-verse exposition. There are 10 excursuses picking up on major themes of the letters. The commentary is essentially exegetical,[20] and little is said about the relevance of the text to the contemporary church and world.[21] Pseudonymity is virtually taken for granted, and the letters are dated some time after AD 80.

The comments tend to offer simply the author's own well-considered understanding; there is an almost complete absence of references to other scholars and the reader will not easily discover where Collins is giving us his own opinions or drawing on those of others, and what his verdicts on their work are. This means that the commentary is mildly unhelpful to students, but they will find it easier to read than the fuller volumes.

Collins majors on placing the text in its contemporary background by offering a very full set of examples of agreements and contrasts with writings from the

---

[20] Collins also has an article expounding the three theological sections in Titus on the same lines as in the commentary.

[21] Preachers must do their own work in applying the text, but this is true of most of the works under review (my own included).

Hellenistic world.[22] Where other commentators sometimes tend simply to give references, leaving the poor student to hunt for them, Collins frequently summarizes or quotes the material, and in this way he does a magnificent job in helping the reader to get the feel of the world of thought in which the Pastoral Epistles were composed. There is a complete index of ancient sources. The student who wants to actually see the usage of much of the moral vocabulary of the letters in a judicious selection of Hellenistic texts will find this volume a boon.[23]

H.-W. NEUDORFER

This German volume on 1 Timothy offers for each section of the text a precise translation, a general introduction, a verse-by-verse exegesis with appropriate excursuses where necessary, and a brief summing up which draws attention to the continuing significance of the text. Neudorfer defends the Pauline authorship of the letter and the traditional identification of its recipient. He opts for a post-first-Roman-imprisonment location with composition at Nicopolis or possibly Ephesus. Following Fuchs he finds a "ring composition": chaps. 1 and 6 with their opening and closing parallel structures form a framework for the letter, which contains instructions for the whole congregation directly from Paul ("I wish . . .") in chaps. 1–3 and then indirectly through Timothy ("Command and teach . . .") in chaps. 4–6.

The commentary is an excellent, succinct guide for students who have some knowledge of Greek, with points of interest and significance throughout the discussion. For example, Neudorfer attempts to estimate the actual proportion of people over 60 in the population at the time: just under 5 percent (and scarcely anybody over 80). This puts the discussion of the widows (11.6 percent of the letter!) into its social context and gives some idea of the relative size of the problem. There is a lengthy excursus on the reference to homosexuals in 1:10. Roloff's claim that in the Pastorals the preacher Paul of his authentic letters becomes the preached Paul is refuted by noting that in such passages as 1 Cor 11:1 and 1 Thess 1:6 Paul presents himself as an example. The question of the identity of Paul's God with the Allah of Islam is discussed in connection with 2:5. However, the hermeneutical questions raised by 2:8–15 are not really discussed.

Neudorfer rightly draws attention to various remarks in the letter which are less intelligible if it is a pseudonymous composition from well after the time of Paul. I am not so sure about his endeavors to explain some of the (for Paul) unusual terminology and concepts as being appropriate for Hellenistic readers rather than Paul's usual audiences: in what ways was Timothy (or his congregation at Ephesus) any different

---

[22] For an example of detailed work of this kind, see J. A. Harrill's article on the background to the term "kidnappers" (1 Tim 1:10), i.e. "slave-traders," a group held in low esteem, even in a slave-owning society, for all manner of vices.

[23] The teaching on the Christian attitude to wealth in the context of Hellenistic ideas is explored by Byrne, "1 Tim 6:6," arguing that the author of 1 Timothy takes over the concept of self-sufficiency from the ancient world but simultaneously endeavors to implant the gospel in the life of the world.

from the readers of Pauline letters to Corinth or Ephesus or wherever else Paul wrote to? (Nor is such "Hellenistic" language characteristic of the writings of Luke, who is seen as possibly Paul's secretary.)

B. WITHERINGTON III

Witherington's work comes as part of his two-volume set on what he regards as *Letters and Homilies to Hellenized Christians* (the others are 1–3 John and 1–2 Peter; a separate volume deals with letters and homilies for Jewish Christians, namely Hebrews, James, and Jude). He argues that the three Pastoral Epistles form a group written toward the end of Paul's life (hence their similarities to one another) and that the distinctive style is due to their being put together by Luke, so that they "reflect a combination of Pauline and Lukan style," noting some overlaps of vocabulary with Luke–Acts. He holds to the view that the early church would not have accepted pseudonymous writings if it knew them to be such, and that the character of the letters is such that, if they were pseudonymous, they were deliberately intended to deceive readers regarding their authorship. In other words, they are either successful deceptions or are authentic. The voice is the voice of Paul. The treatment extends to 350 pages, which gives the commentator reasonable scope for an informative and readable treatment. Although Witherington sticks to exegesis rather than application, he provides an excellent basic discussion for preachers to build upon.

B. FIORE

The commentary series Sacra Pagina provides the interface between Roman Catholic scholarship and the needs of the church. It is intended for a wide range of readers but is essentially a middle-length clear exposition that looks for the "religious meaning" of the text and is "shaped by the context of the Catholic tradition," aiming "to provide access to Sacred Scripture for all the Christian faithful." The format is that of translation of units of text followed by detailed notes and "interpretation" (that tends to be not much more than a summary of the text) and short reading lists. Fiore is a student of A. J. Malherbe, and therefore the commentary gives plentiful references to Greco-Roman literature and brings out the way in which the Epistles provide moral examples for the readers. There is some attention to the ways in which early writers interpreted the Pastoral Epistles, such as Ambrosiaster, Augustine, Chrysostom, and Jerome, and some very brief comments on contemporary relevance. Unlike Collins, Fiore gives lists of sources rather than actual citations, leaving one wondering what the ordinary reader is meant to do with them. The treatment is generally sound and offers no surprises.

W. L. LIEFELD

All of the commentaries discussed so far are primarily exegetical with little concession to the needs of the preacher or Bible study leader who wants to find out what the Pastoral Epistles have to say to the contemporary reader as the word of God. This need is supplied by the New International Version Application Commentary. Here the treatment of each section of text is organized into three parts: Original Meaning, Bridging Contexts, and Contemporary Significance. The rationale is that exposition is based on sound exegesis of the original meaning. Then comes the attempt to discern what is timeless in the timely word spoken in its original context; and finally there is the attempt to apply the timeless word to the contemporary context. Although this basic hermeneutical procedure has been subject to some criticism, I believe that it is fundamentally sound. Certainly it is put to good use in Liefeld's work here. He adopts Pauline authorship and offers a nontechnical exegesis that is primarily concerned with the theological and ethical teaching of the letters. This is a down-to-earth treatment by a skilled scholar-expositor that picks up the important themes in the Pastoral Epistles and encourages preaching about them.

A. KÖSTENBERGER

The treatment by A. Köstenberger is part of the revised *Expositor's Bible Commentary*, which means that it is intended to be succinct (just under 140 pages) and to cater to the needs of preachers. Nevertheless, it is essentially exegetical and gives a helpful basic explanation of the letters, using the format of an introductory "overview" of the passage, followed by a running "commentary" and a short set of "notes" on Greek words; there are some bibliographical helps, parallel references, and occasional comments on application (and the dangers of misapplication); the "notes" provide a specialized discussion of key words or concepts, as well as helpful resource information. The constraints of the series permitted only very brief "reflections" on 1 Tim 2:9–15; 5:3–16; 6:2b–19; 2 Tim 2:1–7; 4:1–8; Titus 1:5–9. Although the three letters are treated separately, each with its own "introduction," the introduction to 1 Timothy in fact covers all three letters and the other two get only a brief summary and outline. It is a great pity that an able scholar has not had more scope to develop his approach; the commentary is succinct but not as comprehensive as some of the more technical commentaries. Preachers will find this commentary helpful and may go to the more technical commentaries for further help.

R. SAARINEN

R. Saarinen's commentary on the Pastoral Epistles (with Philemon and Jude) in the Brazos Theological Commentary on the Bible has three elements. It is partly a distillation of insights from the bigger commentaries into a readable exposition that concentrates on their theology. Alongside this helpful digest it also brings in from time to time the contributions of such expositors as Chrysostom and Calvin. The author's own contribution lies in situating the letters within the context of ancient teachings on moderation, mental disorders, and generosity, and his background in Scandinavian Lutheranism affords a fresh perspective that may not be familiar to North American evangelical readers. Saarinen is not uncritical of what he sees as the Pastor's misogynism and argues that following literally his tendency to accommodate church practice to contemporary social standards may achieve today the opposite effect from what was intended. This is a stimulating study that helpfully and sympathetically challenges some traditionalist approaches without being the last word on the subject. The author does not bring any surprises in exegesis but recognizes the openness of the text to different interpretations between the evangelical and catholic poles. He brings the problems of the text to life and offers a useful stimulus for discussion in the classroom or the Bible study group.

G. T. MONTAGUE

The latest offering in the Catholic Commentary on Sacred Scripture is a simple pastoral exposition by a scholar who has the needs of the preacher and Bible study leader in mind. He adopts a traditional view of authorship, briefly but capably defended, and explains the text carefully and adequately. He is particularly good at placing the letters in their contemporary context and noting important moments in their "effective history," and draws out their modern relevance and application in a manner that is fresh and gracious while always remaining close to traditional Roman Catholic teaching. This makes the commentary less useful for Protestant readers, but it is good to see how much agreement there is on the basic understanding of the gospel and the urgency of evangelism.

J. TWOMEY AND P. GORDAY

A new series entitled Blackwell Bible Commentaries offers not a commentary in the traditional sense but a compendium of interpretations of the text from the ancient to the contemporary period. The aim is to illustrate the influence wrought by the text and the varied ways in which it has been expounded, its difficulties perceived and tackled or ignored, not only by commentators and theological writers but also in literature generally, and from every conceivable school and ideology. Unlike some such studies (including Gorday), which simply reproduce extracts on one verse after another, Twomey's work manages to turn the commentary into more of a running exposition of how successive sections, verses, and themes are treated. The author is a professor of English literature who specializes in the reception of the Bible in literature but has also done his theological homework pretty thoroughly (though he missed Gorday). The result is fascinating, as in the page on Demas which refers to Chrysostom, Calvin, John Flavel, John Bunyan, Charlotte Brontë and Shane Johnson. The author may have his own views on the comparative merits of the insights (or lack thereof) of the many writers cited, but he keeps them to himself and is generally content to inform and entertain his readers: let them make their own judgments! This is riveting stuff and for many of us will open up new horizons.[24]

PART II: SPECIFIC APPROACHES AND TOPICS

THE STRUCTURE OF THE LETTERS

R. VAN NESTE

Rhetorical analysis of the letters is attempted by R. Van Neste. His thesis was written in part as a riposte to the work of J. D. Miller, *The Pastoral Letters as Composite Documents* (Cambridge: CUP, 1997), in which it was argued that there is no coherent argument or clear development of thought in the epistles; they are collections of independent, disparate units loosely stitched together like some of the Jewish wisdom literature; brief fragments of Pauline letters have formed the basis for growing collections of material that are fundamentally incoherent. Miller's thesis is not persuasive, as the fact that many commentators have found it possible to expound the letters as basically coherent documents shows. Nevertheless, the great variety of analyses of the letters offered by commentators shows that their structure is not always self-evident. Van Neste takes up the kind of tools forged by G. H. Guthrie for his analysis of the Letter to the Hebrews, looking for syntactical and rhetorical pointers to continuity and discontinuity, and thereby arriving at an analysis of structure that can claim to be based not just on an assumed train of thought but on objective observations of structural devices and, therefore, reflecting the intention of the author. The results may not appear to be earthshaking in that no radically different understanding of the discourse structure emerges, but the study confirms that there is a coherence in each of the letters and offers a more refined analysis of it than in any previous investigations.

D. J. CLARK

The brief study of Titus by D. J. Clark goes straight into discourse analysis and offers a very careful, detailed examination of the syntactical structure. Among its interesting suggestions is the proposal that 1:15a is a quotation from the false teachers with which Paul disagrees. Clark distinguishes three main sections in the letter, 1:5–13a; 1:13b–3:8a; and 3:8b–11; this is rather different from my own analysis (1:5–16;

---

[24] I regret that I have not been able to see P. Gorday's contribution to the series *Ancient Christian Commentary on Scripture*. His volume, which also covers Colossians, 1 and 2 Thessalonians, and Philemon, is a collection of excerpts from early Christian writers arranged on a verse-by-verse basis. It thus covers part of the field that is traversed in Twomey's more comprehensive work.

2:1–15; 3:1–11) and from that by Van Neste (1:5–9; 1:10–16; 2:1–3:8; 3:9–11) and shows that the debate over structure is by no means over. The main novelty here is the break at 1:13a/b (also made by the New American Bible) on the basis of the new command to Titus in 13b, but at the cost of breaking the link with the description of the opponents in vs. 10–12.

L. A. JERVIS

Somewhere on the boundary between structure and theology is the contribution of L. A. Jervis. She argues that previous studies have tended to see the Paul of 1 Timothy as a quasiforensic authority, laying down the instructions in the letter, or as an ethical paradigm. Rather, she proposes, Paul should be seen as a "poet" who establishes the "story" that is foundational for the community by means of the confessional statements that are closely associated with him (1 Tim 1:15; 2:5–6; 3:16). These confessions tell a story in which Christ is central, referring to his saving work, Paul is the one who passes on this story, and the church is the body that accepts this story and lives by it. The claim, it should be carefully noted, is not that Paul here writes poetry (as opposed to prose) but that he functions like a poet in telling a foundational story. This is a suggestive attempt to explain the underlying rationale of the letter. Jervis begins by looking for the statements that are closely tied to mention of Paul himself in the letter. But since 1 Tim 1:15 is a "trustworthy saying," the question arises as to whether the other sayings similarly described here and in 2 Timothy may have a similar function or whether their existence might modify the thesis significantly.

K. D. TOLLEFSON

An unusual approach is taken by K. D. Tollefson who has studied the phenomenon of revitalization in the secular world and applied the insights to biblical study: "the past and present values, customs and beliefs—which produce dissonance arising from the distortions that exist between them—are analyzed and recombined into a new synthesis, a new mazeway, or a new Gestalt" (146). A visionary (Paul) experiences a conversion (Titus 1:1–3); he communicates his blueprint for change to the rest of the society (Titus 1:4); he appoints leaders and organizes the followers to implement change (Titus 1:5–9); he devises strategies to counter internal resistance (Titus 1:10–16); the vision is transformed into the ordinary life of the people (Titus 2:1–3:7); and the society is encouraged to integrate these new values into its life and make them routine (Titus 3:8–15). In this way Tollefson argues that the various parts of the letter fit together into a coherent whole.

LITERARY APPROACHES

W. A. RICHARDS

Richards' work on difference and distance in post-Pauline Christianity applies literary methods to the study of the letters with the aim of exploring them as individual compositions, each with its own character, rather than as three parts of a single literary enterprise. He wants to place them individually in their broader contexts in the early church, and therefore to free them from being seen in the light of their relationships to the authentic Paul or to one another. He concludes that the three letters were independent projects by three different authors over what may have been a lengthy period of time (50–150 CE); they belong to different contexts in the early church.

Richards argues that they are best understood as (fictitious) letters rather than belonging to some other genre. He analyzes their characteristics: the dramatis personae, the openings and closings, the use of "clichés" (recurring qualifying phrases) and "topoi" (frequently discussed themes), and structural elements (opening lines, summaries, transitional phrases, use of traditions and stock material). This approach can be profitably used in analysis of any New Testament and early Christian letters, whether real or fictitious.

The conversation between Paul and Titus is meant to be overheard, as it establishes the authority of Titus and introduces Paul to the congregations. Richards has difficulties with the descriptions ("virtue lists") of the elders/bishops and thinks that 1:7–9 may be an addition. In chap. 2 he argues that probably the Christians in the community were not slaveowners, since this category is not addressed. In discussing the two "hymns," as he calls them, he draws interesting parallels (as he does elsewhere) with the Odes of Solomon. Titus is seen as being like an official deliberative letter akin to Pliny's letter to Maximus. Part of its aim is to replace a traveling prophetic type of local church leadership with a presbyterian one. This assumption, that the existing ministry came from traveling prophets, is not provided with any backing and is speculative.

Second Timothy with its large cast of actors (Paul's supporters and opponents) and many imperatives presents Paul as a model for Timothy to follow. The tone is warmer and friendlier than in Titus. This, then, is not an official deliberative letter like Titus, but more like a literary deliberative letter akin to the pseudonymous letters of Socrates. It is not a "testament," and it is not clear that Paul is about to die. The references to Timothy as a third-generation Christian suggest that the letter is two generations later than Paul.

First Timothy is more concerned with conflict between groups and classes. It has a high incidence of third-person imperatives (but also the emphatic address in 6:20), stating what Timothy is to teach and urge. The real problem in the church emerges clearly in chap. 6, wealthy members acting as patrons and sponsoring the false teachers. Timothy himself is treated not so much as a subordinate or deputy of Paul (like Titus) but rather as a successor. The letter has an "apostolic parousia" in 3:14–16, and Richards argues for a triplicate structure (1:3–3:13; 3:14–6:2; 6:3–19), where each section has denunciation of opponents, authorization of Timothy in a "charge" given to him, and instructions that he is to convey (e.g. 6:3–12; 13–16; 17–19). This is a "letter-essay," akin to such essays by Epicurus. It speaks to the community on its own authority. It summarizes Paul's earlier teaching so that Paul himself has by now "become 'scripture.'" It is something like a "cover letter" for the Pauline correspondence.

There are thus three types of letters, with three different types of named recipients from three different kinds of "Paul," and intended in reality for three different sorts of implied recipients. Paul is portrayed as elder, pastor, and teacher. The letters are seen as by different authors since it is hard to see these roles as compatible with one another. The letter to Titus is concerned with restructuring the community; 2 Timothy faces a community in danger of dissolution under threat of persecution; 1 Timothy collects advice for a church leader faced by a church where wealth is creating problems. Titus can be placed with Colossians and 1 Clement; 2 Timothy with 2 Thessalonians and 1 Peter; 1 Timothy with Ephesians and 2 Peter.

Despite much useful observation, the main thesis fails to convince. The author has taken little account of the resemblances between the letters; much of what he sees as characteristic of the individual letters is paralleled in the others. In particular, it seems to me that the theologies expressed in the letters and the way in which they are presented are recognizably the same, even if there are some puzzles in it (like the curious total absence of κύριος from Titus). No explanation is given as to how letters so like one another could be produced by different people over so long a period of time. It is right to establish the different contexts and purposes of the letters, leading to the different styles of presentation, but this could equally well be explained as the work of one person addressing different situations and colleagues in appropriate ways. If the letters are dated as late as he proposes, the functions of Timothy and Titus as the named recipients becomes all the more puzzling.

S. C. MARTIN

S. C. Martin's work is concerned purely with 2 Timothy, regarded as a pseudonymous writing, and its thesis is that it is to be understood as Paul's "testament" in the same way as Deuteronomy is to be seen as Moses' testament, handing over his authority to Joshua and summarizing his teaching. Martin sees a deliberate typology being worked out. He notes the references to Moses in 2 Tim 2:19 and 3:8–9, where his authority is challenged (like that of Timothy), and he compares Moses' laying hands on Joshua (Num 27:18–23; Deut 34:9) with Paul doing the same to Timothy. The titles of "servant of the Lord" and "man of God" are held to be evocative of Moses, and the admonition to "be strong" (2 Tim 2:1) is to be seen in the light of Deut 31. The testamentary form of 2 Timothy as a whole lends strength to the argument. In the following chapters the picture of Moses in Judaism is researched at length, showing how he is seen variously as prophet, lawgiver, and suffering intercessor. In the final chapter it is argued that Paul is seen in these three ways in 2 Timothy. Paul functions as a prophet rather than being given this title. It is proposed that Paul (rather than Jesus) is to be seen as the "prophet like Moses" (Deut 18). His teaching is placed over against that of the "teachers of the law" who are his opponents, claiming positions of leadership over against him.[25]

Martin's position is noted by Johnson in the course of a discussion in which he rightly identifies 2 Timothy as a personal paraenetic letter, rather than a farewell discourse or testament.[26] There is a clear difference in categorization here. Certainly Paul is facing the prospect of death in this letter, but he still expects to see Timothy again. On the hypothesis of Pauline composition, this is a paraenetic letter. But if the letter is post-Pauline, then although the compiler knows that Paul is dead, nevertheless he still uses the form of the paraenetic letter and maintains the scenario of Paul dealing with an ongoing situation.

C. A. SMITH

Over against this approach stands the work of C. A. Smith, who argues that 2 Timothy 4:1–8 has the literary form of a charge with five elements: a first-person verb, a second-person addressee, a statement of authority, the content of the command, and the implications of obedience (or disobedience). In this case modifying elements are added to the basic pattern. The author then compares the passage with farewell and testamentary speeches, arguing that they have a very different structure. Paul is not looking forward to his imminent death but reflecting on the trial that he has undergone, his libation being his preaching at the trial, and expressing his confidence of release despite the strenuous time that he has undergone. Timothy's own fidelity is not in question and the tone is more one of encouragement.

M. HARDING

Harding sees the Pastorals positively as attempts to preserve the Pauline legacy and reformulate it through persuasive rhetoric for a new situation.[27] The Pastor is "not just as a theologian of the Pauline tradition, but as a creative and persuasive *communicator* of the Pauline heritage in his social context." He used the whole corpus of ten letters in an attempt "to bring to speech and mediate to the church of his day

---

[25] Collins, 181–85, also accepts the categorization of 2 Timothy as testamentary but has not picked up on the Moses/Joshua typology that is distinctive to Martin's position; he has evidently been working independently of Martin.

[26] Johnson, 321.

[27] He follows his teacher J. C. Beker in exploring the strategies used by the "heirs of Paul," but he holds that Beker's evaluation of the letters underestimates them.

the Paul of the whole corpus—the Paul of a wider tradition." Harding compares the epistles with "the traditions of epistolary moral exhortation and the rhetoric of persuasive speech."

Although the epistles follow the general pattern of Pauline letters, their theology differs from that of Paul in various ways; the realization of the possible delay of the epiphany of Christ for a long time required that the church develop a virtuous and commendable life based on God's saving intervention in Christ. The Pastor also created an image of Paul in which he is recognizably authoritative and therefore the teaching given in his name is to be accepted by the churches. He uses various devices to get his message across: the superior status of the writer; the existing relationship of friendship; the device of "reminder" of what has already been taught; the use of examples, particularly of suffering, both positive and negative, including that of the writer himself; the use of various subsidiary modes of friendly exhortation, notably protrepsis, admonition, rebuke, and consolation. The actual instruction is governed more by the need to coexist with secular society than by the expectation of the parousia. Paul and the Pastor have different ethical agendas; here Harding is more sympathetic to Dibelius's understanding of the letters than are some contemporary scholars (Schwarz, Towner, Kidd). He sees more of a strategy for survival than a commitment to mission. Nevertheless, there is no capitulation to secular values and mores: although it was doubtless the wealthier members who became leaders, the stress is on their moral and spiritual qualities for office. In a broad sense 2 Timothy in particular shows characteristics of the testamentary genre (cf. T. Simeon and 2 Peter) including the following: historical review of the author's life; ethical exhortation; prediction of the future, and (in the NT) imparting of apostolic teaching; moral exhortation; representation of the author as a model of faithful Christian witness; and prediction of coming false teachers.

Although Harding fully recognizes that the epistles are letters and not speeches, he uses the familiar threefold analysis of types of speech, that is, judicial, deliberative, and epideictic. Liturgical materials function epideictically, reminding the readers of what they already experience, deepening that experience, and establishing rapport with them.

It would be an interesting exercise to examine the undisputed letters of Paul in terms of these several types of features, since I suspect that one would be able to document many of the traits that are to be found in the Pastoral Epistles. For Harding, of course, the process going on here is different from what we have in the direct persuasion of Paul to his actual readers since for him here we have "double pseudonymity" in which a writer (the Pastor) uses an assumed *persona* (Paul) to address his own contemporaries under the guise of fictitious recipients (Timothy and Titus). Nevertheless, his approach shows that the epistles can be profitably approached from this perspective of examination of their rhetorical methods.

PSEUDEPIGRAPHY AND AUTHORSHIP

In addition to the discussion in the commentaries there have been a number of studies devoted to the broader question of the use and legitimacy (or illegitimacy) of pseudepigraphy in the early church.[28] I discuss here contributions from the conservative side of scholarship.

T. L. WILDER

In his monograph (summarized in his article) T. L. Wilder raises a hypothetical question. Suppose for the duration of this inquiry that those scholars are right who argue that there are examples of pseudonymous letters in the New Testament. If so, which of the following options is most likely? (1) They were not meant to deceive their original readers but did in fact do so. (2) They were not meant to deceive their original readers and did not in fact do so. (3) They were meant to deceive their original readers, and did in fact do so. The hypothetical theoretical possibility (4), that they were meant to deceive, but did not succeed in doing so, is not an option. Wilder produces evidence that (despite assertions to the contrary) the concept of literary property did play a role in the ancient world. Next, he shows that there are some parallels between the disputed NT letters and paraenetical pseudonymous letters in the Greco-Roman world. Third, he gathers together the evidence that from the second century onward Christians did not accept apostolic pseudepigrapha and regarded them as deceptive. Fourth, he shows the importance attached to apostolic authorship and authority, and he argues that the attitudes of the first- and second-century churches were the same (despite the claim of some that the first-century church was less restrictive). Fifth, he argues that the disputed New Testament letters contain personal details and the like that give them the appearance of authenticity; in other words, if they are not authentic, the pseudonymous authors endeavored to give the impression of authenticity. On the basis of these arguments Wilder concludes that it is most likely that, if there are pseudonymous writings in the New Testament, they would have been intended to deceive the readers regarding their authenticity (and did succeed in doing so until the era of modern criticism). Wilder himself holds that there are no pseudonymous writings in the New Testament, and what his thesis aims to exclude is the possibility that there were nondeceptive, pseudonymous writings in the New Testament.

---

[28] The tendency among many (but not all) scholars who treat the Pastorals as pseudonymous is to assume that this conclusion is now so well established as to require no extended discussion. But see further below. On the assumption that the letters are pseudonymous, Burnet, "Pseudépigraphie," claims that pseudepigraphy is not "an innocent play on the author's name" but "a genuine literary technique," and argues that 2 Timothy shows actualization of a concrete past situation whereas 1 Timothy and Titus demonstrate "anachronism" in which a present situation is transferred into the past to gain the authority of a figure from the past.

J. DUFF

These findings are paralleled in the simultaneous, independent work of J. Duff.[29] He also demonstrates the importance of the concept of literary property. He studies the concept of authorship and shows that there was a close connection between authorship and authority in Judaism. Likewise, he confirms that there was no discontinuity between first- and second-century Christianity over the link between authorship and authority, so that pseudonymity would have met with disapproval throughout this period. If pseudonymous works were accepted, it was because they were wrongly believed to be authentic. Such works were intended from the beginning to deceive their readers.

A. D. BAUM (1)

A third contribution to the topic is the German thesis by A. D. Baum. It helpfully includes as an appendix a collection of the significant relevant ancient sources in their original languages and in German translation. He summarizes his work as follows: "a statement was considered authentic if merely the wording did not come from the person to whom the statement was attributed. However, a statement was not considered to be authentic if the content did not come from the alleged author."[30] Put otherwise, "If the content comes from Paul, it is authentic even if the wording comes from somebody else." This formulation allows for an amanuensis writing up Pauline content in his own words. But Baum denies that a composition by a follower of Paul after his death would have been regarded as a composition with no intent to deceive unless the content stemmed entirely from Paul and it was not cast in the form of a letter written in specific circumstances.

The positive importance of these three contributions is that they show good reason to reject the view espoused by D. Meade that the early church was "soft" on deceptive pseudonymity in the first century and that its attitude hardened only later.[31] However, they leave some issues open or capable only of probable conclusions in view of the complexity of the issues. These include the existence in the context of the early church of works not by the authors whose names they bear. There is not only the phenomenon of Jewish apocalyptic but also the question of the authorship of considerable tracts of the Old Testament that are anonymous or that are a blend of composite authorship and later editing and expansion.[32] In the latter case, we are

---

[29] This brief summary is dependent on Duff's own abstract of his thesis; I have not seen the full work.

[30] From the author's own English summary of his argument (Baum, *Pseudepigraphie*, 195).

[31] D. G. Meade, *Pseudonymity and Canon. An Investigation into the Relationship of Authorship and Authority in Jewish and Earliest Christian Tradition* (WUNT 39; Tübingen: J. C. B. Mohr [Paul Siebeck], 1986).

[32] Many contemporary conservative evangelical scholars recognize that the composition of the Pentateuch was not the work of Moses, even if traditions stemming from him are incorporated. Since the Pentateuch does not identify its author but is strictly anonymous, this may seem not to matter very much and not to be a parallel to the issue at stake here. But the clear implication is that not every statement attributed to Moses (e.g., in the promulgation of laws) necessarily comes from him but may include later revisions and additions, and this raises the same kind of questions regarding authenticity.

looking at works that already in the first century belonged to hoary antiquity and were doubtless generally regarded as being by their "obvious" authors (if there was one). In the former case, there is as yet no clear solution, although Duff argues that intentional "literary fiction" is not necessarily the right answer. Among the views specifically targeted by Baum is the kind of proposal that I myself have offered. His argument is that there is no basis for the practice of allonymity and that the suggestion of a fluid boundary between works written by a secretary during Paul's life time and compositions by a follower thereafter cannot be substantiated.

What is not provided, however, by any of these writers is any sort of way of dealing with the situation posed by any actual writings that have found their way into the canon although they were not written by the persons to whom they are attributed.

R. RIESNER

The possibility that Luke, that is, the erstwhile companion of Paul and author of Acts, was somehow involved in the compilation of the Pastorals, whether before or after Paul's death, is currently proposed by various commentators (e.g., Johnson; Neudorfer) and has now been strongly defended by R. Riesner.

He attempts to neutralize various apparent differences from Acts. First, the Pastorals are directed to an innerchurch situation and therefore develop more fully the topic of heresy that Acts, written more with a missionary aim, knows but mentions only in passing (but in an emphatic way) in Acts 20:28–31. Second, Acts is not concerned with church order, but what it does say about overseers/elders and laying on of hands fits the picture in the Pastorals. Third, although the Pastorals say little about the work of the Holy Spirit, what they do say does reflect the same teaching as in Acts (Titus 3:5–6!), and their silence may be due to desire to give no encouragement to the pneumatic enthusiasm of the opponents of Paul. Fourth, Acts does recognize the apostleship of Paul, despite its virtual disuse of the title.

There are similarities. Both Luke–Acts and 1 Timothy have a strong interest in widows and describe them in similar terms. The use of medical language is common to both sets of documents. And the allusions to the teaching of Jesus in the Pastorals tend to be closest to the traditions recorded in Luke.

Riesner notes the role played by Luke along with Mark in the situation described in 2 Timothy 4. And he argues very briefly that the situation of 1 Timothy and Titus does not fit the period after the end of Acts. He also remarks that Pauline authorship was never questioned in the early church, and a second-century dating is very improbable. The Epistles show undeniable differences in language and theological expression from Paul, but they have many similarities in language and theological

---

Similar considerations apply to other Old Testament writings where the presence of material from writers other than the named writer is generally accepted. Even so ultraconservative a scholar as E. J. Young allowed that Ecclesiastes was not penned by Solomon despite its opening verse.

expression with Luke–Acts. Following E. E. Ellis, Riesner argues that the differences from Paul in the Epistles are largely due to the use of preformed traditions that are "reminiscent of the Jerusalem church" and the use of these helps to account for the admitted differences from Lukan language and style.

Some weaknesses need to be addressed:

(1) Riesner does not interact with the problem of language and style to any great extent. He seems to think that it is sufficient to claim that much of the difference from Luke's own style can be attributed to the use of preformed traditions and presumably Pauline materials. But is this really compelling? If the vocabulary links with Paul are weak, then the links with Luke are certainly no stronger. Moreover, the extent of the traditional materials is pretty certainly exaggerated by Ellis. Johnson links new vocabulary with topics otherwise untreated by Paul (or by Luke), but this will not explain some of the major differences where Pauline vocabulary is lacking or new vocabulary is used instead.

(2) One area that now cries out for research is the nature of the argumentation. For example, Witherington's commentary makes considerable use of Donelson's analysis of cases of enthymemic argument and inductive and illustrative paradigms in the Pastorals. For Donelson an enthymeme is a syllogism with one of the elements omitted and to be supplied by the audience. Donelson finds them used in salvation statements, characterization of the religious life, and appeals to entrusted tradition.[33] Whether or not this is a correct classification of the arguments, the crucial point is that neither Donelson nor Witherington offer any examples of these types of argument from the authentic letters of Paul (or from Luke–Acts[34]). Are the modes in the accepted letters of Paul and the Pastorals of the same kind, or do they fall into different groups?[35] What evidence is there for the same mind working in the same way in the authentic letters of Paul and the Pastorals?

A. D. BAUM (2)

The question of vocabulary and style is investigated in a fresh analysis by Baum.[36] He first of all cites the statistics that show clearly that the Pastorals both individually and as a corpus display a richer vocabulary proportionate to their lengths than the rest of the Pauline corpus. This is true not only of their use of distinctive words not used in the 13-letter corpus outside the Pastorals but also of their use of words

---

[33] L. R. Donelson, *Pseudepigraphy and Ethical Argument in the Pastoral Epistles* (Tübingen: J. C. B. Mohr [Paul Siebeck], 1986). The definition of enthymemes is a somewhat controversial matter. Aune, *Dictionary* (s.v. "Enthymeme"), 150–57, gives bibliography and offers some warnings concerning the weaknesses that he detects in the research so far.

[34] But, because of the difference in genre, usage of enthymemes in Luke–Acts is not very likely, except in the speeches in Acts.

[35] See P. A. Holloway, "The Enthymeme as an Element of Style in Paul," *JBL* 120 (2001): 329–39.

[36] Baum, "Semantic Variation."

shared with the rest of the corpus. Defenders of their authenticity should not deny this feature.

His novel approach is to argue that in Titus (chosen as a test case) there are 83 distinctive words but some 70 of them have virtual synonyms in the rest of the Pauline corpus, so that it would be possible to write a version of the letter using a more limited but much more Pauline vocabulary. Baum then compares the characteristics of oral speech with written speech and notes that the latter generally has a greater vocabulary than the former, and that this is due to the greater amount of time available during written composition compared with a spontaneous speech. So the difference between the Pastorals and the other letters can be attributed to the author (whether Paul or somebody else) having more time at his disposal while composing them. Were the Pastorals written by Paul himself whereas the other letters were dictated orally? If so, this argument from a non-Pauline vocabulary should not be seen as having any weight.

Baum is to be commended for the caution with which he presents his conclusions. Although he has not tested 1 Timothy and 2 Timothy in the same way, the results could well be similar. There are some difficulties, however. The synonyms suggested are not always sufficiently close to be convincing. We still have somebody writing with a vocabulary that indicates a process of thought different from that of the other letters. Further, we need to come up with a scenario that explains convincingly how this additional time for composition was available for these three letters and not for the others.

Also, there is the crucial point, which Baum recognizes, that this increase in distinctive vocabulary is matched by a diminution in the number of particles and pieces of connective tissue noted by Harrison and others. (Harrison listed 112 particles used elsewhere in the corpus but not used in the Pastorals). In correspondence Baum notes that genre can affect the use of particles,[37] but, granted that this is the case, it is not clear to me that the various letters ascribed to Paul vary so much in genre from one another.[38]

THE PASTORAL EPISTLES IN NEW TESTAMENT THEOLOGY

Most of the recent crop of New Testament theologies that organize their treatment around the individual documents and authors (rather than offering a thematic treatment of the New Testament as a whole) contain discussions of the Pastoral Epistles as a group rather than individually.[39] I mention two examples.

---

[37] He cites J. Blomqvist, *Greek Particles in Hellenistic Prose* (Lund: Gleerup, 1969), 137, 140.

[38] Klinker-de Klerck, "The Pastoral Epistles," is a succinct catalogue of some of the points at issue in regard to authenticity but does not advance the discussion.

[39] See below for Herzer's criticism of this practice of not examining the three letters individually for their possibly unique contributions. A notable exception is provided by F. Thielman, *Theology*, who devotes separate chapters to each of the letters. Against the background of false teaching, 1 Timothy deals with right doctrine, right conduct, congregational worship, and leadership of God's household. Titus has the same background of perverse teaching; the letter treats of

G. STRECKER

G. Strecker notes that their christology "draws upon a living, progressing Pauline tradition and develops it even further." Although there is a development toward "church hierarchy," the church structures "remain open to the free working of the Spirit (e.g., 2 Tim 1:14 and elsewhere)." Further, Strecker emphasizes that the Pauline tradition is "still perceptible in the distinction between indicative and imperative, or in the conviction that the 'grace of God' ($\chi\acute{\alpha}\rho\iota\varsigma$) that represents the main principle of Christian action has played a role in the formation of the theological profile typical for the Pastoral Letters."[40] The theology is at bottom Pauline (and common early Christian!) but somehow coming to expression in different ways. Although he handles the Pastorals as a group and discusses their christology and ecclesiology, there is no attempt to sum up their general character.[41]

F. MATERA

Matera handles the letters in a single chapter entitled "A Theology of the Pauline Tradition," which assesses their positive contribution to the maintenance of the deposit of faith received from Paul. For Matera, this positive role is to some extent counterbalanced by various gaps and omissions in their theology and some elements that he regards as regressive. What is important here is not that the theology can be regarded as compatible with Paul's theology, but that the accents are different:

> One looks in vain in the Pastorals for Paul's profound analysis of the human condition, which portrays humanity under the powers of sin, death, and the law. Nor does one find Paul's paradoxical theology of the cross, or his apocalyptic vision of the parousia, when the general resurrection of the dead will occur and the kingdom will be handed over to God, even though the Pastorals complain that some are claiming that the resurrection of the dead has already taken place. The Pastorals refer to the Spirit, but the Spirit no longer plays the same dynamic role that it does in Paul's correspondence. Finally, the church is no longer viewed as the body of Christ or the temple of God, and there is no discussion about its relationship to Israel or to the future of Israel.

On the other hand:

> The theology of the Pastorals, however, maintains the essential element of the Pauline deposit: the manifestation of God in Jesus Christ, salvation by

---

knowledge and conduct and especially "making the Savior attractive," but surprisingly the distinctive christology and soteriology of Titus receive little mention. Second Timothy is concerned with enduring hardship for the gospel and guarding the gospel from false teaching: Paul's gospel of the grace and power of God revealed in the midst of suffering shines clearly through. In a later chapter that synthesizes Pauline theology, the Pastorals are cited particularly with reference to persecution and the church's relationship to the unbelieving world in the last days (441–44, 456–57) but not much otherwise.

[40] Strecker, *Theology*, 586, 589, 593–94.

[41] It must be remembered, however, that Strecker's work was left unfinished and had to be completed by an editor.

grace rather than by human effort, the relationship between the indicative of salvation and the moral imperative, and the hope that there will be a future appearance of the Savior. The enduring contribution of these letters is to have solidified the Pauline inheritance. By claiming Paul as the one from whom they have ultimately received the deposit of faith, they have made the Pauline tradition an integral element of the church's faith.[42]

CHRISTOLOGY AND SOTERIOLOGY

G. A. COUSER

The centrality of *theo*logy, that is, the understanding of God (the Father), has been increasingly recognized in the New Testament generally in a number of recent works. G. A. Couser argues that the descriptions of God in 1 Tim 1:17 and 6:15–16 are not irrelevant descriptions of a distant, transcendent God but are carefully crafted, corresponding portrayals of the God who is Savior (cf. 2:3–7; 4:10) and who is able to act in sovereign power in redemption; he saves in the way described in the letters and not in some other way than that taught by Paul and Timothy.[43]

H. STETTLER

H. Stettler, *Die Christologie der Pastoralbriefe*, takes its place alongside two other works that fall just outside our period.[44] Where Lau's work concentrated on the concept of epiphany and the use of tradition, and Läger emphasized the Pastor's virtual incorporation of Paul, his conversion, and his preaching in the saving event itself, Stettler has undertaken a broader task. She gives a careful exegesis of all the relevant passages (with excellent summaries at each stage) and then attempts a synthesis of the exegetical material; this combination of approaches enables her to do justice to each text in its immediate context and then in the context of the Pastoral Epistles as a whole.

Stettler argues that the Pastor held a christology of preexistence and incarnation but he expressed it using fresh forms of language. In response to the claim that he has hellenized Christian theology and drawn up his christology in terms of contrast with the worship of pagan deities, she shows that his thinking is thoroughly grounded in Hellenistic Judaism and is formulated so that it will get across to the Hellenistic world. The Christology is thoroughly Pauline in its essential structure despite the differences in expression. The Epistles display a considerable degree of dependence on

---

[42] Matera, *Theology*, 257, 258. Also worth consulting is F. Matera, *New Testament Ethics: The Legacies of Jesus and Paul* (Louisville: Westminster John Knox, 1996), 229–47, for his treatment of the ethics of the Pastorals in greater detail.

[43] Cf. his unpublished thesis, "God and Christian Existence in 1 and 2 Timothy and Titus" (Ph.D. diss.; University of Aberdeen, 1992).

[44] A. Lau, *Manifest in Flesh: The Epiphany Christology of the Pastoral Epistles* (Tübingen: J. C. B. Mohr [Paul Siebeck], 1996]); K. Läger, *Die Christologie der Pastoralbriefe* (Münster: Lit, 1996).

the authentic Pauline Epistles, taking their phraseology and teaching and reexpressing it to meet new situations. The opposition represents an early form of Gnosticism with a Docetic emphasis, and the Pastor responds to this with his emphasis on the manhood of Jesus Christ and the fleshly reality of his resurrection.[45] She traces his use of Son of man traditions (linked to the concept of the suffering Servant) and also of some Johannine strands of expression. The Pastor generally does not cite traditions, which might be separated by analysis from his own material, but rather is himself responsible for most of the material that has a traditional flavor, and this flavor is due to his own creative use of the traditions. The stature of the Pastor as a theologian is correspondingly enhanced by this analysis of his methods.

The author is to be commended for her demonstration that the Pastor's use of "in Christ" is fully in harmony with that of Paul (even if the phrase is not used in such a wide manner). There is also her insistence that the doctrine of justification is essentially that of Paul. What she has not done is to consider whether the three letters show individually distinctive features, and whether it is methodologically correct to examine them all together and indiscriminately. This methodological question is taken up by G. Wieland.

G. WIELAND

Wieland's monograph deals with the use of the "salvation" word group in the letters and is a careful exegetical examination of all the relevant texts; each letter is treated independently so as not to read ideas from one letter into the others without adequate justification.[46] The author is concerned primarily with synchronic study and does not explore to any extent the development of the ideas and their background. He produces a carefully nuanced exegesis of the material that throws fresh light on the texts. He considers the use of traditional language and Hellenistic formulations. There is some discussion of the views of recent scholars including those who see a decline from the soteriology of Paul, although more might have been done in this respect. His conclusion is that soteriology occupies a central position in the letters. In 1 Timothy there is stress on the universality of the scope of salvation over against an exclusivist, ascetic heterodoxy; in 2 Timothy the doctrine is closely related to the need to encourage faithful, costly ministry in the face of harsh opposition; and in Titus there is the nurturing of a sense of Christian identity and community based on the appropriation of Old Testament soteriological categories and an emphasis on the consequent ethical transformation. In each case the doctrinal undergirding makes

---

[45] However, a case can be made out that the opposition is rather a combination of a mistaken understanding of Paul's own teaching coupled with a strong Jewish-Christian element that majored on speculative exegesis of the Old Testament associated with ascetical practices; on this alternative view it is not so obvious that the Pastor was combating a heretical or skewed understanding of the person of Jesus.

[46] Wieland, therefore, should not fall under the criticism that Murphy-O'Connor, "Pastoral Epistles," 632–33, directs against H. Stettler.

the paraenesis effective. These are obviously different emphases and not differences in content or character. Would it then be fair, we might ask, to say that any statement about soteriology found in any one of the three letters could equally well appear in any of the other two? Or are the Christologies as divergent as has sometimes been suggested?

C. E. HO

This unpublished thesis[47] tackles the question of whether the outlook represented in the letters can rightly be termed "missionary." At first sight, this may seem to be a complete misnomer, since they are so taken up with the internal problems caused by the opposition to Pauline doctrine, spirituality, and morality in the congregations. Nevertheless, the underlying theology is a theology of salvation, and it is significant that Timothy is designated an "evangelist"; although the stress may be primarily on his pastoral role, it would be wrong to strip this term of its basic significance of being a missionary. The stress on prayer for all people and on God's will for all people to come to a knowledge of the truth fits in with this; although it has been denied, the stress on godly living and adopting a positive attitude toward the surrounding society appears to stem from a missionary motivation rather than simply from the desire to maintain a low, conformist profile in order to avoid persecution.[48]

R. FUCHS

Fuchs is a German pastor who has pursued an unusual approach to the Epistles over several years. Stylistically his material is far from easy reading,[49] but essentially he is an advocate of straight Pauline authorship on the basis of J. van Bruggen's reconstruction of Paul's missionary travels in and around Ephesus, and he argues at length for the distinctiveness of each of the three letters in terms of structure, vocabulary, style, and content. The letters are thus not to be seen as complementary parts of a separate corpus within the Pauline letters as a whole but as individual letters for special occasions like the other Pauline letters. For example, he notes the absence of ἀγάπη in the body of Titus, as contrasted with its importance in 1 and 2 Timothy; φιλία is used instead, and this ties in with Titus being written for newly converted Hellenists for whom ἀγάπη was Jewish-biblical and Jesus-language that they would not have understood (contrast the Greek language in Titus 3:4,15). The different uses of designations for God and Jesus are related to the different situations addressed. "Savior" is frequent in Titus but occurs only once in 2 Timothy, whereas Lord is

---

[47] Ho, "Do the work of an evangelist."

[48] The same position is taken by P. Trebilco (unpublished paper), who compares the rather different attitude to the world in Revelation. He points out that Titus 2:13 polemicizes against certain features of society—there is no uncritical acceptance of its standards and way of life—but the main motivation for closer relationships with society was missionary (1 Tim 6:1–2).

[49] See the helpful (German) summary in the review of his book by J. Buchegger.

absent from Titus, as is the formula "in Christ." Titus prefers "Jesus Christ," but 1 and 2 Timothy have "Christ Jesus." These differences are related to Timothy being a Hellenistic-Jewish missionary, whereas Titus is a Hellenistic-Gentile missionary with a Gentile audience.[50]

THE CHURCH, MINISTRY, AND ETHICS

S. R. NORTH

S. R. North has written a thesis entitled *"Presbuteroi Christianoi*: Towards a Theory of Integrated Ministry," which I know only from its summary by the author in a brief report. He wants to date 1 Timothy and Titus as authentic letters of Paul shortly after 1 Corinthians. "Bishop" is a member of the house-church responsible for maintaining order in it, a "first among equals." "Elders" is a broad term of respect for leaders. "Apostles-prophets-teachers" and "bishops-elders-deacons" were one and the same group with the latter nomenclature not replacing the former until late in the first century. There is much that is novel and controversial in the reported conclusions of this thesis, but I cannot comment further on a thesis that I have not seen.

L. OBERLINNER

L. Oberlinner, author of a profound theological commentary on the Pastoral Epistles, has addressed the theme of Hellenism and hellenization in the letters.[51] He covers three areas.

First, he notes how the Pastor wants to hold fast to the *Christology* that he has learned from a collection of Pauline letters but nevertheless works it out differently. Here he goes over familiar territory with regard to the use of "Savior" and "epiphany." He distinguishes two questions. First, why is the title of Savior so dominant? Is this due to the influence of the outside world or to an inner-Christian development (or to both)? Second, what difference did it make to the Christian congregations that their preaching now used a term that was current both inside and outside the church? Similar questions arise with the use of epiphany, and here Oberlinner notes the risks that accompany the use of terms current in the ruler-cults of the ancient world.

Second, the *ecclesiology* is reflected in the lack of direct address to the church and the use of the concept of the household in which a single person held a position over the others and expected submission from them. The authority of the paterfamilias was decisive in the concept of the household in the contemporary world. Whereas in Paul the house is simply the meeting place for the church, now the household controls the structure. The ἐπίσκοπος has full authority over the congregation.

---

[50] On Christology, see also the discussion of L. Oberlinner below.
[51] Oberlinner, "Öffnung zur Welt."

Finally, he looks at the *ethics* of the letters. There is a strong tendency to urge conduct that would be approved by the surrounding world, including the subordination of wives and slaves. The aim is not to be different from the world but to be like the world. The qualities required of wives are similar to those in the Pythagorean tradition. The commendation of prudence (σωφροσύνη) as a very general quality ties in with ancient ethics.[52]

Oberlinner's case fits in with the conclusions that can be drawn from Collins's commentary. It is difficult to deny that hellenization is going on. This, incidentally, is one powerful reason for not viewing the Pastoral Epistles as straightforward authentic letters of Paul, particularly if they are thought of as letters composed at intervals between his other letters: why should Paul tend to hellenization only in these letters to his associates?[53]

In a later article[54] Oberlinner contrasts the way in which Paul sees the whole congregation responsible for its life (admittedly with charismatic leadership) with the shift to the congregational leaders as the authorities for preservation of the saving knowledge of the gospel and the refutation of those who would corrupt it. The concept of the church as household with a man at its head who conforms to Roman secular standards for rulers gives the leader unquestionable legitimation. "Teaching" becomes a key concept (in contrast to Paul). These developments may have been justified in the author's situation, but they have led to a *Wirkungsgeschichte* which has restricted proclamation and teaching to (male) leaders, and this needs careful examination.[55] One question is whether the concept of the church in the Pastorals should be seen more in terms of development or discontinuity compared with Paul.

D. G. HORRELL

D. G. Horrell's study of the use of ἀδελφός, "brother/sibling," in the Pauline corpus notes the comparative sparseness of this designation for fellow-believers in the Pastoral Epistles and the development of οἶκος terminology; this indicates a shift from a more egalitarian society to the concept of the church as "a stratified and hierarchical community led by those men who lead their human households well" (309). Horrell is careful to nuance his case and to avoid false absolute contrasts, but

---

[52] In an examination of the virtues associated with eldership, Mappes, "Moral Virtues," has queried whether the qualities desiderated in Christian leaders are essentially those approved in the secular society of the time and insists that they are more specifically Christian and stand in deliberate contrast to the vices castigated in the lives of the opponents. This is a useful cautionary note against overemphasizing any conformity to secular society on the part of the church. See, however, Paschke, "*Cura Morum*," for evidence that the "care of manners" practiced by the Roman censors provides an apt historical background for the qualities desiderated in the bishop and deacon lists.

[53] One will need to ask whether the explanations offered by Fuchs are satisfactory.

[54] Oberlinner, "Gemeindeordnung."

[55] Oberlinner writes as a Roman Catholic layperson.

he may be in danger of assuming that the concept of brotherhood conveyed a more egalitarian ethos than was actually the case in the ancient world.[56]

P. TREBILCO

The most ambitious discussion of the Pastoral Epistles as sources for the history of the early church comes in this detailed survey of the church in Ephesus right through into the second century. Trebilco associates the Pastorals, Johannine Letters, and Revelation with this Christian center (along with Ignatius's letter to the Ephesians). His survey of authorship and date (c. 80–100) comes to conclusions similar to my own. First and Second Timothy were probably sent to Ephesus to a Christian group that included strong opponents of some aspects of the Pauline teaching that they have developed in wrong directions under some Jewish influence (cf. Acts 20:30). Whereas other scholars have tended to explore the background situation in order to throw light on the letters, Trebilco attempts to identify the situation of the letters and then use the letters to throw more light on the situation. He does the same for the Johannine Letters and Revelation. He takes up five issues: the relation of the readers to the wider culture, their attitude to material possessions, the role of leadership and authority, the role of women, and their self-understanding as reflected in how Christians referred to themselves. Finally, in this analysis he asks how the different Christian traditions and communities in Ephesus related to one another. Some at least of this material would fit letters written to any Hellenistic center, but Trebilco shows that it is apposite for Ephesus in particular. Noteworthy is his recognition of the missionary aspect of acculturation and use of language that would be familiar in the Hellenistic environment and also of the counter-cultural features emerging from the gospel (opposing the imperial cult and the worship of wealth).

Like Horrell, Trebilco traces the decline in the use of "brothers" to the development of a more hierarchical leadership and to the development of a household model of the congregation that has a hierarchical structure. He also discusses the development of the term "believer" and links it to the growing importance of the concept of "the faith" as the body of traditional doctrine; what is believed has come to be important as the basis of Christian identity. There is an interesting contrast with the Johannine Letters where "children of God" is more prominent. Indeed, a number of mutual influences between the two different groups of believers to whom these letters were sent are suggested.

I. H. MARSHALL

I myself may well be in danger of trying to find in the Epistles a picture of the congregation and ministry that is more congenial to my own predilections.[57] I have

---

56 I owe this suggestion to an unpublished paper by A. D. Clarke.
57 Marshall, "Congregation and Ministry."

argued for a somewhat different picture in which there is more stress on the plurality of ministerial and leadership activities and roles in the letters. It is important to remember that congregational structures inevitably reflected the structures of the synagogue and of secular life, and we must beware of reading back our modern patterns of community and leadership and finding justification for them (and them alone) in Scripture; at the same time we should not downplay the elements in the New Testament that were beginning to transcend the contemporary culture.

So far, however, as the lack of address to the congregations is concerned (cf. Oberlinner above), to my mind this is adequately explained by the fact that here we have letters to congregational leaders. We should remember that Paul himself did exercise considerable control over his own congregations, and his colleagues would behave similarly. The authority of the paterfamilias was an accepted datum in the ancient world; its application in the church may be due to the withdrawal of a figure like Paul himself from oversight over the congregations that he had founded and the increasing role of local leadership. In other words, the distant single leader (Paul) would tend to be replaced by a local single leader.

An important question is whether the material about elders implies a plurality of leaders in any given congregation. On the one hand, this is the most natural explanation of the teaching in 1 Timothy 5. Titus 1:5 could be interpreted of the appointment of elders (plural) in each town or of one elder per town. The analogy of the synagogue favors the former interpretation, and the shift to the singular in Titus 1:6–7 is natural. On the other hand, it is arguable that the singular form "overseer" in contrast to the plurals "deacons and "women" in 1 Timothy 3 implies a single leader. It can be argued also that the imagery of the steward (οἰκονόμος) implies one person in control rather than several, but it should be noted that in Ignatius, *Polycarp* 6, apparently addressed to believers in general, the recipients are described collectively "as God's stewards and assessors and ministers."

WOMEN IN THE PASTORAL EPISTLES

Controversy over this theme shows no signs of subsiding.[58] I mention two monographs and then list some shorter contributions.

J. M. HOLMES

The monograph by J. M. Holmes, *Text in a Whirlwind*, develops four main points: (1) the immediate context, (2) the broader context of the passage in the

---

[58] Attention is naturally centered on 1 Timothy 2. The problems of 1 Tim 5:3–16 are handled by Tsuji, "Zwischen Ideal und Realität": he argues that the author's view is that not all women who were regarded as widows at this time were to receive care from the church. He adopts the view of some earlier scholars that such "widows" included younger women who had never been married at all, and the author was rejecting the ascetically oriented false teaching that was encouraging them to continue a celibate life as "widows" who were provided for by the church.

letter, (3) the relevance of parallel teaching, and (4) the nature of the theological foundation.

(1) The immediate context: the whole of 2:1–3:13 deals with the character of believers (and leaders) and not with what they do in the congregational meeting. Hence vv. 8–12 deal with the character of those who pray and do not necessarily deal with learning in the congregation. The aspect of the verbs is significant and yields the translation "I also permit a woman neither constantly to direct, nor to dominate a man. She should be tranquil."

(2) The broader context: nothing suggests that the teaching in 2:9–15 has anything to do with an alleged connection between the women and false teaching. The women were not deserting traditional female roles. Hence 2:9–15 is of universal and not just local application.

(3) The relevance of parallel teaching: 1 Cor 14:33b–35 is a quotation from a Corinthian letter to which Paul replies with a rejection in v. 36. Hence this passage is extremely problematic as background to 1 Tim 2.

(4) The theological foundation: vv. 13–15 (the "trustworthy saying" of 3:1a) is a citation of Jewish material. Holmes rejects the usual passages cited as possible background (Sir 25:24; *Apoc. Mos.*[59]). As it stands, the passage is concerned purely with Eve's entry into a state of transgression. Verse 15 states that she (Eve) could expect to be saved through the (ongoing process of) child-bearing (culminating in the coming of the Messiah) set in train by her union with her husband, provided that they (Adam and Eve) were to live appropriately in faith.

In short, the passage teaches that woman "must dress appropriately, learn obediently and tranquilly, and not constantly . . . go on and on [at anyone?] or . . . play the dictator over a man." The author is reminded of a Jewish "saying which captures such mutual male-female responsibility to live godly lives, a saying which recalls that both Adam and Eve must live in faith, love and holiness with good sense if the promise of Gen. 3.15 were ultimately to be fulfilled" (300). Later the passage was misunderstood to apply to congregational meetings, the influence of the teaching rejected in 1 Cor 14 worked in the same direction, and the traditional understanding of the passage arose. It follows that Genesis is not used to give a scriptural basis for the silence of women in church.

Holmes's work certainly shows up weaknesses, not necessarily fatal ones, in the more traditional type of exegesis of the passage. Scholars have always recognized that the chapter is concerned with the behavior of men and women in their ordinary life outside the congregational meeting, but this does not mean that their behavior

---

[59] On this text see the detailed study by Heininger, "Die 'mystische' Eva," who argues that it does not present Eve as subordinate to Adam.

within the meeting is excluded from consideration (as Holmes seems to come near to saying). To say that "the Author has chosen to prohibit the *continual* practice of those actions, not the actions themselves" (94) is casuistic and unconvincing. Nor is the nature of the problem that is being addressed exactly clear. The biggest problems concern the novel proposal regarding the origin and function of 1 Tim 2:13–15. If the passage is interpreted as Holmes takes it, its relevance to the preceding verses is far from obvious, the original interpretation of the "child-bearing" is not likely to have been apparent to the readers, and the reference of v. 15b to Eve and Adam is surprising.

A. MERZ

The most challenging work to the conservative type of understanding of the letters comes in a monograph by A. Merz, which develops an "intertextual study." Sadly it is so laden with technical jargon that it is well-nigh incomprehensible and untranslatable. Fortunately we have an English position paper summing up her approach in a symposium on intertextuality, and there is a good and full analysis in the German review by H. Sturcke.[60]

Her thesis is that the author of the Pastorals is interacting with the Pauline corpus of letters at every turn. Somewhere around AD 100 he produces his own corpus of three letters to counteract the existing Pauline corpus. He pretends to be Paul, but the readers are not meant to know this; this is deceptive pseudonymity, and the deception is essential to the author's purpose. His aim is to take up Pauline teachings, themes that need to be modified for his own time or even corrected. His purpose is not to replace the existing Pauline letters (which he clearly knows and echoes) but to add to the corpus further Pauline letters that show how the others are to be interpreted. This procedure is seen in two areas in particular. First, Paul's teaching about the brotherly relationships between slaves and masters (Philemon) needs to be corrected to show that it does not affect the hierarchical structure of society. Second, and more importantly, the equality of men and women in salvation needs to be corrected by noting the second-class situation of women in creation, their priority in sin, and their normative route to salvation through child-bearing. The procedure is justified by appeal to the theories of intertextuality, which bring out the effects in both directions: the author writes under the effects of the Pauline letters and his readers are aware or are made aware of this, but at the same time his writing as if he were Paul alters their understanding of these earlier writings; a principal aim of the Pastorals is to impose a new interpretation on teaching in the existing Pauline epistles, and in the author's situation this involved a strenuous assertion of hierarchical structure and

---

[60] Merz, *Selbstauslegung*; idem, "Self-Exposition"; cf. Sturke, "Review of A. Merz." There is also a summary article in German from the author (Merz, "Amore Pauli"). For a related but apparently independent approach, based on the work of M. Bal and focusing on Titus, see J. W. Marshall, "'I Left You in Crete.'" So far I know of no scholar who has interacted critically with Merz's views in any detail.

submission to authority. No doubt this was done from a position of loyalty to Paul and the desire to make his teaching relevant to the author's dangerous situation, but he achieves it by using "the reference-text-oriented functions of intertextuality to modify statements of the orthonymous pretext corpus under the fiction of being their author" (Sturcke's wording). This is not "conscious falsification," but nevertheless the author "is guilty of deceiving his readers and likely himself." It follows that there are serious implications for the canonical status of the letters.

OTHER CONTRIBUTIONS

P. H. Towner has given a helpful survey of the radical feminist and the biblical feminist approaches, unfortunately in a rather inaccessible journal, and made some pertinent criticisms of each of them.[61]

Contrasting views are presented in dialogue by the two essayists in Beck and Blomberg's symposium. L. L. Belleville presents an egalitarian understanding of the passage. She emphasizes that 1 Timothy is a corrective document in many respects, dealing with specific things that were not right in the church. Calm, quiet behavior is required of the women. She argues that teaching was an activity, not an office, and was required of all believers (Col 3:16; Heb 5:12). The verb αὐθεντέω does not refer to the ordinary exercise of authority but to domination or gaining the upper hand, and what is condemned is not ordinary teaching but teaching in which women were trying to dominate men. The women were being deceived by the false teachers (hence the reference to Eve's deception by the serpent).[62] The complementarian view is presented by T. R. Schreiner, but he offers essentially a repetition of his previously published views.[63]

B. W. Winter has argued that the background to the passage is the rise of a "new" kind of wife in the higher levels of society who claimed for herself as a woman of pleasure the same sexual freedom as her husband claimed and used forms of contraception and abortion to avoid having to raise children. The letter calls Christian wives not to follow this example.[64]

K. Giles has advanced the thesis that the complementarian view as it is presented nowadays is not in fact the traditional understanding of the passage in that its appeal to the concept of women having different roles from men is a novelty and is inappropriate for understanding the rationale of the biblical teaching. His critique is answered in detail by A. J. Köstenberger, and Giles responds to his criticisms.[65]

---

[61] Towner, "Feminist Approaches."

[62] Belleville, "Women in Ministry." See also her other contributions, "Exegetical Fallacies" and "Teaching and Usurping Authority."

[63] Schreiner, "Women in Ministry."

[64] Winter, "The 'New' Roman Wife."

[65] Giles, "Critique, Part I"; "Critique, Part II"; Köstenberger, "Response"; Giles, "Rejoinder."

The problems of the passage occur on the levels of both exegesis and exposition. While there is a growing consensus between so-called complementarians and egalitarians on some aspects of the exegesis, there remain issues where there is still no agreement. It may be suspected that both sides in the debate look for support for those exegetical decisions that favor their own overall understanding of the place of women in the church today. Answers to questions regarding whether the teaching here is a response to a particular problem or is intended to be of general application tend to be tied to different understandings of the original purpose of the passage. At the same time, the question as to how the passage is to be applied today is differently answered.

Here the work of W. J. Webb is of great importance with his attempt to produce objective criteria for seeing the teaching of particular biblical passages as culturally relative and to argue for a redemptive trajectory in the Bible that justifies our going beyond Scripture but always in the direction prescribed by Scripture.[66]

The whole question of women is placed in a wider context by G. C. Streete in her examination of the motif of asceticism (ἄσκησις) as a key to understanding what is going on in the letters. The pattern of behavior advocated in the letters is not opposed to society so much as to individual desire; self-control is inculcated as the way for the church to survive as a corporate institution, and therefore it is understood as submission to the communal rules rather than to a personal ideal of conduct. The asceticism that is advocated is not in regard to food, drink, sexual activity, and family life, but rather subjection to the life of the community in which each person has their proper place. But we may wonder whether it is helpful to call this "asceticism"; what is the alternative?[67]

The ongoing conversation within conservative circles is reflected in the more or less simultaneous publication of an encyclopedic survey of objections to the complementarian view by W. Grudem and the symposium edited by R. W. Pierce and R. M. Groothuis, both of which contain material bearing directly on the passage. Still more recent is the Wheaton conference volume edited by M. Husbands and T. Larsen with contributions from different angles, including my own discussion of 1 Timothy 2.[68]

THE INDIVIDUALITY OF THE PASTORAL EPISTLES

A number of the studies mentioned already take care to investigate the Epistles independently of one another rather than as a group with common characteristics. This approach is developing in momentum.

---

[66] Webb, *Slaves*. His thesis is strongly attacked by Grudem, *Evangelical Feminism*.

[67] Streete, "Askesis."

[68] Grudem, *Evangelical Feminism*; Pierce and Groothuis, *Biblical Equality*; Marshall, "Women in Ministry"; Husbands and Larsen, *Women, Ministry and the Gospel*. The contribution to this last volume by J. M. Hamilton Jr. is notable for its gracious appeal to the two sides within evangelicalism to listen to one another.

J. W. AAGESON

J. W. Aageson focuses on what the early church did with the memory of Paul and how this affected its image of him. The Pastorals play an important role here in that if they are not by Paul himself, they are an example of appropriation of him by later writers with a different theology from his, and then in turn they become an important part of the written legacy ascribed to him, which influenced later writers in their picture of him. A whole range of important questions arises when the scene is surveyed from this fresh perspective. Aageson compares what he identifies as the patterns of theology in each of the three letters with one another and with the indubitable Paul. First Timothy is built around the concept of the household of God. Second Timothy is more concerned with the activity of God and the paraenesis that results from this. Titus is concerned more with the gospel. Comparisons are instituted between the letters. First, attention centers on images of God and Christ. First Timothy and Titus identify God as Savior (unlike Paul), and Titus stands out from its companions by not using κύριος for Christ. The household motif shapes 1 Timothy. The stress on godliness and fitting into the real world found in 1 Timothy and Titus is absent from 2 Timothy, which expects rather trials and suffering. The letters show more agreement on truth, knowledge, and faith. There is opposition with false teachings in 1 Timothy and Titus, but in 2 Timothy the problem is more one of persecution and concomitant suffering. Second Timothy is not concerned with the appointment of leaders and the necessary qualities to be found in them, but with the need for sound teaching to be passed on to the next generation.

It is then claimed that 1 Timothy relates most closely to 1 Corinthians, 2 Timothy to Philippians, and Titus to Galatians. But 1 Timothy and Titus show patterns that are substantially different from those in Philippians (e.g., the lack of personal affection and friendship). Both Galatians and Titus are concerned with the Jewish law, but the manner of engagement is significantly different. What drives Galatians theologically is different from 1 Timothy and Titus. There are also significant differences from 1 Corinthians (body versus household, centrality of resurrection, new emphasis on truth). On the basis of this discussion, Aageson states that we cannot conclude that the same author wrote Philippians and 2 Timothy (still less 1 Timothy and Titus), but rather that 2 Timothy is by a different author from 1 Timothy and Titus (which are assumed to be by the same author). This is a restatement of the by-no-means-novel observation that 2 Timothy is the closest to the accepted Pauline Epistles. As has been said before, if 2 Timothy did not keep such questionable company (1 Timothy and Titus), the task of defending its Pauline authorship would be much easier. Aageson, however, is arguing that it is least likely that Paul wrote the three Pastorals, more possible that Paul wrote only 2 Timothy, and even more likely that all three are non-Pauline but by two different authors.

This sets the stage for an examination of the images of Paul. Paul is presented as a figure of authority (apostle) and a teacher who incorporates the true gospel. Paul is used to sanction the model of the church as a household. The result of this is the beginning of a canonization process that attributes authority to the Pauline writings and to the Pastorals themselves that are presented as if they were part of that collection. Contrast the Paul of Acts who is not a teacher or writer of letters concerned to rebut heresy but a missionary calling others to follow his example of suffering. There is no likelihood that the author of Acts also wrote the Pastorals! The developed theology of Colossians and Ephesians does not figure in the Pastorals, and these documents stand closer to the authentic epistles.

Aageson is well aware that the different circumstances of each of the letters may play a role in determining the theological emphases, patterns, and nuances, but it seems to this writer that he does not take this factor sufficiently into account in his discussion of their mutual relationships, nor does he take note of the different nuances and perspectives even within the corpus of authentic letters, where we see Paul responding to different situations and needs. The questions that he is asking are valuable, but the answers probably need to be more sophisticated.

J. HERZER

A whole series of articles on different aspects of the letters comes from J. Herzer.[69] It commences in 2004 with a survey of recent commentaries (Oberlinner; Quinn; Quinn and Wacker; Johnson; and Weiser). He depicts the consensus view up to this point in time as one that treats the letters as constituents of a group and as pseudonymous compositions from a date well after that of Paul himself. But this consensus is breaking down. All along there has been a conservative wing attributing the letters directly or indirectly to Paul. It has now gained some respectability by its adoption in respect of some or all of the letters by Johnson and Murphy-O'Connor who cannot be accused of theological parti pris. Herzer sees no reason to question the assumption of pseudonymity, but he draws attention to the individuality of the three letters and questions whether they were written as a deliberate corpus and intended to function as one. In this and the succeeding articles he draws attention to distinctives and attempts to show that there are subtle differences between the letters that may be indicative of different authorship and situations. He notes how Johnson identifies evidences concerning the nature of the letters that may be drawn from only one of them and then applied to the whole group. This applies to the ecclesiology, the characterization of the opponents, and the picture of Paul. Herzer observes how Richards sees 1 Timothy as a later school production that is dependent on 2 Timothy and Titus. He is not convinced by Johnson's attempt to place the letters in the lifetime of Paul. He raises the question of the viability of a theory of transparent school compositions over

---

[69] The best place to start with Herzer for English-speaking readers is "Rearranging the 'House of God.'"

against deceptive pseudepigraphy. He suggests that viewing the letters as a corpus to establish how and why they were composed has not succeeded. The virtue and vice lists need fuller investigation in the light of ancient moral philosophy. He also raises the question of what audience is being addressed by commentators.

In subsequent articles Herzer has begun to take up some of these particular issues.

(1) *The opponents.* Herzer questions whether we can assume the unity of the Pastorals and use evidence from all three to build up a composite picture of the opponents.[70] He experiments by looking at them separately and claims that the opponents are Jews from outside the church in Titus, Christians in 2 Timothy, and Gnostics who have left the church in 1 Timothy; 1 Timothy picks up motifs from the other letters. All this leads Herzer to argue for a late date for 1 Timothy and to allow that Titus and 2 Timothy could be authentic Pauline letters (presumably at least so far as this motif is concerned).[71]

(2) *Ecclesiology.* Herzer questions the assumption that "household of God" is the governing motif in all three letters (as made for instance by Horrell and Roloff). He begins with 1 Tim 3:15, the only place where the actual phrase is used. Herzer questions whether exegetes have read the notion of a household into the other letters. He suggests that in 1 Timothy the phrase (οἶκος) refers to the congregation as a temple whose task is to protect the truth of the faith rather than as a community structured according to household codes. The concern is not with structure but with the appropriate kind of behavior. The language in 2 Tim 2:20 (οἰκία) is only that of an illustrative metaphor, and in Titus 1 there is a plurality of presbyters/overseers without a hierarchical structure. The writer of 1 Timothy took the word from 2 Timothy and combined it in a more general manner with motifs from Titus. The letters can thus be put in the order Titus , 2 Timothy, and, after a longer period, 1 Timothy.

(3) *Piety* (εὐσέβεια). The same differentiation appears here. For Titus and 2 Timothy there is a clear understanding of piety as the basic way of life rooted in Christ, but it is not a concept or a central motif. It resembles the Greek concept in which piety is especially related to the relationship to God. But in 1 Timothy it is not expressly

---

[70] This may be the place to mention Pietersen, *The Polemic of the Pastorals*, which makes this assumption. The author proposes that the opponents portrayed in the Epistles were charismatics who justified their practices by appealing to an image of Paul as a thaumaturge. The Pastor's aim is partly to replace this image and to depict Paul as essentially a teacher; the letters are the equivalent of a status degradation ceremony which discredits the opponents themselves. It may seem odd that this kind of charismatic activity was present in a church that shows signs of institutionalization, but Pietersen draws attention to contemporary congregations where charismatic activity and institutionalization flourish side by side. The merit of this work is its careful discussion of the nature of the opposition in the letters. Whether Paul was actually being seen as a thaumaturge is not so obvious to me. Nor am I sure that the opponents are attacked as sorcerers rather than as deceivers. The nature of the opponents seems rather broader to me in the light of the attacks on their asceticism and immorality, their misinterpretation of the Old Testament, and their openness to the temptations to materialism; there is no clear criticism of any specifically Spirit-inspired or Spirit-empowered behavior (signs and wonders) on their part. Pietersen would also need to consider whether Herzer's criticism is valid of approaches of this kind.

[71] Herzer states that Baur based his view of pseudonymity on the (late) Gnostic character of the opponents and saw the letters as a corpus, although the evidence for the presence of Gnosticism came primarily from 1 Timothy alone.

related to God and has more to do with loyalty to the rulers and is more of an objective concept that can be taught and is "useful." It is close to Roman *pietas*.

Herzer notes other problems that afflict the corpus theory. How would the corpus have functioned? In what order would the letters have been read? Could the readers have identified theological motifs that could be gained only by adding together the materials from three letters? Would the pseudonymity apparatus have worked effectively for people who knew other Pauline writings? Would the readers have recognized their own situations and responses to them across three letters written to different situations? Have the varied types of pseudonymity been sufficiently taken into account? Might there be some partial authenticity?[72]

Herzer's work is still under way; he has announced the publication at some time of a monograph that will presumably incorporate the material in these essays, and he is also known to be working on a commentary. As yet there has not been any full interaction with him that I am aware of, apart from an essay by G. Häfner, who defends the hypothesis of the production of the Pastorals as a literary corpus to be read in the order 1 Timothy—Titus—2 Timothy.[73]

CONCLUSION

This essay is nothing more than a record of ongoing research and study in which there has been much further illumination of the issues raised by the Pastoral Epistles, but we remain as far from a consensus as ever. The following important methodological issues have emerged as important for future study.

(1) A number of writers are emphasizing the individuality of the Pastorals as three separate compositions with their own distinctive characteristics and theological developments while yet belonging together as a group. Put otherwise, the three letters clearly stand together within the 13-letter corpus as being somehow different from the others and showing common characteristics among themselves. Yet they are individual writings and attention needs to be focused on their distinctives. This is recognized both by scholars who believe in one author (Fuchs, Towner, and Wieland) and by those who believe in more than one author (Aageson, Richards).

The point is taken up by Herzer who notes how the consensus view in German scholarship that assumes the unity of the Pastorals as a corpus is strongly questioned by Johnson (as also by other English-speaking scholars). Herzer does not accept Johnson's standpoint on Pauline authorship but claims that his challenge to the consensus as regards unity of authorship and composition as a deliberate tripartite corpus must be taken very seriously. Fuchs finds subtle, fine distinctions between the Pastorals which are related to the particular audiences and circumstances that are addressed in

---

[72] Herzer, "Rearranging the 'House of God,'" 564–66.
[73] Häfner, "Das Corpus Pastorale." Oberlinner, "Gemeindeordnung," 295, also maintains the unity of the corpus but without reference to Herzer's challenge.

each case. He has rightly drawn attention to some remarkable differences that other scholars have not noticed or have passed over as insignificant, but he does not argue for differences in authorship; after all, he is the defender of authorship by a versatile Paul who adapts himself to different readers.

What must not be overlooked, however, is that despite these subtleties there is a good deal in common between the letters that at the same time distinguishes them from the other letters by or attributed to Paul:

- The absence of fatherhood language.
- The use of "Savior," both of the Father and of Christ.
- The use of virtue and vice lists involving the use of long strings of nouns.

Some defenders of Pauline authorship claim that the absence of these same notable items of Pauline theology from the Pastorals as a group is due simply to their not being required by the different subject matter and is therefore not remarkable. The fundamental question, however, is not just why they are not explicit but rather whether the same Pauline way of theologizing as is expressed by these items is still forming the underlying structure of the author's thought.

Alongside this question of theological unity there are the broader questions of the contexts of the letters, their purpose of the letters, and their manner of composition. Can one synthesize the indications concerning the nature of the opponents visualized in each of the three letters? If we have three letters that display undeniable literary similarities that distinguish them as a group from the other letters in the Pauline corpus, does this not demand that the group forms a co-text for each of its components? Were conditions in Crete (or "Crete") the same as in Ephesus (or "Ephesus")?

(2) The historical setting (real or fictitious) of the author(s) continues to be a very open question with four types of setting all enjoying some support:

(a) A setting in the course of Paul's missionary work with 1 Timothy and Titus coming from his missionary travels and 2 Timothy from his imprisonment.

(b) A setting in the period after Paul's being taken to Rome and around the date of his death. There is not a lot of difference between a setting just before or soon after his death (especially if Pauline material is incorporated in the letters).

(c) A setting later in the first century when changed circumstances had led to the need to rehabilitate Paul or to use his name to call the church back to orthodoxy.

(d) A setting in the second century (whether for some or all the letters) when the situation is rather more different.[74]

The problem is caused partly by our lack of knowledge. The career of Paul himself is full of so many gaps and uncertainties that it is hard to argue against a postulated setting for the letters somewhere in it. The circumstances at later dates are even more opaque. Likewise the situations regarding the development of church organization and rise of opponents are blurred, and it is arguable that almost any period is possible.[75]

(3) There is a strong polarization between conservative scholars who see the letters as essentially offering an appropriate development of Pauline theology for the new situation toward or after the close of his life and active missionary work and those who see in them a radical rewriting of Pauline theology generally associated with a later date.

On the one hand, more conservative scholars tend to adopt a reading of the letters that sees them as fundamentally in line with the authentic Paul with divergences (e.g., on the place of women) being contextual. The effect is that the letters are interpreted as parts of a Pauline collection. Conversely, there may be a tendency to interpret Paul himself in the light of the letters and to see him as a tamer theologian than he actually was.

On the other hand, more radical scholars tend to adopt readings that distance the letters from Paul and highlight differences and contradictions. Thus Merz in particular wants to see in the letters a deliberate attempt to rewrite Paul on such issues as slavery and women with the purpose of countering Paul's own teaching by a fictitious creation in which the impression is given of Paul correcting himself by withdrawing what he has said on the equal standing of all believers in Christ; in so doing the author was attempting to deceive his readers (and succeeded in doing so) and at the same time was probably deceiving himself into thinking that he was truly expressing what Paul would be saying if he were still alive. The historical Paul is more a champion of women, and the Pastor is an opponent with a generally biased opinion of them.[76]

The curious thing is the way in which the general lines of interpretation of 1 Timothy 2 in particular are shared by some conservatives, who insist that under no conditions can universal prohibitions of women teaching and exercising authority be explained as temporary and local rather than applying to the church today, and radical feminists, who agree on this exegesis (and, if anything, perhaps express it the more strongly) but then proceed to question its canonical authority for the church today. It is an extraordinary alliance of opposites.

(4) For all students of the letters the question of the image of Paul that is presented is a matter for investigation. If they are post-Pauline, how does the construction of

---

74 So M. Hengel and A. M. Schwemer, *Jesus und das Judentum* (Tübingen: Mohr Siebeck, 2007), 13–14.
75 Important here is the question whether Gnosticism is proved to be part of the background of one or more of the letters.
76 Cf. the earlier work of U. Wagener, *Die Ordnung des »Hauses Gottes« Der Ort von Frauen in der Ekklesiologie und Ethik der Pastoralbriefe* (WUNT 2.65; Tübingen: J. C. B. Mohr [Paul Siebeck], 1994).

the picture of Paul relate to the historical Paul and to the images developed in other post-Pauline writings, including Acts.[77]

(5) What, then, is the place of the Pastorals in studies of Pauline theology? The "usual" critical approach is to treat the various deutero-Pauline writings separately from Paul and largely to ignore them in developing a total picture of Pauline theology. How far do more conservative scholars find that their picture of Paul is colored by the Pastoral Epistles, compared with the picture offered by scholars who rigorously refrain from letting the Pastoral Epistles affect their understanding of Paul? We saw how even for Matera the Pastorals lack the profundity of Paul and have significant omissions from his theology. The presentation by Merz proposes that Paul, seen without the shadow cast by the Pastorals, has a more radical understanding of the new creation with its relativizing of the hierarchical structures of ancient society. By breaking free from a traditional picture of Paul's own theology, which depended on a synthesis of material from the whole corpus of 13 letters, it may be possible to see the Paul of the seven generally acknowledged letters as a bolder and more creative theologian.

A further area would be the question of congregational structures and the question whether office is stifling charisma (note Strecker's qualification).

Some scholars tend to regard the letters as later works that fall away from the theological richness of Paul himself and to disparage the Pastor's efforts as second-rate. Others consider comparison with Paul in his different situation to be inappropriate, and they would rather explore how the Pastor has taken over the Pauline tradition and reused it in ways appropriate to the changed situation, be it in the later first century or later still.

(6) Implicit in much of these discussions is, of course, the problem of authorship. Scholars who might be disposed to ignore conservative contributions to the debate as special pleading from a theological position are perplexed by the new defenses of conservative positions by Johnston and (for 2 Timothy) by Murphy-O'Connor, scholars who cannot be accused of conservative theological bias dictating their scholarship.[78] A more open position is taken by Herzer coming from the tradition where pseudonymity is taken for granted and also by some scholars from the more conservative tradition (such as Towner, who explicitly leaves the question open).

There is a clear polarization between the two types of interpretation. The more traditional tendency to relate the letters closely to Paul, whether as direct compositions or as material written in his name by another hand, and to see their theology as having essentially Jewish-Christian roots has been given solid scholarly backing. Streete's comment that pseudonymity is the view of "nearly all modern commentators

---

[77] Cf. Marguerat, "Paul après Paul."

[78] I am not suggesting that the conclusions of conservative (or of radical) scholars are necessarily biased by their theological position. Whether the proponents are conservative or radical, their arguments must be assessed and evaluated academically.

on the Pastoral Epistles"[79] is somewhat exaggerated (cf. Johnson's comment noted above). Nevertheless, the view that the letters are considerably later pseudonymous compositions continues to have powerful support and cannot be airily dismissed by conservative scholars.

What appears to be largely lacking is any genuine dialogue between scholars belonging to these two camps. Merz speaks of the growing strength of conservative evangelical forces in the USA and more widely and thinks that this is a backward move that leads nowhere.[80] More wisely and realistically Bassler comments that probably neither view can be fully demonstrated. Regarding her own work she writes:

> The commentary should convince careful readers of either persuasion that both the "majority consensus" *and* T.'s interpretation rest on largely hypothetical historical reconstructions, that *both* positions about authorship are "unproven" and each can be regarded as "reasonable," that there are more points of contact between these letters and the undisputed letters than is generally acknowledged, that there are also significant differences that this reading ignores or underplays, and, finally, that these are, on any reading, fascinating little letters.[81]

The nonpolemical tone of this comment is to be welcomed, as is her refusal to say that Towner takes up his position because he belongs to a conservative tradition and therefore can be ignored as somebody with whom reasoned debate is impossible.

(7) This and the other essays in this volume cannot be regarded as bringing discussion to any kind of closure. Rather they constitute a contribution to the setting of an agenda with a wide spectrum of participants and an invitation to take part.

---

[79] Streete, *op. cit.*, 315.

[80] Merz, "*Corpus Pastorale*," 276.

[81] Bassler, review of Towner (*CBQ* 69 [2007]: 599).

BIBLIOGRAPHY OF RECENT LITERATURE ON THE PASTORAL EPISTLES

The references to articles in periodicals are mostly taken from a trawl through *New Testament Abstracts* 1999–2008, omitting items that appear to be on a devotional level. The abbreviations generally follow SBL guidelines. The vast bibliography on 1 Timothy 2 and related issues is not included. And I personally have not consulted everything listed—not by a long way! This list is material for selective use in an agenda, not an achievement.

COMMENTARIES

Baugh, S. M. "The Pastoral Epistles." Pages 444–511 in volume 3 of *Zondervan Illustrated Bible Background Commentary*. 4 vols. Edited by C. E. Arnold. Grand Rapids: Zondervan, 2001.

Bénétreau, S. *Les Épîtres Pastorales: 1 et 2 Timothée, Tite*. Commentaires Évangeliques de la Bible. Vaux-sur-Seine: ÉDIFAC, 2008.

Collins, R. F. *1 & 2 Timothy and Titus: A Commentary*. The New Testament Library. Louisville: Westminster John Knox Press, 2002.

Drury, C. "The Pastoral Epistles." Pages 1220–23 in *The Oxford Bible Commentary*. Edited by J. Barton and J. Muddiman. Oxford: Oxford University Press, 2001.

Dunn, J. D. G. "The First and Second Letters to Timothy and the Letter to Titus." Pages 775–880 in volume 11 of *The New Interpreter's Bible*. 12 vols. Edited by L. E. Keck. Nashville: Abingdon, 2000.

Fiore, B. *The Pastoral Epistles: First Timothy, Second Timothy, Titus*. Sacra Pagina. Collegeville: Liturgical Press, 2007.

Gorday, P. *Colossians, 1–2 Thessalonians, 1–2 Timothy, Titus, Philemon*. Ancient Christian Commentary on Scripture. Downers Grove: IVP, 2000.

Johnson, L. T. *The First and Second Letters to Timothy: A New Translation with Introduction and Commentary*. Anchor Bible. New York: Doubleday, 2001.

Keegan, T. J. *First and Second Timothy, Titus, Philemon*. New Collegeville Bible Commentary. Collegeville: Liturgical Press, 2006.

Köstenberger, A. "1 Timothy," "2 Timothy," "Titus." Pages 487–625 in volume 12 of *The Expositor's Bible Commentary* Rev. ed. 13 vols. Edited by T. Longman III and D. E. Garland. Grand Rapids: Zondervan, 2006.

Liefeld, W. L. *1 and 2 Timothy, Titus*. The NIV Application Commentary. Grand Rapids: Zondervan, 1999.

Marshall, I. H. (in collaboration with P. H. Towner). *A Critical and Exegetical Commentary on the Pastoral Epistles*. International Critical Commentary. Edinburgh: T&T Clark, 1999.

Montague, G. T. *First and Second Timothy, Titus*. Catholic Commentary on Sacred Scripture. Grand Rapids: Baker Academic, 2008.

Mounce, W. D. *Pastoral Epistles*. Word Biblical Commentary. Nashville: Nelson, 2000.

Neudorfer, H.-W. *Der erste Brief des Paulus an Timotheus*. Historisch Theologische Auslegung. Wuppertal: Brockhaus/Giessen: Brunnen, 2004.

Perkins, P. "Pastoral Epistles." Pages 1428–46 in *Eerdmans Commentary on the Bible*. Edited by J. D. G. Dunn and J. W. Rogerson. Grand Rapids: Eerdmans, 2003.

Quinn, J. D., and W. C. Wacker, *The First and Second Letters to Timothy: A New Translation with Notes and Commentary*. Eerdmans Critical Commentary. Grand Rapids: Eerdmans, 2000.

Saarinen, R. Pages 19–196 in *The Pastoral Epistles with Philemon and Jude*. Brazos Theological Commentary on the Bible. Grand Rapids: Brazos Press, 2008.

Towner, P. H. *The Letters to Timothy and Titus*. New International Commentary on the New Testament. Grand Rapids: Eerdmans, 2006.

———. "1—2 Timothy and Titus." Pages 891–918 in *Commentary on the New Testament Use of the Old Testament*. Edited by G. K. Beale and D. A. Carson. Grand Rapids: Baker Academic/Nottingham: Apollos, 2007.

Twomey, J. *The Pastoral Epistles Through the Centuries*. Blackwell Bible Commentaries. Malden, Mass./Oxford: Wiley-Blackwell, 2009.

Weiser, A. *Der zweite Brief an Timotheus*. Evangelisch-Katholischer Kommentar zum Neuen Testament. Düsseldorf: Benziger/Neukirchen-Vluyn: Neukirchener, 2003.

Witherington III, B. Pages 23–390 in *A Socio-Rhetorical Commentary on Titus, 1–2 Timothy and 1–3 John*. Volume 1 of *Letters and Homilies for Hellenized Christians*. Downers Grove: IVP Academic/Nottingham: Apollos, 2006.

MONOGRAPHS AND ARTICLES

Aageson, J. "The Pastoral Epistles and the Acts of Paul: A Multiplex Approach to Authority in Paul's Legacy." *LTQ* 40 (2005): 237–48.

———. "The Pastoral Epistles, Apostolic Authority, and the Development of the Pauline Scriptures." Pages 5–26 in *The Pauline Canon*. Edited by S. E. Porter. Leiden/Boston: Brill, 2004.

———. *Paul, the Pastoral Epistles, and the Early Church*. Peabody: Hendrickson, 2008.

Arichea, D. C. "Translating Hymnic Materials: Theology and Translation in 1 Timothy 3.16." *BT* 58 (2007): 179–85.

Aune, D. E. *The Westminster Dictionary of New Testament and Early Christian Literature and Rhetoric*. Louisville: Westminster John Knox, 2003.

Baum, A. D. *Pseudepigraphie und literarische Fälschung im frühen Christentum. Mit ausgewählten Quellentexten samt deutscher Übersetzung*. Tübingen: Mohr Siebeck, 2001.

———. "Semantic Variation Within the *Corpus Paulinum*: Linguistic Considerations Concerning the Richer Vocabulary of the Pastoral Epistles." *TynBul* 59:2 (2008): 271–92.

Belleville, L. L. "Exegetical Fallacies in Interpreting 1 Timothy 2:11–15." *Priscilla Papers* 17 (2003): 3–11.

———. "Teaching and Usurping Authority: 1 Timothy 2:11–15." Pages 205–23 in *Discovering Biblical Equality: Complementarity without Hierarchy*. Edited by R. W. Pierce and R. M. Groothuis. Downers Grove: IVP, 2004.

———. "Women in Ministry." Pages 75–154 in *Two Views on Women in Ministry*. Edited by J. R. Beck and C. L. Blomberg. Grand Rapids: Zondervan, 2001.

Berding, K. "Polycarp of Smyrna's View of the Authorship of 1 and 2 Timothy." *VC* 53 (1999): 349–60.

Blanchard, Y.-M. "'Toute Écriture est inspirée' (2 Tim 3, 16). Les problématiques de la canonisation et de l'inspiration, avex leurs enjeux respectifs." *RSR* 93 (2005): 497–515.

Blecker, I. M. "Die parathēkē rettenden Wissens nach den Pastoralbriefen." Pages 237–39 in *Rettendes Wissen. Studien zur Forgang weisheitlichen Denkens in Frühjudentum und im frühen Christentum*. Edited by K. Löning. Alter Orient und Altes Testament 300. Münster, 2002.

Bligh, M. C. "Seventeen Verses Written for Timothy (2 Tim 4:6–22)." *ExpTim* 109 (1998): 364–69.

Buchegger, J. Rezension von R. Fuchs. *Unerwartete Unterschiede. Müssen wir unsere Ansichten über die Pastoralbriefe revidieren? Jahrbuch für Evangelikale Theologie* 18 (2004): 248–51.

Burnet, R. "La pseudépigraphie comme procédé littéraire autonome: L'exemple des Pastorales." *Apocrypha* 11 (2000): 77–91.

Byrne, P. J. "1 Tim 6:6: 'A Window on the World of the Pastorals.'" *Proceedings of the Irish Biblical Association* 24 (2001): 9–16.

Capper, B. J. "To Keep Silent, Ask Husbands at Home, and not to Have Authority over Men. (1 Corinthians 14:33–36 and 1 Timothy 2:11–12) The Transition from Gathering in Private to Meeting in Public Space in Second Generation Christianity and the Exclusion of Women from Leadership of the Public Assembly." *TZ* 61 (2005): 113–31, 301–19.

Clark, D. J. "Discourse Structure in Titus." *Bible Translator: Technical Papers* 53:1 (2002): 101–17.

Clark, R. "Family Management or Involvement? Paul's Use of προΐστημι in 1 Timothy 3 as a Requirement for Church Leadership." *Stone-Campbell Journal* 9 (2006): 24–52.

Collins, R. F. "The Origins of Church Law." *Jurist* 61 (2001): 134–56.

———. "The Theology of the Epistle to Titus." *ETL* 76 (2000): 56–72.

Coupland, S. "Salvation Through Childbearing? The Riddle of 1 Timothy 2:15." *ExpTim* 112 (2001): 302–03.

Couser, G. A. "God and Christian Existence in the Pastoral Epistles: Toward Theological Method and Meaning." *NovT* 42 (2000): 262–83.

———. "'The Testimony about the Lord,' 'Borne by the Lord,' or Both? An Insight into Paul and Jesus in the Pastoral Epistles (2 Tim. 1:8)." *TynBul* 55 (2004): 295–316.

D'Angelo, M. R. "Εὐσέβεια: Roman Imperial Family Values and the Sexual Politics of 4 Maccabees and the Pastorals." *BibInt* 11 (2003): 139–65.

De Villiers, P. G. R. "A Pauline Letter and a Pagan Prophet." *Acta Patristica et Byzantina* 11 (2000): 74–92.

———. "'Empty Talk' in 1 Timothy in the Light of its Graeco-Roman Context." *Acta Patristica et Byzantina* 14 (2003): 136–55.

———. "Heroes at Home: Identity, Ethos and Ethics in 1 Timothy within the Context of the Pastoral Epistles." Pages 357–86 in *Identity, Ethos and Ethics in the New Testament*. Edited by J. G. van der Watt. BZNW 141. Berlin: de Gruyter, 2006.

Dowd, S. "'Ordination' in Acts and the Pastoral Epistles." *PRSt* 29 (2002): 205–17.

Downs, D. J. "'Early Catholicism' and Apocalypticism in the Pastoral Epistles." *CBQ* 67 (2005): 641–61.

Duff, J. N. "A Reconsideration of Pseudepigraphy in Early Christianity." D.Phil. thesis, University of Oxford, 1998.

———. "A Reconsideration of Pseudepigraphy in Early Christianity." *TynBul* 50:2 (1999): 306–309 (abstract of D.Phil. thesis, University of Oxford, 1998).

Ellington, J. "Problem Pronouns in Private Letters." *BT* 50 (1999): 219–27.

Ellis, E. E. *The Making of the New Testament Documents* (Leiden: Brill, 1999): 406–425. (Originally published as "Traditions in the Pastoral Epistles." Pages 237–53 in *Early Jewish and Christian Exegesis: Studies in Memory of William Hugh Brownlee*. Edited by C. A. Evans and W. F. Stinespring. Atlanta, Scholars Press, 1987.)

Faber, R. "'Evil Beasts, Lazy Gluttons': A Neglected Theme in the Epistle to Titus." *WTJ* 67 (2005): 135–45.

Fatum, L. "Christ Domesticated: The Household Theology of the Pastorals as Political Strategy." Pages 175–207 in *The Formation of the Early Church*. Edited by J. Ådna. WUNT 183. Tübingen: Mohr Siebeck, 2005.

Fitzmyer, J. A. "The Structured Ministry of the Church in the Pastoral Epistles." *CBQ* 66 (2004): 582–96.

Frary, S. W. "Who Was Manifested in the Flesh? A Consideration of Internal Evidence in Support of a Variant in 1 Tim 3:16a." *EFN* 16 (2003): 3–18.

Frenchkowski, M. "Pseudepigraphie und Paulusschule: Gedanken zur Verfasser-schaft der Deuteropaulinen, insbesondere der Pastoralbriefe." Pages 239–72 in *Das Ende des Paulus: historische, theologische und literaturgeschichtliche Aspekte.* Edited by F. W. Horn. BZNW 106. Berlin: De Gruyter, 2001.

Fuchs, R. "Bisher unbeachtet — zum unterschiedlichen Gebrauch von ἀγαθός, καλός und καλῶς in den Schreiben an Timotheus und Titus." *EurJTh* 15 (2006): 15–33.

———. "Ist 'die Agape das Ziel der Unterweisung' (1. Tim 1,5)? – zum unter-schiedlichen Gebrauch des agap- und des fil- Wortstammes in den Schreiben an Timotheus und Titus." *Jahrbuch für Evangelikale Theologie* 18 (2004): 93–125.

———. "Eine vierte Missionsreise des Apostels Paulus im Osten? Zur Datierung des ersten Timotheusbriefs und des Titusbriefs" (forthcoming).

———. *Unerwartete Unterschiede: Müssen wir unsere Ansichten über die Pastoralbriefe revidieren?* Witten: Wuppertal R. Brockhaus, 2003. (See J. Buchegger above).

Gerber, C. "Antijudaismus und Apologetik. Eine Lektüre des Titusbriefes vor dem Hintergrund der Apologie *Contra Apionem* des Flavius Josephus." Pages 335–63 in *Josephus und das Neue Testament. Wechselseitige Wahrnehmungen.* Edited by C. Böttrich and J. Herzer.Tübingen: Mohr Siebeck, 2007.

Gerber, D. "1Tm 1,15b: L'indice d'une sotériologie pensée prioritairement en lieu avec la venue de Jésus?" *RHPR* 80 (2000): 463–77.

Giles, K. "A Critique of the 'Novel' Contemporary Interpretation of 1 Timothy 2:9–15 Given in the Book, *Women in the Church* Part I." *EvQ* 72 (2000): 151–67.

———. "A Critique of the 'Novel' Contemporary Interpretation of 1 Timothy 2:9–15 Given in the Book, *Women in the Church* Part II." *EvQ* 72 (2000): 195–215.

———. "Women in the Church: A Rejoinder to Andreas Köstenberger." *EvQ* 73 (2001): 225–45.

Gill, M. *Jesus as Mediator: Politics and Polemic in 1 Timothy 2:1–7.* Oxford/New York: Peter Lang, 2008.

Gourges, M. "La première lettre à Timothée, témoin d'une 'domestication' et d'une adaptation de la foi et de l'expérience ecclésiale." *ScEs* 56 (2004): 5–18.

Gray, P. "The Liar Paradox and the Letter to Titus." *CBQ* 69 (2007): 302–14.

Grubbs, N. C. "The Truth about Elders and Their Children: Believing or Behaving in Titus 1:6?" *Faith and Mission* 22 (2005): 3–15.

Grudem, W. *Evangelical Feminism and Biblical Truth: An Analysis of 118 Disputed Questions.* Leicester: Apollos, 2005.

Häfner, G. *»Nützlich zur Belehrung« (2 Tim 3,16). Die Rolle der Schrift in den Pasto-ralbriefen im Rahmen der Paulusrezeption.* HBS 25. Freiburg: Herder, 2000.

————. "Das Corpus Pastorale als literarisches Konstrukt." *ThQ* 187 (2007): 258–73.

————. "Die Gegner in den Pastoralbriefen und die Paulusakten." *ZNW* 92 (2001): 64–77.

————. "Schriftauslegung und »gesunde Lehre« in den Pastoralbriefe. Von der Problematik eines spannungsfreien Verhältnisses." Pages 171–98 in *Die Bedeutung der Exegese für Theologie und Kirche*. Edited by U. Busse. QD 215. Freiburg: Herder, 2005.

Hahn, F. Pages 367–84 in Volume 1: Die Vielfalt des Neuen Testaments, *Theologie des Neuen Testaments*. 2 vols. Tübingen: Mohr Siebeck, 2002.

Harding, M. *Tradition and Rhetoric in the Pastoral Epistles*. New York: Peter Lang, 1998.

————. *What Are They Saying About the Pastoral Epistles?* New York: Paulist, 2001.

Harrill, J. A. "The Vice of Slave Dealers in Greco-Roman Society: The Use of a Topos in 1 Timothy 1:10." *JBL* 118 (1999): 97–122.

Heidebrecht, D. "Reading 1 Timothy 2:9–15 in Its Literary Context." *Directions* 33 (2004): 171–84.

Heininger, B. "Die 'mystische' Eva. 1 Tim 2,8–15 und die Folgen des Sündenfalls in der *Apokalypsis Mosis*." *BZ* 46 (2002): 205–21.

Helm, P. "John Calvin on 'Before All Ages.'" *TynBul* 53 (2002): 143–48.

Herzer, J. "Abschied vom Konsens? Die Pseudepigraphie der Pastoralbriefe als Herausforderung an die neutestamentliche Wissenschaft." *TLZ* 129 (2004): 1267–82.

————. *Constructing Pseudonymity: The Pastoral Epistles between Claim and Criticism* (forthcoming).

————. "»Das Geheimnis der Frömmigkeit« (1 Tim 3,16): Sprache und Stil der Pastoralbriefe im Kontext hellenistisch-römischer Popularphilosophie – eine methodische Problemanzeige." *ThQ* 187 (2007): 309–29.

————. "»Das ist gut und nützlich für die Menschen« (Tit 3,8). Die Menschenfreundlichkeit Gottes als Paradigma christlicher Ethik." Pages 101–20 in *Eschatologie und Ethik im frühen Christentum: FS G. Haufe*. Edited by C. Böttrich. Frankfurt: Peter Lang, 2006.

————. "Die »Verheissung des Lebens« (1 Tim 4,8) im Spannungsfeld zwisssschen öffentlicher Verantwortung und persönlicher Hoffnung." Pages 300–11 in *Leben – Verständnis. Wissenschaft. Technik*. Edited by E. Herms. Gütersloh: 2005.

————. "Juden – Christen – Gnostiker: Zur Gegnerproblematik der Pastoralbriefe." *Berliner Theologische Zeitschrift* 25 (2008): 143–68.

————. "Rearranging the 'House of God': A New Perspective on the Pastoral Epistles." Pages 547–66 in Empsychoi Logoi—*Religious Innovations in Antiquity: Studies in Honour of Pieter Willem van der Horst*. Edited by A. Houtman et al. Leiden: Brill, 2008.

Ho, C. E. "Do the Work of an Evangelist: The Missionary Outlook of the Pastoral Epistles." Ph.D. thesis, University of Aberdeen, 2000.

Hock, A. "Equipping the Successors of the Apostles: A Comparative Study of the Ethical Catalogues in Paul's Pastoral Letters (1 Tim 1:9–10; 6:4–5; 2 Tim 3:2–4; Tit 3:3)" *EstBib* 64 (2006): 85–98.

Holmes, J. M. *Text in a Whirlwind: A Critique of Four Exegetical Devices at 1 Timothy 2.9–15* (Sheffield: Sheffield Academic Press, 2000).

Horrell, D. G. "From ἀδελφοί to οἶκος θεοῦ: Social Transformation in Pauline Christianity." *JBL* 120 (2001): 293–311.

Howell, D. N. "God-Christ Interchange in Paul: Impressive Testimony to the Deity of Jesus." *JETS* 36 (1993): 467–79.

Husbands, M. and T. Larsen, *Women, Ministry and the Gospel: Exploring New Paradigms* (Downers Grove: IVP Academic, 2007).

Huttar, D. K. "AYΘENTEIN in the Aeschylus Scholium." *JETS* 44 (2001): 615–25.

———. "Causal *gar* in 1 Timothy 2:13: A Response to Linda L. Belleville." *Journal for Biblical Manhood and Womanhood* 11 (2006): 30–33.

Irwin, B. P. "The Laying on of Hands in 1 Timothy 5:22: A New Proposal." *BBR* 18 (2008): 123–29.

Jacobs, M. M. "On 1 Timothy 2:9–15: Why Still Interpret 'Irredeemable' Biblical Texts?" *Scriptura* 88 (2005): 85–100.

Jervis, L. A. "Paul the Poet in First Timothy 1:11–17; 2:3b–7; 3:14–16." *CBQ* 61 (1999): 695–712.

Johnson, L. T. "*Oikonomia Theou*: The Theological Voice of 1 Timothy from the Perspective of Pauline Authorship." *HBT* 21 (1999): 87–104.

Kartzow, M. B. "Female Gossipers and Their Reputation in the Pastoral Epistles." *Neot* 39 (2005): 255–72.

Keener, C. S. "Women in Ministry." Pages 27–73 in *Two Views on Women in Ministry*. Edited by J. R. Beck and C. L. Blomberg. Grand Rapids: Zondervan, 2001.

Keller, B. R. "1 Timothy 6:5 (Variant)—'Withdraw Yourself from Such [People].'" *WiscLuthQuart* 97 (2000): 291–96.

Kidd, R. M. "Titus as *Apologia*: Grace for Liars, Beasts, and Bellies." *HBT* 21 (1999): 185–209.

Kim, H. B. "The Interpretation of μάλιστα in 1 Timothy 5:17." *NovT* 45 (2004): 360–68.

Klinker-De Klerck, M. "The Pastoral Epistles: Authentic Pauline Writings." *EurJTh* 17:2 (2008): 101–8.

Köstenberger, A. J. "Women in the Church: A Response to Kevin Giles." *EvQ* 73 (2001): 205–24 (with rejoinder by Giles, pp. 225–45).

Lemcio, E. E. "Images of the Church in 1 Corinthians and 1 Timothy: An Exercise in Canonical Hermeneutics." *Asbury Theological Journal* 56 (2001): 45–59.

Looks, C. *Das Anvertraute bewahren: Die Rezeption der Pastoralbriefe im 2. Jahrhundert.* München: H. Utz, 1999.

Malherbe, A. J. "Paraenesis in the Epistle to Titus." Pages 297–317 in *Early Christian Paraenesis in Context.* Edited by J. Starr and T. Engberg-Pedersen. Berlin: de Gruyter, 2004.

Mappes, D. A. "The Heresy Paul Opposed in 1 Timothy." *BSac* 156 (1999): 452–58.

———. "Moral Virtues Associated with Eldership." *BSac* 160 (2003): 202–18.

Markschies, C. "Apostolizität und andere Amtsbegründungen in der Antike." Pages 296–334 in *Das kirchliche Amt in apostolische Nachfolge, I: Grundlagen und Grundfragen.* Edited by T. Schneider and G. Wenze. Freiburg, 2004.

Marshall, I. H. "Congregation and Ministry in the Pastoral Epistles." Pages 105–25 in *Community Formation in the Early Church and in the Church Today.* Edited by R. N. Longenecker. Peabody: Hendrickson, 2002.

———. "Some Recent Commentaries on the Pastoral Epistles." *ExpT* 117 (2006): 140–43.

———. "Women in Ministry: A Further Look at 1 Timothy 2." Pages 53–78 in *Women, Ministry and the Gospel.* Edited by M. Husbands and T. Larsen. Downers Grove: InterVarsity Press, 2008.

Marshall, J. W. "'I Left You in Crete': Narrative Deception and Social Hierarchy in the Letter to Titus." *JBL* 127:4 (2008): 781–803.

Martin, S. C. *Pauli Testamentum: 2 Timothy and the Last Words of Moses.* Rome: Gregorian University, 1997.

Martin, T. W. "Entextualized and Implied Rhetorical Situations: The Case of 1 Timothy and Titus." *BR* 45 (2000): 5–24.

Meier, J. P. "The Inspiration of Scripture: But What Counts as Scripture? (2 Tim 1:1–14; 3:14–17; cf. 1 Tim 5:18)." *Mid-Stream* 38 (1999): 71–78.

Merkle, B. L. *The Elder and Overseer: One Office in the Early Church.* SBL 57. New York: Peter Lang, 2003.

———. "Paul's Arguments from Creation in 1 Corinthians 11:8–9 and 1 Timothy 2:13–14: An Apparent Inconsistency Answered." *JETS* 49 (2006): 527–48.

Merz, A. "Amore Pauli: Das Corpus Pastorale und das Ringen um die Interpretationshoheit bezüglich des paulinischen Erbes." *ThQ* 197 (2007): 274–94.

———. *Die fiktive Selbstauslegung des Paulus: Intertextuelle Studien zur Intention und Rexeption der Pastoralbriefe.* Göttingen: Vandenhoeck und Ruprecht/Fribourg: Academic Press, 2004.

———. "The Fictitious Self-Exposition of Paul: How Might Intertextual Theory Suggest a Reformulation of the Hermeneutics of Pseudepigraphy?" Pages 113–32 in *The Intertextuality of the Epistles: Explorations of Theory and Practice.* Edited by T. L. Brodie et al. Sheffield: Sheffield Phoenix Press, 2006.

Mills, W. E. *Pastoral Epistles.* Bibliographies for Biblical Research 14. Lewiston, N.Y.: Mellen, 2000.

Mitchell, M. M. "PTebt 703 and the Genre of 1 Timothy: The Curious Career of a Ptolemaic Papyrus in Pauline Scholarship." *NovT* 44 (2002): 344–70.

Mühlsteiger, J. *Kirchenordnungen. Anfänge kirchlicher Rechtsbildung.* Berlin, 2006.

Murphy-O'Connor, J. "Pastoral Epistles." *RB* 108 (2001): 630–35.

Nadar, S. "Paradigm Shifts in Mission: From an Ethic of Domination to an Ethic of Justice and Love. The Case of 1 Timothy 2:8–15." *Missionalia* 33 (2005): 303–14.

Nelson, P. G. "Inscription to a High Priestess at Ephesus." *Journal for Biblical Manhood and Womanhood* 12 (2007): 14–15.

Neyrey, J. J. "'First,' 'Only,' 'One of a Few,' and 'No One Else': The Rhetoric of Uniqueness and the Doxologies in 1 Timothy." *Bib* 86 (2005): 59–87.

North, S. R. "*Presbuteroi Christianoi*: Towards a Theory of Integrated Ministry." *TynBul* 51:2 (2000): 317–20.

Oberlinner, L. "Gemeindeordnung und rechte Lehre: Zur Fortschreibung der paulinischen Ekklesiologie in den Pastoralbriefen." *ThQ* 187 (2007): 295–308.

———. "Öffnung zur Welt oder Verrat am Glauben? Hellenismus in den Pastoralbriefen." Pages 135–63 in *Der neue Mensch in Christus: Hellenistische Anthropologie und Ethik im Neuen Testament.* Edited by J. Beutler. Freiburg: Herder, 2001.

Owens, M. D. "Should Churches Ordain the Divorced and Remarried?: An Examination of *mias gynaikos anēr* in the Pastoral Epistles." *Faith and Mission* 22 (2005): 42–50.

Paschke, B. A. "The *cura morum* of the Roman Censors as Historical Background for the Bishop and Deacon Lists of the Pastoral Epistles." *ZNW* 98 (2007): 105–19.

Patsch, H. "The Fear of Deutero-Paulinism: The Reception of Friedrich Schleiermacher's 'Critical Open Letter' Concerning 1 Timothy in the First Quinquennium." *JHC* 6 (1999): 3–31.

Payne, P. B. "1 Tim 2.12 and the Use of οὐδέ to Combine Two Elements to Express a Single Idea." *NTS* 54 (2008): 235–53.

Pierce, R. W. and R. M. Groothuis, *Discovering Biblical Equality: Complementarity without Hierarchy.* Downers Grove: IVP, 2004.

Pietersen, L. K. *The Polemic of the Pastorals: A Sociological Examination of the Development of Pauline Christianity.* JSNTSup 264. London: T & T Clark International, 2004.

Polaski, S. H. "'Let No One Despise Your Youth': The Deconstruction of Traditional Authority in the Pastoral Epistles." *LTQ* 40 (2005): 249–63.

Poythress, V. S. "The meaning of μάλιστα in 2 Timothy 4:13 and Related Verses." *JTS* 53 (2002): 523–32.

Price, R. M. "Schleiermacher's Dormant Discovery." *JHC* 9 (2002): 203–16.

Prior, M. "Revisiting the Pastoral Epistles." *ScrB* 31 (2001): 2–19.

Reuter, R. *Die Pastoralbriefe (The Pastoral Epistles).* Teil 2 of *Synopse zu den Briefen des Neuen Testaments (Synopsis of the New Testament Letters).* ARGU 6. Frankfurt: Peter Lang, 1998.

Richards, W. A. *Difference and Distance in Post-Pauline Christianity. An Epistolary Analysis of the Pastorals.* Studies in Biblical Literature 44. New York: Peter Lang, 2002.

Riesner, R. "Once More: Luke–Acts and the Pastoral Epistles." Pages 239–58 in *History and Exegesis: New Testament Essays in Honor of Dr. E. Earle Ellis for His 80th Birthday.* Edited by S.-W. Son. New York/London: T & T Clark, 2006.

Roose, H. "Dienen und Herrschen: Zur Charakterisierung des Lehrens in den Pastoralbriefen." *NTS* 49 (2003): 440–46.

Scholtissek, K., ed. *Christologie in der Paulus-Schule. Zur Rezeptionsgeschichte des paulinischen Evangeliums.* SBS 181. Stuttgart: Katholisches Bibelwerk, 2000. (See chapter by T. Söding.)

Scholz, S. "Christliche Identität im Plural. Ein neutestamentlicher Vergleich gemeindlicher Selbstverständnisse." Pages 66–94 in *Biblische und Theologische Erkundungen.* Edited by A. Deeg. Göttingen: Vandenhoeck & Ruprecht, 2007.

Schreiner, T. R. "Women in Ministry." Pages 175–235 in *Two Views on Women in Ministry.* Edited by J. R. Beck and C. L. Blomberg. Grand Rapids: Zondervan, 2001.

Schröter, J. "Kirche im Anschluss am Paulus. Aspekte der Paulusrezeption in der Apostelgeschichte und in den Pastoralbriefen." *ZNW* 98 (2007): 77–104.

Seesengood, R. P. "Contending for the Faith in Paul's Absence: Combat Sports and Gladiators in the Disputed Pauline Epistles." *LTQ* 41 (2006): 87–118.

Smith, C. A. "A Study of 2 Timothy 4:1–8: The Contribution of Epistolary Analysis and Rhetorical Criticism." *TynB* 57.1 (2006): 151–54. (Thesis abstract)

———. *Timothy's Task and Paul's Prospect: A New Reading of 2 Timothy.* Sheffield: Sheffield Phoenix, 2006.

Smith, K. and A. Song, "Some Christological Implications in Titus 2:13." *Neot* 40 (2006): 284–94.

Standhartinger, A. "*Eusebeia* in den Pastoralbriefen. Ein Beitrag zum Einfluss römischen Denkens auf das entstehende Christentum." *NovT* 48 (2006): 51–82.

Stettler, H. *Die Christologie der Pastoralbriefe.* Tübingen: Mohr Siebeck, 1998.

Strecker, G. "Sound Doctrine—The Pastoral Letters." Pages 576–94 in *Theology of the New Testament.* Berlin: De Gruyter/Louisville: Westminster John Knox, 2000.

Streete, G.-C., "Askesis and Resistance in the Pastoral Letters." Pages 299–316 in *Asceticism and the New Testament*. Edited by L. E. Vaage and V. L. Streete. New York: Routledge, 1999.

Stuhlmacher, P. Pages 1–53 (passim) in volume 2 of *Biblische Theologie des Neuen Testaments*. Göttingen: Vandenhoeck und Ruprecht, 1999.

Sturcke, H. Review of A. Merz, *Die fiktive Selbstauslegung des Paulus: Intertextuelle Studien zur Intention und Rexeption der Pastoralbriefe*. *RBL* 3 (2005): http://www.bookreviews.org/pdf/4322_4304.pdf.

Sumney, J. L. "'God our Savior': The Fundamental Operational Theological Assertion of 1 Timothy." *HBT* 21 (1999): 105–23 (cf. *LTQ* 33 [1998]: 151–61).

Tamez, E. "1 Timothy and James on the Rich, Women, and Theological Disputes." *Concilium* 1 (2002): 49–58.

———. *Struggles for Power in Early Christianity: A Study of the First Letter to Timothy*. Maryknoll: Orbis, 2007.

Theobald, M. "Paulus gegen Paulus? Der Streit um die Pastoralbriefe." *ThQ* 187 (2007): 253–57.

Thurston, B. "The Theology of Titus." *HBT* 21 (1999): 171–84.

Tollefson, K. D. "Titus: Epistle of Religious Revitalization." *BTB* 30 (2000): 145–57.

Torres, M. L. "Pauline Vicissitudes and 2 Tim 3:11." *Hermeneutica* 2 (2002): 45–59.

Towner, P. H. "Feminist Approaches to the New Testament. With 1 Timothy 2:8–15 as a Test Case." *Jian Dao* 7 (1997): 91–111.

Towner, P. H. "The Portrait of Paul and the Theology of 2 Timothy: The Closing Chapter of the Pauline Story." *HBT* 21 (1999): 151–70. (Translated into German by Rudi Fuchs, "Das Paulusbild und die Theologie des 2 Timotheusbriefes: Das Schlusskapitel der Paulusgeschichte." *Jahrbuch für Evangelikale Theologie* 18 [2004]: 128–44).

Towner, P. H. "The Pastoral Epistles." Pages 330–36 in *New Dictionary of Biblical Theology*. Edited by T. D. Alexander and B. S. Rosner. Leicester/Downers Grove: InterVarsity Press, 2000.

Trebilco, P. "The Early Christians and the World Out There: Reflections on Revelation and the Pastoral Epistles" (unpublished paper).

———. *The Early Christians in Ephesus from Paul to Ignatius*. Tübingen: Mohr Siebeck, 2004. (Incorporates in chap. 12, pp. 553–88, the two articles listed above).

———. "What Shall We Call Each Other? Part One: The Issue of Self-Designation in the Pastoral Epistles." *TynB* 53:2 (2002): 239–58.

———. "What Shall We Call Each Other? Part Two: The Issue of Self-Designation in the Johannine Letters and Revelation." *TynBul* 54:1 (2003): 51–73.

Tsuji, M. "Zwischen Ideal und Realität: Zu den Witwen in 1 Tim 5.3–16." *NTS* 47 (2001): 92–104.

Upton, B. G. "Can Stepmothers Be Saved? Another Look at 1 Timothy 2.8–15." *Feminist Theology* 15 (2007): 175–85.

Van der Toorn, K. "In the Lions' Den: The Babylonian Background of a Biblical Motif." *CBQ* 60 (1998): 626–40.

Van Neste, R. *Cohesion and Structure in the Pastoral Epistles.* JSNTSup 280. London/New York: T& T Clark International, 2004.

———. "Structure and Cohesion in Titus: Problems and Method." *BT: Technical Papers* 53 (2002): 118–32.

Wall, R. W. "1 Timothy 2:9–15 Reconsidered (Again)." *BBR* 14 (2004): 81–103.

Waters, K. L. "Saved through Childbearing: Virtues as Children in 1 Timothy 2:11–15." *JBL* 123 (2004): 703–35.

Wayment, T. A. "Two New Textual Variants from the Freer Pauline Codex (I)." *JBL* 123 (2004): 737–40. (On Titus 1:10.)

Webb, W. J. *Slaves, Women and Homosexuals: Exploring the Hermeneutics of Cultural Analysis.* Downers Grove: InterVarsity, 2001.

West, G. "Taming Texts of Terror: Reading (against) the Gender Grain of 1 Timothy." *Scriptura* 86 (2004): 160–73.

Wieland, G. *The Significance of Salvation: A Study of Salvation Language in the Pastoral Epistles.* PBM. Milton Keynes: Paternoster, 2006.

Wieland, G. M. "Roman Crete and the Letter to Titus," *NTS* 55 (2009): 338–54.

Winter, B. W. "The 'New' Roman Wife and 1 Timothy 2:9–15: The Search for a *Sitz im Leben*." *TynBul* 51:2 (2000): 285–94.

Wilder, T. L. "New Testament Pseudonymity and Deception." *TynBul* 50:1 (1999): 156–58.

Wilder, T. L. *Pseudonymity, the New Testament, and Deception: An Inquiry into Intention and Reception.* Lanham, MD: University Press of America, 2004.

Wolters, A. "A Semantic Study of αὐθέντης and Its Derivatives." *Journal for Biblical Manhood and Womanhood* 11 (2006): 44–65.

NAME INDEX

184, 205, 207, 208, 272,
291, 316
Erickson, M. J.   49, 174

Faber, R.   316
Farrer, A. M.   182
Fatum, L.   316
Fee, G. D.   9, 13, 211, 23, 45,
70, 87, 107, 108, 111, 113,
119, 120, 127, 129, 130,
132, 135, 137, 140, 141,
142, 144, 147, 148, 149,
155, 148, 182, 183, 186,
211, 257
Fiore, B.   87, 104, 154, 167,
258, 269, 279, 313
Fitzgerald, J. T.   89, 260
Fitzmyer, J.   106, 114, 118,
316
Flew, A.   237
Floor, L.   182
Fowler, F. G.   98
Fowler, H. W.   98
Frary, S. W.   316
Freedman, W.   215
Frenchkowski, M.   317
Fuchs, R.   278, 296, 298, 308,
315, 317
Fung, R. Y. K.   126, 178
Furnish, V.   125

Garland, D.   230, 313
Gealy, F. D.   86, 102
Gebauer, R.   126
Gehring, R. W.   68, 81, 173,
175, 176
Genade, A. A.   88
Gerber, C.   317
Gerber, D.   317
Gibson, R. J.   87
Giles, K.   10, 182, 303, 317,
319
Gill, M.   317
Glasson, T. F.   116
Gnilka, J.   182
Goguel, M.   182
Goodwin, M. J.   116, 157
Goppelt, L.   182, 242
Gorday, P.   269, 281, 282, 313
Gordon, T. D.   10, 18
Gore, C.   182

Gourges, M.   317
Grabbe, L. L.   217
Gray, P.   317
Grelot, P.   182
Griffin, H. P.   13, 183, 185
Grimes, J.   96
Groothuis, R. M.   321
Grubbs, N. C.   317
Grudem, W.   174, 191, 193,
304, 317
Guthrie, D.   2, 3, 8, 12, 13,
14, 29, 30, 32, 33, 34, 35,
36, 42, 45, 47, 86, 97, 98,
110, 111, 183, 185, 196,
228, 282

Häfner, G.   85, 86, 308, 317,
318
Hagner, D. A.   215
Hahn, F.   182, 262, 318
Hall, D. R.   127
Hamilton, J. M., Jr.   304
Hanson, A. T.   12, 255, 45,
84, 85, 86, 89, 105, 111,
113, 182, 199, 200, 201,
202, 204, 206, 208, 209,
213, 216, 238, 257
Harding, M.   167, 268, 286,
287, 318
Harmer, J. R.   187
Harrill, J. A.   278, 318
Harris, W. V.   78
Harris, M. J.   144, 161
Harrison, P. N.   42, 72, 292
Harvey, A. E.   181, 184, 211,
213
Harvey, J. D.   91
Hasler, V.   113, 121, 154
Hatch, E.   177, 180, 182
Hawthorne, G. F.   28, 30,
32, 33
Haykin, M.   110, 126
Heckert, J.   108
Heidebrecht, D.   318
Heininger, B.   318
Helm, P.   318
Hendriksen, W.   212
Hengel, M.   310
Herzer, J.   268, 269, 273, 292,
306, 307, 308, 311, 318
Hetzler, C.   88

Hilgenfeld, A.   34
Ho, C. E.   x, 254, 296, 319
Hock, A.   319
Hoehner, H.   28
Holloway, P. A.   291
Holmes, J. M.   268, 300, 301,
302, 319
Holmes, M. W.   187
Holtz, G.   182
Hooker, M. D.   210
Horrell, D. G.   319
Horsley, G. H. R.   109
Houlden, J. L.   101, 168, 264
Howell, D. N.   319
Hurtado, L. W.   109
Husbands, M.   319
Huther, J. E.   128
Huttar, D. K.   319

Irwin, B. P.   319

Jacobs, M. M.   319
Jay, E. G.   188
Jeremias, J.   45, 121, 132,
181, 242
Jervis, L. A.   319
Johnson, L. T.   11, 12, 17, 43,
44, 45, 68, 70, 71, 76, 78,
92, 99, 100, 106, 155, 167,
170, 182, 185, 196, 257,
258, 268, 269, 271, 272,
273, 275, 276, 281, 286,
290, 291, 306, 308, 312,
313, 319
Jones, D. W.   231

Kaiser, W. C.   135
Karris, R. J.   86, 87
Kartzow, M. B.   319
Käsemann, E.   102, 177, 178,
182
Kee, H. C.   242
Keegan, T. J.   313
Keener, C. S.   319
Keller, B. R.   319
Kellum, L. S.   52
Kelly, J. N. D.   45, 111, 113,
119, 127, 132, 182, 183,
185, 189, 196, 201, 225,
242, 258, 262
Kertelge, K.   182

SUBJECT INDEX

Scripture Index

Genesis

2–3   *204*
2:8   *206*
2:9–10   *206*
2:9–15   *206*
2:11–15   *206*
2:18   *205*
2:20   *205*
2:21–25   *205*
3:1–7   *205*
3:15   *205*
3:15–16   *157*
3:16   *205, 206*
4:3–4   *206*
5:13–14   *206*
12:13   *48*
18:18   *262*
21:33   *113*
22:18   *262*
26:4   *262*
26:7   *48*
27:19   *48*

Exodus

2:14   *184*
3:6   *114*
7–14   *217*
13:21–22   *255*
15:18   *113*
19:4–6   *133*
19:5   *145, 210, 222*
19:16–22   *114*
20:2   *135*
20:14   *23*
22:21   *136*
23:9   *136*
33:20   *114*
33:23   *114*
34:6   *208*

Leviticus

1:3   *250*
19:33–34   *136*

19:36   *135*
24   *202*
24:16   *202*

Numbers

4:16   *17*
14:28   *115, 254*
15:40   *135*
16   *203, 204*
16:2   *203*
16:5   *128, 150, 201, 203*
16:26   *202*
16:26–27   *128*
23:19   *133*
27:18–23   *285*

Deuteronomy

4:20   *210*
5:15   *136*
5:18   *23*
6:4–6   *139*
6:18   *250*
6:20–25   *135*
7:6   *145, 210*
7:6–8   *136*
9:4–6   *136*
9:26   *217*
10:17   *217*
10:18–19   *136*
10:21   *135*
11:1–8   *135*
14:2   *145, 210*
15:15   *136*
17:6   *207*
18   *286*
19   *212*
19:15   *207, 208*
19:15–20   *207*
24:18   *136*
24:22   *136*
25:4   *200, 212*
26:18   *210*
29:2–9   *135*

31   *286*
31:15   *255*
32:15   *244*
34:9   *285*

Joshua

3:10   *115, 254*
23:7   *202*

Judges

8:23   *113*
13:22   *114*

1 Samuel

10:19   *244*
21:2   *48*

2 Samuel

7:23–24   *210*

Ezra

7:12   *217*

Esther

4:17   *217*

Job

9:32–33   *216*

Psalms

6:8   *202*
10:16   *113*
21   *209*
22   *209*
22:2   *209*
22:9   *209*
22:17   *209*
22:22   *209*
22:28   *209*
24:5   *109, 244*
26:9   *109*

26:13   *109*
28:4   *217*
29:10   *113*
34:14   *202*
34:19   *208*
39:11   *134*
47:7   *113*
47:8–9   *113*
56:3   *134*
61:5–8   *109*
62:14   *217*
64:5   *109*
64:6   *155*
65:5   *155*
66:7   *113*
67:2–5   *262*
77:5–55   *135*
83:3   *254*
90:2   *113*
93:1–2   *113*
93:18   *134*
97   *113*
101:7   *48*
104   *133*
104:2   *114*
104:6   *133*
104:31   *113*
104:43   *133*
117:2   *113*
130:8   *210*
135:2–3   *217*
146:10   *113*

Proverbs

2:6   *148*
3:7   *202*
14:5   *48*
24:12   *217*

Isaiah

6:5   *114*
8:7   *113*
12:2   *244*
26:13   *128, 150, 202*

332

1:7 *127, 146*
1:9 *29*
1:12 *259*
1:12–13 *146*
1:17 *29*
1:19 *36*
1:21 *151*
1:25 *36*
1:27–30 *127*
1:28 *29*
1:29 *259*
2:1 *29*
2:2 *29*
2:3 *29*
2:5–11 *29, 32*
2:6 *29*
2:6–8 *35*
2:6–11 *209*
2:9 *29*
2:9–11 *140*
2:10 *29*
2:12 *29, 73*
2:17 *179*
2:19 *29, 196*
2:20 *29*
2:22 *63*
2:24 *36*
2:25 *33, 179*
2:27 *29*
2:28 *29*
2:30 *29, 179*
3 *32*
3:2 *29, 248, 257*
3:2–3 *31*
3:3 *126*
3:4–11 *209*
3:5 *29*
3:6 *31*
3:8 *29*
3:9 *31*
3:10 *29*
3:11 *29*
3:12–16 *32*
3:13 *29*
3:14 *29*
3:15 *29*
3:17 *29*
3:18–19 *248, 257*
3:20 *29, 109, 143*
4:1 *29*
4:2 *33*

4:3 *29, 127*
4:8 *29*
4:10 *29*
4:11 *29*
4:12 *29*
4:15 *29*
4:18 *33*
4:21–23 *147*

Colossians

1 *206*
1:7 *179, 180*
1:15–17 *35*
1:19 *145*
1:24 *209*
1:27 *109*
1:29 *254*
2:8–23 *248*
3:1–17 *223*
3:9 *48*
3:12 *133*
3:16 *303*
3:18–4:1 *67, 68*
4:3 *147*
4:7–18 *147*
4:12 *179, 180*
4:16 *5*
4:17 *179, 180*
4:18 *5, 36*

1 Thessalonians

1:6 *259, 278*
1:9 *254*
2:1–2 *259*
2:14 *115, 259*
3:2–3 *196*
3:4 *259*
3:13 *116*
4:2 *58*
4:12 *246*
4:14 *114*
4:16 *114, 116*
5:12 *35, 180, 188, 196, 198*
5:12–13 *179*

2 Thessalonians

1:6–7 *114*
1:6–8 *116*

2:2 *36*
2:8 *4, 112*
2:15 *58*
3:6 *58*
3:7–8 *19*
3:17 *5, 36*

1 Timothy

1 *114*
1:1 *2, 108, 113, 114, 116, 125, 126, 133, 138, 139, 155, 164, 165, 166, 169, 244, 266*
1:1–2 *59, 138*
1:1–3:13 *223*
1:2 *58, 93, 110, 138, 147, 151, 175*
1:3 *9, 11, 32, 54, 59, 61, 62, 81, 82, 94, 99, 110, 138, 196, 214, 249*
1:3–3:16 *13*
1:3–4 *13, 52, 55, 57, 59, 108, 110, 139, 196*
1:3–5 *58, 78*
1:3–7 *56, 57, 78, 95, 96, 98, 99*
1:3–10 *249*
1:3–11 *111, 138, 155, 248*
1:3–16 *248*
1:3–20 *55, 58, 59, 60, 82, 93, 94, 96, 108, 111, 173*
1:4 *31, 57, 69, 70, 79, 94, 96, 115, 124, 132, 226, 249*
1:5 *54, 58, 71, 111, 115, 214, 229*
1:5–6 *93, 94*
1:6 *58, 95, 96, 114, 115, 117, 224*
1:6–7 *122, 249*
1:6–10 *155*
1:7 *31, 54, 94, 96, 98, 111, 114, 132, 224, 226*
1:8 *71, 98, 111, 257*

1:8–9 *98*
1:8–10 *71*
1:8–11 *54, 98, 99, 215*
1:9 *118, 201*
1:9–10 *81, 89, 94, 111*
1:10 *29, 71, 99, 122, 123, 138, 214, 266, 278*
1:10–11 *214*
1:11 *58, 79, 99, 100, 111, 112, 113, 133, 138, 169, 214, 249, 266*
1:11–12 *70*
1:11–17 *109, 118, 119, 122, 123*
1:12 *81, 99, 100, 109, 138, 249, 250*
1:12–14 *249*
1:12–16 *169, 249*
1:12–17 *90, 99, 100, 112, 114, 138, 250, 266*
1:13 *96, 99, 100, 112, 114, 125, 229, 249, 258*
1:14 *58, 70, 99, 138, 224, 229, 250, 266*
1:14–16 *208, 209, 250*
1:15 *58, 79, 80, 99, 100, 110, 112, 113, 114, 115, 116, 122, 138, 139, 140, 141, 152, 216, 250, 258, 266, 283*
1:15–16 *156*
1:15–17 *141*
1:16 *99, 100, 109, 112, 113, 114, 116, 119, 125, 140*
1:17 *93, 100, 109, 112, 113, 114, 139, 294*
1:17–19 *86*
1:18 *55, 58, 79, 80, 94, 108, 110, 115,*

335